ALSO BY LYNN PICKNETT AND CLIVE PRINCE

The Templar Revelation

The Stargate Conspiracy

Turin Shroud—In Whose Image?

ALSO BY LYNN PICKNETT, CLIVE PRINCE,
AND STEPHEN PRIOR

Double Standards

War of the Windsors

Friendly Fire

ALSO BY LYNN PICKNETT

Mary Magdalene: Christianity's Hidden Goddess

The Secret History of Lucifer

The Sion Revelation

The Truth About the Guardians of Christ's Sacred Bloodline

LYNN PICKNETT AND CLIVE PRINCE

A TOUCHSTONE BOOK
PUBLISHED BY SIMON & SCHUSTER
New York London Toronto Sydney

TOUCHSTONE
Rockefeller Center
1230 Avenue of the Americas
New York, NY 10020

Designed by Jan Pisciotta

Manufactured in the United States of America

ISBN-13: 978-0-7432-6303-0
ISBN-10: 0-7432-6303-0

For

Craig Oakley

"Love and honor"

Acknowledgments

Many friends and colleagues have contributed to the gestation, writing, and production of this book. We would like to thank the following people especially:

Craig Oakley—who shared our experiences from the beginning and for being a devoted friend through good times and bad.

Jeffrey Simmons—for being our agent and our friend.

Our friend and colleague the late Stephen Prior—for encouraging and supporting us and cheering this book on. And Francesca Prior for warm hospitality and friendship.

At Simon & Schuster: Nancy Hancock, Sarah Peach, and Martha Schwartz.

For help with research and information:

Geoffrey Basil-Smith, Robert Brydon, Andrew Collins, Simon Cox, Nigel Foster, "Giovanni," Jerry Jardine, Hannah R. Johnson, Joy and John Millar, Dr. Steven Mizrach, Guy Patton, Graham Phillips, Keith Prince, Rat Scabies, Mick Staley, and Caroline Wise.

For support, encouragement, and help in various ways:

Vida Adamoli, David Bell, Debbie Benstead, Bali Beskin, Geraldine Beskin, Ashley Brown, Jayne Burns, Yvan Cartwright, Karine Esparseil, Carina Fearnley, Stewart Ferris and Katia Milani, Charles and Annette Fowkes, Susan Hailstones, Sarah Litvinoff, Jane Lyle, Vera and Michael Moroney, Lily and David Prince, Lucy Smith, Lou Tate, Sheila and Eric Taylor, and Joe Webster, David Trotter, and the crew of the late lamented Edge (especially our own Society of Angels—Leda Kalleske, Jess Roper, and Daisy Lythe) for helping to restore sanity!

And the staff of the British Library; the British Newspaper Library; the British Library of Political and Economic Science; St. John's Wood Library; Institut Français (London); Bibliothèque Nationale, Paris; and The Information Service of the French Embassy in the United Kingdom.

Contents

Introduction

When we presented our discovery of the secret symbolism in Leonardo da Vinci's paintings in our 1997 book, *The Templar Revelation: Secret Guardians of the True Identity of Christ*, little did we realize that we were making a significant contribution to a remarkable phenomenon of the twenty-first century. Not only did our book directly inspire Dan Brown to weave his blockbuster *The Da Vinci Code* (2003) around the concept of da Vinci's love of hidden heresies and dangerous codes, but we were taken aback to realize that in doing so we had also assisted at the birth of a new, impassioned wave of interest in the truth about the origins of Christianity.

A central part of Brown's fiction is the notion that there exists an age-old French society, the Priory of Sion, whose task it is to protect the sacred bloodline of Jesus and Mary Magdalene—the implications of which are truly shocking to those who remain true to the traditional teachings of the Church. The inevitable backlash against all the subjects raised in Brown's book has seen the Priory of Sion roundly trounced, dismissed once and for all as a straightforward hoax.

However, we became increasingly dissatisfied with either extreme—complete acceptance of everything claimed by or on behalf of the Priory or blanket dismissal—for two reasons. While there is evidence that the Priory is a modern creation, rather than the ancient and venerable secret society it is supposed to be, there is considerably more to it than a simple hoax. As our continuing research has found, the Priory really *is* important, but for rather different reasons.

This has given us the golden opportunity to present our ongoing investigation into the Priory of Sion. And unexpectedly, we found this work converging with other, quite independent, lines of research, specifically those that led to our 1999 book, *The Stargate Conspiracy*, which dealt with a little-known but extremely influential politico-occult movement known as *synarchy*. As we delved into it even deeper, we found ourselves unexpectedly back in the underground stream that also sweeps the Priory of Sion along. Even the research for our book on the "secret history" of the Second World War, *Friendly Fire: The Secret War Between the Allies* (coauthored with the late Stephen Prior, and Robert Brydon, 2004), became surprisingly relevant, as certain power struggles in wartime France provide an important backdrop to *The Sion Revelation*.

The second reason for our writing this book is much wider in scope, and to us more important: those who defend the traditional religious views against Dan Brown's book argue that if they can prove the Priory of Sion is a hoax, then the deeper issues—such as the reality of the "forbidden" gospels, the relationship between Jesus and Mary Magdalene, and the centuries-long Church cover-up of such inconvenient evidence about the Christian religion—can also be condemned and dismissed. This is utter nonsense.

Whatever else can be said about Brown's book, it has brought some fundamental questions about spirituality and religion to a massive and even secular international audience and sparked off far-reaching debates. It has even been pointed out that it has revived on a grassroots level the same bitter debate that raged in the formative years of the Christian religion. The major split was between the two fundamentally different visions of the faith: the Gnostic view, in which the individual forges his or her own relationship with God and is therefore responsible for his or her own salvation, and the priest-led faction that became the Church—in which the Church alone holds the keys of the Kingdom. It is a battle that the Church believed long won, but now the fissure lines are reopening as the floor is cleared for either a new, informed debate or a fight—and all due to the unlikely influence of an airport thriller!

Obviously, for some reason and in some mysterious way, Dan Brown has tapped into the prevailing zeitgeist, but this phenomenon can only exist because people have a deep inner *need* to excavate beneath the traditional religious certainties. But Brown is by no means its only popular manifestation. J. K. Rowling's young wizard Harry Potter scintillates with Gnostic daring, and—as many commentators point out—

the movie series *The Matrix* draws directly on ancient Gnostic concepts, dressing them up as science fiction, with elements from the Priory of Sion's mythos also having pride of place. While *The Matrix*'s sacred city of "Zion"/Sion is not unique to Priory lore, it is hard to find another source for the character called the Merovingian.

The true story of the Priory is rather different from Brown's version, but it *is* highly significant, disturbing, and even alarming. And it carries us along into a dark and intriguing world where a great many other uncomfortable facts, both religious and political, will have to be faced.

LYNN PICKNETT
CLIVE PRINCE
LONDON
September 2005

PART ONE

Illusion

CHAPTER ONE

TRUE LIES

FACT: The world's fastest-selling book is Dan Brown's 2003 novel, *The Da Vinci Code.*

FACT: A modern-day Grail quest, Brown's thriller is based on the secrets surrounding the French-based secret society the Priory of Sion (more properly, Prieuré de Sion), allegedly devoted to upholding the sacred bloodline of Jesus and Mary Magdalene.

However, in the case of the "Priory" (as we will boldly call that intriguing organization for short), although facts may be hard to come by, they lead into a world that is considerably stranger than even Mr. Brown's fiction.

The Priory of Sion[1] takes center stage in *The Da Vinci Code* as the underground order whose astounding secrets are threatened by powerful enemies and which the heroic Robert Langdon and Sophie Neveu must prevent from falling into the wrong hands. Despite the acclaim, astonishment, and downright horror—depending on one's point of view—which greeted these secrets worldwide, basically Brown's thriller merely revivifies an old controversy. In fact, everything about the shadowy Priory of Sion—even its very existence—has been hotly debated in the English-speaking world since the early 1980s, and in its homeland of France for at least a decade before that.

In the novel, the Priory is presented in the guise by which it has become best known (at least in Britain and the United States), as a centuries-old secret society that exists to preserve and protect certain potentially explosive facts and which has exerted a behind-the-scenes influence on European history for centuries and continues to do so today. Readers and seekers new to the subject positively salivate over Brown's description of the Priory as "a modern goddess worship society, keepers of the Grail, and guardians of ancient documents."[2] What on earth can pagan goddesses have to do with the quintessentially Christian Holy Grail? What possible documents could prove such a connection? The allure is irresistible.

The major secret the Priory is allegedly sworn to protect is the existence of a bloodline—a family descended from no less than Jesus Christ himself and his *wife,* Mary Magdalene. Of course, the very existence of such a family would—if it could be proven—undermine the foundations of Christianity. To believers Jesus was God incarnate, a lifelong celibate who had neither need of nor desire for an intimate relationship (certainly not with a woman believed to have been a prostitute). Because of its explosive potential, the secret has been kept away from prying eyes by the Priory of Sion, for the Church would stop at nothing to remove this threat to its power base and its age-old stranglehold over its flock.

In Brown's book, the Priory has three main, interrelated duties: to protect the sacred bloodline of Jesus, to safeguard the tomb of Mary Magdalene, and to preserve documents that prove the true story of Jesus and his lineage.

Brown goes further and makes the Priory a repository of another strand of forbidden knowledge: the importance and power of the sacred feminine as embodied in ancient pagan goddess worship, linked to the concept of sacred sexuality—akin to today's Eastern Tantric rituals. As *The Da Vinci Code* includes sex rites in the Priory's ceremonies, the reader is left reeling: how could Jesus Christ, embodiment of divine chastity, possibly be linked to *sex,* not only as a personal act of passion and emotional commitment but also as a religious *sacrament,* equal in holiness to baptism and the Mass?

All of these challenging and, to many people, completely alien ideas have contributed to elevating an airport paperback to the status of revelatory history, almost of theology—particularly in the United States. Astonishingly, reading a thriller has now become a personal religious experience, the sort of epiphany one is supposed to receive only at the hands of the Church or the clergy.

The key locations of the novel—the Louvre Museum and the church of St.-Sulpice in Paris, and Scotland's Rosslyn Chapel—have been swamped with tourists, mainly from America: indeed, the Louvre has seen a 50 percent increase in visitor numbers, while the exasperated officials at St.-Sulpice have posted a notice at the entrance declaring that absolutely *no* secrets are to be found within. Internet forums dedicated to discussing *The Da Vinci Code*'s central contentions have mushroomed—Yale University has even created an online course on the subject. Brown's book has generated a whole industry of "unauthorized guides," such as Dan Burstein's *Secrets of the Code* and Simon Cox's *Cracking the Da Vinci Code,* which attempt to explore, amplify, or discredit the underlying concepts. At the time of this writing, in summer 2005, at least a dozen have been published.

As all this is unheard of for any new book, let alone a "mere" thriller, it has taken the publishing world completely by surprise. Even Brown himself seems astonished at the unique phenomenon he has unwittingly spawned.

And witness the astonishing reaction of the Church itself: in March 2005 Cardinal Tarcisio Bertone, Archbishop of Genoa—formerly a leading contender for the papacy—announced that he has taken it upon himself to provide the Church's opposition to Brown's book, leading a campaign to refute its "fables."

Behind the Sensation

With or without his intention, Dan Brown has succeeded in bringing to a whole new audience a number of important issues, which, while familiar to specialist researchers, are seldom discussed at a more popular level. These include the origins of Christian dogma, particularly the extent to which it was invented by the Church for political, rather than spiritual, ends; how equally valid but "heretical" alternative interpretations of Christianity were ruthlessly suppressed and evidence that challenged the established dogma was covered up by the Church; alternative views of the nature of Jesus—in particular that he was a mortal man who married and fathered children; the suppression of the sacred feminine—universally accepted before the advent of the patriarchal religions of Judaism and Christianity; and the sacramental nature of sex.

While Brown used these ideas as background, skillfully weaving them into the narrative of his fast-paced adventure, they have grabbed the attention—and imaginations—of millions of readers round the globe. Enthused and astonished by his revelations, they, too, now have a quest: to discover for themselves just how true those concepts really are. Suddenly the world is brimming with keen-eyed historical detectives who will no longer tolerate ecclesiastical conspiracies, cover-ups, or even old-fashioned clerical arrogance, smugness, and condescension. And whatever else *The Da Vinci Code* inspires, surely that can never be a bad thing.

Brown drew his ideas from several sources, but one of his two main inspirations was *The Holy Blood and the Holy Grail* (*Holy Blood, Holy Grail* in the United States)—a controversial international best seller in its own right, having remained in print for nearly a quarter of a century—written by Michael Baigent, Richard Leigh, and Henry Lincoln in 1982. Brown's other major source was our own *The Templar Revelation: Secret Guardians of the True Identity of Christ,* published in 1997. These titles, together with other sources,[3] appear on the bookshelves of *The Da Vinci Code*'s villain Sir Leigh Teabing—the name is so odd because it comes from those of two authors of *The Holy Blood and the Holy Grail,* one as an anagram.

The distinctive common ground between *The Holy Blood and the Holy Grail* and *The Templar Revelation* is the great genius of the Italian Renaissance Leonardo da Vinci (1452–1519)—incidentally, he should be known as Leonardo and not da Vinci (although common usage has now made it inevitable that even we will succumb from time to time). Allegedly he was the Priory of Sion's Grand Master for the last nine years of his life, a claim largely accepted by Baigent, Leigh, and Lincoln.

Brown drew from *The Holy Blood and the Holy Grail* the core concept of the existence and survival of the bloodline of Jesus and Mary Magdalene and its protection by the Priory (prompting Baigent and Leigh to initiate legal action against the publishers of *The Da Vinci Code,* ongoing as we write). Brown blended the bloodline concept with ideas and discoveries sourced from *The Templar Revelation.* In particular, he drew the key notion of secret information "encoded" into the symbolism of Leonardo's paintings, such as *The Last Supper* and *The Virgin of the Rocks,* from our first chapter, "The Secret Code of Leonardo da Vinci."

The importance of sacred sexuality and reverence for the Feminine along with the essentially *pagan* background of Jesus' teaching are also central features of our book. They are absent from *The Holy Blood and the Holy Grail* but actually fit rather awkwardly with some of its central themes, based as they are on the idea that Jesus' authority came from his status as the legitimate King of Israel and that he was primarily a political figure who never intended to start a new religion.

Finally, Brown's book reveals that the physical secret guarded by the Priory of Sion—literally its Holy Grail—is the actual body of Mary Magdalene. However, while we muse about this in *The Templar Revelation,* in the absence of hard evidence it is impossible to take the notion any further.

"Fact"?

However, while Brown's blockbuster has undoubtedly presented many provocative and exciting ideas to the startled gaze of the world's readers, many of those who have spent decades researching these interrelated subjects are often somewhat taken aback by the misconceptions he perpetuates, especially where the Priory of Sion is concerned (although in fairness all he ever intended to do was write a work of fiction).

Brown's portrayal of the purpose and history of the Priory of Sion, if not its rituals, is one that will be familiar to readers of *The Holy Blood and the Holy Grail* and its 1986 sequel, *The Messianic Legacy* (which explored some of the religious implications and the modern-day activities of the Priory in greater detail). But disconcertingly, the fact is that most of the historical material about the Priory on which those books are based is hardly objective—it ultimately derives from the Priory itself.

The major source of information on the Priory of Sion is a series of documents that were lodged in France's national library, the Bibliothèque Nationale in Paris, in the 1960s and have become known collectively as the "Dossiers Secrets" (Secret Files). Building up the story piece by piece, they clearly originated with the Priory (although it has always maintained a discreet distance from the Dossiers, finally dissociating itself from them completely—as we will see). According to the Dossiers Secrets, the Priory of Sion was founded nearly a thousand years ago, at the time of the Crusades, enjoying an unbroken existence ever since and being presided over by some of the greatest names in history.

Baigent, Leigh, and Lincoln—through their own research into the claims made in the Dossiers Secrets—largely accepted this story, and although *The Da Vinci Code* is fiction, Dan Brown has compounded the acceptance by making this bald statement up front, on a preface page headed "Fact":

> The Priory of Sion—a European secret society founded in 1099—is a real organization. In 1975 Paris's Bibliothèque Nationale discovered parchments known as *Les Dossiers Secrets,* identifying numerous members of the Priory of Sion, including Sir Isaac Newton, Botticelli, Victor Hugo, and Leonardo da Vinci.

However, even this short paragraph contains some startling errors. In "*fact,*" far from being romantic old parchments, many of the Dossiers Secrets are actually typewritten! The Bibliothèque Nationale did not "discover" them: the documents were deposited there by their creators, to be found later by researchers—and even then they were more or less directed to them. And this happened in the 1960s, not 1975.

This collection of documents is indeed remarkable, if only for the fact that it has inspired two of the most widely read and hugely controversial books of recent years, *The Holy Blood and the Holy Grail* and *The Da Vinci Code.* And yet, superficially at least, there is a good case that the Dossiers Secrets are an elaborate fabrication—in other words, *that the Priory of Sion is a hoax.* But, as we will see, nothing is certain about that tricky organization, which still has the power to surprise or even shock.

A Heated Debate

Opinion has split into two camps: those who accept the history and purpose of the Priory of Sion as told in the Dossiers Secrets (and elaborated in *The Holy Blood and the Holy Grail*) and those who dismiss the whole thing as a charade. For the latter camp, the Priory has no real substance apart from a handful of shady individuals who actually perpetrated the hoax, and it certainly had no existence whatsoever before the modern era.

However, while the skeptics do undoubtedly have the weight of evidence on their side, in our view it is a serious mistake to dismiss the Priory for that reason alone—at least until certain major questions have been answered. First and most obvious is simply why the perpetrators expended so much effort on their hoax. For make no mistake, if it is a hoax, the Priory of Sion is as intricate a hoax as any in history, and if only for that reason is worthy of further scrutiny. In fact, it was this central paradox that inspired us to continue our research into the Priory after the publication of *The Templar Revelation.*

Of course, even if two or three people came together and decided to call themselves the Priory of Sion for their own amusement, it "exists." Indeed, perhaps becoming a victim of its own success, the organization has in just this way spawned many imitations—"Priories of Sion" that are incontestably the products of one or two individuals with nothing better to do. As the (official) Priory's general secretary, Gino Sandri, said in 2003, "The assertion that the Priory of Sion doesn't exist frankly amuses me as, to our knowledge, one can count at least eleven around the world."[4]

The real question is whether the Priory is *important.* Does it really possess age-old secrets that would, if revealed, fundamentally change our view of Christianity and even our basic concept of its founder? And does the Priory have any real influence in the world today—as it claims?

There are other, less important questions, such as the extent of its membership. (Not that a society has to be particularly large to wield considerable influence—even a handful of people can be mighty powerful, providing they are in the right place at the right time.) However, our extensive research has led us to believe that the Priory of Sion *should* be taken seriously—despite all the controversy and doubts. Our own experience makes us go even further: we now realize that it would be a grave mistake to underestimate the Priory's very real power and influence. But why? What are the arguments for a real and active Priory of Sion?

The Popular Version

Focusing first on the "pro-Priory" camp: the most widely known version of the Priory's history and purpose is given in *The Holy Blood and the Holy Grail,* which can be summarized as follows:

Jesus and Mary Magdalene were man and wife, and had children.

After the Crucifixion, Mary and the children fled to France, where their descendants took root. Eventually they married into a dynasty of Frankish kings, the now-legendary Merovingians, who established their rule over parts of what is today France, Germany, Belgium, and the Netherlands between the sixth and eighth centuries. However, they were betrayed and usurped by a new dynasty, the Carolingians—with the support of the Roman Church, which knew the secret of the Merovingians' origins and feared what would happen to its carefully crafted doctrines if the existence of Jesus' descendants, with all that implied, were to become known. The key event in this usurpation was the murder of King Dagobert II in 679—although he was not the last Merovingian king, as is frequently assumed.

However, according to Priory sources, Dagobert's infant son, Sigebert, believed by history to have perished soon after his father, survived the overthrow of the Merovingians. He was hidden in the Languedoc region in the south of France—specifically in what is today the legendary village of Rennes-le-Château, close to the foothills of the Pyrenees. He and his descendants were protected by those who knew the secret of his family's origins, a group that eventually became formalized as the Order of Sion, a secret organization formed at the end of the eleventh century to advance the bloodline's interests. The Order of Sion was founded in Jerusalem by one of the leaders of the First Crusade, Godefroy de Bouillon (Godfrey of Bouillon)—allegedly one of Dagobert's descendants.

The popular version, as largely retold in *The Da Vinci Code,* goes on: The Order of Sion was in turn behind the creation of the fabled Knights Templar, the order of "warrior monks" who dominated the Holy Land and Europe for nearly two hundred years following their foundation in (or around) 1118. However, in 1188 there was some kind of schism between the two orders and they went their separate ways.

The Priory of Sion—as it eventually became—outlived the demise of the Templars in 1307, surviving through the centuries to the present day, presided over by a succession of Grand Masters that included some of the most illustrious names in European history (mingled with some rather more obscure personalities), such as the British Sir Isaac Newton, Robert Fludd, and Robert Boyle, and the Italians Botticelli and Leonardo da Vinci. In more recent times some rather surprising personalities from the world of literature and the arts have purportedly presided over the Priory: Victor Hugo, Claude Debussy, and Jean Cocteau. These nineteenth- and twentieth-century Grand Masters were all French. The Priory of Sion claims to have been the power behind many of the most important movements in European esotericism, such as the Rosicrucians, and further back even to have been the guiding hand behind figures such as Joan of Arc and Nostradamus. And even today it pursues its aim of restoring the "sacred bloodline" of the Merovingians to power in France—indeed, in Europe.

That is the reconstruction according to the authors of *The Holy Blood and the Holy Grail.* The Dossiers Secrets acknowledge that the purpose of the Priory is to protect Dagobert II's bloodline, but this is because, they say, it represents the legitimate royal family of France. The Priory's ultimate aim is to restore the Merovingians to the French throne (which is nothing if not ambitious). The added significance of the Merovingian dynasty—that it was itself descended from Jesus' children—is *not* found in the Dossiers Secrets but was the original hypothesis of Baigent, Leigh, and Lincoln. (However, the Dossiers Secrets do claim that the Merovingians were descended from the House of David.)

Many enthusiastic followers of Baigent, Leigh, and Lincoln's books (Dan Brown included) seem to have no idea that not only has the Priory *never* made the claim of descent from Jesus but has explicitly disavowed that hypothesis, as we will see.

The Case for a Hoax

The case for the Priory being a hoax pure and simple is straightforward. First, far from its having a pedigree stretching back nearly a thousand years, there is no documentary evidence whatsoever that it existed before 1956! And no historians or researchers specializing in the occult or secret societies had ever heard of the Priory of Sion before it became a topic of discussion in the 1970s. While this lack of hard evidence does not necessarily prove that the Priory did not exist in the past—after all, the most successful secret society would remain totally unknown to outsiders—surely it would have left *some* trace of its continuing presence.

In its defense, the Priory claims to have operated through "fronts"—other societies and groups, such as the secretive seventeenth-century

Catholic cabal the Company of the Holy Sacrament (Compagnie du Saint-Sacrement)—which *are* known to history. But there is no independent corroboration of this claim: we simply have to take their word for it.

Second, there are undeniable mistakes in the historical scenario outlined in the Dossiers Secrets that reveal many of its key claims to be false. Although we will examine them later, briefly the fatal flaws all relate to what is supposed to be the Priory's very reason for existing—the survival of the Merovingian dynasty. Very early in our research we concluded that there was something decidedly suspicious about the whole Merovingian business. This was partly because of the problems with the historical material in the Dossiers but also because of some glaring logical problems with the "bloodline" scenario: it is simply impossible to prove beyond reasonable doubt that any person currently alive is the direct descendant of Dagobert II—still less of Jesus himself!—and in any case simple mathematics shows that there would be millions of members of the "sacred bloodline" around today, an exponential dilution of both blood and sacredness that would render it considerably less than special.

Then there are the serious questions about the person most associated with the Priory—certainly its public face—in its modern-day incarnation: the enigmatic Pierre Plantard (also known somewhat grandiloquently as Pierre Plantard de Saint-Clair, among other aliases he adopted with great facility during his long career).

Plantard was named as one of the Priory's officers on its official debut in 1956 and continued to be its public face from the 1960s to the end of the 1980s. At the time of the publication of *The Holy Blood and the Holy Grail,* for which he supplied information, he was the Priory's Grand Master. Going further, the Dossiers Secrets suggested—and Plantard later explicitly claimed—that he was, in fact, the modern representative and personification of the bloodline, the direct descendant of Dagobert II. Of course, the implications were intended to be impressive, not to say sensational. If the Merovingians were indeed the rightful French royal family, then Plantard was the true, if uncrowned, King of France. And if the central hypothesis of *The Holy Blood and the Holy Grail* is correct, then Plantard was also the direct descendant of Jesus.

Like the Priory itself, Plantard inspires extreme views and equally extreme passions. To some, he was a distinguished initiate who possessed some of the greatest secrets of all time, *the* man who literally embodied the long-obscured truth about Christianity. To others, however, he will always be simply a cheap—and outrageous—confidence trickster.[5]

On the one hand, Baigent, Leigh, and Lincoln were clearly impressed, writing of their first meeting with him in 1979: "M. Plantard turned out to be a dignified, courteous man of discreetly aristocratic bearing, unostentatious in appearance with a gracious, volatile but soft-spoken manner. He displayed enormous erudition and impressive nimbleness of mind—a gift for dry, witty, mischievous but not in any way barbed repartee. . . . For all his modest, unassertive manner, he exercised an imposing authority over his companions."[6] And the French writer Gérard de Sède—who will play a significant part in this story—said of Plantard: "[He is] tall, thin, he eats little, neither drinks nor smokes and when he is our guest never has the first course [clearly a revealing factor to a Frenchman]. There is in him at the same time the scholar, the poet, and a slightly diabolical ironist."[7]

On the other hand, Plantard's detractors have accused him of everything up to and including being a Nazi sympathizer and a pedophile. One recent commentator writes, "It is often hard in the case of Plantard to find the line between what is known and what is a good story."[8]

Plantard, who died in 2000 at the age of eighty, was at best a shadowy figure, at worst an obviously dubious character. Secretive, elusive, yet charming, he admittedly more than matches the ideal profile of a con man—or, it must be said, an intelligence officer: the skills needed by both are not dissimilar. He was certainly involved in some suspicious ventures, including shady financial dealings. But most damning of all is the alleged fact that, some seven years before his death, Plantard admitted under oath that he had invented the whole thing.[9]

The leading skeptic and debunker of both the Priory in general and Plantard in particular is the British researcher Paul Smith, who has been hot on the trail for more than a decade.[10] Over the years Smith has done a superb job of doggedly unearthing and presenting original documents relating to the Priory and Plantard. (His particular triumph was getting the file on the latter from the Paris Prefecture of Police.) Undoubtedly, given the strident tone he routinely adopts when denouncing Plantard,

Smith is an anti–Priory/Plantard zealot. But most important, his argument that the whole Priory affair was Plantard's scam fails to answer certain crucial questions, as we will see.

So the absence of any independent documentary evidence for the Priory's existence before the 1950s, taken together with the problems about its historical claims, may appear to give the skeptics the upper hand, but nothing about the Priory is ever clear-cut.

Murkier and Murkier

For many people, the evidence that the Priory has lied—ever, on any subject—automatically means that it can be dismissed out of hand. But this attitude ignores some major aspects of the conundrum.

The Priory of Sion was not the sole invention of Pierre Plantard, nor was he its one and only member. Even if it was all a fraud, he had coconspirators. He never worked alone: when the Priory made its first appearance in official records in 1956, there were at least three others involved. Plantard's most famous collaborator, from the early 1960s until his death in 1985, was Philippe, Marquis de Chérisey. And the Priory has survived Plantard: it continues to operate under its general secretary, Gino Sandri, who first met Plantard in the early 1970s and has been involved with the Priory since 1977. Any theory that seeks to explain the Priory away as a hoax of Plantard's also has to account for the involvement of these people—and many others.

Plantard and his companions maintained the deception for more than thirty years, with considerable effort. Yet nobody, not even Paul Smith, has been able to offer a satisfactory reason for such a tenacious and prolonged scam. The most obvious motive—money—can be discounted. Not only is there no evidence that Plantard made anything but modest sums from the affair, but there are occasions on which he *could* have capitalized on it but signally made no attempt to do so. If he was solely a con man, why didn't he just forget it and move on to something much more lucrative?

In fact, it would have been only too easy to turn the Priory of Sion into a moneymaking machine. The world of noble and chivalric orders (which the Priory claims to be, albeit a secret one) is plagued by fraud and deceptions. There are numerous organizations, either new inventions or alleged revivals of defunct historical orders, with no legitimate basis whatsoever. These self-styled orders have been created either by individuals with a *folie de grandeur,* for whom this is the only way to achieve status, or as means of taking money off the unwary—and they exist aplenty—who will pay handsomely for entry into such orders, to use grandiose titles and ranks and wear the robes and insignia (all at a price, of course). Provided the order has the right cachet to attract members (or rather subscribers), it can mean relatively easy pickings: in some countries, such as Italy and (with certain qualifications) France, which no longer recognize royal or noble prerogatives, charging people for admission to an order claiming a spurious pedigree is not even illegal.

Yet the Priory can offer more than this. It is considerably more than merely a neochivalric order with fancy-sounding ranks and grades: it has the added advantage of initiating its members into an order that, as many millions of people around the world now believe, will—eventually—let them in on some of the greatest secrets of all time. To many it seems irresistible, and is the most obvious motive for creating such an elaborate hoax (after all, it would hardly be the first time such a thing has happened). And yet there has never been the slightest suggestion that anybody has been ripped off in this way, or that the Priory has solicited membership for a fee—and there are many ready to pounce should such an allegation even be whispered. Few self-styled orders have been in such a perfect position to exploit gullible wonder seekers as the Priory was after the success of *The Holy Blood and the Holy Grail*—yet Plantard not only failed to do so but actually backed off as more and more interest in the society was generated.

Even two skeptical British writers, Bill Putnam and John Edwin Wood, while discounting Plantard and de Chérisey's claims, pronounce themselves perplexed on the *point* of it all: "The amount of effort that the . . . two expended in inventing the puzzles, the genealogies and the fake history is immense . . . [but] financial gain does not appear to have been their motive."[11] Others have suggested that it was some kind of elaborate practical joke; if so, we're still waiting for the punch line.

Divine Comedy

In fact, perhaps there will never be a punch line. An increasingly popular suggestion of recent years is that the whole Priory of Sion affair was not just an elaborate practical joke but a joke as surrealist performance art in which there is no tagline—literally art for art's sake (a kind of parallel to the concept of crop circle hoaxes).

An American Priory of Sion researcher, the anthropologist Dr. Steven Mizrach, has even identified the French surrealist tradition that flourished in the 1960s known as Oulipo, in which "hoaxes" involving complex codes and cryptograms, hidden symbolism in paintings and literature, and ingenious wordplay would be devised as *pure art,* then let loose upon an unsuspecting public to see how it would react. (One of the points of the exercise was never to reveal it was essentially just a joke.) According to Mizrach, Jean-Pierre Deloux, Plantard's journalist associate in the 1970s and '80s, belonged to a branch called Oupolipo, which used the formula of detective novels in its artistic ruses.[12]

Despite being one of the most satisfying explanations of the whole affair—since it accounts for the hoaxers' otherwise inexplicable failure to exploit their creation—like all theories, this one fails to explain everything, especially Pierre Plantard's *political* activities in the 1940s and '50s, in which he embroiled the Priory of Sion and its forerunners. But although surrealism was by no means Plantard's style, it was very much that of his "partner in crime" in the 1960s, Philippe de Chérisey, an actor and writer who had worked with one of France's great surrealist humorists, the "French Goon" Francis Blanche.

However, the two apparently opposite explanations (of serious intent and a surrealist hoax) are not actually mutually exclusive. If, as we increasingly believe, the Priory was a front and the Dossiers Secrets an exercise in *misinformation*—we will develop this more fully later—then who better to employ on it than an "oulipist"? And although the popular image of occultists is of granite-faced fanatics and humorless cranks engaged in weighty (if pointless) rituals, in fact humor has always had pride of place in their extraordinary activities.

The great historian of Renaissance esotericism Dame Frances Yates, in her study of the origins of early-seventeenth-century Rosicrucianism, *The Rosicrucian Enlightenment,* discusses their use of humor. Johann Valentin Andreae, regarded by many as the best candidate for the author of the famous Rosicrucian Manifestos, described his own mystical writings as a *ludibrium*—a kind of theatrical jest. But Yates identifies an underlying serious intent: "This may not be, with him, always a term of contempt. In fact if one examines the passages in Andreae's writings about the RC [Rosicrucian] brothers one finds that, although a frequent way of denigrating them is to refer to them as mere players, comedians, frivolous and foolish people, yet at other times he highly praises players, plays, and dramatic art generally, as socially and morally valuable."[13] She also notes: "It is Andreae's strong interest in the drama which helps to explain the *ludibrium* of Christian Rosencreutz and his Fraternity as, not a hoax, but a dramatic representation of a profoundly interesting religious and intellectual movement."[14] And Dr. Christopher McIntosh agrees, writing: "The Rosicrucians embodied [their] vision in a brilliantly created mythology with a strong element of playfulness."[15]

The concept of such "divine comedy," treating very serious matters with a seeming lightheartedness, is found in other aspects of the occult. In 1616 the renowned esotericist Michael Maier entitled a major treatise *Lusus serius*—"Serious Game"—and the idea continues to be expressed today in the form of "chaos magic."

And of course da Vinci, who Yates believes prefigured distinctly Rosicrucian qualities, embodied the occultists' belief in the importance of "divine comedy"—in his paintings and in his many hoaxes, jokes, and illusions, which so fascinated those who met him. But few could doubt that under the gaiety and lightness of touch, Leonardo da Vinci was utterly, even awesomely, *serious.*

Inventing Sion

The favored explanation of most advocates of the "hoax pure and simple" theory is that Plantard was a mythomaniac who actually believed his own fantasies about being the rightful King of France. (Presumably the reason for this explanation is the complete absence of any evidence that Plantard made money out of his promotion of the Priory.) In other words, Plantard was basically delusional, either really believing in his royal rights or with a grip on reality so slender that he believed he could fool France into giving him its crown.

However, there is no denying that the Dossiers Secrets, as Putnam and Wood acknowledge, were put together with great effort and, we emphasize, with considerable historical—and psychological—skill. While examining the Priory's historical claims, time and again we would reach the point of dismissing the entire thing as a hoax—usually when turning up another blatant falsehood—then some obscure piece of information would surface, making a connection that would cause us to think again.

An enormous amount of effort has been put into creating the story told in the Dossiers Secrets, composed of truths, half-truths, and lies, woven together to make an enticing whole. Some elements of the story can be proven to be wrong—either because of a genuine mistake or because they have been distorted, "spun," or even invented. But despite what the Priory's detractors say, not all of it is invention or distortion.

The whole has been put together *thematically* rather than logically, and it is the way the key themes emerge and recur during research that impresses most. To take one example (others will follow throughout): the list of purported Grand Masters in the Dossiers Secrets contains the name of the celebrated René d'Anjou—Good King René—one of the great patrons of the early Renaissance. His presence on the roll of Grand Masters added yet another major historical figure who would impress readers with the importance and seriousness of the Priory. However, Baigent, Leigh, and Lincoln discovered that René was particularly fascinated with the theme of Arcadia, and, as we ourselves found, he also had a passionate interest in the legends of Mary Magdalene's life in southern France, for example ordering excavations of key sites in an attempt to find her tomb.[16]

However, the Dossiers list as René's successor his rather less well-known daughter, Iolande de Bar. She married one of René's knights, Ferri, the lord of the important pilgrimage center of Sion-Vaudémont in Lorraine, where she spent most of the rest of her life. The mountain of the tellingly named Sion-Vaudémont has been deemed sacred since pre-Christian times, originally in honor of the goddess Rosemerta but by Iolande de Bar's day dedicated to Our Lady of Sion, a cult centering on her votive statue, to which the Dukes of Lorraine had paid homage since at least the early Middle Ages. There was also the Abbey of Notre-Dame de Sion, to which was attached the chivalric order called the Knights or Brotherhood of Sion founded by Ferri's grandfather in

December 1396.[17] (According to Baigent, Leigh, and Lincoln, these knights were connected with the Abbey of Notre-Dame de Mont Sion in Jerusalem that the Priory of Sion claims as its birthplace some two hundred years earlier, but we have been unable to verify this.)

Is this the elusive evidence for the Priory of Sion as a tangible, historical organization? Of course, it makes perfect sense that a knightly order would have been attached to this important abbey (similar orders were fashionable at that time) and that it would bear the name of the place where it was founded. On that basis there is nothing particularly surprising about the existence of the fourteenth-century Knights of Sion, and no specific evidence to connect them with today's Priory of Sion or any of the organizations that it claims as an ancestor.

But the significant thing is that this connection is not spelled out in the Dossiers Secrets: Iolande de Bar's name simply appears on the list of Grand Masters, prompting researchers to delve further into information about her, thereby discovering a knightly order of Sion. Either the connection is genuine or this trail has been laid with consummate skill more or less to compel researchers to find the connection for themselves, making it all the more convincing for that reason. (The third possibility, pure coincidence, might work for one particular connection, but there are so many other examples that we can disregard it as an explanation.)

The trail of connections continues. . . . Sion-Vaudémont's status as a pilgrimage center suffered as a result of the French Revolution, but in the 1830s three brothers—all Catholic priests—Léopold, François, and Quirin Baillard, made it their life's work to restore it, along with its "twin," Mont Sainte-Odile in Alsace, about sixty miles away, as a sacred center.[18] This they did with great skill and success, raising money from as far away as the United States to reestablish the monastery on Sion-Vaudémont. Curiously, the three brothers then became followers of the controversial mystic Eugène Vintras (1807–1875), who founded a sect called the Church of Carmel, in which men and women were given equal status and which incorporated sexual practices into its rituals. Unsurprisingly, he—and the Baillard brothers—were roundly condemned and excommunicated by the Pope (Léopold recanted on his deathbed and was reconciled with the Church). Thus Sion-Vaudémont in comparatively recent times became a center of heresy and sex rites.[19]

At the beginning of the twentieth century, this curious tale was used as the basis for a book by the great French novelist Maurice Barrès (although not particularly well known in Britain, he was one of France's most influential writers), *La colline inspirée* (*The Inspired Hill*, 1913). The novel opens with the expulsion of a religious fraternity, the Oblates of Sion, from the mountain. And oddly, Barres's story bears many striking similarities to the real mystery of Rennes-le-Château, with which the Priory of Sion claims to have been intimately associated. Barrès was also deeply involved in the occult revival that swept the Paris salons at the end of the nineteenth century.

When such a chain of connections happens once, it is clearly interesting—even suggestive—but not enough on which to base a conclusion. But when it happens repeatedly—following avenues of research that appear quite separate but end up with the same individuals, at the same key sites, and dealing with the same religious, esoteric, or artistic themes—it rapidly becomes impressive. Such chains of connections become downright dizzying after a while and naturally lead researchers to the view that something genuine lies behind it all—that the Priory really has had a hand in all these things, over the course of centuries, and now teasingly lays them out for researchers to follow. This is what happened in the case of Baigent, Leigh, and Lincoln—although they rejected certain claims made by the Dossiers Secrets and Pierre Plantard. But, of course, there is also the possibility the Dossiers Secrets were deliberately designed to create exactly this impression, weaving together otherwise unrelated occurrences that just happen to have something (such as the name Sion) in common and that reinforce one or another of the major themes of the Dossiers. Even so, if this explanation is correct, a huge amount of research, knowledge, and skill has been employed, arguing against the accusation that it was all just a simple money-spinning ploy. (Many of Plantard's detractors claim not only that he was the principal author of the hoax but also that he was of below-average intelligence: given the amount of work behind the Priory of Sion story, clearly both accusations can hardly be true.)

This is also an example of the *psychological* skill employed in creating the story told in the Dossiers Secrets. The creators have used other such tricks, particularly by incorporating themes and symbols that possess a potent emotional charge: in other words, archetypes. As Baigent, Leigh, and Lincoln write in *The Messianic Legacy:*

> Insofar as we, in our researches, have come to know the Prieuré, we have encountered an organisation which, in full consciousness of what it is doing—and, indeed, as a matter of calculated policy—activates, manipulates and exploits archetypes. Not only does it traffic in familiar and traditional archetypes—buried treasure, the lost king, the sacredness of a bloodline, a portentous secret transmitted through the centuries. It also, quite deliberately, uses itself as an archetype. It seeks to orchestrate and regulate outsiders' perceptions of itself as an archetypal cabal—if not, indeed, *the* archetypal cabal. Thus, while the nature and extent of its social, political and economic power may remain carefully veiled, its psychological influence can be both discernible and substantial. It can convey the impression of being what it wishes people to think it is, because it understands the dynamics whereby such impressions are conveyed. . . . We are dealing with an organisation of extraordinary psychological subtlety and sophistication.[20]

The Priory both tricks and teases. It leads researchers on, and when it decides the moment is right, for mysterious reasons of its own, easily sends them round in circles, no doubt laughing its collective hat off. No one can afford to believe everything it says, but—as experience has taught us personally, as we will see—it would often be a mistake to disbelieve it either. We have to treat *anything* and *everything* the Priory says with caution.

We also have to treat with caution a great many pronouncements about that peculiar secret society. Opinions on the Priory tend to be divided into stark black-and-white, positive-negative alternatives: either everything it claims is true, or it is all a heap of cheap lies. But of course real life isn't like that.

Experience in other fields shows that just because a group or organization has lied, exaggerated, or misrepresented information, it should not automatically be rejected as unimportant. (After all, the Blair government still presides over the United Kingdom.) To take an obvious example, a major part of the work of intelligence and security agencies, such as the CIA, involves the composition and dissemination of *misinformation*—official lies, in other words—but nobody would argue that if those lies were exposed, the CIA could and should be disregarded as an organization of no consequence, or the rest of its activities be always and forever considered insignificant. In fact, the more it takes it upon itself to lie, the more most people believe it *should* be taken seriously.

Telling untruths is not necessarily always judged to be a bad thing: it depends on why they are told (and, indeed, whose side one is on). Deception operations—official hoaxes—played a major part in winning the Second World War, diverting enemy resources and attention, and distracting attention from genuine operations. In dealing with the Priory of Sion, and the claims it has disseminated through either the Dossiers Secrets or other means, exactly the same methods should be employed as in analyzing the activities of intelligence agencies. The two have much in common.

One crucial point above all others is often overlooked when examining the Priory of Sion: no secret society—ancient or modern, whether a massive global organization or just a few coconspirators in France, and whether its intentions are serious or fraudulent—would reveal anything about itself in public *unless there was an advantage in doing so.* Therefore the test of anything it does choose to reveal—perhaps even more important than whether it is factually true—is *why it has been revealed.* Who was it aimed at—the general public or a specific group? And why does the Priory want that target audience to believe these things to be true? Until such questions have been answered, the solution to the mystery remains as elusive as the Holy Grail itself.

Bearing all these considerations in mind, we find ourselves in the no-man's-land between the two extreme views. On the one hand, there are those who uncritically accept all the Priory's claims, building their theories and hypotheses on its every pronouncement, no matter how contradictory or ridiculous; on the other, there are those who automatically sneer at anything and everything it says simply because the Priory seems to enjoy being contradictory and ridiculous on *some* occasions. However, the crucial point is that both sides ignore any evidence that fails to fit their preferred solution—the saying about babies and bathwater is most often true when applied to the Priory! But for us, neither camp offers a satisfactory solution to the riddle.

These are the purely logical reasons why we take the Priory of Sion more seriously than many (but, we stress, considerably less literally than many others). However, we have other, more practical reasons for this approach.

In some respects we speak from personal experience of the Priory. Individuals connected with it have supplied us with extremely arcane and unlikely information that, against all the odds, proved to be correct. Indeed, it is no exaggeration to say that, albeit indirectly, we owe our ten-year joint writing career to the Priory of Sion—hardly an insignificant matter in our lives! From our own contact with the organization, we know it is worth taking seriously. Whatever else it may or may not be, take it from us, it would be a grave error to dismiss the Priory as a straightforward hoax.

Meeting the Priory

It began in 1990, during our unfolding research into the Shroud of Turin, when we were contacted by an individual who only ever used the pseudonym Giovanni (Italian for John). We received several letters from this mystery man—initially kept in our "cranks" file but soon earnestly pored over as we became genuinely intrigued—culminating in a single meeting with him in London in March 1991.[21]

It was an exciting, if somewhat tense—not to say *in*tense—encounter. Probably in his mid- to late forties, Giovanni looked very similar to the British actor Tom Conti (the Greek café owner in the movie *Shirley Valentine*), with a mane of graying dark hair and slightly crumpled designer clothes. He spoke English fluently but with a marked Italian accent, and had a way of closely observing us without being too obvious, like a private eye or an intelligence officer. His eyes laughed before the rest of his face, constantly twinkling no matter how serious his words. Occasionally he would make a dramatic, expansive gesture with elegant hands unadorned by rings, but mostly his physical mannerisms were unexpectedly subdued—odd, one might think, for an Italian. Perhaps he had been expertly trained to discipline his body language.

Giovanni claimed to be an Italian member of the Priory of Sion, although of course we had no way of checking or verifying this. What we were able to verify independently was that he was familiar with Europe's esoteric "underworld." He identified certain individuals, in Britain and abroad, who he said were either fellow members of the Priory or members of related esoteric societies—and in some (but by no means all) cases we were intrigued to discover we could confirm this. So Giovanni's secret society "credentials" checked out—at least in that respect.

In particular Giovanni named two leading figures in British publishing, both already known to us. Presumably he chose them for that very reason: after all, it would be easier for us to corroborate his information about them. In one case we were able to confirm that the person concerned had—unexpectedly—an interest in esoteric matters that included active involvement in secret groups. In the other case, we uncovered a much stronger indication of membership of the Priory itself, also being impressed by his connections with the international world of high finance. (The Priory claims to be heavily involved with the global banking fraternity, but of course any halfway decent faux society would make such a claim.)

Disappointingly, we never discovered Giovanni's true identity. Although at one time we thought we had worked it out, this turned out to be a red herring—probably a deliberate setup. But he did claim to represent a schismatic faction within the Priory, intent on leaking certain information into the public arena. (And rather deflatingly, it seemed that we were not his first, or even second, choice: apparently he had attempted to bring his information to the attention of other Shroud of Turin researchers before us.) At the time we treated this as a bit of flim-flam employed deliberately to heighten the sense of the dramatic: indeed, virtually everything about our contact with Giovanni was highly theatrical, no doubt to draw us in—and, of course, to remain vivid in our memories. But we were amazed and excited to discover from information that emerged years later that he may well have been telling the truth.

Giovanni's ostensible reason for contacting us was, as we have mentioned, our research into the Turin Shroud, about which he claimed to have inside information as a Priory man. According to him, the Shroud was indeed a fake (as the 1988 carbon dating had famously demonstrated). But he claimed to know who the faker was: *no less than Leonardo da Vinci,* alleged by the Priory to be one of its Grand Masters. He also claimed to know *how* Leonardo had created the then still-mystifying image on the Shroud, through a process of what he called "alchemical imprinting"—in other words, a primitive form of photography. But perhaps most staggering of all was Giovanni's statement that Leonardo had used his own face for that of the man on the Shroud, the very image believed by devout millions over the centuries to be none other than Jesus Christ.

Giovanni presented these three dramatic pieces of information to us as clues in a work of historical detection, lines of research that we could and should either prove or disprove through our own efforts. (Later we realized this is the magical adept's traditional method of teaching, although it also has much in common with the training of intelligence officers.) As matters turned out, it was not a job for shirkers—nor, as we were to discover, for either the pious or the squeamish.

Da Vinci's Devilish Relic

Much to our own astonishment, we were able to provide evidence even for some of Giovanni's most apparently ridiculous claims. We presented the results of our detective work in our first book, *Turin Shroud—In Whose Image?* in 1994 (revised and updated in 2000 with the subtitle *How Leonardo da Vinci Fooled History*).

However, we were not the first to propose that Leonardo was the Shroud's master faker: others had already acknowledged that he fitted the profile of the hoaxer perfectly. It had to be someone capable of devising a method of creating the image that still refused to yield its secrets (the carbon dating told us the Shroud was a fake but nothing about how the image was imprinted). Yet to our amazement we were to discover a host of circumstantial evidence that put him squarely in the frame, being in the right place at the right time, having shady dealings with the Savoy family who owned the Shroud, and so on.

As for how the image was created, we were able to use a very basic photographic process—employing a camera obscura (the forerunner of the modern camera, with which Leonardo is known to have experimented) and easily obtained light-sensitive substances—to produce our very own "Shroud," bearing all the supposedly miraculous characteristics of the allegedly holy relic. At almost precisely the same time, the South African professor Nicholas Allen did exactly the same thing (in fact, employing an even simpler process than ours but also using a camera obscura).

Finally, only dyed-in-the-wool and desperate believers that the Shroud is genuinely that of Jesus—known as Shroudies—are unable to see the resemblance between the man on the Shroud and Leonardo. One of the most amusing acknowledgments came in 2001, during the filming of a television documentary on our theories for the National Geographic Channel (the award-winning *Leonardo: The Man Behind the Shroud?*).[22] For balance, the program makers interviewed several believers, including the Italian artist Luigi Mattei, who makes superb life-size sculptures based on the Shroud's image. Although a passionate believer in its authenticity, while demonstrating his artistic techniques before the camera, apropos of nothing, the artist offered the statement that he had always been struck by the similarity between Leonardo and the man on the Shroud. Of course, the resemblance between the two reinforces the first contention: that Leonardo was the genius responsible.

Along the way we also discovered that certain families who were involved in the "Great Holy Shroud scam" turned out to be the same dynasties that feature in *The Holy Blood and the Holy Grail* as being connected with the Priory of Sion.

All this was very odd. Although we had made the da Vinci connection before Giovanni arrived on the scene—in fact, it was why he contacted us—another tip-off he gave us also turned out to be correct. This suggested that the Priory (assuming Giovanni really was a member) did have access to "inside information" about Leonardo. Even then, we were well aware of the question marks that hung over the Priory's historical claims, but this seemed to confirm that they possessed *some* hidden or lost esoteric knowledge, some genuine secrets about heretical individuals of the past.

We were also aware of the view that the Priory comprised a mere handful of members who kept the thing going simply for their own amusement or as part of a wider concerted scam: but if so, where did Giovanni fit in? Perhaps he really belonged to some other society or esoteric group and had merely *pretended* to be an emissary of the Priory. But why? How could he benefit from such a subterfuge?

However, the second avenue of research prompted by Giovanni's cloak-and-dagger intervention was to turn out to be even more extraordinary.

Disciples of the "Other Christ"

At our single landmark meeting, Giovanni had largely confined himself to the subject of the Shroud of Turin. Although he made some gnomic statements about the Priory past and present, he always avoided answering our direct questions on the matter (as indeed should any self-respecting member of a secret society). But with his parting shot he brought up another subject, a most peculiar non sequitur at the time, in the form of a question: "Why are our Grand Masters always known as John? . . . This is no small point, but it is *the key.*"

We were to discover that that one little question contained a major hint about a secret that far eclipses Dan Brown's hypothesis in its potential to unsettle—even shock. Twelve years on, we can categorically state that our own research has revealed that Giovanni possessed information that opened the portal to a truly cataclysmic secret, one that certainly—and truly sensationally—presents a challenge like no other to the established Church. Indeed, to the very basis of the Christian religion.

According to the Dossiers Secrets, the Grand Masters of the Priory of Sion take the "official" name of Jean (French for John—Jeanne/Joan/Joanna if the Grand Master is female), in much the same way each Pope takes a new name on his election. Leonardo, for example, appears on their lists as Jean IX—John the Ninth. No explanation was forthcoming for this apparent elevation of the name John. No previous researchers have attempted to find out more about this tantalizing subject.

Our work on Leonardo and the Shroud had naturally inspired us to know more about what had motivated him to create the ultimate hoax (and one of the most successful in history). It was clear that the answer lay in his religious and spiritual beliefs, which are acknowledged to have been heretical. (Many people assume that, as the "first scientist," Leonardo must have been a nonbeliever, an atheist rather than a heretic, but in fact nothing could be further from the truth.)

It rapidly became clear—for reasons we explain in the first chapter of *The Templar Revelation*—that Leonardo was virtually obsessed with St. John the Baptist. Half of his surviving religious works of art include that rather intimidating New Testament figure—and we were to find that many of the remaining paintings and sketches include *symbolic* references to John even when he is not physically present in the composition. In other words, wherever possible, Leonardo included John the Baptist in his paintings, even if sometimes doing so meant employing some artistic license in the interpretation of the theme he was commissioned to paint: he simply added a reference to John via the clever use of veiled symbolism. Clearly, the Baptist was overwhelmingly important to Leonardo for some secret but very special reason.

The key symbol in what soon became apparent as his subtle subversion is what we call the "John gesture"—the right index finger pointing heavenward—seen most obviously in the last painting Leonardo produced, *St. John the Baptist.* But crucially, it is also made by characters in other paintings as a device to give John a physical presence in works in which Leonardo could not otherwise justify his inclusion.

The other striking, and decidedly heretical (to say the least), aspect of Leonardo's "Johannite" obsession was that he clearly regarded the Baptist as not merely important in the context of Jesus' life and mission. Discussing Leonardo's *Virgin of the Rocks,* which depicts the infant Jesus and John the Baptist, Ilse Hecht of the Art Institute of Chicago observes: "John is transformed from a bystander to a person equal to Christ, an innovation which reached the utmost limits of the spiritual content of the motif and could only be achieved by an artist like Leonardo who had only loose ties to the dogma of the Church."[23]

The notion of considering John, the supposed herald of Jesus, as somehow equal to Christ is astounding enough. But over a decade of research has led us to believe that Hecht actually understated the case. To Leonardo there was no equality about it: that deeply heretical and slyly audacious artist really believed John to be *superior* to Christ.

All this presented us with a major clue as to which John the Priory of Sion meant. So, too, did this apparent belief in John's superiority over Jesus. According to the Dossiers Secrets, the first Grand Master of the Priory of Sion, a Norman nobleman called Jean de Gisors, took the title Jean II. But this presented another conundrum. Why begin with John the *Second*—and in any case, who was John the First? The French historian Jean Markale summarizes the Priory's odd explanation that Jean de Gisors took this title because "the title Jean I was traditionally reserved for Christ."[24] But why on earth should Christ be honored by being called John?

Slowly a new and challenging picture began to emerge, although considerably more research was needed before the whirling kaleidoscope fragments finally settled into a comprehensible image. Dead center is the heretical movement known as Johannitism, which did indeed revere John the Baptist above Jesus, even regarding him as the "true Messiah" or "true *Christ.*" (The Greek *christos,* simply a translation of the Hebrew *Messia*—meaning Anointed One—carried a very different meaning from the one later imposed on it by Christian tradition. The holder of this divine mandate was expected to be and behave in ways that were radically different from modern Christian belief.)

As we soon discovered, the real relationship between John the Baptist and Jesus Christ also requires a bold and committed effort of will to comprehend after centuries of obfuscation, cover-up, and conspiracy. Far from being a lone voice crying in the wilderness, John had his own disciples: indeed, the evidence is that Jesus himself began as one of them. There is no question that some—perhaps a majority—of John's disciples regarded *him* as the Christ, and not all switched their allegiance to Jesus after John's execution by Herod Antipas. Neither is there any doubt that the Baptist's movement continued in rivalry to Jesus' even after the Crucifixion. In fact, heretical sects revering John the Baptist as Christ are recorded in the Middle East, as Dositheans (after one of their leaders, Dositheus), for a full *five centuries* after the foundation of Christianity. All this can be found in the New Testament itself and the chronicles of the early Church.

Unpalatable though it may be to many Christians, the fact is that John and Jesus were *rivals,* as were their respective followers. This goes a long way toward answering the question that the seeker after truth will ask sooner or later: why is St. Stephen, and not John the Baptist, Christianity's first martyr? Indeed, a few moments' thought will reveal that John is not really regarded as a Christian saint at all.

There is more: John's followers—the Johannites—did not die out in the Middle East. They actually survive to this day, as the world's only living Gnostic religion, a sect and people known as the Mandaeans, who call their priests Nasoreans. Until recently, their main home was the wetlands of southern Iraq and Iran, the scene of much persecution by Saddam Hussein. Although after the first Gulf War in 1991 many dispersed to other places around the world—Florida, Australia, the Netherlands, and even London—the main community still lives in Iraq, centered in the southern town of Nasiriyah (a name clearly derived from

Nasorean).[25] Now targeted by Islamic fundamentalists, the Mandaeans can also expect little help from the West, as they are not Christian either. They revere John the Baptist as their great prophet—and not only reject Jesus but utterly and vehemently despise him as the usurper of John's movement and his rightful leadership.[26]

Scholars are generally agreed that the Mandaeans are genuinely the descendants of the immediate followers of John the Baptist, forced east and south by persecutions first by Christians and then by Moslems. Although naturally much changed after nearly two millennia of wandering in the wilderness, they still retain a strong memory of their origins.

The Mandaeans may have been known to Europe only since the 1700s, but they are recorded in Arab writings—including the Koran, where they are called Sabians—in the intervening years, making it clear that they are the "Church of John," which disappeared from Western records in the late 500s. In fact, one Arab writer at the end of the eighth century specifically states that the Mandaeans are descended from the same Dositheans who were recorded as revering John the Baptist as Christ as late as the sixth century. And clearly the Mandaeans were once much more widespread, with communities throughout the Holy Land and Middle East until at least the time of the Crusades, after which a wave of Moslem persecution drove them south.

The evidence is overwhelming: there is no question that the "John movement"—those who regarded John the Baptist as the rightful Messiah—survived in the Middle East. The assumption is that it was eradicated in the West, or more accurately the Mediterranean world under Christian control, by the early Church. (Communities of John followers in Asia Minor are actually recorded in the Acts of the Apostles.) But if so, how could Leonardo—and others, as we found—have been aware of these beliefs in the second half of the fifteenth century, when the Arab world was largely closed to Europeans?

Intriguingly, Johannitism either reentered Europe during the Crusades, when communications with the Middle East reopened, or had survived, deep underground, as a secret heresy that used the Crusades as an opportunity to go in search of its roots. We concluded that Mandaeanism—or Johannitism—was the major secret of such groups as the Knights Templar.

There are more tantalizing clues: certain European esoteric traditions that have existed since at least the turn of the nineteenth century assert that the Templars did indeed derive their secret doctrines from an encounter with a sect termed the "Johannites of the East" or the "Church of John of the East." Although without supporting evidence, of course, mere traditions fail to *prove* anything, but when added to the evidence we uncovered about Crusader knights—including the Templars—encountering the Mandaeans and absorbing some of their beliefs, they are extraordinarily intriguing. And significantly, *the Priory of Sion is unashamedly linked to those very same traditions.* The French authority Jean-Pierre Bayard, in his *Guide to Secret Societies and Sects,* specifically describes the Priory as a "Johannite order."[27]

Of course, if the "secret" of the Priory is that it is Johannite, then clearly it is a very different animal from the secret society described in *The Holy Blood and the Holy Grail,* which argues that it exists to protect the descendants of Jesus Christ—John's great rival!

It was an almost heart-stopping moment when we realized the true significance of our own brush with the Priory. Giovanni's seemingly throwaway line about the Grand Masters always being called John had proved to be the key to something of such immense importance that without a flicker of hyperbole it can truly be said to challenge the very basis of the Christian religion.

The Schism

If the Priory is a modern, postwar hoax, how and why did Giovanni set us on a trail that proved so evidential? It could hardly be just coincidence. Clearly, Giovanni had been confident enough that, once on the trail, we would uncover hard evidence to corroborate his claims. And as we were not well-known researchers in those days, his belief in us could hardly have been based on our track record. The facts had to speak for themselves, and when we found them, they shouted loud and clear. The implication was that, as a member of the Priory, Giovanni already knew these things to be true. Therefore the Priory *did* have access to genuine historical "inside information." And therefore it couldn't be a modern hoax—could it?

Leaving aside queries about Giovanni's true identity or the organization he may have represented, the obvious question was: why did he choose us to reveal such sensitive and even sensational information? It had to be for the Priory's own benefit, not ours. Perhaps we were being used as the channel through which Leonardo's master hoax would finally be appreciated for what it was, and as a means to encourage people to ponder on the Johannite heresy—and its extraordinary implications. Perhaps. But was there anything about the whole business that would benefit the Priory more immediately?

One obvious reason was that these revelations would provide some independent corroboration of the Priory's historical existence. Generally, the historical reconstruction, based on the Dossiers Secrets and presented in *The Holy Blood and the Holy Grail* and *The Messianic Legacy*, had largely gone unchallenged; the controversy had mostly centered on the religious elements, particularly the putative relationship between Jesus and Mary Magdalene. However, by 1990 doubts were beginning to surface about the veracity of the Dossiers Secrets' historical claims. If the Priory could be proved to possess or have access to some inside information—something nobody on the outside had ever known—about one of those it claimed as Grand Master, perhaps it would help to reestablish some credibility.

At least that was how we reasoned at the time. However, we had no way of knowing then that there was a much more specific reason for Giovanni to have contacted us during the years 1990–91. The Priory was in turmoil.

Giovanni told us he was part of a schismatic faction—a "dissident" group—within the organization. Specifically, he said that it believed the current leadership was moving the organization away from its original raison d'être and beliefs. He complained about the interference of "politics"—presumably infighting. In fact, he said for political reasons the leadership was trying to "rewrite its history." Apparently it was a time of real danger: throughout his contact with us, he stressed he was taking grave personal risks by feeding us this information.

Not unnaturally, we took this with a large pinch of salt—as just some extra spice to jolly us along and a convenient explanation for his clandestine approach. (As we will see, the Priory has indeed used *fake* schisms as covers for changes of direction.) However, although we would not be aware of it for nearly ten years, in that at least he was telling the truth. There really had been a major schism.

In 1989, Pierre Plantard (returning as the Priory's Grand Master, having resigned five years earlier) had changed the plot entirely. In letters to members and in the pages of the Priory's internal bulletin, *Vaincre* (*Conquer*), he retracted the version of the Order's history in the Dossiers Secrets. (In fact, Plantard had always carefully avoided directly endorsing the Dossiers and, although few were convinced, retained just enough "plausible deniability" to get away with such an abrupt disavowal.) He replaced it with a far less interesting story, but in any case, after he admitted the original was a lie, who would believe anything he said?

Plantard now claimed that the Priory of Sion dated not from the eleventh century after all but from the eighteenth; it had no connection with the founding or subsequent history of the Knights Templar; the list of Grand Masters that appeared in the Dossiers Secrets was "false"—although he still maintained it was correct after 1766. Most significant of all, Plantard not only dissociated himself from the "Jesus bloodline" theory put forward in *The Holy Blood and the Holy Grail* but positively mocked it.[28] (We will examine the reasons behind this abrupt and bizarre change of mind more fully later.) The fact that Plantard had changed the "official" version of the Priory's origins and history in 1989 was not widely known until the end of the 1990s, when its letters and bulletins began to circulate among researchers. Even now, surprisingly few enthusiasts of *The Holy Blood and the Holy Grail* seem to be aware of it. Naturally, however, there are several extremely far-reaching implications of this shift.

First, if as many believe the whole thing was a hoax masterminded by Plantard, why abandon it just when it was beginning to pay off? After all, millions of readers around the world had accepted the claims in Baigent, Leigh, and Lincoln's two books—the historians' and genealogists' scorn hardly cut much ice with their most devoted fans. Although this was precisely the time to exploit the story for all it was worth, Plantard not only pulled back but also actively dissociated from it both himself and the society over which he claimed to preside.

Paul Smith has suggested that the 1989 makeover was part of a comeback bid by Plantard, but this makes no sense at all.[29] Plantard had never actually gone away, and although he had already sold his hoax to a huge worldwide audience, here he was apparently inventing a new, contradictory story that effectively outed the first version as a lie!

In any case, the new version was at first restricted to just a small audience, posing another perplexing question. If the Priory has no members (apart from Plantard's fellow plotters), to whom were these letters and their bulletin being circulated?

Finally, this astonishing volte-face provides a convincing explanation for Giovanni's sudden appearance in our lives. Plantard had instigated a new policy, replacing the "cover story"—including the list of Grand Masters—which had been carefully built up and maintained for some twenty-five years with something very different. If individual members disagreed with the change in policy, perhaps they attempted to undermine it by leaking information that supported the *original* cover story, kick-starting a new impetus. The most obvious way to do this was to appear to release a few more of the Priory's supposedly ancient secrets to handpicked independent researchers, in much the way Plantard had appealed to Baigent, Leigh, and Lincoln. (The pattern is basically the same: the authors of *The Holy Blood and the Holy Grail* were already pursuing their research when Plantard arrived on the scene and gave them, depending on one's point of view, information or misinformation that pointed them in a particular direction.) Our own Priory "mole" appeared to show that the organization *did* possess information about one of its historical Grand Masters—who appeared on the list Plantard now disowned.

But again there was the obvious question: how could a fictitious organization with no members suffer a schism?

A Shift in Perception

After *The Templar Revelation,* we changed—or rather clarified—our view of the Priory of Sion. Our experience suggested that its membership extended beyond the confines of Pierre Plantard and his immediate circle: there was not only Giovanni himself but also the two British men he had mentioned, whom we were able to corroborate as members—or at least as members of some similar esoteric society. But our being able to point to a handful of members did nothing to prove it was truly an ancient secret society or to answer the very real questions about some of its historical claims.

In *The Templar Revelation* we kept to the neutral ground between the Priory as a modern creation and an older organization, *some* of whose historical claims checked out. We speculated that perhaps there *had* been a historical secret society—not necessarily calling itself the Priory of Sion—and that the modern Priory had access to some of its archives. This scenario provided a neat answer, but unfortunately we had no way of telling whether it was correct.

However, the more we delved, the more we came to favor another conclusion, one that made more sense of the apparent contradictions. It occurred to us that the Priory of Sion as such *is* a modern invention but that it was created as a front for other societies that *are* known among politico-occult secret societies in Europe. We summarized this idea in the revised edition of *Turin Shroud—In Whose Image?*[30] and have elaborated on it on various platforms since.

Essentially, we changed our minds because we knew from our study of the sources of various esoteric ideas and traditions woven together in the Dossiers Secrets (details will be given later) that the Priory was connected with other secret societies already known to researchers—and that did date back, if not to the Crusades, then at least 300 years. This scenario was reinforced as we uncovered specific connections between those societies and individuals linked to Plantard and the Priory.

This evidence could point in one of two ways: either the Priory was behind those other societies (i.e., they were fronts for the Priory) or these societies were behind the Priory. In the mid-1990s, at the time of writing *The Templar Revelation,* we were inclined toward the first option, but further investigation made us realize that the latter was correct. Significantly, other researchers, independently and for quite different reasons, have been drawn to similar conclusions. We will explain how and why we reached this conclusion as the story unfolds.

International Treasure

Much of the Priory's lore—like that of many similar societies—gives pride of place to the Knights Templar, so we must be careful at the outset to separate the facts (such as they are) from the huge amount of highly embroidered fiction.

Many people today know about the various mysteries—real or imagined—surrounding the Knights Templar, mainly through their enduring appeal in popular culture. For example, they feature virtually without explanation in the 2004 movie *National Treasure,* in which they are portrayed as guardians of a great treasure and the progenitors of Freemasonry, but those are only two of the secrets with which they have been associated.

There are genuine mysteries and uncertainties about the Order of the Temple, which is hardly surprising given the secrecy with which it carefully shrouded itself over its two centuries of existence. Indeed, mystery envelops virtually everything about the Knights Templar, from their origins to their dramatic demise.

The Order was founded in the years following the First Crusade, which successfully captured Jerusalem and large parts of the Holy Land, although there is considerable uncertainty about the exact circumstances in which the Order began. The Templars' creation is usually dated to 1118, but the evidence suggests it was actually a year later that nine French knights, led by Hugues de Payens, the Templars' first Grand Master, took a vow to protect the pilgrimage routes in the Holy Land—a function widely regarded, on purely practical grounds, as a cover story.

The formal foundation of the Templars took place a decade later, in 1128, when—under the patronage of the incredibly powerful Bernard of Clairvaux, head of the Cistercian Order and the true power behind the papal throne—the Order received its own Cistercian-based Rule that was later approved by Pope Innocent II. It was then that they were granted their distinctive regalia and uniform—the white tunic, to which the red *croix pattée* was added later—and took their formal name, the Order of the Poor Fellow Soldiers of Christ and the Temple of Solomon (*Ordo Pauperum Commilitonum Christi Templique Salominici*), or simply Templars. (The title derives from the fact that Hugues and his companions were given quarters in the al-Aqsa mosque in Jerusalem, then believed—incorrectly—to be on the site of the Temple of Solomon.)

Quite literally, the Templars were warrior monks, taking the usual monastic vows of poverty, chastity, and obedience and living the religious life in every other way—except that they had special dispensation to fight and shed blood. And it was in the military aspect of their calling that they soon excelled, becoming the utterly terrifying special forces of their day.

The Order also became incredibly wealthy, as kings and nobles all over Europe stood in line to donate gifts of land and property. And its role and activities extended beyond the purely military: as rich pilgrims and noblemen gave them money for safekeeping, the Templars developed much of what became the modern international banking system. Warriors, influential ecclesiastics, prototype bankers, and diplomats, they held an importance in Europe and the Holy Land in the twelfth and thirteenth centuries that is impossible to overestimate; the Order was the most powerful institution after the Church itself, and seemingly untouchable. But pride, of which the Templars undoubtedly possessed a superabundance, was soon to come before an almighty fall.

As the result of a plot hatched by the King of France, Philippe IV ("the Fair"), the Templars' utter ruin came suddenly, brutally, and catastrophically. Local representatives throughout his kingdom received sealed orders to raid every Templar property without warning at dawn on Friday, October 13, 1307, arresting all the knights. Philippe claimed he had discovered that the Templars, the order that existed solely to protect and fight for Christendom, was in reality a hotbed of heresy and devil worship. The Knights were charged with blasphemous acts: denying Christ, spitting and trampling on the cross at their chapter meetings, as well as institutionalized homosexuality. It was said that they worshiped an idol called Baphomet, in the shape of a disembodied head. Eventually, after a lengthy trial, the Order was dissolved by Pope Clement V in 1312, and two years later the last Grand Master, Jacques de Molay, along with other leaders, after languishing in prison for seven years, was slowly roasted to death on the Île de la Cité, near Notre-Dame Cathedral in central Paris.

Although it has long been believed that the charges against them were trumped up and that Philippe was really only after their riches, the latest historical research indicates that—whatever the truth of the charges against the Templars—Philippe actually believed them. But even if money grabbing was his motive, he was signally unsuccessful. When the Pope closed down the Order, he commanded that its estates and property be given to its rival, the Knights Hospitaler (properly the Order of the Hospital of St. John of Jerusalem, today's Knights of Malta). And the Templars' great treasury in Paris, known as the Temple, was found to be largely empty when the King's men forced an entry, fueling theories—as hyped in *National Treasure*—that at least some Templars somehow knew about the impending raids and had spirited away their treasure. Most of these theories assume it was not simply of great material value but included sacred objects—perhaps the Ark of the Covenant, or the Holy Grail itself.

The final mystery concerns the fate of the Templars after the Order was disbanded. Did it continue underground to pursue its mysterious agenda? Or perhaps the Templars maintained a clandestine existence to avenge themselves on the two institutions—the French monarchy and the Church of Rome—which had so brutally ended their days of glory. Another now-famous theory is that Freemasonry emerged from the secret society established by the Templars.

(Despite the popular perception of the entire order being rounded up, tortured, and massacred, in fact only a handful of Templars—about 150—were executed or died under torture. The vast majority—over 90 percent, amounting to about 14,000 people, including 1,000 knights—went free. In the paradoxical way of medieval ecclesiastical justice, only those who maintained their innocence were tried and sentenced to either death or imprisonment, those who confessed to the charges being absolved of their sins and released. Outside France, most Templars were not even questioned, let alone tortured for confessions, and—as their vows were still binding—they were allowed to join other chivalric or monastic orders. In Spain and Portugal, the Order basically just changed its name and carried on as usual.)

In France today, new secret societies realize they stand no chance of being taken seriously unless they claim some intriguing link with the medieval Templars—usually imagined rather than real.

Inside French Minds

Essential to an understanding of the story of the Priory of Sion is the recognition that it is predominantly not Western, not even European, but resolutely and entirely *French.* Many British and American researchers have veered wildly from the mark by trying to judge facts and events by the criteria of their own countries and cultures. Anglo-Saxons beware: if you want to understand the Priory, you have to see through French eyes—as we soon learned.

Moreover, as we discovered, the Priory of Sion story is intimately connected with some of the most important political and social events in modern French history—particularly the great trauma of the World War II Nazi Occupation, from 1940 to 1944.

France, like some other European countries, such as Italy, is rather more conspiratorially minded than Britain or the United States (although both seem to be rapidly catching up). This is because of France's long history of conspiracies and secret cabals, results of its many historical power struggles, particularly after the nation was polarized between republicans and monarchists following the French Revolution of the late eighteenth century and Napoleon's Empire. Secret societies are taken much more seriously in France, rather than seen as merely sources of polite amusement, as they tend to be in the United Kingdom or the United States. In fact, secret societies of all kinds—religious, political, criminal, and "occult"—have played a not inconsequential part in French society for centuries.

In continental Europe there also exists a twilight underworld where far-right groups, organized crime, security and intelligence agencies, and "initiatory" societies meet and merge. Probably the most famous example is the Masonic lodge P2 (Propaganda Due)—with which the Priory of Sion has been linked—which is probably best remembered for its involvement in the collapse of the Vatican bank, the Banco Ambrosiano, which led to the murder in London of "God's Banker," Roberto Calvi, in June 1982.

At its height, P2 had a membership of around a thousand, which included more than forty members of the Italian Parliament; three Cabinet ministers; the heads of the Army, Navy, and Air Force; and the chiefs of intelligence and counterintelligence; besides judges, policemen, and many leading businessmen and financiers. With such an august membership, the P2 lodge room even became a kind of shadow government, with its founder and Grand Master, Licio Gelli (although unelected and unknown to the general public), one of the most powerful men in Italy—even in Europe. The group had links with far-right terrorist groups, the Mafia, and the CIA—which shared P2's aim of crushing the Italian Communists—and may have been the conduit through which the CIA channeled funds to anti-Communist groups. (It has been suggested that the CIA actually created P2, but its origins are too obscure to be certain one way or another.)

Another example of the workings of this murky world is an organization called the Service for Civic Action (Service d'Action Civique, or

SAC), which may well have some connection with the Priory of Sion. The SAC emerged from the *service d'ordre*—an internal group responsible for party discipline and security—of Charles de Gaulle's Rally of the French People (Rassemblement du Peuple Français, or RPF) in the immediate postwar years. The *service d'ordre* was made up of former members of the Resistance and military, police, and intelligence officers, all utterly devoted to the General, and was originally founded to protect Gaullist candidates and provide security at RPF meetings and rallies.

As de Gaulle disbanded the RPF at the beginning of 1953, its *service d'ordre* also ceased to exist—at least officially. But in reality its members formed a clandestine network that agitated and plotted to return de Gaulle to power, including attempts to destabilize the Fourth Republic, which they achieved in 1958. Once in power, in January 1960, de Gaulle formally established the SAC, which soon became a peculiar semiofficial organization: effectively a state security agency with wide-ranging powers and a close relationship with other police and security agencies, which nevertheless owed its allegiance to one political party and creed alone.

Described as the "praetorian guard of the Gaullist movement,"[31] the SAC was essentially there to protect de Gaulle and keep him in power, which meant keeping a watchful eye on his political opponents and, where necessary, undermining or discrediting them, often by using dirty tricks and smear campaigns. More important, the appearance of the anti–de Gaulle terrorist Secret Army Organization (Organisation de l'Armée Secrète, or OAS)—composed of former or serving Army officers sworn to take revenge on the General for granting Algeria independence in 1962—gave the SAC a significant enemy, which threatened both de Gaulle and the security of the State, to pit itself against. At its height the SAC is said to have been thirty thousand strong and organized at regional and local levels throughout France.

Despite its highly charged role and the fact that its existence was a matter of public record—it even published its own journal, *Service d'Action Civique*—the SAC kept a very low profile, and many French people were unaware of it. De Gaulle never mentions it once in his memoirs, and few biographers of him or other leading Gaullist politicians refer to it.

However, when de Gaulle left office in 1969, the SAC began to lose its sense of purpose. Although continuing to protect other Gaullist politicians and the ideal of Gaullism itself, it started to drift—dangerously. Many politicians, particularly Interior Minister Raymond Marcellin, were wary of such a loose cannon, seeking any opportunity to clip its wings or even close it down. It lost members and funding. But it is always a volatile situation when a well-organized and semiclandestine organization loses its raison d'être; it will inevitably find other outlets to fill the void.

In certain areas, such as Marseilles, the SAC already had connections with organized crime gangs. But now the relationship between the two began to blur, with some SAC members making the most of opportunities provided by their cover to engage in lucrative criminal activities, such as drug and arms trafficking. But to Anglo-Saxon eyes, they formed a much stranger chain of associations.

In 1970 the SAC established an even more clandestine operation, to be used for tasks that required greater secrecy and plausible deniability in case anything went wrong. It did this under the innocuous-sounding Technical and Commercial Studies (Études Techniques et Commerciels, or ETEC), under the control of Charly Lascorz. In fact, ETEC worked closely with the intelligence departments of the police and Ministry of the Interior, and with the French equivalent of MI5, the Directorate of Internal Security (Direction de la Surveillance du Territoire). With the main aim of infiltrating political organizations, Lascorz initiated such an operation against what seems to be an unlikely target. Of the many organizations today that proclaim themselves the heirs of the medieval Knights Templar—either literally or as perpetuators of their original ideals—the largest and most influential, with Grand Priories in many countries, is the Sovereign and Military Order of the Temple of Jerusalem (SMOTJ). ETEC successfully infiltrated the French Priory of the SMOTJ by engineering the election of its man General Antoine Zdrojewski, the former chief of the Polish Resistance in France, as the new Grand Prior. But it was Lascorz who gave the orders.[32]

There were several reasons for infiltrating the Templars. As the SMOTJ tended to appeal to the upper echelons of society—the bosses—it could be used to infiltrate the police, the Army, the media, and so on. Indeed, according to François Audigier, author of an intensive study of the SAC, the SMOTJ already had links to various intelligence services.[33] But it was also a source of funds—new recruits to the SMOTJ were expected to pay handsomely for their honors and regalia, money that funded both ETEC operations and Lascorz's lifestyle. (His secretary and girlfriend was a former Miss France.) Then, as the 1982 exposé *On the Orders of the SAC* (*Aux ordres du SAC*) by the journalist Serge Ferrand and the former ETEC agent Gilbert Lacavelier explains: "The 'ennobling' of ETEC by the Order of the Templars marked the start on a course to a frantic free-for-all that would find expression in an incredible succession of frauds."[34]

Besides lining his own pocket, Lascorz held extreme right-wing views and had no scruples in using both ETEC and the SMOTJ to advance his highly questionable ideology. In April 1971 he established the Union for the Defense of Liberty and Rights (Union pour la Défense des Libertés et des Droits), described by Audigier as "an explosive blend of an embryonic party of the extreme right and Templar Freemasonry."[35] This in turn forged links to other extreme-right groups across Europe, particularly in Germany—using the already-existing network of the SMOTJ, according to Lecavalier.

However, Lascorz had overreached himself: the SAC's opponents in the government leapt at the opportunity to teach it a lesson by using ETEC as an example. Lascorz was arrested—he escaped but was rearrested in Spain and extradited—and sentenced to three years for fraud (although he served less than half his sentence).

The wheels-within-wheels nature of this affair is confusing but typical of that shadowy world. The SAC creates a front organization, ETEC, which infiltrates and takes over the SMOTJ, which it then uses to infiltrate other organizations. Also typical is the admix of several organizational and personal agendas: the SAC's official function to protect Gaullism, Lascorz's political ambitions, the objectives of the far-right groups, and the SMOTJ's Templar ideal, besides straightforward criminality to finance the other agendas.

The SAC suffered an even greater decline—basically becoming irrelevant to French politics and drifting yet further into crime and militant extreme-right activities—after the advent of Valéry Giscard d'Estaing as President in 1974. Matters came to a head when, on the night of July 17–18, 1981, as the result of an internal feud, a former SAC member and police inspector, Jacques Massié (also reportedly a SMOTJ Templar), was shot dead, along with his wife, his eight-year-old son, and three others, at their house in Auriol in Provence.

The resulting official inquiry into the SAC, which reported to Parliament in May 1982, found that the organization—still with some 4,600 members—was deeply involved in criminal activities, citing 120 examples ranging from counterfeiting and drug trafficking to prostitution and detailing its connection with eleven murders or attempted murders. Although President Mitterrand ordered its dissolution in July 1982, the SAC may not have ended there: several experts believe it continues to exist—even more secretly.

The SAC and P2 are just two examples of those highly dubious complex interrelations, very much the world in which the Priory of Sion operates.

Accepting l'Occulte

Another major cultural difference in France is that the "occult"—what we prefer to call the "esoteric"—is viewed more reverently, and is even more prominent in everyday life than in more mundane and cynical Britain, as a glance at the occult section of any French bookshop will reveal. In the United Kingdom the "Mind, Body, and Spirit" sections of major booksellers will chiefly comprise sanitized "New Age" titles: more committed seekers have to patronize one of the excellent specialist shops such as London's Atlantis or Watkins' Bookshops; in France books and magazines dealing with the most abstruse forms of esotericism are more readily available—and are snapped up by droves of eager occultists. In Britain and the United States, those who pursue metaphysical disciplines or perhaps an interest in alchemy or ceremonial magic tend to be regarded either as cranks or as walkers on a distinctly dark side, but to the French, alchemists and ritual magi are generally much more acceptable—almost, in some circles, viewed as mere hobbyists.

It has long been so. In the Parisian salons of the late nineteenth and early twentieth centuries, the worlds of art and the occult mingled seamlessly. The presence on the Priory's list of Grand Masters of world-famous French writers and musicians such as the novelist Victor Hugo and the composer Claude Debussy still tends to raise eyebrows among British readers. Imagine the sensation if, say, Charles Dickens, Edward Elgar, or Gilbert and Sullivan were revealed to have headed a somewhat murky British secret society! (The innocently hilarious goings-on of the Pickwick Club and the Mikado would rapidly take on a more sinister hue.) But in France such an association barely warrants a Gallic shrug. French novelists, poets, artists, and composers of the nineteenth and early twentieth centuries were steeped in esoteric ideas (we have already met Maurice Barrès). One celebrity of direct relevance to the Priory of Sion story is the internationally celebrated opera singer Emma Calvé (1858–1942), who was also a leading light of Paris's esoteric world and the enthusiastic lover of several of its prominent members. (Perhaps, however, this is merely a matter of image. Society movers and shakers in British and American circles, such as the shipping heiress Emerald Cunard, who was a very close friend of the infamous British ritual magician Aleister Crowley, also drifted elegantly from artistic salon to magic temple via a succession of rumpled beds.)

Although a little less openly admitted, in France an interest in esoteric matters even extends to the hardheaded world of politics (but again it is largely a matter of image—many prominent British and American politicians have also pursued their unorthodox interests: for example, in the United States Henry A. Wallace, Franklin Roosevelt's vice president, participated in parapsychological research, while in the United Kingdom the early-twentieth-century Prime Minister Arthur Balfour was an ardent devotee of Spiritualism).

It is against this background of almost casual blending of occultism and politics that we can begin our investigation into the Priory of Sion.

However, in order to uncover the Priory's true motives and beliefs, we have to go back to the beginning—or at least the earliest date at which the verifiable documentary evidence unequivocally reveals the society to exist. Inevitably, there will be surprises and not a few shocks.

CHAPTER TWO

BEHIND THE THRONE

While the skeptics do a splendid job of throwing the baby out with the bathwater, having discovered the Priory of Sion's seemingly shameless capacity to be economical with the truth, we have found that the Priory *is* still very much worthy of study, as is its enigmatic figurehead, Pierre Plantard. What he and his associates got up to in the Second World War will prove particularly intriguing. But first, let us examine the *official* birth of the Priory of Sion.

On May 7, 1956, the subprefecture at Saint-Julien-en-Genevois in the *département* (administrative region) of Haute-Savoie—on the border with Switzerland, not far from Geneva—received a request for registration[1] from the officials of an "association" calling itself the Priory of Sion, subtitled CIRCUIT. The request was signed by its president, the twenty-one-year-old press correspondent André Bonhomme, who also declared his alias of Stanis Bellas, and its general secretary, Pierre Plantard (calling himself Chyren—a name taken from the prophecies of Nostradamus), who gave his profession as journalist. The headquarters of this then unknown association were declared to be a house called Sous-Cassan in the nearby town of Annemasse—in fact, Plantard's own address. The registration forms listed two other officials: Vice President Jean Deleaval, a French draftsman living in Geneva, and Treasurer Armand Defago, a technician also from Plantard's town.[2]

The registration of the Priory of Sion was formally announced in the government's *Journal Officiel* on June 25, 1956—with its brief, and possibly tongue-in-cheek, description of the society's aims—"study and mutual assistance." It would be hard to sound any blander.

"A big thing out of nothing"

Of the four "founding members" of the Priory of Sion, apart from Plantard only the president, André Bonhomme, has ever been traced. Always reticent and publicity-shy, after 1956 he appears to have had no further connection with the affair until August 1973, when he wrote to the subprefecture at Saint-Julien declaring that he had resigned as president of the "Association du Prieuré de Sion."[3]

In 1996 Bonhomme told the BBC: "The Priory of Sion doesn't exist anymore. We were never involved in any activities of a political nature. It was four friends who came together to have fun. We called ourselves the Priory of Sion because there was a mountain by the same name close by. I haven't seen Pierre Plantard in over twenty years and I don't know what he's up to, but he always had a great imagination. I don't know why people try to make such a big thing out of nothing."[4]

Damning Plantard utterly with that "great imagination" comment, Bonhomme's bluster surely protests too much. In any case, it all depends on one's definition of *fun.* Was this statement, like so many others connected with the Priory, a double bluff, carefully constructed misinformation intended to keep away all but the most dogged or plank-thick researchers?

As French law requires a copy of each association's constitution and rules to be deposited with the subprefecture, to be available for public inspection, the Priory of Sion dispatched a copy of its statutes with its registration. As might be expected, they make interesting reading. They explain that the subtitle CIRCUIT stands for Chevalerie d'Institution et Règle Catholique et d'Union Indépendante Traditionaliste (Knighthood of Catholic Institution and Rule and Independent Traditionalist Union). The society's bulletin would also be called *Circuit.*[5]

Its aim was "the constitution of a Catholic Order, intended to restore in a modern form, while retaining its traditionalist character, the ancient chivalry, which, through its actions, promoted a highly moralizing ideal and the element of constant improvement in the rules of life and the human personality." In pursuit of this ideal, the society's most immediate aim was to establish "a Priory, which will serve as a center of study, meditation, rest, and prayer," on the nearby Montagne de Sion. This is the first explanation of the name Priory of Sion—and very straightforward it seems, but then appearances can be deceptive. Their chosen location of the Col du Mont Sion is a fairly modest peak of 2,500 feet, some twenty miles from Plantard's home at Annemasse and five miles from Saint-Julien.

The statutes declare that membership is open to all Catholics over the age of twenty-one (then the age of majority in France) who share the society's aims. Once inside the Priory, the newcomer faced nine grades, each with a maximum membership—three times more than the next highest grade, giving a total *potential* membership of 9,841. (Although critics dismiss this as far too grand, the statutes never claim that the society actually has all those members. It was just its preset limit.) The highest grade—the equivalent of Grand Master—is *Nautonnier,* "navigator" or "helmsman." (The grades then become notably more chivalric: Seneschal, Constable, Commander, Knight, Squire, Valiant, Crusader, and Novice.) As in the best-regulated esoteric societies, the Priory's grades are impressively complex, being organized into 729 Provinces, twenty-seven Commanderies, and a kind of executive council called the Arche "Kyria" consisting of the top four grades—forty members in all.

However, why Priory and why Sion? Now that it is so evocative to millions across the globe, it seems incredible that the name Priory of Sion had anything other than a magical creation—although the facts, while typically complex and even contradictory, are somewhat different. As we have seen, the society's first aim was simply to create a monastic-style priory on the Montagne de Sion. The society was named after the place. *C'est tout.*

The explanation had transmuted into something rich and strange by the time it appeared in the Dossiers Secrets, ten years after the registration. Now we are told the Priory took its name from the Abbey of Notre-Dame de Mont Sion, founded in Jerusalem in the wake of the First Crusade—much more historic and romantic! Of course, this may simply have been typical Priory mythmaking, seizing on another, more enticing Sion to fit their bill. However, we uncovered evidence (which will be discussed later) that the creators of the Priory had the Jerusalem abbey in mind from the start.[6] In that case, either the nearby Col du Mont Sion was just a coincidence or—less likely—the society deliberately based itself in that area because there was a conveniently named mountain nearby.

There is an intriguing literary parallel: the creation of a monastic retreat on a mountain named Sion seems to have been inspired by Maurice Barrès's novel *La colline inspirée,* which in turn was taken from the real-life activities of the Baillard brothers on Sion-Vaudémont in Lorraine (described in the last chapter). The game playing has already begun.

Priory itself is an odd choice of name for a society, more usually being used to describe a society's or order's subdivision, often geographical. Today several "neo-Templar" organizations claim descent from the medieval Knights Templar, or at least aim to continue their ideals, the most prominent being the Sovereign and Military Order of the Temple of Jerusalem. As neo-Templar orders usually organize themselves into Priories and Grand Priories in various locations, the name *Priory* of Sion could well hint heavily at an affiliation—real or imagined—with the mysterious and swashbuckling Templars of old.

Paul Smith suggests that the inspiration for organizing orders of chivalry into priories originated with the esotericist Paul Le Cour, who is mentioned in both earlier and later Priory-related material. But in both cases a priory is merely part of the organization, not the whole thing.

The name Priory of Sion is even more puzzling because in 1956 the society preferred the alternative CIRCUIT—and in any case, its journal of the same name covers nothing remotely related to chivalric priories. Insisting on calling itself the Priory of Sion seems fairly pointless, certainly at that stage in its evolution.

Between the Lines

About a dozen issues of the free publication *Circuit,* edited by Plantard, were produced during 1956. For those seeking age-old cover-ups and conspiracies, the *Bulletin of Information and Defense of the Rights and Liberty of Low-Rent Housing* (*Foyers HLM—inhabitations à loyer modéré*—council housing in Britain, or public housing in the United States)—will be a huge disappointment. It is staggeringly mundane and even boring, merely a litany of local authority cock-ups, tenants' protest meetings, and horror stories about living conditions. Sometimes it is sublimely banal, even bathetic, consisting of adverts for pencils; lists of bakers, doctors, and pharmacies open on Sunday; and quizzes for council estate children. There is absolutely no hint about the Templars' glory days in Jerusalem. For example:

> The scandal breaks of the *Cités d'Urgence* [postwar temporary housing estates]; 168 families protested outside the Prefecture in Mantes in Seine-et-Oise, declaring that the homes built last year and in April were [already] in danger of collapse.
>
> At Chelles-les-Coudreaux, houses are actually lifted up by tree roots! The estate's distress only adds to the general indignation felt.
>
> Then it's the turn of Drancy, La Courneuve, Pavillon-sous-Bois, Saint Étienne, Annecy, pitiful cases that we cannot describe owing to lack of space.[7]

Apart from Annecy, none of the places is anywhere near Annemasse or even in the Haute-Savoie—most are close to Paris.

The quizzes seem rather tough for young children—suspiciously so, one might think. For example:

> What is the name of the French statesman, counselor to the Parliament in Paris, superintendent of Finances, then Chancellor of France, who was born in the Puy de Dôme and proclaimed three ordinances celebrated for their very enthusiastic sentiment of Liberty and Equality?[8]

Apart from a solitary article arguing for a new system of astrology with thirteen signs—later something of a preoccupation with Plantard—there is nothing esoteric at all in the pages of *Circuit.* So what on earth was it about?

The Priory of Sion was legally registered, first and foremost, to produce *Circuit,* yet the journal's subject matter bears no relation whatsoever to the group's registered aims. The publication is glaringly, even ludicrously, irrelevant and inconsequential. If the Priory of Sion was really all about fighting for the rights of council tenants, why didn't it simply say so on its registration forms and forget all the high-flown stuff about Catholic chivalry?

The registration could have been a means of providing legal cover for producing *Circuit,* but then why bother? After all, a fairly tedious publication about council houses has no need for cloak-and-dagger activities. Even as a hoax it makes no sense—and certainly not as the "fun" alleged by André Bonhomme. (Unless Annemasse is a *really* dull place!)

There must be more to *Circuit* than meets the eye—and it seems that there was. As we stared at the everyday articles about rising damp and buying pencils in bulk, something began to niggle at us, something strangely familiar. A pattern was emerging—for example, in the remorseless singling out of particular locations, publishing of contact addresses and telephone numbers, and veiled references to political figures . . . Then it hit us. *Circuit* read exactly like the publications of the wartime Resistance.

Their every move watched by both Nazi occupiers and their collaborators, the French freedom fighters would hide contact details, coded instructions, and so on under a mass of apparently innocuous material—such as day-to-day civic events. *Circuit* even states it is part of a network of similar local groups working in defense of *foyers HLM*.

But what with André Bonhomme's reticence and the mystery surrounding the identity of the Priory's two other officers, the only line of further inquiry is Pierre Plantard himself, and getting to know him would be no easy task.

The Godfather

Pierre Athanase Marie Plantard was born in Paris on March 18, 1920, only child of another Pierre—who died when Pierre junior was just two—and Amélie (née Raulo). Adding to the fog surrounding everything about him, throughout his long life Plantard used various aliases and variations of his name, most famously from 1972 styling himself Pierre Plantard de Saint-Clair, claiming that he was the legitimate holder of the title of Comte de Saint-Clair (from Saint-Clair-sur-Epte, a village about thirty miles northwest of Paris). This linked him to the radiant aura of the illustrious Anglo-Norman St. Clair/Sinclair family, holder of an important place in British, and particularly Scottish, esoteric traditions: they are famously connected with the Knights Templar, the origins of Freemasonry, and the enigmatic Rosslyn Chapel near Edinburgh. But was Plantard really the heir to this title?

Plantard gave Baigent, Leigh, and Lincoln a copy of his birth certificate, which certainly cited his father as Pierre Plantard de Saint-Clair,

Comte de Saint-Clair and Comte de Rhedae. (According to some, Rhedae was the ancient name for Rennes-le-Château.) However, when the three authors wisely obtained a copy of Plantard's birth certificate from the appropriate *mairie,* they found his father to be simply Pierre Plantard—a humble valet.[9]

When Baigent, Leigh, and Lincoln confronted Plantard with this in Paris in 1984—hoping to catch him out—without missing a beat he smoothly explained that the certificate had been lodged in the *mairie*'s files during the Nazi Occupation in order to hide his father's true status from the Germans, who regarded aristocrats with particular suspicion. In fact, this was a common enough practice, although the authorities were unable to say whether it applied in Plantard's case.

Another source of information—a police report from February 1941, shortly before Plantard's twenty-first birthday—also identified his father as a valet and his widowed mother as a cook for upper-crust households.[10] To further muddy the waters, according to Pierre Jarnac, one of the most meticulous French researchers into the Priory of Sion mystery, Plantard senior was a wine merchant—although of course he could simply have changed his job.[11]

Most skeptics need look no further than the police report. But that may be being less than fair—after all, if the Plantards had gone to the lengths of falsifying their details to avoid Nazi suspicion, they would naturally stick to the story when questioned by the police. But of course it is much more logical that the son of a valet would pretend his father was really a count than vice versa. Also, it is common practice in the esoteric world to claim some fancy-sounding title—usually without the slightest justification. Once again, though, things are never quite so simple where Plantard and the Priory are concerned.

The birth certificate that Plantard showed to Baigent, Leigh, and Lincoln was not a forgery, as many assume, but actually an amended certificate issued in 1972, when the registration of his birth was changed. This is confirmed by the fact that on Plantard's passport—obtained using the new birth certificate—he was Pierre Plantard de Saint-Clair, Comte de Saint-Clair et Comte de Rhedae. If the certificate was a forgery, Plantard would have been in serious trouble, at least when the story emerged in the French edition of *The Messianic Legacy.* Besides the original registration of Plantard's birth, the register includes an officially certified amendment, dating from August 1972. Although anyone can legally change his or her name by *acte unilatéral*—the equivalent of the British deed poll—significantly his *father's* details were also changed: Pierre Plantard senior was not only holder of the two aristocratic titles but now an architect. Such a complete makeover was way beyond the scope of an *acte unilatéral.*[12]

Clearly in 1972 Plantard produced something that convinced the relevant authorities that the original registration of his birth was incorrect, particularly about his father's status. But what it was remains unknown. Perhaps his document was a forgery; maybe he smooth-talked the officials; perhaps he bribed someone in a high place. But our only legitimate conclusion is an open verdict: the situation is certainly not as clear-cut as the skeptics would have us believe.

Even returning to his birthplace to change the registration also required unnecessary effort on Plantard's part—he had adopted aliases before without going to such trouble. For some reason, in 1972 it was important to him to establish the new form of his name *officially.*

But was Plantard really a count twice over? Perhaps not. Comte de Rhedae is particularly suspect. On the one hand, Rhedae was an ancient Visigothic town in the Languedoc area of southern France that some believe was the site of today's Rennes-le-Château, but even so the name Rhedae has remained unused for the best part of a millennium. On the other hand, some levelheaded researchers, such as the French historian Jean Markale—by no means credulous about the Priory of Sion—happily accept Plantard's aristocratic credentials.[13]

Perhaps he was entitled to them, perhaps he wasn't—in fact, nobody knows how many titles existed before the French Revolution at the end of the eighteenth century, or even what they were. As the British Bible on all matters aristocratic, Burke's Peerage, points out: "There is and there never has been any register, in France, for the regulation of titles. Various methods have been tried to bring some order into all of this; none has been successful. In any case, many owners of the most revered and ancient titles could not, now, produce any reliable documentation to prove their claims."[14]

Since the Revolution, the French government has been relatively indifferent to the use or appropriation of aristocratic titles (other than for fraudulent purposes). Before the Revolution, a title went with the land, not the person—noble status was neither conferred nor removed by the granting or loss of a title. If the land changed hands, the title went with it. Plantard could claim to be comte of the two places only if he owned *terrain titré* in Saint-Clair-sur-Epte and Rhedae, which would be particularly difficult as nobody knows for certain where Rhedae was! (It is rather like claiming the title of Count of Camelot.) But while *terrain titré* is required by Burke's Peerage before it will acknowledge the right to a title, frankly it is somewhat unlikely that under the Fifth Republic of 1972 the authorities would have cared.

On balance, Plantard *probably* invented his aristocratic credentials—if only because the Rhedae title is so unlikely. But even so, this invention needs to be put in perspective. Although his detractors argue that his insistence on an aristocratic pedigree shows he must have been a fantasist with delusions of grandeur and should therefore be instantly and completely dismissed, adopting aristocratic titles for good old-fashioned social climbing is a relatively common practice in France and not necessarily a sign of either mental instability or pathetic insignificance. Even Valéry Giscard d'Estaing, former President of the country (1974–1981) and more recently architect of the controversial European constitution, benefited from much the same practice: the d'Estaing title was adopted by his grandfather to improve the family's image.[15] Le roi Giscard (King Giscard), as he was called by his opponents, also had monarchist pretensions—something of which Plantard was to be accused—reinstating royal protocol to the French presidency and demanding the same status as a monarch as head of state.

The critics also argue that if Plantard lied about his aristocratic status, then nothing else he says can be trusted—but the converse is, presumably, that if he really was the legitimate Comte de Saint-Clair, everything he uttered would be the unvarnished truth! And yet Plantard's closest confederate in the 1960s and '70s, Philippe de Chérisey—who is equally vilified by the same critics—was unquestionably the legitimate holder of the title Marquis de Chérisey. The skeptics want it both ways.

A Mysterious Mentor

Plantard's entry into the world of esoteric and neochivalric orders—a burgeoning scene in France, lurking not far beneath the surface of polite society—happened, according to his own account, through an encounter with the curious, controversial, and shadowy character Georges Monti, who rapidly became his mentor. Plantard says he was a fourteen-year-old schoolboy when he was introduced to Monti in 1934 by his family doctor, Camille Savoire, an eminent physician and philosopher, as well as a prominent Freemason.[16]

As usual, skeptics have poured scorn on this account, without much reason. Plantard associated himself with Monti from at least 1942, and although the older man was a player in the European esoteric world in the first decades of the twentieth century, he was relatively unknown outside specialist circles, especially in the early forties. To have known of Monti at all, Plantard would have had to belong to such circles, even if he invented their actual relationship. But why fabricate a closeness to Georges Monti of all people—a man with a distinctly dubious reputation?

By all accounts, Monti (1880–1936) was a dark star of the occult world: amoral and self-centered, he used the esoteric underground for self-aggrandizement. Moving purposefully through those intense, incense-riddled circles, he wormed his way to the top of most of the secret societies, seeking out their secrets and bolstering his personal influence. Using one of his many aliases, Comte Israël Monti, he even managed to inveigle membership in the B'nai B'rith, the exclusively Jewish system of Freemasonry, although not only was he not Jewish but by all accounts he was rabidly anti-Semitic.

Born in Toulouse—traditionally a major center of French occultism—Monti was brought up by the Jesuits (having been abandoned by his parents) but rebelled against their strict discipline, being attracted at an early age to the esoteric underworld. From there he gravitated to the Paris salons, where art and the arcane mingled promiscuously, first making his mark in the early 1900s as secretary to the important esotericist Joséphin Péladan. He was also closely associated with another leading occultist, Dr. Gérard Encausse (Papus), who dispatched him on a secret mission to Egypt in 1908.[17]

Once established in his chosen milieu, Monti carved his ascent through the esoteric brotherhoods of France, Italy, and Germany—where his involvement with the Ordo Templi Orientis (OTO), a neo-Templar society dedicated to sexual rites, brought him into contact with the controversial British occultist Aleister Crowley (1875–1947), who dominated the OTO in the 1920s and '30s. Monti has even been described as Crowley's French representative. The Parisian poet and esotericist Anne Osmont (1872–1953) wrote that Monti approached her for help in setting up a French branch of the OTO in the 1920s.[18] He also became involved in espionage—always a surprisingly common activity for leading occultists—essentially for his own benefit, becoming a double agent for the French and the Germans during and after the First World War. Monti died in suspicious circumstances—probably of poison—in Paris in October 1936, a few days after the bulletin of the Grand Lodge of France denounced him as an impostor and Jesuit spy. All in all, he was an interesting role model for the young and impressionable Plantard.

The elusive Monti characteristically clung to the shadows, his name seldom surfacing even in the annals of the French occult world. The connection between Monti and the young Plantard therefore not only shows that the latter was part of the esoteric scene in the 1930s but—tantalizingly—also links him with the "golden age" of nineteenth and early-twentieth-century Parisian occultism.

The Roots of the Vine

Plantard's teenage years coincided with a particularly turbulent era in modern French history. As in most of Europe, in France the era between the two world wars saw great political polarization and internal upheaval, affecting the victors of the First World War as much as the losers. Everyone was scarred by the hostilities: for example, almost all families in Britain had lost a brother, son, husband, or sweetheart in the mud and guts of France and Belgium. Some villages had lost all their young men. Almost a whole generation was either wiped out or mutilated. It was hell on earth, utterly unimaginable to us today, and left the survivors demented with grief and reeling with shock. To them there was only one motto that mattered: *Never again.* But how to achieve peace? How to regain their nations' strength and power?

Suddenly politics mattered. Millions were questioning the old order while traditionalists and conservatives defended it even more fiercely, and grave tension simmered between the two new, violently opposed ideologies emerging from the ruins of war. The Russian Revolution of 1917 created the first Communist state, not only providing impetus to left-wing revolutionary groups throughout Europe but also offering the new Soviet Union as a base to support, encourage, and fund fellow travelers. At the other extreme, the triumph of Mussolini's Fascists in Italy in 1922—a reaction to the rise of Communism—had created a model and inspiration for similarly inclined groups elsewhere in Europe. But then in 1933 came the meteoric rise of Hitler's bully boys in Germany, electrifying all extreme-right groups—including those in France. The stage was set for the second great apocalypse of the twentieth century.

Like many other post–Great War nations, France was sunk in introspection, posing hard questions about both its past and its future. Some wanted to create a bold new world based on modern scientific, industrial, and political developments; others considered that all France's problems were the direct result of ignoring the lessons of her history and traditions. And as ever, the French were haunted by their very own profound, recurring dilemma: had they really been right to end their monarchy? Could they ever shake off the guilt of the bloodlust that had led to the barbarous deaths of King Louis XVI and his queen, Marie Antoinette, under the flashing blade of the guillotine?

Things were bad. But matters were worsened by the global recession caused by the Wall Street Crash of 1929. Although the French weathered it better than most Europeans, they still suffered a steep rise in unemployment and the unrest that accompanies economic uncertainty, especially in an era before welfare or state benefits. The people were poor, exhausted—and terrified. The history of France showed that this was a very dangerous combination for a government that was becalmed and stagnant—no single party able to command enough support to take decisive measures. The government changed every few months. In this seething caldron of communists, socialists, radicals, and fascists, it was hardly the best time to be a moderate.

A particularly influential movement was the extreme-right nationalist, royalist, and Catholic Action Française, founded by Charles Maurras (1868–1952), together with its daily newspaper—also entitled *Action Française*—in 1899. Between the wars Action Française influenced many important conservative figures—both General de Gaulle and Marshal Pétain—but it eventually went down with the Vichy regime, whose National Revolution attempted to act on its principles in 1944.

Maurras may have been an ultratraditional Catholic, but he was also vehemently anti-Semitic, drawing a clear distinction between the traditions of the Catholic Church and its Jewish antecedents. He considered the true repository and guardian of the Christian faith to be the Church and its dogma, *not* the Bible, declaring, "I am not going to leave this learned procession of Fathers, Councils, Popes, all the great men of the modern élite, to tie myself down to the gospels of four obscure Jews."[19]

John Laughland points out in his study of François Mitterrand's presidency, *The Death of Politics* (1994), that the relationship between the political left and right in France is different from the British version, largely because, paradoxically, the right has absorbed as much of the "Revolutionary tradition" as the left, to produce what Laughland calls the "subversive Right." He writes: "Vichy was to prove the apotheosis of the peculiarly French mixture of Left and Right. Few ostensibly right-wing movements can have embraced nationalist and socialist ideas as clearly as Marshal Pétain's government, except perhaps the Nazis themselves."[20] Laughland further identifies two political currents that have emerged from the subversive Right: one politically organized and active, exemplified by Action Française, and the other "a more nebulous body of opinion, inspired by the writings of the Romantic nationalist Maurice Barrès and the anti-Semitic Édouard Drumont."[21]

Especially after the rise of Nazism, when France had two fascistic neighbors, its streets were thronged with demonstrations, marches, and countermarches that often turned into physical clashes between opposing political groups. Politically motivated violence was common.

As usual, it was the young people who led direct action in the marches and demonstrations, and the street battles that followed. Youth groups of all political persuasions found themselves highly esteemed by the movers and shakers. Action Française boasted its own youth organization, the Camelots du Roi (the King's Street Peddlers), and there was the Croix de Feu (Cross of Fire), founded and led by Colonel François de La Rocque, which by October 1935—when it agreed to renounce violence—had around 2 million members, some surprisingly illustrious.

Tensions came to a head on February 6, 1934, with the worst outbreak of violence on the streets of Paris for seventy years. While the Chamber of Deputies was in session, a right-wing demonstration in the Place de la Concorde grew until, augmented by ex-servicemen, it numbered some 40,000, who threatened to attack the Chamber. Opening fire, the police and guards killed sixteen protesters (and three bystanders) and injured 650. The police suffered one fatality, with nearly 1,700 injured.[22] Although it could easily have escalated into a coup d'état or even full-scale civil war, le sixième février still entered into the vocabulary of the time—and even caused Prime Minister Édouard Daladier to resign.

After the trauma of February 1934, the dust settled, and eventually a left-of-center coalition government, the Popular Front, was established in June 1936 under Léon Blum. But this only inflamed extreme-right hostility; not only did Blum's government depend on the Communist Party to survive but Blum himself was Jewish and, it was widely believed (probably incorrectly), a Freemason.[23] The belief, shared with the Nazis, that Freemasonry is a Jewish-controlled institution was typical of right-wing ideology in the France of the 1930s—and the inevitable background to Plantard's career.

Under the Popular Front, right-wing extremism became the province of clandestine terrorist groups, such as the dreaded Cagoule (Hood), which carried out political assassinations and bombing campaigns in Paris. The capital was living through another Terror.

Shocked to the core, the French suddenly realized that their country needed to become much more moderate, at the same time somehow placating its volatile youth. Jules Romains's Ninth of July Movement (Mouvement du 9 Juillet) was surprisingly successful at persuading the leaders of the opposing youth organizations to discuss their differences face-to-face in an attempt to find some way of working together for the good of France. Romains wrote, "The vaster and more distant objective was to give France a new constitution, stemming from the old, identical to it in its republican spirit and in its absolute respect for the rights of man, but cleared of some defects, and better adapted to modern needs; in a word, more dynamic—a constitution that the youths could love and defend with energy because it would be their work."[24]

Another youth organization intent on persuading young people to cooperate rather than beat one another to a pulp was the Estates General of Youth (États Généraux de la Jeunesse), also founded in the wake of February 6 by one Jeanne Canudo. A few years later this would develop into a Europe-wide movement, the Estates General of European Youth (États Généraux de la Jeunesse Européenne). As we discovered, both these organizations would turn out to be particularly relevant to our Priory of Sion investigation.

Gangly seventeen-year-old Pierre Plantard played his own part in this burgeoning scene in 1937 by founding an organization called the French National Renewal (Rénovation Nationale Française), together with its free weekly bulletin, *The French Renewal* (*La Rénovation Française*) with a circulation of 10,000 (according to official files). He also established the Catholic Youth Group (Groupement Catholique de la Jeunesse), running religious youth clubs in Paris. These related projects assumed several names (a standard Plantard trick), such as the French Union (Union Française) and Youth of France (Jeunesse de France).[25]

According to Pierre Jarnac, in the midst of all this, in 1939 Plantard went to university to study archaeology; there he met Philippe de Chérisey (although their collaboration only really began in the early 1960s). At some point around this time Plantard also worked as a sacristan at the church of St.-Louis d'Antin in Paris.[26] But as Jean-Luc Chaumeil, who worked closely with Plantard in the 1970s, noted, the key to understanding him was the loss of his faith after working at the church, when "he became an atheist and regretted it."[27]

After the Fall

However, if Plantard thought his career would run smoothly, he—like millions of others—was to be brought up sharply by the great French trauma of war with Nazi Germany in September 1939. Not yet reconciled to the horror of the 1914–1918 war, the French faced another monstrous invasion of their soil. The blitzkrieg attack on the Low Countries began on May 10, 1940, rapidly becoming a humiliating debacle for both British and French forces. Beaten back to the beaches of Dunkirk, the British Army was forced to abandon the continent, standing helpless as the Germans advanced to the very shores of Britain's only ally. Inevitably, France had to surrender, making terms with its old rival for dominance in continental Europe. In its third war with Germany in a century, the proud French nation had to accept the occupation of two-thirds of its country by the Nazis. Suddenly both sleepy villages and festive cities echoed to the rumble of foreign tanks and the brutal slapping of thousands upon thousands of goose-stepping feet.

One of the heroes of the First World War, Marshal Henri-Philippe Pétain, commander of the victory at Verdun, was asked to take over the government of the country, based in the spa town of Vichy—originally as a temporary measure pending a return to Paris. Although many overseas observers were surprised at the leniency of Hitler's terms (under the circumstances), the country was divided into the Occupied zone and Vichy rule. The Third Republic, in place since 1870, was dissolved. Instead, Marshal Pétain presided over the French State—as it happened, with a future of just four uneasy years.

In London, a hitherto unknown brigadier general, Charles de Gaulle, decided that destiny had anointed him to restore Gallic honor. On June 18, 1940, he made his legendary radio broadcast known as "*L'Appel*"—"The Call"—for "French resistance," for ordinary noncombatants on the ground in France to impede the Nazi war machine in any and all ways possible. From the London BBC studio, so near geographically yet so far in many other ways from his beloved Paris, de Gaulle declared himself leader of France.

To understand Plantard and the Priory's background, it is necessary to ignore the temptation to color this emotive period with the black-and-white certainty of hindsight. At the time people had no way of knowing what was going to happen and which side was going to win the war. (Indeed, until the end of 1941 most objective people would have put their money on the Germans.)

Today there is a particularly polarized view of the situation in France during the war: the Free French and the Resistance equaled good (with reservations about the Communist Resistance); Vichy French equaled bad. But the reality was considerably more complex: indeed, the notion that not actively resisting amounted to collaboration is something of a postwar luxury. For example, Jean Cocteau—a celebrity not unconnected with the Priory of Sion, as we will soon see—simply ignored the Occupation, carrying on his artistic and social life as usual, and although denounced as a collaborator after the Liberation, he was cleared by an official investigation. However, critics of all and everything connected with this story still label him a collaborator—while at the same time denying he had any connection with the Priory of Sion!

Misconceptions—or rather oversimplifications—abound, but the situation was constantly changing in response to new developments. For example, French fascists who had seen eye to eye before the war were now divided, some believing that in the long term the Occupation was a good thing, as it would allow French fascism to triumph and eventually there would be no need for German control: the two countries would be allies in a fascist Europe. Others, no matter how favorably they viewed Nazism, were affronted by their country being under the domination of *any* foreigners, wanting the Germans out as soon as possible.

Only a minority of politicians, officials, and officers in the armed forces actively welcomed close ties with Nazi Germany. (Naturally they tended to rise to the top in Vichy.) Most were horrified by what had happened to France, but, like it or not, Vichy *was* the legally constituted government, so even though they might naturally have sided with the Allies and de Gaulle, they reluctantly accepted its authority.

The period of autonomous self-rule by the Vichy regime—subservient to Germany only in matters relating to the wider war—in which Pétain and his government made all the decisions, lasted from July 1940 to November 1942. In response to the Allied seizure of French North Africa, Operation Torch, in that month, the Germans—fearing that France might turn against them—moved into the Vichy zone and took direct control of it. After that, although Pétain remained in office and his government stayed nominally in charge, it was the Germans who actually decided on government appointments and so on. (In other words, Vichy can be called a German "puppet" only after November 1942, not before.)

Today, of course, we see de Gaulle as the hero who defied Hitler and risked all for his nation's honor, and Pétain as the villain—the arch-Nazi sympathizer, Hitler's puppet. But that was emphatically not how most French people—or even many Allies—viewed Pétain at the time.

Few French people had even heard of de Gaulle—he was given his first public office, undersecretary of state for national defense, just ten days before France's capitulation—and, of course, not many happened to be tuned in to the BBC to hear "*L'Appel.*" It took some time for news of his defiant stand to filter throughout France.

As the writer Jean Blum puts it, "In 1940, two personalities called on the French to follow them, a great statesman and a traitor. In 1945, these two illustrious chiefs had preserved the scene but exchanged their roles."[28] When France fell, while power was transferred to Pétain both constitutionally and legally, de Gaulle was actually condemned to death by a French court as a deserter and traitor for rebelling against the legitimate government.

Unthinkable though it is now, back then many French citizens regarded Pétain as their national savior, the hero who had prevented their total subjugation and enslavement, allowing France to retain some remnant of independence and self-determination. That was always Pétain's defense—he had struggled hard with Hitler to maintain France's sovereignty—which of course, after the war, was taken as an attempt to wriggle out of blame. But, it must be stressed, this was how many—perhaps most—French people saw him at the time. Even after the Germans *did* occupy the Vichy zone in November 1942, this view of the Marshal remained widespread.

In fact, even after the war many held the view that that France's survival had needed both de Gaulle and Pétain—a recurring image was that Pétain was France's shield and de Gaulle was its sword—but politically such subtleties were impossible in the post-Liberation atmosphere. For the sake of unity, Pétain had to be cast as the villain, tried, and imprisoned. (He was sentenced to death, but the sentence was commuted to a Napoleon-like life imprisonment on the Ile d'Yeu, eleven miles off the Brittany coast, where he died in 1951.)

Another misconception is that Pétain and his government were simply puppets or stooges of the Nazis, with no authority of their own. Although this was true after November 1942, before then Pétain resolutely pursued his own agenda for France, accommodating Hitler's wishes only when absolutely necessary.

Legally and constitutionally, Pétain's government *was* the legitimate government of France—technically, Vichy had authority over the whole of France, but in practice its laws and decrees were subject to German approval in the Occupied zone. De Gaulle possessed only a *moral* claim to be the leader of the French people. Vichy was recognized as legitimate by the Roosevelt administration in the United States, which maintained formal diplomatic relations with Pétain's government up until the Operation Torch landings. Even then FDR (who loathed de Gaulle and refused to recognize him as leader of France until forced by circumstances to do so in October 1944) hoped that a deal could be done with Pétain that would leave him in control of a liberated France, in order to ensure continuity of government. Even after the D-Day landings, some high-ranking Americans still wanted to keep Pétain in power.[29]

Vichy's legitimacy was even recognized by Churchill's government—it was Vichy that broke diplomatic relations with Britain, not the other way round, when the Royal Navy attacked the French fleet at Mers el-Kébir in Algeria two weeks after France's surrender. And Churchill maintained clandestine communication directly with Pétain well into the war, making a secret deal to scale down British pressure on Vichy France if he minimized his cooperation with Hitler.[30]

Crucially, Pétain and his government had the option of sitting the war out quietly until it was obvious which way things would go. However, Pétain had his own firm ideas about what was needed to halt the moral decline of France, grasping the opportunity to declare a "National Revolution" that he believed would regenerate the nation. This was entirely his initiative: it had nothing to do with the Nazis.

Pétain's vision of the spirit and destiny of France and how it should be restored to greatness was, in fact, surprisingly similar to de Gaulle's—both had been greatly influenced by Maurras's Action Française.[31] Perhaps this oneness of purpose is not so surprising. Before the war de Gaulle and Pétain—student and master at the military academy at Saint-Cyr—had been close, de Gaulle subsequently ghostwriting books on military strategy for the older man. Pétain was even godfather to de Gaulle's son Philippe (who was named after him).[32] Indeed, had their geographical situations been reversed in June 1940, they could easily have swapped roles. The major difference between the two men lay in means rather than ends: while Pétain rose above democracy, cannily de Gaulle realized he would never achieve anything worthwhile without carrying the people with him.

The embarrassingly swift Fall of France caused a crisis of conscience and confidence among the French. Besides having to accept brutal and alien masters in two-thirds of the country, some 1.8 million Frenchmen languished in POW camps in Germany or the Occupied zone. To some extent hostages to ensure France's cooperation, there was much anxiety about their fate.

Many saw all this not merely as the *result* of France's moral decline but as a form of *punishment* for it. France was suffering for its past sins—but this also presented an opportunity for redemption or purgation. (Some of de Gaulle's followers even likened him to a sacrificial Christ, taking France's suffering on his own shoulders.) Many saw the great "sin" as the all-too-bloody end of the monarchy. These included one of those prisoners of war, a young Sergeant François Mitterrand, who after his escape (or release, depending on the version) wrote an account for a Vichy journal of his transportation to Germany (tellingly entitled "Pilgrimage to Thuringia"—*pilgrimage?*), in which he recounted the feeling of stunned shock and bemusement he shared with his companions. He describes how he regarded the defeat as the result of France's long moral decline and declares, "I thought that we, the heirs of 150 years of errors, were hardly responsible."[33] It was all downhill from the Revolution of 1789.

Those very specific circumstances and the mood of wondering despair, indelibly linked to the almost mystical urge for national redemption, provided the prequel for Plantard's rise to Priory prominence.

In the Thick of It

When war broke out Plantard was nineteen, living in the Place Malesherbes in the Seventeenth Arrondissement of Paris with his widowed mother. He had yet to be called up for military service. In December 1940, using the alias Varran de Vérestra, he wrote to Pétain, pledging his support against the "terrible 'freemasonic and Jewish' conspiracy" that threatened to bring "appalling carnage to France and to the world." Plantard believed that the war itself had been "created by the Jews." He declared that he led a group of around a hundred youths who were at the Marshal's disposal. According to the police, the letter was sent through an intermediary with contacts in Vichy, a M. de Brinon—so at least it was no random madman's approach.[34]

Plantard has been seriously criticized for expressing such sentiments—and, of course, rightly so. His fervent anti-Semitism is difficult to square with the later Priory of Sion's claim to have some ill-defined connection with the House of David—not to mention Plantard being allegedly the descendant of Jesus himself!

However, while not seeking to excuse him, perhaps a little more context will help clarify the picture. In fact, the existence of a "plot" by Jews and Freemasons would hardly have constituted shocking news to Pétain or those around him. Just as in Nazi Germany, the idea that all France's ills were caused by Jews was a cornerstone of Pétain's ideology. Anti-Semitic laws, relegating France's Jews to second-class citizenship, had already been passed, and the suspicions about Freemasonry would culminate in its ban in February 1942. Whether Pétain seriously believed in the "conspiracy" or was using these two usual suspects of the far right as convenient scapegoats and targets is uncertain. Where Plantard is concerned, employing such terms would have been a means of currying favor with the new regime. Of course, even self-seeking anti-Jewish posturing is bad enough.

But clearly his letter set off alarm bells. The immediate result was that Vichy's Interior Minister ordered a police investigation of de Véréstra and his background. Their report of February 1941 survives, acknowledging that Plantard had been involved in several youth organizations of his own creation, such as the French National Renewal (with about a hundred members in 1937) and the Catholic Youth Group, and that in October 1940 he had applied for permission to resume publication of the prewar *French Renewal.* It was refused.[35]

The report's conclusion is a glittering prize to those who dismiss Plantard's entire career as the product of his own mythomania. In particular, it describes him as "*illuminé et prétentieux.*" The word *illuminé* depends very much on its context: literally meaning "lit up," when applied to, say, a poet, it means "inspired"; more generally it means "visionary"; when used pejoratively—as it clearly is by the police investigator—essentially it means a crank.

The full verdict reads: "Indeed, Plantard, who boasts of being in contact with numerous men of politics, appears to be one of those *illuminés* and pretentious young people, heads of more or less fictitious groups, wanting to give themselves importance and who take advantage of the current movement in favor of youth to attempt to get themselves taken into consideration by the government." At least it shows that Plantard was ambitious.

The Conquering Hero

Plantard's next venture was much more intriguing and directly relevant to his subsequent career with the Priory of Sion. He became editor of

Vaincre (*Conquer*), the organ of the Alpha Galates Order (Ordre Alpha Galates)—of which he was Grand Master. (The title *Vaincre* was revived for the Priory of Sion's in-house journal in 1989.)

Vaincre's covers were emblazoned with a banner declaring the Order's purpose: "for a young knighthood." Alpha Galates aimed, it said, to revive the chivalric ideal among French youth, and *Vaincre* was its vehicle for doing so. As editor, Plantard first took the name Pierre de France, although he favored the more impressive Pierre de France-Plantard in later editions.

Six issues of *Vaincre* were produced between September 1942 and February 1943, copies of which survive in the Bibliothèque Nationale. Although only four pages long—paper being scarce during the war—it was professionally typeset, printed, and illustrated on high-quality paper, by Poirier Murat in Paris's Rue du Rocher.[36] Published on the twenty-first of each month, it had a circulation that increased from 1,400 to 4,500 by the final issue. Like the later *Circuit,* it was given away free, which poses the question of who financed it. It could hardly have been Plantard himself: as far as can be ascertained, he was living off his widowed mother at the time.

Many of the same questions hang over Alpha Galates as were later raised about the Priory of Sion: was it simply a fiction created by young Plantard or an authentic quasi-chivalric order with many members and, perhaps, real influence and power?

"Alpha Galates" alludes to the "First Galatians" or Gauls (the Galatians to whom St. Paul addressed his New Testament epistle were descended from Celtic settlers from Gaul)—with perhaps an element of "top-class or superior Galatians." Judging by the contents of *Vaincre,* the name was intended to invoke the spirit of France's mythical ancient past.

The Order's statutes, dated December 27, 1937, are printed in *Vaincre.* Although there is no record of its being officially registered then, Plantard's French National Renewal was formed at around the same time, implying a connection between the two organizations.[37] (In fact, Alpha Galates was officially registered in September 1944, after the Liberation—now aiming to provide aid for young people who had suffered under the German Occupation.)

The statutes present Alpha Galates' aims in terms as nebulous as those of the later Priory of Sion, but basically it sought to engender knightly and patriotic ideals through mutual support and group activities. Like the Priory, it was structured on chivalric lines, consisting of nine grades, from Brother to the ultragrand His Druidic Majesty. The Order was divided into two sections, the Legion and the Phalanx, and organized administratively into Arches and Provinces—all exactly the same as the Priory. Once again, an order's headquarters were at Plantard's address: this time in the Rue Lebouteux in Paris's Seventeenth Arrondissement.

However, despite its declared political neutrality, there is one disturbing regulation: "The Order is rigorously closed to Jews and to any member who is recognized as belonging to a Judeo-Masonic order." Clearly this is consistent with Plantard's anti-Jewish and anti-Masonic stance as expressed in his letter to Pétain.

Pieced together from *Vaincre,* the history of the Alpha Galates Order seems to be as follows: appalled by the events of sixième fevrier 1934, the distinguished legal professor Louis Le Fur was advised by his friend the Comte de Moncharville to write to Georges Monti. Six months afterward he was initiated into the Order. (Much later—in 1989—it was stated that Monti founded Alpha Galates actually on the key date of February 6, 1934.) Clearly, the implication was that he was both founder and first head of the Order. By the time of the first publication of *Vaincre,* the Grand Master was the Comte de Moncharville, presumably having succeeded Monti on his death in 1936. However, according to Le Fur, in September 1942, de Moncharville resigned in favor of Pierre Plantard.[38]

Critics often doubt that someone of Plantard's immaturity—then just twenty-two—could have assumed the authority of Grand Master. But the whole point of *Vaincre* was that it was aimed at the *young,* and who better to have at the helm than a keen twenty-two-year-old?

(Many others were pursuing the same ideas at the time, predominantly the Uriage schools, founded by the Catholic cavalry officer Pierre Dunoyer de Segonzac in 1940. This movement is the subject of John Hellman's *The Knight-Monks of Vichy France* (1997), and its parallels with Plantard's work are explored by Guy Patton and Robin Mackness in their *Web of Gold* (2000). Hellman writes: "Vichy's National Revolution abounded in mystical Catholic army officers, residing in imposing country chateaux, who were determined to reorient French youth."[39])

The Comte de Moncharville appears to have been Maurice Moncharville, also a professor of law, who had traveled extensively in the Far East; in the 1910s and '20s he was prominent in the French community in Siam (modern Thailand), and in 1912 he was the founder and first president of a cultural organization called the Committee of the French Alliance in that country. (There appears to be no such animal as a Comte de Moncharville—but of course, there is *nothing* definitive about French titles.)

Vaincre features articles by various members of Alpha Galates, some using real names, some pseudonyms. Apart from Pierre de France-Plantard, there are Le Fur, Moncharville, Robert Amadou, Dr. Camille Savoire, Jacques Brosse, and the esoterically inclined poet Gabriel Trarieux d'Egmont.

The hyperskeptic Paul Smith makes the extraordinary claim that *all* the articles in *Vaincre* were actually written by Plantard, and that none of those whose names he used, either as contributors or as Alpha Galates members, had ever heard of him, specifically listing Monti, the celebrated aviator Jean Mermoz, Savoire, Le Fur, Moncharville, Amadou, and Brosse.[40] But as Monti and Mermoz, for example, both died in 1936, one wonders how Smith can be so sure they had never come across Plantard.

The claim that Plantard wrote the entire magazine is demonstrably incorrect. Robert Amadou, for one, acknowledges that he knew Plantard and was initiated into the Alpha Galates Order in 1942 (aged eighteen), and that he wrote an article on chivalry for the October edition of *Vaincre.*[41] And as several of the articles are attributed to Louis Le Fur, one of France's greatest professors of law, using his name would have been particularly foolhardy—especially since the Occupation had done nothing to emasculate France's legal system.

This presents Plantard in very distinguished company indeed: clearly he is hardly a lone madman who fabricated the whole thing. Nevertheless, it is highly unlikely that at the tender age of twenty-two he had the kind of authority over such figures as Le Fur, Savoire, and Moncharville that a Grand Mastership would usually imply. We suspect that it was actually the other way round: those elderly but venerable men gave the orders but needed a young man as the face of their youth-oriented project. The ambitious and impressionable Plantard was their front man.

Who were these shadowy men of Alpha Galates? Just what kind of company was young Plantard keeping? The eminent legal professor Louis Le Fur (1870–1943) was right-wing but not extremely so, and a supporter of the Vichy regime, in which he held office. Even so, in his 1922 book *Races, Nationalities, States,* Le Fur attacked the alleged supremacy of the Aryan race—in fact, all theories of racial superiority—writing: "It is a theory without any certifiable scientific facts: it rests on postulates that are not even always in accord with each other, and one can affirm that it constitutes both an anti-scientific doctrine and a regression for humanity."[42] Significantly, Le Fur was a leading advocate of European unity, which he had pursued with his prewar think tank, Energie.

Plantard claimed he had met Monti through Camille Savoire (1868–1951), an eminent physician, holder of the Grand Cross of the Légion d'honneur, a philosopher and political theorist (described as a "propagandist for the cause of peace"), as well as a prominent Freemason. However, he was to switch his allegiance to a particular form of Freemasonry—the Rectified Scottish Rite—which is rather different from the mainstream version. In March 1935 he formed one of its governing bodies, the Grand Priory of the Gauls—an interesting name for two reasons—of which he remained Grand Prior until his death.[43]

Another of *Vaincre*'s well-known contributors was Robert Amadou (b. 1924), an authority on esotericism, Freemasonry, and parapsychology. He, too, belonged to the Rectified Scottish Rite, having been secretly (because of the wartime situation) initiated into its Alexandrie d'Égypte (Alexandria of Egypt) lodge in Paris in June 1943.[44] Before *Vaincre*'s appearance, he had already joined another significant society, the Martinist Order, into which he was initiated in 1942 by another celebrated writer on the esoteric, Robert Ambelain. Amadou was elevated to its highly secret interior order, the Silencieux Inconnus (Unknown Silents, or S.I.), in September that year, under the name Ignifer.[45] Amadou's involvement with these prestigious orders at the same time as Alpha Galates suggests that the latter enjoyed a similarly high status.

Amadou was also at school with Plantard's main postwar collaborator, Philippe de Chérisey—who wrote to the British researcher Geoffrey Basil-Smith in 1983: "The great specialist of the Martinist school is Robert Amadou. We were at school together; I suppose we are not on the best terms now."[46] We can hazard the guess that it was de Chérisey who introduced Amadou to Plantard.

Another young player on the same scene, Jacques Brosse (b. 1922), who wrote articles for *Vaincre* also on chivalry, would go on to become a well-known writer and philosopher, an exponent of Zen Buddhism and other forms of Eastern mysticism, a leading environmentalist, and one of the pioneers of experimentation with psychoactive drugs for mystical purposes. He was the friend of luminaries such as Carl Jung, Aldous Huxley, and—interestingly—Jean Cocteau (whose name recurs in relation to the Priory of Sion).

Vaincre also names as a former member of Alpha Galates Jean Mermoz, France's leading aviator—compared by many with Charles Lindbergh—who died in 1936 aged thirty-five. While his membership of Alpha Galates is impossible to verify, Mermoz (who shared Lindbergh's extreme-right ideas) was a leading member of Colonel de La Rocque's French Social Party (Parti Social Français), successor to the Croix de Feu.[47]

On the front page of the first edition of *Vaincre* there are a number of endorsements—quotations by various prominent individuals on the theme of chivalry. Although not claimed as members, clearly they were deemed desirable as associates of Plantard and Alpha Galates, or vice versa. One or two have somewhat sinister connections.

The prominent journalist Henry Coston writes (his emphasis): "Speeches are all very fine, but what use are they? You see, what is needed in our Homeland is action, a *chivalric action,* free from political intrigues." And Marshal Louis Franchet d'Espéréy adds his voice: "An Order of Chivalry, but it is the foundation stone of a nation, France is rightly lost for having replaced its *Chevaliers by Cavaliers.*"

Before the war, Marshal Franchet d'Espéréy (1856–1942)—one of France's most eminent soldiers—had been secretly involved with the right-wing terrorist network the Cagoule. Henry Coston (1910–2001), was also an extreme right-winger, who although a definite collaborator astonishingly managed to rehabilitate himself after the war.

The 1936 edition of the *Dictionnaire national des contemporains* (*National Dictionary of Contemporaries*) describes Coston as "one of today's youngest journalists and certainly the youngest director of a newspaper." In fact, he entered the world of journalism at the tender age of sixteen in 1927, already secretary to the Villeneuve-sur-Lot section of Action Française. After working for several newspapers, mainly the *Express du Midi,* he went to Paris to revive *La Libre Parole,* defunct since

1924. He also founded the *Éditions Nationales,* in which, according to the *Dictionnaire,* "he published under his signature some works on 'Judaism and Freemasonry.' "[48] He also founded the Franciste movement, which, in Coston's own words, was of "national and socialist tendencies."[49]

After the Liberation of Paris, Coston fled to Germany, but he was arrested in Austria in 1946. Having served a prison term for collaboration, he returned to journalism, founding Clubinter Presse and in 1952 La Librarie Française. In 1955 he published his first book since the war, the ominous-sounding *Financiers Who Run the World* (*Financiers qui mènent le monde*), before launching the review *Lectures françaises* in 1957.

Coston was extraordinarily prolific, editor of the four-volume *Dictionary of French Politics* (1967), in which—never a modest man—he included an entry for himself, also author of textbooks on journalism. One of his major obsessions was with the notion—as stated by Prime Minister Édouard Daladier in 1934—that France was controlled economically and politically by just two hundred families. Before the war, Coston stressed their alleged Jewishness, but in his 1960 book, *The Return of the "200 Families,"* the alleged Jewish connection was conspicuous by its absence—partly because even he could hardly pretend that this supposed Jewish elite had come through Hitler's war unscathed; in fact, perversely, he blamed many of the two hundred families for backing the Vichy regime so enthusiastically.

However, his output before and during the war made his views rather clearer. In 1937 he wrote *The Jews Against France,* in which he trotted out the usual fulmination against the notorious Protocols of the Elders of Zion—allegedly evidence for a Jewish conspiracy to rule the world that was, in fact, a hoax perpetrated in 1905 by the Russian secret police to foment anti-Semitism—particularly railing against Freemasonry. During the Nazi Occupation, Coston wrote *Jewish Finance and the Trusts* (1942), and in 1944 he edited and contributed many of the articles in a rabidly anti-Semitic, very glossy magazine with the unambiguous, not to say infantile, title *I Hate You!* (*Je vous hais!*), in which he upheld the authenticity of the Protocols of the Elders of Zion. He also blamed Jewish interests for backing the United States against Hitler, whom he portrayed as the defender of the Aryan race (in the words of one of the other contributors, "Hitler, the liberator, promoter of the defense of the Aryans").[50] Coston saw the war as "the ultimate phase of the age-old struggle that Judaism has conducted against the non-Jewish peoples."[51] (Utterly jaw-dropping after all the Nazi pogroms—not to mention the Holocaust, then in full, horrific flood.) He blindly trots out the usual hate-filled lines: the Jews control the theater, cinema, and the press, they're spies, et cetera, et cetera. It goes without saying that Coston maintained the old conspiracy theory that "Freemasonry is of Jewish origin."[52]

However, after all that acid racial bile, in his 1967 *Dictionary of French Politics,* under the entry "Jew," Coston actually sympathizes with the Jewish people for the "persecutions of which they were the victims in the course of the centuries, in antiquity, in the Middle Ages, and in the twentieth century—the last to date, the most odious and murderous, at the time of Hitler"—though still carefully and perversely pointing out, without making any particular point, the predominance of Jews in certain key fields, such as the press and advertising.[53]

Back in 1944, Coston was proudly writing with his usual egotistical twist, "After an eclipse of some years during which anti-Semitism remained dimmed, the name of Henry Coston, in 1927, brought about the reawakening of the anti-Jewish campaign with a *Libre parole nationale.*" He also boasted of forming the "particularly anti-Masonic" *Cahiers de l'Ordre* in 1929. And in an article entitled "The Enjewishment of France" (*L'enjuivement de la France*), on the history of Judaism in France, Coston makes this significant statement:

> The Visigoths and the Burgundians took measures in respect of them [the Jews], and the Council of Vannes, in 465, forbade priests from frequenting the sons of Israel. The Merovingian kings Clotaire II and Dagobert II were even more severe: the first withdrew from them the right to litigate against a Christian, and the second repressed them in his states.[54]

This is particularly disturbing: Dagobert II, later to be the Priory of Sion's great mystical folk hero, is revered here because of his anti-Semitism by someone with whom Plantard is happy to be associated—someone who also actively endorsed *Vaincre* and the Alpha Galates Order itself. This is not quite the noble romanticism of *The Da Vinci Code*!

However, demonstrating the elusive and paradoxical nature of *Vaincre,* this apparent outrage is balanced by the inclusion of another name, that of a German diplomat who, of all those mentioned in *Vaincre* as members of Alpha Galates, has attracted the most attention because of the potential implications of his membership—Hans Adolf von Moltke. Described as a "master in our Order," he appears, in an extraordinary statement in an article by Le Fur in the January 1943 issue of *Vaincre*, to endorse Plantard:

> I have the pleasure to say, before my departure for Spain, that our Order has at last found a chief worthy of it in the person of Pierre de France.
>
> It is therefore with total confidence that I depart to perform my mission; for while not deluding myself about the perils I run in discharging my duty, I know that until my last breath my watchword will consist in recognition of Alpha and fidelity to its chief.[55]

Why should such an eminent and well-connected German diplomat use such unequivocal language in backing a young, untried man like Plantard? Naturally, critics have suggested that the quotation is a fake—even that Le Fur never wrote the article. But cavalierly attributing such quotations to an important German, via a professor of law, would have been very risky. Von Moltke was to die suddenly less than two months after the publication of this issue of *Vaincre,* but no one could know that—so faking the endorsement would have been asking for trouble. And, as always, we need to ask what Plantard stood to gain for his agenda by exploiting such a name: what were *Vaincre*'s readers supposed to make of it?

A career diplomat from a prominent family, Hans Adolf von Moltke was German ambassador to Poland from 1931 to 1939 (already in harness before the Nazis came to power). He was then appointed ambassador to Spain—the departure referred to in Le Fur's article—against his wishes, according to his cousin Count Helmuth James von Moltke, who wrote that "When he raised objections, he was told to choose between Madrid and a concentration camp."[56] He died of appendicitis in Madrid in March 1943.

However, Hans Adolf's relationship to Helmuth James von Moltke links him to the anti-Hitler "resistance" in Germany, particularly the

Kreisau Circle (this was the Gestapo's term—the group itself had no formal name). This was formed by Helmuth James von Moltke and Peter Yorck von Wartenburg at the former's estate at Kreisau in Silesia.

The Kreisau group was not overconcerned with ousting the Nazi regime (although it was in contact with other groups that were, most especially the "resistance" cell centered on Colonel Claus von Stauffenberg, which mounted the failed July 1944 bomb plot to assassinate Hitler), being more concerned with planning for the reorganization of postwar Germany. Yorck von Wartenburg believed it would actually be beneficial for Germany under the Nazis to suffer a heavy defeat, as a kind of purging of the German psyche. But their ambitions went further—not just for the rebuilding of Germany but for the creation of a new Europe. Perhaps significantly, the Kreisau Circle is known to have had an agent in Paris from late 1942, although his or her identity has never been uncovered.[57]

Hans Adolf von Moltke was not only a cousin of Helmuth James but also married to von Wartenburg's sister Davida—so he certainly had connections to the leaders of the Kreisau Circle. But was he actually a part of it? And if so, did Plantard and Alpha Galates know?

Baigent, Leigh, and Lincoln argue that von Moltke's appearance in *Vaincre* shows a connection between Alpha Galates and the anti-Nazi movement in Germany. However, despite his link to the leaders of the Kreisau Circle by family and marriage, there is no direct evidence that Hans Adolf shared their convictions or aims.

Nevertheless, it seems too much of a coincidence that the Kreisau Circle's long-term agenda of creating a federal Europe was shared by Alpha Galates—as we will see—suggesting at least some form of coordination with the German "united Europe" lobby.

Predictably, views of *Vaincre* are nothing if not polarized. Those who take Plantard seriously emphasize the association with those such as von Moltke, whereas Plantard's critics seize on the link with the likes of the arch-anti-Semite Coston. Perhaps a closer examination of the periodical will shed some light on the matter.

Inside Knowledge

Always a peculiar publication—at least to Anglo-Saxon eyes—*Vaincre* was a heady and promiscuous mix of esoteric ideas and political agendas. On the quasi-mystical side, the main focus was on the distant past—ancient wisdom traditions, particularly of the Celts, and the reality of the lost continent of Atlantis. Moncharville's series of articles claimed that when Christianity obliterated the Druids, the "Atlantean tradition" was preserved by monks who used it when creating the Order of Galates, the brother order of the Cistercians. It was obviously a favorite theme: one Auguste Brisieux (possibly a pseudonym taken from a nineteenth-century Breton poet) wrote that survivors from Atlantis had established themselves in Brittany. The work of the astrologer and "Atlantologist" Paul Le Cour (1871–1954)—whose 1937 book, *The Age of Aquarius* (*L'Ere du Verseau*), greatly influenced the New Age movement—is frequently cited, although there is no suggestion he was personally involved in Alpha Galates. It should be remembered that such "alternative" ideas can crucially influence the real world—after all, similar notions lay at the root of Nazi ideology, even inspiring the Party's meteoric rise to power in Germany.

However, the most controversial aspect of *Vaincre* remains its politics. Later Plantard claimed it was a "Resistance journal," but his detractors maintain it was pro-Vichy—or even pro-Nazi. (Although there was a Resistance publication called *Vaincre*, this was probably just a coincidence: after all, *Conquer* was rather an obvious title for a wartime magazine.)

Certainly, Plantard presented the authors of *The Holy Blood and the Holy Grail* with a statement apparently from *Vaincre*'s printer, Poirier Murat, vouching that the publication was a "Resistance journal."[58] Perhaps Murat should be taken seriously—as a Chevalier of the Légion d'honneur and a leading figure in the French Resistance. At least, that is, according to Plantard when he produced the endorsement. However, when we checked with the relevant authorities we found that there was no record of Murat ever being awarded the Légion d'honneur.[59] So it appears Plantard was simply lying. This also calls into question the claim that Murat was a hero of the Resistance, which rests on Plantard's word.

Vaincre's emphasis on a "new knighthood" that would fight for the renewal of France *could* be taken as a veiled urging to rise up against the Nazi occupiers, but there are other interpretations. In fact, like many other organizations of that time and place, *Vaincre* was largely focused on a future France that would be blissfully independent, thanks to either an Allied victory or a reconciliation with a Nazi-dominated Europe. *Vaincre*—"conquer/conquest"—referred not to the Nazis but to France itself. Whatever happened, it was assumed that Pétain would still be in power when the dust settled.

Not only was *Vaincre* dedicated to Pétain, but it also declared Alpha Galates to be "solely devoted" to his service and that of France. In the first number, Plantard's editorial expressed admiration for the Vichy leader as—tellingly—the first man since the fall of the monarchy capable of uniting the French people. But of course being pro-Pétain did not automatically equate with being a collaborator—not until after the war, that is.

Although right-wing, *Vaincre* was anticapitalist: in the first issue Pierre de France wrote that Alpha Galates' vision of the country was based on "the cooperation and harmony of the people, united in a true socialism, banishing forever the quarrels created by capitalist interests." And he writes of the new movement to achieve this (his emphasis): "It must first of all be united, grouped together; it must be numerous, that is to say forming a Great Order of chivalry, because if we are *numerous and disciplined, we will be strong, because if we are strong we will be feared and can conquer,* that is to say impose on the masses a doctrine and an ideal." But what exactly was Plantard advocating? A paternalistic, hierarchical society certainly—but would it also be a dictatorship? After all, the Nazis were National *Socialists.*

Vaincre was nothing if not ambitious. Its "young knighthood" would have counterparts throughout Europe, the foundation for a "United States of the West." An often reproduced illustration from *Vaincre*'s first number shows a knight on horseback, carrying a flag bearing a symbol that later became the seal of the Priory of Sion, riding confidently on a road marked "États-Unis d'Occident" (United States of the West) toward a rising sun that encircles the sign for Aquarius, a reference to the coming astrological age. The road begins with the date 1937—when Alpha Galates was allegedly founded—while the sun is marked "1946," presumably the year when some program was scheduled to culminate. (One side of the road is marked "Brittany" and the other "Bavaria," implying that the United States of the West would be run by France and Germany.)

As might be expected, *Vaincre*'s politics were distinctly ambiguous: sometimes it is even unclear whether the writers approve or disapprove of their own chosen subjects. For example, Auguste Brisieux writes that "preparations for Hitler's coming to France have been going on since 1934, following the setback of February 6." But was it a "setback" for Alpha Galates or for its enemies? And was the Nazis' arrival in France deemed a good or a bad thing?

In fact, *Vaincre* sat firmly on the fence about Nazism and the Occupation, keeping its comments to the minimum—when they are mentioned, it is only in vague and ambiguous terms. In one of the few direct references to the Führer, in the January 1943 edition, Plantard wrote, "I want Hitler's Germany to know that every hindrance to our projects undermines it, as the Resistance of Freemasonry ruins German strength." However, he seems to have meant this as a warning to the German occupiers not to impede the Order. (It is true that the Germans appear to have been suspicious about *Vaincre* and Alpha Galates.)

Understandably, *Vaincre*'s strong and often nauseating anti-Semitic streak has prompted accusations of pro-Nazism. However, as the example of Poland—the most rabidly anti-Semitic country in Europe before it was virtually destroyed by the Germans—shows, it was possible to be anti-Jewish while also being anti-Nazi. Tragically, anti-Jewish sentiment was rife throughout Europe, and many who opposed German expansion and the rest of Nazi ideology at least agreed on that.

Plantard later defended himself by saying that *Vaincre* had to adopt such a tone to avoid raising German suspicions, hastening to point out that the collaborationist journal *Au Pilori* attacked *Vaincre*—and himself personally—in November 1942.[60] But that misses the point: if it had chosen to ignore the issue entirely, *Vaincre* would have emerged with much less ambiguity and potential blame.

Yet a curious fact suggests that something else was simmering away beneath the surface. In *Vaincre*'s January 1943 edition, an article by the pseudonymous Brisieux singled out the Jewish industrialist Fould for criticism, both as a Jew and as a Mason. Gaston Marie Achille Fould (1890–1969) was a member of a prominent Jewish banking family and grandson of the eminent Achille Fould, Napoleon III's Finance Minister. But fifteen years later Plantard and Fould would be working side by side on the Manifesto to the French (Manifeste aux Français), another "renewal of France" movement formed in the wake of General de Gaulle's return to power in 1958.[61] What this means is uncertain, though it does suggest that to some extent Alpha Galates was pursuing an agenda it deemed above even the politics of the Occupation. But what could possibly persuade the Jewish banker to cooperate with Plantard, editor of the apparently anti-Semitic *Vaincre*? What secret agenda could be big enough to mitigate such a personal and even racial insult?

On the subject of Freemasonry, although *Vaincre* usually took a hostile line, again there are ambiguities. Sometimes the magazine seems to approve—after all, some of its own were Masons. However, French Freemasonry is far from a homogeneous and unified movement, boasting several rival forms, each with its own governing body. The predominant branch—the one Vichy attacked—comes under the authority of the Grand Orient of France. But other bodies govern lodges with different systems or rites, such as the Grand Lodge of France and the National French Grand Lodge (Grand Loge Nationale Française, or GLNF). The chief difference among them is their attitude to God: the Grand Orient is, as befits republican France, neutral on the subject (the reason it remains unrecognized by the United Grand Lodge of England, which insists Masons believe in *a* god). While the GLNF is similarly theist, the Grand Lodge of France dedicates its work *solely* to the Great Architect of the Universe.[62]

However, during the Occupation, there was another important—though small—group, the Grand Lodge of the Rectified Rite (Grand Loge du Rite Rectifié), which represented the Rectified Scottish Rite (which, despite its name, has little connection with Scotland). Although it merged with the GLNF in 1958, it was still autonomous in 1942—and it included the Alpha Galates Masons: as we have seen, Camille Savoire created and presided over its Grand Priory of the Gauls. This resolves the apparent contradiction in *Vaincre:* it was possible to attack the Grand Orient while still belonging to the Rectified Rite. Alpha Galates and *Vaincre* could even represent an internecine struggle within French Freemasonry—the Rectified Scottish Rite's war on the Grand Orient.

However, the nature of the relationship between Rectified Scottish Rite Freemasonry and Alpha Galates is tantalizingly murky. The Order could have been a front or recruiting ground for the Rite, or perhaps they just shared similar aims. But as we discovered, this Masonic connection significantly underpins not just Alpha Galates but the Priory of Sion itself.

Entering the Priory

In his 1984 letter of resignation as Grand Master of the Priory of Sion, Plantard referred to his induction into the Order on July 10, 1943, on the recommendation of Abbé François Ducaud-Bourget[63]—but this seems to be a nonstarter as there is no proof that the Priory even existed at that time. However, the priest Ducaud-Bourget definitely did, and he is rather interesting.

An ardent royalist and ecclesiastical traditionalist, Ducaud-Bourget (1897–1984) founded the Universal Union of Catholic Poets and Writers (Union Universelle de Poètes et Écrivains Catholiques) and the review *Matines.* He was conventual chaplain of the Sovereign Military Order of Malta—the chivalric order descended from the medieval Knights Hospitaler that still enjoys a special status with the Vatican—between 1947 and 1961 and was awarded the Resistance Medal for his work during the war.[64] However, reflecting the paradoxical nature of the time, he was also a favorite of Pétain's: in fact, Ducaud-Bourget was Pétain's choice as the next Archbishop of Paris (the Catholic Church's highest authority in France).[65] (Later Ducaud-Bourget was reputed to have been Grand Master of the Priory in the 1960s.)

Maurice Moncharville's death in February 1943 seemed to spell the end for *Vaincre:* the periodical folded within the month, revealing that perhaps he had been its true driving force and financial backer, although there may have been an element of fear after the Germans' direct takeover of the Vichy government. Certain activities were no longer tolerated. While Alpha Galates might have made the right noises to the Nazis about Pétain and even the Occupation, not to mention Jews and Freemasons, it was still a quasi-chivalric body connected to a form of Freemasonry. As the tide suddenly turned against Germany in the wider war and its grip on the Occupied territories tightened, such connections were enough to attract suspicion.

Within a year of *Vaincre*'s end, Plantard was sent to prison for four months, again for reasons unknown. Once again the story is tantalizingly tortuous.

Plantard himself volunteered the information that he had spent time in Fresnes prison, near Paris, between October 1943 and February 1944, allegedly because of his Resistance activities. He also claimed to have been tortured by the Gestapo. This version of events appeared as well in an article by his first wife, Anne-Léa Hisler, in 1960 and in the printer Poirier Murat's alleged 1955 statement. In 1989 Plantard was even to claim—somewhat despicably—that he had been imprisoned for helping Jews obtain false papers, and that his release had come about through the intervention of Count Helmuth James von Moltke. This is highly unlikely: von Moltke had been arrested by the Gestapo the previous month and remained in prison until his execution a year later.[66]

Plantard's detractors claim that he was imprisoned for quite a different reason, perhaps some irregularity with *Vaincre* or running an unregistered society.[67] However, the fact that eight months elapsed between the last issue of *Vaincre* and his imprisonment argues against a direct connection with the publication. Besides, police reports in 1945 (after the Liberation) and 1954 state that, according to their files, Plantard did not have a criminal record, indicating that it was not the French authorities who were responsible for his imprisonment (which would have been the case if he had been running an unregistered society). Nobody knows the exact reason for his sentence.

The 1945 report, referring to his assorted requests to put Alpha Galates and other organizations on record, states: "These various requests, and perhaps his attitude toward the Occupation authorities, earned him an incarceration of four months in the prison at Fresnes."[68]

This is the nearest we have to an official explanation for Plantard's arrest and detention; while frustratingly short on details, it does indicate that he was regarded as an actual or potential nuisance by the German authorities. His sentence seems to have been something of a short, sharp shock to clip the wings of a cocky, power-hungry young man.

At least this is in Plantard's favor: it was the *Germans* in Paris who sought his arrest, unlikely for a collaborator or a known sympathizer. (Plantard's mother also told the 1945 investigators that the Gestapo, not the French police, had arrested her son.) But although being imprisoned by the Nazis is a long way from actually being a Resistance hero, reinvention of one's wartime past was hardly uncommon (as we have seen with Henry Coston). In fact, much more eminent people—even the future President Mitterrand—created yet more fabulous fantasy pasts for themselves when the facts were considerably less heroic.

Postwar Plantard

Little can be traced of Plantard's activities in the years between the Liberation and the registration of the Priory of Sion. In December 1945 he married Anne-Léa Hisler, although totally unnecessary mystery and evasion surround his marriage, as they do everything else in his life. He claimed they divorced in 1956, but in fact they were still living together in the mid-1960s—and it seems they remained man and wife until Anne-Léa's death in 1971.

According to her biographical sketch of her husband from 1960, they moved to Switzerland, near Lake Leman, in 1947.[69] According to official files, by 1951 he was back in France, having settled in Annemasse, where Pierre Jarnac claims he worked as a draftsman, although Plantard declared he was a journalist on the Priory of Sion's registration form, perhaps because it sounded more impressive.[70]

What *is* known is that Plantard was involved in some questionable financial dealings for which he received a six-month sentence. But the rest is shrouded in mystery, as researchers soon hit the wall of France's privacy laws, which are among the strictest in the world. Releasing information concerning someone's criminal record to a third party (apart from police and other government agencies) is strictly prohibited.

This is what we do know: in the 1980s Plantard became embroiled in certain very heated controversies, complete with threats of legal action. An anonymous circular concerning his alleged criminality sent to French and British researchers included this allegation:

> Is there any need to recall that in 1952, Pierre Plantard illicitly carried out transfers of gold ingots from France to Switzerland (to the Union des Banques Suisses) for more than ONE HUNDRED MILLION [francs] and that he went before the criminal court for fraud . . .[71]

When Baigent, Leigh, and Lincoln confronted Plantard with this, he admitted to having organized the gold transfers but said that doing so had not been against the law at the time (although it became illegal later). He claimed the gold was to fund a network of groups that were planning General de Gaulle's return to power. Of course, Annemasse, being on the Swiss border, would have provided an ideal base for such activities.[72]

The anonymous writer had implied that the gold transfer was directly connected with Plantard's prosecution for fraud, but while this is not the case, he *was* prosecuted for some form of financial impropriety in 1953. We know this from a letter in the Saint-Julien subprefecture's Priory of Sion file from Annemasse's mayor on June 8, 1956, which states that in December 1953 Plantard was sentenced to six months' imprisonment for *abus de confiance*—abuse of trust. Essentially this means embezzlement, diverting funds, or abusing one's position as a trustee (or similar) of somebody else's assets. But who the injured party was and exactly what Plantard did remain frustratingly obscure, as is any potential connection with the bullion transfers. All this does, however, reveal that Plantard had a dubious reputation with money.

The anonymous circular of 1983 makes another allegation regarding Plantard's morality:

> Then in 1957, not divorced from his former wife, he had a girlfriend of eighteen (the age of majority then being twenty-one) and that [sic] the parents brought a complaint against him.

Odd though it may seem today, in those days parents were legally responsible for children up to twenty-one, the rather elderly age of majority. Also at that time the moral climate in France—probably in reaction to the upheavals of the war—was bordering on puritanical: homosexuality and all forms of promiscuity were decidedly frowned on. And apparently here was the thirty-seven-year-old Plantard, a married man, having an affair with an eighteen-year-old girl—whose parents had filed an official complaint against him. It may sound bad, but surely it came nowhere near the full-blown police investigation for *détournement des mineurs,* "corruption of minors," of which Plantard's enemies accuse him. Worse, some such as Paul Smith describe the offense as "*child* corruption"—with the inevitable implication that Plantard molested a young child—without giving the precise details (or evidence for any other similar accusation).[73] Perhaps significantly, none of these critics made such claims while Plantard was alive.

But the 1983 denunciation made another allegation:

> This affair [of the eighteen-year-old], like the others, was ∴ hushed up, as Pierre Plantard was at the beginning of 1958 the secret agent of de Gaulle, assuming the secretariat of the Committees of Public Safety.

The ∴ sign symbolizes Freemasonry, suggesting that de Gaulle's Masonic supporters hushed the matter up—and that, during that period at least, Plantard had friends in high places.

But was Plantard really a "secret agent" of de Gaulle or the Gaullist movement? Certainly he would seem to have been: he claimed the gold transfers to Switzerland were intended for the pro–de Gaulle network, and there is also solid evidence not only that Plantard was a secret agent but also that he played a key role in one of the most important events in France's postwar history: de Gaulle's triumphant return to power and the creation of the Fifth Republic.

Recalled to Life

In August 1945 a triumphant Charles de Gaulle strode dramatically at the head of his troops into an ecstatically liberated Paris—brilliantly circumventing Roosevelt's plan to have France ruled by an Allied military government. Having run rings round the American President, de Gaulle now had himself proclaimed and accepted as the President of France's provisional government (i.e., the caretaker government until the dust settled).

De Gaulle's vision of France went far beyond the overthrow of the Nazis: he, too, truly believed that his beloved nation was sick to its soul. He was deeply opposed to a return to the prewar system of government; in his view, under the old Third Republic the political parties had enjoyed far too much power, resulting in frequent changes of government and difficulty in getting anything done. He wanted to rewrite the constitution to give more power to the Head of State—i.e., the President, previously largely a figurehead. To the committed monarchist de Gaulle, getting rid of the King had been an almost sacrilegious error—a sin and a crime. He would have brought the monarchy back, but as doing so would have caused an outcry approaching civil war, he sought the next best thing: a presidency with the powers of a monarch, effectively an elected king.[74]

However, as de Gaulle soon realized that his dream France was never going to materialize, he resigned on January 20, 1946. On October 13 a referendum endorsed the new constitution of the Fourth Republic, but not convincingly, as only about one-third of the people voted in favor (9.2 million for, 8.1 million against, 8.4 million abstained). But de Gaulle was right; government was chaotic: between 1946 and his return to power in 1958 there were no fewer than twenty-four governments and seventeen prime ministers.

In April 1947 de Gaulle launched his own political party, the French People's Rally (RPF), appropriating the emotive Free French symbol of the Cross of Lorraine. However, after a disastrous performance in the 1951 elections, he dissolved the RPF, withdrawing from public life to his house at Colombeyles-Deux-Églises in the Haute-Marne, on the edge of the Forest of Clairvaux, just forty miles from Domrémy, birthplace of another legendary savior of France, Joan of Arc. Ostensibly, he was writing his war memoirs—not so much to keep him occupied but, like Churchill, to ensure his version of the events would be preserved for posterity. But really he was waiting for the call that he was certain would come for him to resume his unique destiny. As he admitted:

> For the next six years, from 1952 to 1958, I was to devote myself to writing my War Memoirs without intervening in public affairs, but never for a moment doubting that the infirmity of the system would sooner or later lead to a grave national crisis.[75]

To everyone else de Gaulle's return seemed improbable. At the end of 1955, less than 1 percent of the population said that they hoped he would become President; in July 1956 this was 9 percent, and even as 1958 began his admirers still accounted for only a meager 13 percent. The great war hero was suddenly a has-been.[76]

By contrast, de Gaulle enjoyed a great deal of support in the armed forces, and those admirers were continually urging him to make a dramatic move. Marshal Alphonse Juin, one of France's leading commanders, wrote to him in May 1956 that the time had arrived for him to make a "solemn appeal" to the nation, as he had done in 1940. De Gaulle's firm but friendly rejection is telling: "For the moment I believe that, for me, silence is the most impressive attitude . . . if I speak one day, it will be to take action. When I am sure, we will be together once again."[77]

De Gaulle's strategy of biding his time, waiting for the great crisis that would have France begging him to return, eventually paid off.

To many French people, their country's decline was humiliatingly exemplified by the loss of their empire. Before the war France had possessed important colonies and protectorates in North Africa (Algeria, Morocco, and Tunisia), Central Africa, and French Indochina (modern Vietnam, Cambodia, and Laos). Although the countries of French Indochina won their independence in 1954, much worse was the agitation for independence that followed in Algeria.

France had held relatively nearby Algeria for so long, and so many of its nationals had settled there, that it was regarded virtually as part of France itself. But then came the unthinkable: it had to assign an increasing flood of troops to Algeria in an attempt to quell the growing clamor for independence. Finally, when the government appeared to be caving in, the colony's civilian and military leaders took over, creating a Committee of Public Safety. (Although Comité de Salut Public is customarily translated as Committee of Public Safety, making it sound like some pressure group for the prevention of accidents, to the French, *salut public* has the much more high-minded connotation of "national salvation.") This was a very French form of coup d'état based on lessons learned from the Revolution. The self-appointed committees took over the running of towns, ostensibly to maintain law and order during a crisis, but in reality to seize power.

Formed in Algiers, the Committee took control of the Algerian capital on May 13, 1958—essentially a takeover by Gaullist Army officers in defiance of the government in Paris. Not surprisingly, Prime Minister Félix Gaillard resigned. But then the rebellion threatened to spread to France itself (Metropolitan France, to distinguish it from its North African possessions). As the Army rose up against the government, civil war and a military dictatorship seemed to be imminent. A figure who had remained aloof from the situation and who could reconcile the opposing sides was needed. De Gaulle once again saw himself as, in his words, "the chosen instrument"[78] to save France, this time from itself.

The Algerian military told him that unless he took control, there would be military incursions into Metropolitan France itself: indeed, intelligence revealed that the invasion was planned for the night of May 27–28, with four thousand paratroopers poised to take control of Paris. On May 24 troops from Algiers landed in Corsica, while Committees of Public Safety seized power in Ajaccio, Calvi, and Corte. A network of committees, working closely with local Army commanders, also appeared in the major cities of France.

The British historian Michael Kettle noted of de Gaulle's role: "Things were as bad as in 1940. But to save France this time, he would have to be Pétain as well as de Gaulle. He knew that he was being called on as almost a trinity: as king, subconsciously by nearly all; as dictator, by many in the army and among the right; and as democratically elected Prime Minister, by a growing number in the country."[79]

As the nation held its breath, de Gaulle returned to Paris for discussions with the politicians. After being elected Prime Minister by the National Assembly on June 1, he formed a government, of which only two ministers—Michel Debré (Justice) and André Malraux (Information)—were known Gaullists. The next day—after a carefully stage-managed threat to resign and plunge the nation back into chaos—he was granted full powers to reform the constitution. The main architect of the new constitution was Debré, the new President de Gaulle's first prime minister.

De Gaulle finally achieved his dream of reshaping the constitution, establishing the Fifth Republic. The September 1958 referendum was decisive: 80 percent were in favor (on a turnout of 85 percent). Two months later, on December 21, 1958, de Gaulle was elected the first President of the Fifth Republic. (In fact this was the first time he had ever stood for election to public office.)

Although de Gaulle claimed the President would arbitrate between the various governmental branches, in reality he alone controlled national policy. John Laughland points out that "the powers enjoyed by the French President are unequalled by those of any other politician in the Western world."[80]

De Gaulle had swept back to power, to his destiny, with the mandate to reshape France as he had always wanted, because of the convenient uprising in Algeria—at least that is what the history books say. The truth was rather more complex. De Gaulle's supporters, especially in the military, had been poised to take advantage of any crisis—or had perhaps even engineered it.

There is no doubt that there was a behind-the-scenes plot—a conspiracy—to bring de Gaulle back. What has never been established is whether he was aware of it or even its prime mover. He always professed that he knew nothing. But then he could hardly say otherwise. He claimed:

> The crisis that broke out on May 13 in Algiers did not . . . surprise me in the least. Nevertheless, I had played no part whatsoever either in the local agitation, or the military movement, or the political schemes which provoked it, and I had no connection with any elements on the spot or any minister in Paris.[81]

He acknowledged that the Governor-General of Algeria, Jacques Soustelle, had been one of his closest associates during the war and in the RPF, and that various other former associates had promulgated the idea in Algeria that he should be called upon to take power. But he insisted, "They did so without my endorsement and without having even consulted me."[82]

But surely it is beyond belief that the astute de Gaulle could have remained unaware of such high-profile plotting. Either he adopted a Nelsonian "I see no ships" attitude or he was kept fully informed but cannily maintained the required level of plausible deniability. Otherwise it could have been said that de Gaulle had conspired with the Army to take control of France—unthinkable!

As we saw in Chapter 1, the RPF had an internal *service d'ordre,* which was to become the SAC. Although it was officially nonexistent between 1953 and 1958, it is hard to believe that it was content to kick its heels—especially while de Gaulle's military devotees were feverishly preparing for his triumphant return.

Merry and Serge Bromberger, in their 1959 book, *The 13 Plots of the 13 May* (*Les 13 complots du 13 mai*), identify the small group of de Gaulle supporters who planned the events. They included Jacques Soustelle, whom they say adopted the tactics of the Wooden Horse of Troy by returning to Algiers, and Michel Debré.[83]

This being France, the situation becomes complicated, because despite official denials of any plotting, there were in fact *two* plots (besides several subplots) which involved the Army and Committees of Public Safety, both of which went into action on May 13, 1958. The other major conspiracy was by an anti–de Gaulle faction that wanted to engineer a military takeover. It had the same objectives and employed the same methods—the only difference being one wanted de Gaulle and the other emphatically did not.

The other conspiracy was masterminded by the arch-intriguer Dr. Henri Martin, who had been one of the founders of the prewar Cagoule. He, with a number of generals and another great conspirator, the Belgian Pierre Joly, formed a group with the unlikely name the Grand O, which the Brombergers called "the new Cagoule."[84] Fomenting a crisis, the Grand O carried out a campaign of bombing in Algeria in 1957. The center of the plot was Saint-Étienne (one of the locations mentioned in *Circuit*), headquartered at the house of the former Resistance worker Thérèse Obertaud (wartime code name Gladys), where a police raid on the night of May 16–17, 1958, found a cache of machine guns and other arms. Over the following days, similar large hoards were found in the Loire and Puy-de-Dôme.[85]

As a final convolution, the network of Committees of Public Safety established in France itself was effectively shared between the two groups of conspirators as they involved both pro– and anti–de Gaulle factions. And as it became clear that popular support was with the General, the Grand O conspirators eventually threw their lot in with him anyway.[86] Therefore the main problem with the plot to return de Gaulle is that it is exceptionally difficult to know after the event who was motivated by what.

The Mysterious Captain Way

In 1964 Anne-Léa Hisler wrote that the Committees of Public Safety operated under the command of Marshal Alphonse Juin and that the ruling committee consisted of Michel Debré, André Malraux, and Pierre Plantard, "known as Way." She quotes from de Gaulle's letters to Plantard ordering the disbanding of the committees.[87] If true, this marks Plantard out as a very significant player indeed. (Unfortunately, nobody has ever been able to establish the authenticity of these letters, as the originals have never been seen.) Although it would be tempting to dismiss this as typical Plantardian flimflam, in fact there is good evidence to believe it.

On May 18, 1958, foreign media agencies such as the American United Press received a release announcing that a Committee of Public Safety was operating in the Paris area.[88] This was obviously big news. On June 6—five days after de Gaulle was voted in as Prime Minister—an article appeared in the national daily *Le Monde* with the headline "How Many Committees of Public Safety Are There in France?" It quoted Léon Delbecque, one of the men who had set up the original Algiers committee, who said that that committee would continue and that a national committee would soon be established, referring to the "three hundred and twenty Committees of the Metropole" (i.e., 320 committees were poised to seize power throughout France). Committees were already officially acknowledged in Toulouse, Tarbes, Lyons, and the Rhône. In an electrically charged atmosphere, a communiqué had been issued by the Central Committee, in the name of Captain Way, declaring:

> The Committee of Public Safety must express the wishes of the people, and it is in the name of liberty, unity, and solidarity that all the French must participate in the work of reconstruction of our country; all the volunteers who have followed our appeals for fifteen days must be present today and help General de Gaulle. Patriots, to your posts, and trust in the man who has already saved France: General de Gaulle.[89]

Three days later *Le Monde* stated that Committees of Public Safety now existed in and around Paris and in fourteen other *départements.* And the newspaper now had more information on the mysterious Captain Way, the National Committee's secretary, who had written to them under his real name—Plantard. (He took the alias from his telephone number, which could be dialed by spelling "WAY" and "PAIX.") The letter states:

> The Central Committee was created on May 17, and its object was propaganda and providing liaison among all the Committees of Public Safety in France.

> Considering that France is a land of liberty, that each has the absolute right of his convictions, our action is outside all politics, exclusively on the patriotic level, to bring our maximum strength to the renewal of France.
>
> In this way we have declared in a letter of May 29 to M. General de Gaulle that "we conform strictly to the directives we receive from the authorities."[90]

The article also reported on a new communiqué from the National Committee and signed by its President, J.-E. Gavignet, a former Resistance leader who had been deported to Dachau: "Between May 16 and May 18 our Committee founded provisional Committees of Public Safety in six arrondissements of Paris, twenty-two communes of the Seine, Seine-et-Oise, and Seine-et-Marne, and in fourteen metropolitan departments." *Le Monde* described Plantard as an accountant for a Paris business, while he himself mendaciously claimed to be a "former deportee," presumably to borrow some reflected glory from Gavignet's wartime trauma.

Finally, seven weeks later, *Le Monde* announced that the Central Committee had folded, reproducing a communiqué from Way:

> The dissolution is made of the Central Committee of Public Safety for the Paris region, which leads the Committees of Public Safety in Paris and other localities, thereby freeing the activists who responded to the call of May 17.
>
> The Central Committee's officials have resolved to form federations of the movement of the Manifesto to the French [La Manifeste aux Français], 139, Rue Lafayette, Paris (Tenth Arrondissement), the national rally whose program ensures the defense of the country and of liberty.
>
> For the bureau of the Committee
> Captain Way[91]

The paper comments:

> [Of] the "Movement of the Manifesto to the French," which succeeds the committee . . . M. Pierre Plantard is secretary of propaganda, and one finds among its members the names of MM. Achille

Fould, industrialist; Paritsch, journalist; Maurice Du Parc, . . . and Dr. Paul Baron.

So at least Plantard had colleagues. It was certainly no one-man band. (But curiously, Achille Fould had been singled out for criticism, as both a Jew and a Freemason, in the January 1943 issue of *Vaincre*. His association with Plantard in 1958 seems too coincidental, suggesting that the wartime publication—even his denunciation—had actually been part of some elaborate, long-term game.)

In other words, less than two years after the public debut of the Priory of Sion and *Circuit*, Plantard really did play a key role in the events that thrust de Gaulle back to power. However, it seems he was just an organizer and issuer of statements, not a decision-making mover and shaker.

Of course one's head reels. Surely, as Plantard was pro-*Pétain* during the Vichy period, he was the last person to work so keenly for de Gaulle's cause. However, it was by no means as incongruous as it might first seem to switch allegiance from wartime marshal to leader of the Free French. As we have already noted, de Gaulle and Pétain harbored similar visions of France's future—they were enemies not because of differing principles but because of their individual situations after the Fall of France. There is the added complication that Plantard might have been part of Henri Martin's Grand O conspiracy, which began as an anti–de Gaulle plot but switched sides.

Plantard's and Hisler's claims check out. The only controversy is that they name Michel Debré and André Malraux as leaders and claim that the committees were controlled by the senior military veteran Marshal Alphonse Juin. In fact, these three were de Gaulle's closest supporters—he records that at the end of May, in the lead-up to the critical parliamentary vote, "Marshal Juin, for his part, came to assure me that the Army was behind me as one man."[92] (Juin does seem to have been involved in the behind-the-scenes plotting, especially as he held no official post in the armed forces at that time).[93]

Officially the trio had no connection with the events that brought about de Gaulle's return until after the Algerian coup, and then only in an aboveboard way. Nevertheless, committees *had* been established throughout France ready to be mobilized once the crisis broke—and *some* high-ranking Gaullist must have controlled them. But he could never be identified—officially de Gaulle was simply swept along by events. The clamor for him to return had to be seen as totally spontaneous. Whoever really ran the committees would have to work through front men, middlemen, and intelligence cutouts. Perhaps not surprisingly, Malraux in his memoirs claims to have been astonished at what unfolded, writing that when asked how he thought de Gaulle would return to power:

> "Through a conspiracy of the military in Indo-China," I answered. "They think they're using him but will get their fingers burnt." It was not the Indo-China army, and when my prophecy proved almost right I was staying in Venice, absolutely certain that nothing was going to happen.[94]

Naturally, Malraux returned hotfoot to Paris and two days later was summoned by de Gaulle, who although not yet in power offered him the post of Minister of Information. Ever the action man, Malraux wanted something more challenging, such as running the Algerian hot spot, but he was refused.

Assuming his testimony is accurate, if Malraux was out of the country, not expecting the coup in Algiers, he could hardly have helped orchestrate the wider conspiracy to bring back de Gaulle. However, his appointment as Minister of Information—i.e., propaganda—which lasted for the few months while de Gaulle established himself, would have provided convenient cover and opportunity for managing grassroots support. After all, that was the committees' main business.

It is interesting that when Anne-Léa Hisler's booklet was submitted to the Bibliothèque Nationale, Juin, Malraux, and Debré were not only all still alive but also in positions of authority, yet no action was taken against either her or Plantard.

1956 and All That

Besides Plantard's involvement with the Committees of Public Safety, other clues link him with de Gaulle: the 1952 bullion transfers coincide with the dissolution of the RPF and the establishment of the clandestine network to prepare the way for the General's return. It is even possible to suggest that Plantard was working in some way for—or with—the organization that later became the SAC, or the Grand O network. So was the registration of the Priory of Sion and its magazine *Circuit* in 1956—two years before de Gaulle's return—also part of this long-term plan for the destiny of France, perhaps even the whole of Europe?

Confusion surrounds not only *Circuit*'s content but also the supposed raison d'être of the Priory of Sion (according to its 1956 registration). As we have seen, *Circuit* bore a remarkable similarity to the typical Resistance publication: covertly maintaining contact among scattered partisans and supplying them with coded instructions while its network of clandestine groups operated under the cover of housing associations. In fact, some locations mentioned in the first *Circuit*'s council house news were where Committees of Public Safety were said to be operating just two years later.

In 1980 a Belgian magazine article about the Priory of Sion quoted an alleged member (Lord Blackford) as stating that the 1956 Priory was merely a breakaway group from the "real," much older Priory and that it had been "dissolved after the events of 1958 in France."[95] It all forms a remarkably consistent pattern.

Gino Sandri gives the current official line on the Priory's 1956 registration as this: "The association created in Annemasse responded to its time, in that place, to a precise aim. It was . . . if you prefer, a sort of exterior circle. A similar function was allotted to the Order of the Alpha Galates created in 1934 in Paris."[96] So the Annemasse Priory and Alpha Galates *were* fronts, if we can believe Sandri.

A year after de Gaulle's momentous return, Plantard produced *Circuit* again—or rather, he produced another publication with the same name. But apart from their title, the two *Circuit*s have virtually nothing in common. This version made no connection with the Priory of Sion/CIRCUIT, proclaiming itself the "publication of social, cultural, and philosophical studies" of the Federation of French Forces (Fédération des Forces Françaises)—a completely fictitious organization. Significantly, there was no attempt to register the Federation, as required by law. The reason for registering the Priory of Sion in 1956 appears to have been to legitimize the publication of the bizarre original *Circuit*, but in 1959 Plantard seems to have felt safe dispensing with this nicety, producing a magazine that advertised itself prominently as the Federation's "cultural periodical." With de Gaulle now in power, did he consider himself immune from hostile official action, at least on that score?

The new *Circuit* ran to at least nine monthly issues, the first dated July 1, 1959, with a circulation of about fifteen hundred—or so it claimed. It was produced from Plantard's address in the Avenue Pierre Jouhay in Aulnay-sous-Bois (which Anne-Léa Hisler cited as the headquarters of the Committees of Public Safety), a northeastern suburb of Paris. At first, like the earlier version, *Circuit* was cheaply typewritten and copied—but soon it was professionally produced, just like *Vaincre.*

Obviously the new publication was really a continuation of the wartime journal: there are even frequent references to previous numbers of *Vaincre,* almost as if it had never ceased. The overall tone is patriotic, appealing for French unity with exhortations to revive the spirit of the Resistance. *Circuit* Mark Two also outlined sweeping plans for the reorganization of France's central and local government. And, as in *Vaincre,* the ideal of a united Europe is stressed; this time, it is a United States of Euro-Africa—including the surviving European colonies, chiefly French North Africa. The 1959–60 *Circuit* also shares with *Vaincre* an overt esotericism, with articles on symbolism and astrology (again proposing a thirteenth sign, Ophiuchus the serpent bearer, between Scorpio and Sagittarius).

Both Anne-Léa Hisler and her husband wrote for the resurrected magazine—Plantard under his own name and that of Chyren. But what was the new *Circuit* really about, and who was it aimed at? Baigent, Leigh, and Lincoln suggest it may have been intended to maintain contact between the cells of the now-disbanded Committees of Public Safety.[97] This makes sense if, as we believe, the 1956 *Circuit* passed coded messages between local cells that would emerge as Committees of Public Safety when the time came. Now that they had achieved their goal, the committees had been disbanded, but logic—and common sense—dictates that the machinery had to be kept in place in case it should be needed again. Of course, the more secure de Gaulle became, the less likely it would be to be called upon.

Taking Stock

Given what we know of Plantard's pre-1956 career—and his involvement in the dramatic events of 1958—if we were asked to assess the raison d'être of the Priory of Sion in, say, 1960, we would have to conclude it was a front for those who had plotted de Gaulle's return to power. They were probably connected either with the General's "praetorian guard," the SAC, or with the Grand O.

As for Plantard's role—first in Alpha Galates and then in the Committees of Public Safety—he was essentially the front man, the public face. He seems to have had a gift for creating and organizing groups, though less so for maintaining them. And although he issued communiqués and wrote editorials, the ideas they expressed seem to have originated with others, who preferred to keep themselves in the background. While his name and photograph appeared on the first page of *Vaincre* as Editor and Grand Master of Alpha Galates, in reality Plantard seems to have been more of a figurehead, with more senior individuals behind him. This pattern was repeated in the Committees of Public Safety.

We have also noted the 1941 police report that stated Plantard was adept at creating "more or less fictional" societies. If, as we were becoming increasingly convinced, the Priory of Sion was established as some form of front, what better qualifications were needed for the front man?

At this point, it is telling what has *not* been mentioned. There is nothing about Merovingians, Knights Templar, or lost treasure. No claim to a thousand-year pedigree or the existence of a sacred bloodline. Nothing of the potent later mythos that was to become so familiar through *The Holy Blood and the Holy Grail* and *The Da Vinci Code.* Although articles on the esoteric appear in the later *Circuit,* between June 1956 and July 1959 the focus is strictly political and social.

But if the Priory of Sion was registered as a cover for *Circuit,* itself seemingly a front for an underground Gaullist network, the big question is: was the society created for this purpose, or did it already exist? The evidence as it stood in 1960 suggested the former—but then there are the so-called Cocteau statutes.

"Astonish me!"

In 1980 it was claimed that the statutes deposited with the Saint-Julien subprefecture in 1956 were effectively just dummies for the record, while the real statutes were not for public consumption. The writer and journalist Jean-Luc Chaumeil, who devoted a great deal of time and effort to researching the Priory of Sion in the 1970s, produced a copy of what he claimed were the real statutes. These added a whole new dimension to the controversy, as they bore the signature of the man who was said to be Grand Master in 1956: the famous poet, playwright, artist, and filmmaker Jean Cocteau.[98]

At least the story is consistent: the *Circuit* of June 3, 1956, refers to a forthcoming meeting to discuss the statutes, and the Cocteau version is dated two days later. (The original statutes are dated a month earlier.) Priory documents from 1981 also refer to its last convention being held on June 5, 1956.

Cocteau's name was first linked with the Priory in 1967, perhaps suspiciously four years after his death—but of course the head of a truly secret society would hardly have advertised the fact in his lifetime. Cocteau's name appears as the most recent Grand Master on the list in one of the Dossiers Secrets deposited in the Bibliothèque Nationale. It follows two other names from the world of the arts and literature: Victor Hugo—whose novels include *Les Misérables*—allegedly Grand Master from 1844 to 1885, and the composer Claude Debussy, from 1885 to 1918. Cocteau is said to have taken over the Priory in 1918, when he was twenty-nine, and to have presided over it for the rest of his life.

But is Cocteau's signature genuine? Unfortunately, this is yet another dead end. The signature appears authentic, but forging signatures is not particularly difficult, especially when specimens are so easy to obtain, as with someone as famous as Cocteau. On the one hand, Baigent, Leigh, and Lincoln took the signature to be the real thing, using it to make certain deductions about the Priory—but if the signature is a fake, then of course those deductions are invalid. On the other hand, if we assume (in the absence of evidence that the document existed before the end of the 1970s) that it is a fake and *that* assumption is wrong, then any conclusions we extrapolate from it would be equally wrong. It is all very frustrating.

Authentic or not, the statutes make their own contribution to the controversy. They declare the *founding* of the Sionis Prioratus or Priory of Sion, although stating that it follows the "usage and customs" of an original but defunct Order established by Godefroy de Bouillon in 1099.

The membership must never exceed 121 (although it does not say whether there *were* or *are* that number), a much more reasonable tally than the nearly 10,000 of the other statutes. There are also said to be 243 "free brothers" known as "valiants" (*preux*) or the Children of St. Vincent, without voting rights—a separate but affiliated order said to have been formed in 1681.

Membership is open to adults who accept the society's aims and constitution, regardless of gender, race, politics, or religion—i.e., it is not exclusively Catholic, a fundamental contradiction between the two sets of statutes. However, membership is also *hereditary:* each member is allowed to bequeath his (or her) grades and titles—bizarrely including even the Grand Mastership—to their son or daughter.

There are five grades, with titles similar (but not identical) to those of 1956: Nautonnier, Crusader, Commander, Knight, and Squire. Here, the top three grades constitute the executive council of the Arche Rose-Croix (rather than Kyria).

Plantard later explained the existence of two—blatantly contradictory—sets of statutes dating from the same time as the result of a schism. In 1979 he wrote to the researcher Jean Robin: "The Priory of Sion created at Annemasse in 1956 by André Bonhomme has not existed since 1962; it was only a split of members of another Priory of Sion, which was produced in 1956 by the intransigence of Jean Cocteau."[99] Other information disseminated by the Priory amplified this: Cocteau wanted to make certain changes to the statutes that antagonized some of the members.[100] The explanation may appear to work, but it fails to be entirely convincing.[101]

Still, is there any evidence that Cocteau was really involved with the Priory, or at least with known members? And if he was never actually involved, why did the hoaxers choose him of all people? The flamboyant and dissolute Cocteau was hardly an obvious choice to lend credibility to the society's historical and esoteric claims.

Jean Cocteau (1889–1963) was one of the stars of twentieth-century French culture. Born into a solidly bourgeois family, he entered the milieu of the Parisian salons in the 1910s, mixing—and working—with luminaries such as Serge Diaghilev, Pablo Picasso, and Erik Satie, collaborating with the last two on the ballet *Parade* in 1917. He also knew and stayed with Maurice Barrès, writing a memoir of one visit when they discussed the Baillard brothers during the First World War.[102] In both life and art, the ever creative Cocteau certainly did his best to fulfill Diaghilev's injunction on their first meeting in 1913: "Astonish me!"[103]

Cocteau's career progressed from poet—he described poetry as "religion without hope"—through playwright to maker of dark and sardonic mythological art-house movies. Basically an artist and designer, Cocteau led an excessive personal life that was the complete antithesis of his bourgeois background: he was not only homosexual but also, for a large part of his life, a habitual drug user.

He was also mad about the unexplained or downright weird. His biographer Patrick Mauriès writes: "In his latter years he had become fascinated with UFOs (calling them 'saucers') and claimed he was the first 'parapsychological' poet."[104] He wrote the foreword to one of the first, and classic, French studies of UFOs, Aimé Michel's *Lueurs sur les soucoupes volantes* (1954, published in English as *The Truth About Flying Saucers*). He was also keenly interested in the controversial "catastrophist" theories of Immanuel Velikovsky, calling *Worlds in Collision* "indispensable."[105]

However, perhaps his greatest preoccupation in the last decade of his life was the paradoxical nature of time. He considered the experiences related in *An Adventure* by the English academics Charlotte Moberly and Eleanor Jourdain—who claimed to have experienced a "time slip" in the grounds of the palace of Versailles that plunged them back into the eighteenth century—as "the most important of our time."[106]

It was his passion for the vagaries and meaning of time (which runs through his haunting and peculiar last film, *The Testament of Orpheus—Le testament d'Orphée,* 1960) that underpinned his interest in parapsychology and the paranormal (psi). He wrote in his 1954 journal:

> The *psi* phenomena belong to a world, a plane, where the notions of determinism, of cause and effect, are no longer valid. (Jung.)
>
> Paranormal phenomena are transcendent in relation to time and space.[107]

While we personally have no problem with the reality of the paranormal, unfortunately there is nothing to connect Cocteau's psi research with the Priory as an organization. In fact we are stuck with considerably more basic questions than that. Is there any evidence at all to link Jean Cocteau with the Priory of Sion, particularly with the supposed upheavals and reorganizations of summer 1956? After all, if they were anything like as dramatic as we have been led to believe, they must have been very time-consuming for their Grand Master.

As far as we can establish, Cocteau spent most of that critical year in his villa in Saint-Jean-Cap-Ferrat, near Nice, working on two frescoes, for the chapel of St. Peter in the nearby fishing village of Villefranche-sur-Mer and, rather incongruously, for the Register Office farther up the coast in Menton, on the other side of Monte Carlo.

Although the three volumes of his journal published since 1983—under the title *The Definite Past* (*Le passé défini*)—take us only up to 1954, Cocteau made it known that he always intended them for publication.[108] Clearly, therefore, they would hardly include any of the juicier bits he wanted to keep from the public. Whether potentially in the "juicy" category or not, there are no references to the Priory of Sion or its associates, such as Plantard. But then again, if Cocteau was doing his job properly as the head of a secret society, we would hardly expect to find him committing it to paper. However, we were excited to discover—as we will explain later—that Cocteau does refer to people and subjects that were to assume a huge significance as our investigation proceeded.

He knew Debussy, his alleged predecessor as Grand Master—they were both frequenters of the great Paris salons—but then a hoaxer would have selected public figures whose paths were known to have crossed. Of those figures from Plantard's early years, Cocteau's most direct connection was with Robert Amadou, a member of Alpha Galates and contributor to *Vaincre.* Cocteau corresponded with Amadou—both wrote forewords to the 1959 French edition of Moberly and Jourdain's now-classic time-slip book.[109]

At the time of *Vaincre,* Cocteau carried on artistic business as usual in occupied Paris. Mauriès comments: "Cocteau can scarcely be said to have distinguished himself, by either his actions or the soundness of his judgment, during the war years."[110] This was (and is) enough to brand him a collaborator in some people's eyes, but he had also been unwise enough to write a salute to the fascist artist Anno Becker in 1942. Although cleared of active collaboration, Cocteau remained a pariah (perhaps paradoxically) to the far right for the rest of his life.

However, although no direct evidence can be found to link Cocteau with the Priory or Alpha Galates, he was such a complex personality that the idea of his involvement or even his Grand Mastership can never be dismissed out of hand. For example, in *Jean Cocteau and His World* (1987), Arthur King Peters writes of his now-famous mural in London painted in 1960: "In the Soho district of London, Cocteau's murals for the Church of Notre-Dame de France include certain curious bits of iconography, such as a black sun emitting black rays, that are sometimes associated with the Prieuré de Sion, a secret religious society in which Cocteau was purported to have been Grand Master."[111] Peters, at least, resists the temptation to reject the notion, presumably because it is unwise to disregard anything about such a multifaceted artist and paradoxical character. Undoubtedly, the symbolism in the mural *is* very significant, as we will see shortly—although Peters can offer no explanation for it.

One person who happily shed light on this for us was the artist, actor, and singer Alain Féral, who as a young man worked with Cocteau. A member of the 1960s band Les Enfants Terribles, named after the play that made Cocteau famous, Féral has been described as the older man's protégé. In 1984 he settled in the village of Rennes-le-Château, where he set up his artist's studio. But Féral made it clear to us that Cocteau was his mentor, philosophically or spiritually—perhaps even esoterically—rather than artistically.

Even so, Féral was quite specific that Cocteau had *not* been Grand Master of the Priory of Sion—in fact, from his own research, he condemned the entire list of Nautonniers as a fabrication. But far from dismissing the whole thing as a cheap hoax using the great man's name in vain, Féral asserted that there were good and specific reasons for Cocteau's name appearing on that list, just as there were for all the other names. Yes, it was a fabrication, but it was neither random nor meaningless. In fact, it had been meticulously crafted.

This was most intriguing. Cocteau was involved in something esoteric—but not the Priory of Sion (at least in its public form). Again, we were drawn to the idea that the Priory we knew was some kind of cover or front for something else—either to put some distance between researchers and the real organization or to divert them from its real activities. And while there is no direct evidence to link Cocteau with Plantard or the Priory, a study of the artist's works reveals very similar preoccupations and themes.

We have already referred to Cocteau's weird mural in central London's "French Church"—Notre-Dame de France in Leicester Place, off Leicester Square—which is described in detail in our previous book.[112] There are significant resonances between this mural and other artistic works connected with the Priory's story. For example, the design is clearly based on the geometry of the pentagram, as is Nicolas Poussin's *The Shepherds of Arcadia,* which recurs in the mystery.

We were excited to discover that Cocteau's symbolism in the French Church mural parallels Leonardo's in *The Last Supper,* a similarity that was both unexpected and astonishing, especially as the two artists both appear on the list of the Priory's Grand Masters, five hundred years apart.

As we explained in Chapter 1, it was Leonardo's obsession with John the Baptist—as expressed in the symbolism of his paintings, particularly the "John gesture"—that led us to uncover the whole Johannite heresy. It was therefore extraordinary to read the closing passage of a short essay that Cocteau contributed to a 1959 book on Leonardo. Cocteau refers to an earlier poem, *Homage to Leonardo,* repeating its last two stanzas and explaining: "They say better than this short piece what Leonardo inspires in me and the fraternal love I bear for him." The final verse clearly refers to Leonardo's *St. John the Baptist* and the John gesture describing how his index finger *dexterously* points the way to a mysterious realm in which da Vinci is triumphant.[113]

In fact, Cocteau was named after John the Baptist—as is the custom in France, he celebrated the saint's day of June 24 as a kind of second birthday[114]—perhaps prompting a fascination with the Baptist that led into full-blown Johannitism.

Cocteau was also preoccupied with the relationship between myth and history—a recurring theme of Priory members—writing:

> In my estimation, I prefer the mythologist to the historian. Greek mythology, if one immerses oneself in it, is of more interest than the distortions and simplifications of history, because its lies remain

> unalloyed with reality, while history is an alloy of reality and lies. The reality of history becomes a lie. The unreality of the fable becomes the truth.[115]

Words that could almost be the blueprint for the Priory of Sion.

Making Myths

The theme of myth taking precedent over historical fact arises again in another prominent individual's alleged relationship with the Priory of Sion. André Malraux was one of several illustrious names who, like Cocteau, were claimed as Priory men in the early 1980s, after their deaths.[116] Even so, perhaps the putative Malraux connection can shed some light on the turbulent 1950s—when he and Marshal Alphonse Juin were allegedly particularly prominent. As Plantard's wife said that together with Michel Debré they were responsible for the Committees of Public Safety—although the Priory has never claimed Debré as a member—the next stage in our effort to make sense of the Sion story is to examine the lives and careers of these two men.

The Algerian-born Marshal Alphonse Juin (1888–1967) was a professional soldier who spent much of his career in North Africa, rising to the rank of general in 1938. On the outbreak of Hitler's war a year later, he commanded a motorized infantry division in France and was captured in June 1940 but released by the intercession of General Maxime Weygand (the Supreme Commander of British and French Forces until the French surrender), returning to command troops in Morocco. Succeeding Weygand as Commander in Chief of French Forces in North Africa under the Vichy regime, Juin exploited his position to lend clandestine support to the American-led Operation Torch landings in Algiers and Morocco in November 1942, after which he led the Free French in the Tunisian campaign before commanding the French Expeditionary Force in Italy, experiencing the hell of Monte Cassino. As de Gaulle's Chief of Defense Staff, he was by his side on D-Day and at the liberation of Paris.

Juin's glittering career was by no means over with the end of the war. After four years as Resident General in Morocco, he became Commander in Chief of NATO Land Forces in the Central European Theater

Command, taking control of all British, Dutch, Belgian, French—and even American—troops in Germany.

In 1953 Juin was accorded the highest honor France can offer its military heroes, the rank of Marshal of France. This award is so prestigious that, once conferred, it can never be removed—even Pétain remained a marshal. But Juin did not approve of the way postwar France was being run or the increasing materialism of Western society.[117] Tired of the battles he had to fight with politicians over European defense, he retired, at his own request, on October 1, 1956.

During de Gaulle's years of retreat at Colombey, many Army officers saw Juin as a sufficiently august substitute, urging him to exploit his position to cause the government to tumble in order to take over. However, the loyal Gaullist Juin refused: in any case, he knew de Gaulle was just waiting in the wings to resume his place in the spotlight.[118]

Clearly Juin was a highly principled, devoted, but hardly blind Gaullist, but does that mean he was also a Priory man?

"Not a writer—an event"

And what of the other major figure named by Madame Plantard as a prime mover in the Committees of Public Safety? André Malraux (1901–1976), whose best-known work is *The Human Condition* (*La condition humaine,* 1933), was an intriguing blend of artist and action man, a novelist and adventurer whom de Gaulle appointed Minister of Cultural Affairs, a post he held for ten years from 1959. He always possessed an indefinable aura: as William Righter notes in *The Rhetorical Hero* (1964): "Malraux entered the European consciousness not as a writer but as an event, as a symbolic figure somehow combining the magical qualities of youth and heroism with a sense of unlimited promise." Righter adds, "From the beginning he was mythologized."[119] Always something of an Indiana Jones, Malraux flew over the Arabian desert in 1934 in a quest to locate the Queen of Sheba's legendary palace.

Malraux first came to public attention as the result of an escapade in Cambodia (then in French Indochina) in 1922, when he was twenty-one. After exploring the Khmer temples with his first wife, Clara (née Goldschmidt), and a friend, Louis Chevasson, Malraux was arrested with the latter for stealing bas-reliefs, intending to sell them in America.

Malraux was sentenced to three years, while Chevasson got eighteen months. Back in Paris, when Clara roused the intelligentsia—including celebrities such as André Gide and André Breton—the press enthusiastically took up their case. The resulting outcry was too strong for the French administration in Cambodia: the adventurers had their sentences commuted.

A committed Communist and antifascist, Malraux fought for the Republicans during the 1936–1939 Spanish Civil War. However, he broke with the USSR when the Russians signed the Nazi-Soviet Pact in August 1939—clearing the way for war in Europe. Now Malraux was an ardent anti-Stalinist.

Like Cocteau, Malraux had a flexible attitude to the relationship between factual truth and myth—which he extended to his personal history, making it even more difficult to get to know the real man. His biographer Robert James Hewitt says drily of Malraux's autobiographical writings—tellingly entitled *Antimemoirs* (1967)—that they are "not . . . altogether factual,"[120] while a chapter in François Gerber's 1996 study of Malraux's relationship with de Gaulle is entitled "Malraux Mythomaniac." And perhaps we should remember William Righter's opinion: "Of course, much of the legend of Malraux is only doubtfully true."[121]

This welter of uncertainty—increasingly familiar after Plantard and Cocteau—especially applies to Malraux's wartime experiences. However, while Malraux told as many lies and exaggerations about his past as Plantard, one is regarded as a serious statesman and the other as a con man. Perhaps it depends on how successful the lies were.

An experienced aviator, Malraux enlisted at the outbreak of the Second World War but, with the usual perversity of the authorities, was assigned to a tank unit. He was wounded and captured in June 1940, although a few months later, with the help of his half brother Roland, he escaped from a POW camp in Sens (not too dramatically: he was allowed out to work on a farm). Together with the poets Jean Grosjean and Jean Beuret, he made for the Vichy zone, where he met up with Jean-Paul Sartre, Simone de Beauvoir, and the journalist Emmanuel d'Astier de la Vigerie. Once among such sympathetic intelligentsia, Malraux returned to novel writing.

There is something of a mystery about Malraux's involvement with the Resistance and British intelligence. Both of his half brothers, Roland

and Claude Malraux, were working for the now-famous British sabotage and clandestine operations organization the Special Operations Executive (SOE). Although this brought André Malraux into regular contact with British agents (or French nationals working for the British) from the summer of 1942, he appears not to have been active in the Resistance himself. He seems to have been content to write and live quietly with his girlfriend Josette Clotis and their young son. (He was separated from Clara, whom he later divorced.) The political historian Janine Mossuz writes in *André Malraux and Gaullism* (1970): "The year 1943 remains rather mysterious for those interested in André Malraux's past. And one only truly picks up his trail in 1944."[122]

Puzzlingly, although according to official papers Malraux did nothing for the Resistance or SOE until March 1944, he was still trusted to communicate with and even meet British and French agents. Normally this would have been strictly forbidden for obvious security reasons. Despite being technically an escaped POW, he was able in May and September 1943 to travel to Paris, where he had meetings with members of the Resistance and even the SOE agent Harry Peulevé.[123] Several of those who knew Malraux at the time believed he must have had a beyond-top-secret role. One French SOE agent, Serge Ravanel, recalled a conversation with him in November 1943 that implied strongly he was in direct contact with the British, from which Ravanel inferred Malraux was actually working for some other British intelligence organization, such as MI6 (SOE's great rival, it ran its own European networks).[124]

It was only in March 1944, after the arrests of his half brothers—drawing unwanted attention to him—that André actively entered the Resistance. Claude died under torture, and just a few weeks afterward Roland, along with Harry Peulevé, fell into the hands of German intelligence. Days later another *résistant* friend, Raymond Maréchal—a fellow freedom fighter from his Spanish Civil War days—was killed in an ambush.

Tellingly, Malraux's Resistance career began at the top, as Colonel Berger—named after a character from his *Walnut Trees of Altenburg* (*Les noyers de l'Altenburg,* 1943), who, in turn, was given his mother's maiden name. Perhaps coincidentally Altenburg is in Alsace-Lorraine—as Malraux points out in his *Antimemoirs,* a few miles from the "sacred mountain" of Saint-Odile, the twin of Sion-Vaudémont, on which the Baillard brothers had established their religious community.[125] Some commentators note the striking similarities between the adventures of the fictional Berger and Malraux's claimed experiences in 1944, but was life really following art? Or was Malraux deliberately creating his own myth?[126]

Initially assigned to lead the Resistance in the Dordogne area, on July 22, 1944, Colonel Berger was wounded in an ambush, then imprisoned at Toulouse. Had the war not been at its end, undoubtedly he would have been tortured—probably killed—but he was fortunate: the Germans abandoned the prison as the Allied threat drew closer.

In the last month of the war (April 1945), as Malraux wrote proudly in his *Antimemoirs:* "It was the Alsace-Lorraine brigade that recaptured Saint-Odile."[127] As the commander of those twenty thousand troops, he must have felt a particularly strong sense of Fate that he of all people should liberate what he clearly regarded as a sacred place. Exactly why he revered Saint-Odile remains a mystery—he was not an Alsace man himself. At the end of the war, Malraux received the Médaille de la Résistance, the Croix de Guerre, and, tellingly, the British DSO (Distinguished Service Order).

There was something of a media sensation when Malraux, a famous longtime supporter of the extreme left, suddenly announced he was backing the (to say the least) conservative General de Gaulle. But in reality there was no big mystery; as Janine Mossuz wrote: "His gaullism proceeded neither from chance or doctrine: it was a faith in the advent of another world that only Charles de Gaulle could construct."[128] Although theirs was an unlikely friendship and collaboration, Malraux was close to the General, who wrote in his memoirs, "To my right I have, and will always have, André Malraux."[129]

Malraux first met de Gaulle in August 1945 and was appointed Minister of Information in his provisional government in November 1945 (the same month in which his much-loved partner, Josette, was killed in a train accident). He left that post when de Gaulle resigned in January 1946. Involved in de Gaulle's RPF—advocating the concept of Euro-Africa, so central to Plantard's revived *Circuit*[130]—Malraux actually devoted most of his time between the General's two periods in power to writing books on art. In 1948 he married his half brother Roland's widow, the concert pianist Marie-Madeleine Lioux.

Although Malraux knew Jean Cocteau, in those circles it would have been much more surprising if they had never met. However, considering that he was a great admirer of Leonardo da Vinci, it may be significant that the paintings he praised most were *The Last Supper* and *The Virgin of the Rocks.*[131] Some even thought Malraux shared certain characteristics with the Florentine genius: his biographer William Righter sees Malraux unequivocally as the descendant of "that Renaissance image of man as work of art . . . whose supreme exemplars were so often artists: Leonardo and Michelangelo, or Leon Battista Alberti."[132]

Mona Lisa's Escort

Apart from his putative involvement with the Committees of Public Safety, Malraux resumed his job as Minister of Information briefly, in January 1959 becoming Minister for Cultural Affairs, a post he held for the next ten years, leaving office with de Gaulle. However, his role as Minister of Culture was no sinecure or cozy reward for services rendered. It was a vitally important part of de Gaulle's program for the renewal of the French nation. Essentially, it was Malraux's task to reinvent France, or at least to create a new national myth as an emotional focus for the people, healing the wounds of the past and rallying the country around de Gaulle. He duly devised festivities and commemorations that, according to François Gerber in *Malraux–de Gaulle: The Nation Regained* (*Malraux–de Gaulle: la nation retrouvée,* 1996), "celebrated the cult of the nation."[133] Just as de Gaulle was re-creating France politically, Malraux was resurrecting its traditions and culture; in the words of Herman Lebovics in *Mona Lisa's Escort: André Malraux and the Reinvention of French Culture* (1999), his aim was "cultural reformation."[134]

Extending the idea overseas, Malraux took French culture to the world, in January 1963 personally escorting the *Mona Lisa* to the United States, where it was seen by 1.7 million Americans in Washington and New York and feted by the Kennedys. Behind this celebration of French high culture was a distinctly political agenda: at that time de Gaulle was locked in a battle with the Kennedy administration over military superiority in Europe—banning U.S.-controlled nuclear missiles from France on the same day as he famously vetoed Britain's entry into the Common Market. At least the tour would assert France's *cultural* superiority. (Despite Leonardo's Italian origins, the French have always regarded him as one of their own and the *Mona Lisa* as a vital part of their cultural heritage.)

The ultimate expression of the revivified French soul came when

Malraux presided over the transfer of the ashes of the Resistance hero Jean Moulin—who died while being transported to Germany after suffering unspeakable Gestapo torture—to the Paris Panthéon, the "temple of the republic dedicated to the 'Great Men' of the nation."[135]

Malraux was to receive the same honor, his body being reinterred in the Panthéon on November 23, 1996, the twentieth anniversary of his death. Perhaps nothing encapsulates his curiously Cocteauesque—and possibly Prioryesque—thinking as this statement of his from 1955: "I believe that the task of the next century, in the face of the most terrible threat mankind has ever known, will be to reintegrate the gods."[136]

The Emerging Pattern

The Priory of Sion in the 1950s was not merely the province of French activists. Although it properly belongs to a later stage of the story, it is useful to summarize the alleged role of certain key British businessmen, first made public in Baigent, Leigh, and Lincoln's *The Messianic Legacy.*

These four men were prominent figures in London's ancient financial area (known simply as the City), mainly in banking, insurance, and shipping: Captain Ronald Stansmore Nutting, OBE—a former MI5 officer; Viscount Frederick Leathers—wartime Minister of Transport and a close friend and business associate of Sir William Stephenson (codenamed Intrepid, he ran wartime British intelligence operations in the USA); and Major Hugh Murchison Clowes, DSO. But most significant of all was the Earl of Selborne (Roundell Cecil Parker), who as Minister of Economic Warfare from 1942 to 1945 was responsible for the Special Operations Executive. The Selborne family acknowledge that after the war he was involved in European royalist movements.[137]

As usual, the weakness in the story is that the claims were made so long after the (alleged) event and there is no independent evidence to link these individuals with either Plantard or the Priory. But their names were certainly not chosen randomly.

Plantard was able to produce copies of the men's birth certificates and signatures on notarized legal documents relating to the transfer to London, in 1955 or '56, of supposedly important parchments concerning the Merovingian affair (to be discussed in Chapter 5). However,

Baigent, Leigh, and Lincoln's detective work established beyond question that the relevant parts were forgeries—which had been appended to the *genuine* signed and notarized documents. Exactly when the fake parts were added is impossible to tell, other than that it was after 1964 and before they were circulated in 1983. But for our present purposes, the important question is: how did Plantard acquire the original legal documents, which unquestionably date from the mid-1950s?

The notary, Patrick J. Freeman, established that the original documents were drawn up to accord with a French decree requiring every representative of a foreign insurance company working in France to supply a specimen signature and a copy of his birth certificate, all legally notarized.

However, the Cocteau statutes specify that members of the Priory of Sion have to provide specimen signatures and copies of their birth certificates—Plantard even claimed that this was precisely what caused the 1956 "schism." (This is another reason why it is so frustrating that the authenticity of the Cocteau statutes remains unproven.)

There are only two alternatives. The first is that Plantard acquired the copies he showed Baigent, Leigh, and Lincoln—and Freeman's document—from the archives of the Priory of Sion, implying that the four London businessmen *were* members. The second is that he got them from French government files, which were originally lodged with the Ministry of Economics but which, by the time of those authors' inquiries, had been passed to the Ministry of Justice.[138]

There is no way of telling which alternative is correct—although the latter seems simpler. But whichever it is, this was no crude hoax. Either the four British men were members of the Priory of Sion, or Plantard (and/or his colleagues) had access to extremely confidential government files.

But why these four men? Why would they have wanted to join the Priory of Sion? Or, alternatively, why had Plantard (or whoever) selected from the government files those particular individuals out of the many British people—and people of other nationalities—who had to register under the new decree? Tellingly, all four were directly involved in some capacity or other with wartime British intelligence operations, specifically with SOE. But in order to know this, the Plantard cabal would have had to have had inside knowledge of that enclosed and fanatically secretive world.

A pattern is emerging—after all, André Malraux was mysteriously linked with SOE and other British intelligence departments. Although not conclusive, it involves intelligence agencies operating in France during the Second World War, particularly during the last months of the Nazi Occupation. In the 1950s this group turned seamlessly to clandestine operations to engineer General de Gaulle's return to power.

Whatever was going on, its underlying themes seem to be basically monarchist, patriotic, somewhat mystical, esoteric, and perhaps artistic—but not *necessarily* extreme right-wing. Whatever "they" were up to, its heart and soul was utterly focused on the greater glory of France. No matter who or what stood in their way.

Meanwhile, within months of playing his part in de Gaulle's restoration, and editing the new incarnation of *Circuit,* Plantard had moved on to fresh pastures. He now turned his attention to the mystery surrounding the tiny hilltop village in the south of France named Rennes-le Château.

CHAPTER THREE

A Tale of Two Treasures

While still engaged on the second version of *Circuit,* Pierre Plantard arrived in the environs of Rennes-le-Château in the Languedoc area of southern France with devious intent. During the previous few years the village had attracted some publicity as the scene of a baffling treasure hunt, but soon Plantard's scheming ensured that Rennes-le-Château and its bizarre mystery would become inextricably entwined with the Priory.

Even on Plantard's first visit, the tiny, out-of-the-way village no doubt struck him as tantalizingly peculiar, almost like a set from one of Cocteau's more surreal films noirs. But beyond the somewhat sinister style, as he and many others were to discover, there was real substance to the mystery.

Even a casual visitor might find the village shrouded in a distinctly theatrical air. In those days, the hotel-restaurant La Tour (the Tower), owned by Noël Corbu, was a curious baroque-style villa called the Villa Béthanie (Bethany Villa), whose ornamental garden ended in a terrace with a dramatic view over the valley of the river Aude and which is dominated by a two-story mock Gothic tower called the Tour Magdala. These and other similarly unexpected buildings in Rennes-le-Château, now somehow unreal in their faded, stagy grandeur, were built on the minute instructions of the former village priest Abbé Bérenger Saunière, during his term of office, between 1885 and his death in 1917. Saunière (whose name was purloined by Dan Brown for the character of the curator of the Louvre—and Grand Master of the Priory of Sion—Jacques Saunière) remains at the center of an intransigent mystery. Where did this humble country priest—members of whose profession in that time and place were usually as poor as church mice—find the money to build such an impressive *domaine*, his own little hilltop empire? What inspired him to decorate his church so oddly, almost sacrilegiously, with Stations of the Cross that run counterclockwise and include a small black boy, a man in a tartan kilt, and a woman in a widow's veil? And why is a stone outside the church door inscribed with an upside-down cross?

Pierre Plantard was drawn to Rennes-le-Château's weirdness as if by a magnet. According to Antoine Captier, who married Noël Corbu's daughter Claire: "According to a document from 1959, Monsieur Corbu was already in contact with Monsieur Plantard. He did not say why he came to Rennes-le-Château nor how he knew of the story."[1]

Possibly Plantard had been visiting the area for two or three years beforehand; certainly he continued to explore the countryside and to research the mystery—befriending many people who had known Saunière, besides local researchers and historians—for at least five years. In many of those excursions he was joined by his old university friend Philippe de Chérisey, by then an actor. Exactly when de Chérisey began to accompany Plantard is far from certain, but it is known he visited the area from at least 1961.[2] Plantard later claimed—without offering a shred of evidence—that he had first visited Rennes-le-Château in 1938, at the age of eighteen.[3]

The local historian, curator of Carcassonne Library, and leading member of the Society of Arts and Sciences of Carcassonne René Descadeillas (1909–1986) wrote discreetly about Plantard's visits (although not actually naming him): "He was an individual difficult to define, colorless, secretive, wily, not lacking in loquacity, whom those he approached said was unknowable. He did not follow conventional medical treatment. One also wonders about the reasons for his repeated appearances, as he appeared even in winter."[4]

Although his detractors assume he invested so much time familiarizing himself with the Rennes-le-Château affair as homework for some scam, he seems to have been genuinely interested in the treasure story. It was at least five years before he attempted to exploit it—even though in the meantime he had successfully orchestrated nationwide publicity for another tale of treasure—pursuing avenues of inquiry that had escaped other researchers and treasure hunters and that were only vaguely relevant to the core question of Abbé Saunière's fabulous wealth.

Plantard managed to turn the other treasure story, a much more opportunistic enterprise, into a national cause célèbre, or at least a seven-day wonder. This was the strange mystery of Gisors, which led to the first appearance of the Priory of Sion in a mainstream publication.

The First Treasure Story

Gisors lies about forty-five miles northwest of central Paris—on a clear day the white dome of Montmartre's Sacré-Coeur can be seen from the top of the castle—in the valley of the river Epte.

For five centuries after the Vikings invaded Normandy in the 900s, Gisors was a disputed border town. The Treaty of Saint-Clair-sur-Epte of 911 brought an uneasy cessation of hostilities between the Norsemen and the Frankish kings, recognizing the Viking leader as Count of Rouen—his descendants becoming not only Dukes of Normandy but Kings of England after 1066. As the river Epte came to mark the border between two kingdoms, depending on the circumstances, Gisors (on the Anglo-Norman side) was either fought over or used as a point of rendezvous between the two sides. The château was built as a border fortress on the orders of William Rufus at the turn of the twelfth century, although it has been much modified over the centuries, being taken by the French a hundred years later and remaining in their hands for the next two centuries.

The town of Gisors also possessed a sacred elm tree—so old it was held up by iron rods and so large it took nine men holding hands with arms outstretched to encircle it. (It may be significant that a similar elm—with which the Gisors tree was compared—was found in Paris, on the boundary between the Paris Temple and the church of Gervais and St. Proteus. Gisors's parish church is dedicated to the same saints.)[5] It was this tree, and the field where it stood, which marked the traditional meeting place between warring factions or nations.

The surname of a sixteenth-century priest of Gisors, Pierre Neveu, became that of *The Da Vinci Code*'s Sophie (granddaughter of a Saunière, of course priest of Gisors's twin in Priory mythology, Rennes-le-Château).

Like most ancient castles, Gisors has attracted its share of legends, such as the one concerning Blanche d'Evreux (1332–1398), the White

Queen (Reine Blanche), wife of Philippe VI of France, whose family home was the château at Neaufles-Saint-Martin (about three miles away). The story goes that the two castles are linked by a tunnel, which Blanche used to escape a siege. (Blanche—said to be the patron of the alchemist Nicolas Flamel—appears on the list of Grand Masters of the Priory of Sion as Jeanne III, and Flamel as her successor.) There are also tales of a magically protected treasure hidden in this tunnel.[6]

The castle's towers have evocative names: the Tour du Diable (the Devil's Tower), Tour du Gardien (the Guardian's Tower), and Tour du Prisonnier (the Prisoner's Tower). The walls of the last bear the scratched name of one Nicolas Poulain. Imprisoned as the Queen's lover, he is said to have escaped by digging a tunnel to the fabled underground passageway.

There may be something in these tales. While the three-mile passageway to Neaufles-Saint-Martin might be fictitious or perhaps more of an exaggeration, in fact a honeycomb of tunnels does link the keep to the church and various houses in the town of Gisors. This even includes an underground chapel, dedicated to St. Catherine (a particular favorite of the Templars), recorded in documents of the time but whose precise location has since been lost.[7] Other tunnels came to light as the result of Second World War bombing (in 1940 by the Germans, in 1944 by the Allies). The archaeologist Eugène Pépin has also written authoritatively of a "network of underground caves" beneath Gisors.[8]

In March 1950, after discovering four stone sarcophagi near the church, workmen broke through into a vault leading to a crossroads between two tunnels, lined with skillfully constructed limestone blocks. Although this find was reported by the archaeologist Eugène Anne, remarkably the vault was simply sealed up after it was inspected.[9] (At that time practical considerations were more important than mere historical interest: Gisors had suffered badly from the bombing and urgently needed to be reconstructed.)

Under the Occupation, the Germans turned the castle into a workshop for repairing tanks, including an underground storage cistern that held fifteen thousand liters of petrol. Because of its importance to the enemy, Gisors was also a center for the Resistance. But despite the exigencies of twentieth-century warfare, the town always exuded a romantic, quasi-mystical air.

It is said that at the beginning of 1944, a German military mission arrived to excavate, searching for something specific.[10] But while this evokes colorful pictures of Indiana Jones and the occult-minded Nazis chasing powerful sacred relics, if the Germans knew something of great significance lay beneath the castle, why wait to search for it?

However, at the end of the war one Roger Lhomoy (1904–1974)—the château's caretaker, gardener, and guide since 1929—claimed to have made an important discovery at Gisors. At the beginning of 1944, together with his friend M. Lesenne, Lhomoy began secretly digging at night. (Apparently before the war he had often clandestinely explored historical sites, selling whatever he happened to find.) With the possibility of cave-ins, it was a risky business, and on one occasion he injured himself, but by the time the Germans pulled out in June 1944, he had successfully reached fifty feet down. Then he broke through into a chamber, which he describes as a Roman chapel, a hundred feet long, thirty feet wide, and fifteen feet high:

> Immediately on my left, near the hole through which I had passed, there was an altar of stone, as well as its tabernacle. On my right, all the rest of the building. On the walls, halfway up, supported by corbels of stone, statues of Christ and the twelve apostles, life-size. Along the walls, placed on the ground, stone sarcophagi two meters [six and one-half feet] long and sixty centimeters [two feet] wide: there were nineteen. And in the nave, what my lamp illuminated was incredible: thirty coffers of precious metal, arranged in rows of ten. And the word *coffer* is inadequate: I should speak rather of cupboards laid down, cupboards each of which measured 2.5 meters [8 feet] in length, 1.8 meters [6 feet] in height, 1.6 meters [5¼ feet] wide.[11]

Mr. Spielberg would have been impressed. Lhomoy announced his discovery to the town councillors in March 1946, inviting them to see for themselves. Together with the local fire chief, Émile Beyne, they penetrated as far as the tunnel entrance but refused to proceed because of the apparent danger, instead ordering a team of German prisoners of war to seal it up.[12]

Undeterred, in July 1946, Lhomoy secured permission from the Secretary of Fine Arts to excavate further, but he also needed permission from the local authorities, who not only owned the château but also were his employers. They refused. In 1952, when he got backing from two Parisian businessmen, a hotelier named Lelieu and a manufacturer called Guiblet, the council asked for an impossibly high payment of one million francs as insurance against possible damage.[13]

There the story rested for more than a decade, until renewed publicity attracted Pierre Plantard onto the scene—and then, predictably, the mystery grew and grew. This also marked the Priory of Sion's debut in popular literature.

However, even before Plantard arrived, it is clear there was a genuine mystery about this affair. There are only two possible explanations: either Lhomoy really did find what he claimed but for some reason this was covered up, or quite simply, he invented the whole story. Although most commentators have plumped for the latter, there is something odd about the whole business: unless he was mentally ill, why would Lhomoy invent a story that could easily be disproved by investigating the hole, into which he actually invited local councillors? And even if the authorities suspected he was pulling their legs, surely they would at least want to check the coffers, which just *might* be filled with treasure after all.

This was the line taken by Jean Markale in *The Templar Treasure at Gisors* (the title of the English translation of his 1986 book, *Gisors et l'énigme des templiers*). While dismissing the claims made by Plantard and his associates, Markale poses the question "Why, even if Lhomoy lied, did those with official authority visibly prevent the continuation of his explorations that may have provided proof, if only proof that he was a liar?"[14] Markale also writes:

> According to the private confidences he shared, Roger Lhomoy gave the impression of having been encouraged in his research by an ecclesiastic. This is not impossible. We know a certain number of clergy members in the region took an interest in the history of Gisors and knew of the existence of a crypt in which chests were stored, though having no precise information concerning the nature of these chests.[15]

Enter a Key Player

It is at this point that a prime mover in the story of the Priory of Sion makes his appearance. Gérard de Sède de Lieoux—although he dropped the aristocratic appendage—was born in 1921 of a prominent Gascon family he claimed was descended from that of Clement V, the Pope who ordered the dissolution of the Templars. After reading philosophy at the universities of Paris and Toulouse, he was a member of the Resistance during the war before joining the French Forces of the Interior, and he received citations for the liberation of Paris. He died in 2004.

De Sède began as a poet of some promise in impressive company—in 1942 his small collection *L'Incendie habitable* (*The Habitable Fire*) was chosen to be published in a series by La Main à Plume, the other eleven poets including luminaries such as André Breton and Pablo Picasso, the latter writing about his painting *Guernica.* (Incidentally, Picasso lived for a time at Gisors.)[16]

After the war, de Sède entered journalism, eventually becoming diplomatic correspondent for a major press agency, although adding variety to his life by taking up pig farming in 1956 (continuing with his journalism, chiefly for *Ici-Paris,* as a sideline). He met Lhomoy in 1959.

In the 1960s de Sède produced two books that owed something to Plantard's influence and could even be viewed as essentially Priory propaganda, one concerning Gisors and the other Rennes-le-Château: *The Templars Are Among Us* (*Les templiers sont parmi nous,* 1962) and *The Gold of Rennes* (*L'Or de Rennes,* 1967). These earned him considerable criticism as either Plantard's partner in crime or a sensationalist who was reluctant to let the facts get in the way of a good story—and happy to trot out anything Plantard told him as long as he thought it would sell. However, this assumption needs to be put in context of his other work around that time.

Between the two Priory books, de Sède wrote *The Cathar Treasure* (*Le trésor cathare,* 1966), a decent and well-researched work on the Cathars—the once-powerful Gnostic Christians who flourished around Rennes-le-Château and were destroyed by a papal crusade in the thirteenth century. And in 1968 de Sède edited *Why Prague?* (*Pourquoi Prague?*), a serious seven-hundred-page book on the Soviet invasion of Czechoslovakia in August 1968. Moreover, he was no Plantard pushover: he merely used aspects of the latter's alleged "inside information" on the mysteries of Gisors and Rennes-le-Château as pointers or tip-offs, reinforcing them with his own research.

Later the two men suffered a serious rift. After essentially bringing him to public prominence and paving the way for *The Holy Blood and the Holy Grail,* de Sède wrote a savage indictment of Plantard as a fantasist in his 1988 book, *Rennes-le-Château: The Files, the Impostures, the Fantasies, the Hypotheses* (*Rennes-le-Château: Les dossiers, les impostures, les phantasmes, les hypothèses*).

Back in 1960 it was de Sède's article in *Ici-Paris* on Lhomoy's (alleged) discovery that brought Plantard out of the woodwork. First came an urgent phone call, followed by a letter announcing dramatically that the article and Lhomoy's claims were dangerously encroaching on areas reserved for "initiates." Plantard warned sonorously (his emphasis): "Gisors, as well as *three other places,* are known to the high initiates to be an ancient sanctuary of the Order of the Temple; now, the secret of the Temple is not lost: it is hidden from the profane. Until more information is available, I do not believe that M. Lhomoy was given the mission of carrying out the search."[17]

Claiming to possess documents revealing the truth about the underground chapel, Plantard declared that the affair should not be publicized. Although when he met de Sède, Plantard announced he was not at liberty to show him the documents, he did produce a plan of the underground chapel, which bore the Templar *croix pattée.* This could have been (and probably was) drawn from Lhomoy's description, but de Sède accepted it because it appeared to be genuinely ancient. Plantard claimed to have found the plan while employed by the Swiss government to research medieval documents in Geneva.[18]

The result was a collaboration with de Sède that led to *The Templars Are Among Us,* which linked Lhomoy's discovery with the medieval warrior monks. In fact, most of the research was solely de Sède's—it was only the notion of a Templar connection that he took from Plantard, who otherwise kept his initiate's mouth firmly shut. However, the latter was credited for drawing the plans and contributing an appendix in the form of answers to questions posed by de Sède, which will be examined shortly.

The theory advanced in de Sède's book—under Plantard's inspiration—was that the coffers Lhomoy saw contained the archives of the

Knights Templar, hidden in Gisors at the time of the Order's suppression in 1307. Or perhaps it was the fabled Templar treasure, which appears to have been spirited away from the Paris Temple shortly before the roundup began (as popularized in *National Treasure*).

Historically, there is little or nothing to justify such a hypothesis, as Gisors has only the most tenuous of connections with the original Templars. True, in 1108–9 the fortress was in the charge of a knight named de Payns—but whether he was the same as the famous founder of the Knights Templar, Hugues de Payens, or a relative or no connection at all remains unknown. When as part of a treaty between France and England (masterminded by Thomas à Becket), it was decided that Gisors was to be placed in the control of a neutral party, the Templars were the obvious choice. Between 1158 and 1161 the castle was under the guardianship of the Order, although this amounted only to the presence of three Templar knights.[19] That sums up the full extent of the link between the château of Gisors and the Templars. In any case, as Jean Markale points out, at the time of the Templar arrests, Gisors belonged to the King and was packed with his soldiers—hardly the best place for the Templars to hide their treasure or secret archives![20]

The only other—extremely tenuous—connection is that some evidence reveals that the Master of the Temple, Gérard de Villiers (the only senior Templar in France to escape), took the treasure to the coast, where he and it could be spirited away by ship. As the quickest route from Paris to the coast runs close to Gisors, de Sède argued that Gérard de Villiers *could* have dropped the coffers off on the way.

Be that as it may, in the minds of the public and the media, de Sède's book established a connection with the Templars that endures—and precipitated an extraordinary series of events.

In May 1962 the donjon was sealed on the orders of the Ministry of Cultural Affairs, whose Minister, we recall, was then André Malraux. In August, the Ministry ordered excavations, which took place in September and October. A curious statement by the Ministry declared them to be "routine excavations" with—it stressed—no connection whatsoever to de Sède's book.[21] Few believed a word of it. By accident or design, the dig was completed on October 12, the eve of the day that had seen the official end of the Knights Templar exactly 655 years before.

The dig generated a huge amount of interest. The Grand Master of one neo-Templar Order, the grandiosely titled Marquis de Guisel de

Vaux, Duc du Val d'Agueda, of the equally grandiose Sovereign and Military Order of the Temple of Jerusalem and Mount Carmel, turned up to stake his Order's claim to any treasure that was discovered. Also on the site throughout was that famous "archaeologist" Pierre Plantard, this time acting as Lhomoy's adviser.[22]

Although the dig found nothing, Lhomoy was allowed into the depths, in front of the assembled media. When he complained that the excavations had stopped just five feet short of the crypt, the officials blithely declared that there was nothing beyond the end of the tunnel. But the affair refused to go away. On January 24, 1963, the magazine *Nouveau Candide* asked:

> Why have they refused Belgian television the right to follow the excavations? Why could a serious film production company, which put an official request to the National Centre of French Cinema for authorisation to film at Gisors, not obtain from the Ministry a firm authorisation or a refusal with an explanation for several months? Why does Freemasonry seem to interest itself so closely in the affair?[23]

When Malraux himself was questioned about it by a senator in February 1963, his written reply was this.

> Although the arguments of a historical nature leave very little room for the confirmation of the hypotheses put forward [the existence of the coffers], I envisage, before they fill in the shaft, the clearing of the last layers of earth, with the aim of lifting all uncertainty on the subject of this affair.[24]

New excavations commenced a year later—in February 1964—this time carried out by a regiment of Army Engineers from Rouen (the grounds being temporarily classified as military terrain specifically for the purpose). After a month it was announced that nothing had been found—although the official statement did acknowledge that the purpose of the exercise was to "verify certain statements relating to the presence of a treasure,"[25] which had been strenuously denied by the Ministry up to that point. On completion of this work, all the excavations were filled with cement, apparently because of the dangers of undermining the keep's foundations.

There is something odd about the whole affair, not least because it had been basically orchestrated, or at least inspired, by Pierre Plantard. He had persuaded de Sède and many others of the validity of a completely unjustified Templar connection—but so successfully that the link between the Order and the château remains a "fact" for many. And officialdom's actions seem to have complemented Plantard's: without the two series of government-backed digs and blatantly contradictory statements by the Ministry, all we would have would be Lhomoy's word and de Sède's book—by no means enough to sustain the story for so long. And the central question is, as Alain Lemeyre asks in *Guide to Templar France* (1975), if Lhomoy was just a mythomaniac, why did the Minister of Cultural Affairs authorize the 1962 dig? Of course the actions of Malraux's department introduce a whiff of conspiracy or cover-up: but did "initiates" in the upper echelons of government really orchestrate the whole thing in order to whisk away the treasure-filled coffers? In any case, Pierre Plantard and André Malraux do seem to have been acting in concert, as if to some carefully stage-managed plan.

Was Plantard—who kept a low profile during this episode as far as the media was concerned—actually steering attention *away* from what was really going on? Strangely, there is independent evidence that predates Lhomoy's claims for the existence of the thirty coffers. A letter written in 1938 by Gisors's parish priest, Abbé Vaillant, to a Paris architect concerns a packet of ancient documents that he had given him for safekeeping, which include "a Latin manuscript dating from 1500 that talks of thirty iron coffers."[26]

(It is interesting that the hero of Malraux's 1933 novel *The Human Condition,* set in China, is Kyo Gisors, the son of a French father and a Chinese mother. Why Malraux chose to give the character that particularly evocative surname is unknown.)

Sion Surfaces

Plantard's appendix to *The Templars Are Among Us* is particularly significant because it included the first references to the Priory of Sion, albeit brief and oblique, in a mainstream publication. (The appendix was deposited as a separate document entitled *Gisors and Its Secret* in the Bibliothèque Nationale in 1961, the year before de Sède's book was published.)

Entitled "A Hermeticist's Point of View," the appendix—which introduces Plantard as both archaeologist and hermeticist—takes the form of an interview. De Sède poses eight questions about the Gisors château, to which Plantard replies noncommittally but articulately, even impressing with his knowledge of esoterica—the tarot, astrology (again using a thirteen-sign zodiac), astronomy, and alchemy. He also reveals a sound grasp of history, quoting from classical writers such as Strabo and scholarly studies of architecture, astronomy, and mathematics. If nothing else, Plantard has done his homework—although what he says is not always correct or true, and it is always very much his own interpretation.

Suspect though the value-added details, said to come from the secret archives of "certain societies," might be, the document is considerably better researched, presented, and focused than most of Plantard's writings in *Vaincre* or *Circuit,* or even his later productions—which strongly implies the work of another hand. (Suspicion immediately falls on Philippe de Chérisey, whose own later writings reveal the same grounding in esoteric and historical subjects.)

Gisors is important, writes Plantard, as the northernmost point of an equilateral triangle projected over France, the other points being Montrevel-en-Bresse (a small town in the Ain, not far from the Swiss border) and Jarnac, near the Atlantic coast. The significance of the triangle is that the town of Bourges marks its center. (Plantard seems to be making the most of the opportunity to ensure future interest in the town—which would become increasingly central to Priory mythology.)

There is no quaintly banal focus on low-cost housing now. The mystical comes through strongly, albeit largely in veiled references and hints—for example, the importance of the great Egyptian goddess Isis, referred to as "the Hidden Mother," and "the two eyes of the octopus," an allusion to secret alchemical processes.[27] (The octopus reappeared as a key symbol in the Dossiers Secrets.) Plantard also talks of the symbolism in Gisors's château design and architecture, littering his replies to de Sède's questions with consciously tantalizing references to "initiates" and "certain societies."

Intriguingly, Plantard explains the origins of the term *Nautonnier* or "helmsman" for the Priory's Grand Masters.[28] As the medieval stonemasons and architects often traveled wherever their skills were required by sea or river, they were known as *nautes constructeurs* (sailor-builders). Paris was home to one of their most important bases. For once, however, it is possible to determine Plantard's source—if not his interpretation.

In 1711, during excavations in the great cathedral of Notre-Dame de Paris, a stone dating back to Roman times was unearthed, bearing an inscription referring to the *nautae parisiaci,* apparently some kind of boatmen who plied the Seine between Paris and Rouen under the patronage of Isis, goddess of navigation. The stone and inscription featured in the 1725 *Histoire de la ville de Paris* (*History of the Town of Paris*) by the celebrated antiquarians Gui-Alexis Lobineau and Michel Félibion. (Later Lobineau's name was exploited to help create the myths surrounding the Dossiers Secrets.)

Clearly, Plantard (or whoever really wrote the appendix) was familiar with this work. But the term *Nautonnier* had already featured in the Priory's 1956 statutes although without explaining its origins, showing that he was at least thinking along these lines five years earlier.

Of course, Plantard brings the Templars into the story, stating the Order was founded in 1128. (Technically he is perfectly correct: although the Order had existed in some form for nine years, it received papal sanction and its official rule only at the Council of Troyes in January 1128.) Plantard writes:

> When the Order of the Temple was founded in 1128, many of its members were recruited from the lay guilds as well as from the regular clergy. On his return from the Crusade, Louis VII brought back with him several monks, initiated in the East, members of the Abbey of Notre-Dame de Sion; while some settled in the St. Samson Priory in Orleans, others integrated themselves with the Order of the Temple; around 1161, discords manifested within the Order, the sovereignty of the Grand Master was no longer unanimously recognized, a schism was in the air, and the English Templars sensed that the breakup of the Order was coming. There still exist in our day secret archives, the property of certain societies, which affirm that in 1188 "the elm was cut" and that one of its branches, the Ormus, having as its emblem a red cross and a white rose, would be the origin of the

> Rosicrucians. In 1188, the members of the Ormus installed themselves at Saint-Jean-le-Blanc, in the priory of Mont Sion, under the protection of the Priory of Saint-Samson of Orléans. They rendered a particular cult to Our Lady. The monastic life never existed there; the activity was that of a formidable initiatory and religious organization that escaped the control of the abbots of Saint-Samson; the last of these, pursued in 1291, found his salvation only in a prompt retreat to Sicily. Soon it was the turn of the Order of the Temple: 1314 came to mark the disappearance of the Order.
>
> After the disappearance of the Order of the Temple, a tradition asserted that, in a secret place—Gisors, perhaps—the Ark, ship of the Nautonnier, was hidden. However, Gisors was not the only place: near Dreux are the ruins of the château of La Roberlière (or La Robardière), built by Robert I and which Pierre de Dreux (Jean III) had designed as a retreat . . . [29]

Plantard elucidates further in a footnote, even suggesting that the Ormus still exists:

> Since 1188, the number of its members has been thirteen, like the signs of zodiac. The supreme Master, called Nautonnier, has always adopted the name John. The first took the name of Jean II. We are today in the XXIst reign of the Johns.[30]

For the moment, it is enough to say that the historical details about the Abbey of Notre-Dame de Mont Sion in Jerusalem, the settling of some of its monks in Saint-Samson of Orléans, and its later association with Saint-Jean-le-Blanc are all absolutely correct and verifiable. Later we were able to identify the actual historical source used for these statements, which made a great deal fall into place. Of course, it is not possible to verify the "initiates' " input, such as the link with the Templars and creation of the mysterious Ormus.

However, the reference to the "cutting of the elm" in 1188 does refer to a real, if obscure, event that took place at Gisors. In that year Philippe II of France and Henry II of England met at the elm to listen to William, Archbishop of Tyre (author of the earliest known account of the origins of the Templars—to whom he was fanatically hostile), who was calling for a Third Crusade.

For some reason, a row broke out between the English and French concerning the ancient, sacred tree, leading to a scuffle that ended with it being hacked down on Philippe's orders. His reason remains obscure, although legend has it that both parties fell out over who should enjoy its shade, while other versions claim it was because of the tree's symbolic importance for the Anglo-Normans.[31] Plantard, however, offers a third interpretation, claiming it was an act of esoteric symbolism, in some way representing a rupture within the Order of the Temple that resulted in a breakaway organization, the Ormus—the French for "elm" is *orme.* (There would have been Templars present, especially as a crusade was on the agenda.)

Tempting though it is to believe otherwise, Plantard did not actually invent a secret brotherhood called Ormus, and the year 1188 was believed to be highly significant in certain esoteric circles long before he penned his account, although it was not linked to the event at Gisors. We will return to this later.

Even though the Priory of Sion lurks behind Ormus, albeit only implicitly, its name does appear, briefly, in Plantard's appendix. To de Sède's question about the presence of signs to guide the "pilgrim" at Gisors, Plantard replies—along with references to specific inscriptions and tombs at the château—that if the pilgrim climbs to the top of the keep at midnight on December 24 and looks toward the constellation of Gemini:

> Then perhaps the miracle will be fulfilled. Like Jacob, the traveler may have a strange dream: "Two Johns will appear to him, one the child of man: the Cernunnos; the other a child of God: the Smertullos, awaiting the third coming; as, in making the inside shine, he sees again John with the shell baptizing Jesus, the dove being present, then again John, the evangelist of the Cross, the beloved in the heart of Jesus."[32]

A footnote gives the reference: "Instruction for the clerks, grade of Commander, Priory of Sion."

Seeing the two New Testament Johns—the Baptist and Jesus' "beloved disciple"—as particularly significant is common enough in the esoteric and Masonic worlds, although the connection with the Celtic deities Cernunnos (god of animals) and Smertullos (ruling deity of the underworld) is new. Masons swear their oath to the "two Saints John"—although why they do so eludes even Masonic historians; it appears to be part of a tradition the movement has absorbed in the mists of time, although its meaning has been lost. But as this apparently baffling Johannite element was there from the beginning of the Priory's emergence into the public domain, presumably they knew why.

All this fits into the developing story of the historical Priory of Sion, some of it being reproduced in the later Dossiers Secrets. But equally important at this stage of our investigation are certain *differences* from the more familiar tale of the Priory's origins and history. First, the name of Godefroy de Bouillon, later said to be the instigator of the Order, has yet to be mentioned (although even fairly cursory delving into the history of the Jerusalem Abbey reveals him to be its founder). Pierre de Dreux is mentioned as a Grand Master—the second, judging by his title of Jean III—but he appears nowhere on the Dossiers Secrets' roll call. Finally, the Grand Master at the time of writing, in 1961, is said to be Jean XXI, whereas famously the Dossiers Secrets gives the then Nautonnier, Cocteau, as the far more symbolically named Jean XXIII. All this suggests a developing mythos, the core of which will remain the same, although the details are still being worked out. But as yet no word about the mystical and magical Merovingians!

Inside Rennes-le-Château

Later the heart of the Priory's self-promotion would be very much its own reading of the mystery of Rennes-le-Château and the unexplained wealth of its priest, Abbé Bérenger Saunière (1852–1917). Thanks to Plantard's efforts, that remote French village is now world famous, its few narrow streets echoing with tourists' Babel chatter—and the arrival of film crews, inspired by Dan Brown either to enthuse over the mystery or to try to debunk it.

Some even believe the whole thing was invented for the local tourist industry. But it is clear that a real mystery was hijacked—blatantly "spun" by the Priory for its own agenda. It is therefore particularly enlightening to examine the Saunière story as it was before Plantard stamped the Priory's image on it, as far as it can be reconstructed from surviving documents and testimony. By seeing what was added—and why—we may get a clearer understanding of what the Priory is really about.

There was great excitement in 2001, when it appeared that, finally, some tangible discovery was about to be made at Rennes-le-Château. In April a Canadian team arrived with ground-penetrating radar equipment—apparently tipped off by the grandson of one of Saunière's workmen, who said he had been told that the priest had buried a chest or box beneath the foundations of the Tour Magdala.

For some reason, most of those involved in the new enterprise were more closely associated with the history and archaeology of the Holy Land: the team was funded by the Merrill Foundation, a private organization usually associated with financing archaeological work in the Middle East. A key figure in organizing the survey was Dr. Robert Eisenman—most famous for his work on the Dead Sea Scrolls—under whom the team had previously worked at Qumran in Israel (where the scrolls were found). The ground scan detected an object around three feet square buried some twelve feet beneath Saunière's tower, as well as signs of a crypt beneath St. Mary Magdalene's church. (This is not such a great revelation—the existence of the burial vault of the Lords of Rennes was already known from historical documents; the location of the entrance is the great mystery.)

It took another two and a half years to organize a dig to find out what the "chest" was, not only because of French bureaucracy—permission being needed from a multitude of government departments—but also because all excavations have been banned by the commune's authorities since 1965. During that time there was a veritable circus, with all kinds of rumors flying around.

A group called Consortium Rennes-le-Château, headed by Eisenman, was created specifically to carry out the work; its Italian archaeologist Andrea Barattolo dramatically suggested that the crypt beneath the church might be the remains of a Celtic sanctuary or even "the acropolis of the Gaulish civilization."[33] (He seems not to have considered the possibility that it was just a . . . church crypt!)

Sensation greeted the arrival of the Italian theologian Dr. Serena Tajé, who was initially reported to work for the Vatican, but this was later denied. In July 2001 *Le Figaro* attributed some astonishing quotations to "*la théologiquement sexy Serena Tajé,*" also termed the "*volcanique théologienne.*" (Clearly it was hardly her intellect that impressed the reporter.) She, too, appeared to be in the grip of a *folie des grandeurs*, speculating, "Perhaps we will discover items concerning the foundation myth of the Church" or "a tangible sign of the presence in this place (a presence attested to by the holy texts) of the judge of Jesus, of that same Herod Antipas who stopped here, in Rennes-le-Château, on the road of exile, in the company of a certain Mary the Magdalenian."[34] Her religious reading must have been somewhat different from the standard version.

Why should anyone really believe that a box buried by a French priest a century ago would contain such gems? Obviously the story still possesses the power to cast a potent spell, even over theologians (no matter how sexy) and archaeologists.

Tajé caused the most astonishment when she was quoted as saying, "I have been given the mission by the Church of destroying any compromising document that we might find." This was later dismissed as a dinnertime joke.

After several delays, in front of cameras from The History Channel and the distinguished company of Eisenman, Barattolo, and Michael Baigent, the excavation beneath the Tour Magdala finally went ahead in August 2003. After all that buildup and feverish press attention, the "chest" turned out to be a stone. That, however, is very unlikely to be the end of the matter: like the pyramids of Giza, the myth of Rennes-le-Château seems to rely on regular doses of excitement rising to hysteria—no matter how undeserved—before subsiding again and so on in an apparently endless cycle.

Ironically, the regional authorities have refused permission to excavate the "crypt" beneath the church—although it is by far the more interesting of the two findings.

But why the consuming interest in what may lie under the village? What could possibly lurk under that soil that could spark such sensation?

A Very Strange Village

Some fifteen hundred feet above sea level, with a population of around one hundred—and even they are remarkably invisible—the village of

Rennes-le-Château is an unlikely theme park, although that is what it is in danger of becoming, thanks largely to Pierre Plantard.

Overlooking the scrubby valley of the river Aude and the village of Couiza, Rennes-le-Château lies about sixty miles from Toulouse and is twenty-five miles south of the medieval walled city of Carcassonne. It is also only forty or so miles from the Spanish border and just off the Roman road from Carcassonne to Catalonia, which remained the main route to Spain until the arrival of the twentieth century and the building of the La Catalane *autoroute.* Although not quite the isolated spot of the imagination, Rennes-le-Château is still small enough not to appear on many maps and relatively difficult to find. In Saunière's day—without cars or even a decent road from Couiza—it must have been tricky to get there, even from just down in the valley. The village was once considerably more important, but it never recovered from being sacked by the Spanish in 1361, followed almost immediately by the horrors of the plague.

Some believe that Rennes-le-Château was once the major Visigoth city of Rhedae, which appears in the annals as the equal of Carcassonne and Narbonne but whose precise location has been lost. Although this theory—first suggested by a local historian in 1880—is widely held by aficionados of the mystery, it is unlikely: Limoux, about eight miles north, is a better candidate, though Rennes-le-Château would still have been an important strategic outpost.[35]

The village has been Rennes, or variations such as Regnes, since at least the mid–sixteenth century. Identifying it with its ancient château (which dates from the 1100s), to distinguish it from its neighbor, Rennes-les-Bains, is comparatively new: until the eighteenth century, the hilltop village was simply Rennes and the spa village in the valley was Bains-de-Rennes.

Saunière was born in Montazels, just across the valley from Rennes-le-Château. His grocer father, Joseph (also known as Cubié), was a respected member of the bourgeoisie, having been mayor and also being steward of the dilapidated château and manager of its flour mill.

Bérenger (as he preferred to be called) was not the only member of the family to choose the priesthood: his younger brother, Jean-Marie Alfred (1855–1905), entered the seminary first. Over the last decade it has become increasingly obvious that Alfred Saunière had at least as important a part to play in the story as his better-known brother. (Ironically, the first articles and books on the Rennes-le-Château affair mistakenly used Alfred's photograph for Bérenger—this still happens today.)

After his ordination and a couple of minor postings, Bérenger Saunière became curé (parish priest) of Rennes-le-Château—which then had a population of about three hundred—in June 1885, when he was thirty-three. His inheritance from his predecessor, Antoine Croc, consisted of a leaky presbytery and a church dating from the tenth century that was clearly about to collapse.

Dedicated to St. Mary Magdalene, the church had once been chapel exclusively to Rennes's lords, while the villagers had their own place of worship until it was destroyed by the Spanish raiders—apparently in the belief that it hid some fabulous treasure. There is a confusion about the dedication of the original parish church: medieval references to both a St. John the Baptist's and a St. Peter's exist, but whether this means that there were once two churches in the village (besides the aristocrats' chapel) or that either church or chapel was rededicated at some point remains unclear.[36] The crypt of the original parish church survives beneath a private building.

Nearly thirty years before, a diocesan survey by the architect Guiraud Cals had concluded that demolition and rebuilding would be less expensive than restoration—and because of lack of funds, only structural repairs that prevented the building actually falling down had been done in the intervening years. The village council had again noted the desperate need two years before Saunière arrived, but there was no money. Neither was there any possibility of him using his own funds to shore up his church: he eked out a living on just seventy-five francs a month. Even the presbytery was so uninhabitable he had to lodge with a villager.

Saunière's arrival coincided with a period of political turmoil in France that directly concerned the Church and the priesthood. Elections were to take place in October 1885, and a concerted effort was being made by a conservative coalition to bring back the monarchy (which had already been restored and deposed since the Revolution). Once again, the nation was split—although the Catholic Church naturally favored the restoration, as it would be better off under a king and there were already republican rumblings about ending the Church's favored status.

Before the election, Saunière virtually ordered his flock to vote against the Republic, which he decried in a sermon as the work of the devil. But the socialist Radicals won; Saunière was denounced for using his pulpit for political ends and in punishment transferred to a seminary in Narbonne. He returned to Rennes-le-Château in July 1886—absolutely unchastened.

The year 1886 saw another event that was to become an enduring part of the Rennes-le-Château/Priory of Sion legend (not least because it was championed by Pierre Plantard). Saunière's neighboring colleague, the respected Abbé Henri Boudet (1837–1915), a member of the Society of Arts and Sciences of Carcassonne and parish priest of the ancient Roman spa town of Rennes-les-Bains, published a very strange book: *The True Celtic Language and the Cromlech of Rennes-les-Bains* (*La vraie langue celtique et le cromleck de Rennes-les-Bains*). But although the title page states it was published in 1886 and printed by the firm of François Pomiés of Carcassonne, researchers have discovered that the printer had already gone out of business. What does this mean? (Why is *nothing* in this story ever straightforward?)

Boudet's book puts forward the novel—not to say surreal—theory that the universal language and mother tongue of the ancient world was *English!* As "proof" the priest offered interpretations of words that out-Python Monty: for example, he claims that the biblical Sodom derived from *sod-doom*—"condemnation [doom] on the soil [sod]."[37] Turning to his own locality, he dredges up translations so lunatic that one suspects he *must* be joking: apparently in all seriousness he argues that the local peak of Cardou was named when people pondered how to maneuver their carts over it—"Cart, how?"[38] Quite. But were the ancient Gauls so stupid they never thought of calling it "why don't we go round it instead"?

One might expect such mad etymology from a barely literate peasant who was obsessed with the few words of English he had somehow acquired, but not only was Boudet an accomplished antiquarian but he also possessed a degree in English.[39] The sheer absurdity of his book has prompted many researchers to suspect that its true purpose was something else entirely—perhaps some kind of code. As Jean Markale puts it succinctly, "So many stupidities written in one book by someone who was obviously not an idiot does merit some examination."[40] But since the work became an integral part of the Rennes mystery (perhaps not incidentally thanks to Plantard) in the 1970s, nobody has ever penetrated its cipher, if that is what it is.

Digging, Delving, and Decoding

Back in harness in Rennes-le-Château, Saunière began to try to repair his ailing church, scraping together money from wherever he could find it. The village authorities gave him a small sum for the most pressing repairs, and there was a legacy of six hundred francs from one of his predecessors. But a more important source of funds was a donation by the Comtesse de Chambord of one thousand francs. (Twenty years later, when confronted by his bishop to account for his wealth, Saunière inflated this to three thousand francs).[41] It must have been one of her last acts, as the Comtesse died in May 1886. But who was she, and why did she give Saunière the money? More to the point, how had she even heard of him?

Marie-Thérèse, Comtesse de Chambord (1817–1886), was a most distinguished woman, being a member of the venerable Habsburgs, the imperial family that ruled over the Austro-Hungarian Empire, and the widow of the chief pretender to the throne of France, Henri de Bourbon, Comte de Chambord (1820–1883), who had died three years before. Marie-Thérèse's husband had lived as a virtual exile in Habsburg Austria. The Emperor, Franz Josef, the most powerful man in Europe, was autocratic, rigidly disciplined, and unyieldingly proud of his family's status and heritage. Indeed, he harbored ambitions to extend his dynasty's power and influence, ultimately to reign over the whole of Europe. Clearly, his endorsement of the Comte de Chambord was part of this grand design—after all, if Chambord had become King of France, he would have been very much in the Emperor's debt.

However, this straightforward explanation is complicated by the fact that the Royalist party Saunière spoke out for in the 1885 elections supported the Orléanist *rivals* to the Bourbon (legitimist) claim that the Comtesse's husband had represented—so she should hardly have been keen to hand over money to that particular obscure Languedocian priest.[42] Most commentators assume that Saunière came to the Comtesse's notice via his brother, Alfred, who had already carved out a name for himself as a smoothly diplomatic teacher and preacher in various Jesuit establishments, although he never actually joined the Order.[43]

There were other, unexpected connections between the tiny Languedocian village and the heir to the Bourbon throne. The Comte de Chambord's tutor had been Armand de Hautpoul-Félines—so loyal to the cause that he refused payment. He later became the Comte's traveling companion, visiting London with him in 1843. The last noble family to rule Rennes-le-Château, until the Revolution, were the Hautpouls—Armand was the nephew of and heir to the last lord of Rennes-le-Château, the Marquis d'Hautpoul.[44] (Perhaps significantly, one of Philippe de Chérisey's aristocratic predecessors, another Marquis de Chérisey, was a member of the Comte de Chambord's intimate circle.)[45]

As an intriguing parallel, René Descadeillas—a leading debunker of the Saunière story—notes that it was also a donation from the Habsburg court in Vienna that began the Baillard brothers' work in Sion-Vaudémont in the 1830s, as featured in Maurice Barrès's *La colline inspirée*.[46]

Saunière started to put this money to good use repairing and renovating St. Mary Magdalene's church—and it is here that matters become famously complex, obscure, and mysterious. Reconstructing events after so long—especially after so much speculation, theorizing, and deliberate distortion—is of course exceptionally difficult; it is also frustratingly impossible to be definite about some key events. What follows is our own reconstruction, based on surviving documents and eyewitness testimony that was recorded *before* the mystery reached a wider public.[47]

When Saunière started restoring the church in 1887, he first replaced the old altar. This was possible thanks to another gift, from a Madame C. from Coursan near Narbonne, a former resident of Rennes-le-Château who had vowed that if she recovered from a serious illness she would give the church a new altar. The seven-hundred-franc altar was delivered in July 1887, as attested by surviving invoices and other documents.[48]

Naturally this replaced the old altar—basically a flat stone slab fixed into the wall at one end and supported at the other by a very old stone pillar, carved in an elaborate design featuring a cross. Although it is now famed in Rennes lore as the Visigoth pillar, informed opinion is that it is actually Carolingian, from around 800 C.E. (about three centuries after

Visigoth rule in the region).[49] Inside this pillar a cavity was found containing documents of some kind, rolled up in wooden tubes, as several of the workmen later remembered. René Descadeillas, who interviewed some of them, writes:

> The majority of witnesses report that in pulling out the entablature, they brought to light a cavity filled with dry ferns, in the middle of which rested two or three wooden cylinders: these contained manuscript documents on parchment. The curé took them. He declared that he would decipher, read, and translate them if he could. The rumor did the rounds of the locality. The mayor asked the curé for the translation. A little while afterward, the latter entrusted to him a translation written in his own hand. The text related, it is said, to the construction or repair of the church altar, which is plausible. We do not know what became of this document, just as we do not know where the translation has gone.[50]

This is significant because—as we will see—what were claimed to be these very parchments, bearing enigmatic coded messages, were circulated in the late 1960s. However, hiding objects or writings while consecrating altars was a common enough practice.

At around this time—it is impossible to be precise—Saunière also had the stone flooring replaced, leading to another discovery that either was significant then or was later to assume significance. During the raising of the old stone flags—some of the village children who helped were still alive when Descadeillas went to investigate—a large stone, in front of the altar, was found to bear a very damaged bas-relief on its underside. Although it is known today as the Knights' Stone (*Dalle des Chevaliers*), this may be a misnomer: the two scenes it depicts are hard to make out, apart from a mounted horseman carrying something, but experts believe the scenes relate to hunting. Estimates of its age vary from the eighth to the thirteenth century.[51]

Once again, something was found. Claire Captier, Noël Corbu's daughter, based on what the villagers told her in the 1940s and '50s, writes: "It was under this stone . . . that Abbé Saunière found an *'ouille'* (pot) full of precious objects, such as pieces of gold."[52] One of the foster sisters of Saunière's servant, Marie Dénarnaud, also saw this pot, and she told Descadeillas about it in 1957.[53] Presumably the stone covered an interment, and the pot had been buried with the deceased. But whatever it was, this alone could hardly account for Saunière's great wealth.

Some claim a link between the two discoveries, suggesting that one of the documents from the altar directed Saunière to this stone, which is why he had it raised. However, this sounds more like a later rationalization: after all, the floor was being replaced anyway.

Clearly there was some form of burial under the stone—both ancient and, judging by its position in front of the altar, important. Although there are also claims that the stone concealed the entrance to a crypt, as Saunière completely replaced the floor with new slabs, it is now hard to tell. However, when Noël Corbu and others—including the then mayor—dug on this spot in the late 1950s, they found only earth and bones.[54]

A third possible location for a discovery comes from the testimony of Saunière's bell ringer, Antoine Captier, who (according to his family) said that during renovation work he noticed a gleam from an old wooden baluster they had moved and found a phial hidden inside. Inside this in turn was a rolled parchment, which he gave to the priest. He heard no more about it.[55] Although this episode is undated, clearly it happened during work of some kind, but then renovation took place over several years. Again, the baluster survives: the hollow—concealed behind a removable sliver of wood—is very small.

So far we have three possible locations for Saunière's putative find, and even the discovery of a cache of gold coins. However, the priest was still living modestly and making repairs to the church using identifiable sources of income—grants, donations, and loans. At this stage there was no mystery about it.

Saunière then turned to the replacement of the stained-glass windows beginning in September 1887 with a few at a time, ordered from Henri Feur of Bordeaux.

A more important change occurred when the priest moved in with the Dénarnaud family, newcomers to the village from nearby Espéraza. At first Madame Dénarnaud acted as his housekeeper and servant, but later (some time between 1888 and 1892) their daughter Marie (who was twenty in 1888) took over—also becoming his greatest confidante.

In August 1890 various essential repairs began on the church and presbytery; these continued for a few years, funded by a variety of donations, grants, payments to say honorary masses, and even loans. By September 1891, Saunière had already spent a healthy 2,661.50 francs, dwarfing his salary of just 450 francs a year.

With great ceremony on June 21, 1891, he installed a new statue of Our Lady of Lourdes outside the church—using the ancient stone from the altar as its plinth. Curiously, Saunière had the stone erected upside down, thereby inverting the cross carved on it—clearly not a mistake, as it also bears the Alpha and Omega symbols, making it very obvious which way up it should be. As Jean Blum writes, the idea that this was ignorance or carelessness on Saunière's part is "unacceptable, pure and simple."[56] Of course inverting the most sacred symbol of the Christian religion is more than an eccentricity, being usually associated with sacrilege amounting to the satanic. Obviously this was part of some plan—but what was it? What message could he possibly be trying to convey?

Saunière also had the words MISSION 1891 carved on the stone: obviously referring to the year, but what the mission was is unknown. Some interpret it as "*mis*" (placed) and "*Sion*"—i.e., it was put there by the Priory of Sion in 1891—but this is pure speculation.

There are several other indications that for some reason Saunière considered the year 1891 important, although nobody knows why. However, it could be significant that he made a collage—found in his papers by the Corbus—of two illustrations from the periodical *La Croix*. The first shows three cherubs carrying a child heavenward, with the caption "The year 1891 passes into eternity with the fruit of which they speak below." Beneath this a second picture shows the three wise men bringing their gifts to the baby Jesus.

Something did happen in 1891, although three months *after* the erection of the statue. On September 21, Saunière recorded the following in a terse one-line diary entry summing up the day's events: "Letter from Granès [a nearby village]. Discovery of a tomb. Rain in evening."[57]

That the discovery was significant is revealed by his activities over the subsequent days. First, he stopped the ongoing renovation work in the church (which suggests that the tomb had been discovered *inside* the church, not in the churchyard). A week later he left abruptly on a "retreat," according to his diary traveling to Carcassonne and Luc-sur-Aude, a village about two miles north of Rennes-le-Château. The next day he recorded: "Saw curé de Névian—Chez Gélis—Chez Carrière—Saw Cros and Secret."[58]

Névian is a somewhat distant village near Narbonne—presumably its parish priest had traveled to this meeting. By contrast, Abbé Antoine Gélis was one of Saunière's nearest clerical neighbors, parish priest of the village of Coustassa, across the Sals valley from Rennes-le-Château. The elderly Gélis was to be found murdered savagely and mysteriously six years later. Carrière is unknown. Cros was the diocese's Vicar-General—a good friend of Saunière's. Not surprisingly, mention of the "Secret" has made a great many mouths water, prompting theories that Saunière visited the priests to confide in them about something astonishing he had found in the tomb. Disappointingly, however, Secret is actually a surname in France, or alternatively, as Bill Putnam and John Edwin Wood suggest plausibly, it could be an abbreviation for *secrétaire:*[59] perhaps Saunière saw Cros and his secretary—suggesting it was something other than a social call.

Although he returned to his parish on October 2, Saunière did not resume rebuilding until two weeks later—and then, as he noted, he made an "agreement with new masons." Why halt the work and then employ new workmen? Was it then, perhaps, that the entrance to the vault beneath the church had been discovered? In the parish register for 1694–1726 there are several references to such a crypt, which was open at that time. For example, in March 1705, Anne Delsol, sister-in-law of the then Baron of Rennes, Henry d'Hautpoul, was interred "in the tomb of the Lords that is next to the baluster." In 1724 Henry de Vernet was interred in "the tomb of the Lords."[60]

Although Paul Saussez of the Consortium Rennes-le-Château recently revived the theory that Saunière's riches came from finding the way into the Hautpoul tombs, discovering the tomb hardly made the priest rich overnight. He still had to borrow a small sum from Mme. Barthélémy Marre in November 1891.[61] (Incidentally, his diary entries stop abruptly on April 12, 1892—frustratingly, just as the plot thickens.)

There is another puzzle concerning the vault. Why and when it was sealed remains unknown, but certainly when the last Baron of Rennes died in 1753 in Limoux, he was buried there and not in the village. However, his widow, who survived him by nearly thirty years, lived and died at Rennes-le-Château and, puzzlingly, was buried not in the family vault but in the graveyard. Was there no room in the crypt?

Since 1422, when the last heiress of the previous noble family to hold Rennes, the Voisins, married Pierre-Raymond d'Hautpoul, his family (from just north of Carcassonne) had been lords of Rennes. In the eighteenth century they also acquired the title of Marquis de Blanchefort, an enigmatic ruin a little under three miles from Rennes-le-Château, usually referred to as a château but, judging from the remaining foundations, not really much more than a watchtower.

The last Lord of Rennes and Blanchefort was François d'Hautpoul (1689–1753), who married Marie de Nègre (or de Négri) d'Ablès[62] in 1732 and had three daughters (their only son died in childhood). Dame Marie survived her husband by nearly thirty years but during her long widowhood maintained very unhappy relations with her daughters; one, Gabrielle, even took legal proceedings against her for "degradation to the goods and of the château of Rennes," deterioration of the furniture and effects of the inheritance.[63]

When Dame Marie died on January 17, 1781, her spinster daughter Elisabeth inherited, becoming Mademoiselle de Rennes, but just eight years later the Revolution brought an end to the privileges of aristocracy. By the mid–nineteenth century the château of Rennes and its lands were in other hands.

The parish priest at the time of Marie de Nègre's death—Saunière's predecessor by a hundred years—was Abbé Antoine Bigou, who had held that post since 1774. It was he who oversaw her funerary rites and who had her tombstone—a monument now at the center of the mystery—erected. (Condemned as a "recalcitrant priest"—one who opposed the Revolution—in 1790, Bigou fled to Spain, where he died four years later.)

Although Marie's tombstone was to become marvelous material for the Priory's spin doctors, there is something genuinely odd about it. The simple lines of her epitaph are riddled with errors, surely far too many to be explained by poor workmanship. (However, the details of Marie's death—the date, her age, and so on—are correct, as confirmed by the registration in the diocesan archives.) It is supposed to read: "Here lies Noble Marie de Nègre d'Ablès, Dame d'Hautpoul de Blanchefort, aged sixty-seven, deceased on XVII January MDCCLXXXI. Requiescat in Pace [Rest in Peace]." But there are wrong letters, omitted letters, letters peculiarly raised or lowered from the main text. To pick out the most blatant, d'Ablès has become d'Arles, the second C in the date is an O, and most breathtakingly, the incorrect break in the Latin phrase on the penultimate line—"Requies catin"—makes "catin," at that time a term for a prostitute or trollop!

CT GIT NOBLe M
ARIE DE NEGRE
DARLES DAME
DHAUPOUL DE
BLANCHEFORT
AGEE DE SOIX
ANTE SEPT ANS
DECEDEE LE
XVII JANVIER
MDCOLXXXI
REQUIES CATIN
PACE

The mistakes are so blatant that many have assumed them to be some form of coded message, probably left by Abbé Bigou. The Priory was to exploit the concept unashamedly.

The tombstone itself no longer exists—but it was still there in Saunière's day, although lying broken in a corner of the graveyard where the priest himself had thrown it. Indeed, it was Saunière who erased the enigmatic inscription, perhaps trying to hide its hidden message. He was too late, however: a copy had been made, in June 1905, by members of the Society of Arts and Sciences of Carcassonne, who published the description and diagram in their journal a year later. However, although the wording of the inscription is almost certainly verbatim, as Putnam and Wood point out, in the diagram it appears to have been composed using standard compositors' type—not a feature of the original![64] Presumably changed out of convenience by the printers, this alteration makes it impossible to tell what the stone really looked like. Although this has no effect on attempts to "decode" the inscription, it does seriously hamper the theories based on measurements between various points on the stone.

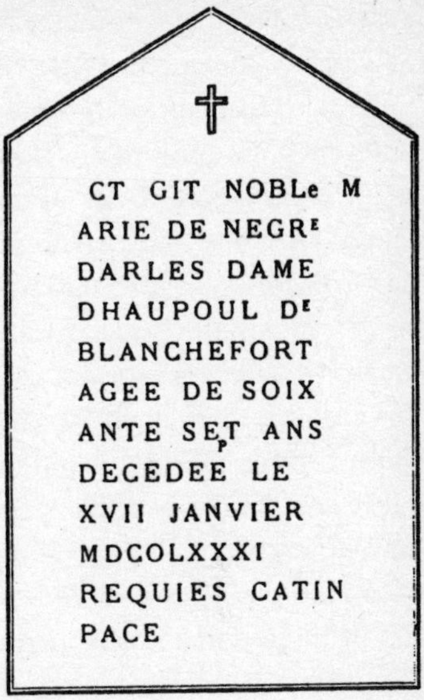

The idea that Saunière erased the inscription to hide its secret—assuming it was in some way connected to the source of his wealth—also needs to be put in context. By the time the visiting antiquarians recorded it in 1905, Saunière had been a wealthy man for several years. Yet it was only after their visit that he destroyed the inscription—so clearly he had no major anxiety that someone else would find the clue. There are other possible reasons for him removing the text (perhaps to avoid embarrassing questions about why he had despoiled the grave of the village's last noble patron).

Mystery is piled upon mystery by the claim that Marie de Nègre's grave had *two* stones, the other being a horizontal slab bearing an even more enigmatic inscription featuring the *Et in Arcadia ego* motto. For now, we will simply note that it seems the second stone never existed but was rather an invention of the 1960s.

Another pair of tombstones poses similarly awkward questions—however, this time they are undeniably for the same person, Paul-Urbain, Marquis de Fleury (1778–1836), in the cemetery of Rennes-les-Bains. The first tombstone wrongly gives his birth date as May 3, 1776, while the second commemorates the transfer of his body to another spot in the graveyard and states that he died on August 7, 1856, aged sixty! What on earth was going on?

Curiously enough, this Comte de Fleury was the grandson of Dame Marie de Nègre of Rennes and Blanchefort: Marie's youngest daughter, Gabrielle d'Hautpoul de Blanchefort, married the Comte de Fleury, and Paul-Urbain was their son.[65] How odd that the tombstones of two members of the same family should continue to tantalize with their weird errors—if indeed that is what they are.

Saunière's Mysterious Trips

By the end of 1892, Abbé Saunière was behaving undeniably oddly, frequently traveling outside the area without permission from his superiors. He even left a number of stock letters for Marie Dénarnaud to send out in reply to any correspondence while he was away, saying he was busy and would write a proper reply as soon as he could. Saunière was covering his tracks.

According to the villagers, he would take the train from Couiza south toward Perpignan—outside his diocese—but where he went from there nobody knows. He did sometimes stay at a small hotel in Perpignan, the Eugène Castel, but he appears to have used it more as a base for wider forays.[66]

Rumor places him in Spain and Paris—and even England twice[67]—but Claire Corbu, owner of the priest's surviving papers, declares, "We have found nothing that gives us the least indication as to the destination and aim of Abbé Saunière's journeys."[68] The most controversy centers on whether or not Saunière made a trip to Paris, as this was to become an integral part of the legend. In particular, it is claimed he mingled in the capital with members of occult groups, including the esoterically minded opera singer Emma Calvé—who is even said to have become his lover. But in fact there is no specific evidence that he ever visited the French capital. What was once regarded as the best evidence, a set of photographs bearing the name of a Paris photographer, has fallen by the wayside since it was conclusively proven that they are likenesses of *Alfred* Saunière. The only other tangible clue is a glass Eiffel Tower found by the Corbus after Marie's death in a collection of mementos—but was it a souvenir or a gift? There was also a street map of Paris, although it seems to date from nearer 1913. But of course, if Saunière had money to burn, the obvious place to enjoy doing it would have been the European capital with the naughtiest twinkle in its eye. Perhaps the unorthodox priest from the dusty little hamlet so far to the south really did savor a welcome break in Paris, far away from his disapproving superiors.

The French researcher André Douzet claims to have evidence that places Saunière in Lyons in May, June, and September 1898 and the early summer of 1899. He has reproduced copies of invoices for the hire of carriages in the city, although these show the hirer to be simply one "Monsieur l'Abbé Saunière"—perhaps some other priest entirely, or even the ubiquitous Alfred.[69]

Desecration and Redecoration

As we have seen, by 1905 Marie de Nègre's gravestone was apparently thrown in a corner of the graveyard by Saunière. Exactly when he did so is not known, but it is likely to have been during 1895—when he and Marie Dénarnaud were engaged in some very dubious activities in the cemetery. Three times in March 1895 the villagers made written complaints—which survive—to the local subprefecture that for reasons they were unable to fathom Saunière had been moving and destroying gravestones and disturbing their relatives' graves. They dismissed Saunière's claim that he was just tidying the place up—some villagers remember seeing holes some ten feet deep. Indeed, he had to build an ossuary—still there in one corner of the graveyard—to contain the bones he had turned up during his digging. Considering that this was desecration on a large scale, if perhaps incidental to the priest's main activity—whatever that might have been—the reaction of the villagers was if anything surprisingly mild. Certainly to outsiders the whole business is more than a little creepy.[70]

Saunière's next project was the redecoration of the church, undertaken between 1896 and 1897. The various statues, including the bizarre staring-eyed demon that holds up the water stoup and the large bas-relief taking up the western wall, along with the Stations of the Cross, were the work of Giscard of Toulouse, who signed the contract in November 1896. (When complete the church was blessed by Saunière's Bishop, Félix-Arsène Billard, on the day of Pentecost, at the beginning of June 1897.)

The decoration is certainly odd—but is this because of Saunière's lack of taste or because he was trying to tell us something? If so, what on earth was it? The inscriptions and decoration of the church's porch and tympanum have inspired a great deal of comment, debate, and speculation. Undeniably, they are strange, not only because of what they include but also because of what they leave out.

Some—such as Putnam and Wood—have glibly dismissed the very notion that there is anything odd about Saunière's decoration of the church. However, many French specialists find it odd: the art historian Jean-Claude Danis has listed no fewer than ninety anomalies within the church, which should be taken seriously.[71] Each individual anomaly *might* have a mundane explanation, but the overall picture is one of conscious design.

Famously, the porch bears the Latin motto "*Terribilis est locus iste,*" usually translated as "This place is terrible"—terrible in the sense of awe-inspiring. (Some English books have it as "This place is accursed," which is just plain wrong.) In itself, it is actually not as surprising as many make out, being the first part of a biblical quotation—the second part follows immediately below, arched above the doorway. These are the words uttered by Jacob when he has his vision of the ladder to heaven—in the King James Version, "How dreadful is this place! This is none other but the house of God, and this is the gate of heaven." Surely it makes perfect sense to find this quotation at the entrance to a church.

Even so, there is something peculiar about it, because the first part is actually *wrong* (and priests, particularly in those days, had to know Latin). The literal translation is "*Your* place is terrible"—*iste* means "of yours." Was Saunière for some reason distancing himself from his congregation—perhaps even from the Christian religion?

On either side of the *Terribilis* quotation is the first part of another biblical saying: "*Domus mea domus orationis vocabitur*"—"My house shall be called the house of prayer." But the second part is missing—the quotation, from the words of Jesus when he casts the moneychangers from the Temple (Matthew 21:13), should continue "but ye have made it a den of thieves." Why draw attention to this saying, then leave out the whole point? Taken together, the two quotations have an unnerving effect, as if Saunière is saying, "You have made *your* place a den of thieves."

However, there may be a fairly rational explanation: under a deal or concordat Napoleon concluded with the Catholic Church, the state became responsible for paying the clergy and maintaining the churches. Parish priests were regarded as civil servants. While this might have been a good financial arrangement for the Church, effectively it made individual churches the property of the Republic, which is why Saunière had to rent his presbytery from the village authorities. (After the separation of church and state in 1905, the government took over responsibility for maintaining churches, but the Church had to pay the priests.) These inscriptions could be a sign of Saunière's disapproval of the gradual secularization of the Church in France.

This political outrage also may have spilled out into the unusual design for the water stoup. The (in)famous demon statue, life-size and crouching on one knee just inside the door, is usually referred to as Asmodeus (a demon who guards buried treasure). Staring in apparent outrage or horror, he is holding up the holy water stoup beneath four angels making the sign of the cross under the legend *"Par ce signe tu le vaincras"*—a slightly odd version of the celebrated "In this sign you will conquer," here being "In this sign you will conquer him [or it]." What was Saunière trying to suggest by changing such a familiar phrase in this way?

Tellingly, in the sermon that landed him in such trouble, Saunière said about the Republicans: "They are the devil to be defeated; they are to be brought to their knees beneath the weight of religion and the baptised. The sign of the cross is victorious and with us!"[72] Despite all the reams of highly colored speculation about the water stoup, this does seem a likely explanation—although there may be other levels of interpretation.

Placing the holy water stoup on the devil, or a demon, is not unique in France—a similar motif was used in the church of Montréal, a village about fifteen miles north of Rennes-le-Château, and Jean Markale cites another in Campénéac in Brittany.[73] But it certainly creates a jarring effect in Saunière's church, especially with so many other anomalies to puzzle over. (Incidentally, the French equivalent of the English idiom "to stick out like a sore thumb" is "to stand out like the devil in a holy water stoup.")

A large bas-relief on the western wall shows Jesus delivering the Sermon on the Mount, but there on the grass is a small bag that has burst open to spill out gold coins—a somewhat unorthodox rendition of the Gospel scene.

Here the Stations of the Cross run counterclockwise, opposite to the traditional direction: while it may not actually be unique, it is sufficiently unusual to attract comment. And there are odd touches: there are a woman in a widow's veil, a child clad in a tartan kilt, and other anomalous figures carrying out presumably meaningful actions.

The final touch was the painting of Mary Magdalene on the front of the altar, the work of an anonymous artist from Carcassonne, but Saunière and his priest friend Joseph Courtaly made the finishing touches themselves.[74] This was in homage to the saint whom Saunière clearly revered with a special intensity, naming his library and house after her alleged homes in Magdala and Bethany respectively.

So far the priest had spent his extra money on the church, but there were signs that by this time cash was coming in thick and fast, more than he knew what to do with.

Horror—and Riches

A few months after the completion and rededication of the church, a horrific event shook the neighborhood. On the night of October 31, 1897, seventy-year-old Abbé Antoine Gélis, parish priest of Coustassa for forty years, was brutally murdered in his presbytery, his skull caved in by someone he had apparently welcomed into his house. The culprit was never caught, and the killing was seemingly motiveless—bizarrely, the only things taken were the contents of a travel satchel, although the murderer could easily have found just over one thousand francs in various drawers.[75]

Then a few days later the investigating judge, Raymond Jean, found another thirteen thousand francs that Gélis had hidden in various places in his presbytery and church. Jean also discovered that the old priest had recently invested between fifteen and twenty thousand francs.[76]

Whether Gélis's murder had any connection with the Rennes-le-Château affair—Gélis had been one of the priests visited by Saunière after his "discovery of a tomb" six years before—is unknown, but it certainly shows that the area was home to some very peculiar and brutal happenings. (Until he was found to have an unshakable alibi, suspicions immediately fell on Joseph Pagès, Gélis's nephew, who was related to Saunière by marriage—but then it was a small world.) Both Saunière and the apparently crazed etymologist Boudet attended Gélis's funeral on November 3, 1897.

By now Saunière was rolling in money, which he clearly determined to spend on himself rather than the church. In 1898 he began to buy up land in the village on which to build his lavish *domaine,* although he did so in other people's names, mostly that of Marie Dénarnaud.

The priest had several bank accounts and dealings with financial institutions in Paris, Toulouse, and Perpignan. There is even evidence suggesting that he had an account in Budapest. In late 1899, when the subprefecture investigated him, it returned the following somewhat contradictory report: "M. Abbé Saunière is in a well-off position. He has no family responsibilities. His conduct is good. He professes anti-government opinions. Attitude: militant reactionary. Notice: unfavorable."[77]

In 1900 work began on a baroque two-story house, which Saunière named the Villa Béthanie (after Bethany, the New Testament residence of Mary, Martha, and Lazarus). He explained it was intended to be a home for retired priests, although it was never actually used as such. But oddly Saunière never even moved into it himself; although he used it for entertaining important guests, he continued to live in the presbytery, for which he paid the commune a peppercorn rent of twenty francs a year.

Like every other self-made Victorian, Saunière splashed out on the creation of impressive grounds, building an ornamental garden, complete with a terrace looking over the landscape. But his finishing touch was the famed Tour Magdala, which he used as a library (its oak bookshelves alone cost ten thousand francs in 1908). He stocked it well, not just with religious and theological works, as might be expected, but also with books on politics, history, and geography. He also subscribed to a number of magazines and journals. The work was finally completed in 1908.

He became an obsessive and voracious collector—of books, stamps, postcards, apparently anything he could lavish money on. He had two dogs, the weirdly named Faust (presumably after the notorious medieval scholar who had sold his soul to the Devil) and Pomponnet, besides two pet monkeys, Capri and Mora. As for the enigmatic Marie Dénarnaud—he ordered the latest fashions from Paris for her: not quite the traditional way for a country priest to treat his housekeeper.

Having reserved the Villa Béthanie for entertaining, the priest and his housekeeper behaved like Oriental potentates: surviving invoices for the vast quantities of food and, especially, drink make astonishing reading. Rum was imported from Martinique, wine and brandy were downed as if entertaining Roman emperors of particularly immoderate habits. And then there is the matter of *who* Saunière entertained in such style. Naturally, local worthies and dignitaries flocked to enjoy such lavish hospitality, but other guests are much more intriguing.

They included the artist and politician Henri Dujardin-Beaumetz (1852–1913), later Undersecretary of State for Fine Arts—although in fact he and Saunière had been friends since a previous posting in Alet-les-Bains, and Dujardin-Beaumetz was at that time a local politician representing Limoux. Yet their friendship is still somewhat surprising, as Dujardin-Beaumetz was not only a republican and Radical but also a Freemason of the La Clémente Amitié lodge.[78]

From a thank-you letter that survives in Saunière's papers, apparently one of his guests, a M. Bousquet, came from as far away as the village of Bayons in Provence near the Italian border.[79] Also found among the priest's papers was a greeting card from the Duc and Duchesse d'Auerstadt, while another eminent visitor was the author Andrée Brugière, who styled herself the Vicomtesse d'Artois.[80]

Another intriguing name at Saunière's table is that of the Marquise du Bourg de Bozas, from an important family with esoteric connections. Her presence is explained by her relationship with the priest's brother, Alfred, since 1893 a teacher at the Petit Séminaire in Narbonne, where, in the words of the researcher Franck Marie, "His dissolute life caused a scandal."[81] The Marquise's name—besides those of several other women—was linked with Alfred, who would end in disgrace as an alcoholic, defrocked priest.

But the most controversial alleged guest of Saunière's was the celebrated soprano Emma Calvé (1858–1942). Not only was she the most famous person allegedly to have dined with the "humble" priest but her connections with the steamy and often dark world of the occult have not unnaturally inspired some heated speculations.

Born Rose-Emma Calvet in Decazeville in the Aveyron (later changing the spelling of her surname, mainly so English audiences could pronounce it), she made her professional debut in 1881, going on to enjoy a thirty-year career as a huge international star, touring virtually every corner of the world. From 1892, each year she starred at the Royal Italian Opera in London's Covent Garden (for a vast ten thousand francs a month), living in the then rather louche area of St. John's Wood. During her first summer in London, she also received an invitation to sing for Queen Victoria, which she repeated annually—sometimes at Windsor Castle, sometimes at the monarch's quaint Scottish retreat, Balmoral. (Clearly Calvé was a great favorite: Victoria even commissioned a bust of her.)

In addition to her acclaim in conventional circles, Calvé was a leading light of the Parisian occult salons, originally through an interest in spiritualism—then very much in vogue in Paris and largely popularized in literary and artistic circles by Victor Hugo.

A key figure in that heady and intense milieu was Dr. Gérard Encausse, known as Papus, whose immediate circle of like-minded friends included some surprises, such as the Nobel prize–winning physiologist Charles Richet, the astronomer Camille Flammarion, and Colonel Albert de Rochas, director of studies at the important École Polytechnique. Calvé's biographer Jean Contrucci writes: "Emma Calvé frequented these spirits, as scholarly as they were nonconformist, and if she only occasionally perceived the superficial aspects of her friends' researches, she absorbed their certainties, sharing their theories in confidence and devoting herself, in public as in private, to occultism."[82]

As Contrucci also notes of the time that this bond was formed:

> Papus, despite the abundance of his hair, had nothing of the "old fogey" [*vieille barbe*]: he was twenty-five, and his youth was not unconnected with the interest that the ladies had in him. And, despite the virtues of the disinterest he had the [good] sense to "advertise," he was not sorry to see the most beautiful shoulders and eyes in

> Paris at his lectures. There was nothing like it for bringing in new members than to see, in the first row of the audience, Mlle. Sarah Bernhardt, and the poetess and composer Augusta Holmes with the "Valkyrian" blond mane that contrasted with the jet-black hair of Emma Calvé, from whom beauty radiated.[83]

(After a first invitation in 1895, Calvé would celebrate every summer solstice at Camille Flammarion's house, in the company of Papus, Colonel de Rochas, and Richet.[84] As we will see, these highly regarded scientists possessed some weird beliefs, which she perhaps shared and which were to become surprisingly influential among the men who ran Europe.)

The Paris occult world centered on two establishments—which complemented rather than rivaled each other: the brilliantly named Bookshop of the Wonderful (Librairie du Merveilleux), set up by Papus in the Rue de Trévise, and the Bookshop of Independent Art (Librairie de l'Art Indépendant) in the Rue de la Chaussée-d'Antin. Emma Calvé frequented both. Contrucci writes of the Bookshop of the Wonderful:

> The back room also served as the headquarters of the Martinist Order, revived by Papus in 1891 [it was actually about 10 years earlier], which meant to perpetuate the spirit of chivalry and that of the New Gnostic Church, of which Papus was "bishop." One finds around him, apart from his disciples, Paul Sédir, Paul Adam, Victor-Émile Michelet, other renowned occultists whom Emma frequented or met often: Stanislas de Guaïta, reviver of the Rosicrucians under the name of the Cabalistic Order of the Rose-Cross, who studied the Bible from an esoteric angle, Joséphin Péladan (the *sâr* Péladan), and also the curious or "fellow travelers," such as Charles Maurras, Villiers de L'Isle-Adam, Maurice Barrès, . . . Huysmans, Catulle Mendès, Victorien Sardou.[85]

Of course two of these names leap out at us: Maurice Barrès, whose *La colline inspirée* seems to have set the scene for the Priory of Sion, and most astonishingly, Charles Maurras, founder of the incredibly influential, and ultra-Catholic, Action Française.

The Bookshop of Independent Art was the creation of Édouard Bailly, who was dedicated to encouraging an interest in esoteric ideas and promoting new musical and artistic talent. It was more for artists, as Contrucci notes:

> The end of the afternoon would see rubbing shoulders, along the shelves of the bookshop, Claude Debussy and Erik Satie, Toulouse-Lautrec and Félicien Rops, Odilon Redon and Edgar Degas, Pierre Louÿs and Henri de Régnier, Mallarmé, dropping by from Condorcet, where he taught English, Paul Le Cour and Joris-Karl Huysmans, the Catholic yet *luciferan* esotericist . . .[86]

It was here that Emma Calvé met one of her most famed lovers, the novelist Jules Bois, author of *The Wedding of Sathan* [*Satan*] (*Les noces de Sathan*). As Contrucci writes: "If Calvé toppled into occult practices and active esotericism, she owed it in large part to Bois, even if he only reinforced what was already in gestation."[87]

An interesting name to encounter here is Claude Debussy (claimed by the Priory as a Grand Master), composer of much poignantly haunting music, such as the famous *Clair de Lune.* He and Bois planned to collaborate on a stage version of *The Wedding of Sathan,* but when it fell through Bois worked with Erik Satie instead.[88] Calvé knew Debussy through their shared musical as well as esoteric interests, and she was also acquainted with Jean Cocteau's parents.[89]

Now a rich international star, Calvé bought her own castle, the eleventh-century Château de Cabrières, near Millau, not far from her birthplace. She wrote in her first autobiography (published in 1922): "It saw the horrors of the religious wars and was the refuge of a certain group of Knights Templar."[90] Perhaps unsurprisingly, the castle was rich in esoteric lore: apparently the fabled Book of Abraham the Jew—which allegedly enabled Nicolas Flamel to make the Philosopher's Stone and achieve the mysterious alchemical "Great Work"—was once kept there.[91]

In 1896 Mlle. Calvé made what she described as a "pilgrimage" to Saintes-Maries-de-la-Mer, one of the prime sites of the Mary Magdalene cult in Provence.[92] Perhaps she had a sisterly feeling for a woman whose name was so intimately associated with unorthodox morals and even, more controversially, with goddesslike fascination.

All this would be particularly interesting *if* Calvé had been a guest of Saunière's, as the Priory's version of the Rennes-le-Château story makes much of. But was she really his dinner guest? If not, how did her name become linked with his?

In fact, there is no definite evidence, even from letters or other documents, to show that Emma Calvé ever visited Rennes-le-Château, or that Saunière met her in Paris. But before we dismiss her as a convenient device of the later mythmakers to connect Saunière with the Parisian occultists and, in particular, Debussy, it should be stressed that the claim *predated* the Dossiers Secrets. It is based on the testimony of villagers who, long before the mystery received any widespread publicity, claimed to have seen her in the village, as even the arch-skeptic René Descadeillas acknowledges.[93] At the very least this shows that Calvé's name inspired the later myth rather than the other way round. (And Contrucci, writing in 1989, acknowledges that she could have easily traveled down to Rennes-le-Château during her summer retreats at Cabrières, about a hundred miles away.)[94]

Decline and Fall

All good things come to an end—the very best things usually sooner rather than later—and Saunière's hedonistic hilltop life was no exception, barely outlasting the completion of his *domaine.* His last "year of splendor" arrived in 1908, when the finishing touches were put to the Tour Magdala, although he was already struggling to pay for the work.

The catalyst seems to have come when the local bishop changed six years before. Until then, Mgr. Félix-Arsène Billard seems to have acted as Saunière's protector, or at least chosen to look the other way from his subordinate's activities. (In fact, there is evidence that Billard himself was engaged in some dubious financial dealings.) But he died in 1902 and was replaced by Paul-Félix de Beauséjour, who soon grew curious about how one of his parish priests could legitimately afford such a life of unashamed luxury.

However, de Beauséjour was only part of the problem: whatever its source, Saunière's money was drying up. It is tempting to link this reversal of fortune to Alfred's steep decline and death, after his drinking and womanizing had attracted more than a little criticism. Dismissed from the priesthood and mortally sick, he returned to his home village of Montazels in 1904—bringing one Marie-Émilie Salière to look after him. (Moving into the diocese presumably brought him, and therefore his brother, to the Bishop's attention.) He died on September 9, 1905.

Something connected with Alfred's demise caused friction between Bérenger and his family; soon afterward he made out a will leaving everything to Marie Dénarnaud, specifically stating that he did this because of "the little trust I have in my relatives, whose conduct has been very reprehensible on the death of my brother A.S., deceased at Montazels."[95] (Perhaps significantly, Saunière specified that on Marie's death everything should go to the Bishop of Carcassonne, but in a *later* will made out in 1912, after the Bishop's actions against him—in which he pointedly describes himself as "*former* curé of Rennes-le-Château"—this condition was dropped.)[96]

A more cynical motive for the Bishop's interest may have been connected with the separation of Church and State in December 1905: if it could be shown that Saunière's personal *domaine* had been bought with money that was rightfully the Church's, then the diocese could stake a claim to it.

The row with de Beauséjour was to rumble on for several years and end up in the Court of Rome, the highest ecclesiastical court in the Catholic Church. At first Saunière haughtily refused to explain his source of wealth, basically telling the Bishop it was none of his business. Then he resorted to producing flagrantly false accounts, inflating the sums he could legitimately explain (for example, the Comte de Chambord's 1,000 francs miraculously became 3,000). In July 1911 he produced a list of expenses totaling 193,000 francs, almost exactly equaling his alleged income. Even though, in Descadeillas's words, this was "an enormous sum for that period,"[97] from surviving invoices and correspondence, it appears the real amount was about three times greater still.

Saunière claimed that his money had been amassed from a multitude of sources: small economies here and there, the sale of postcards to tourists, all adding up to one massive implausibility. Indeed, with his lavish lifestyle so well known, it is astonishing that he dared claim to have made any economies, large or small. But he also admitted that he had received many donations from wealthy individuals and families, adding: "My brother, being a preacher, had numerous connections; he served as the intermediary for these generosities."[98] (This would explain why Bérenger's fortunes declined after Alfred's death.) But, he insisted, these gifts had been made under a promise of secrecy, and he would not break that confidence: except in a few cases where a donor had given openly, as with the Comtesse de Chambord, he refused to say who had made the donations, or how much they had given. (This is very odd: on the whole it is unlikely that donors would demand to have their kindness kept secret from the bishopric.)

Faced with such insubordination, in January 1909 de Beauséjour removed Saunière to a new parish, Coustouge, a tiny, remote village thirty or so miles away. Rennes-le-Château's mayor wrote to the Bishop supporting Saunière, declaring that his replacement would mean "a deserted church and religious ceremonies replaced with civil ceremonies."[99] (It was remarkable how the villagers' loyalty had increased since Saunière had come into money.)

The row rumbled on until July, when Abbé Henri Marty was sent to take over the parish. But the mayor's prophecy came true: while the church itself was empty, worshipers sought out the makeshift altar in the Villa Béthanie where Saunière continued to administer the sacraments. He had simply refused to leave the village, eventually tendering his resignation. Officially he was no longer the parish priest of Rennes-le-Château after June 1, 1910. One of his closest friends wrote to him at around this time:

> You have had the money, it is not up to anybody to penetrate the secrecy that you keep; you have spent it as you pleased, this concerns only you . . .
>
> If someone gave you the money under natural secrecy, you are obliged to keep it, and nothing can release you from this secrecy except solely the person who gave it to you, and even in that case, you must see if the revelation they authorize you to make does not bear a moral prejudice, and in that case you must still keep quiet . . .[100]

Saunière was summoned before a tribunal in Carcassonne in October 1910, accused of trafficking in masses. Although he was found not guilty—through lack of evidence—his insubordinate attitude and refusal to reveal the source of his income earned him a sentence of *suspens à divinis,* forbidding him from administering the sacraments. The outraged Saunière invoked his right of appeal to the Court of Rome, but the sentence stood. In July 1915 it was announced in the diocesan journal:

> It is for the diocesan administration of Carcassonne deeply painful, but a pressing duty, to indicate to the faithful that M. Abbé Saunière, former curé of Rennes-le-Château, currently residing in the same place, has, by sentence of the *Officialité* [the ecclesiastical court] dated December 5, 1911, been deprived of his sacerdotal powers, that he must therefore no longer celebrate the holy sacrifice, and that, from now on, he cannot acquit the fees for masses that are entrusted to him.[101]

During all this time, the once-wealthy priest was actually short of money: his papers reveal that he was even trying to sell the *domaine* to pay off his debts, but he failed to find a buyer and was overdrawn at the bank. (Marie continued paying the interest after Saunière's death.)

Curiously, however, the money seemed to start flowing again just before his death; at least he started making plans for more building work that would have cost a total of 8 million francs: increasing the height of the Tour Magdala, building a new 130-feet-high tower and an outdoor baptismal pool, and adding a chapel to the cemetery. He was also planning to pay for piping a water supply to the village (presumably for the pool) and constructing a proper road to Couiza. The latter was for his benefit, as he planned to treat himself to an unheard-of luxury for that part of France in 1917, a motorcar.[102] Of course he may simply have been indulging in fantasy or planning what he would do with money he was expecting to roll in. He may not have actually possessed the necessary funds.

Inevitably, the strain—not to mention the period of exceptionally good living—had taken its toll. Saunière was very sick in the last years of his life, sometimes confined to bed for weeks at a time. No doubt desperate about his health, he made a trip to Lourdes in 1916.

There is a little mystification about his death. He died on January 22, 1917, in his sixty-fourth year, following what sounds like a stroke—some think a heart attack—after collapsing on the terrace of his *domaine* a few days earlier. How many days before is unclear, but although at some point the date of January 17—with its somewhat puzzling significance in Priory mythology—became fixed, in fact, there is no specific evidence for this.

Saunière was buried in the churchyard on January 24, 1917, but only after a curious ritual took place: "Put in an armchair in the sitting room [of the Villa Béthanie], [his corpse] remained there on display for a whole day, covered in a blanket with red pom-poms. In veneration, those who came cut off a pom-pom and took it away."[103] This, at least, was according to Noël Corbu, who produced the first account of the affair in the late 1950s.

Because of Corbu's commercial interest in building up the mystery, his account is generally treated with a pinch of salt—undoubtedly he embroidered certain parts of it—but at least this shows that the "pom-pom" ritual was not a later invention by the Priory of Sion mythmakers. (While villagers paying their respects is perfectly understandable, the business of the red pom-poms remains a mystery. Did it possess a special significance, or was it a spontaneous gesture of respect and affection?)

When Saunière died, the villagers recall Marie Dénarnaud repeating over and over, "My God! My God! Monsieur the curé is dead . . . now everything is finished."[104] What was the "everything"—her own somewhat equivocal relationship with the priest or something on a grander scale altogether, some long-term plan or plot? Certainly, she was seen burning papers in the park after Saunière's death.[105] (There are also claims that she burned large quantities of banknotes after the Second World War, when the currency changed, but this may be a garbled memory of the earlier event; if Marie possessed large quantities of banknotes, she had refused to touch them during the previous thirty years.)

Postmortem

Marie remained devoted to Saunière, visiting his grave every day and every night for the rest of her long life. Throughout the years, she steadfastly refused to answer questions about him.

In fact, Marie was trying to find a buyer for the property from at least 1925 through the intermediary of Abbé Eugène Grassaud.[106] But in the uncertain climate of the interwar years, nobody was interested in a weird property in such an out-of-the-way location.

A friend of Marie's, Mme. Vidal—to whom the former housekeeper lent the Villa for her wedding night—recalls an enigmatic conversation. Marie had made the apparently melodramatic statement "With what Monsieur the curé has left, one could feed all of Rennes for a hundred years and it would still remain!" To which Mme. Vidal replied sensibly: "But if he left you so much money, why do you live as a pauper?" Marie: "[As] to that, I cannot touch it! (*A aquo ni tusti pas!*)." Saunière's great confidante refused to elaborate.[107]

In late 1944 and early 1945, Spanish members of the Resistance were sheltered in the *domaine,* presumably with Marie's knowledge and permission. This presence would seem to be directly connected with the gruesome discovery in March 1956 of three bodies buried in the grounds dating from about that time; Corbu and his companions were led to that spot by a dowser called in to attempt to locate Saunière's "treasure."[108] (Opinions are divided between whether the dead men were Resistants killed by the collaborationist Milice or vice versa.)

Noël Corbu and his family moved into the area—to Bugarach—in 1942, after which he wasted no time in befriending Marie. On July 22, 1946, she gave the *domaine* over to him in return for being allowed to live out the rest of her life there. In fact, it was something of a dream come true: she had been searching for such a solution for her old age for many years.

Perhaps Corbu's acquisition of the property was the result of a deal with the Church, still keen to get its hands on the *domaine.* It has been suggested that Corbu was interned after the Liberation for black marketeering, and the Church—through the intermediary of Resistant Abbé Gau—offered to have him released in return for persuading Marie to sell him the property, which he would then turn over, or sell on, to the diocese. But Corbu apparently reneged on this deal, keeping the *domaine* for himself. Although there is no proof of this, the first writer to mention it, Jean-Luc Chaumeil in *The Treasure of the Golden Triangle* (1979), cites the testimony of a local priest, Abbé Maurice-René Mazières, the former president of the Society of Arts and Sciences of Carcassonne.[109] If this is accurate, then clearly the Church regarded Saunière's *domaine* as significant. And, of course, it is interesting for the implications about Corbu—according to many skeptics, the outright inventor of the Rennes-le-Château mystery.

Corbu's daughter Claire (who married the grandson of Saunière's bell ringer, also Antoine Captier), records Marie telling her father, when he was having business difficulties (his interests in Algeria were going under): "Don't worry yourself so much, my dear Noël . . . one day I will tell you a secret that will make you a rich man . . . very rich!"[110] Claire

Captier dates this to around 1949. Unfortunately, Marie became senile in her last years, before dying of a stroke in January 1953.

Noël Corbu then turned the villa into the Hôtel-Restaurant La Tour, which opened on Easter Day 1955; there he began to entertain his guests with the first accounts of the Saunière affair. Then he committed it to writing, before finally tape-recording it to play to visitors. Clearly Corbu capitalized on the mystery to attract customers to his out-of-the-way hotel-restaurant—who can blame him?—and was behind the first major burst of publicity, in 1956. But did he, as many allege, actually *create* the mystery? Or did he merely build up something genuine in the annals of the village?

The Saunière story was the subject of a series of articles in the regional newspaper, *La Dépêche du Midi,* in which the priest was dubbed the "billionaire curé" (*curé aux milliards*) and his fortune given as an improbable 50 billion francs. (The articles were illustrated with a Paris portrait of Alfred Saunière.)

From there the mystery steadily became better known, initially within the treasure-hunting fraternity (always very well represented in France) but finally achieving national publicity thanks to a television program in 1961 and inclusion in the popular mystery writer Robert Charroux's *Treasures of the World* a year later. The publicity brought treasure hunters flocking to the village with a motley crew of mediums and dowsers, to dig all over the place, with or without permission. In the end, the commune authorities banned excavations in 1965.

Discrepancies, Questions, Puzzles

That is how the Rennes-le-Château story stood before it was hijacked by the writers of the Dossiers Secrets. Those already familiar with the mystery may have noticed some apparent omissions: for example, where are the coded parchments, bearing mysterious messages? Where is the connection with Poussin's *Shepherds of Arcadia* and an enigmatic monument that once stood beside the road to Arques? So successful is the Dossiers Secrets' version that it is easy to assume these aspects have always been integral parts of the story. However, we have been careful to include only those elements that featured before Plantard became involved, in order to see how he changed the story to fit the Priory of Sion's agenda.

The Saunière mystery boils down to two questions: Where did his money come from? And what, if anything, was he trying to convey by the weird decoration in his church?

First, how much money did the priest actually make—or rather spend? Although he had been able to pay for quite substantial work on the church in the preceding ten years, his inexplicably lavish spending really began only in the mid-1890s. This was when he packed the church with unnecessary decoration before buying up the land for his *domaine,* clearing it, and constructing his buildings and gardens, as well as undertaking the extraordinarily opulent entertaining. The building work was completed in 1908, although for the final year or two he struggled to pay for it.

Although Saunière claimed to his bishop that his *domaine* had cost him 193,000 francs, surviving documents—invoices, orders, and correspondence—show he spent at least 660,000 francs, and as his papers are incomplete, the true figure is undoubtedly more.[111] It is difficult to be precise about the modern equivalent, but taking into consideration inflation, the change in relative values of goods over time, and the vagaries of the exchange rate—not to mention revaluations of the French currency itself—the best estimate is in the region of 1.5 to 2.0 million pounds sterling.[112]

Even if we take the higher figure—to allow for incomplete documentation and spending on perishables such as food and drink—Saunière spent about 2 million pounds during a ten-year period. It may not make him the "billionaire priest," but 150,000 to 200,000 pounds a year is still way beyond what would be expected to line the pockets of an average Languedocian priest. At least that part of the mystery was not cobbled together out of thin air.

The immediate—and perhaps still most popular—assumption was that Saunière had found a treasure trove. (However, Noël Corbu's theory that it was the treasure of Blanche of Castile is certainly wrong).[113] Although some of the weirder elements of the story may be the results of projecting some mystical significance onto physical treasure, Indiana Jones style, throughout history the area around Rennes-le-Château does seem to have acted as a magnet for sacred treasures.

In the third century B.C.E., the treasure from the venerable Oracle of Delphi was pillaged by Gauls from southern France, some of whom settled in Asia Minor, becoming the biblical Galatians, while others returned home, presumably taking their booty with them.[114] Then there is the sacred treasure from the Temple of Jerusalem—including the holy Menorah (seven-branched candlestick) carried off by the Romans during the Jewish Revolt and plundered in turn from Rome in 410 by Visigoths based in the Languedoc. And of course, their lost, or rather mislaid, city of Rhedae was somewhere around Rennes-le-Château. The Temple treasure then disappears from history.

Today, of course, the Jerusalem artifacts would possess not merely material and religious but also *political* significance for the State of Israel. Indeed, it was reported in the press in December 1972 that Israeli agents had visited the area to investigate—and Pierre Plantard later explicitly stated that the Priory of Sion is the guardian of the Temple treasure. This solution to the Saunière mystery still has its advocates, such as Guy Patton and Robin Mackness in *Web of Gold.* (Of all possible historical treasures, the Jerusalem treasure enjoys the best case for being hidden in the locality of Rennes-le-Château.)

Then there is the putative and fabled treasure of the Cathars, the heretical Christian sect that flourished in the area for two hundred years until their brutal suppression by the Albigensian Crusade in the early thirteenth century. The last major Cathar stronghold to fall was the mountaintop fortress of Montségur in the Ariège, some fifty miles west of Rennes-le-Château. In 1244, after a lengthy siege, the heretics negotiated a deal by which, if they were allowed time—probably to celebrate one of their holy days—they would surrender to the Inquisition, willingly (even gladly) giving themselves up to the flaming pyre. The siege ended on the night of March 15–16, 1244, with the grisly culmination as expected.

However, the episode is still hedged around by rumor and myths. In fact, not only Cathars were in the castle at the end—a political dimension to the "crusade" meant local lords and their soldiers were also inside, resisting the Crusaders. Besides, not all the heretics preferred death to denying their faith: after recanting, some were imprisoned at Carcassonne. From the captured soldiers and survivors, the Inquisitors expertly extracted the information that between two and four heretics had been selected to escape the massacre, by being either lowered down the cliff on ropes or hidden under the castle floor to slip away later. All these witnesses agreed that the purpose of their escape was to save the Cathar treasure, because they possessed the secret of its location.[115] Perhaps significantly, the surrender of Montségur was negotiated by Ramon d'Aniort—then Lord of Rennes-le-Château.[116]

The Templars make an almost mandatory appearance in the mystery, being fabled as guardians of treasure: a reputation they may have earned because of something they acquired in the Holy Land (some say the Ark of the Covenant)[117] or at least the fabulous wealth they had amassed during the two centuries of their existence. Some argue that the Paris Temple treasure, rather than being spirited out of France by ship at the suppression in 1307, went southward to important Templar properties in the Languedoc. As Roussillon was then part of Spain, the Templar holding at Le Bézu, some three miles from Rennes-le-Château but under the Roussillon Templars' authority, was beyond the reach of the hostile French king, Philippe the Fair. (Evidence suggests that after the fall of the Holy Land, the Templars sought to create their own "kingdom" in the Languedoc, which remained their heartland.)

Documents reveal that in 1147, Pierre de St. Jean, lord of Rhedae or Rhedez, entered the Order of the Temple and by the 1160s had become a very prominent figure in the regional Order.[118] If, some argue, Rhedae was actually Rennes-le-Château, this would definitely link the Templars and the village. *If*. . .

Sacred artifacts aside, there are plenty of candidates for treasures of a more worldly kind. As the Romans once mined gold and other precious metals from the hills around Blanchefort, an undiscovered vein could still exist.

In 1340, at Le Bézu, the King's men arrested two knights, Guilhem Catala and Pierre de Palajan, who were illegally minting gold coins. Although the coins were counterfeit in the sense that they were unauthorized by the King, their gold content was better than that of the official coins. But where did the gold come from?[119]

Many valuable objects have been found in the area over the years: in the eighteenth century a 44-pound ingot made from partially melted gold Arab coins was found on the plateau between Rennes-le-Château and Blanchefort. In 1860 a 110-pound gold ingot was discovered in the area. Slightly later, in Saunière's time, a gold statue was found near the Ruisseau de Couleurs, a watercourse at the bottom of the hill on which

Rennes-le-Château stands. Analysis of a gold bracelet found near the village in the 1970s proved it to be of East African origin, presumably having entered the region with the Moors.[120] And as we have seen, Saunière himself found a pot of gold coins beneath the Knights' Stone.

The area around Rennes-le-Château is also rich in folktales of treasure (as are many ancient sites), most intriguingly associated with the château of Blanchefort. A local legend tells of a young shepherdess who chanced upon the devil counting his money—specifically, for some reason, nineteen and a half million gold coins. Perhaps this is based on some scrambled memory of the Roman gold mines. Another folktale describes how the shepherd boy Ignace Paris was tortured to death by the Lord of Rennes to make him reveal where he had found a hoard of gold coins. This story is illustrated on the confessional Saunière had installed in the church.

Any of these tales could be the solution to the mystery of Saunière's wealth, but in the final analysis they all rest on speculation—and certainly none accounts for the *irregularity* of his cash flow.

Many researchers prefer a more mundane explanation, their favorite being that Saunière was abusing his office by "trafficking in masses"—taking payment from people outside his parish to say masses for deceased relatives, a practice allowed by the Church but only under strict conditions (priests had to turn the money over to the diocese to be distributed among all the priests). This was René Descadeillas's favored explanation (although originally he considered it to account for just *part* of the mystery); it resurfaced more recently in *The Treasure of Rennes-le-Château: A Mystery Solved* (2004) by Bill Putnam and John Edwin Wood.

There is no doubt that Saunière was taking considerable amounts of money to say masses, in fact, for far more masses than he could possibly say. He received numerous small payments, usually of between 1 and 10 francs—which still sometimes totaled as much as 150 francs a day—via the post office at Couiza. The requests came from France, Belgium, Italy, Switzerland, and Germany.[121]

However, even this simple, if unsavory, solution fails to account for the priest's wealth: Saunière was spending considerably more than he received from this source. In any case, what was so special about Saunière, or Rennes-le-Château, that so many people from so far away wanted him to say masses for their departed loved ones? Jean Markale thinks that the requests for masses were just a by-product of Saunière's "grand plan"—whatever that was.[122] These small sums were augmented by larger donations from wealthy individuals, the first, as we have seen, from the Comtesse de Chambord with Alfred acting as intermediary—although Saunière refused point-blank to provide any details.

Although the large donations and the smaller fees for masses probably do account for Saunière's fortune, besides the irregularities in his cash flow, particularly after Alfred's death, there is still a mystery: what was so special about him that people showered money on him by every post?

It has been suggested that Saunière was accruing a fortune from charging for "Masses of Vain Observance," essentially a form of magical spell casting, perhaps for amatory purposes,[123] which would explain why his "customers" sought him out as offering a special service. But maybe it was something more mundane, perhaps even criminal: for example, could Saunière, in his village conveniently close to the Spanish border, have acted as the equivalent of a money launderer? In his book on the Gélis murder, Jacques Rivière points out that the Languedoc would have been a logical place for the monarchists—then in a very precarious position—to have squirreled away funds for a fight back and that priests (also reeling before the new wave of anticlericalism) were the logical people to safeguard such funds.[124] Although this suggestion is plausible, like most aspects of this affair, in the absence of solid evidence it has to remain speculation.

In *The Templar Revelation,* we suggested that Saunière was being paid by outsiders to search for something known or suspected to be hidden or lost in the village or the surrounding area. In our view, this possibility best fits the facts, although once again there is no specific proof. Others, too—Jean Markale, for example—have been drawn to this idea. As to *what* the priest might have been looking for, the problem is that there are too many candidates: Markale suggests Saunière was being paid to search for the Hautpoul family archives on behalf of the Habsburgs.[125]

Where the Rennes-le-Château mystery is concerned, conjecture is all too easy—the checkered history of the area and village provides plenty of fruitful ground for speculation. But it must be remembered that skeptics often speculate as much, and sometimes just as wildly, as "believers" in the heady atmosphere generated by both the genuine mystery and the skills of Priory spin doctors.

The fact remains that there are aspects to Saunière's life and activities that should never be lightly dismissed—unanswered questions that skeptics tend to ignore completely. *Something* was going on, into which the Rennes story neatly fits.

The Mysterious Archduke

One undisputed fact immediately and dramatically lifts the Saunière story beyond the mundane affair of a greedy provincial priest: as even Descadeillas acknowledges, Saunière was visited regularly by none other than a Habsburg archduke.[126] But why should a member of one of the oldest and most revered imperial families of Europe flog all the way on terrible roads to the dusty Languedoc to see an obscure parish priest?

The locals frequently spoke about the visits of "*l'étranger*" (the foreigner) or "the Austrian." When word of the visits reached the local subprefecture—who were very wary, as relations with Germany were shaky and spy scares were common—they interviewed the visitor, and their report was sent to the Deuxième Bureau (the French MI5) in Paris.

The visitor turned out to be none other than Archduke Johann Salvator von Habsburg (1852–c. 1890), the youngest of the ten children of Léopold II, Grand Duke of Tuscany, and a cousin of the powerful Austro-Hungarian Emperor, Franz Josef.

Johann Salvator claimed that while traveling to Spain in 1888 he had taken a wrong turning at Couiza, ending up in Saunière's village. This is unlikely, to say the least: even today it would be hard to mistake the turning, and in Saunière's day the road up to Rennes-le-Château was just an anonymous and uninviting track. But whatever the reason for his visit, he clearly liked the place, returning in 1889 and 1890. Interestingly, the Archduke's explanation for his journey was that "no longer believing in the security of his family, he had come to find a refuge in Rennes, and to prepare for his family to go there."[127]

It has been suggested that there was some connection between the Archduke's visits and the gift from the Comtesse de Chambord—herself a Habsburg. Descadeillas speculates, not unreasonably, that as the Comtesse de Chambord might have bequeathed other regular payments to Saunière, the Archduke may have visited to see that he was using the funds properly. Descadeillas also suggests that the Austro-

Hungarians may have assigned the priest the task of building them a refuge near the Franco-Spanish border.[128] Although the hypotheses fit the facts, as usual, direct evidence is conspicuous by its absence—and (again as usual) there are more questions than answers. As we have seen, Markale alternatively suggests the Archduke's visit was connected with Saunière's search for the Hautpoul family archives. However, in both scenarios Johann Salvator is a Habsburg agent.

However, the Archduke's extraordinary life means that his connection with Saunière can point in one of two opposite directions. Very much the maverick of the family, he renounced his titles and privileges, committed the unpardonable sin of marrying a commoner—the ballerina Ludmilla "Milli" Stubel—in 1890, changed his surname to Orth (from his Austrian castle), and attempted to live an incognito, if hardly normal, life as a qualified ship's captain on the high seas. Furious, the supremely authoritarian Emperor Franz Josef not only disowned him but in October 1889 even banned him from setting foot in Austria.

Orth's life ended like something out of a novel when the ship on which he and Milli were sailing to South America disappeared off Cape Horn in July 1890. But inevitably there are theories that he faked his death and lived out the rest of his years in obscurity in Norway. Therefore his three known visits to Rennes-le-Château in the years 1888–1890 could have been as an envoy of the family or, alternatively, part of his preparations for his own disappearance. (In fact, he was already using his alias before the last of these visits.) In other words, he could have been acting equally for or against the Habsburgs.

Whichever scenario is correct, two such unlikely events—a flow of wealth from a mysterious source and the visits of a colorful Archduke, himself no stranger to intrigue—make the skeptics' claims that Saunière was merely involved in dubious financial dealings appear lame in the extreme. But although it is difficult to believe there was no connection between Johann Orth and Saunière's later activities, the Archduke's visits happened before the priest came into any sizable sums of money and before his "discovery of a tomb" and the rest of the complex and fabled story.

Today's Habsburgs have shown an interest in the affair: in 1975 Archduke Rudolf of Austria visited Rennes-le-Château and Carcassonne, where he discussed the story with Mgr. Georges Boyer, the retired Vicar-General, and Abbé Mazières, a local historian. Although when questioned about this by Jean Robin, Rudolf was evasive—even claiming he had been discussing another Archduke entirely—Mgr. Boyer confirmed that Johann Salvator had indeed visited Rennes and stated, puzzlingly, that he wanted to found a retirement home for "elderly artists" there.[129] (Curiously, this echoes Saunière's alleged ambition to build a similar institution for retired priests. Both men must have believed the air at Rennes to be particularly healthy.) In a letter to Robin in February 1976, the current head of the family, Otto von Habsburg, said he knew nothing about Saunière or Rennes-le-Château, merely that he had visited Carcassonne several times and that he frequently passed through the area en route to Spain.[130]

Something was going on—yet the connection between Saunière and the maverick Archduke who became Johann Orth and allegedly disappeared at sea, while established fact, is perhaps weirder than anything even Pierre Plantard could dream up. (And significantly, he made no attempt to exploit this particularly colorful connection.)

There are other signs that Saunière was up to something, including two enigmatic references in letters he and Marie received. The first is in a letter to Saunière from an elderly colleague, Abbé Gazel, priest of Floure (near Carcassonne) written on May 27, 1914. Ostensibly, Gazel—who clearly has not seen Saunière in many years—gives his best wishes for Saunière's saint's day, but after the customary platitudes and inquiries about the younger priest's health, the writer suddenly asks:

> Have you news of St. John? Me, I haven't known anything for some time. After the death of Abbé Bastide, I wanted to take it [or "him"] back from Bonbania, but he refused, telling me that he contents himself with St. John, one of the Consolations that parish gives him.[131]

And shortly after Saunière's death, a friend wrote a similarly enigmatic letter to Marie:

> At this time, my dear friend, since you do not wish to receive at your home, in order to do the job which you know about, Mr. [*sic*] de St. Jean, you may want me to come [instead].[132]

The Gnostic Revival

Saunière is also connected with another important trend of the time, the revival of Gnostic ideas, particularly their Cathar manifestation. This partly came about because of the "rediscovery" of Gnostic thinking through new scholarship and because the burgeoning nationalist movement in the Languedoc sought to maintain its distinct historical heritage and traditions, of which the Cathars were a central part.

There were several more or less authentic attempts at "Cathar Church" revivals, but one of the most important—and earnest—was that of Déodat Roché from nearby Arques. As, according to Antoine Captier in 2001, one of Roché's brothers was Saunière's physician while another acted as his notary, it is very unlikely that Saunière was not aware of the Roché family connection with neo-Catharism.[133]

The area buzzed with pride in ancient beliefs and past glories: another local luminary with a mission was Prosper Estieu (1860–1939), an Occitan nationalist whose political and artistic work invoked the Troubadours and the undying spirit of Cathar Montségur. In the 1890s he founded schools to teach the Occitan language and culture in Carcassonne and Montségur. And from 1896 to 1909—while he was the village schoolteacher—he published the uncompromisingly entitled periodical *Mont-Ségur,* actually from Rennes-le-Château (*Rennes-lo-Castel* in Occitan).[134]

Obviously, in the burgeoning world of mystical and traditional revivals, the Rennes-le-Château area was a force to be reckoned with, and whether or not Saunière was actively involved in these campaigns, he would certainly have been well aware of them. However, there are other, particularly intriguing connections, specifically between the noble families of the region and certain secret societies.

The Masonic Connection

As we have seen, the two key families in the area were those of the last Lady of Rennes, Marie de Nègre d'Ablés, Dame d'Hautpoul et de Blanchefort, and the Fleurys of Rennes-les-Bains. The two dynasties had intermarried several times, the most interesting such union from our perspective being that of Marie's daughter Gabrielle to Paul-François-Vincent, Comte de Fleury. Their son was Paul-Urbain de Fleury of the mysterious gravestones of Rennes-les-Bains.

It must be stressed that these families were not obscure country gentry from a backwater of France but were extremely influential—and not just in their own area. One factor in their eminence was that during the Hautpouls' fiefdom of Rennes-le-Château, the seat of the bishopric was at Alet (now Alet-les-Bains), a small town less than five miles up the main road.[135] So Abbé Bigou and the Hautpouls were virtually on the doorstep of the Bishop, no small consideration given their extraordinary effect on nineteenth-century Catholicism in France.

A measure of the status—and connections—of the de Fleury family in Saunière's day is that Hubert Rohault de Fleury was the key figure in the revival of the Catholic cult of the Sacred Heart (Sacré-Coeur). Based on the visions of a seventeenth-century nun from Paray-le-Monial, Marguerite-Marie Alacoque (later canonized), it was revived by Rohault de Fleury in the 1870s as the focal point of Catholic monarchism, particularly the legitimist cause—in other words, it was a religious cult with a definite political dimension. When Rohault de Fleury's brainchild, the "flagship" Sacré-Coeur basilica in Paris's Montmartre, was built, the largest contributor of funds was the Comte de Chambord. (Clearly infected with enthusiasm for the cult's message, Saunière also placed a statue of Jesus displaying the Sacred Heart on the front wall of his Villa Béthanie.)

In this way, the Rennes-le-Château/Rennes-les-Bains area was linked through its noble families to major political-religious movements in France and to the Chambord—and therefore Habsburg—cause. This begins to put quite a different complexion on the story of the humble country priest who supposedly stumbled onto something in an obscure village, especially when his dealings with a Habsburg archduke are also taken into account. However, there are other mysteries connected with these families—indications that they were involved in some highly secret activities—which are just as tantalizing as the more obvious links with either the Saunière affair or the later Priory of Sion enigma.

For example, take the will of François-Pierre, Baron d'Hautpoul of Rennes, which was registered on November 23, 1644, by the notary of Espéraza—a little under two miles from Rennes-le-Château—Michel

Captier. Although the existence of this will is well documented, there is something very odd about it. It was discovered in 1780 by one of Captier's successors as Espéraza's notary, Jean-Baptiste Siau, but when the Hautpoul family asked for it, he refused to part with it on the grounds that "it would not be prudent on my part to give up a will of [such] great consequence."[136] Unfortunately, what was so significant about this will—and what happened to it—is unknown. It was last heard of in April 1781 (the Revolution being the most obvious explanation for its disappearance).

After Marie de Nègre died, a row erupted among her three daughters over the inheritance of the family titles and the land that went them. The eldest, Elisabeth—who never married and lived the rest of her life in Rennes-les-Bains—refused to allow her sisters access to the family documents relating to the titles on the grounds that to do so would be "dangerous" and it would be best first "to decipher them [the documents] and distinguish which is a title of the family and what is not."[137] This implies that the Hautpoul archives contained documents that were not only in some way difficult to read—presumably either in an ancient and/or foreign language or perhaps in code—but also, as Jean Markale points out, not necessarily even the property of the family.[138]

Frustratingly, nobody knows the full nature of the Hautpoul archives, but it seems too coincidental that the noble family of the village that would be the focus of the Saunière mystery should have possessed such apparently dark secrets. This realization led Markale to conclude that the priest was being paid to try to locate the Hautpoul archives, which—like many other aristocratic papers—would have been hidden at the time of the Revolution and ensuing Terror.

However, another clue may be found in the involvement of these families in certain very significant forms of Freemasonry. In the 1830s three men from the Hautpoul family—Eugène, Charles, and Théobald—were members of the highly controversial La Sagesse Masonic lodge of Toulouse, the only one of the city's eight lodges affiliated to the Grand Orient that supported the claim of Comte de Chambord to the throne of France.[139] (As we have noted, Armand d'Hautpoul-Félines was Chambord's tutor.)

The La Sagesse lodge was the direct antecedent of another important esoteric society, one of several Rosicrucian revivals of the nineteenth century, the Order of the Rose-Cross of the Temple and Grail

(Ordre de la Rose-Croix du Temple et du Graal), founded in Toulouse around 1850 by the scholar and alchemist Vicomte Louis Charles Édouard de Lapasse (1792–1867).[140]

A later Grand Master of the Rose-Cross of the Temple and Grail was Joséphin Péladan (1859–1918), whose secretary, we recall, was Georges Monti, Plantard's mentor. In 1888 Péladan also founded another Rosicrucian society, the Cabalistic Order of the Rose-Cross (Ordre Kabbalistique de la Rose-Croix), with the Alsatian Stanislas de Guaïta (1861–1898), who was idolized by Maurice Barrès, so much so that he devoted a book to de Guaita's memory after his early death. Papus (Gérard Encausse), a spiritual mentor of Emma Calvé, was also a member.

The Web Tightens

The Hautpouls were also connected with the creation of the Rectified Scottish Rite, which was founded at an important Masonic gathering—the Convent of the Gauls—in Lyons in 1778. One of the Convent's prime movers was Alexandre Lenoir, the brother-in-law of Jean-Marie-Alexandre d'Hautpoul (whose granddaughter Claire also married into the Fleury family).[141]

Originally a highly secretive Masonic system (although becoming a little less so with the passage of time) and more commonly known today as the Rectified Scottish Regime, the Rite implanted itself particularly strongly in Switzerland.[142] (It is not to be confused with the other "Scottish" system, the Ancient and Accepted Scottish Rite, which is especially popular in the United States. Besides the title, the two have little in common.)

The Rectified Scottish Rite possesses six grades, organized into two open classes and one secret, interior order. The highest of the secret grades is Knight Beneficent of the Holy City (Chevalier Bienfaisant de la Cité Sainte, or CBCS)[143]—a euphemism for Templar, while the Holy City is Jerusalem or Zion/Sion. Those who attain this grade become "knights" and take Latin noms de guerre.

However, at least in the eighteenth and nineteenth centuries, there was an even higher, yet more exclusive and secret class, called the Profession (*Profès*), comprised solely of those of the rank of Knight Beneficent. Even that was further divided into the *Profès* and the *Grand Profès.*

The purpose of the Profession was to study and meditate on "the doctrine set out in the texts (secret instructions)."[144] Michel Gaudart de Soulages and Hubert Lamant write in their *Dictionary of French Freemasons* (1995): "This class has, apparently, disappeared, or, if it still exists, carries on . . . a very discreet existence."[145]

According to Gérard de Sède, Paul-Urbain de Fleury not only was a member of a Grand Orient lodge in Limoux but also held the rank of Knight Beneficent—having attained the top rank of the Rectified Scottish Rite.[146] Jean-Luc Chaumeil has related both the inscription on de Fleury's tomb—"*Il est passé en faisant le bien*," meaning broadly "He spent his time doing good," a clear reference to "Bienfaisant"—and the oddity about the dates, to the symbolism of the Beneficent Knight of the Holy City.[147]

Of course that these aristocrats should be Freemasons is not particularly remarkable—what is surprising is their connection with the Rectified Scottish Rite, which though important, is relatively small compared with the more mainstream forms of Freemasonry. But what it lacks in size, the Rectified Scottish Rite clearly makes up for in power.

Dame Marie de Nègre d'Ablès's family was also connected with forms of Freemasonry that operated outside the mainstream. In 1815 one of her relatives, Gabriel Mathieu Marconis de Nègre, founded in Montauban the mother lodge of a new rite, the Disciples of Memphis, part of the "Egyptian Rites" of Freemasonry—those that advocate and explore the possible ancient Egyptian origin of Freemasonry. The Montauban lodge was established by former members of the French Mission in Egypt, who had—apparently—been initiated into some form of Masonic or quasi-Masonic society in Cairo.[148] The Rite of Memphis, as it became known, is more usually associated with Gabriel's son, Jacques-Étienne Marconis de Nègre (1795–1868), who expanded the Order.

Although Marconis de Nègre's Rite of Memphis seems quite different from the Rectified Scottish Rite with which the Hautpouls were associated, the difference is only superficial: we discovered that in fact they share a common origin and are essentially two faces of the same movement (which we explain more fully in Chapter 6). And there are specific connections between key individuals in both systems—a trail that leads to Bérenger Saunière's brother, Alfred.

Jacques-Étienne Marconis de Nègre affiliated his Rite of Memphis with another society, the Philadelphes,[149] which had been established in

Narbonne by François, the Marquis de Chefdebien d'Armissan (1754–1814), a cavalry colonel, Knight of Malta, and very high-ranking and influential Mason. Before this, he too had been instrumental in creating the Rectified Scottish Rite, of which he reached the grade of Knight Beneficent, taking the name Franciscus, Eques a Capite Galeato.[150] For this reason there was a close relationship between the Rectified Scottish Rite and the Philadelphes.

The Marquis de Chefdebien d'Armissan's new secret society, the Philadelphes (also known as the Original Rite, or *Rite Primitif*), was devoted to the acquisition and study of esoteric knowledge, particularly the secrets of other Masonic systems. Intriguingly, Jean-Pierre Monteils described the Philadelphes as "one of the most mysterious secret societies of the time,"[151] while Marconis de Nègre wrote of its Rose-Cross grade: "The first chapter of the Rose-Croix possesses knowledge that, in some regimes, establishes the Masonic cult; the second chapter of the Rose-Croix is the depository of very curious historical documents; the third chapter deals with all Masonic knowledge, physical and philosophical; the fourth chapter deals with all parts of science that they call occult or secret."[152] This becomes all the more significant in the light of Alfred Saunière's career.

During the 1890s, besides teaching at the seminary in Narbonne, Alfred became tutor to the children of the then Marquis de Chefdebien d'Armissan (who, probably not coincidentally, had been an intimate of the Comte de Chambord).[153] But Alfred was to leave under a cloud, sacked for some misdemeanor. According to a descendant of the Chefdebiens, Aynard de Bissy, he was dismissed for stealing documents from the family's archives—which, given the connection between the Chefdebiens and the Philadelphes and the purpose of the Philadelphes, is more than a little interesting.[154] Was Alfred intent on extricating Masonic deep doctrine when he ransacked his employer's files? If so, was it for his own elucidation, or would the papers be pored over by cabals of shadowy brothers?

To sum up this tantalizingly incestuous Masonic situation: in the late eighteenth and early nineteenth centuries, three closely related secret societies—the Rectified Scottish Rite, the Philadelphes, and the Rite of Memphis—were all intimately involved with the three major families in the Rennes story—Hautpoul, Fleury, and Nègre—along with the Chefdebiens of Narbonne. And of the priestly Saunière brothers, one became curé of the last possession of the Hautpoul-Nègres and the other worked for the Chefdebiens. All this strains coincidence beyond the breaking point.

Even so, the plot thickens. It was due to Alfred that Rennes-le-Château's priest encountered the Marquise du Bourg de Bozas, who, according to Emma Calvé's biographer Jean Contrucci, was "linked to Papus and the Martinist Order."[155] And, as we will see, the Martinists had some quite extraordinary beliefs.

The famed but enigmatic Papus (Gérard Encausse) ran his Martinist Order from the Bookshop of the Wonderful when occultism was at its most fashionable among bohemians and thrill seekers. He had founded this secret society in the 1880s to perpetuate the mystical philosophy of Louis-Claude de Saint-Martin (1743–1803), with a secret inner order, reserved for the highest initiates—the rather ominously named Silencieux Inconnus (Unknown Silents, or S.I.).[156]

However, there was, and is, a particular connection between Martinism and the Rectified Scottish Rite: Saint-Martin himself was elevated to Knight Beneficent in October 1785 (as Eques a Leone Sidero) and then into the more highly secret rank of Profession.[157]

Some remarkable individuals belonged to Papus's circle, but that the Marquise du Bourg de Bozas should be connected to his Order is hardly surprising, as she came from a family steeped in esotericism. She was descended from a president of the Toulouse Parliament (before the Revolution the region was semiautonomous) whose family were great patrons of the occult: Saint-Martin himself stayed with them in Toulouse in 1776 and 1777, and also with their son, Mathias du Bourg, in the Haute-Garonne. (The du Bourgs were also related to the de Joyeuse family, lords of Rennes-le-Château's neighboring village of Couiza.)[158]

These connections were clearly extremely significant, even apparently being reflected in Saunière's weird decoration of St. Mary Magdalene's church, which as many researchers—including ourselves—claim is Masonic. However, while some dismiss such a connection completely, others such as Jean Markale, accept its presence but deny Saunière was behind it (on the rather naïve grounds that the Church forbids priests to be Masons). Markale suggests that the stonemason who supplied the statues and Stations of the Cross, Giscard of Toulouse—unsurprisingly, a Freemason—was responsible for the symbolism.[159]

Whoever was behind it, much of the symbolism is common to all forms of Freemasonry, but several researchers have independently discerned images that are specific to the grade of Knight Beneficent of the Holy City, the highest grade of the Rectified Scottish Rite.[160]

This is rather unexpected: whatever trail we follow relating to Rennes-le-Château and the two brothers Saunière, we end up with the two related societies, Rectified Scottish Rite Freemasonry and the Martinist Order—*precisely the same societies that we connected with the Alpha Galates Order.* (Robert Amadou was a member not merely of both but also of their secret inner orders, entering the Martinist Order's S.I. in September 1942—at the time of his involvement with Alpha Galates—and in May 1966 attaining the Rectified Scottish Rite's Knight Beneficent grade and taking the name Eques ab Aegypto.)

Is it just a coincidence that the two secret societies that were so prevalent around Rennes-le-Château should surface again in connection with Alpha Galates, the forerunner of the Priory of Sion?

Plantard's Plan Unfolds

Pierre Plantard spent a great deal of time in the Rennes area from around 1959, sometimes alone and sometimes with Philippe de Chérisey, exploring the countryside and becoming acquainted with noteworthy locals such as Noël Corbu and Abbé Joseph Courtaly, who had known Saunière. (Courtaly's name was later used to add spurious credibility to the Dossiers Secrets.)

However, by all accounts Plantard was as interested in Rennes-les-Bains as he was in Rennes-le-Château, and in Abbé Boudet as much as Abbé Saunière—which is particularly intriguing, as at that time only Rennes-le-Château and the straightforward mystery of Saunière's wealth had received any widespread publicity. It was not until the 1970s and '80s that parallel enigmas, such as those connected with Boudet and Gélis, came to light. It was Plantard himself who was largely responsible for adding Boudet and his enigmatic, not to say apparently insane, *True Celtic Language* to the Rennes-le-Château jigsaw, by overseeing the publication of a facsimile edition in 1978. In this at least, Plantard seems to have been ahead of the game.

Although his detractors assume he was familiarizing himself with the story to use as background for his grand hoax, Plantard appears to have been genuinely interested in it, uncovering leads—such as the Boudet connection—which had eluded other researchers. It was also at least five years before he attempted to do anything with this mystery. Gisors absorbed all his energy at that time.

Later, in 1967 and 1972, Plantard bought several plots of land on the plateau close to the Château Blanchefort and the strange outcrop known as the Rocque Nègre[161]—surely an odd move if he had merely created a hoax with nothing substantial behind it. Obviously he *cared* about the area, even at a personal level.

And what can we make of the fact that independent investigation of the Rennes-le-Château affair consistently brings us back to the same secret orders that we already discerned hovering in the background of the Alpha Galates Order, the wartime precursor of the Priory of Sion? Was this just a remarkable coincidence, or was it an indication that there is a genuine connection between the Priory and the Saunière affair that predated Plantard's arrival on the scene?

But before scrutinizing those intimately involved secret groups, let us turn our attention to how Plantard and the Priory of Sion unashamedly pressed the Rennes-le-Château mystery into the service of their own agenda.

CHAPTER FOUR

"HIDDEN GOLD, HIDDEN BLOOD"

The Rennes-le-Château mystery was hijacked as the convenient vehicle for a major development in the presentation of the Priory of Sion, mainly through the now-famous Dossiers Secrets, the series of documents deposited in Paris's Bibliothèque Nationale between 1964 and 1967, which gradually built up a potent mythology—the origins, history, and purpose of the Priory.[1] However, other events played out in the public domain would also assume their part in creating what was to become the most widely known aspect of the Priory's alleged raison d'être.

The Dossiers Secrets were no mean achievement: first they harnessed the Rennes-le-Château mystery and introduced and developed the idea of the survival of the Merovingian bloodline—according to them, the secret discovered by Saunière. Then the Priory of Sion was introduced, allegedly its avowed purpose to protect and to promote the interests of that bloodline. The Dossiers also emphasize the significance of the Plantard family as the direct descendants of the last Merovingian kings, laying a trail that eventually arrives at Pierre Plantard's father and the registration of the Priory of Sion in 1956, before inevitably ending with Pierre Plantard, the Merovingian heir—and therefore pretender to the throne of France.

However, nowhere in the Dossiers Secrets is it made explicit that the Priory of Sion exists to protect the Merovingian survivors, and even this is implicit only because both subjects are cleverly juxtaposed. The sole specific link is that the Priory claims (or claimed then) that it was founded by Godefroy de Bouillon, who was supposedly of Merovingian descent.

The information is fed piece by piece, enticing readers to make their own connections between references in different documents—allowing them to experience carefully stage-managed "eureka!" moments as the wider picture is unveiled. But logically the trail can lead only in the way they want us to go.

Most people with an interest in this subject accept that the Dossiers Secrets were largely the creation of Pierre Plantard, with assistance from Philippe de Chérisey. However, Plantard always denied any connection with them: when he resigned as Grand Master of the Priory of Sion in July 1984, his resignation letter cited as one of his reasons for stepping down "all the publications, press articles, books, and multigraphed documents deposited in the Bibliothèque Nationale that implicate me, reproduce the Priory of Sion's texts, and use my name fraudulently."[2]

In 1985, after Pierre Jarnac repeated the assumption of Plantard's authorship in his *Histoire du trésor de Rennes-le-Château* (*History of the Treasure of Rennes-le-Château*), he received this sharp rebuke:

> . . . why should you associate me so absolutely with the works of Mr. [*sic*] Philippe de Chérisey? Why try, in this way, to attribute a dozen eccentric works or publications to me? What would you say if I, in my turn, claimed that you were, quite simply, the author of this crazy collection![3]

So Plantard blamed it all on de Chérisey, who had conveniently died a few months earlier. But although Plantard seems to protest too much—few, including ourselves, take his characteristically self-righteous disavowals seriously—in fact there is no direct evidence to connect him with the Dossiers. At the very least he scrupulously maintained a distance that allowed him plausible deniability should he ever need it (and he did exploit it). But, more significantly, the evidence indicates that there was at least a third guiding hand behind the Dossiers Secrets.

Virtually everyone who knew and worked with Plantard agreed that he had neither the intelligence nor the mental focus to devise such an intricate story and sustain it over a long period—as we observed with his appendix to Gérard de Sède's *The Templars Are Among Us*. Perhaps he had the basic ideas, but the research, narrative skill, and intellectual stamina needed to build this story up over the course of several years were beyond him. Most researchers assume that the brainpower and skill belonged to de Chérisey—in any case by far the sharper, and much more passionate about intricate mind games, the Dossiers Secrets' defining characteristic.

Some later "Priory" documents can definitely be attributed to de Chérisey—some even bear his name—but how much he actually contributed to the core Dossiers Secrets is uncertain. De Chérisey himself seems to have treated the whole thing as a kind of surrealist prank: as Gérard de Sède writes in his 1988 book, his contributions were concocted "with a certain courage, much humor, and . . . reveal a fertile poetic-Romanesque imagination more than a vulgar imposture."[4] But there are also signs of at least one other hand in the creation of the Dossiers.

After savagely denouncing Plantard as a fantasist and fraud—besides dismissing the whole Merovingian survival fable as pure invention—de Sède acknowledged that many of the Dossiers Secrets either were not in Plantard's style or were, frankly, too clever for him. Calling the Dossiers Secrets the "apocrypha of Rennes-le-Château," he writes:

> The problem—as there is one—is that in order to forge this delirious myth, its authors must have had access to learned sources that necessitated long and difficult research. . . . We therefore have an affair of people possessing a solid university training and rather extensive knowledge, which immediately excludes certain authors of rickety language and uncertain spelling who are in the foreground. Consequently, there is a certain mystery in the extravagance of the apocrypha of Rennes-le-Château.[5]

"Certain authors" and their "rickety language and uncertain spelling" are clearly references to Plantard, whose written style was infamously somewhat idiosyncratic. As do we, de Sède concludes that Plantard was merely the front man—somebody else was masterminding the Dossiers Secrets. (De Sède came to the same conclusion about Plantard's *Vaincre*/Alpha Galates period, writing of "others, preferring the shadows, pulling the strings.")[6] This was also the view of the writer who, to a large extent, succeeded de Sède, Jean-Luc Chaumeil. In the 1970s, Chaumeil produced articles and a book based on material provided by Plantard and de Chérisey that were largely supportive of their claims, although his subsequent rejection of Plantard as a hoaxer erupted into an acrimonious public row. But despite that, even as recently as 2001, Chaumeil said: "I think that Plantard was manipulated. . . . Like all those who are manipulated, he was also flattered by this story . . ."[7]

Discussing some of the Dossiers' key documents by the pseudonymous Henri Lobineau, the Carcassonne historian René Descadeillas—so deeply affronted by the distortions to his beloved region's history that he dedicated himself to redressing the balance, and certainly no Plantard fan—observed about their language: "What strikes the reader of this text is the heaviness of the phrasing. Probably it is the work of an individual who practices both French and German. . . . For us, the Swiss origin of this bizarre document is not in doubt."[8]

Plantard was a Parisian born and bred; de Chérisey was Belgian. Everyone assumes that one or both were solely responsible for composing the Lobineau documents—yet it appears that a shadowy Swiss, who remains unidentified, was involved. There are several references to Switzerland in the Dossiers, and copies of some of the documents were posted to researchers from Geneva—a city repeatedly linked to Plantard since immediately after the war. There is also evidence—see later—of at least two more confederates, apparently British, who took a significant role in events.

Summing up the central paradox of the Dossiers Secrets, de Sède writes that they are "both crude and scholarly," concluding, "One does not give oneself so much trouble for the sole pleasure of mounting a gigantic hoax."[9] Indeed. For those reasons we believe that the Dossiers Secrets were not a hoax pure and simple. The fact that there are other individuals in the shadows reinforces not only our suspicion that Plantard was merely a front man but also our conclusion that the Dossiers Secrets were designed from the start as *misinformation.*

A Mission to Lie

Although the Americans call it *dis*information—the best version has got to be the delirious French *intoxication* or *intox*—misinformation is deliberately disseminated false information (i.e., lies), either to make the target audience believe something that is untrue or to divert attention away from something that *is* true—or, often, both. The classic example is the deceptions practiced by both sides, but most successfully by the Allies, during the Second World War: for example, the buildup of forces for the Operation Torch landings in North Africa, which were protected by leaking information to the Nazis that the real target was Norway.

However, the most effective misinformation is far more than just a convincing lie. Inevitably, some *true* information—elements that can be verified in order to make the story as a whole seem credible—has to be included. When the exercise is intended to conceal genuine facts, then the game becomes even more complex and multileveled. For example, if data in the public domain could lead to dangerous or classified information, false trails are laid to divert attention somewhere else entirely. (In Operation Torch, as the forces and their activity could hardly be hidden from the Germans, the Nazis had to be prevented from discovering *why* they were being amassed by creating misinformation pointing toward an invasion of Norway.) Often the misinformation involves several trails, so that if enemies see through one, another takes its place, until in the end they become so confused that even if they do stumble on the secret, they have no idea what to believe. The most subtle version is when the *true* secret is disguised as misinformation. There have been instances where the enemy has actually possessed genuine information but dismissed it, perhaps the most far-reaching example being Stalin's refusal to believe that Hitler planned to attack the Soviet Union in June 1941, despite the mountain of evidence.

We believe the Dossiers Secrets were intended as just this kind of misinformation, designed as diversions from genuine secrets while eventually performing the ultimate trick of discrediting *themselves* so that more conventional investigators would naturally dismiss the whole thing as fit only for crackpots and cranks. It works on two levels: either researchers give up completely, or if they persist they find themselves chasing Merovingians—ending up labeled cranks or fools themselves. This scenario accounts for the paradox of the great skill and effort behind the Merovingian fable, as opposed to the transparent nonsense of the eventual payoff. It's a merry dance.

But if the Dossiers Secrets were an exercise in misinformation, who were they aimed at? Not the general public: as the six documents were deposited singly in the Bibliothèque Nationale, although technically in the public domain they were still not exactly public. The exercise was to culminate in a successful book—Gérard de Sède's *The Gold of Rennes*—but it was almost entirely about Rennes-le-Château, devoting just three pages to the Merovingian survival story and making no mention at all of the Priory of Sion. Rather than the Dossiers Secrets being designed to lead to de Sède's book (as we originally suspected), it seems that de Sède's book was intended to lead *certain* readers to the Dossiers Secrets.

It was only six years after the publication of *The Gold of Rennes,* and nearly a decade after the first Dossiers, that a magazine picked up on the files, thrusting the Priory of Sion and its Merovingian pretensions into the spotlight. If the object of the exercise had really been to orchestrate publicity for the Priory and Plantard's spurious claim to the French throne, surely they could have moved more quickly, especially given the success of de Sède's book. There is only one logical conclusion: the Dossiers Secrets were aimed at individuals or groups *within French esoteric secret societies.*

The sage Jean Markale muses:

> While "one train can definitely hide another" in the Rennes-le-Château affair, we no longer know who is hiding whom or who is manipulating whom. Manipulation necessarily took place, even if we do not believe in the existence of certain "philosophical brotherhoods." These names have had the good sense to remain in the shadows, assume borrowed names, or even infiltrate existing groups that are perfectly orthodox. This is why the Priory of Sion appears to be a red herring. It is intended to hide something, to divert attention, which is very clear with respect to the Saunière affair.[10]

As we were dissatisfied with the knee-jerk dismissal of the Dossiers Secrets as a straightforward hoax and sought a scenario that resolved their essential paradoxes, we were particularly intrigued when in 2003 the current Priory spokesman, Secretary-General Gino Sandri, said that the famous copies of the parchments allegedly found by Bérenger Saunière were created as a means of "diverting attention in order to protect other documents." He added that it was "a real campaign aimed at an individual or a society active in the field of the occult."[11] (Of course, given the Priory's celebrated slipperiness, it would be foolish to take this as absolute confirmation of our theory—but it is interesting nevertheless.)

A cover story used a decade before with quite a different purpose has been resurrected—but like all misinformation, it also contains nuggets of hard fact.

The Murky Merovingians

The first of the Dossiers Secrets was a booklet entitled *Genealogy of the Merovingian Kings and Origins of Various French and Foreign Families of Merovingian Stock* (*Généalogie des rois mérovingiens et origine de diverses familles françaises et étrangères de souche mérovingienne*).[12] Although it was placed in the Bibliothèque Nationale in January 1964, its imprint reads, "Geneva, 1956." Baigent, Leigh, and Lincoln as well as others have taken this date at face value, concluding that this document—based on the parchments allegedly discovered by Bérenger Saunière—predates Pierre Plantard's visits to Rennes-le-Château. But there is no evidence that this document existed before 1964.

The supposed author is a genealogist named Henri Lobineau, although obviously this is a pseudonym. Certainly Plantard was familiar with the work of the eighteenth-century historian Gui-Alexis Lobineau; Paris's Rue Lobineau—named after him—which runs past the important church of St.-Sulpice (later with its own starring role in the story) is another possible inspiration. Bearing in mind Descadeillas's observation that the author of this document was Swiss, it is worth noting that the Dossiers Secrets say Henri Lobineau lived in Geneva—but although the Place du Mollard was real, the house number turned out to be nonexistent.

The full title of the document is self-explanatory: *Genealogy of the Merovingian Kings and Origins of Various French and Foreign Families of Merovingian Stock, After Abbé Pichon, Dr. Hervé, and the Parchments of Abbé Saunière, Curé of Rennes-le-Château.* In other words, Lobineau has ostensibly drawn together these three sources (augmented by others cited in the work) to produce a definitive "family tree" of the Merovingian descendants. In fact, Lobineau even claims to have culled his facts from another—real—individual who was to have a central role in the unfolding drama: "The genealogical tables of Abbé Pichon and Dr.

Hervé, supplemented by Abbé Saunière . . . were kindly communicated to us at our request by Monsieur Abbé Hoffet, 7 Rue Blanche in Paris (9th), in 1942." As we will see, Hoffet surfaces repeatedly in this story.

Pichon and Hervé were genuine historians and genealogists, although as far as can be ascertained they wrote nothing on the Merovingians. (The Dossiers allege that Abbé Pichon produced his genealogy in 1809 on the orders of Napoleon.) But of course the most intriguing part is the reference to the "parchments of Abbé Saunière."

There is no doubt that Saunière *did* find parchments hidden in the altar pillar in 1887—but this is the first suggestion that they were in any way historically significant and that there was an implicit connection between this discovery and his subsequent wealth. Sensationally, Lobineau alleges that the parchments contained genealogies tracing the descent of the Merovingians *after* their supposed extinction in the eighth century.

The booklet consists of a series of genealogical tables showing the Merovingian descent and highlighting the emergence from it of several important families, such as the Ducs de Lorraine and Comtes de Bar. The meticulously compiled tables are mostly correct, but only the parts that link these families with the Merovingians are relevant—unfortunately, they are also consistently the most dubious. Adding to the problem, Lobineau's notes and glosses amplifying or explaining certain points are often extremely gnomic, although when they are put together with information from later documents certain mouthwatering connections begin to emerge.

One of the most important tables is number 5, showing the descent of the Merovingians from their semilegendary founder, Merovée, customarily known in English as Merovech (proclaimed King of the Franks in 448; the dynasty was named after him) to Dagobert I (602–638). At the height of the Merovingians' power, around 560, while they possessed the whole of France except for Septimania (which included Rennes-le-Château, then in the hands of the Visigoths) and Brittany, technically Dagobert I was not, as Lobineau has it, "King of France," but merely King of the Franks.

This table is also headed with the bold non sequitur "One day the descendants of Benjamin left their lands, some remaining. Two thousand years later Godefroy IV became King of Jerusalem and founded the Order of Sion." The following scenario, explaining the connection between these two apparently wildly disparate statements, emerges from Lobineau's notes:

The Franks over which the Merovingians ruled originated as a Germanic tribe known as the Sicambrians (which is correct); but according to Lobineau, the Sicambrians themselves came from one of the tribes of Israel, the Benjamites, who left Palestine and migrated first to Arcadia in Greece, then via Italy over the Alps to the lands along the Rhine. Although this is more questionable, Baigent, Leigh, and Lincoln show such a migration route was not impossible.[13] But this suggests only that it *could* be true, not that it *is*—and the fact is that the Dossiers Secrets are the sole evidence.

However, although Lobineau claims the Merovingians were ultimately of *ethnically* Israelite origin—but not also followers of Judaism—he says that up to Clovis they were "pagan kings of the cult of Diana." (Clovis, who reigned from 481 to 511, converted to Christianity in 496, but a later document in the collection states he did so only "out of necessity."[14]) In fact, Israelites worshiping pagan deities is not as odd as it might sound: in the period of the alleged migration, with Judaism as we know it still a future development, the Israelites did indeed worship several other gods and goddesses. From the Old Testament it even appears that the Benjamites were the most "pagan" of all the Tribes—actually a source of friction with the others—worshiping a goddess who could easily have been assimilated to Diana in later times. Although not proving Lobineau correct, this does show that some serious thought went into the documents. It also helps explain how the apparently anti-Semitic Plantard could have felt comfortable with a scenario that emphasized a Jewish—or at least Israelite—origin for the Merovingians.

But what possible connection could there be with the second part of Lobineau's statement, about Godefroy IV becoming King of Jerusalem two thousand years later? The "illustrious" Godefroy IV is the Duc de Bouillon—a land in Lorraine—and also Duke of Lower Lorraine, who was one of the leaders of the First Crusade and was allegedly offered—but declined—the crown of Jerusalem after the holy city was captured in 1099. (When he died a year later, his brother Baudouin accepted the title.) The historian John C. Andressohn writes in his *The Ancestry and Life of Godfrey of Bouillon* (1947): "Fortune smiled upon Godfrey of Bouillon: a second son, he inherited, by a chance that is rare in history, a duchy from his uncle; by chance he became the ruler of Jerusalem."[15]

As Lobineau points out, in ancient times Jerusalem stood on the Tribe of Benjamin's land—indeed, it produced the first King of Israel, Saul. And to an extent Godefroy de Bouillon was only taking what was rightfully his—as Lobineau's genealogies show that Godefroy was of Merovingian descent.

This is where the mythmaking truly begins. Lobineau's central claim—and that of the whole Dossiers Secrets—is that the Merovingian line did not die out, as history records, but survived in secret. According to conventional history, the Merovingians were replaced by the Carolingians—originally their own senior officials, the Mayors of the Palace (*maior domus*). The changeover took place in 751, when—with the sanction of the Church—Pépin (Pippin) the Short, Mayor of the Palace to the last of the dynasty, was proclaimed king. A new royal house was born.

The Dossiers Secrets' version of a secret survival begins with a Merovingian ruler of *one* of the three Frankish kingdoms, Dagobert II (known as Dagobert the Young), who, just three years after winning his throne from a rival, died mysteriously while hunting on December 23, 679—probably assassinated on the orders of his Mayor of the Palace, Pépin the Fat. It would not have been surprising, for Dagobert was profoundly unpopular, as the chronicler Stephanus notes: "[He was] destroyer of cities, despising the counsels of the magnates, reducing the people with taxation, like Rehoboam, son of Solomon, being contemptuous of God's churches and their bishop"[16]

Dagobert II's single son and heir, the three-year-old[17] Sigebert, disappears from history at the time of his father's death, presumably also murdered, although some argue that Pépin locked him away in a monastery for the rest of his life.[18] But according to Lobineau, Sigebert not only survived but escaped Pépin's clutches, being carried off by his mother's family to the relative safety of Rennes-le-Château, or Rhedae, as the Dossiers call it unequivocally. (As this allegedly happened in 681, presumably he was hidden somewhere else for two years.) The place was chosen because it was the homeland of his mother, Dagobert II's second wife, Gisèle (or Gislis), daughter of Béra II, the Comte du Razès. Sigebert (referred to as Sigebert IV, as if he had officially acceded to the throne) eventually succeeded his grandfather as Comte du Razès. His descendants therefore represent the secret continuation of the Merovingian line of descent—the now-fabled bloodline of Dagobert II.

This Sigebert—on whom the whole Merovingian story hangs—was given the title *rejeton ardent* (ardent offspring), a note explaining that he represented a "new stock issuing from the Merovingian Kings, the Plant-Ards or Rejeton-Ardent."

Lobineau also claims that Dagobert II had already transferred a large part of his treasure to Rhedae to finance his campaign to conquer the Aquitaine area of central and southern France. Therefore the "secret" of Rennes-le-Château comprises both the secret of the Merovingian survival *and* the location of a treasure—keeping everyone happy!

Seven generations after Sigebert IV, in the late ninth century, Sigebert VI (nicknamed Prince Ursus) is said to have lost the title of Comte du Razès after an attempt to oust Louis II. By the thirteenth century the family had been reduced to "simple peasants"—but the main line of descent bore the magic name Plant-Ard.

According to Lobineau, Godefroy de Bouillon "was the issue of the cadet branch of Sigebert IV," so through Godefroy the Merovingians not only briefly recaptured some of their former status but even surpassed it by becoming rulers of the ultimate kingdom—Jerusalem. (Their moment of glory was brief, as Jerusalem was recaptured by the Moslem Saracens in 1187, although the title continued to be used by their descendants in Europe. As it happens, it eventually passed to Archduke Johann Salvator's branch of the Habsburg family. The title now technically belongs to Otto von Habsburg, but it is of course meaningless.) Other tables in this collection link the bloodline with the families of Saint-Clair and Gisors, among others, taking it up to the last years of the sixteenth century.

So this was allegedly the secret discovered by Abbé Saunière that made him so rich: the parchments—which bore the seal of Blanche of Castile—found in the Visigoth pillar contained information on the Merovingian survival. (An interesting touch, as Noël Corbu had already popularized the idea of Saunière finding Blanche of Castile's treasure—one of the few suggested treasures with *no* historical support whatsoever—and clearly the authors of the Dossiers Secrets felt uneasy with the idea of abandoning this strand entirely.) Saunière took the parchments to Paris to consult Abbé Hoffet, who, although still a teenager, was already noted as a gifted linguist and paleographer. Also referring to Pichon and Hervé's earlier works, Hoffet was able to draw up the

Merovingian line of descent to the present day. He had passed this information on to the pseudonymous Lobineau.

But what of Dagobert's treasure? Lobineau implies it was the source of Saunière's wealth—but it was also his downfall, as the treasure is cursed: only the rightful descendant of Prince Ursus can touch it without coming to grief. Lobineau writes, "This is the legend from which the gospel, in the parchments, finds itself cursing the miscreant who dares steal a fragment of this treasure." Lobineau also implies that the curse was responsible for Saunière's decline, his Bishop's hostility, and ultimately, the priest's death.

The essentials of the Merovingian survival myth and its connection to the Rennes-le-Château mystery are all in this first document, although there are only isolated references to the Priory of Sion, which has yet to be elaborated. However, there are mentions of the Abbey of Notre-Dame de Mont Sion in Jerusalem—which appeared in Plantard's Appendix to *The Templars Are Among Us* nearly three years before—and its foundation by Godefroy de Bouillon (which is historically correct). But in the next document the Priory of Sion is given a much more prominent and active role.

It was a year and a half—August 1965—before the second installment—*The Merovingian Descendants, or the Enigma of the Visigoth Razès* (*Les descendants mérovingiens ou l'énigme du Razès wisigoth*) by Madeleine Blancasall, which added extra detail about Saunière and the parchments[19]—was lodged in the Bibliothèque Nationale. This and the Henri Lobineau work are self-referencing, each ostensibly backing up the other: Blancasall frequently refers to and quotes from Lobineau as an authority.

The pseudonym Madeleine Blancasall clearly derives from the Rennes-le-Château church and the two rivers overlooked by Blanchefort, the Blanques and Sals. The work is also supposed to have been translated from the German by one Walter Celse-Nazaire—presumably named after the church of St. Nazaire and St. Celse in Rennes-les-Bains. The introduction states that it is intended exclusively for the "Association Suisse Alpina"—apparently a reference to the governing body of Swiss Freemasonry, the Grand Lodge Alpina. (Another Swiss connection: as we have seen, René Descadeillas noted that the author of at least some of the Dossiers Secrets must have been from Switzerland.)

This is the story in brief as told in the Blancasall Dossier: The secret of the Merovingian survival was known to, and guarded by, the Hautpoul family of Rennes-le-Château. On her deathbed, the last of this family, Marie de Nègre d'Ablès, Dame d'Hautpoul et de Blanchefort, having no one else to pass it on to, entrusted the secret to her confessor, the village priest, Abbé Bigou. She directed him to a hiding place in the remains of the old St. Peter's church, where he found wooden tubes, sealed with wax, containing four parchments bearing "litanies to Our Lady" and "coded Gospels" of Luke and John. Bigou was able to decode them using another document given to him by Dame Marie. Because of the political climate as the clouds of revolution gathered, the priest realized that the "secret" could be passed on only in a similarly veiled form—he chose to do so through the enigmatic inscription on Marie's headstone. He also hid the parchments back in their wooden containers in the Visigoth pillar of the altar of St. Mary Magdalene's church.

A century later Bérenger Saunière arrived in Rennes-le-Château. At the beginning of 1891, two representatives of the Priory of Sion arrived to inform him that a great secret was hidden somewhere in his parish, relating to a legendary treasure. (How the Priory of Sion knew this is left unexplained, as is the question of if they knew the secret of the Merovingian survival, how they lacked the documents to prove it.) Saunière set about searching for this secret under cover of renovating the church and—in February 1891—found the parchments in the altar pillar where Bigou had hidden them.

Faced with the enigmatic documents, Saunière took them to Bishop Billard of Carcassonne, who advised him to take them to Paris to consult the young Abbé Émile Hoffet, even advancing him the funds to do so. According to this account, Hoffet was then a priest at the Church of the Trinity, living in the Rue Blanche.

Neatly drawing everything together, Blancasall writes of Hoffet:

> It was he who enabled Abbé Saunière to find the secret of Rennes. It was also he, fifty years later, on visiting Gisors, who gave the guardian Roger Lhomoy information concerning the famous thirty coffers deposited in a St. Catherine's chapel. Abbé Hoffet was then very alert despite his eighty years, and all his life he had attempted to establish a legitimate line of descent of Dagobert II, the saint, that is to say a Merovingian line down to our day.

Hoffet decoded the messages hidden in the parchments, claiming as "payment" the document with the "litanies to Our Lady." A key passage of Blancasall's work reads:

> On the advice of Abbé Hoffet, the curé of Rennes went to the Louvre Museum to contemplate the works of Poussin and Teniers, as the *en claire* text after decoding delivered this message: Shepherdess no temptation, that Poussin and Teniers have the key—Pax DCLXXXI [681]—by the cross and this horse of God—I finish off the demon guardian at noon—blue apples. [*Bergère pas de tentation, que Poussin et Teniers gardent la clef—Pax DCLXXXI—par la croix et ce cheval de dieu—j'achève ce daemon de gardien à midi—pommes bleues.*][20]

This marked the emergence of a new element, which has attracted more attention than any other in the Dossiers Secrets, if not the whole Rennes-le-Château mystery. In the decades since, many minds have been exercised trying to work out the meaning of these strange statements. What are the blue apples? What do the two painters Nicolas Poussin and David Teniers have to do with it? In fact, according to this version, these enigmatic lines were directions to various places in the vicinity of Rennes-le-Château, which led to Dagobert's treasure.

Blancasall's narrative then describes how, immediately on his return to Rennes-le-Château, Saunière erased the inscription on Marie de Nègre's gravestone (implying a connection between the inscription and the parchments), helped by Marie Dénarnaud.

Blancasall has provided an explanation for Saunière's discovery and his wealth. But what about his strange decoration of Rennes-le-Château's church? She explains: "The shadow of the mysterious Priory of Sion hovered over Rennes-le-Château and the Abbé faithfully obeyed," following its design of the church's decoration in order to *hide* any clues Bigou might have left. In other words, it means nothing, being designed to misinform and confuse—which is interesting in itself. (Could this have been a double bluff, to persuade researchers it was pointless trying to decipher the symbolism of the church decoration?)

Another new element is introduced: the Knights' Stone raised by Saunière—called here the "stone of the two horses"—is said to have covered the tomb of Sigebert IV and his two successors, Sigebert V and

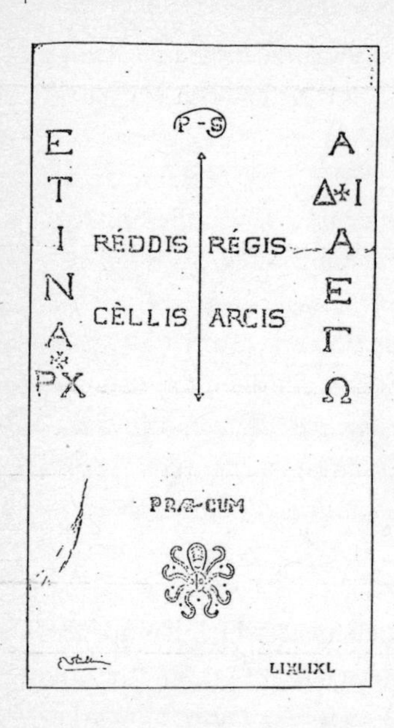

Béra III. The stone itself is alleged to commemorate the flight of the infant Sigebert to Rhedae/Rennes-le-Château in 681 (the year also featured in the parchments).

The Blancasall document includes drawings of the Knights' Stone and Marie de Nègre's headstone, both credited to the archives of the Society of Arts and Sciences of the Aude—correctly, as it happens. But it includes a third drawing, credited to the same source but this time falsely, of what is supposedly a *second* stone that covered Marie de Nègre's grave. Its most interesting feature by far is the *Et in Arcadia ego* motto—curiously, in ancient Greek lettering—as well as the Latin words *Réddis Régis Cèllis Arcis,* which are open to several interpretations. The other key features of this stone are the initials P-S (Priory of Sion?) at the top and at the bottom the Latin word *prae-cum,* a common feature of medieval tombs that means "pray for me." Unfortunately, there is no reliable evidence that this stone ever really existed.[21]

On Saunière's lavish entertaining at the Villa Béthanie, Blancasall writes: "Personalities of all kinds followed one another there: Emma Calvet [*sic*], the great opera singer, the pretty Vicomtesse B. d'Artois, as well as other ladies whose wealthy families still exist in the region." But the priest also had many male guests—why the emphasis on *ladies*?

For once, this is correct. Where Emma Calvé is concerned the author of the document is not inventing new and sensational elements but relating the story as told in the village before the mythmaking began.

Blancasall writes of the last year of Saunière's life:

> At the end of 1916, a great decision was taken by the curé of Rennes: he would preach "a new religion" and "undertake a crusade in the *département*." He dismissed the representative of the Priory of Sion who came to visit him. He said he would receive no other orders

> than those of Jean XXIII, the last Merovingian descendant. He began to assemble 8 million francs-or [gold francs—equal to 10 francs] in banknotes. Panic reigned in the Bishopric of Carcassonne, while the prelates in the Vatican were disturbed by this situation. The Priory of Sion welcomed the affair coldly, and political circles judged this undesirable maneuver as outright war.[22]

This is the first mention of January 17, 1917, as the day on which Saunière was allegedly mortally struck down. On his deathbed, we are told, "the priest asked for Jean XXIII the Merovingian to come to him. But he would not go." This Jean XXIII was Jean Plantard—the cousin of Pierre Plantard's father. Blancasall sums it up: "Such is the secret of the Razès; a genealogy and a treasure made Abbé Bérenger Saunière a billionaire curé."

Some extra genealogical tables, attributed to Lobineau but not included in the earlier work, show the line of descent from Dagobert I to one Pierre V—Pierre Plantard's father. The final table is genuinely that of Plantard's family from the second half of the eighteenth century—but there is a conspicuous leap after the previous one, which ends about a hundred years before.

Another idea introduced here—and accepted unquestioningly by many ever since—is that one of the Grand Masters of the Knights Templar, Bertrand de Blanchefort, came from the family that owned Blanchefort near Rennes-le-Château. This is patently untrue: Bertrand de Blancquefort, the seventh Templar Grand Master (presided c. 1156–1169), came from a village near Bordeaux and had no connection with the Blanchefort near Rennes-le-Château.[23] But of course this association manages to crowbar the dashing and mysterious Templars—always good value—into the story.

Dan Brown Would Be Proud

Although certain modifications were made in later documents, essentially these two documents elaborated the whole story of the Merovingian survival and its revelatory solution to the Rennes-le-Château mystery. As yet, the exact nature, role, and purpose of the Priory of Sion remain unexplained—that would come later. But it is time to pause and evaluate what we have so far. First, the explanation of the Saunière mystery.

The account is well researched—certainly the most detailed version of the affair up to that time (although with some distinctly dubious additions) with several items of information dug out of local archives. Blancasall also quotes from Saunière's letters—but this is not so surprising as Plantard knew Noël Corbu, who owned his papers.

Marie de Nègre's strange headstone is now the focus of the story, and its reproduction has been unearthed from a sixty-year-old local society journal. As there is something genuinely odd about the inscription on her gravestone, whatever else Blancasall might have done with this, he or she did not actually invent it. However, Blancasall *does* appear to have fabricated the existence of a second inscribed stone from this grave, which features the *Et in Arcadia ego* motto.

Attention is also drawn to the priest of Rennes-les-Bains, Abbé Henri Boudet, and his weird book, *The True Celtic Language and the Cromlech of Rennes-les-Bains,* for the first time—although the exact significance is not explained. Whether or not it truly deserves a place in the Saunière story, finding this long-forgotten book was in itself quite an achievement.

And the solution it offers to the Saunière mystery is quite ingenious—as the plot of a novel, with a liberal helping of artistic license and a side order of ingenuity to fill in the holes, Dan Brown himself would be proud of it. The gaps may be filled by alleged inside information known only to the Priory of Sion, but generally its internal logic hangs together surprisingly well. The loose ends are skillfully tied up: for example, by making Abbé Hoffet the bridge between Saunière and Lobineau. But it also includes telltale mistakes.

According to this account, Saunière made his discovery in the Visigoth pillar in February 1891, after the visit of two Priory men. But independent sources reveal that the discovery can be dated to 1887, and the Knight's Stone was raised during the renovations of 1888 or '89, not 1891. And here Saunière is said to have erased the inscription on Marie de Nègre's grave immediately after his return from Paris, again in 1891, whereas in reality it was still there to be copied by the visiting antiquarians fourteen years later. Moreover, Abbé Émile Hoffet was not a priest at the Church of the Trinity in 1891—in fact he was serving outside France at that time—and while the Rue Blanche address given in both documents *was* his, it was from a much later period of his life. These slips reveal the claim that all this is based on inside information possessed by the Priory to be dubious to say the least.

But the reason for these errors is instructive: they are not the author's own blunders but have been forced on him or her because of an attempt to create a consistent story out of very different elements, just as novelists often skip over holes in their plots and hope nobody notices. And because the only properly researched account at that time was Descadeillas's *Note on Rennes-le-Château and Abbé Saunière*—and that was only for the Carcassonne archives, not for publication—there was little chance that these anomalies would be picked up. The gamble paid off: it was many years before the publication of primary sources enabled researchers to spot the flaws.

The reason for the discrepancies in the dates arose from having to pinpoint 1891 as the year the first key events took place, for two reasons. First, of course, Saunière himself highlighted 1891. But more important was its connection with Abbé Hoffet—the device that linked those events and Lobineau.

"No whiff of sulfur"

Abbé Émile Hoffet was a real person, who certainly had the right credentials for inclusion in the Priory of Sion story. Born in Alsace (then in Germany) in 1873, he studied for the priesthood at the Junior Seminary of Our Lady of Sion—at Sion-Vaudémont in Lorraine, the evocatively named holy place at the center of this story.[24]

Hoffet continued his novitiate in Saint-Gerlach in the Netherlands, where he entered the order of the Oblates of Immaculate Mary in August 1892. After his ordination in Liège, Belgium, in 1898, his career took him to Corsica, Rome, and several posts in France before he settled in Paris, where he remained more or less until his death in 1946. For a time he taught at Notre-Dame-de-Lumières at Goult, not far from Avignon in Provence, which is named after a Black Madonna statue that the Priory of Sion later singled out as one of its most important objects of devotion, although without offering a word of explanation. Pierre Plantard was to state: "The Black Virgin is Isis and her name is Notre-Dame-de-Lumières."[25] Surely this is the most perfect encapsulation of the sacred feminine—yet coming from Plantard, what does it mean? Anything, nothing, or everything?

Although a priest, Hoffet enjoyed mixing in Paris's esoteric and artistic circles, being a particularly good friend of Debussy—through whom he knew Emma Calvé. Her biographer Jean Contrucci writes:

> Emma knew Abbé Émile Hoffet, an oblate, like her a close friend of Debussy, well. This slim young man, barely twenty, was a living encyclopedia: a renowned polyglot, paleographer, and cryptographer. To his scholarly reputation, Abbé Hoffet added that of being an occultist of the highest order. Esotericism had no whiff of sulfur for this fashionable and cultivated priest, since there is a Christian occultism . . . which allows research into mediumship or spiritism to cohabit with the certainties of faith.
>
> Emma and Abbé Hoffet often had the opportunity to debate the subjects for which they had a passion in the surroundings of meetings organized at the Bookshop of Independent Art, which was equally familiar to Debussy.[26]

There may be slightly more to it than that. Hoffet had close links to the editors of the traditionalist *Revue Internationale des Sociétés Secrètes*, founded in 1912 and dedicated to exposés and warnings about the activities of "occult" orders and cults. Perhaps he infiltrated those circles to clandestinely gather inside information for the exposés. Moreover, according to Jean Robin, Hoffet also knew Georges Monti—the founder of the Alpha Galates Order and Plantard's mentor.[27]

It is important to realize that none of Hoffet's connections—with Notre-Dame de Sion in Lorraine, Debussy, Calvé, or Monti—appears in the Dossiers Secrets, but they have been uncovered by independent researchers eager to discover more about him.

As Hoffet was well known in religious and esoteric milieus between the wars, but not outside those circles, clearly the author of the Lobineau and Blancasall documents was familiar not only with his life and career but also with the occult scene. And as he died in 1946, Hoffet could easily have known Plantard—especially since they both knew Monti.

However, the eagerness to associate Hoffet with the Saunière story created a problem—he was only twelve when Saunière arrived at Rennes-le-Château, and fourteen or fifteen when the curé found the parchments. Saunière was hardly likely to travel to Paris to consult some obscure, callow youth! To compensate, the discovery of the parchments was taken forward to 1891, when the admittedly precocious Hoffet was a more reasonable eighteen.

Actually, Hoffet was not even near Paris at the crucial time; he was serving his novitiate in the Netherlands. Of course he could have visited Paris in 1891 or '92—but then how did Mgr. Billard know he would be there? (Later Dossiers Secrets claim that Hoffet only accidentally became involved with Saunière's parchments while visiting a friend in Paris, but this merely underlines the logistical problem.)

Basically Blancasall and Lobineau's version of the Saunière story is fatally flawed, as is the alleged involvement of Abbé Hoffet—seriously damaging the idea of him as the conduit through which Lobineau learned about the Merovingian survival. But even so, this story has been carefully crafted using genuine inside information—in-depth research in Rennes-le-Château and a sound knowledge of Hoffet's life and career. And despite all the understandable criticism, it is still the best-known version of the Rennes-le-Château mystery. But even the Saunière mystery is just a device: the real story concerns the Merovingian survival. So how well does *that* stand up to scrutiny?

The Merovingian Myth

Although the Merovingians played an important role in the formation of France, they could never appear in its history as such because there simply was no French nation in their day—so when the Dossiers Secrets refer to Dagobert I and others as "King of France," they are plain wrong. And as we have seen, the Merovingians' territories did not cover all of modern France and also spilled out into what is now Belgium and parts of the Netherlands and Germany.

Originally France, or Francia, was simply a dukedom that included Paris. When the last of the Carolingian dynasty—the Merovingians' supplanters—died without an heir in 987, the Duke of France, Hugues Capet, was elected king. It was only after this that the term "France" was used of the king's entire domain, and then by extension of the nation as a whole. Even so, the Merovingians hold an important place in French hearts as essentially the founders of what was to become the nation, primarily at an emotive and mythical level very similar to the place of the Angles and Saxons in the history of England: although their rule did not extend to the whole of what is today England (still less Britain) and it is nearly a thousand years since the last Saxon was deposed by the Norman dynasty, the nation still calls itself Angleland—or England.

The appeal of the seductive mythic past is why General Charles de Gaulle could write on the first page of his memoirs covering the years of his presidency: "The legitimacy of a governing power derives from its conviction, and the conviction it inspires, that it embodies national unity and continuity when the country is in danger. In France, it was as a result of war that the Merovingians, the Carolingians, the Capetians, the Bonapartes, the Third Republic all received and lost this supreme authority."[28]

This puts the Priory of Sion's claim that the Merovingian survivor is the rightful or legitimate King of France into context. On the one hand, it appeals to the powerful archetype of the Lost King—like the resonance of the British with Arthur, their "Once and Future King," but even more potent to the French (especially after their soul-searching over the assassination of Louis XVI and Marie Antoinette). But on the other hand, a modern Merovingian pretender, even if able to prove his heritage beyond dispute—difficult to say the least—would be able to stake no claim whatsoever to the long-cold throne of France. He would have no more persuasive case than an English descendant of Alfred the Great. Too much history has passed to make such a proposal even remotely realistic.

As the Franks' lands consisted of the kingdoms of Austrasia, Burgundy, and Neustria, only a ruler of all three could legitimately be called King of the Franks. Dagobert I, for example, who had the right credentials, was a true King of the Franks, whereas his grandson Dagobert II was only King of Austrasia.[29] Although some of the Merovingian kings reigned over all three, on their deaths the lands were divided among their sons.

Failure to understand this principle has led to unnecessary mystification about Dagobert II, particularly when lists of "Kings of the Franks" jump from Dagobert I to Dagobert III without mentioning Dagobert II—prompting claims that he has been maliciously airbrushed out of history. In reality, the constant unifying and breaking up of the three kingdoms creates a nightmare for anyone trying to keep track of the various kings: Dagobert I was King of the Franks, Dagobert II of Austrasia only, whereas Dagobert III was once again King of all the Franks.

This highly divisive pattern of inheritance meant that the Merovingian period was no Golden Age of wise and benevolent rule by a succession of divinely mandated kings but very unromantically an era of constant internecine warfare and intrigue, as ambitious members of the dynasty struggled to seize as much Frankish land as possible. Kings were frequently assassinated. But if one individual succeeded in winning all three kingdoms, they would be dispersed again immediately after he died, and the whole bloody business would start all over again. In effect, the Merovingian period saw a roller coaster of alternating union and fragmentation of the three kingdoms.

In fact, the concept of a main line of Merovingian descent—legitimately passing on power from father to firstborn son—at the heart of the Dossiers Secrets is largely a fiction anyway: with the historical Merovingians, power was passed on as much by custom, conquest, and intrigue as by birth. But what makes Dagobert II so special?

Despite the popular impression, Dagobert II was *not* the last Merovingian king. The dynasty continued for another seventy years, until Childeric III was deposed in 751 by Pépin the Short, with the support of the Pope. This is especially significant as it was the first time the Church had claimed the right to appoint kings, thereby asserting its superiority over secular rulers. Pépin established what became known as the Carolingian dynasty, after its most famous king, Charlemagne (Carolus Magnus), proclaimed Holy Roman Emperor on Christmas Day 800.

Although Baigent, Leigh, and Lincoln write, "The main line of Merovingian descent had been deposed with Dagobert II. To all intents and purposes, therefore, Dagobert's assassination may be regarded as signalling the end of the Merovingian dynasty,"[30] this is a considerable overstatement. The subsequent rulers—including six kings of all the Franks—were as much Merovingians as was Dagobert, basically being descended from Dagobert II's uncle Clovis II, who, although the younger of two brothers, had inherited the kingdoms of Burgundy and Neustria. (It is true, however, that the last Merovingian rulers were largely figureheads—puppets controlled by the Mayors of the Palace, who held the real power. These final monarchs were known as the *rois fainéants*, translated by Baigent, Leigh, and Lincoln as "enfeebled kings" but more accurately as "lazy kings.")

Although a somewhat obscure monarch, Dagobert II was declared a saint some two centuries after his death (but only by the Frankish clergy; his name does not appear in today's Catholic canon), with a feast day on December 23, apparently because his body, interred in a chapel at Stenay, miraculously repelled a Viking raid. At least this shows that even after the dynasty's eclipse there was believed to be something special about Dagobert and, presumably, the Merovingian dynasty as a whole. After this his relics became the focus of a cult at Stenay. However, there is a major irony about the Dossiers Secrets' claims—the ultimate Merovingian hero, Dagobert II, may actually have been not a Merovingian at all but an impostor.[31]

He had a particularly complicated life, even by Merovingian standards. His father—or rather, presumed father—Sigebert III of Austrasia, being believed to have no children, had adopted the son of Grimoald, his Mayor of the Palace, proclaiming him his heir. Twenty years after Sigebert III's death, after much internecine strife, the throne of Austrasia was again vacant and the subject of a power struggle. In 676 a young man abruptly appeared from the British Isles, his supporters among the Austrasian nobles claiming he was actually Sigebert III's son.

The story was that, after Grimoald's son was adopted by Sigebert, the Queen had found herself pregnant with Sigebert's child. To stop him claiming the throne, Grimoald had the young boy secretly exiled to Ireland, where he grew up in a monastery. It was said all memory of Dagobert's existence had been erased—even his mother thought he was dead. But now here he was, twenty-five years old and claiming his birthright. While some Austrasian nobles accepted him, others refused to acknowledge him, so for three years, until his death, he battled to establish his credentials.

The exile's return is, of course, deeply suspicious. So, too, is the explanation of where he had been for two decades: given the practices of the time, surely it is far more likely that Grimoald would have had the infant Dagobert summarily killed rather than packed off to Ireland.

If one wanted to invent a conspiracy theory about Dagobert II, the most obvious one would be that he was not actually Merovingian. Admittedly, there is a particularly neat irony in the Merovingian impostor Pierre Plantard claiming descent from a Merovingian impostor. Maybe that was the point.

More Merovingian Myths

Had Sigebert IV survived, he could have staked a legitimate claim to the throne of Austrasia but not to the other Frankish kingdoms. But the Dossiers Secrets allege that when the rest of the Merovingian dynasty was extinguished, the line descended from Sigebert was the sole representative of the true kings of the Franks—and hence of France.

Most of Lobineau's genealogies are accurate: only certain parts are questionable—but these are precisely the most important parts as far as the Priory's version is concerned. The basic Merovingian genealogy, for example, is correct—it can even be established which history books it came from—but a second wife of Dagobert II called Gisèle is an added extra. Records of Dagobert's time are sketchy, and although the existence of his son Sigebert is acknowledged, Dagobert II is known to have had only one wife, Matilda, who was actually an Irish princess. In fact, his second marriage to Gisèle of the Razès, who gave birth to Sigebert, is mentioned *only* in the Dossiers Secrets. Presumably Gisèle was invented to make the crucial connection with Rennes-le-Château.

Of course, the believers argue that this story drew on genuine inside information, secret archives or documents not known to mainstream historians. But the errors are dead giveaways, and obviously the additions are complete fabrications.[32] The major problem is they allege that Gisèle is the daughter of Béra II, the second Comte du Razès—a little tricky as he took that title in 845, more than a century and a half after his alleged grandson's birth![33] And in any case, there was no Comte du Razès in Sigebert's day: the title was created by Charlemagne, who bestowed it on William of Gellone, one of the most illustrious figures of the time, who passed into legend as the epitome of the chivalrous and pious knight.[34] (As it happens, William of Gellone is a significant player in *The Holy Blood and the Holy Grail*'s reconstruction of history, as part of the Merovingian bloodline, although he is conspicuous by his absence in the Dossiers Secrets' version of the Merovingian descendants. The files certainly missed a trick there!)

Then there is the claim that Godefroy de Bouillon—another great hero of his time—was of Merovingian descent (although not of the main branch), and that this was why he saw the crown of Jerusalem as rightfully his. The notion that Godefroy could trace his ancestry back to the Merovingians is now so widespread and so often repeated that it is almost established history. And yet it is patently untrue.

Godefroy (or Godfrey), Comte de Bouillon and Duc de Lorraine (1061–1100), was, as we have seen, a leader of the First Crusade, which successfully captured Jerusalem in 1099. His brother military leaders allegedly offered him the title of King of Jerusalem, but the evidence suggests that all he was really offered was the role of Advocate of the Holy Sepulcher. (Godefroy died a year later, and his brother Baudouin—or Baldwin—became the first King of Jerusalem.)

According to Lobineau, Godefroy's Merovingian ancestry came about because his paternal grandfather, Eustache, Comte de Boulogne, was the son of Hugues Long Nose, the younger brother of the direct Merovingian descendant. But according to the usual biographies and genealogies, Eustache's ancestry on his father's side goes back to the Mayors of the Palace of Neustria—and to Charlemagne! Moreover, on his mother's side, Godefroy was also a direct descendant of Charlemagne, therefore from the dynasty that *usurped* the Merovingians. As the historian John C. Andressohn writes: "Godefroy de Bouillon was the scion of illustrious ancestry. Both the paternal and maternal branch claimed descent from Charlemagne, an assertion which seems substantiated."[35] In other words, Godefroy was mostly—and proudly—Carolingian, and there is no evidence—outside the Dossiers Secrets—that he had any Merovingian blood at all.

The Lobineau genealogies also obscure the fact that Godefroy had an older brother, Eustache, Comte de Boulogne,[36] by placing him to Godefroy's right on the chart as if he were a *younger* brother. Of course, if (as later Dossiers Secrets claim) the Priory of Sion had manipulated events to set a Merovingian descendant on the throne of the Holy City, by rights they should have chosen Godefroy's older brother.

The Holy Blood and the Holy Grail claims that Godefroy was the only Crusade leader to sell all his lands, property, and possessions before leaving for the Holy Land, suggesting that he knew in advance he would be proclaimed King of Jerusalem. But as the British historian Jonathan Riley-Smith writes: "Until he took the cross he had not shown any marked piety and it is clear from the terms of the mortgage agreements he drew up that in 1096 he had no definite intention of settling in the East."[37] In reality Godefroy pawned his possessions to the Bishops of Liège and Verdun to raise money for the Crusade, on the understanding that they would be redeemable either by himself when he returned (with the expected booty) or, if he died on the expedition, by his brother.[38]

Godefroy also funded his crusade through a protection racket imposed on the Jewish communities in Cologne and Mainz, which he persecuted brutally until each town agreed to pay him five hundred pieces of silver to buy his bully boys off.[39] This is hard to reconcile with Godefroy being not only of Jewish descent but also fully cognizant of the fact.

Baigent, Leigh, and Lincoln also claim that Godefroy was the first person to be offered the crown of Jerusalem. In fact, contemporary chronicles show it was initially offered to Raymond, Comte de Toulouse, and it was only when he declined it—because he wanted to return home—that Godefroy was considered. Poor Godefroy: it gets worse. Not only is it certain that Raymond of Toulouse was the first to be offered the crown but the contemporary chronicler Albert of Aachen states that it was then offered to—and declined by—*all* the other Crusader leaders before Godefroy accepted it. As Andressohn writes: "Unflattering as it may be to him, Godefroy by the merest chance became the ruler of Jerusalem, the real source of his later fame."[40]

All this fatally undermines the Dossiers Secrets' claims concerning Godefroy. But why did they go to such lengths to link him with the Merovingians? Of course, there was the cachet of the title King of Jerusalem being associated with the Priory of Sion—as well as the implicit compliment that the secret society had the power to engineer such a high-level election, and perhaps even to manipulate the whole crusade for its own purposes. But the documents also claim that Godefroy was the founder of the "Order of Sion" in 1090.[41]

Godefroy did establish an Abbey of Notre-Dame de Mont Sion in Jerusalem, which did indeed boast an associated order of knighthood. How did the author or authors of the Dossiers Secrets discover this rather abstruse piece of information? We will be returning to this question later.

A unique feature of Lobineau's genealogies is that they become *less* detailed the nearer they approach the present day: those of the Comtes du Razès—uncheckable by any independent source—are replete with details of the families into which they married. But after about 1500 the marriages of the males in the direct Merovingian line become a little vague—just a list of the wives' names. Clearly, by this point the family is a complete fiction, so Lobineau has to avoid linking them with anyone whose life can be verified.

"This very closed club"

But if, as we believe, the whole Merovingian business was essentially *misinformation,* where did the idea come from? Obviously the Merovingians were chosen because they exude a particularly sexy mythic resonance, but was the idea of restoring them to the throne of France original or did the Priory of Sion borrow—or even inherit—it?

There is a clue in a small book called *The Enigma of Rennes* (1978) by Philippe de Chérisey, which includes a purported interview with an elusive (and possibly nonexistent) character called Henri de Lénoncourt, quoting him as saying: "A Merovingian Party has existed for sixty years: the Cercle du Lys, the true founder being Johann Stefan von Habsburg, called 'Monsieur de Chambord,' but Simone de Beauvoir, in her book *La force de l'âge,* gave another founder: Lionel de Roulet; this very closed club has three or four hundred members in Paris."[42]

The attribution of the "Merovingian Party" to Johann Stefan von Habsburg—apparently a mistake for Johann Salvator—seems to be an attempt at mystification, but in fact the party was founded by one Lionel de Roulet. (Somewhat cheekily, the revived 1989 *Vaincre* named him as a member of the Priory of Sion.)

A pupil of the famous existentialist philosopher Jean-Paul Sartre—who called him "my disciple"—Lionel de Roulet married Simone de Beauvoir's sister Hélène in 1942. In the second volume of her autobiography, *La force de l'âge* (1960, the English edition entitled *The Prime of Life*), de Beauvoir wrote of events in 1934:

> While Sartre was away I gave philosophy lessons to Lionel de Roulet, who was now living in Paris. He and a few friends had founded a so-called Merovingian Party, which advocated, by means of posters and pamphlets, the return of Chilperic's descendants to

> the throne. I scolded him for giving up, as I found, far too much time to such nonsense; but he had a natural talent for philosophy, and I felt very warmly towards him.[43]

This was clearly the inspiration for the Priory's Merovingian fantasy, but how did the Dossiers Secrets' masterminds know about this somewhat obscure prewar movement? The answer seems to lie, once again, in wartime intelligence agencies.

In May 1940, when war broke out in earnest, Lionel de Roulet and Hélène went to Lisbon, where he worked for the Institut Français. Although he made it known only shortly before his death, while there he was involved in intelligence operations. As neutral Portugal provided a vitally important channel for British and Free French agents to infiltrate deeper into Europe, de Roulet's job was basically to organize their passage—risky, as German agents were also busy in Lisbon—in the words of the Beauvoir sisters' biographer Claudine Monteil, "with more discretion than courage."[44] Obviously his work meant a close association with SOE.

Immediately after the war, de Roulet was dispatched to the Austrian capital, Vienna (then in the Soviet Zone), working for the Foreign Ministry as "counselor responsible for information"—in other words, intelligence gathering.[45] After that the de Roulets settled in Alsace, where Lionel worked for the Council of Europe until the 1980s. In the 1960s he was particularly concerned with education and youth organizations, rising to Assistant Director-General of Cultural Relations in the Council of Europe. Of course de Roulet's connection with wartime intelligence work and SOE, and with a Merovingian revival, *may* be purely coincidental. . . .

Stone Tapes

The next installment of the Dossiers Secrets appeared in the Bibliothèque Nationale in May 1966. Attributed to one Antoine l'Ermite—another transparent pseudonym, St. Anthony the Hermit, whose feast day is the mysteriously "magic" January 17, being one of the saints' statues Saunière placed in his church—it is entitled *A Merovingian Treasure at . . . Rennes-le-Château.*[46]

The nine-page pamphlet is mostly—cheekily—a direct facsimile of the chapter on Rennes-le-Château from Robert Charroux's *Treasures of the World,* with just one or two minor changes. For example, whereas Charroux records one of the villagers saying that Saunière's secret is to be found "at the bottom of a tomb," l'Ermite renders it as "on a tomb." But its main purpose is to reproduce the stones that gel with the developing myth—Marie de Nègre's headstone and the Knights' Stone. The latter is supposedly copied from an unidentified book, with the caption "Carolingian tombstone (771) found in 1882–83 under the altar of the Roman church of Rennes-le-Château, the ancient, much declined, capital of the Comte du Razès." The drawing is dated 1884. This is nonsense: Saunière, who arrived in the village only in 1885, raised the Knights' Stone in 1887 or '88.

The stone slab bearing the *Et in Arcadia ego* motto, (supposedly) from Marie de Nègre's grave, is reproduced once more, but this time with a source: "Plate taken from *Engraved Stones of the Languedoc* by Eugène Stüblein, printed in Limoux—1884—Library of M. Abbé Joseph Courtaly at Villarzel-du-Razès (Aude)." Very specifically it references page 189 of Stüblein's book.

The rest of the pamphlet tells the familiar story of the discovery of the four parchments relating to the Merovingian genealogy—but with one new piece of information: before they were placed in the altar by Bigou, the parchments were found "attached to the will of François-Pierre, Baron d'Hautpoul, of Rennes and registered on November 23, 1644, by Captier, Notary of Espéraza (Aude)." As we have seen, this will did exist, although its significance, while obviously great, remains somewhat baffling. The explanation given here is that the *"Actes Captier"* were genealogies of the Merovingian survivors, implying that they ended up with Bigou, who then inserted them into the altar pillar, where they were eventually found by Saunière.

But how did they find their way into the Dossiers Secrets? A note in the Antoine l'Ermite pamphlet explains that in 1961 they were given to "Alpina" by Abbé Joseph Courtaly of Villarzel-du-Razès—the same priest who as a young man had helped Saunière to paint the bas-relief of Mary Magdalene on the church altar. A sick man, Courtaly retired to the village where he was born, Villarzel-du-Razès, in the summer of 1961, and often took the waters at Rennes-les-Bains; it was there that he frequently met Pierre Plantard.[47] But he had died in November 1964, a year and a half before this document surfaced in the Bibliothèque Nationale.

Less than a month after the deposition of the Antoine l'Ermite work, Courtaly's name was hijacked to bestow a spurious provenance on another series of reproductions, copies of figures allegedly from the book mentioned by l'Ermite, *Engraved Stones of the Languedoc* (*Pierres gravées du Languedoc*), which included the following explanation, signed and dated by Courtaly (at Villarzel-du-Razès, April 1962):

> The book of Eugène Stüblein, Limoux 1884 edition, having become very rare, and being perhaps one of the rare owners to have it in his library, I owe it to myself to satisfy the numerous requests from researchers to make a reproduction of the book's plates, nos. 16 to 23 on the villages of Rennes-les-Bains, Rennes-le-Château, and Alet.

(The deposition slip was signed by Antoine l'Ermite, his address given as a hotel in Paris's Seventeenth Arrondissement.)

Unfortunately, the book never existed, although its alleged author, Stüblein (1832–1899), was a real man, who spent most of his life in the Aude. A celebrated meteorologist, he also wrote on local antiquities, including two books on Rennes-les-Bains, published in 1884 and 1886. But in all his well-cataloged output, there is nothing entitled *Engraved Stones of the Languedoc.*[48]

If there is still any room for doubt, the Dossier repeats a telltale mistake from Antoine l'Ermite: the sketch of the Knights' Stone bearing the signature "Stüblein" with the caption "Stone from the sepulcher of Princes Sigebert IV, Sigebert V, and Béra III in the St. Magdalene church." But we know Saunière was not even assigned to Rennes-le-Château until 1885—the year after the supposed publication of Stüblein's book—and the carved side of the stone remained facedown until the renovations in 1887–88. Besides, how did Stüblein know that this covered the graves of the Merovingian survivors, as this was supposedly the secret discovered by Saunière from the parchments?

A Hint of Heresy

In November 1966 a new document, comprising just a few papers, was deposited in the Bibliothèque Nationale. This took the form of a polemic, a riposte by "S. Roux" to certain statements of one Lionel Burrus, although obviously its real purpose was to leak the true identity of Henri Lobineau.[49]

For the first time a note of heresy creeps into the Merovingians' survival story. So far they have been treated as the unjustly deposed kings of France, but now the Roman Church is said to be afraid of the Merovingians for some dark secret they *could* reveal about Catholicism . . .

First there is a copy of an article allegedly from the *Geneva Catholic Weekly* (*Semaine Catholique Genevoise*), although there has never been any publication of that title. Ascribed to Lionel Burrus, it is entitled "*Faisons le point* . . ." ("Taking Stock . . ."). Tellingly, copies were sent to researchers with a known interest in the affair, including René Descadeillas. They were postmarked Geneva, where Lionel Burrus's family was prominent—but he had died in a car crash at the age of twenty in September 1966, two months before this document appeared.[50] A distinct pattern is emerging.

The purported Burrus, who claims to represent an organization called the Swiss Christian Youth, reveals Henri Lobineau to be Leo R. Schidlof, who had recently died in Vienna (on October 17—nineteen days before the document arrived at the Bibliothèque Nationale). Burrus is supposed to be defending the recently deceased man from an attack made in a "Roman Catholic bulletin" accusing him of being "pro-Soviet, a notorious Freemason, [and] preparing [the ground for] a popular monarchy in France." The motive for this attack, says Burrus, is the Vatican's loathing for the Merovingians' descendants, who "have always been at the bottom of heresies, since Arianism, passing through the Cathars and the Templars to Freemasonry." (The belief that Jesus was a mortal man, not the Son of God, Arianism was rejected by the Roman Church—by vote—at the Council of Nicaea in 325. It was declared a heresy and its adherents persecuted, although it remained popular in areas outside Rome's control. The Visigoths were devotees.)

Leo Schidlof was actually an authority on miniatures, author of the comprehensive (and ironically enormous) *The Miniature in Europe in the 16th, 17th, 18th, and 19th Centuries.*[51] Although born in Austria, he lived in London between 1948 and 1966 and died on a trip to Vienna. But was he also Henri Lobineau? No researcher has ever established the slightest connection between him and the Priory of Sion, still less the Dossiers Secrets, or that he possessed a special interest in the Merovingians, or for that matter even genealogy. This conveniently recently deceased individual was used to give Henri Lobineau an identity, presumably to preempt awkward questions about his existence. (As both Schidlof and Burrus were fairly well known, we can assume notice of their deaths was taken from the newspapers.)

Revealing their labyrinthine thought processes, the Dossiers' creators seized the opportunity to introduce a "correction" to their previous story. Although Burrus repeats the line that Schidlof got the Merovingian survival details from Abbé Hoffet, there is now an amendment: "Abbé Hoffet did not receive, in 1892 [*sic*] at the age of nineteen the mission of translating the parchments of Bérenger Saunière. . . . We have before our eyes the contents of the German text, and here is the exact translation: 'My friend Hoffet pursued his studies in 1892 in Paris and met, in the course of a dinner at Ane's, the curé Saunière; he was nineteen, this was his first step into the Merovingian affair. Saunière had been sent by Mgr. Billard of Carcassonne . . . to Abbé Bueil, Director of St.-Sulpice, and Monsieur Ane was his nephew . . .' Henri Lobineau therefore never wrote that Saunière went to get Abbé Hoffet, who was not yet ordained a priest, to translate his parchments!"

It is correct that in 1892 (the year to which the event has shifted seamlessly from 1891) Hoffet was still a novice, and he was ordained only six years later. But the original Henri Lobineau account *did* say that. Suddenly aware of their mistakes, the composer or composers of the Dossiers Secrets seized this golden opportunity to invent a correction, pretending it had been an error in translation but also enabling them to inject the evocative church of St.-Sulpice into the developing story.

S. Roux duly submitted a rejoinder, entitled "The Rennes-le-Château Affair: A Reply to Monsieur Lionel Burrus," basically repeating and amplifying the claims about Schidlof—and the Merovingians—as rebuffed by Burrus. Roux maintains that Schidlof was "a dignitary of the Grand Lodge Alpina in Switzerland, and did not hide his sentiments of friendship with the States of the East, which did not prevent him from being a very good Swiss secret agent and also an honest and good man." He suggests that at the time of his death, Schidlof was "preparing in Austria a future Franco-Russian accord"!

Another document, deposited a few months later, identified Roux as the alias of Abbé Georges de Nantes.[52] This was distinctly risky—not only was de Nantes very much alive at the time but he was fairly notorious as the ultratraditionalist Catholic priest who had the temerity to declare Pope Paul VI a heretic for his liberal views. Questioned by French researchers, Abbé de Nantes denied that he was the author of this tract—or that he had any knowledge of the Rennes affair.[53]

Roux alleges that because they were cheated out of their rightful throne by a conspiracy of the Carolingians and the Church, "the [Merovingian] descendants have, since Dagobert II, always been secret agitators against the royal power in France and the Church. They were also supporters of all heresies. The return to power of a Merovingian descendant would be for France the proclamation of a popular state allied to the Soviet Union, with the triumph of Freemasonry." In other words, the "underground" Merovingians have traditionally supported any heretical movement simply because they, too, hate the Church.

Roux plants another little seed that was to flower a few months later, in one of the most perplexing episodes of the whole Rennes-le-Château affair. After repeating the claim that the Eugène Stüblein extracts had been reproduced by Abbé Courtaly, he adds, "This priest also gave reproductions of the genealogy of St. Dagobert's descendants to M. Fatin, of Rennes-le-Château, to the International League of Antiquarian Booksellers, 39, Great Russell Street, London, to Antoine l'Ermite, et cetera."

At the time Roux's document surfaced, Marius Fatin, the owner of the château in Rennes-le-Château, was still alive—although he was to die within a few months, in early 1967. Between the wars Fatin served in the merchant navy, in 1920 settling in the Lebanon (then a French protectorate), where he founded the Overseas School of the Levant (École Outre-Mer au Levant) for the children of French settlers.[54] During the war he joined the Free French of the Levant, assuming an important role in de Gaulle's movement. Describing him as a "companion of the liberation," Jean Blum says he "featured among the faithful within the faithful of General de Gaulle."[55] Indeed, according to the villagers, Fatin received a greeting card from the General every year. He was also described as "an archaeologist and high-ranking Freemason[56]—a connection that was to become more significant over the following few months. He had taken over Rennes's crumbling château in 1946, as the postwar dust was settling.

To add to the confusion, in the late 1970s another candidate was suggested as the real Lobineau: one Henri, Comte de Lénoncourt, who had allegedly taken the name from his street, the Rue Lobineau in Paris—and was also, again allegedly, a friend of Schidlof. According to Philippe de Chérisey, Lénoncourt supposedly died in 1978 at the age of 87—but, as usual, before the identification was made public. However, although Baigent, Leigh, and Lincoln accept Lénoncourt as Lobineau, our best efforts and those of other researchers in the United Kingdom and France have failed to produce any evidence that this particular Comte de Lénoncourt ever existed. As the last recorded holder of the title was born in 1872, he would have been an unlikely 106 in 1978.[57]

In a further twist, Gino Sandri now claims that Comte de Lénoncourt was an alias of a former SOE agent, who served in occupied France and Switzerland during the war and who composed the genealogies under another pseudonym, Henri Lobineau. Sandri identifies him only as Monsieur N., an acquaintance of Leo Schidlof's, which is why his name was used earlier. [58] As ever, this should be taken with a large pinch of salt.

Another Intriguing British Connection

The last of the Dossiers Secrets, *The Secret Files of Henri Lobineau* (April 1967), was again a collection of various papers. Although we will deal more fully with it in the relevant place, for now we should consider one particular paper because it relates to the important letter, dated July 2, 1966, to Marius Fatin ostensibly from the International League of Antiquarian Booksellers in London—a real organization—as a follow-up to a visit by two of its representatives:

> After our visit last week to your château of Rennes, and before leaving France, we have the great pleasure to be able to inform you that your château is indeed historically the most important in France, as this residence was the refuge in 681 of Prince Sigibert [*sic*] IV, son of

> King Dagobert II, who became Saint Dagobert, as well as their descendants, the Comtes de Rhédae and Duc [*sic*] du Razès.
>
> Facts attested to by two parchments bearing the seal of Queen Blanche of Castile . . . with the will of François Pierre d'Hautpoul, registered on 23 November 1644 by Captier, Notary, in Espéraza (Aude), documents bought in 1948 by our League with a part of the library of Mr. Abbé E. M. Hoffet, 7, Rue Blanche in Paris, who got these documents from Mr. Abbé Saunière, former *curé* of Rennes-le-Château.
>
> The tombstone of Sigibert IV features in the book of Stüblein, Limoux 1884 edition, and was found in St. Magdalene's church in Rennes-le-Château. . . .
>
> Your château is therefore doubly historic!

Unfortunately the two signatures are indecipherable.

Of course, the summary and confirmation of all the major features of the story so far are far too neat. Franck Marie and Pierre Jarnac have established beyond any doubt that this letter is a fake: not only has the League repeatedly denied any knowledge of this affair, but the letter was written on a letterhead it used only between 1948 and 1950.[59] (Although curiously, the letter says that the League acquired the parchments in 1948, when it was still using the letterhead.)

The obvious conclusion is that it is a straightforward fake, employing the Dossiers Secrets' usual trick of backdating it after Marius Fatin's death to give spurious credibility to the idea that the famous parchments were now owned by the International League of Antiquarian Booksellers in London. After all, the copy appeared in the Bibliothèque Nationale only in April 1967, although it received more publicity than most of the Dossiers Secrets: a month later *La Dépêche du Midi* blazoned the headline "HISTORICALLY THE MOST IMPORTANT IN FRANCE"—THE CHÂTEAU OF RENNES CONDEMNED TO DISAPPEAR.

But . . . a photograph of Marius Fatin holding the letter appears in Jean-Luc Chaumeil's 1979 book *The Treasure of the Golden Triangle.* This means that the letter *did* exist when Fatin was still alive, although the photograph proves nothing except that someone took a snap of him looking at a copy—and the identity of the photographer is not stated. But as the letter refers to a visit by two British representatives of the League, it would be very odd to show Fatin the copied letter if they had never arrived. Moreover, Marius Fatin's son Henri—who continued to live there after his father's death—has never complained that the letter is a fake nor declared that there was no such visit, either at the time of the *Dépêche* article or whenever it has been quoted in the intervening years.

This is very perplexing: the letter is unquestionably a fake, yet the Fatins' behavior suggests that it was a follow-up to a genuine visit. Of course, it would be easy enough for two people to turn up *claiming* to be from the International League—but they would have to be, or at least pass as, Englishmen. This rules Plantard out, and although the actor de Chérisey could perhaps have pulled off an adequate impersonation, both men were known in the village from earlier visits. (The villagers have long memories for faces, as we know from experience.) An alternative is that Marius Fatin himself was involved in the scam, but there is no evidence for this. In any case, the inference would be the same—Plantard and de Chérisey were not acting alone.

Yet again, what on earth was going on? It seems to be another deception designed to bestow apparent credibility on the Merovingian survival story, this time laying a trail to London. But there is an inevitable conclusion: just as Plantard and de Chérisey appear to have had at least one confederate in Switzerland, two others were apparently British. In any case, whatever was happening was a group exercise rather than the effort of a single mythomaniac, as the critics are so fond of believing.

The Mystery of the Red Serpent

By far the most mysterious and compelling of the Dossiers Secrets is the curious work entitled *The Red Serpent* (*Le serpent rouge*), subtitled "Notes on St.-Germain and St.-Sulpice of Paris."[60] Very different from the previous documents, having no overt connection with either Rennes-le-Château or the Merovingian survival (although the links exist for the cognoscenti), it is a collection of pages copied from other works relating to the church of St.-Sulpice in the Saint-Germain-des-Prés district of Paris's Left Bank. But the haunting prose poem at the beginning has attracted the most attention of all the Dossiers Secrets.

Mystery—or rather mystification—surrounds both the date and the authorship of the document and introduces a distinctly macabre note. Dated January 17, 1967, the work as a whole is attributed to Pierre

Feugère, Louis Saint-Maxent, and Gaston de Koker, although the prose poem is ascribed to Saint-Maxent alone. The deposit slip, signed by the former gendarme Feugère, is dated February 15, 1967, but the official stamp bears the date March 20. The difference between the two dates is particularly important—the three purported authors were alive on the first but were *all dead* by the second.

All three men hanged themselves during the night or early morning of March 6–7, 1967: Saint-Maxent and de Koker on the evening of March 6, and Feugère at around six o'clock the next morning. This appears to be yet another example of whoever was behind the Dossiers Secrets purloining the names of the recently deceased—as with Abbé Courtaly, Leo Schidlof, and Lionel Burrus. This time, however, the motive seems to be different: whereas the others were used to block further investigation by employing the names of people no longer in any position to confirm or deny anything done or said in their name, this time a new and urgent note of danger, mystery, and excitement is introduced.

After meticulously investigating these deaths, Franck Marie concluded that the three men not only had no link with *The Red Serpent* or anyone involved with the Priory of Sion but also: "No known link at the time unites these three men. For this reason, three routine inquiries into *suicide* were undertaken by the police, separately" (his emphasis).[61] Moreover, he established that *The Red Serpent* and the *dépôt légal* form were typed on the same typewriter, which was also used for Dossiers Secrets written before and *after* the deaths (*The Merovingian Descendants* of 1964 and *The Secret Files of Henri Lobineau* of April 1967).

Clearly, attributing *The Red Serpent* to these three men was a hoax. The obvious explanation is that the real authors noted the convenient tragedies, used their names, then backdated the deposit slip. But there is one distinctly gruesome element suggesting that there might be more to it. The title page of *The Red Serpent* gives the addresses—all correct—of the three alleged authors in, respectively, Pontoise, Argenteuil, and Ermont, all very close suburbs of northwest Paris. (Argenteuil and Ermont are about two miles apart, and Pontoise about ten miles from both.) Presumably three identical but *unrelated* suicides within a ten-mile radius of each other on the same night are something of a rarity (unless Paris's suicide rate is ridiculously high). Either there *was* some connection among the three deaths that the police never discovered or it was a one-in-a-million coincidence.

If there was an undetected link among the three men, this implies that the real composer of *The Red Serpent* was aware of it. In any case, it is hard to write off this complex setup as "just" a hoax.

The Serpent Speaks

The Red Serpent's opening prose poem comprises thirteen "verses," each relating to a zodiac sign (plus a thirteenth, Ophiuchus, the serpent bearer), whose meaning is veiled and gnomic, representing a pilgrimage or initiatory journey. The object of the quest is to find a sleeping beauty, equated with both Isis and Mary Magdalene—both obviously iconic and archetypal representatives of the sacred Feminine.

Those familiar with the area around Rennes-le-Château and Rennes-les-Bains will understand most of the cryptic allusions. For example, the second verse (Pisces) refers to "the nautonnier of the undying ark, impassive like a column on its white rock, peering toward the south [*midi*], beyond the black rock," referring to Blanchefort and the nearby Rocque Nègre. The sixth verse, Cancer, refers to a black-and-white mosaic floor to which both Jesus and Asmodeus direct their gaze, obviously a description of the interior of Rennes-le-Château's church. In the context of a holy water stoup, the verse also uses the phrase *Par ce signe tu le vaincras*—with its anomalous *le*, found uniquely there.

The eighth verse, Virgo: "I am like the shepherds of the celebrated painter Poussin, perplexed before the riddle: '*Et in Arcadia ego* . . . ' " is another reference to Poussin's *Shepherds of Arcadia*, to which we will return shortly. There are also allusions to the painter Eugène Delacroix and the "sign" he left in "one of the three tableaux in the Chapel of Angels," clearly referring to his paintings in St.-Sulpice, creating a further tantalizing trail.

Another example, from the tenth verse (Scorpio), speaking of Jean-Jacques Olier, St.-Sulpice's builder (emphasis as in the original): 'I understand the truth, *he has passed* [*il est passé*], but also doing *good* [*en faisant le bien*] to him, as well as *he* of the flowery tomb [*tombe fleurie*]." We recall that Paul-Urbain *de Fleury*'s tomb in Rennes-les-Bains cemetery also bore the inscription "*Il est passé en faisant le bien,*" meaning broadly "he spent his time doing good." Only someone with a detailed knowledge of the area would understand.

The remainder of *The Red Serpent* consists of pages copied from other books—as far as can be determined all genuine—mainly relating to St.-Sulpice or the nearby St.-Germain-des-Prés. (There are also genealogical tables and maps that serve no particular purpose other than to crowbar in the all-important Merovingians.)

Clearly the authors are implying—or contriving—a link between Rennes-le-Château and St.-Sulpice, but was the latter dragged into the story by accident or by design? What is so special about this Parisian church? Unlike Rennes-le-Château, St.-Sulpice was already well established on the esoteric map of France, featuring prominently in J.-K. Huysmans's novel about Satanism in nineteenth-century France, *Down There (Là-bas,* 1891). He frequented the same occult salons as Emma Calvé—whose biographer Jean Contrucci described him as "the Catholic yet *luciferan* esotericist."[62]

Although there has been a St.-Sulpice on the site since at least the thirteenth century, originally it was just a small parish church within the grounds of the Abbey of St.-Germain-des-Prés. The saint after whom it was named, Sulpice or Sulpicius, was a seventh-century bishop, therefore of the Merovingian period—in fact he was Bishop of Bourges, the town chosen as the mystical center of France in Plantard's piece for *The Templars Are Among Us* back in 1961. St. Sulpice's feast day is January 17, which for reasons never explained recurs in the Dossiers Secrets.

However, the current imposing church—covering about the same area as Notre-Dame de Paris—dates from the seventeenth and eighteenth centuries.[63] The driving force behind this perhaps overambitious project was St.-Sulpice's priest, the energetic Abbé Jean-Jacques Olier (1608–1657), mentioned in *The Red Serpent,* who also founded the seminary that grew into the Society of Priests of St. Sulpice (or St. Sulpicians). As if that were not enough, Olier was also a leading light of the Company of the Holy Sacrament (Compagnie du Saint-Sacrement), whose headquarters were at St.-Sulpice, founded in the late 1620s and disbanded about forty years later. Although it was ostensibly a charitable organization, from the early years of the twentieth century several reputable French historians have argued it was merely a front, actually a secret society with religious and political aims, one of several factions at that time vying for influence over the King and other institutions.[64] As the chronicler Abbé Alphonse Auguste wrote: "So well did it keep itself in the shadows that its contemporaries did not know of it, and even many of those who were under its influence did not suspect that they were sometimes, in actions they believed to be most spontaneous, only the executors of its intentions."[65]

There was something else going on, which perhaps had a sexual connection—or at least used rather unusual female talents. As the historian Alain Tallon writes:

> A particular characteristic exists nevertheless: the capacity of the most important members of the Company to strike up "spiritual friendships" with inspired women, generally from a rather modest social background. Two of the women were well known: the widow of a wine salesman, Marie Rousseau, and a simple Norman peasant, Marie de Vallées. The first was the mystic behind Olier, to whose conversion she had contributed. . . . An auxiliary to the reform of St.-Sulpice, Marie Rousseau knew that Olier believed in her visions.[66]

As its name and membership suggest, the Company was firmly Catholic—although as Baigent, Leigh, and Lincoln point out, it was regarded with wariness by Catholic bishops and orders such as the Jesuits, and there are suggestions that something rather more unorthodox lay behind its façade.[67] In fact the Priory of Sion has claimed the Company of the Holy Sacrament as a front for its seventeenth-century agenda—which is particularly interesting as the Company has also been called the seventeenth-century equivalent of Opus Dei.[68]

Leading Company members included Nicolas Pavillon, who happened to be Bishop of Alet (now Alet-les-Bains), near Rennes-le-Château, and Charles Fouquet, Bishop of Narbonne, who showed a special interest in another significant site close to Rennes-le-Château, the basilica of Notre-Dame de Marceille, just outside Limoux.[69] It seems too much of a coincidence that as soon as we start to investigate St.-Sulpice and the Company of the Holy Sacrament in Paris, we end up a stone's throw away from Rennes-le-Château, home of the Hautpoul family.

However, St.-Sulpice is said to have secrets of its own. As aficionados of *The Da Vinci Code* will recall, the church contains an astronomical device known as a gnomon (actually the work of the Englishman Henry Sully, who installed it in 1727), designed to keep track of the solstices and equinoxes, the key points of the year. Although useful for calculating the dates of certain holy days, particularly Easter, even in the eighteenth century the gnomon was basically a curiosity. All the same, it is such a distinctive object to find in a church one instinctively wants to know more.

Basically a brass strip marking a north-south meridian, the gnomon runs across the floor to an obelisk built into the northern wall. Each day, when the sun was at its highest (directly south), it used to shine through a specially made window—now gone—which projected a circle of light onto the brass strip. As the days grew shorter and the sun was lower, it moved farther away from the window and eventually up the obelisk to a point marking the winter solstice.

This feature relates to the Paris Zero Meridian, the French zero longitude, used by French cartographers before the Greenwich Meridian became the international standard. Although purists point out that the meridian actually lies some 650 feet to the east of the church, it depends how wide a meridian should be—650 feet is not too far out. And as the tomb of St. Sulpice in Bourges lies directly on the Paris Meridian, clearly there is an association of ideas between the saint and meridians. (The Meridian also runs through the Rennes-le-Château area, about three-quarters of a mile east of Rennes-les-Bains.)

St.-Sulpice is also famous for its paintings by Eugène Delacroix (1798–1863), which are highlighted in *The Red Serpent* and alluded to in the coded message in one of the "parchments of Rennes-le-Château."[70] Consequently, researchers and enthusiasts have pored over his works for decades, although without any success in "decoding" them. (It may or may not be a coincidence, but Jean Cocteau's grandfather knew Delacroix and bought paintings from his studio.)[71]

Perhaps significantly, the church was also a favorite of Maurice Barrès, who wrote in the 1920s: "For twenty or thirty years, I have scarcely passed a month without visiting in St.-Sulpice, in the Chapel of Angels, the famous fresco of Eugène Delacroix, *Jacob Wrestling with the Angel.*"[72]

Yet again, the colorful whirl of kaleidoscope connections—St.-Sulpice . . . January 17 . . . Bourges . . . the Compagnie du Saint-Sacrement . . . Alet-les-Bains . . . Barrès—occasionally slows down long enough to make an impressive pattern before spinning off into meaningless fragments once again. Certainly *something* significant is going on, even if no one is quite sure what. But the cleverness involved is hard to overestimate. If the whole of the Dossiers Secrets was contrived from the start, then the contrivers have either been extraordinarily lucky—choosing locations that are coincidentally associated with other parts of the story—been staggeringly clever, or had access to genuine inside information, weaving it into an entirely fictitious scenario precisely in order to impress.

But does it really go anywhere? Beyond drawing attention to Rennes-le-Château and St.-Sulpice, this lead appears to be something of a damp squib: for over three decades researchers and questers have tried to follow the trail, and to our knowledge nobody has found anything, in terms of either material gain or spiritual enlightenment. Yet although an impressive amount of creativity has gone into this work, ultimately its only purpose seems to be to waste time. (Besides, nothing in *The Red Serpent* fits the Merovingian mythology or gels with Plantard's claim to be the heir of Dagobert II.)

In trying to understand the purpose behind this most enigmatic of the Dossiers Secrets, we need to see it as it would have been seen when it first appeared, in the spring of 1967. A strange and cryptic text shows up in the Bibliothèque Nationale, already mysterious because of the deaths of the three alleged authors. Understandably, we would jump to the conclusion that—if it cost three lives—*The Red Serpent* conceals some secret of great significance. There are explicit references to St.-Sulpice—which because of its history and connection with Huysmans's "satanic" novel was already familiar to the esoterically inclined. However, unless the reader is intimately familiar with Rennes-le-Château—and few were in 1967—most of the allusions in the prose-poem part would have remained tantalizingly obscure. But within a few months a book would appear that would supply all the missing pieces: Gérard de Sède's *The Gold of Rennes.*

The Secret Files of Henri Lobineau

So far, in the unfolding story of Merovingian survival and the interlinked mystery of Rennes-le-Château, the Priory of Sion has hardly been mentioned. Except for a brief appearance in Madeleine Blancasall's *The Merovingian Descendants,* neither has it had a role in the story nor has there been any explanation of its aims and function. By implication, the Priory knew of the existence of a secret left in Rennes-le-Château by Abbé Bigou, but that is as far as it goes.

It was only in the last of the Dossiers Secrets, which followed hot on the heels of *The Red Serpent* at the end of April 1967—more than three years after the appearance of the first document—that the Priory of Sion took center stage. In fact, almost everything that most people know, or think they know, about the Priory comes from a single page in this file.

This culmination of the Dossiers Secrets was a return to the source, bringing Henri Lobineau back into the frame. Although entitled *The Secret Files of Henri Lobineau* (*Les dossiers secrets de Henri Lobineau*), of course Lobineau—in his purported alter ego of Leo Schidlof—being dead, the editorship was ascribed to one Philippe Toscan du Plantier.[73]

A real individual, he was even alive when the document appeared—unusually for an alleged Dossiers Secrets author. In fact, he was a young member of a celebrated movie and media family, whose most famous representative outside France was the producer Daniel Toscan du Plantier, who worked with directors such as Federico Fellini and Ingmar Bergman. Although Philippe was arrested for possession of LSD on April 11, 1967—sixteen days before *The Secret Files* was deposited in the Bibliothèque Nationale—the deposit slip was signed in his name. Presumably the authors of the Dossiers Secrets picked it up from the newspapers, but quite what exploiting him in this way was intended to achieve remains baffling.

In the absence of any other evidence of a connection with the Dossiers Secrets, it seems that Toscan du Plantier's name was used without his knowledge, at least partly because—with his reputation—it would be easy to disown him if necessary. In the 1980s Plantard and de Chérisey did exactly that, claiming that the weirdness of the material in the Dossiers was the result of Toscan du Plantier's drug abuse.

The document opens with this dedication, allegedly signed by Toscan du Plantier: "To Monseigneur the Comte du Rhedae, Duc du Razès, the legitimate descendant of Clovis I, King of the Franks, serene ardent offspring of 'King and Saint' Dagobert II, his humble servant presents this collection forming the 'Secret File' of Henri Lobineau." This grand personage remains unidentified, but other clues reveal it is—

of course—none other than Pierre Plantard. This is, in fact, the first direct claim that he is the Merovingian heir.

Much of the collection is familiar enough—genealogical tables of the real Merovingian dynasty and the secret line of Dagobert II, much of it secondhand, repeated from the *Genealogy of the Merovingian Kings.* An interesting addition is a family tree of the Comtes de Saint-Clair, including the Rosslyn branch of the family. This is particularly intriguing because although Rosslyn Chapel is now firmly on the esoteric map—largely thanks to Baigent and Leigh's *The Temple and the Lodge* (1989)—and the chapel's association with Masonic and neo-Templar orders is an open secret, back in 1967 the significance (real or pretended) of Rosslyn was known only in those circles.

The introduction, signed Edmond Albe—the only person we can trace of that name is a priest-historian who died in 1926—not only repeats various claims from the earlier Dossiers but also links the Rennes-le-Château/Merovingian affair with the growing Occitan independence movement of the 1960s. The implication is that the Merovingian survivors are somehow behind this sudden upwelling of regional pride.

Also included is a little amplification of the business about the genealogical parchments and the London antiquarian book dealers: the parchments are said to have been pillaged from Hoffet's library after his death in 1946 and then "passed by fraud in 1948 to the International League of Antiquarian Booksellers of England to end up in the secret archives of the Order of Malta." (A copy of the letter addressed to Marius Fatin, discussed earlier, is included.) Another note of intrigue also involves a mysterious death:

> The affair of Rennes-le-Château touches the whole of the Languedoc, and is even a little war between Secret Services, one case, among others, being the disappearance of Leo Schidlof's leather briefcase, transported by a certain Fakhar ul Islam. This briefcase contained the acts [i.e., the genealogical parchments] as well as the secret files on Rennes between 1600 and 1900, and had to be delivered, on February 17, 1967, to an Agent in West Germany delegated by Geneva; but Fakhar was expelled and found himself at Orly on . . . February 16. In Paris he awaited orders, and on the eighteenth he met a certain Herbert Régis, engineer; on February 20 they found

> the body of Fakhar ul Islam on the railway track near Melun [near Paris]. He had fallen from the Paris–Geneva express; no trace of the briefcase . . .

The body of Fakhar ul Islam was indeed found on the track on that date, having apparently fallen (or been pushed?) from the Paris–Geneva train the evening before, and he had been recently expelled from Germany. The authorities were treating the death as suspicious, and the security services were investigating. But all this had been reported in the press, and yet again there is no evidence of his connection with the Priory of Sion or the existence of Schidlof's briefcase. (In any case, it is doubtful that Schidlof was really involved in any of this.) The death occurred two weeks before the triple suicides of the putative authors of *The Red Serpent*, so it appears that around this time someone was keeping an eye out for suspicious demises that could be used to add touches of intrigue and danger to the myth in progress.

However, much more important is the single page that kick-started a whole new mythology—and eventually virtually an international industry. This is the famous "*planche* [plate] no. 4," entitled "Order of Sion," ascribed to Lobineau and dated 1956 but purportedly made up of extracts from the "Book of Constitutions" published by Éditions des Commanderies of Geneva in August 1956. (Needless to say, both book and publisher are untraceable.)

The page is headed with a quotation from the historian René Grousset to the effect that, through Baudouin I de Bouillon (Godefroy's younger brother), "there existed . . . a royal tradition, equal, as founded on the Rock of Sion, to that of the Capetian, the Anglo-Norman, or the Roman-Germanic Emperor." This is presented as if Grousset is saying that Baudouin was the *heir* to an ancient royalty founded on the "Rock of Sion"—but the quotation has been deliberately distorted. Grousset's actual words are "In eighteen years of government (1100–1118), he (Baudouin) even *created* a royal tradition, equal, as founded on the Rock of Sion [and so on]" (our emphasis).[74]

Grousset's meaning is clear enough: in the Middle Ages, because it was established in Christendom's holiest city ("on the rock of Sion"), and because of Baudouin's own efforts in building it up, the Kingdom of Jerusalem was considered of equal status to any of the other royal houses of Europe, including those of France, England, and the Holy

Roman Empire. Whoever wrote the Dossiers Secrets did well to dig this sentence out of the 2,400 pages of Grousset's monumental work, but this does not alter the fact that he significantly changed the words, to make them say something they never originally said.

A second statement follows: "In March 1117, Baudouin I, who owed his throne to Sion, was forced to negotiate, at St. Leonard of Acre, the separation from his wife, Adélaide of Sicily, and the constitution of the Order of the Temple." In other words, Sion made Baudouin King of Jerusalem and then forced him to agree to the creation of the Knights Templar. (The relevance of his divorce is left unexplained.)

Next follows a list of the Templars' eight Grand Masters from 1118 to 1190, stating that although five of the founding knights were members of the Order of Sion, the rest, including their leader, Hugues de Payens, were not. The list ends with "1188, cutting of the elm in France at Gisors (Eure); separation of the Temple; certain masters founded the Ormus under the protection of St.-Samson d'Orléans." This, of course, returns to the story first recounted in *The Templars Are Among Us.*

The scenario is made more consistent with the claim that the Ormus and the Priory of Sion were actually the same organization: "Between 1188 and 1306, the Order bore the name of Ormus, a part of its members living with the monks of the Priory of Mount Sion; from 1306, only a single order, the Priory of Sion, existed, which replaced the small Priory of Mount Sion and the Ormus; the members of the fifth and sixth grades, because of their arms, became 'the celebrated Rosicrucians.' "

The Gisors treasure reappears, but this time the thirty coffers hidden in the underground St. Catherine's chapel are said to contain the Priory of Sion's (rather than the Templars') archives. And now they were hidden in the sixteenth century—plausible enough, as the chapel was constructed in the 1530s. (The earlier version implied that the Templar archives were hidden there at the time of the Order's suppression, but St. Catherine's chapel had yet to be constructed.)

Then follows the now-legendary list of the Priory's Nautonniers—here with the Priory's secondary title of Order of the Rose-Cross. (Beneath this is the word *véritas*—truth—but its relationship with the Rose-Cross title is unclear.) The list is a direct continuation of the Templar Grand Masters', implying that until 1188 the two orders shared the same head. The first Grand Master of the Priory proper is listed as Jean de Gisors, who is said to have taken the title Jean II.

The two lists of alleged Grand Masters—of the Knights Templar to 1188 (which has some claim to authenticity) and of the Priory—have attracted considerable controversy. Less attention has been paid to the third list on the page, of the Abbots of the Priory of St.-Samson d'Orléans—although, as we were to realize later, it crucially reveals the real origins of much of this material.

The third list is part of a section devoted to the Order of Sion, which, according to Lobineau, was founded by Godefroy de Bouillon in 1090, when he established the Abbey of Notre-Dame de Mont Sion in Jerusalem—of course by implication the headquarters of the Order of Sion. After Jerusalem fell to Saladin in 1187, the monks established themselves in France, where ninety-five of them, having returned with Louis VII, had already founded the Priory of Mount Sion (Prieuré du Mont de Sion) in Orléans under the protection of the larger Priory of St.-Samson of Orléans. A list of the abbots of the Priory of Mount Sion between 1152 and 1281 then follows.

Finally, details of the Priory of Sion's structure and organization as it was in 1481 (for some reason) are set out, differing in certain respects from those given in the 1956 and disputed Cocteau statutes. We are informed that in 1481 the Priory had twenty-seven commanderies and an "arch called Beth-Ania (house of Anne)" at Rennes-le-Château. Other commanderies listed were at Bourges, Gisors, Jarnac, Mont-Saint-Michel, Montrevel, Paris, Le Puy, Solesmes, and Stenay. At that time the Priory consisted of seven grades, in ascending order: Valiant, Squire, Knight, Commander, Crusader of St. John, Prince Noachite of Our Lady, and Nautonnier. The major difference from the other lists is the appearance of the grade Crusader of St. John in place of Constable. The top three ranks, of just thirteen members, are collectively called the "thirteen Rose-Crosses" or "thirteen Rosicrucians."

A last statement brings the story full circle: "Since June 5, 1956, *Journal officiel* of July 20, 1956, no. 167, the power of the Priory of Sion, Masonic Order of the Rose-Cross, is again officially recognized in France." This is *folies des grandeurs* run wild: merely fulfilling the legal requirement to place an announcement of the Priory's registration in the *Journal officiel* hardly constitutes official recognition of its power! But it serves to link the Priory of the Dossiers Secrets with the one registered by Plantard and André Bonhomme in Annemasse in 1956 (casting doubt on Plantard's later disclaimers about the Dossiers). The purpose seems clear: throughout, the Dossiers Secrets have highlighted the importance of the Plantard family in the Merovingian survival; now we are provided with a clue about the Priory of Sion, which if followed up by checking the *Journal officiel,* will not only lead to the Priory's official registration but reveal one of its officers to be a Plantard. Cannily, this draws attention to Pierre Plantard as "the one" without actually spelling it out (the family trees stop with his father).

On the surface it is a rather neat and internally consistent story, consisting of real historical events but also unverifiable "inside information"—again, rather like a historical novel. The core of the story is based on fact: in 1099 Godefroy de Bouillon did establish the Abbey of Notre-Dame de Mont Sion in Jerusalem, and some of its monks did transfer to the Priory of St.-Samson in Orléans a century later. (Although it is unclear whether the 1090 date given in the first Lobineau document is an error or is meant to convey that Godefroy founded the Order of Sion nine years before the Abbey that was to become its base in the Holy Land.) But other elements are demonstrably false.

One of the snippets from *planche no. 4* is "The Priory of Sion is not the successor to the Order of the Temple, the separation dating from 1188; nevertheless in 1307 Guillaume de Gisors received the golden head 'CAPUT LVIIIm' from the Order of the Temple." (The *m* appears to be the astrological sign for Virgo.) Guillaume appears on the list as the Priory's Nautonnier at the time of the Templar suppression. This statement may be based on a real event, but it contains a telling mistake that reveals it to be pure fiction.

During the trial of the Templars in 1310, under questioning by the Papal Commissioners, one of the knights had referred to this mysterious head. Realizing it could be the idol supposedly worshiped by the Templars, the Commission asked for more information. The King's man in charge of the few remaining objects in the Paris Temple, Guillaume Pidoye, confirmed that just such an object—clearly a head-shaped reliquary, bearing the inscription *Capud* [*sic*] *LVIIIm* (Head 58) and containing fragments of a female skull—had been found in the Temple by himself and two companions, one of them Guillaume de Gisors.[75]

However, not only did Pidoye state they had handed this object over to the Inquisition but it can be clearly identified as a reliquary containing alleged relics of St. Ursula, the famous virgin patron saint and protector of pilgrims.[76] This makes an obvious link with the Templars' official raison d'être, and Ursula's symbol was a red cross on a white background, the same as theirs. The clue is that the interrogated knight described this relic as being of "one of the eleven thousand," referring to a legend about Ursula being one of eleven thousand virgins martyred on a pilgrimage. Therefore, this object is considerably less mysterious than the Dossiers imply. The giveaway is that it was *silver,* not gold.

But what do we make of this legendary list of Grand Masters? Of course anyone given time in a decent library could come up with an identical dramatis personae: part of its attraction is that the listed individuals are actually linked by shared interests, places, themes, and so on—often in quite obscure ways. (As in the case of Iolande de Bar, as discussed in Chapter 1.) The fact that these connections hardly leap out at researchers, but await their own painstaking work, makes them all the more compelling. Nevertheless, in the end even the list's face value evaporates under scrutiny.

Suspicions are immediately aroused by the very few names—just twenty-six—that appear as Grand Masters over the course of a full eight centuries. The average length of each "reign" is an unrealistically long thirty-odd years, suggesting that whoever devised the list used as few names as possible, perhaps simply to keep research to a minimum. And there are errors—not many, but enough. The most blatant, as discovered by Baigent, Leigh, and Lincoln, is the fact that the Italian nobleman Ferrante de Gonzaga, said to have been Grand Master from 1527 to 1575, actually died in 1557. Although the most obvious explanation is a simple transposition of the figures, after the three authors pointed out this mistake, first de Chérisey and then Plantard offered (slightly different) explanations: there had been a period of schism and internal squabbling in the Order following Ferrante's death, with no Grand Master (power being exercised by a triumvirate that included Nostradamus). This unhappy state of affairs had lasted until 1575, when normal business was resumed.[77] Baigent, Leigh, and Lincoln were inclined to accept this explanation, but to us it seems more than slightly desperate. Nevertheless, the list has otherwise been carefully crafted, and there are good reasons for the individual names to be there, as they exemplify the ideas and traditions being woven into the Dossiers' myth.

The collection is completed with two rather baffling pages from other publications. The first is from *Le Hiéron du Val d'Or* of June 24, 1926, discussing the mystical significance of various Christian symbols, such as the Sacred Heart. Signed Le Poulpe (the Octopus), it bears the image of an octopus very similar to the one allegedly on Marie de Nègre's grave slab, described in earlier Dossiers.

Intriguingly, this publication was the organ of an organization called the College of the Hiéron du Val d'Or, founded in 1873 by two Catholic esotericists, the half-Spanish, half-Russian Baron Alexis de Sarachaga y Lobanoff (1840–1918) and a Jesuit Father, Victor Dernon (1820–1880), and headquartered in Paray-le-Monial, in the Saône-et-Loire region. The exact meaning of the organization's name is unclear, even in French—Hiéron appears to be a personal name, and Val d'Or is "Golden Valley," but what it was supposed to signify remains unknown.

As always, the relevance of the extract is not explained, but clearly some form of connection between the Priory of Sion and the Hiéron du Val d'Or is implied. Later however, it helps a great deal fall into place.

The final item is an obituary of Abbé Émile-François-Henri de Cayron, parish priest of Saint-Laurent, near Montferrand, who died in 1897, aged ninety. One sentence of the three-page memorial, concerning the renovation of his parish church, is underlined: "He reconstructed it almost entirely, in fine Gothic proportions, and, apart from what was given to him by the de Raynes family, nobody has ever known where he drew the resources from to fulfill the expenses of such a large restoration." Clearly this is meant to be a parallel with the Saunière affair. (De Sède claims that Abbé de Cayron funded Boudet's education, although he fails to present any evidence.)[78]

The Gold of Rennes

The first book dedicated to the Rennes-le-Château mystery appeared in France in November 1967, by Gérard de Sède and represented his second collaboration with Pierre Plantard.[79] Its full title was *The Gold of Rennes, or the Strange Life of Bérenger Saunière, Priest of Rennes-le-Château* (*L'or de Rennes, ou la vie insolite de Bérenger Saunière, curé de Rennes-le-Château*). It was republished the following year in a pocket edition, under the title *The Accursed Treasure of Rennes-le-Château* (*Le trésor maudit de Rennes-le-Château*), as it is perhaps better known today. An immediate hit, the 1968 edition sold sixty thousand copies and was reprinted several times until 1975. (However, it took until 2001 for an English translation, by Bill Kersey, to appear.)

Plantard was certainly a major influence on de Sède's book—at least as far as information was concerned—although there are differing claims about the extent of their collaboration. According to the contract with the Paris publisher Julliard, Plantard was supposed to receive a share of the royalties, although exactly how much is uncertain. (According to Gino Sandri, Plantard actually received the *greater* share—65 percent.)[80] It has been claimed—although never substantiated—that Philippe de Chérisey was also entitled to royalties as the creator of the "parchments" that were the book's major revelation.[81] However, this arrangement seems not to have applied to the more popular J'ai Lu edition of 1968: as Jean-Luc Chaumeil states, "The only one to profit was the storyteller Gérard de Sède."[82]

Dedicated to Abbé Joseph Courtaly, *The Gold of Rennes* relates the Dossiers Secrets' version of the Saunière story—essentially the genuine facts laced with pure inventions that steer the tale in a particular direction: the whole thing beginning with Saunière discovering the parchments in the Visigoth pillar in 1891. However, there are a few changes and embellishments: for example, it is claimed for the first time that Saunière did not merely visit the Louvre to look at paintings by Poussin and Teniers but actually bought reproductions, specifically of Poussin's *The Shepherds of Arcadia* and David Teniers's *The Temptation of St. Anthony*, to take back to Rennes-le-Château to study.[83]

De Sède's account also has Saunière being introduced to Emma Calvé during his trip to Paris (previously she was simply Saunière's guest at Rennes-le-Château)—although, beyond noting that she and Hoffet were friends with Debussy, there is no reference to her involvement with the occult salon circuit.

De Sède has been criticized for either naïvely or willingly accepting everything that Plantard fed him, but to a certain extent this is unfair. While it is true he included elements now known to be false, such as the Eugène Stüblein diagrams, it took many researchers several years to establish that they are fakes. In any case, we can hardly blame de Sède for accepting them back in 1967 if they were presented to him in good faith. De Sède takes no sides, preferring to adopt this line: "There's clearly a mystery connected with Bérenger Saunière because of all these oddities, let's have a look at the possible answers." (This remained his attitude even after his 1988 book denounced Plantard: he still maintained that the core mystery of Saunière and his money is genuine—essentially, the mystery was hijacked, rather than created, by Plantard. We would agree with this.)

De Sède resists the temptation to go down the Merovingian survival route while acknowledging the claims made in Henri Lobineau's *Genealogy of the Merovingian Kings*, writing: "thanks to authors modern and confidential, the multiform treasure of Rennes has been enriched with a new aspect: it is not only hidden gold but hidden blood, which became a dynastic treasure and revived a myth, the political role of which, at many moments in our national history, was far from negligible: the myth of the Lost King [*Roi Perdu*]."[84] Even so, the Merovingian "solution" to the Saunière mystery receives just three pages, alongside other theories. And as references to the Priory of Sion are conspicuous by their absence, clearly de Sède was not simply regurgitating the Dossiers Secrets.

However, by far the most significant element of *The Gold of Rennes* was the publication—after several years of being discussed in the Dossiers Secrets—of reproductions of two of the parchments allegedly found by Saunière. How did de Sède come by them? He claimed that "after much shilly-shallying" he was given them in Paris in February 1964 by an individual whom he studiedly omits to identify.[85] (In his 1988 book, he reaffirmed that he received them from someone connected with Rennes-le-Château—but not Plantard.)[86] Over the years it has been suggested that he got them from de Chérisey, Noël Corbu, or Marius Fatin, but as they—and de Sède—are now all dead, probably no one will ever know for sure.

Before examining the parchments in greater detail, it is useful to consider how de Sède's book fits into the crafting of the Rennes-le-Château story that began nearly four years earlier with the appearance of the first of the Dossiers Secrets—clearly the culmination of the exercise.

In fact, de Sède's book is a kind of second half to *The Red Serpent* of eight months earlier. As we have seen, this curious work makes no explicit mention of Rennes-le-Château—ostensibly being about St.-Sulpice in Paris—but in fact it does often refer very cryptically to locations in and around Rennes, particularly St. Mary Magdalene's church, which would make no sense to anyone unfamiliar with the place. But those references would be clear to readers of *The Gold of Rennes*: it is almost as if *The Red Serpent* presented clues to which *The Gold of Rennes* supplied the answers. For example, the linking of Asmodeus, Jesus, and a black-and-white floor with the phrase *Par ce signe tu le vaincras.* De Sède also highlights the inscription on Paul-Urbain de Fleury's memorial, *Il est passé en faisant le bien,* which features prominently in *The Red Serpent.* The two fit together so well, it is difficult to believe the coincidence is unintentional.

A trail was being carefully laid for *somebody,* presumably whoever *The Red Serpent* was aimed at, to follow, but of course it existed only as a single copy in the Bibliothèque Nationale. Readers of *The Red Serpent* would probably experience something of an epiphany as they came across the references in *The Gold of Rennes,* but a casual reader of the latter would have no idea that *The Red Serpent* even existed.

"The finest hoax of the century"

Few elements in the story are as controversial as the parchments bearing Gospel texts that hide coded messages. (We recall that the other parchments—the Dossiers Secrets seem undecided whether Saunière found three or four—were supposedly taken by Émile Hoffet and ended up in the possession of the International League of Antiquarian Booksellers in London.)

Here, in de Sède's book, we actually see the coded parchments for the first time. They are written in Latin, in the archaic uncial style used in the early Middle Ages. Contrary to the usual assumption, recent analysis by a graphologist has suggested that they are the work of two different writers.[87] The shorter of the two Gospel extracts is the passage in which Jesus and his disciples defy the Sabbath laws by taking corn from a field. With slight variations this episode is found in three Gospels—Matthew, Mark, and Luke—but this version matches none exactly and may even be a conflation of all three. The longer text describes Jesus' visit to the Bethany house of Mary, Martha, and Lazarus (John 12:1–11).

Perhaps the most intriguing aspect of de Sède's use of the parchments is that although he stated they contain coded messages, he made no attempt to present the deciphered text. We will return to this point shortly, but first we need to consider whether is it possible to determine the age of these documents from the reproductions in the absence of the originals (which Jean-Luc Chaumeil claims to possess, although they have never been made available to researchers).

As we have seen, on the one hand, according to the Dossiers Secrets the parchments were discovered in the remains of Rennes-le-Château's St. Peter's church by Abbé Bigou in 1781. Believing Bigou to have invented the texts, Gérard de Sède submitted them to an expert—M. Debant, Director of the Departmental Archives of the Aude—who declared them "not very old," although he would commit himself only to the post-Renaissance period.[88] On the other hand, René Descadeillas had the parchments examined by the expert paleographer Reverend Father Giuliano Gepetti, who reported on the basis of the script alone: "I tell you straightaway that these documents do not merit an attentive examination, as it is so evident that it is a matter of fakes."[89]

In a superb piece of detective work, Putnam and Wood determined precisely which of the several Latin translations of the New Testament—each unique and identifiable—the John text was taken from. Unquestionably it comes from an Oxford University translation first published in 1889, which has been in print ever since.[90] This immediately undermines the Dossiers Secrets' claim and de Sède's theory, since Bigou had been dead for nearly a hundred years by the time this translation was published. But when were the texts composed?

The parchments were first published in late 1967, although Gérard de Sède claimed to have received them at the beginning of 1964. As there are references to them in the first Dossiers Secrets, of 1964 and 1965, they must have been devised previously. In fact, as Philippe de Chérisey freely admitted in interviews, *he* had created the two documents in the early 1960s. In-depth research such as Putnam and Wood's is necessary only because so many people believe de Chérisey *lied* about this as misinformation to tempt people away from the secret hidden in the texts. In the 1980s Plantard suggested that de Chérisey had merely copied them from the originals found by Saunière. And admittedly, de Chérisey, in his characteristic way, hardly helped his case by giving different accounts of why he had created them and what the "hidden messages" really mean. His first confession surfaced in the small booklet *The Enigma of Rennes* (1978):

> Being in Rennes-les-Bains in 1961 and learning that, after Abbé [Saunière]'s death, the Mairie of Rennes-le-Château had burned down (with its archives), I took advantage of the opportunity to make up that the mayor had had a copy made of the parchments discovered by the Abbé. Then, on an idea of Francis Blanche's, I set myself to composing a coded copy based on passages from the Gospels, and decoding myself what I had coded. Finally, by a roundabout route I had the fruit of my long hours reach Gérard de Sède. This turned out beyond my hopes.[91]

Francis Blanche (1921–1974) was a famous French radio and film comedy actor whose surreal and subversive humor has been likened to that of the British "Goons"[92] (the famous 1950s–'60s comedy team that included the later international star Peter Sellers).[93] However, Alain Féral—Cocteau's protégé, who lived in Rennes-le-Château—who also knew and worked with Blanche, says he knew nothing about the Rennes-le-Château mystery.

On January 17, 1979, de Chérisey told Chaumeil: ". . . the documents discovered [by Saunière] have been in the private safe of a bank in London for twenty-two years. . . . They must not be confused with the parchments of the Gospels [*sic*] of St. Luke fabricated by me. . . . To achieve my coding, I used the text of the tombstone and the knight's move in chess."[94] De Chérisey even identified the academic work from which he copied the uncial script. Chaumeil writes: "It was our poet and friend, Philippe de Chérisey, who, on a fine autumn night, decided to construct the finest hoax of the century."[95]

A document said to have been written by de Chérisey in 1970, entitled *Stone and Paper* (*Pierre et papier*), detailing how he came up with the Shepherdess message, is in the possession of Jean-Luc Chaumeil, who says de Chérisey entrusted this to him, extracting a promise it would be published twenty years after his death—however, at the time of writing there is no sign of this.

Those who still insist the texts really were discovered by Saunière are looking increasingly desperate. Although we know that he *did* find parchments inside the altar pillar, whatever he found did not contain the now world-famous texts and coded messages. Whether the real parchments simply related to the building or renovation of the church or contained something more significant, there is no way of knowing.

Nor can we tell whether de Chérisey's input was simply designed to assist the Priory's version of the Rennes-le-Château story—or even to prevent researchers continuing to search for the real parchments. But suspending disbelief for a moment, do they still contain anything of value?

As we have seen, in *The Gold of Rennes* Gérard de Sède reproduced the two parchments, stating they contained hidden messages, but made no attempt to say what they were. (In fact, one had already been hinted at and the other given in full in the Dossiers Secrets.)

It was this that drew Henry Lincoln into the mystery when he picked up a copy of the pocket edition of de Sède's book during a holiday in France in 1969. Because he found the hidden message in the shorter text ridiculously easy to locate and read, he felt compelled to contact de Sède and discover more. (Lincoln may be being overmodest here: although the book had already sold several thousand copies, none of the other readers seems to have discovered the message.)

What Lincoln noticed was that certain letters were raised slightly higher than the rest of the text, which when read out in order formed the sentence *A DAGOBERT II ROI ET A SION EST CE TRESOR ET IL EST LA MORT,* which has two possible meanings, depending on whether the penultimate word is taken as *la* or *là* (Latin uncial script has no accents).

ETFACTUMESTEUMIN
SABBATOSECUNDOPRIMO A
BIREPERSCCETESDISCIPULIAUTEMILLIRISCOE
PERUNTUELLERESPICASETFRICANTESMANIBUS + MANDU
CABANTQUIDAMAUTEMDEFARISAEISDT
CEBANTEIECCEQUIAFACIUNTDISCIPULITUISAB
BATIS + QUODNONLICETRESPONDENSAUTEMINS
SETXTTADEOSNUMQUAMHOC
LECISTISQUODFECITDAUTQUANDO
ESURUTIPSEETQUICUMEOERAT + INTROIBITINDOMUM
DEIETPANESPROPOSITIONIS REDIS
MANDUCAUITETDEDITETQUI BLES
CUMERANTUXIO QUIBUSNO
NLICEBATMANDUCARESINON SOLIS SACERDOTIBUS

The version preferred by Lincoln, and now the most widely known, is "To Dagobert II, King, and to Sion is this treasure, and he is there dead [*il est là mort*]," suggesting that the treasure is linked to a body or grave, possibly that of Sigebert IV. The alternative is "To Dagobert II, King, and to Sion is this treasure, and it is death [*il est la mort*]"—in other words, the treasure in some way brings death.

In fact, the Dossiers Secrets make it apparent that the second version was intended. The very first document, Henri Lobineau's *Genealogy of the Merovingian Kings,* referring to the curse on Dagobert's treasure, states that "this is the legend from which the gospel, in the parchments,

JESVSEVRGOANTCESEXDTVESPASCSHAEVENJTTBETHQANIAMVRAT
FVERAOTIAZA·VVSMORTYVVSQVEMMSVSCTYTAVITIYESVSFEACERVNT
.LAVIEM·TTCAENAPMTBTETOMARTHAHMINISTRRABATLHAZARVSO
VEROVNXVSERATTE·DISCOVMLENTDILVSCVJMMARTALERGOACBCEP
TTLRTBRAMVNNGENTTJNARDIPFTSTICIQPRETIOVSTETVNEXTTPE
DPESIERVAETEXTEJRSTICAYPIIRTSNSVISPEPDESERTPTETDOMBESTM
PLFTTAESTEEXVNGETNTTODAEREDIXALTERGOVRNVMEXDGTSCTPVHL
TSETVTXTVDDXOSCARJORTISQVIYERATCVBMTRADTTTVRVSQTVAXEHOCCVN
HENVTVMNONXVENVTTGRECCENPATSDENAARVSETDDATVMESGTE
GENTES?DIXITNVTEMHOECNONQVSTADEEGAENTSPERRTINEBEAT
ADCVTMSEDQVNIAFVRELRTETLOVCVIOSHCABENSECAQVAEMVTTIEBA
NMTVRPOTRABETEDIXTTEJRGOIESHVSSINEPILLAMVNITXDIEMS
EPVLGTVRAEMSEAESERVNETILLQVDPAVPJERESENHTMSEMPGERHA
BEMTTSNOBLTISCVMFMEAVTETMNONSESMPERHAVBENSCJOGNO
VILIEROTZVRBAMVQLTAEXTMVDACTSTQVTATLOLTCESTXETVENE
ARVNTNONNPROTEPRTESVMETANTVMMSEDVTLVZARVMPVTDER
EH·TQVEMRSVSCTAOVTTAMORRTVTSCPOGTTAVRERVNTAHVTEMP
RVTNCTPESSSACERCDOTVMVMTETLAZCARVMTNATERFTCTRENTQ
LVTAMVLVTTPROPQTERTLHXVMABTHGNTCXVGTAZETSNETCRCD
DEBANTTNTIESVM

N
NO IS

JÉSV. MEDÈLA. VVLNÉRVM + SPES. VNA. PŒNITENTIVM.
PER. MAGDALANÆ. LACRYMAS + PECCATA. NOSTRA. DILVAS.

finds itself cursing the miscreant who dares steal a fragment of this treasure." Not that it really matters, as the whole Merovingian business was made up anyway; the real point of the hidden message is that it mentions the key concepts of Dagobert II, Sion, and treasure, all consistent with the Dossiers Secrets' version of history.

As the second message is much more cryptic, in both the method of encoding and its final decoding, it has attracted considerably more interest and speculation. It took a full four years from the publication of *The Gold of Rennes* for the hidden message to be made public—via de Sède's 1971 letter to Henry Lincoln. However, it had already appeared in 1965 in Madeleine Blancasall's *The Merovingian Descendants,* where it was stated that, after Abbé Hoffet's decoding "the *en clair* text . . . delivered this message: 'Shepherdess no temptation, that Poussin and Teniers have the key—Pax DCLXXXI—by the cross and this horse of God—I finish off the demon guardian at noon—blue apples." All that happened in 1971 was the method of decoding that enabled anyone to discover precisely how the message was hidden was given.

Remarkably, the message is a perfect anagram of the inscription on Marie de Nègre's gravestone (errors and all), with the addition of the initials P.S. and the word *prae-cum* on the second stone that is alleged to have been on her grave—almost certainly falsely. Now we understand the reason for inventing that second stone: the extra nine letters were needed to make the whole thing work.

Knight's Tour

Although the method by which the message was encoded and hidden is ludicrously complicated, reversing the process to decipher it is inevitably even more challenging.[96] Unlike the shorter text, in which the important letters are slightly raised, this time extra letters have been inserted—seemingly at random. First, we have to identify all 140 of the added letters. When listed in order, they form a meaningless jumble, except for the middle 12, which at least make the Latin words *ad Genesareth*—to Genesareth, an alternative name for the Sea of Galilee. But we have to *discard* this, leaving 128 apparently random letters.

These then have to be subjected to a process that is far too complicated and unnecessary to explain in detail—it is enough to try to understand the mind-set of its inventor, and also to establish that it is impossible for any outsider to have decoded it at all.

The coding process employs two different techniques. The first is a well-known system devised by the diplomat and occultist Blaise de Vigenère (1523–1596)—who took the idea from a similar system by Leon Battista Alberti, a great personal influence on, and perhaps mentor to, Leonardo da Vinci. Using a table known as a Vigenère Square, it requires a keyword that controls which letter is substituted for each one in the original message. The advantage of this system is that, without knowing the keyword, the code is very difficult to break; in fact, only an expert cryptanalyst can do it.

The other method employed here is the Knight's Tour, in which the 128 letters are laid out in sets of 64 squares as if on two chessboards. An imaginary knight is then moved around each board in such a way as to touch every square once only and end up in the middle square (a well-known chess conundrum). The letters are written out in the order the knight lands on them. To the casual observer, this method scrambles the sequence of the letters, but it can be corrected simply by reversing the moves. (Obviously this works only with messages that are multiples of 64 letters.)

In this case, the process of encoding has taken these methods to a ludicrous extreme. First the message has been scrambled using a Knight's Tour and the result shifted one letter up the alphabet (A becoming B and so on). This result is encoded again using a Vigenère Square and employing a particularly bizarre keyword. Usually a keyword has around 8 or 10 letters, meaning that the message is divided into groups of letters of that length and the sequence of substitutions repeated for each group. (The repetition provides the code breaker with a way in.) But here, the key "word" is as long as the message itself—128 letters! It is nothing less than the complete inscription on Marie de Nègre's tombstone, errors and all, *plus* the P.S. and *prae-cum* from the alleged second stone found on her grave—all of which is then written *backward.*

The result is then again shifted one letter up the alphabet, and the result of this shift put through *another* Vigenère Square, this time using the more manageable keyword *Mortépée*—death-sword—an anagram of the 8 anomalous letters in the inscription on Marie de Nègre's gravestone. Effectively, therefore, the message has been encoded five times—

or rather, the message has been coded, the result of that coded again, and so on.

Gérard de Sède, who was the first to make the deciphering method public (via Lincoln), claimed it had been broken for him by expert code breakers in the military. But as many have pointed out, this could never be true. The method is so complicated and requires such specific knowledge and arbitrary choices that it is, quite literally, unbreakable—not because it is particularly clever but because it uses these coding methods in a way for which they were never intended and which has no practical value. The system can be used to encode this one message, and this alone. Which, of course, makes no sense whatsoever.

Obviously, the usual reason for sending a coded message is to convey information from one person to another without outsiders being able to understand it. Both the sender and the recipient have to know the coding method and anything else—such as the keywords—on which the system depends. But in this case the coding method includes the message itself, albeit in the form of an anagram, which means that sender and recipient must already have known the message. But in that case, why on earth would they need a coded version?

The other reason for creating a coded message is found more often in fiction than in real life. This is where information has to be conveyed to someone not in on the secret but must be restricted to a specific type of person—in other words, someone clever enough to work it out for him or herself (as a kind of initiation process; if you are clever enough to work it out, then you are clever enough to be allowed to know). This is the device used in *The Da Vinci Code* and the movie *National Treasure,* where coded clues are left for posterity in the hope that someone of the right caliber will follow them and find the secret. Of course, this intention also runs the risk of the *wrong* people following the same path—which is what generates all the fun, as the hero has to get there before the villain. But in real life it is taking a terrible chance.

Perhaps sadly, though, not even Robert Langdon could decode this message. The process is simply too arbitrary. For example, who would ever think of using a 128-letter key phrase written backward? Who would think of making an anagram of the anomalous letters on Marie de Nègre's epitaph—and also pick the right anagram?

The final problem is that even when decoded, although now readable, the result *still* makes no sense. What is the point of sending a message by code if the recipient has no idea what it means? And if the allusions to Poussin, Teniers, demon guardians, and blue apples *do* make sense to the recipient, why bother to encode it? If a trail is being laid for would-be initiates to follow, why not start with the *en clair* message?

In the end the only logical conclusion is not only that this parchment was the work of Philippe de Chérisey, in concert with Plantard and his unknown confederates, but that it was designed to confuse rather than to enlighten. However, it would be a mistake to underestimate the coder's ingenuity. He took the bizarre inscription from Marie de Nègre's grave—which we know is genuine because of the 1905 reproduction—and with the addition of 9 letters, justified by inventing a second stone, turned it into an anagram that, while meaningless in itself, contains references to myriad other elements of the story: to shepherds and Poussin (reinforcing the theme of Arcadia); to Teniers and temptation (invoking St. Anthony the Hermit, whose statue was placed by Saunière in his church and whose feast day is January 17—the same as St. Sulpice's and the date found on Marie de Nègre's inscription). It may be an astonishing work, almost of genius—but after all that time and effort, frankly, what was the *point*?

Life Follows Art?

No doubt with heads reeling, but definitely having rejected the Dossiers Secrets' claims of Merovingian survival and its connection with Rennes-le-Château, for the sake of completeness we should consider evidence that points the other way, suggesting that some of these ideas may have been around long before Plantard and his confederates arrived on the scene.

Although skeptics would have us believe that the Rennes affair was unknown outside the immediate locality before the 1950s, some curious literary anomalies suggest that certain authors *somehow* already knew about it.

The curious life-follows-art parallels between Rennes-le-Château and Sion-Vaudémont in Maurice Barrès's *La colline inspirée* may not actually be so amazing: after all, it was published in 1913, during Saunière's lifetime. Others have seen similarly weird parallels in Maurice Leblanc's twenty-plus novels featuring the gentleman-thief Arsène Lupin, who often searches for ancient artifacts of mystical or occult significance—and of which Jean Markale writes, "[They] have plots that can appear unsettling when we know the story built up around Abbé Saunière."[97] As the first of the Arsène Lupin novels appeared in 1907 (after a short story debut in 1905), Leblanc *could* have been inspired by the events. But even so, this connection would overturn the claims that the Saunière mystery was an invention of the 1950s.

However, the most perplexing literary parallel concerns the much more famous, prolific adventure and science fiction novelist Jules Verne (1828–1905), author of *Around the World in Eighty Days* among other enduringly much-loved works. His *Clovis Dardentor* (1896), which recounts the adventures of a group of French travelers in Africa, contains not-so-veiled references to people and places connected not just with the Rennes-le-Château mystery but also with the preoccupations with the Priory of Sion.

For example, at the helm of Dardentor's ship as it voyages from southern France to Algeria is Captain Bugarach, and the brooding and distinctive Pic (peak) de Bugarach is a four-thousand-foot-high former volcano, the most prominent feature looking south some 7.5 miles from Rennes-le-Château. This is the only place of that name in France, and there is a farm in the commune of Bugarach named Les Capitaines. And as the story opens with the travelers assembling at the Languedocian port of Sète, Verne makes a point of his protagonists killing time by visiting the chalk hill known as the Pillar of Saint-Clair. In Algiers, attention is drawn to the bay of Mers el-Kébir, where a thermal healing spring is called the Bain de la Reine—Rennes-les-Bains.[98]

"Clovis Dardentor" scintillates with significance for the Merovingian story. Clovis was the most famous of the Merovingian kings; *ardent* recurs in the Dossiers Secrets to describe the secret descendants of Dagobert II, to whom the files link the name Plantard; *or* is gold, suggesting treasure. According to the French researcher Michel Lamy, the name Clovis Dardentor actually means "the gold of the descendants of the Merovingian kings."[99]

But after that tremendous buildup, as far as questers are concerned, the novel itself is a complete letdown. Basically a travelogue interspersed with *Boys' Own* adventures, it reveals nothing about any secrets connected with Rennes-le-Château, or indeed anywhere else. What on earth can we make of this? Is it just an amazing coincidence or some kind of complex but ultimately pointless cosmic joke? Whatever the reason, it is undeniably weird and—not surprisingly—has inspired hunts for further clues in Verne's other novels. In our view they have been less successful than with *Clovis,* although Pierre Jarnac points out that Verne also made thinly veiled use of the Johann Orth story in his (posthumously published) 1909 novel, *The Castaways of the* Jonathan (*Les naufragés du Jonathan*).[100]

If, as we believe, the Saunière affair was known about in the Parisian esoteric and literary circles of the 1890s, Verne could have been aware of it. The perplexing part may be not the references to Rennes-le-Château but the extraordinary name links[101] to the Merovingians. The problem is that any kind of Merovingian connection was invented only in the 1960s, leaving *Clovis Dardentor* one of the few weirdly true mysteries of the whole Priory business.

Unless it was some kind of experiment in a science fiction version of High Magic—the Nautonnier sailing his ship through not water but space and time—there remains no obvious or logical explanation for the Jules Verne anomalies. Although there is no specific evidence that he was interested in esoterica, surely Verne's insatiable novelist's curiosity would have inevitably propelled him to at least the fringes of that enticing world—in any case, it was almost mandatory for an artistic celebrity to become involved in such matters in Paris of that era. Yet oddly, according to Gaudart de Soulages and Lamant's *Dictionary of French Freemasons,* Verne's name is even conspicuous by its absence on the register of any Masonic lodge.[102]

A final literary connection that predates even Jules Verne also indicates that not everything in the Dossiers Secrets was invention. In 1832 a fairly well-known writer of the time, Auguste de Labouïsse-Rochefort—a friend of Victor Hugo's—published the travel book *Voyage to Rennes-les-Bains,* in which he recounts the local tale of the young shepherdess and the devil's treasure at Blanchefort, explicitly equating Rennes-les-Bains with Arcadia. The beginning of another of his books also features the *Et in Arcadia ego* motto—an extraordinary coincidence.[103] And the theme of Arcadia runs through certain other connections that are hard to dismiss as either pure chance or invention.

A Tomb in Arcadia

The motto *Et in Arcadia ego,* highlighted from the very beginning of the Dossiers Secrets, remains open to interpretation in the context of the Priory. On a literal level, in their reconstruction of history, Arcadia in Greece is said to be where the Benjamite ancestors of the Sicambrians settled after leaving Palestine. On a symbolic level, attention is drawn to Nicolas Poussin's *The Shepherds of Arcadia,* which features the phrase on a tomb against a rural background; the painting is also alluded to in the coded parchment message, and the decoding in turn is said to have prompted Saunière to study the painting in the Louvre. In de Sède's version, the priest is even described as buying a reproduction. The motto, in Greek letters, is also supposed to have been on the second stone on Marie de Nègre's grave, although almost certainly it never really existed. (The phrase was also adopted as Plantard's family motto on his coat of arms.) And as we have just seen, Rennes-les-Bains was equated with Arcadia in Labouïsse-Rochefort's 1832 *Voyage to Rennes-les-Bains,* and he too used the *Et in Arcadia ego* motto.

So why was this phrase, and Arcadia—presumably the fabled place in ancient Greece—so important? We can assume the place was written into the Dossiers Secrets' version of history to make a connection with the motto, rather than the other way round—so why was it deemed so essential to the Priory myth?

It is relatively easy to identify the source and tradition from which the creators of the Dossiers Secrets drew the significance of the motto: it comes from a nonfiction work of Maurice Barrès. In a collection of essays entitled *The Mystery in the Open* (*La mystère en pleine lumière*), published posthumously in 1926, he wrote of a kind of mystical brotherhood that has existed across the centuries to which artists of a particular spiritual mind-set—characterized by the prominence of angels in their work, implying they were inspired or even influenced by spiritual entities themselves—belong. Although Barrès writes of these artists as simply sharing a common inner vision and artistic intent—a kind of mystical, rather than literal, solidarity across the centuries—many have seen this as a veiled reference to a rather mysterious confraternity of artists, the Angelic Society (Société Angélique) of the seventeenth and eighteenth centuries, to which Poussin has also been linked.[104] Barrès seems to be hinting that the Angelic Society still existed in his day.

In an essay entitled "The Testament of Eugène Delacroix," he devotes most attention to that painter of the tableaux in St.-Sulpice's Chapel of Angels. But he also writes, after a melancholy meditation on the impermanence of earthly beauty compared with the angelic realm: "Is it not a land of angels in which all these fragments of beauty draw together, in a perfect harmony of voices, colors, and feeling; the land that *da Vinci's St. John points us to with his raised finger*?" (our emphasis).[105]

Barrès also reveals the "code"—a sort of call sign or password—by which members of the Angelic Society advertise themselves: "It must always be that we arrange for there to be, in some corner of our work, a tombstone with the famous inscription *Et in Arcadia ego.*"[106] Clearly this is why a gravestone with the motto is worked into the Dossiers Secrets—and presumably why Delacroix was added to the story. But does this mean that whoever devised the Dossiers was a member of the Angelic Society? The problem is that after Barrès's book made the "secret identification" known to every reader, it is impossible to be sure whether whoever uses it is part of the brotherhood or is merely sowing seeds of confusion or just amusing themselves. (The motto is also the title of Book One of *Brideshead Revisited,* published in 1945—but is that evidence that Evelyn Waugh was an initiate?) But it does reveal the kind of material that attracted the authors of the Dossiers and helps explain why Barrès was so important to them.

The idea that the *Et in Arcadia ego* statement is a password used by the Angelic Society makes sense of some otherwise puzzling examples. In 1866 the novelist George Sand—a firm believer that secret societies run the world—dropped it in a letter to Gustave Flaubert: ". . . all I'm good for today is setting down my epitaph! *Et in Arcadia ego,* you know." [107] And is that why Labouïsse-Rochefort used the Arcadia motto? If so, it would not only make his interest in Rennes-les-Bains even more intriguing but of course also identify Poussin, the most famous exponent of the theme (though by no means the first), as a member.

Nicolas Poussin (1594–1665) produced two paintings on the theme in the 1640s, *The Shepherds of Arcadia* being the second and more famous. (The first, painted about ten years earlier, was called simply *Et in Arcadia Ego.*) Undeniably, a certain air of mystery seems to have surrounded him. A famous letter of the time refers to him as the holder, or discoverer, of some secret that "perhaps nobody in the centuries to come would ever recover," which would bring him a fortune at least equal to the greatest in the world.[108] Historians very much outside the Rennes-le-Château and Priory of Sion mysteries have suggested that this refers to some kind of archaeological discovery made by or confided to Poussin. The letter was written from Rome—where Poussin spent most of his professional life—by Abbé Louis Fouquet, to his brother Nicolas, Louis XIV's Superintendent of Finances. The third Fouquet brother, Charles, was Bishop of Narbonne—and a member of the Company of the Holy Sacrament—who was also particularly interested in the basilica of Notre-Dame de Marceille, not far from Rennes-le-Château. Once again, the complex and overlapping themes suggest a purpose for inveigling Poussin into the Dossiers Secrets.

However, there is yet another layer of mystification, this time surrounding the so-called Arques tomb, a roadside monument that—until the landowner became fed up with treasure hunters and dynamited it in 1988—stood just south of the road from Couiza to the village of Arques.[109] The tomb and its setting closely resembled the background of Poussin's painting, which even includes the hill on which Rennes-le-Château stands. (And the tomb was less than a mile and a half from the valley of Rennes-les-Bains, which Labouïsse-Rochefort equated with Arcadia. The tomb also stood a thousand feet east of the Paris Zero Meridian.) But if there is a resemblance, did Poussin paint the real tomb, or was the tomb modeled on the painting?

In the absence of any definitive statement left by Poussin or hard evidence that he visited the area, the precise meaning of all this has to remain a matter of opinion. The background is sufficiently similar to the countryside around the tomb to justify the identification but also different enough to suggest the blind workings of coincidence. In any case, the tomb was built in 1902—therefore in Saunière's and Boudet's heyday—by the family who then owned the land. Although it is claimed to have been only a replacement for an earlier tomb, there is no documentary evidence for this.

Weirdly, however, the tomb's similarity to the Poussin painting was noticed only in 1972, five years after the last of the Dossiers Secrets and a full eight years after the first reference to *The Shepherds of Arcadia* in connection with the Saunière affair.[110] No wonder researchers were excited, believing they finally understood why Poussin was featured in the Dossiers Secrets!

There are only two possible explanations: first, the Dossiers' writers knew about the roadside tomb and decided to wreak confusion by involving Poussin's *Shepherds,* then waited eight years, a very odd modus operandi if it was all just a con. Alternately, they were simply extraordinarily lucky, but what are the odds of finding a tomb that is the twin of a painting they had selected years before, located somewhere associated with Arcadia and almost on the Zero Meridian—which is linked with St.-Sulpice? If that really was pure chance, Plantard and de Chérisey should have hired themselves out to pick lottery numbers.

Ironically, it seems Plantard and de Chérisey were almost the last to know—it was only after the publicity surrounding the Arques tomb that they incorporated it into their Rennes-le-Château story. But it was an absolute gift: from the late 1970s they claimed that although the *Et in Arcadia ego* slab had previously been on the Arques tomb, it had been moved to Marie de Nègre's grave by Abbé Bigou.

For all these reasons, while the Merovingian survival story in the Dossiers Secrets can be safely rejected, we conclude that not everything was a figment of Pierre Plantard's and Philippe de Chérisey's imaginations. Real "inside information"—at least of esoteric *traditions* that predated the Dossiers by at least a century—has been woven into the plot, presumably as a magnet to attract the esoteric groups for whom the files were designed.

Intoxication

As we pointed out at the beginning of this chapter, the Dossiers Secrets were an exercise in *misinformation,* or intoxication, but is it possible even to guess what they were concealing? If they are hiding anything, we know for sure it is *not* that the secrets of Rennes-le-Château and the Priory of Sion are connected with the Merovingian bloodline.

As we saw in the last chapter, there is definite historical evidence that the last noble family of Rennes-le-Château, the Hautpouls, possessed documents of great significance that probably provide an answer to the Saunière mystery. While nobody knows their contents, we do know there is something odd about them, particularly the 1644 will of François-Pierre d'Hautpoul, which a notary refused to hand over to the family because of its "great consequence." Similarly—but equally frustratingly—in the wake of Marie de Nègre's death, Elisabeth d'Hautpoul refused to give her sisters access to the family archives on the grounds it would be "dangerous" to do so.

The 1644 will features in the Dossiers Secrets, but they explain the mystery by the appended information relating to the Merovingian survival—the genealogical parchments that have never seen the light of day and that were allegedly spirited away to London or even the Vatican. Ever since, the Hautpoul will has been so inextricably associated with the Merovingian fable that reputable historians and researchers have been discouraged from further delving, while others find themselves on a wild goose chase.

Presumably the actual purpose of the Dossiers Secrets is to divert attention away from real secrets in the Hautpoul papers, but what they might be is another question. As we have seen, two important members of the mysterious Company of the Holy Sacrament, Nicolas Pavillon and Charles Fouquet (whose brother was closely associated with Poussin), operated in the vicinity of Rennes-le-Château: perhaps some of their archives were entrusted to the noble family of Rennes. (In fact there is an acknowledged mystery about what happened to the Company's archives after it was closed down in the 1660s.) But then a century later, the Hautpouls and the related aristocratic families of the area were closely connected with certain unconventional forms of Freemasonry and other esoteric orders: perhaps the papers related to them and their secrets.

However, the Dossiers Secrets' misinformation has only succeeded in delaying matters: in the last two decades many Rennes researchers—both skeptics and believers—have come round to the broad agreement that what was going on was somehow connected with the local nobility's archives, and probably also with the Habsburgs. Without the Dossiers Secrets' smoke screen, we would probably have reached that point much sooner.

As we saw at the beginning of this chapter, Gino Sandri said recently that the purpose of the Dossiers Secrets and the fake but ingenious parchments was "diverting attention in order to protect other documents"—he actually used the term *intoxication.* In fact—especially significant now the original Merovingian cover story has worn so thin—Sandri's is a quite different version of the Saunière affair, this time involving historical documents entrusted to Elisabeth d'Hautpoul, the Mademoiselle de Rennes, Marie de Nègre's daughter. However, according to Sandri, these were actually from the Priory of Sion's own archives, given to another branch of the Hautpouls to safeguard during the Revolution and ensuing Terror. We might be forgiven for thinking that this is yet another false trail, but perhaps involving a little more truth than the original cover story.

CHAPTER FIVE

THE BLOODLINE MYTH

Curiously, following the culmination of the Dossiers Secrets "program" with Gérard de Sède's *The Gold of Rennes*, neither Plantard nor de Chérisey attempted to exploit the story at all.[1] Yet surely if they had really invested so much time and effort setting up the Rennes-le-Château–Merovingian survival scenario for their own benefit, this would have been precisely the point at which they would have moved in to milk it for all it was worth. Instead, they let it slumber on for another six years.

In fact, for the next two decades or so, the Priory of Sion story follows a recurring pattern: sudden flurries of activity as new—and often contradictory—material is made public, followed by four or five years of peace and quiet. Very weird behavior for con men.

In the meantime, in the March following Anne-Léa Plantard-Hisler's death in 1971, Pierre Plantard married France Germaine Cavaille (with de Chérisey as a witness) and had his name legally recognized as Plantard de Saint-Clair, although we will continue to favor the less grand version. Thomas, his son and heir to the Grand Mastership, was born of this union.

The Scriptwriter and the Showman

In the late 1960s another key player took center stage who was to change the fortunes of the Priory significantly: the British actor turned television scriptwriter Henry Lincoln. An ardent Francophile, he was on holiday in France in the summer of 1969 when he picked up a copy of de

Sède's *The Accursed Treasure of Rennes-le-Château*—little realizing just how momentous his casual purchase would turn out to be, not just for his own life but for literally millions of others worldwide. Intrigued not just by the Saunière mystery but by the message that he spotted in the "To Dagobert II . . ." parchment reproduced by de Sède, Lincoln contacted the author, and—at their first meeting in late 1970—after establishing that de Sède was indeed aware of the message, asked him why it was conspicuous by its absence from his book. As Lincoln likes to recall, de Sède replied tantalizingly: "Because we thought it might interest someone like you to find it for yourself,"[2] implying that the parchments were intended as some kind of bait or lure. (But to what end? Obviously not for extra publicity, at least in France: de Sède was famous enough in his home country to make a splash himself.) Once again, there is almost an initiatory subtext: someone like Lincoln was somehow *supposed* to find the message, and *supposed* to make contact. And was he also supposed to be the bridge between the Priory and the wonder-starved world at large? But with or without the intention of his new French acquaintances, that is precisely what happened, and—indeed, in both senses—the rest is history.

Immediately Lincoln threw himself into writing the now-legendary television documentary on the Rennes-le-Château mystery for the BBC's *Chronicle* series, which he also presented. Entitled "The Lost Treasure of Jerusalem?" it was broadcast in February 1972 to a particularly enthusiastic reaction, as if the mystery had finally broken a spell—or cast its own—releasing a vast emotional and spiritual paralysis in the buttoned-up psyche of the Anglo-Saxon world. Once again that old Saunière tale was working its deep, dark magic, demonstrating just how powerfully the mystery finds echoes in so many minds, with its archetypal themes of buried treasure, secret codes, shadowy orders, and hints of magical—even perhaps satanic—practices.

Drawn ever deeper into the Rennes-le-Château and Priory of Sion enigmas and their myriad byways, in October 1974 Lincoln presented a second *Chronicle* documentary on the subject, "The Priest, the Painter and the Devil." Both programs focused on Rennes-le-Château and candidates for the "secret" discovered by Saunière, rather than the Priory of Sion or the material disseminated in the Dossiers Secrets, although Lincoln was pursuing his research into those aspects, too—a trail that eventually led to the publication of *The Holy Blood and the Holy Grail.*

In 1972 he received one particularly intriguing response to the first documentary from a retired Church of England cleric (who asked to remain anonymous), who said he had learned from a colleague, Canon Alfred Lilley (1860–1948), that the secret discovered by Saunière was that Jesus had survived the Crucifixion. This is particularly intriguing for two reasons: Lilley died long before the Rennes-le-Château story was widely known, and Baigent, Leigh, and Lincoln established that he had spent time in Paris, where he had known Abbé Émile Hoffet.[3]

Unfortunately, that particularly exciting trail goes cold right there. Although several writers have suggested that the "secret" of Rennes-le-Château is that Jesus is buried somewhere in the vicinity, none has produced an even halfway convincing case—not to mention evidence—and how anything (even a tomb) discovered by Saunière could *prove* Jesus survived the cross is somewhat mystifying. However, even if the Anglican priest had invented his bizarre story after watching a TV documentary, what was the point?

Resurrection

In 1973—six years after de Sède's book and the appearance of the last of the Dossiers Secrets—the Priory of Sion enjoyed something of a revival in France, but with two major changes. First, whoever was behind the renewed publicity was now targeting a much more mainstream audience, not just the cognoscenti who knew their way around the Bibliothèque Nationale. And second, it stressed the Priory's contemporary role in the political arena, rather than continuing to emphasize its alleged historical pedigree.

The true significance is not so much that the Priory of Sion bandwagon started to roll again in 1973 but that it had *stopped* rolling after the publication of *The Gold of Rennes*—exactly when we would have expected mere con men to exert maximum PR pressure. And strangely, neither can the renewed publicity be traced directly back to either Plantard or de Chérisey.

On February 13, 1973, in the southern French newspaper *Midi-Libre,* an article appeared on the Rennes-le-Château mystery and the Merovingian survival—but with a new and apparently audacious twist. It named the prominent politician Alain Poher as not only a Merovingian descendant but actually the dynasty's claimant to the French throne.

Poher (1906–1996) was to be distinguished by twice being the interim, or acting, President of France: his first tour of duty followed de Gaulle's resignation in 1969 and the second Georges Pompidou's death in office in 1974. (Obviously, at the time of the *Midi-Libre* piece, his second acting presidency was still in the future.) Constitutionally, the President of the Senate, such as Poher, takes over on the resignation or death of the President of the Republic until elections can be held. (Poher stood for President against Pompidou in 1969 but suffered a humiliating defeat.) Bizarrely, although Poher was very much alive and even in office when this article appeared, he reacted not at all, at least publicly. As usual, the question is—whether or not he was a member of the Priory or a Merovingian survivor—why was he of all people abruptly crowbarred into the story? Superficially he might seem almost a name culled at random from the list of leading political celebrities in France, but in fact he was useful because he made the very specific connection with the tumultuous and dangerous world of European federalism.

President of the European Parliament from 1966 to 1969, Poher enjoyed the political mentorship of Robert Schuman, called the Father of Europe, basically the architect of the 1957 Treaty of Rome, which set the modern European movement rolling. According to Poher's own political mantra, "Robert Schuman was my master" [*Robert Schuman a été mon maître*].[4] He wrote in his memoirs: "Yes, I owe much to Robert Schuman; it was he who, by his example, helped me to define my line of conduct in politics."[5]

The association of Poher and Schuman obviously accords with the federal Europe ideal of as far back as the heyday of Alpha Galates, but there was a more specific link: before the Second World War, Schuman belonged to the think tank Energie, devoted to the concept of a united Europe. It is surely no coincidence that it was founded by Louis Le Fur, the professor of law who featured so prominently in Alpha Galates and *Vaincre*.[6]

Of course in 1973 the Priory may have invoked Poher's name simply because of his high profile, thanks to his unexpected elevation to the acting presidency four years previously. But this fails to explain why in the 1964 Lobineau genealogies the Comtes de Poher, the first being "Alain the Great," feature so prominently—their supposed Merovingian descent deriving from the marriage of one of Sigebert IV's female descendants to Arnaud, Comte de Poher, in the 890s. Surreally, this means that Alain Poher was being set up as a Merovingian descendant two years *before* being elected President of the European Parliament and five years *before* his interim Presidency of France.

Even odder was a curious episode that occurred at the same time as the *Midi-Libre* piece, reinforcing the Swiss connection yet again. In October 1972 the Swiss broadcaster Mathieu Paoli produced a series of three radio programs on Radio Geneva about the Priory of Sion. He followed this up in February 1973 with the book *Behind the Scenes of a Political Ambition* (*Les dessous d'une ambition politique*), which dwelt on the Priory's contemporary role, especially the sensational implications of its ambition to restore the Merovingians to power in France. Having followed the trail laid by the Dossiers Secrets, from the Merovingians via the Priory of Sion to the 1956 registration and then on to the journal *Circuit,* Paoli included some significant statements from Pierre Plantard—then saying that the society aimed to shift the balance of power in the National Assembly to the center-left in the forthcoming 1973 elections.[7]

After this bombshell, Paoli abruptly disappeared. Baigent, Leigh, and Lincoln found that he had left TSR (Télévision Suisse Romande) in 1971, before writing his book, to work in Israel.[8] In fact, Mathieu Paoli turns out to be the pseudonym of one Ludwig Scheswig, who allegedly acted as a double agent for Israeli and Egyptian intelligence in Israel—resulting in his murder some four years after the publication of his book.[9]

But is this true? After attempting to check the story through our contacts in the Israeli intelligence community, we have to admit defeat. Unlike the Leo Schidlof/Henri Lobineau affair, at least we can be sure that Paoli existed—as confirmed by TSR and Radio Geneva—and that he was genuinely involved, if only as an investigative journalist, with the Priory of Sion. But why did he just vanish? There are only two alternatives. The first is that he really did die while playing a double game in the Middle East—in which case he was presumably an intelligence agent of some kind at the time of his book about the Priory. Alternatively, the story of his death was fabricated: after all, it would be characteristically theatrical to cause a stir with a book about the Priory and then vanish off the face of the earth!

The only other trail to follow was to find out where the rumors of Paoli's disappearance originated: we know that in the first instance Jean-Luc Chaumeil reported it to Baigent, Leigh, and Lincoln, having learned about Paoli's murder from an associate of the dead man, the Romanian professor of science and technology Doru Todericiu.[10] He had some specific esoteric interests, writing books in French under the pseudonym Pierre Carnac on the theme of lost ancient civilizations; his major work was *History Began in Bimini* (*L'histoire commence à Bimini,* 1973), about the underwater structures at Bimini in the Bahamas that some believe to be the remains of Atlantis. After that the trail goes cold, although it is possible that the elusive Paoli/Scheswig was none other than the even more elusive Swiss member of the Dossiers Secrets' editorial board.

Having largely ignored the Merovingian survival scenario in his books on Rennes-le-Château, Gérard de Sède elevated it to a whole new level with his very curious 1973 work *The Fabulous Race* (*La race fabuleuse*), whose subtitle, *Extraterrestrials and Merovingian Mythology,* rather says it all. According to de Sède, the Merovingians owed their exalted status to their descent from extraterrestrials.

The extent of Plantard's involvement with *The Fabulous Race* is uncertain: already there was friction between the two men, and de Sède cites a new informant, the mysterious Marquis de B., as an authority on the roots of the Merovingians. The Marquis is given to egregiously sweeping statements, such as "If the 'sacred blood' of the Merovingians, which renders their hereditary genetic marks tangible, testifies to a very ancient crossing with a species, the evolution of which began on another planet and continued for a certain time on ours, then, as astonishing as it appears to you, *the descendants of extraterrestrials formerly reigned over France*" (original emphasis).[11] Astonishing indeed.

At the end of 1973, the Priory of Sion boasted its first major exposure, when the editor of the Paris review *Le Charivari* assigned Jean-Luc Chaumeil to contribute a piece based on the Dossiers Secrets. The society's spin doctors must have been ecstatic: the October issue was entirely devoted to the Priory, even reproducing a number of key documents for the first time—for example, the 1956 (Annemasse) statutes and an "interview with the lost king": who else but Pierre Plantard de Saint-Clair?

A poet and painter who turned to journalism and magazine editing to make a living, Chaumeil was already interested in the Rennes-le-Château mystery after having read de Sède, but it was the *Le Charivari* assignment that established him as a leading figure in Priory research who nevertheless—like de Sède—shifted from being an admirer of Plantard to end up denouncing him. (But both men always maintained a soft spot for de Chérisey.) As Chaumeil said in his most recent reminiscence of his dealings with Plantard:

> There were a thousand questions; as for the replies, they were allusive, irritating in many respects, always carefully organized, perhaps too carefully. . . . This individual was cheerful nevertheless, full of humor, a little bit *illuminé.*[12]

One *Le Charivari* "scoop" that turned out to be nothing of the sort was its splash of the "treasures of Rennes-le-Château," with photographs supplied by Mathieu Paoli. These showed golden, bejeweled plate and vessels allegedly found by Saunière and sold secretly via the Banque Fritz Dörgé in Budapest to the Habsburgs that were now supposedly in Switzerland (and, somewhat confusingly, now said to be owned by followers of the mystic Rudolf Steiner). At least this is plausible, as Saunière was in contact with the bank, but the pictures turned out to be of something quite different: the hoard of sixth-century treasures discovered at Petrossa, Romania, in 1837 and now in the Bucharest museum. (Despite this disappointing setback, the Romanian connection may still be significant through the link between Paoli/Scheswig and Todericiu/Carnac.)

At the same time Plantard and the Rennes-le-Château story enjoyed banner headlines in the weekly publication *Pégase,* edited by Chaumeil. Several articles appeared on various aspects of the Rennes mystery: in September 1973 there was a piece on Plantard—who also looked out enigmatically from the cover—entitled "From Jarnac to Gisors," by Michel Vallet, who under the nom de plume Pierre Jarnac was to become one of the most indefatigable researchers into the Rennes-le-Château affair. Even then, Vallet was not entirely won over by Plantard, writing that after learning about Saunière's discovery of treasure, "with some outside assistance, he [Plantard] conceived a fantastic genealogy in which he enthroned himself 'Descendant of the Merovingian Kings' and in consequence sole legitimate descendant of the throne of France.

But he did not stop there; he constituted a secret sect that he entitled the Priory of Sion."[13]

After *Pégase* carried an interview with Philippe de Chérisey the following month, there followed one with "master" Plantard. It was only now that he openly claimed to be the modern representative of the Merovingian bloodline and rightful King of France—previously readers had had to work this identity out for themselves from the Dossiers Secrets' tantalizing trails. For example, in a letter to Chaumeil in July 1974, Plantard declared (with somewhat perverse logic): "I am indeed the direct and legitimate descendant of the line of Sigebert IV, himself son of Dagobert II, King of Austrasia. Let those who contest it prove the contrary!"[14] But bizarrely, after this flurry of publicity, the story went to sleep for another four or five years—until the next flurry.

Quite a Different Caliber

In 1977 another figure who was to play an increasingly important role appeared on the scene: Gino Sandri, who would become—and at the time of writing still is—the Priory of Sion's Secretary-General. According to his own account, he was initiated into the society on Plantard's specific recommendation.[15] (He was also a witness to Jean-Luc Chaumeil's marriage in 1981.)

Sandri is of quite a different caliber than either Plantard or de Chérisey. Despite his long association with Plantard and the Priory of Sion (usually dismissed as a hoax by serious esotericists), Sandri is a respected scholarly writer on mystical and Masonic matters. But there is no reason to doubt his sympathies, for his specialties are particularly revealing.

Everything about Sandri is distinctly Martinist. He writes for *L'Initiation,* the Martinist journal established by Papus (and revived by his son), and was also on the editorial board of the International Center for Martinist Research and Study (Centre Internationale de Recherches et d'Études Martinistes, or CIREM)—along with Robert Amadou, the former Alpha Galates member. Sandri has also contributed to the respected *Renaissance Traditionelle,* the "review of Masonic and Symbolic studies," on the history and rituals of the Rectified Scottish Rite and the Order of the Gold and Rose Cross.

Once again we found ourselves contemplating the Martinist Order and the Rectified Scottish Rite, and once again their particularly intimate relationship with the Priory is underlined. However, this time the cozy enclave also includes the Order of the Gold and Rose Cross, whose close association with the Rectified Scottish Rite would become even more obvious.

Whether or not Sandri's emergence acted as a catalyst, the story began to develop again at around this time. The first move was the publication of a six-page pamphlet in July 1977, by Éditions Dyroles in Toulouse, of *The Circle of Ulysses* (*Le cercle d'Ulysse*) by the pseudonymous Jean Delaude—Jean de l'Aude or John of the Aude—none other than Philippe de Chérisey. (A real Jean Delaude wrote articles on Rennes-le-Château in *La Dépêche du Midi* in 1974, but this appears to be a genuine coincidence.)[16]

The Circle of Ulysses completely undermines the Dossiers Secrets' version of the Merovingian-Plantard bloodline: "While it is correct that Sigebert found himself named as ardent offspring [*rejeton ardent*], it has never been written that he was the son of King Dagobert II of Austrasia. On the contrary, there is no doubt that he was the son of Béra II and the grandson of Wamba, proclaimed King of the Visigoths in 672." Even by the Priory's standards, this is bizarre. It is as demonstrably wrong as the original—there is still no evidence that Sigebert ever existed, let alone had a significant father—but as he supposedly sired the line that led to Plantard, if he was *not* Dagobert's son, then that line was *not* Merovingian. Yet again, de Chérisey and Plantard are toying with us—almost as if testing to see if the public would *still* swallow the Merovingian story, despite such glaring anomalies and abundant hard historical evidence to the contrary. But the pseudonymous Delaude also started another strand of the story that was to resurface dramatically later:

> On the death of Abbé Bérenger Saunière, on January 22, 1917, his niece, Mme. James, who lived in Montazels, expressed her resentment [that] she had for her whole inheritance only ". . . that old bumf that nobody can read, and a book from the *Magasin pittoresque* collection, that's all. . . ." In October 1955, she sold the parchments for 250,000 old francs to two Englishmen: Captain Ronald Stansmore and Sir Thomas of the International League of Antiquarian Booksellers. . . .

> The so-called manuscripts presented by Gérard de Sède are fakes. The original was fabricated in 1961 by the Marquis Philippe de Chérisey and deposited in May 1962 with Maître Bocon-Gibot. Gérard de Sède therefore possessed only a photocopy, reproduced in his book *The Gold of Rennes.* Better yet, this same Marquis added spice to his joke by publishing in June 1971 . . . a work on Rennes with the decoding of the original. This work bore the name of *Circuit.*

The story concerning Madame James and the two Englishmen (the Antiquarian Booksellers of London) was to develop into an intriguing subplot. Actually Bertha Jammes, she was indeed Saunière's niece, daughter of his sister Mathilde and her husband, Jean Oscar Pagès.[17] Beyond that, however, the tale rapidly disintegrates under scrutiny, as we will see.

"Bastard rites"

Returning to the activities of today's Priory of Sion, *The Circle of Ulysses* named Abbé François Ducaud-Bourget as Cocteau's successor as Grand Master, going on to make some startling statements about the Priory's current agenda: "What is the Priory of Sion preparing? I do not know, but it represents a power capable of confronting the Vatican in the days to come. Mgr. Lefèbvre is a very active and formidable member, capable of saying: 'You make me Pope, I will make you King.' "

The linking of two prominent churchmen to the Priory of Sion is astonishing—especially as both were still alive at the time the allegation was published, and this time not in writings tucked away in the Bibliothèque Nationale. Archbishop Marcel Lefèbvre was a very controversial Catholic "reactionary traditionalist,"[18] a prewar member of Action Française who had brazenly criticized and even defied Pope Paul VI, to the point that he was threatened with excommunication. Believing that Paul (and his predecessor John XXIII) had sacrilegiously modernized and liberalized the Church, Lefèbvre was particularly outraged by the Pope's enthusiasm for a new form of the Mass in 1969. In response to his suspension from office in June 1976, after he refused to accept the changes, he railed against the new "bastard rites, bastard sacraments, bastard priests," declaring that "if the Pope is in error, he ceases to be Pope," and continued to celebrate the old-style Mass in public places, including a wrestling hall. He had already established a power base at a seminary he founded in Econe in Switzerland.[19]

That was the situation in 1977, when de Chérisey/Delaude astonishingly named him publicly as a member of the Priory of Sion, but equally astoundingly the fiery Archbishop took no action against him, although there was an interesting sequel. In *The Holy Blood and the Holy Grail,* Baigent, Leigh, and Lincoln made much of a statement in August 1976 by one of Lefèbvre's English supporters that the rebel Archbishop had a "powerful ecclesiastical weapon," which was "earth-shaking" and which he would not hesitate to use if the Pope made good his threat and excommunicated him.[20] Although they point out that Paul VI did indeed back down at this time, the sinister implications seem not to be justified, as Lefèbvre's wings had already been effectively clipped by the time *The Holy Blood and the Holy Grail* was written.

A month after his election in October 1978, Pope John Paul II summoned Lefèbvre to the Vatican. Gordon Thomas and Max Morgan-Witts write in *Pontiff* (1983) that after the Archbishop was ushered into a private audience, believing he was to receive some concessions from the new, conservative Pope:

> For fifteen minutes [the door] remains shut. Then it suddenly opens. John Paul stands there. He is holding Lefèbvre by the elbow. The archbishop looks dazed. As they stand in the doorway the pope once more embraces the archbishop warmly. He says, in excellent French, "It will be all right, it will be all right." Lefèbvre nods. He does not speak. . . .
>
> The rebellion Marcel Lefèbvre first proclaimed on 8 December 1965, and which he subsequently cleverly subsidized with well-publicized conflicts, is over.[21]

As the two men were alone, nobody else knows exactly what happened, but from the testimony of Vatican insiders, Thomas and Morgan-Witts argue that John Paul II had threatened to excommunicate Lefèbvre and all his supporters if he continued to criticize the Vatican publicly. Why this threat had failed to work when used by Paul VI, and why Lefèbvre now made no use of his "earth-shattering" weapon (or if he did, why it failed), remains frustratingly unknown.

In 1978 Plantard presided over the "relaunch" of Abbé Henri Boudet's apparently lunatic book, *The True Celtic Language and the Cromlech of Rennes-les-Bains,* as part of the series Classics of Occultism published by Pierre Belfond. It was a facsimile of the original edition, with a lengthy preface by Plantard de Saint-Clair[22] (and a shorter introduction by one of the series's editors, Jean-Pierre Deloux).

Plantard claimed that when his grandfather Charles Plantard had met both Saunière and Boudet in Rennes-le-Château in 1892, the latter gave him a signed copy of his book—which was eventually reprinted for the series, including the dedication (not specifically inscribed to Charles Plantard) and signature.[23] This was treated with some skepticism until in the mid-1990s the British researchers Richard Andrews and Paul Schellenberger found a letter from Boudet in Oxford's Bodleian Library (accompanying a copy of his book) which showed the signature to be genuine.[24] Of course this hardly proves Plantard's whole story, but clearly he did have access to a signed copy of Boudet's long-lost 1886 book.

In the summer of 1979 another major work on the Priory appeared: Jean-Luc Chaumeil's *The Treasure of the Golden Triangle* (*Le trésor du triangle d'or*), which reinforced the Priory's myth according to the Dossiers Secrets—its role as creators of the Templars, protectors of the Merovingians, and so on—linking the society with both Rennes-le-Château and Gisors (two of the points of the "golden triangle," the other being Stenay, sacred home of Dagobert II's relics). The hands of Plantard and de Chérisey, who are quoted extensively throughout, can clearly be detected, although Gino Sandri claims that he also had major input. However—perhaps under Sandri's influence—it also introduced an important new element into the story, relating to the role of Godefroy de Bouillon, although now significantly modified. According to this revised version, besides being of (alleged) Merovingian descent, while in the Holy Land, Godefroy encountered a sect called the Brothers of the Red Cross (Frères de la Croix Rouge) or Brothers of Ormus (Frères d'Ormus). This was founded by Ormus (or Ormessius), an Egyptian priest who was converted to Christianity by St. Mark in 46 C.E., and who established the Sages of Light (Sages de la Lumière) with six colleagues. Later, a school of "Solomonic wisdom" distilled from various Jewish sects, including the Essenes (like the Templars, rather overused candidates for esoteric pedigrees), attached itself to the Sages of Light. Chaumeil relates:

> Palestine conquered, Godefroy learned to understand better these strange Christians who linked themselves to the initiatory traditions of both ancient Egypt and Judaism. Were they not the true Church, pure and great in spirit as its founder wished, and as the Apostle John, his preferred disciple, also wished? . . .
>
> In Godefroy's mind a great design then germinated. Formerly, his forebear Clovis had been the sword and shield of the Church: that of which Christ had entrusted the keys to the apostle Peter, and which came to establish its seat in Rome. He would become the sword and shield of the Church of John, more connected with the Spirit. Thus was born the Order of Sion, the heart of which was situated in the Abbey of Notre-Dame de Sion, in Jerusalem.[25]

The Order of Sion then founded the Templars and

> Thus, in the twelfth century, the instruments, spiritual and temporal, were created to enable the realization of the grandiose dream formed by Godefroy de Bouillon. The Temple would be the servant of the Church of John, and at the same time of the premier, the only legitimate, dynasty.[26]

This account cleverly mingles several key concepts: the Priory of Sion as protector of the Merovingian bloodline now boasts an alluringly mystical gloss, picked up by Godefroy on the crusade and incorporated into his grand design.

Although it had long been absent, this is actually a return to an aspect that was present in the very first published writings on the Priory of Sion, Plantard's appendix to de Sède's *The Templars Are Among Us,* back in 1962. We recall that this highlighted—but failed to explain—the importance of the "two Johns," the Evangelist and the Baptist. The enigmatic use of the name John by the Priory's Grand Masters has also been present throughout the development in the Dossiers Secrets, but here for the first time there is an explicit connection to the Johannites. As Jean Markale comments:

> Thus we are assured that the Priory de Sion [*sic*] was born of the fusion of the Brotherhood of the Red Cross, Essene groups, and Godefroy de Bouillon's group. In this way the Priory of Sion is given a connection to the Johannites. What indeed would become of esoteric sects, prudently called "philosophical circles," if they could not be placed under the protection of St. John? Whether the protector is John the Baptist, or the John who wrote the Apocalypse (John of Patmos), we are assured, is of no importance.[27]

Presumably it was "prudent" to call the esoteric sects "philosophical circles" because they were actually profoundly, perhaps even offensively, heretical. We will explore the claimed relationship of the Priory and the Johannite tradition in the next chapter.

The New Nautonnier

Meanwhile, Henry Lincoln had continued to delve into this affair, and in 1975 he met Richard Leigh, an expatriate American university lecturer with a similar enthusiasm for the esoteric aspects of the mystery, particularly concerning the Templars. Leigh then introduced Lincoln to Michael Baigent, a journalist and photographer from New Zealand who was also fascinated by the Order. (Although habitually referred to as "*les Anglais*" by French commentators, only one of the three is actually British born.) Their agreement to follow up the tangle of trails arising from the Dossiers Secrets and other sources led to *The Holy Blood and the Holy Grail,* which sensationally introduced the Priory of Sion to a massive international audience seven years later. Once those millions were hooked, there was no going back for the Priory.

Before that, the trio were involved in the third of Henry Lincoln's *Chronicle* documentaries. "The Shadow of the Templars," broadcast in November 1979. For the first time the Priory of Sion and Pierre Plantard—who was interviewed on camera—were prominently featured. It was during the research for this documentary that the three authors made contact with Plantard for the first time, their path smoothed by the BBC. This culminated in March 1979 with their first meeting, in a Paris cinema hired for the occasion, arranged through a Paris-based BBC researcher, Jania Macgillivray, via Jean-Luc Chaumeil, although—perhaps appropriately—Plantard's actual television interview was filmed in a surrealist art studio owned by Chaumeil's mother.

Although Plantard claimed that the Priory of Sion was the guardian of the Jerusalem Temple treasure (one of the candidates for Saunière's momentous discovery), he concentrated particularly on the Priory's plans for a political revolution that would pave the way for a restoration of the (or *a*) French monarchy.[28]

Between those meetings and the publication of *The Holy Blood and the Holy Grail,* something momentous happened to the Priory: Pierre Plantard (de Saint-Clair) apparently became its Grand Master. (Previously the only information on his position came from the 1956 registration, in which he was named as General Secretary.) Strangely for the business of a "secret" society, his election to its helm was actually reported in the press on January 22, 1981 (although only in the local and regional newspapers—which, if they operate like British locals, basically happily print anything they receive):

> A true secret society of 121 dignitaries, the Priory of Sion, founded by Godefroy de Bouillon in Jerusalem in 1099, has counted among its Grand Masters Leonardo da Vinci, Victor Hugo, [and] Jean Cocteau; this Order assembled its convent in Blois on January 17, 1981 (the previous convent dating from June 5, 1956, in Paris).
>
> During the present Blois convent, Pierre Plantard de Saint-Clair was elected Grand Master of the Order by 83 votes out of 92 on the third ballot.
>
> The choice of this Grand Master marks a decisive stage in the evolution of the conceptions and spirits in the world, as the 121 dignitaries of the Priory of Sion are all éminence grises of high finance and international political or philosophical societies, and Pierre Plantard is the direct descendant of the Merovingian kings through Dagobert II; his ancestry is legally proven by the parchments of Queen Blanche of Castile, discovered by the curé Saunière in Rennes-le-Château (Aude) in 1891.
>
> These documents, sold by the priest's niece in 1955 to Captain

Ronald Stansmore and Sir Thomas Frazer, were deposited in a safe of Lloyds Bank Europe Limited in London.[29]

Yet as the Priory of Sion is—depending on one's point of view—either a hoax or a cover for some other organization, why did Plantard wait so long to declare himself Grand Master? After all, he had been its spokesman for many years. (Plantard himself said later that the announcement was intended to prepare for the presidential elections due a few months later, which swept Mitterrand to power.) And who was supposed to have been the Grand Master since Cocteau's death in 1963?

Although by now it is clear that the Priory of Sion is a cover, a hollow shell to be filled with whatever would please the shadowy "Them," the question of the purported succession to Cocteau remains a fascinating indication of how the cover story worked and an insight into the mindset of the puppet masters. The last mention of the subject that appeared in the Dossiers Secrets—the 1967 Lobineau documents—had left Cocteau at the helm.

As we have seen, in Delaude/de Chérisey's *The Circle of Ulysses,* Cocteau's successor was named as Abbé François Ducaud-Bourget, who (allegedly) introduced Plantard into the Priory of Sion in 1943. As Ducaud-Bourget was still alive when this was written—and was closely connected with the highly influential Knights of Malta—bandying his name about was perhaps not the smartest idea unless they somehow knew they could get away with it. (Incidentally, Ducaud-Bourget was trained at St.-Sulpice.) But to muddy the waters yet further, there is an alternative version of the succession.

A curious article on the Priory of Sion appeared in the Belgian weekly *Bonne Soirée* on August 14, 1980; it was a translation of an article by Jania Macgillivray written a year or so earlier but doctored to include several items of information not then publicly known about the Priory (and unknown even to Macgillivray). This said that, since Cocteau's death in 1963, leadership of the Priory had resided with a triumvirate of Plantard, Gaylord Freeman, and Antonio Merzagora.[30]

How Macgillivray's original text came to be hijacked in this way is unknown, although suspicions fell on the French translator, credited as one Robert Suffert. Predictably, even that identification is obscured by the usual Priory murk with a smirk, especially when it was alleged it was an alias for Paul Smith, the ultraskeptical British researcher!

Several years later, in October 1985, a new document, *The Mysterious Rennes-le-Château,* was deposited in the Bibliothèque Nationale, naming Jania Macgillivray as the author and with the deposit slip signed by Paul Smith—as he himself acknowledges, a "perfect forgery" of his signature—who was also identified as the translator Robert Suffert. (As Smith pointed out, at least at that time he could hardly speak French, let alone translate an entire article.)[31] Yet in 1987, in a letter to Pierre Jarnac, Plantard again identified Suffert with Smith—a blatant attempt at mischief making.[32]

Beyond France

Plantard's two companions in the triumvirate named in *Bonne Soirée*—later confirmed to Baigent, Leigh, and Lincoln by Plantard himself—for the first time extended the story beyond France and also into the world of international high finance.

Presumably Antonio Merzagora was the Italian banker, an associate of the eminent industrialist Agostino Rocca (1895–1978, who was credited with creating the Italian steel industry in the 1930s and was head of the nationalized steel industry during the Second World War). But the alleged involvement of Gaylord Freeman (1910–1991) implied that the Priory's influence extended even further afield. An extremely important and influential American banker and financier, he was most notably associated with the First National Bank of Chicago, of which he was Chairman between 1969 and 1975 (also playing a key role in establishing its famed art collection). Freeman was also an adviser on the economy to the U.S. government, for example chairing a presidential task force on inflation during the Carter administration.[33]

Predictably, there is no evidence of a link between either of these bankers and Plantard or the Priory, but when *Bonne Soirée* was published and Plantard named them to Baigent, Leigh, and Lincoln, both men were still alive but neither took any action. Either Plantard had an incredible cheek (after all, spreading lies about a very wealthy American banker is asking for trouble) or he felt for some reason he could bandy these names about with impunity.

The "official" line changed again in 1989, when *Vaincre* stated that the Grand Master between 1963 and 1981 had been John E. Drick (1911–1982)—another prominent U.S. banker associated with the First National Bank of Chicago.

Dreaming of the Holy Vine

Baigent, Leigh, and Lincoln's research into the history of the Priory and its guardianship of the sacred bloodline first reached the public in the form of a novel, *The Dreamer of the Vine* (1980) by Liz Greene—a psychologist and astrologer who is also Richard Leigh's sister. Based on the life of the visionary astrologer Nostradamus, it concerns plots to have the Merovingian Guise family set upon the throne of France in the sixteenth century. Although one of the characters is a shadowy éminence grise named Plantard and the Priory of Sion basks in a stellar role, the novel also emphasizes goddess worship and sexual rites as the Priory's main raison d'être—neither of which finds much place in Baigent, Leigh, and Lincoln's works. (Greene was to produce a second novel based on the Priory, *The Puppet Master,* in 1987.)

Although the three *Holy Blood* authors accepted the Dossiers Secrets' Merovingian survival story, they sought another factor to account for the almost religious fervor with which the family had been revered and protected over the centuries other than it being allegedly the legitimate royal family of France. First, they noted the recurring theme of the Holy Grail—long associated with both the Templars and the Cathars—and realized that the medieval Grail romances emphasize the importance of lineage and inheritance, the duty of keeping and protecting the Grail devolving on certain families who were inextricably linked with specific individuals listed in the Priory's Merovingian genealogies. For example, at least according to legend, Godefroy de Bouillon was the descendant of the Swan Knight Lohengrin, who in Wolfram von Eschenbach's Grail saga *Parzival* is the son of the eponymous hero himself. Wolfram's epic also associates the provenance of the Grail story with the Anjou family, which is prominent in the Dossiers Secrets' genealogies and the history of the Priory.

All this prompted Baigent, Leigh, and Lincoln to hypothesize that the mysterious Grail represented a real lineage—a *bloodline.*[34] And they came up with the famous play on words that gave their book its title:

that the word used in some of the early romances to describe the object of the quest, *sangraal* or *sangreal,* has for centuries been broken in the wrong place. Instead of "san greal"—holy grail—it should have been "sang réal"—blood royal.[35] But *whose* bloodline was it?

(In fact, the pun was intentional from the beginning. Most of the first crop of romances simply call the object of the quest a *graal* or, as in Wolfram's version, *Grâl.* It was initially described as the *sangreal* in Robert de Boron's *Joseph d'Arimathie,* written around the turn of the twelfth century, in which for the first time the Holy Grail was explicitly identified as the cup in which Jesus' blood was caught as he hung on the cross. Robert de Boron was aware of the *san greal/sang real* pun, although he intended it as a reference to "real [or true] blood," the blood of Christ preserved in it.)[36]

The penny dropped, according to Lincoln, as he and Richard Leigh were puzzling over the question of why the Merovingians were so important, and Leigh mused that there was "something fishy" about the dynasty. Suddenly there was what must have seemed like an epiphany: as the fish was Jesus' earliest symbol, was *that* actually the answer—was Jesus himself the missing link?[37]

From that apparently startling serendipity, the connections rapidly fell into place. First there were the repeated allusions to Mary Magdalene in the material disseminated by the Priory, which, although possibly referring to the Rennes-le-Château church, in itself raised the question of why that church had been dedicated to her in the first place. The trio discovered she is particularly venerated in the Languedoc because according to legend she lived out her long life in that area after having fled (or been exiled) from Judea following the Crucifixion. As we showed in *The Templar Revelation,*[38] these legends are more plausible than similar tales of biblical figures turning up in unlikely places. Since the Magdalene, too, is associated with the Holy Grail (which she is said to have taken to France), on Baigent, Leigh, and Lincoln's reasoning, it was a bloodline—a child or children—she carried with her. *Christ's offspring.*

The theory had been put forward by New Testament scholars many years before that Jesus and Mary Magdalene were man and wife, and as we discovered, there is no lack of evidence to support the idea of an intimate, even sexual, relationship between the two. (However, we disagree that they were legally married: even the heretical accounts very carefully employ terms such as *partner* or *concubine,* but not *wife* or *spouse.*) Putting this together, Baigent, Leigh, and Lincoln developed the hypothesis that the Magdalene had taken Jesus' children to France, where at some point they married into the Frankish family that transmuted into the Merovingian dynasty. Presumably, given the Merovingians' descent (according to the Dossiers Secrets) from the Israelite tribe of Benjamin, which supplied Israel with its first king, this was intentional. *That* was the secret; *that* was why the Merovingians were deemed sacred—and why the Priory of Sion has guarded the "holy bloodline" ever since: because it is the bloodline of Jesus himself.

However, we emphasize that this was not the claim made by the Dossiers Secrets (which merely traced the Merovingians back to the House of David), although the idea was found in embryonic form in Gérard de Sède's *The Gold of Rennes*—innocently tucked away in a footnote. Discussing the Virgin Mary (in relation to Saunière's statue of Our Lady of Lourdes), de Sède mused: "According to the evangelists, Jesus was, through his maternal line, a descendant of David and Solomon, therefore King of the Jews by blood. This has favored speculation on the possible survival of the privileged human line in which the Messiah was incarnated, speculations reinforced by the incontestable ritual analogy between the anointing of the Jewish kings and the anointing of the coronation inaugurated for Clovis."[39] Was de Sède's apparently throwaway note intended to be the literary equivalent of a message in a bottle tossed out to sea, in the hope that Fate would ensure the message was delivered—one day, somehow?

When *The Holy Blood and the Holy Grail* was published, in January 1982, it generated an enormous controversy on both sides of the Atlantic. Denounced by churchmen and historians (although it had its supporters even within those circles), it was a massive succès de scandale. The book's legions of enthusiastic readers were excited by the heady tale of treasure, mystery, secret societies—and, at its very heart, new and challenging information about the religion that has shaped Western culture. (For good measure they threw in the notion—argued by several scholars before—that Jesus survived the Crucifixion, although in fact it has little or no bearing on their central hypothesis of the survival of his bloodline.) The Priory of Sion had certainly reached a new, international audience—but at the cost of being indelibly linked with the idea that it existed to protect Jesus' descendants. And as far as they were concerned, it was not *fact*—as in *The Da Vinci Code*—that they were guardians of both the secret of the bloodline and its human embodiments.

Indeed, when interviewed on French radio immediately after *The Holy Blood and the Holy Grail* came out, Plantard flatly rejected its theory and the notion that he was a lineal descendant of Jesus Christ.[40] (Presumably, though, he was flattered to discover he was not only the true King of France but also the great-grandson many times removed of God.)

To us, objectively, *The Holy Blood and the Holy Grail* is something of a mixed blessing. While it is frustrating that certain demonstrable historical errors originating in the Dossiers Secrets—such as Godefroy de Bouillon being descended from the Merovingians—have become fixed in people's minds as fact, most of the information and alternative ideas about Jesus and how the Christian Church originated are valid. And, of course, to most readers new and exciting. Baigent, Leigh, and Lincoln took what were essentially breathtakingly daring and novel concepts—including de Sède's message in a bottle—to a massive new audience, who probably would never otherwise have known they existed.

Almost simultaneously with *The Holy Blood and the Holy Grail*, a glossy, lavishly illustrated newsstand publication on Rennes-le-Château and the Priory of Sion—Jean-Pierre Deloux and Jacques Brétigny's *Rennes-le-Château: Secret Capital of the History of France* (*Rennes-le-Château: capitale secrète de l'histoire de France*)—appeared in France. It was described by Pierre Jarnac as a "propaganda brochure in aid of the Priory of Sion and its supporters."[41] Again heavily guided by Plantard, the bulk of the text was taken from articles on the Rennes-le-Château affair in *L'inexpliqué* (the French version of *The Unexplained*)[42] over the previous two years. Like Chaumeil's earlier book, it highlighted the Priory's Church of John connection, which had been almost totally ignored by Baigent, Leigh, and Lincoln.

The Lloyds Bank Affair

A year after the publication of *The Holy Blood and the Holy Grail* came the perplexing episode of the Lloyds Bank documents. In May 1983, Plantard gave Baigent, Leigh, and Lincoln copies of notarized documents dating from 1955 and 1956 that related to the transfer from

France to London of the genealogical parchments allegedly found by Abbé Saunière. Said to be in a safety deposit box in Lloyds Bank, they boldly declared that the parchments contain "proof of the direct descent, through the male line of Sigebert IV, son of Dagobert II, King of Austrasia, through the House of Plantard." The papers went on to name British businessmen involved in the transaction: the Earl of Selborne, Viscount Leathers, Ronald Stansmore Nutting, and Hugh Murchison Clowes, whose signatures and copies of their birth certificates were attached. Moreover, the notarized documents stated that the parchments would be kept for only twenty-five years—until 1981—after which they would revert to Pierre Plantard (Comte de Rhedae and Comte de Saint-Clair).

The doctored 1980 Macgillivray article in *Bonne Soirée* had repeated this story but added that in 1979 the parchments had been returned to Paris, where they were lodged with a bank. (In fact, Baigent, Leigh, and Lincoln discovered that in that year Lloyds stopped offering a safe deposit service—a somewhat abstruse piece of information that shows someone had done his homework.)

As we have seen, although the signatures and birth certificates were genuine, the three authors established that the relevant parts were definitely forged. The telltale mistake in the first document was that the parchments were said to have been lodged with Lloyds Bank Europe—but there was no such thing until 1964. Although no similar clue turned up in the 1955 document, proving one a fake naturally casts considerable doubt on the other. Not only did the British men share business connections, particularly with Guardian Royal Exchange Assurance, but, as we have seen, they all had wartime links with intelligence organizations such as SOE.

As the documents are fakes and the genealogical parchments to which they refer describe a nonexistent lineage, the point of the exercise seems somewhat obscure. Most obviously it would provide apparently independent support for the existence of the parchments, and therefore for the Merovingian survival fable of the Dossiers Secrets. And but for the slip about the name change of the division of Lloyds Bank, no one would ever have known.

However, Baigent, Leigh, and Lincoln believe that Plantard was the *dupe* in all this, because when they pointed conclusive proof of forgery out to him, he was "visibly shocked and upset."[43] In other words, Plantard's belief that he possessed legal evidence for his right to the parchments—which in turn would prove his descent from Dagobert II—had suffered an abrupt and cruel blow. But this supposition works only if he *believed* the Dossiers Secrets, which means he really was seriously deluded, or someone had convinced him that he was the rightful King of France, in which case he was both gullible *and* deluded. Was Baigent, Leigh, and Lincoln's interpretation of his reaction actually right? There is another possibility, of course: perhaps Plantard was simply aghast at being found out.

There are other oddities about this episode. The claim that Saunière's niece Bertha Jammes sold the parchments to "Captain Ronald Stansmore and Sir Thomas" was first made in *The Circle of Ulysses*—almost certainly by Philippe de Chérisey—in 1977. It was repeated the following year in a twenty-page booklet entitled *The Enigma of Rennes* that de Chérisey signed with his own name, in which the two British men were identified, somewhat grandiosely, as "Captain Ronald Stansmore of the British Intelligence Service and Sir Thomas Frazer, the éminence grise of Buckingham [Palace]." (This was repeated in Chaumeil's 1979 book, which described a Ronald Stansmore.)[44] But Stansmore was actually Nutting's middle name, and elsewhere he is called Roland—another apparent gaffe.

The obvious assumption is that these statements were intended to set the scene for the appearance of the notarized documents, and therefore Plantard and de Chérisey already possessed the doctored papers. However, as they included copies of Nutting's birth certificate and full signature (and he signed himself R. S. Nutting), it is very curious that they failed to get his name right, especially because they *were* aware he had worked for M15, which for obvious reasons was not widely known. (Sir Thomas Frazer's role is mystifying, as he plays no further part in the unfolding drama: apart from business connections to the Earl of Selborne, he has no apparent links, still less as the "éminence grise of Buckingham Palace"!)

It seems that de Chérisey and Plantard themselves were being fed bits and pieces of information, which they incorporated into their own material, paving the way for the appearance of the notarized documents. Plantard himself said he acquired them only in 1983, and while it is always a mistake to take his word at face value, if he possessed them earlier, surely he would have exploited them in some way—but he showed them to Baigent, Leigh, and Lincoln a full seven years after "Stansmore's" first appearance in the narrative. Yet again, whatever was really going on, everything seems to have been intended to work toward a *long-term* plan.

The Warning

Toward the end of 1983 an anonymous pamphlet appeared listing Plantard's past misdemeanors. As the tract implied it was the work of Chaumeil, supposedly a flyer for a forthcoming book (which never appeared), Plantard launched a libel suit against him, although in the end the matter never reached court. For his part, Chaumeil has steadfastly maintained that the anonymous campaign against Plantard was a deliberate attempt to frame him. In fact, by smearing Plantard and blaming it on Chaumeil, it seems that some third party was clearly trying to stir up trouble for one or both, although logically Plantard must have been the main target.

The fact that the mysterious "Them" sought to cause this kind of aggravation for Plantard is interesting in itself. Whatever the Priory of Sion may or may not be, the very existence of its enemies means it transcends the level of simple hoax—proving that someone, somewhere, takes it very seriously indeed.

It seems that the Plantard camp was in something of a panic in case certain documents relating to the Priory were about to surface. In January (the seventeenth, of course) 1984, the Priory circulated a *mise en garde*—warning—to its (supposed) membership, informing them about the Grand Master's action against Chaumeil and warning them against any dealings with the latter, otherwise they might find themselves dragged into the whole affair. Clearly this originated with Plantard, who disseminated copies to nonmembers such as Baigent, Leigh, and Lincoln, presumably as insurance—or to preempt a scandal—if certain information or documents came to light.

The *mise en garde* referred to a box of archives apparently stolen from de Chérisey's apartment in 1967, consisting mostly (it was claimed) of correspondence among Jean Cocteau, André Malraux, and Marshal Juin between 1935 and 1955. As the anonymous anti-Plantard leaflet was circulating in the guise of the flyer promoting Chaumeil's forthcoming five-volume work on the "doctrine of the Priory of Sion," Plantard seems to have been afraid it might be based on the missing documents. Alternatively, the circulating archives might be offered to other researchers—most obviously, following the success of *The Holy Blood and the Holy Grail,* Baigent, Leigh, and Lincoln—and the Priory's official warning seems to have been intended to make them wary of "trafficking in documents," or essentially receiving stolen goods.

This exercise in damage limitation begs another question: if the Priory is really just a hoax, what damage could any documents possibly do—unless they *proved* it a hoax, in which case surely Plantard would hardly risk an action for trafficking in them.

However, the *mise en garde* presented one final puzzle. It was signed not just by Pierre Plantard (curiously not de Saint-Clair) but by three others: Gaylord Freeman, John E. Drick, and A. Robert Abboud. Freeman we already know, and from the most recently published version of the Priory's succession of Grand Masters, it seems Drick filled the gap between Cocteau and Plantard. Alfred Robert Abboud (born in Boston of a Lebanese immigrant father) followed Freeman as Chief Executive of the First National Bank of Chicago, and John Edward Drick was one of its executives for over forty years, until his retirement in 1977. Yet again, why their names were circulated on "official" Priory documents that would inevitably be published and would prompt researchers such as Baigent, Leigh, and Lincoln to contact the men, is a mystery. No one has established any direct connection between the banking trio and the Priory, or any of the other societies and orders associated with it. (Indeed, Freeman has explicitly denied membership of the Priory.) And as Freeman and Abboud were alive when the *mise en garde* was circulated—and Abboud still is—what on earth convinced Plantard that he could use their names with impunity? (Just for good measure, until early 1983, when all this material started to circulate, the First National Bank of Chicago and Guardian Royal Exchange Assurance shared the same London offices.)[45]

There is at least one glaring anomaly: Drick had died two years before his signature appeared on the Priory's *mise en garde.* When Baigent, Leigh, and Lincoln confronted Plantard with this in Paris in September 1984, he pointed out that the signatures of all three Americans were actually rubber-stamped, and that in line with Priory policy an officer's signature continued to be used until a replacement took over. (This curious custom seems to be genuine—Pierre Plantard's signature was still appearing on Priory documents nearly two years after his death.) But Plantard knew Drick was dead, volunteering the information before Baigent, Leigh, and Lincoln could spring it on him—making the point of the whole exercise even more puzzling. And how had he managed to acquire the signature stamps of leading Chicago bankers anyway?[46]

To the *Holy Blood* authors, Plantard explained that certain American bankers were involved with the Priory because they supported the concept of a United States of Europe. (Although the United States generally regards a united Europe as an economic rival and a challenge to its global position, certain interests do welcome such a move.)

In October 1984 another smear campaign went on the attack, but this time on the society as a whole rather than just Plantard personally, in a pamphlet signed by one Cornelius entitled *The Scandals of the Priory of Sion* (*Les scandales du Prieuré de Sion*). This linked the Priory to the Mafia and the notorious Italian Masonic lodge P2 besides other political, financial, and criminal conspiracies (including assassinations). It also referred to a high-ranking member of the Priory—clearly Plantard—meeting the Grand Master of P2, Licio Gelli (dating the encounter two days after Plantard's election as Nautonnier and setting it in the rather ordinary Parisian brasserie La Tipia near the Gare du Nord railway station, where he often held meetings).

Either this pamphlet—linking the Priory of Sion with the murky world where organized crime, political intrigue, and secret societies meet—was produced by its enemies (in which case it is interesting the Priory had any) or it was put out by the society itself to bolster its aura of mystery and power, even if of a distinctly shady kind. As usual, we can take our pick. But the appearance of *The Scandals of the Priory of Sion* coincided very neatly with Plantard's bombshell.

Exit Plantard

During 1984 Plantard resigned not just from the Grand Mastership but from the Priory of Sion itself, abandoning the whole ship he had steered with such uniquely tricksy skill and guile. His resignation letter, since widely circulated among researchers, is dated July 10, 1984, although he made no mention of this to Baigent, Leigh, and Lincoln until the end of that year—*after* their meeting in September. The difference is significant: if he really resigned in July, it was before the flurry of anonymous denunciations, but if he backdated his resignation letter, then he resigned *because* of the attacks.

Plantard claimed he left the society not only for health reasons but also because of "certain maneuvers by our English and American Brothers," as well as the appearance in "multigraph brochures deposited in the Bibliothèque Nationale, of *false* or *falsified* documents concerning me" (his emphasis).

He was replaced as Nautonnier by Philippe de Chérisey, at least according to Priory sources, although as always it is impossible to be sure. For example, one letter, dated January 17, 1985, from de Chérisey to Plantard—referring to their rift and his election—cheekily implies that Henry Lincoln was not only somehow linked to Plantard's departure but also closer to the Priory than he acknowledged: ". . . there was no intrigue on my part to obtain your resignation of July 10, 1984, any more that in my election as G ∴ M ∴ [Grand Master] on September 10, 1984. The one responsible was Fr ∴ [Frère, or Brother] Louis Vazart with the Lincoln clique, via Fr ∴ Ginno [*sic*] Sandri."[47] (Although de Chérisey avoids actually calling Henry Lincoln "Brother," obviously the letter was designed to raise nagging doubts about his real reasons for being so interested in these affairs.)

After de Chérisey's sudden death less than a year later, on July 17, 1985—from complications during routine surgery—nothing was really heard officially from the Priory until the relaunch of *Vaincre* in September 1989 and Plantard's return not only to the Priory but to its helm.

The reemergence of *Vaincre* as the Priory's internal bulletin provides proof, if it were needed, of the continuity between the wartime Alpha Galates Order and the later Priory of Sion. But by this time the story of the Priory's origins and history had fundamentally changed, with its explicit rejection of the Dossiers Secrets' scenario, including the now-famed list of Grand Masters. Through letters to members and the new *Vaincre*, Plantard offered another construction of the Priory's origins (based, he said, on "new research" and the rediscovery of long-lost archives supposedly hidden for safekeeping on the outbreak of the Second World War), which placed it not in the Middle Ages, as once claimed so vaingloriously, but as late as the seventeenth or eighteenth century. Nor were the Templars its military arm. Indeed, in the words of

Vaincre, these records show that "the Priory of Sion has no direct or indirect affiliation with the Order of the Temple." The history culled from the Dossiers Secrets—the very basis of *The Holy Blood and the Holy Grail*—is dismissed as a "fantasy lineage," the product of Philippe Toscan du Plantier's drug-crazed imagination. Plantard proudly boasts that he has "put an end to 'a mythology' of false Grand Masters that some claim go back to the Order of the Temple and even to Jesus!" However, the list of Grand Masters from the eighteenth into the twentieth century is still supposedly genuine.[48]

The revised story is that the Priory of Sion is *believed* to have been founded in Rennes-le-Château on January 17, 1681, by the Hautpoul, Fleury, and Nègre families, although the earliest document confirming its existence dates from 1738. In a letter ostensibly to members dated April 4, 1989, Plantard states that the Priory's constitution was drafted by Victor Hugo on July 14, 1870, on the same day that, tellingly, he "planted the oak of the United States of Europe." However, the usual caveats apply. For a start, most of this is based entirely on unverifiable "inside information"—the people named in the foundation story may have existed, but they are too obscure for much to be known about them. In the absence of the actual documents the Priory claims to possess, there is little or nothing to follow up. And in any case, why suppose this version is any more reliable than the Dossiers Secrets'? (We will see the significance of Hugo's planting of the "oak of the United States of Europe" later.)

But what was Plantard really up to? It seems that, with extraordinary guile, rather than mounting an attempted comeback, as his critics assume, what he was actually doing was *closing down* the Priory of Sion business—not exactly what one would expect of a cynically accomplished con man. Having succeeded in reaching an eager international audience with his hoax and now in a position to make a killing by exploiting his Merovingian pedigree and status of Grand Master of what had become, paradoxically, one of the world's best-known secret societies, instead he backed off, lay low for fully four years, and then demolished the edifice that he had so painstakingly constructed over the best part of thirty years.

The story is that Plantard was coaxed back in March 1989 on a temporary basis to sort out some major problems, but having done so he immediately resigned again, this time in favor of his son Thomas Plantard de Saint-Clair (invoking that curious hereditary principle). His second resignation letter is dated July 6, 1989. So even before the outside world knew he was back at the helm, he had gone again.

In his *final* farewell, Plantard claimed he had pushed through certain reforms that had "thwarted the peril of the American section" by separating the European and American memberships into different organizations, leaving the Priory "of a uniquely European nature."

In his letter of July 1989 Plantard refers only obliquely to the identity of the Grand Master who succeeded de Chérisey, saying that, since his resignation in 1984, "two Nautonniers have tried to lead the Priory, both failed and each died from a heart attack, one on July 17, 1985 [de Chérisey], the other on March 7, 1989." (Allegedly Plantard had been asked to act as Grand Master to sort out the problems after these sudden deaths.) But when interviewed by Noël Pinot in *Vaincre* on March 9, 1989, at Avignon, Plantard was more specific: "For a long time the Americans dominated our country, for both financial and economic reasons. Now the order is composed of many members who are major financiers, politicians, directors of important insurance companies, magistrates, which is the ideal circuit of the various actions. And so Patrice Pelat was trapped, and I can still say it here, I keep my deep respect for him despite everything." Roger-Patrice Pelat, a close friend of François Mitterrand who posthumously became embroiled in one of France's biggest financial scandals, did indeed die suddenly of a heart attack on March 7, 1989. We will return to him.

For the last ten years of his life, Plantard chose to remain elusive, dividing his time between Barcelona and Perpignan, deep in Cathar country. During the 1990s any attempts to contact him (including our own in the middle of the decade) or the Priory were neatly fielded by Gino Sandri, who, together with Thomas Plantard, acted as Plantard's protector.

Although unsurprisingly speculation continues to be fevered about Plantard's successor as Grand Master—not to mention the identity of the current Nautonnier—Gino Sandri simply refuses to discuss the topic.[49] (But it seems he has never sought the title himself.) And if, as we firmly believe, the Priory was simply a fictional cover for other societies, such speculation is pointless: even if there is a Grand Master, he or she presides over only a hollow shell.

With a deft touch, some game playing even attended Plantard's death. In April 2000 his son announced his demise to French researchers as if it had just happened, although it had actually occurred on February 3. As Sandri explained (or rather failed to): "Pierre Plantard de Saint-Clair did not wish to end up like Péladan or Georges Monti, victims of poisoning. A strategy was worked out and arrangements made. I can't say any more."[50]

In early 2003 another communication purportedly from the Priory of Sion emerged, signed by Sandri and also by Pierre Plantard as Nautonnier and G. Chyren (presumably maintaining the Priory tradition of using deceased members' signature stamps until their vacancies have been filled). There is one very clumsy mistake: the date is given as December 27, 2003, which obviously should be 2002. Initially it was doubted that this was a genuine communiqué from the Priory—perhaps it was an Internet hoax—although Sandri has since acknowledged it.[51] It reads:

> Conforming to our Book of Constitutions,
>
> This day, at Saint-Denis, the Nautonnier has proceeded with the investiture of members of the Arche. The Head of the Order was restored through his good offices. According to the Tradition, it is formed of a couple assisted by their guardian.
>
> On the threshold of the fateful year 2003, all is therefore arranged for SION's apogee, as the presence of the Woman is indispensable; it is the condition sine qua non as all our members learn.
>
> The Commanderies of Saint-Denis, Millau, Geneva, and Barcelona are in operation. Always according to the Tradition, it is a woman who directs the first Commandery.
>
> The Assembly of Provinces is summoned for January 17, 2003. It will meet in the heart of Paris. The special ceremony for PEACE in the world will be celebrated. Instructions will be given on this subject.
>
> The Order of the Priory of Sion is made up of 9,841 members constituting the CIRCUIT of PEACE.
>
> An office will soon be set up, intended to serve as the official link between the public and the Order of Sion. The Secretary-General is charged with its administration and the publication of the internal bulletin CIRCUIT.

What was all this about? Clearly the Priory was expecting great things of 2003—and by the strangest quirk of fate, it got them, for that was the year in which the Dan Brown phenomenon propelled the society into the global spotlight. But Sandri suggested in October 2003 that it was part of an exercise to smoke out the many pseudo-Priories that have sprung up with the advent of the Internet: "There are cycles that determine the favored moments, which in certain circles they call the circuits. These remarkable instants are propitious for revelations. As far as the Priory is concerned, everything is in order and we move toward a necessary clarification. The false Priories will appear openly, which will favor their implosion."[52]

The DNA of God?

If the Priory had dropped the whole bloodline business, *The Holy Blood and the Holy Grail* started a ball rolling that shows no signs of stopping. And thanks to Dan Brown, these days millions of people the world round believe in the sacred bloodline almost as an article of faith. But while Brown's version was fiction, and in any case it merely highlighted the idea that Jesus was married and had children, whose descendants are still around, there is a whole new raft of books that take the theme and run with it into the most fantastic realms.

The overwhelming weakness in *The Holy Blood and the Holy Grail*'s hypothesis is that it relies so heavily on the Dossiers Secrets and other material disseminated by the Priory. We know that there is next to nothing to support the concept of Dagobert II's bloodline, and if that is nonexistent, then the idea that it might also be Jesus' also crumbles away to nothing before our eyes. However strong the case might be for Jesus' intimate relationship with Mary Magdalene—from which children would almost inevitably have resulted—the evidence for their offspring essentially becoming the Merovingian dynasty or any other identifiable line of descent simply is not there.

The claim that through their Sicambrian ancestry the Merovingians originated with the Israelite tribe of Benjamin is equally unprovable. Yet Baigent, Leigh, and Lincoln write that the Priory of Sion "can establish, quite definitively and to the satisfaction of the most fastidious genealogical enquiry, that the Merovingian Dynasty was of the Davidic line."[53] (In fact, the Dossiers Secrets' claim that the Sicambrian Franks—and therefore the Merovingians—were descended from the Tribe of Benjamin contradicts the concept that the Merovingians were of the House of David, since David actually came from the Tribe of Judah.)

Moreover, the Franks themselves actually claimed descent not from David or the Israelites, or from Arcadia, but from the Trojans. (This belief is common to many other European peoples—for example, the medieval British believed their country was founded by settlers from Troy.) The mid-seventh-century chronicler Fredegar, one of the major sources for the history of the Merovingian dynasty, records the legend that their ancestors were Trojans who followed King Priam from Greece to the Rhine.[54]

Despite these not inconsiderable difficulties, the idea of a sacred bloodline descended from Jesus has taken a firm hold in the alternative history field, being developed far beyond even what was hypothesized, or intended, by Baigent, Leigh, and Lincoln. So why exactly did they believe the Merovingians were so significant, and how does their theory differ from the later developments?

First we need to be very conscious of the distinction between genetic and legal inheritance, although devotees of sacred bloodline theories often mix the two promiscuously. The passing on of specific genetic characteristics from parents to children, and so on down a line of descent, is quite different from legal rights and privileges arising from birth. All the children will share the same genes—which their own offspring will inherit—but only the firstborn male will inherit a title and family seat, or crown. If an illegitimate son is not detected, he will still inherit land, property, money, and titles from his supposed father, even though he possesses none of his genes. Errant children (such as Johann Salvator von Habsburg) can be dispossessed of their birthrights—cut out of a will or stripped of their titles and estates—but not of their genetic inheritance, which is literally in their blood (and all the other cells of their bodies).

Conversely, birthrights—and particularly the right to rule—have never been determined *solely* by birth in any culture. There are always other conditions, such as laws and customs, which also have to be obeyed or fulfilled; most obvious is the emphasis on legitimacy, even though children born of a king's mistress carry his genes as much as those sired on his queen. (Britain's lusty Charles II had thirteen illegitimate children but none within wedlock: had his illegitimate offspring been recognized, the Duke of Buccleuch would now be monarch instead of Queen Elizabeth II.) In all European royal houses, male children counted as more important than female, and in many countries women were entirely forbidden from becoming monarch (which is why the royal house of Britain and Hanover split when Queen Victoria acceded to the joint throne of England and Scotland: as Hanoverian law forbade a woman from ruling Hanover, its throne went to her uncle, the Duke of Cumberland.)

Then there are rules of conduct or behavior, sometimes enshrined in a nation's laws, which override considerations of birth alone. For example, the heir to the British throne loses that status if he or she marries a Catholic. (As a result of this law, when the last Stuart died in 1714, the English and Scottish crown passed to someone who otherwise would have been fifty-second in line to the throne, establishing the Hanoverian line, which transmuted into today's House of Windsor.) In many dynasties, royal status and privileges could be lost by marrying someone from a lower class or caste. This principle reached its arrogant apogee with the complex rules of succession in the Russian imperial house, which removed status from anyone who married outside the gilded circles of royalty and the very top stratum of the aristocracy. This self-defeating rule resulted in the fact that there is nobody alive today who has any claim to the throne lost when Czar Nicholas II and his family were executed after the Russian Revolution. As every surviving member of the dynasty has married outside the prescribed ranks, all of them have lost their claim to the throne. The Bolsheviks would be pleased.

Apart from all these modifications to the simple rule of being born to the right parents, there is one that overrules all others: the sword. Even kings and queens who fulfill every criterion of correct birth, law, custom, and behavior can have their thrones removed by someone with a bigger army, who can establish his or her own family as the new and only legitimate dynasty through might alone (which is how most houses became royal in the first place). War and conquest were as much part of the Merovingian rules of succession as birth and law.

This raises the question of exactly what rights Pierre Plantard was claiming by tracing his descent *specifically* back to Dagobert II (and what rights are claimed on his behalf by Baigent, Leigh, and Lincoln when they extend the line back to Jesus). Clearly, they were rights of legal, not genetic, inheritance: all members of the dynasty shared the Merovingian genes—the distinctive DNA sequences that identified them as members of that family and might even have bestowed on them certain shared physical characteristics. (The "Habsburg lip," which threatened even Marie Antoinette's beauty, is a famous example, while according to the Dossiers Secrets the Merovingians boasted a distinctive birthmark in the form of a red cross between the shoulder blades. Unfortunately there is no independent evidence for this.)

Even according to the Priory, the Merovingian descendants married into or produced some of the most important noble and royal houses of Europe—most significantly the dukedom of Lorraine and then, through marriage in the mid–eighth century, the mighty Habsburgs. If these "Merovingians" became so important and powerful, this weakens, rather than strengthens, the Dossiers Secrets' case. If the Merovingians could attain such status under their own steam, why did they need the shadowy protectorate of the Priory of Sion? According to the Priory's genealogies, the Austro-Hungarian Emperors were of Merovingian descent—but they could hardly be described as powerless nobodies in need of secret guardians. And the Priory of Sion takes no credit for bringing these lineages to power: it exists only to protect the (alleged) descendants of Dagobert II.

In the Dossiers Secrets, the Priory made no claim that there was anything physically or genetically special about the bloodline: it was the fact that it was the *legitimate* royal house of France that marked it out. After the Carolingian usurpation twelve hundred years ago, Dagobert's putative descendants could have claimed they were the nearest blood relatives and therefore heirs to the Frankish kingdoms. But the Dossiers Secrets imply that this legal right was passed down through the centuries and is still valid—which we know is nonsense: the laws changed too many times over the course of that millennium. In any case, to whom could a Merovingian claimant appeal in the twenty-first century?

Besides all the problems about establishing a line of descent from Dagobert II, there are difficulties at the other end of the family tree, with Pierre Plantard himself. Even if there *had* been a secret lineage from Dagobert II, and if it *had* become the Plantard family, Pierre Plantard would still be outside the direct line of succession. This is because his paternal grandfather, Charles Plantard, was the *younger* of two brothers:

the elder, Pierre, would have been the direct heir of Dagobert, as would his son Jean (the Jean XXIII of Saunière's day according to the Dossiers Secrets), our Pierre Plantard's cousin, and then his son, and so on.

To overcome this very basic obstacle, the Dossiers Secrets state that Great-Uncle Pierre, for reasons not explained, signed away his rights in favor of his younger brother, Charles, which means that the title passed down through *his* son, our Pierre's father. (This is offered as an explanation of why Jean XXIII was unable to respond to Saunière's deathbed appeal, because he had been dispossessed of his rights—showing at least that there was an effort to make the whole story consistent.) Unfortunately, bending over backward in this way to explain why Pierre Plantard should have the throne completely undermines the logic behind the concept of the Merovingians' right to rule—the natural inheritance of the eldest son. Having supposedly enjoyed a direct and unbroken male line for twelve hundred years, it spoiled everything by going awry in the last couple of generations.

Despite all this, many people are under the impression that what is being claimed for the bloodline is some form of physical, genetic inheritance that confers something special on those fortunate enough to possess it: Einsteinian intelligence, perhaps, or a Christ-like spirituality—certainly a predestined, even divine right to rule. Presumably this is because of the West's cultural conditioning that there was something inherently special about Jesus, who is now also firmly in the equation.

This was not actually what Baigent, Leigh, and Lincoln claimed at all, although many of their readers seem to have had no problem in making the inference, or at least something very similar. (However, it must be said, posing questions about the Merovingians such as "Why should their blood come to be invested with such immense power?" was asking for trouble.)[55]

Even if the three authors are right about the Merovingians being the lineal descendants of Jesus, as they themselves ask: what does it matter? Paradoxically, if Jesus fathered children, he must have been a mortal man, not partly or wholly divine (thus ending the fundamental split in early Christianity that was resolved by condemning as heretics the Arians, who believed Jesus to be a mortal prophet). While this view might present a challenge to traditional Christians, ironically it also means that there is nothing intrinsically special about Jesus' descendants: if he wasn't divine, neither are they, and they are no more likely to be wiser, nobler, kinder, or more spiritually enlightened than anybody else.

The *Holy Blood* authors answer this conundrum in two ways. First, they argue that Jesus was, literally, the King of the Jews—as the Gospels suggest, a direct descendant of King David and therefore the rightful but dispossessed King of Israel, making his children and their descendants also heirs to that title. (They suggest that is why Godefroy de Bouillon seemed to regard the Kingdom of Jerusalem as his birthright—although, as we now know, that whole episode is profoundly flawed.) But of course staking a claim to reign over the modern State of Israel would be infinitely more difficult even than setting a Merovingian on the throne of France.

Second, Baigent, Leigh, and Lincoln suggest that the Priory of Sion is seeking to capture—or exploit—the *emotional* response surrounding the very concept of a living descendant of Jesus Christ. None of the legalities and the historical and genealogical arguments would matter a jot compared with that particular excitement: the trio argue that the aura or glamour of being of the line of Jesus, and the archetype of the priest-king, would be enough to persuade many people.[56] In other words—although Baigent, Leigh, and Lincoln avoid using the word—it is essentially a *cult* response that is being orchestrated. Followers are swept along by their instinctive feelings. Logic and reason have no part in it. (Again, though, the Priory never sought to use the archetype of Jesus in this way—that was Baigent, Leigh, and Lincoln's own contribution. But their argument applies as much to the *Roi Perdu* of France, although with a considerably more limited appeal.) Of course, if it is hearts rather than minds that the Priory seeks, then there is no requirement for its story to be based on fact—as long as they can *persuade* their audience it is true, the response will be the same.

In the Blood

The idea that certain specific genetic traits can be preserved within, and restricted to, any one identifiable family over such a long period of time is obviously arrant nonsense. Quite simply, after a few generations a family becomes too diffuse and unwieldy, intermarriage ensuring that its genes are spread too widely through the rest of the population.

Assuming that an average generation is twenty years (making sixty-odd generations since Dagobert II and one hundred since Jesus) and that each generation produces an average of two children (probably a very conservative underestimate, given the size of families historically), the "dynasty" will double in size with every generation, so that after ten generations there would be over one thousand members. In around thirty generations the total of this exponential growth would even theoretically exceed the population of the earth! Of course, after the first few generations, many of the marriages will be between distant and not-so-distant relatives, meaning that a host of people have been counted many times over. But even so, there will still be millions of them alive today: truly, we *are* all related, if we can trace our family tree back far enough. And a great many of us would be related to Jesus and Mary Magdalene—possibly we actually are. But before we all get too excited, other factors have to be taken into account.

In March 2003, the *American Journal of Human Genetics* published findings that some 0.5 percent of the world's population—around 16 million men—were descended from Genghis Khan (1162–1227) or his close male relatives. A genetic study of the peoples in the former countries of the Mongol Empire discovered that a specific sequence in the Y chromosome—found only in male DNA—indicating descent from a common ancestor was possessed by 8 percent of those tested. Because of the considerable possibilities for fathering children for Genghis Khan and his lusty, roving male kin, and certain tribes' age-old belief that they are the direct descendants of the great warlord, the scientists concluded that the genetic fingerprint was indeed his. But not all of the sixteen million descendants of Genghis Khan are megalomaniac warlords with a penchant for furry hats.

Of course, certain physical characteristics are transmitted by inheritance, but this transmission is a very hit-and-miss affair, which in any case really works only over a few generations. Once the genes have been well and truly mixed, any specific quality will become common to all, disappear, or manifest only sporadically and unpredictably in individuals now widely separated on the family tree. In other words, no special genetic trait could be restricted to a single family, or even group of families, for anything more than a few generations.

The only way that the hypothetical sacred Merovingian gene could be narrowly confined to a bloodline is by selective breeding: if its sexual activity is strictly controlled and it is allowed to breed only within itself—bearing in mind that even illegitimate offspring will carry the genes outside the family. Not only would that practice cause the usual problems of inbreeding, but in any case this is *not* what the Dossiers Secrets claim, as their genealogies show that members of the bloodline intermarried with other families (as in the connection with Godefroy de Bouillon). As soon as that happens, the "special" gene will spread to other families, so whatever gifts it confers will begin to manifest there, too. And very soon there will be thousands of people with the "gift" . . . and then millions.

Added to that, as until the very recent past almost without exception people married within their own class or caste, royal and noble houses soon became very closely related, so *all* of them would now be genetically Merovingian. (Because of the restricted size of the exclusive royal European "club," its intermarriages—and inbreeding—have been compared with those in a small and isolated village.) Of course, the proliferation of royal bastards born of commoners means that there are many ordinary folk of "royal blood" around today.

The task of preserving the integrity—or purity—of the bloodline would be much easier if the "sacred" gene was passed exclusively through the female DNA, from mother to daughter. Then it would barely matter who the father was, and the problem of illegitimacy threatening the purity of the bloodline would be solved. But then the magic or sacred "it" could be passed on only to daughters, and the Priory of Sion's genealogies emphatically trace Dagobert II's descendants through the *male* line.

On purely logical grounds, the idea of a family being set apart because of its blood—genetic inheritance—is a fiction, although it is one that has served its purpose over the centuries as a way of keeping certain families in positions of privilege.

In most cultures it has always been assumed that birth and inheritance *mean* something, beyond simply inheriting land and possessions. The old idea that breeding will out was deeply ingrained. "Blood" determined people's station in life, particularly the higher up the social scale they were. Kings and priests in particular were believed to receive their mandate direct from God, or the gods: they simply ruled *by right,* by virtue of who they were. However, in the modern world the concept of individuals being special—superior—by virtue of their parents is archaic and outmoded; most no longer believe that abilities, skills, or (especially) fitness to preside over the lives of the rest of the people is passed on by birth. Experience reveals the flaws in the argument: gifted leaders or brilliant minds can—and often do—produce incompetent or dim heirs.

Indeed, even though today we know it is meaningless, on an emotional and archetypal level, the idea of blood being special is still strangely powerful. (Special bloodlines and magical inherited powers routinely crop up in blockbusters such as the Harry Potter and Star Wars series.) Despite our hard-won egalitarianism, we still tend to regard people who can boast an illustrious ancestor as at least more interesting than—or set apart from—the rest of us. (And the converse is true: descendants of notorious figures, such as the Nazi leaders, have to cope with the shameful fallout.) Birth can still, at least, give some, such as members of the Kennedy and the Bush dynasties, a head start.

And of course royalty, crowned and anointed in the presence of God amid ancient panoply into the last bastion of set-apartness, despite being constantly challenged nowadays to prove itself worthy of its inherited rights and privileges, still retains its almost magical glamour. Footage of Elizabeth II's 1953 Coronation, with its soaring music and almost mystically enrapt central figure moving somberly through age-old rituals, can still bring a shiver to the spines of most hardened republicans. *She* is different, *she* is called by God because of her birthright, *she* is our Queen, and therefore we love, obey, and almost worship her. How much more potent, then, if she were descended not merely from German princelings—or through the historical accident of Edward VIII's abdication—but from Jesus Christ himself! Many respond at a profound, almost atavistic level to the notion of superior or, better still, *sacred* blood.

Controversial Claimants

The major popular exponent of a sacred bloodline is the British author Laurence Gardner, who developed it through a series of books beginning with *Bloodline of the Holy Grail* (1996). Gardner works closely with the controversial Prince Michael of Albany—Michel Lafosse—who claims to be the direct descendant of Bonnie Prince Charlie (Charles

Edward Stuart) and hence the head of the House of Stewart [*sic*] and legitimate King of, at least, Scotland, claiming the title King Alexander IV of the Scots. Lafosse was born in Brussels in 1958 and settled in Scotland in 1976, brandishing documents that he insists establish his claim.

The Stuart dynasty lost the throne in the early eighteenth century, as a consequence of the English Parliament declaring the Catholic James II to have abdicated when he fled to the continent in 1688 in the face of the Glorious Revolution led by his Protestant daughter Mary and her husband, William of Orange, who it then recognized as co-sovereigns. When Mary's sister, Anne, died childless in 1714, the royal Stuart line came to an end, and the throne (from which Catholics were now excluded by law) passed to the House of Hanover, forerunner of today's House of Windsor. Many still doubt that Parliament had the authority to depose James II, and consequently some continue to regard the Stuarts as the lawful sovereigns of England and Scotland—especially the latter.[57] The Scottish claim is strengthened by the fact that the 1707 Act banning Catholics from the throne was passed only in the English Parliament, before the union of England and Scotland. According to conventional historical wisdom, the direct line came to an end in 1807 with the death of Henry Benedict Stuart, Cardinal Duke of York—who stated that he was King "by the grace of God, but not by the will of men"—although the right to the title passed to collateral branches of the family and is today with Prince Franz of Bavaria (Francis II to Stuart supporters).

The difficulties in returning even this relatively recent—and arguably unjustly deposed—royal family to the throne underscore the ludicrousness of trying to restore a dynasty as ancient as the Merovingians.

Lafosse bases his claim that while in exile in Rome in 1784, Charles Edward Stuart obtained papal permission to annul his marriage to Princess Louise of Stolberg-Gedern and the following year married the Comtesse de Massillon. It is from their son Edward, Duke of Albany, that Prince Michael claims descent, but the colossal stumbling block is the fact that neither the annulment nor the second marriage is acknowledged by historians or genealogists, and Lafosse has not produced any evidence to persuade them otherwise.

Lafosse's problems are essentially the same as Plantard's: first he has to prove himself the legitimate descendant of the Stuarts, and then he must get them restored to the throne—if that really is his ambition. He has been feted by many groups and individuals on his word alone, generating a sizable support base and public profile (even being invited onto a radio show at the time of the restoration of the Scottish Parliament in 1999 to discuss the devolution of power to Scotland). The genealogist Jerry Jardine writes that "a few years ago he made quite a splash in the USA and Canada by creating Knighthoods, Dame-hoods and other titles in the Order of the Temple of Jerusalem. These titles were not inexpensive. A number of American ladies and gentlemen were displaying their enamelled crosses (similar to the cross of Malta) at the various Scottish Gatherings & Games held in those countries."[58]

This is the essential difference between Lafosse and Plantard: the latter never once attempted to exploit his claim in this way—despite many perfect opportunities. (Ironically, Lafosse told an interviewer in 2004: "I dismiss the Plantard claim.")[59]

Shortly after he first appeared in Scotland in 1976, Lafosse produced two documents that allegedly proved his case: his birth certificate as Prince Michael James Stewart, Comte d'Albanie (plus other titles), and letters from a senior figure in the Vatican Archives confirming the existence of records of the Young Pretender's annulment and remarriage. However, researchers have obtained a statement from the Brussels registrar that the certificate produced by Lafosse was "false" and a denial from the Vatican official, Mgr. Martino Giusti, that he was the author of the letters Lafosse produced.[60] In his turn, Lafosse claims the birth certificates supplied by the Brussels authorities (showing him to have been registered simply as Michel Roger Lafosse) are an "outright forgery," part of an ongoing conspiracy to deny his family's right to the throne currently occupied so uneasily by the Windsors.[61]

Debrett's has pronounced: "We have never seen any proof of his claims, which seem very unlikely. We treat this with a great deal of scepticism." A spokeswoman for the Court of Lord Lyon in Edinburgh, which deals with disputes concerning Scottish titles and heritage, said: "He has produced absolutely no evidence of his claims of his ascent, and until he does I would not recognise him as anything other than Michel Lafosse."[62]

However, some do—apparently—acknowledge his superiority: in 1992 he was elected head of the European Council of Princes, which he calls a "constitutional advisory body" attached to the European Parliament. He alleges that it was formed in 1946 and that until 1992 its head was the hugely influential Otto von Habsburg. But unfortunately the latter has denied any knowledge of such an organization.[63]

As Laurence Gardner writes in his introduction to Prince Michael's *The Forgotten Monarchy of Scotland* (1998) on his election: "The new appointment held political implications for Scotland because, in unanimously electing Michael of Albany, some thirty-two sovereign houses openly proclaimed the continuing *de jure* (rightful) Scots monarchy to an international audience; a royal dynasty which, according to British academic historians, had long been extinct."[64] (Gardner holds the title Presidential Attaché to the Council, as well as being its "appointed Jacobite Historiographer Royal.") Lafosse also stood unsuccessfully as a Member of the European Parliament in the Czech Republic in the elections of 2004.

Privileged Access

The difficulty in corroborating Laurence Gardner's overall thesis is that he relies heavily for key parts of his historical reconstruction on "privileged access" to the private archives of the likes of Prince Michael of Albany and certain chivalric orders. Basically we have to take his word for it not only that these documents say what he claims but that they even exist (just like the Dossiers Secrets' boast to be based on authentic documents that remain inaccessible and invisible to less fortunate mortals).

Gardner also has an interesting way with linguistics and etymology, authoritatively stating alternatives to the standard derivations of words without producing any evidence. For example, in *Realm of the Ring Lords* (2000), he writes: "The Cathars were supporters of the Albigens: the Elven bloodline which had descended through the Grail queens of yore such as Lilith, Miriam, Bathsheba and Mary Magdalene. It was for this reason that, when Simon de Montfort and the armies of Pope Innocent III descended upon the region in 1209, it was called the Albigensian Crusade."[65] Actually, according to received wisdom—and, one might think, common sense—the Cathars were called Albigensians after their favored town of Albi in southern France. Of course received wisdom is by no means always correct, but surely if Gardner has such startling new evidence, he should let us all in on the secret, rather than simply wielding his revised story like a blunt instrument.

Bloodline of the Holy Grail is essentially a new interpretation of *The Holy Blood and the Holy Grail* plus certain new information from those private archives that apparently fill in some of the gaps. Here not only do Jesus and Mary Magdalene marry and have children but we are even told their names—a girl, Damaris (or Tamar); Jesus (II); and Joseph, the "Grail Child" who was taken to Gaul. The blank between that event and the rise of the Merovingians five centuries later is filled in with a genealogical chart showing that Joseph's descendant Pharamond married a Sicambrian princess. Merovée, the founder of the dynasty, was their grandson.

The Dossiers Secrets' unreliable claims about the Merovingian survival through Sigebert IV are repeated, although Gardner adds some original mistakes—describing the historic Dagobert II as the son of Sigebert II, not III as he should be, and Dagobert's son, who was sheltered in Rennes-le-Château, as Sigebert III instead of IV. Here, too, Godefroy de Bouillon is of Merovingian descent. The reappearance of the Dossiers Secrets' errors naturally casts considerable doubt on the accuracy of the "private archives" used by Gardner.

However, in his version Jesus' family was perpetuated in several European families, not exclusively the Merovingians. For example, the bloodline was also established in Britain by Joseph of Arimathea, from which Arthur and the other Kings of Britain were descended. And as the "Grail bloodline" led to the House of Stewart (Gardner's and Prince Michael's preferred spelling), its modern representative is . . . Prince Michael of Albany.

In the final analysis, Gardner's message is essentially political—he writes at the beginning of *Bloodline of the Holy Grail* that it is "a book about good government and bad government."[66] To him the world would be in a much better position if the Grail family were allowed to rule in the way it was intended to as part of the natural order.

In *Genesis of the Grail Kings* (1999), Gardner takes the origins of the bloodline back even further—not to Jesus or King David but to Adam and Eve, and indeed, considerably beyond. Sensation lovers in the United Kingdom can salivate over the subtitle of *The Pendragon Legacy of Adam and Eve,* while American readers relish the even more eye-popping *The Explosive Story of Genetic Cloning and the Ancient Bloodline of Jesus.* In this book, Gardner's "privileged access" provides an open sesame into another archive besides Prince Michael's: that of the Imperial and Royal Dragon Court and Order, a revival of a medieval Hungarian noble order whose Grand Master is the British "His Royal Highness" Nicholas de Vere, who inevitably also claims Merovingian descent.

Unashamedly, Gardner states that the "Grail bloodline" owes its origins to genetic engineering by extraterrestrials that took place in ancient Sumer, creating a superior strain to the humanity they had already created: "Adam"—a new race, not a single individual. (Of course the idea that the Merovingians were partly alien had already surfaced in Gérard de Sède's 1973 book, *The Fabulous Race.*)

Gardner explains that the ETs were the mysterious group of gods called the Anunnaki, who according to Sumerian mythology brought kingship down from heaven: in other words, the "divinely" appointed kings—the Grail bloodline—are the descendants of the genetically altered Adam.[67] (De Vere terms its descendants Dragons and associates "Adam" humanity with the Aryan race, claiming that Aryan means "scion of the wise and noble race"—although he is quick to distance this from the Nazis' beloved Aryan "master race." Although some might think he is missing the point, de Vere dismisses the Nazis as "German peasants" of inferior genetic stock to the *real* Aryans. At least in de Vere's system the Nazis are now the inferior race!)[68]

In this and later books, Gardner introduces the highly controversial subject of "monatomic gold" or "white powder gold," said to be a special form of the metal discovered in natural deposits in Arizona in the 1980s by the farmer David Hudson, who after years of study managed to replicate it in the laboratory. Hudson also claims to have produced monatomic forms of other metals, including silver, with similarly remarkable properties; for them he coined the interesting term Orbitally Rearranged Monatomic Elements, or ORMEs. (Monatomic gold and other elements can now be purchased as rather unusual dietary supplements—in the words of one supplier, to "assist with your personal ascension process.")[69] Hudson promoted these discoveries in the United States in a series of lectures in the mid-1990s.[70]

The list of properties associated with monatomic gold is indeed remarkable. It is said to be a superconductor, to be antigravitational, and to bend space-time—even to teleport into other dimensions. It also acts on DNA to heal any disease or ailment—Hudson and his supporters have claimed many cures of cancer and AIDS. Finally, monatomic elements are allegedly able to cause "spiritual shifts" in consciousness that usher in greater transcendental awareness, enlightenment, and enhanced psychic powers.

If all this sounds too good to be true, it's probably because it is. Not one of these claims has been backed up by any verifiable evidence. The cancer and AIDS patients who were saved by monatomic gold remain anonymous; the scientific laboratories that confirmed the amazing physical properties refuse to be named until they are ready to publish their work; vested political and business interests are trying to hush the whole thing up. And so on. Even so, the remarkably elusive white powder gold is adulated among the New Age subculture, particularly in America. Even the news that Hudson has had multiple heart bypasses has done little to dent their faith in its powers.[71] If one seeks to understand the allure of the Holy Grail, one need look no further. It is as well to remember that the Grail was first mentioned in a medieval best seller. It was fiction.

Following his study of the physical properties of white powder gold, Hudson found evidence it had been known to select groups throughout history: it was the Philosopher's Stone of the alchemists, the Grail stone of Wolfram von Eschenbach, the manna that saved the Israelites in the wilderness, and various other magical substances mentioned in ancient Egyptian and other texts. How Hudson knows this is hard to tell. And in any case his search for historical or mythological precedents is made somewhat easier by the fact that the magical substances he claims as really being white powder gold do not have to be white, powdery, or made of gold. The general idea is that the secret of white powder gold was handed down by the "gods" and has been used ever since by secret elites and priesthoods, who are therefore more enlightened and wiser than the rest of us. Hudson, like Gardner, invokes the (equally questionable) theories of Zecharia Sitchin that the gods of ancient Sumer were, in fact, extraterrestrials who created the human race, and a superior strain of kings, through genetic engineering.

To cap it all, Hudson discovered that he was descended from the Guise family, who appear in the Dossiers Secrets' list of Merovingian descendants—inevitably making him "of the bloodline." He believes this is why he was "fated" to discover monatomic gold.[72]

All these ideas appear in Gardner's work, although he has added others drawn from Nicholas de Vere. Gardner explains that originally the Kings of Sumer were able to extend their consciousness and mental powers by ingesting the menstrual fluids of the Anunnaki priestesses—a substance known as Star Fire. (The term also occurs in the magical rituals of Aleister Crowley, where again it is a substance produced from the vulvas of priestesses, although in this system of a terrestrial kind.) Later, monatomic gold was developed as a synthetic version of Star Fire bestowing the same abilities. (Nicholas de Vere, who acknowledges that he has practiced the Star Fire ritual, dissociates himself from the monatomic gold aspect, declaring, "You are either genetically a Dragon or you are not, and no amount of monatomic gold is going to change your genetic makeup.")[73]

So we see that the major development of the hypothesis in *The Holy Blood and the Holy Grail*—which must seem rather tame in comparison—is that a genetic component, a magical gift that literally comes from the stars, is being claimed for the bloodline. And the various elements of the bloodline—the genetic "creator gods," white powder gold, and of course Prince Michael's claim to the throne of Scotland—are forced into the appearance of a coherent, internally supportive story.

This Merovingian fever reached its apogee in the 2001 book by Jon King and John Beveridge, *Princess Diana—the Hidden Evidence,* which asserted that the Princess of Wales was assassinated by M16 and the CIA not merely because she was about to marry a Muslim but also because she was being "courted" by supporters of the Merovingian bloodline—of which she was herself a member. Apparently this posed such a threat to the future of the British royal family that she had to be done away with. The book and theory are endorsed in a foreword by Prince Michael of Albany.

There may or may not be suspicious circumstances surrounding the death of Diana (which is, fortunately, outside the scope of this book),[74] but the proposal that she was assassinated because she was Merovingian founders immediately as a result of lack of evidence for the line's survival. And in any case, there is still the problem that there would not be anything special about that bloodline even if it had survived. (All this reveals the weakness in the structure around the Merovingian–Anunnaki–white powder gold axis: if one part falls, then the rest crashes down with it—if there were no Merovingian survivors and nothing special about their blood anyway, then at least the motive claimed by the Diana assassination theory is wrong.)

In 2000 there was another addition to the bloodline canon: *Rex Deus: The True Mystery of Rennes-le-Château and the Dynasty of Jesus* by Marilyn Hopkins, Graham Simmans, and Tim Wallace-Murphy. Wallace-Murphy is a well-known writer on Masonic and esoteric subjects who had collaborated with Hopkins on a previous book about Rosslyn Chapel, and Graham Simmans is a British expatriate who lives in Rennes-le-Château. According to this version, Baigent, Leigh, and Lincoln got the right story but the wrong(ish) bloodline: this trio claims that the "bloodline" families are descended from the High Priests of the Temple of Jerusalem.

The hypothesis is based on information supplied by an informant identified only as Michael, who claims to be a member of a select group of families descended from the Davidic and Hasmonaean royal families of Israel and the twenty-four High Priests of the Temple of Jerusalem of Jesus' day. Unfortunately, the evidential documents were lost—tragically having been kept in a desk that was accidentally sold.[75] (Perhaps the present owner might hand them in?)

In this version, Jesus' importance derived from being both heir to the throne of David and of priestly descent, Mary having been ritually impregnated by the High Priest Gabriel (the Gospel story of the Annunciation being a garbled version of this). After that we are on familiar ground: Jesus married Mary Magdalene, and they had children. Jesus' son (James in this version), the heir to the throne of David, was brought to England by Joseph of Arimathea. Godefroy de Bouillon was given the throne of Jerusalem because he was "rightful heir of the Davidic line and a direct descendant of Jesus"[76]—omitting the inconvenient fact that he actually had an older brother, the real "rightful heir."

The place of the Priory of Sion is taken by another secret society, Rex Deus, which was behind the creation of the Knights Templar. (Michael also claimed to be a direct descendant of the Templar founder, Hugues de Payens.) This version of the bloodline also ends with Prince Michael of Albany, who is not only feted as a member of the Rex Deus bloodline but cited as an authority on obscure historical matters. For example, when discussing the theory (long speculated about but unsupported by any specific evidence) that the Templars discovered a cache of scrolls in Jerusalem, Hopkins, Simmans, and Wallace-Murphy write, "HRH

Prince Michael of Albany confirmed this when he described the scrolls discovered by the Templars in their excavations in Jerusalem as 'the fruits of thousands of years of knowledge.' "[77]

Curiously, the *Rex Deus* authors criticize Baigent, Leigh, and Lincoln's bloodline hypothesis—comparing it to fiction—on the grounds they rely too heavily on the discredited Dossiers Secrets (here attributed unquestioningly to Plantard and de Chérisey alone), ending up with the wrong bloodline, the Merovingians.[78] This is particularly ironic as *Rex Deus* itself boasts nothing as tangible as even the Dossiers Secrets behind it, relying simply on the word of Michael. In any case, the authors accept that the bloodline is that of Jesus (and, incidentally, Mary Magdalene) and that the Merovingians were indeed members of the Rex Deus line.

There are some very basic errors in Hopkins, Simmans, and Wallace-Murphy's reconstruction of events at Rennes-le-Château. For example, they date the beginning of Saunière's restoration of his church, and the ensuing discoveries, to 1891, whereas it happened four years earlier. More important, they write: "We accept that Saunière had repeated contacts with Emma Calvé both in Paris and at Rennes-le-Château but it is less certain that he entertained the French Minister of Culture in his remote hilltop village. However, when we examine the alleged contacts between this rural country priest and the Habsburgs, the senior ruling family of Europe, we are on much shakier ground."[79] In fact, the situation is completely the reverse. There is *no* documentary evidence for the Saunière-Calvé connection, this being based solely on the memories of the villagers; of the visits of the *future* Minister for Fine Arts, Dujardin-Beaumetz, there is no doubt—he was a local politician and artist who was a friend of Saunière's before the priest was even assigned to Rennes-le-Château; and the visits of a Habsburg Archduke, albeit a maverick one, are solidly recorded in police and Deuxième Bureau files.

It is rather puzzling why Rennes-le-Château features in the *Rex Deus* story at all, as the authors dismiss the Dossiers Secrets as a hoax and *The Holy Blood and the Holy Grail*'s hypothesis as tantamount to fiction. Hopkins, Simmans, and Wallace-Murphy offer no explanation of where Saunière got his money, indeed do not even hazard a connection between the Rex Deus families and the Saunière affair.

Cult Status

Inevitably, the sacred bloodline concept is perfect for exploitation by would-be cultists. Picking out certain individuals as *destined* leaders—even if their rightful role is not recognized by the powers that be—provides the potential for claimants to that elite to paint themselves as martyrs, conspired against by the enemies of the Truth ("By the grace of God [or the Anunnaki], but not by the will of men"). Presumably it is only a matter of time before somebody emerges to stake such a claim, establishing himself or herself as the leader of a ready-made pseudoreligious cult.

Recent history repeatedly warns of the grisly fate that can await members of even what appear to be harmlessly eccentric cults, as their leaders decide for whatever reason that it is time for them to wind up the enterprise, decreeing that their followers must end their lives (or, if they refuse, have them taken). In Jonestown, Guyana, in 1978, over nine hundred members of the People's Temple took poison, while in 1997 thirty-nine followers of the Heaven's Gate cult willingly, even ecstatically, went on their last journey beyond the stars. Moreover, there were three separate episodes of mass suicide and murders of members of the sinister Order of the Solar Temple.

Indeed, despite all the logical objections to the bloodline theories, a casual surf around the Internet shows that a great many people out there are utterly enthralled by the concept of bloodline families who are different from the rest of us—although the enthusiasts tend to be divided between those who think the "bloodliners" are our hidden saviors and those who regard them as the secret satanic rulers of the world. The idea of the sacred bloodline is also gradually integrating with more traditional New Age beliefs and culture, and claimants are treated with interest, respect, and even a certain awe. But as we have shown, whether in one's view the bloodline is good or bad, the whole concept rests on very shaky foundations indeed. It is a potent modern myth that has developed considerably since *The Holy Blood and the Holy Grail,* extending far beyond what its authors proposed. And more worryingly, the emphasis on an all-powerful heritage can also be seen as a return to the old idea, albeit dressed up in a modern guise, that certain people are superior to the rest of us solely because of the families they are born into.

Surely that is not what our hard-won democracy should be about. (And it is positively dangerous, for if individuals can be superior because of their genetic makeup, then by implication the reverse is true—some of us are *inferior* because of our lineage, physical characteristics, or race. All too recent history has shown what use the criminally insane and unscrupulous can do with such ideas.)

However, the most significant aspect is that Plantard and de Chérisey never tried to exploit this cult potential, either for material gain or for power and influence over others, even though it would have been easy enough to do so. In fact, the two Priory tricksters downplayed the whole business, even taking care to distance themselves from it.

The Story So Far

We have concluded that, contrary to popular opinion, the Priory of Sion *as such* is a fiction, a convenient cover story—perhaps even an illusion. Its specific claims concerning its historical pedigree and supposed purpose since its inception at the end of the eleventh century fall apart when scrutinized, as do the theories that rely on those claims being true. The Priory of Sion is *not* about restoring the Merovingians to power in France: in fact, since the Priory changed the plot so radically in 1989, it is no longer even about being *seen* to be working for a Merovingian restoration.

Pierre Plantard's function was to front the enterprise, to keep the game in play (or more accurately, since the story often went into hibernation for several years, to bring it back into play when needed). Philippe de Chérisey seems to have been chief mischief maker: he certainly relished the labyrinthine mystification and game playing almost as a form of performance art.

Joke it may be, but there was considerable work and a degree of expertise in historical and esoteric matters behind its construction. And there seems to be something substantial behind the illusion. We have found repeated connections to orders and societies that indubitably do exist, and a teasing recurrence of certain themes with no connection to the Merovingian cover story: which may, of course, merely represent another level of misinformation, but it may also provide certain clues about the true agenda of those who really pull the Priory's strings.

But while it is only too easy to say what the Priory of Sion isn't, is it possible to discern what it actually *is*?

In the next chapter we will examine the Priory's "symbolic history" in an attempt to work out what, if anything, it believes in. For now it is important to remind ourselves of the one principle that has remained constant through all the reinventions and game playing: the ideal of a united Europe. This was a major focus of the wartime Alpha Galates Order and *Vaincre,* right through to Plantard's last words on the Priory in 1989, about Victor Hugo "planting the oak of the United States of Europe." Material disseminated by the Priory links it with individuals such as Alain Poher who were prominent in European affairs. This preoccupation can even be seen in Plantard's production, while involved in the Gisors affair, of a small booklet on a subject that, at first, appears incongruous. In 1961 he deposited in the Bibliothèque Nationale a twenty-four-page booklet, attributed to CIRCUIT, with the self-explanatory title *Comparative Tables of Social Charges in the Countries of the Common Market.* Working toward the creation of a federal Europe seems to be a genuine aim and principle at the core of the Priory's thinking, whatever all the other theatrics may or may not be about, as Plantard spelled out to Baigent, Leigh, and Lincoln in September 1984.[80] But the inspirations for such an apparently solid political ambition may seem a little bizarre.

PART TWO

REALITY

CHAPTER SIX

Return to the Source

As we now know, the Priory of Sion attaches itself to certain esoteric groups such as the Templars and Rosicrucians—the usual suspects, which seem to be almost mandatory associates for any secret society that wishes to be taken seriously. (However, unlike most orders, the Priory has never claimed to be a direct continuation of the Templars, merely to have been their colleagues in the past, although still implying strongly that it possesses some of their secrets. And the Priory associates with Freemasonry in only the loosest possible way.)

It seems logical that understanding the strands and connections in the Dossiers Secrets and other Priory material may well reveal something promising, about either the Order's true beliefs (if it has any) or the reasons for its preoccupations. Does the Priory really guard great secrets or possess any knowledge that remains inaccessible to the outside world? If not, what was its source of information? And why did it choose those particular subjects in the first place?

The Woman Jesus Loved

One of the unusual elements is the Priory's emphasis on Mary Magdalene; referring to her somewhat enigmatically in the Dossiers Secrets and elsewhere. Interviewed by Jean-Luc Chaumeil in the late 1970s, Philippe de Chérisey declared (no less enigmatically): "The figure of Mary Magdalene is the key, as she is the hyphen between Marseilles, where she died, or is at least reputed to have died, and Vézelay, where her relics are kept. On the other hand, one finds at Rennes that the church has been dedicated to her since 700, which shows the devotion they bore for her and which is significant for the deciphering of the tomb."[1]

It was this unusually strong reverence for the woman still widely considered to be a reformed prostitute[2] that inspired the three *Holy Blood and the Holy Grail* authors to suggest that the Magdalene was Jesus' wife and progenitor of his bloodline—although as we now know, this was *not* the intention of the authors of the Dossiers Secrets. However, the elevation of Mary Magdalene to such an important position, without any particular explanation, has become one of the most fruitful of the avenues opened by the Dossiers Secrets and other Priory material. It led Baigent, Leigh, and Lincoln—and then ourselves and other researchers, such as Margaret Starbird—to investigate alternative sources of information about her. And what a revelation that has been.

The alternative sources, such as the Nag Hammadi Gospels, show that significant groups of early, Gnostic Christians believed Mary Magdalene not only to be important in her own right as a teacher and preacher but also to have had some kind of special relationship with Jesus, raising important and *valid* questions about the role of women in the religion, not to mention the nature of Jesus himself. The very existence of the Gnostic writings also reveals what biblical scholars have known for generations, that there are texts about Jesus and the origins of Christianity besides the books of the New Testament. In turn, this prompts ordinary nontheologians to ask obvious and major questions about the extent to which the early Church selectively edited and distorted the Christian message. As readers of Dan Brown inevitably find themselves asking, have we been *lied to* about Christianity, and about Jesus himself?

Whatever conclusions one might reach about Pierre Plantard, the Priory of Sion, and the Dossiers Secrets, above all others these questions have seized the imaginations—and ignited the indignation—of fans of *The Holy Blood and the Holy Grail* and *The Da Vinci Code.* As it is very, very unlikely that so many readers would have even known such information exists otherwise, ultimately they have to thank the Dossiers Secrets and other writings by Plantard and de Chérisey for the key to such an exciting but daunting liberation. In that sense at least, that odd couple has done an enormous service for us all.

However, the only-too-easy debunking of other parts of the Priory myth tends to be a disincentive from also investigating these more serious, evidential—and truly challenging—aspects of the story. In fact, this is exactly how traditional Christians seek to protect their age-old dogmas, arguing that if Plantard can be shown to have invented the Priory of Sion, then the Gnostic Gospels and other apocryphal sources can also be safely ignored—which is nonsense. Baigent, Leigh, and Lincoln did not invent the "forbidden" gospels or the case for Mary Magdalene's special place in Jesus' movement, if not his personal life, or the scandal of the selective editing of the original Christian texts. The scholarly case for all this had been set out long before; the *Holy Blood* authors simply found themselves investigating the alternative gospels and other largely ignored material because they were trying to discover why the Priory venerated Mary Magdalene with such intensity. Under all the surreal Priory jokes, contradictions, nonsense, and dead ends lurks something of genuine—even major—significance. And it is because of the Priory of Sion, albeit in the most ludicrously labyrinthine manner, that most of us today know the Church has covered its tracks for two millennia with a tangle of half-truths and outright lies. The importance of this is hard to exaggerate. Yet because of the remorseless—and admittedly often justified—debunking, it is a very special baby that trembles on the brink of exiting unceremoniously with the bathwater.

Another rewarding and profoundly thought-provoking line of inquiry was opened by the Priory's superficially odd association of Mary Magdalene with Isis, the great Egyptian goddess of life, sex, and magic, and the semiheretical European cult of the Black Madonna. Again, following these leads reveals that there is evidence to connect Mary Magdalene, and through her even Jesus himself, with the pagan mystery cults of Egypt.[3] But was this trail laid deliberately by the Priory—or whoever really pulls its strings?

Although many of the Dossiers Secrets' references to Mary Magdalene seem intended to lead to Rennes-le-Château's church rather than to the biblical or historical woman, why were so many churches in that part of France dedicated to her in the first place? In fact, in that region she was and is the object of a cult—even amounting to what several researchers have called the *Church* of Mary Magdalene. The discovery of such a cult leads in two related directions: first, to the legends that she traveled to southern France after the Crucifixion, and second to the discovery that the original basis of her *heretical* cult in the Languedoc (as opposed to the officially sanctioned Catholic cult that displaced it) emerged from information otherwise found only in the long-lost Gnostic Gospels, which must therefore have circulated in France in the first centuries after Christ.[4]

But did the Priory *intend* to lay this trail, or was it just a happy accident? As far as we know, attributing such a significant role to Mary Magdalene has never been an intrinsic part of the traditions of any esoteric society or order, at least from the eighteenth century onward. Although there are some references to female figures with Magdalene-like associations in certain French Masonic lore, they *might* be veiled allusions to her, but they might not. That's as far as it goes. But it is strange that, as Mary Magdalene was a particularly important figure to the medieval Knights Templar, who took an oath to the "obedience of Bethany" and used her name in their absolution, none of the societies claiming to be descended from them seems to have perpetuated this particular tradition. Either their beliefs about Mary Magdalene are very well hidden "deep doctrine" or she was simply never there—casting doubt on their claims to be genuine Templar heirs.

However, the Dossiers Secrets could have drawn on history rather than esoteric lore. Although first presented to the world outside France through *The Holy Blood and the Holy Grail,* the Provençal legends are obviously well known in their homeland, and they—and therefore Mary Magdalene herself and her role in the original Christian movement—have been meticulously pored over, at least during the last couple of centuries. And of course, the discovery in the mid–nineteenth century of texts such as the poetic and revelatory *Gospel of Mary Magdalene*—one of the dozens of texts banned by the early Church—also made her the focus of attention among certain circles.

As we tried to trace exactly when scholarly interest in Mary Magdalene began in France, certain fascinating facts surfaced. The character Stella in Alexandre Dumas's (père's) 1837 play *Caligula* tells her mother that while in Gaul she witnessed the disembarkation of Mary Magdalene and her companions on a beach in what is now southern France, and as a result of an inspirational encounter with the lady herself, Stella changed her name to Mary. When she explains to her mother, "It's the name of a sacred virgin," her mother replies, "But so is the other one."

One of the earliest detailed examinations of the legends of Mary Magdalene in Provence was the monumental two-volume study—by Abbé Étienne Michel Faillon, priest of St.-Sulpice, whose other major work was a biography of Jean-Jacques Olier. A meticulous compendium and analysis of the historical texts, *Unpublished Monuments on the Apostolate of St. Mary Magdalene in Provence* (1848), concluded that the legends were based on a real event—Mary Magdalene really had traveled to France and lived out her long life there—and that she had indeed been an *apostle* in the full meaning of the term. Faillon's book is a plea to restore the Magdalene to her rightful place of glory in the Church, "of which she is the *figure*[head]."[5]

Frustratingly, though, it is impossible to say definitively whether the Magdalene's appearance in Priory lore—and the discoveries that followed—is a lucky coincidence or a result of the fact that the Priory (or its controlling organizations) really guarded a great secret about her. In any case, this, along with the Johannite theme, is by far the most fruitful revelation to emerge from the Priory material. Leaving aside all the time-wasting fantasies about Merovingian bloodlines, *returning* Mary Magdalene to her former status as the beloved companion of Jesus is a breathtaking and enduring triumph for the Priory, whether or not it was intentional.

The Sacred Feminine

Even beyond the maligned but magnificent Magdalene, from the outset the sacred feminine has been an important aspect of the Priory's "doctrines." Highlighting Isis is another major feature of Plantard's 1962 appendix to Gérard de Sède's *The Templars Are Among Us.* And in *The Red Serpent,* Mary Magdalene and Isis are specifically linked. Also, as we have seen, Plantard boldly associated the Black Madonnas of Europe with Isis.

But why choose Isis and not another goddess of the ancient world, such as Diana, Astarte, or Artemis? Does the ancient Egyptian religion play a significant part in the Priory's beliefs, or does it merely hark back to the eighteenth-century "Egyptian Rites" of Freemasonry? Perhaps Isis was chosen because she is still widely thought of as the supreme icon of the sacred feminine, with an exceptionally enduring cross-cultural appeal. But is the Priory using her name in vain, simply as an exotic morsel to tempt the jaded palates of modern seekers?

In unusually straightforward language for a Priory man, Gino Sandri has declared the importance to the society of the feminine in general and the archetypal role of Isis in particular:

> On a fundamental level, it [the Female] is an essential point, unfortunately well hidden. The majority of initiatory societies are often only caricatures, and latent misogyny is a sign of this. Without being able to expand on the subject, I would submit this for your reflection. In many rituals, the applicant is placed in the presence of death and rebirth. Death and transfiguration! Now, in Egyptian mythology, it was Isis alone who was in a position to reassemble the scattered pieces of the body of Osiris.[6]

Such reverence for the sacred feminine is not, of course, unique by any means—most esoteric societies at least pay it lip service, although Sandri's description of the "latent misogyny" of societies that *claim* such reverence is particularly perceptive. In a similar way the Catholic Church boasts about showing respect for motherhood while being notoriously sexist as a matter of principle.

(Perhaps it is no coincidence that the Roman Church was founded by St. Peter, who emerges from the recovered Gnostic Gospels as something of a hotheaded dimwit whose slowness to understand infuriates Jesus and who hates not only Mary Magdalene—whose life he actually threatens—but also "all the race of women." Faithful to his example, his Church remains misogynist to this day. More sensationally, the Gnostic Gospels make it clear that, despite the New Testament's buildup of Peter's alleged importance in Jesus' movement, it is Mary Magdalene and John the Evangelist who are the favorites, and *she* who not only is closest to Christ but knows his innermost secrets—whereas they remain inaccessible to the famous twelve male disciples. Clearly, Jesus revered the sacred Feminine in the person of his beloved Magdalene, whom he called "the All" and "The Woman Who Knows All," but this view was not shared by rough diamonds like Simon Peter, whose devotees maligned and misrepresented the Magdalene for two millennia—and of course, in doing so, *also misrepresented Jesus Christ himself.* What would he say about his "All" being turned into a prostitute, for which there is zero evidence, and almost written out of the New Testament, while the books that sing her praises were condemned as heretical, burnt, or hidden?)[7]

John's Tradition

As we have seen, the Priory also allies itself with the mysterious heretical Johannite tradition in several ways. Although lurking in the background from the beginning, the Johannite element (for example, as the Church of John supposedly encountered by Godefroy de Bouillon) became more central at the end of the 1970s, after the advent of Gino Sandri.

There are several interpretations of the Johannite tradition and its meaning. Usually in European esoteric traditions it is associated with John the Evangelist, Jesus' young disciple, and represents a Gnostic Church in opposition to St. Peter's Church of Rome. Devotees of such esoteric traditions seem to have seized on John's movement because, while recognizing that the Catholic Church—the *only* form of Christianity allowed in Europe before the sixteenth-century Reformation—is flawed, they fight shy of actually challenging the "Gospel truth," the very foundations of the Christian religion. They assume that something went wrong in the succession—that Jesus had bestowed his authority on John, the "beloved disciple," not on Peter, and so it is *that* John's Church that represents the true continuation of the religion founded by Jesus.[8]

Other versions emphasize the role of John the Baptist, yet others of John of Patmos, the traditional author of the Revelation to John. Some believe John of Patmos and John the eponymous Gospel writer to be one and the same anyway (although on textual grounds alone this is very unlikely). Other traditions, as in modern Freemasonry, attribute key roles to both the Baptist and the Evangelist, although without any clear idea why.

However, all branches of Johannitism agree that the Gospel of John is enormously significant, although the attribution of the fourth Gospel to the disciple John is purely traditional. In fact, the Gospel (the only one in the New Testament claiming explicitly to be written by one of Jesus' disciples) is anonymous, the writer simply referring to himself as the "disciple Jesus loved."

Perceptively, Jean Markale notes that heretical forms of Christianity that challenge Rome seem to find it natural to place themselves under the patronage of *a* John—almost as if any John will do.[9] We suggest that this is because of a dim memory—perhaps a memory deliberately dimmed—of something real although incorrectly interpreted by later groups who were ignorant of the full story.

As we now know, there *was* a historical Church of John that *did* pose a major threat to the embryonic Christian movement, and that actually believed John the Baptist was the true Messiah—*and Jesus was his usurper.* Although as we noted in Chapter 1, the John religion not only survived in the Middle East but still survives in the form of the Mandaeans of Iraq, both the movement and the very knowledge of its existence were successfully suppressed in Europe. But memories of a rival Church of John that once existed, and might still exist in the Holy Land, had trickled down to later heretical groups. In our reconstruction, in trying to make sense of this, these groups came up with the hypothesis—entirely logical on its own terms—that Jesus had passed "secret teachings" on to his disciple John, whose own line of priests preserve those secrets, reserved for initiates.

While there is definite historical justification for a rival church founded in the Baptist's name (which existed alongside Jesus' Church for at least five centuries), there is no evidence at all for a movement venerating the Evangelist. The many *traditions* of a secret John the Evangelist Church are much more recent in origin.

The confusion may easily have arisen because, according to John's Gospel, the "beloved disciple" (assumed to be John) began as a disciple of John the Baptist, later switching to Jesus' cult.[10] (This particular part of the New Testament is likely to be true, since in general it tends to downplay the fact that John *had* disciples in the same sense as Jesus.) If the younger John was once a disciple of the Baptist—possibly taking his name after the initiatory rite of baptism—then any secret teachings that were passed down this line are more likely to have been those of John the Baptist. We have also suggested that the confusion between the two Johns may have been deliberate on the part of the "true" Johannites—those who venerate the Baptist—in order to hide their real beliefs behind the more acceptable Evangelist.[11]

Be that as it may, does the Priory scatter Johannite references about simply to prove it is familiar with the tradition? Or does it possess genuine secrets about Johannitism, unknown to anyone else (apart, perhaps, from the Mandaeans)? It is hard to tell—but Giovanni's carefully stage-managed hints about the importance of John successfully acted as a gateway to discoveries about the real conspiracies and cover-ups that have surrounded the Christian Church from the very beginning.

Ironically, what appeared to be a minor question from Giovanni—why the Grand Masters took the name John—led to something major, while one of the Priory's alleged raisons d'être, such as the Merovingian survival, very quickly crumbles into dust. But can we discover where the Priory found its Johannite references?

As we have seen, the Priory's version—which postdated the Dossiers Secrets, first appearing in Jean-Luc Chaumeil's 1979 book *The Treasure of the Golden Triangle*—described Godefroy de Bouillon encountering a "Church of John" that represented true Christianity and, at least partly in revenge for what Peter's "false" Church had done to his Merovingian forebears, deciding to adopt its doctrines.

This is actually a conflation of two similar tales, to which Godefroy de Bouillon has been added to give it a more appealing Merovingian gloss. Both these foundation myths, like the Priory's, purport to explain how an order came into being, identifying its associated traditions and making it legitimate with the required pedigree. As both stories appeared at roughly the same time—about two hundred years ago—it is impossible to tell which one influenced the other, or if either or both used earlier sources.

The first was the foundation myth of a "revived" Order of the Temple that appeared in France in 1804, claiming to be the direct successor of the medieval Knights Templar, which after five centuries underground judged the time was right to reveal itself again. This Order of the Temple, after the usual reorganizations, schisms, and reconciliations, became today's most important and influential neo-Templar organization, the Sovereign and Military Order of the Temple of Jerusalem, one of two main streams of alleged Templar survival, known as the Larmenius transmission (after the first of the supposed secret Grand Masters), as opposed to the Scottish transmission, which we will examine shortly. Unlike the Scottish branch, the Larmenius transmission is non-Masonic, even something of a rival to Freemasonry today.

When this new Order of the Temple was first founded (or, as it would claim, revived), it aligned itself to the Johannite tradition—although subsequently discarding it in favor of conventional Catholicism. Today the Order insists that all members be Christians.[12] Its foundation story claimed that the Templars' founder, Hugues de Payens, had encountered a Johannite "Order of the East" that retained Jesus' true teachings—presumably because he took them from his teacher, the Baptist, but ultimately deriving from the mystery schools of Egypt—as passed on to his disciple John the Evangelist. Of course this is basically the same as the Priory's story, except that in theirs Godefroy de Bouillon takes the place of Hugues de Payens.

Although this is very interesting, unfortunately it is impossible to follow up. No one knows the origins of the Order of the Temple's story—usually it is assumed that the founder simply made it up, although at the very least he seem to have woven earlier traditions together into a coherent narrative. However, the Priory's second foundation myth is more revealing.

The Secret of Ormus

According to the Priory of Sion's original story, between 1188 and the beginning of the fourteenth century, it was known as the Ormus, which is what it called itself exclusively for its first public appearance in 1962. The society was said to have come into being as a result of the mysterious cutting of the elm (*orme*) ritual at Gisors in 1188. They also said that the Rosicrucians emerged from the higher grades of the Ormus.

The name Ormus was actually taken from the lore and traditions of an earlier society, the Rite of Memphis, one of the Egyptian Rites of Freemasonry. (Some commentators believe that Ormus is a form of the name of the Zoroastrian creator-god Ohrmazd, a later version of Ahura Mazda. Perhaps it was originally, but in these traditions the name became associated with Egypt rather than Persia.)

The first of the Egyptian rites was the Rite of Misraïm (Hebrew for "Egyptians"), created in Italy in the 1780s before spreading to Egypt and then being taken to France in 1813 by the three Bédarride brothers (Joseph, Marc, and Michel). However, as it was denounced by the Grand Orient as a danger to state security, attracting the unwanted attention of the police, it wound itself up in January 1823, most of its leaders joining Scottish Rite Freemasonry. After keeping a low profile for a few years, it started up again in the early 1830s.[13]

The Rite of Memphis was originally a lodge within Misraïm, having been established in Montauban in 1815 by Freemasons who had previously belonged to the French Mission to Egypt and who claimed to have been initiated into a Coptic Rosicrucian tradition in Cairo. (This is probably true, except that the society they were initiated into seems to have been a recent import from Italy.) One of this band was Gabriel Mathieu Marconis de Nègre—from the same family as the last Dame of Rennes-le-Château—who was elected Grand Master of the Rite of Misraïm in 1816.[14]

However, the Rite of Memphis was established as a separate system in 1838 or '39 by Gabriel's son, Jacques-Étienne Marconis de Nègre, after he had been expelled twice from Misraïm (once under the name Marconis and once as de Nègre). He gave the Rite its own structure, exporting it to the United States and elsewhere.[15] (Inevitably, being so similar, the two Rites were later united into the single Rite of Memphis-Misraïm, the main figure behind this being no less than the hero of Italian unification, Giuseppe Garibaldi. The rites had, and still have, a large following in Italy.[16] In 1908 Papus became the Grand Master of Memphis-Misraïm in France, a position he held until his death eight years later.)

Jacques-Étienne Marconis de Nègre associated his order with the Philadelphes of Narbonne, created by the Marquis de Chefdebien d'Armissan, which was in turn very closely connected to—basically an offshoot of—the ubiquitous Rectified Scottish Rite Freemasonry.

Not unexpectedly, Marconis de Nègre presented an elaborate foundation myth for his society, probably to be understood only as a metaphorical description of its esoteric, spiritual, and philosophical streams of thought. According to de Nègre, the movement began with an Egyptian priest of Serapis (a later Hellenistic repackaging of the dying-and-rising god Osiris) named Ormus, who was converted to Christianity by the apostle Mark and founded the Brothers of Ormus to perpetuate this hybrid form of the Egyptian mysteries and Christianity. Soon afterward, a third stream, a Jewish school of "Solomonic science," formed from various sects, including the Essenes, joined the Brothers of Ormus. The Brothers of Ormus were also known as the Rosicrucians of the East (Rose-Croix d'Orient), so Ormus and Rosicrucians are linked—just as in the Priory of Sion's version. The secret Brotherhood continued in the Middle East until the time of the Crusades, when its priests were encountered by the leaders of the Templars, who took their doctrines back to Europe: this was the secret "heresy" of the Templars. It was from this stream that the Rite of Memphis claimed descent.[17]

Of course this is essentially the same scenario as in the Priory's Church of John foundation story (and the revived Order of the Temple's "Johannites of the East"), although the details are a little different. In the Memphis version there is no overt Johannitism, and in the Priory version Godefroy de Bouillon takes the role of all the Templar leaders.

According to *The Ritual of the A. & A. Egyptian Rite of Memphis* in the 1880s, the eighteenth degree of the Rite of Memphis, or "Rose-Cross," "was founded in 1188, in Palestine by the Egyptian Priest Comesius, who had been converted to Christianity,"[18] making another parallel with Priory lore. Although the details are different—it takes place in the Middle East, not northern France—certain major associations are present. Key concepts in the Priory's mythos—the link between Ormus, the Rosicrucians, and the year 1188—were there in the "traditions" of the Rite of Memphis long before the Dossiers Secrets. However, the Ormus tale was not even original to Marconis de Nègre, who borrowed it from the German Order of the Gold and Rose Cross (Gold- and Rosenkreutz),[19] which we will examine soon.

Interestingly, while rejecting allegations that the Priory of Sion is a Masonic system or is affiliated with the Freemasons, Gino Sandri acknowledges that in the eighteenth and nineteenth centuries the Priory was behind the creation of certain forms of Freemasonry that were to act as its "exterior circle" (although he says the Priory later cast them loose to follow their own paths), specifically naming the Rite of Memphis.[20] Sandri explains that the Priory created Memphis and, by implication, the other orders connected with it, as fronts. But in fact the Priory borrowed the myth of Ormus from Memphis, not the other way round. The evidence strongly suggests that Sandri's whole statement is also a reversal: these Orders created the Priory as a front.

The Grand Masters

In addition to such mythic elements, the Dossiers Secrets include information that is supposed to be literally historical. For example, the famous *planche* number 4 of *The Secret Files of Henri Lobineau* includes three lists of names: the early Grand Masters of the Knights Templar, the Nautonniers of the Priory of Sion down to Cocteau, and the abbots of the Priory of Mount Sion in Orléans. These were supposedly taken from the Priory's own records and archives, but can any of them be traced back to earlier sources?

In fact, only the second list—the Nautonniers—is unique to the Dossiers Secrets, the other two having already appeared in earlier works. Interesting and well crafted though it might be, not only do we know that this second list is dubious but in any case the Priory itself has disowned it, as in Pierre Plantard's 1989 statements during his reinvention of Priory history.

Were those particular names chosen at random, or was there a specific reason for choosing them? Again, for the most part, they are the usual suspects, selected because of their connections with places or political and/or esoteric movements that the Priory appropriated for its fictional history but also because they form a genuine historical chain of connections. The appearance of the Rosicrucians Johann Valentin Andreae and Robert Fludd and the alchemist Nicolas Flamel, for example, is unsurprising. And although once the name of Isaac Newton may have raised a few eyebrows, most people in this field recognize that besides his pioneering work in mathematics and physics he was a dedicated scholar of unconventional subjects, including alchemy. (Esoteric circles even in the 1950s and '60s would have been aware of this "other" Newton.)

The two most surprising names are Sandro Filipepi (Botticelli) and Leonardo da Vinci, since neither artist has a reputation for occultism as far as mainstream historians are concerned. However, both were at least acquainted with Hermetic philosophy, the esoteric and magical school that underpinned the Renaissance and later flowered in Rosicrucianism. And of course our own research has shown Leonardo to have been steeped in the anti-Christian Johannite heresy.

Does the inclusion of these two Renaissance men indicate some unique knowledge on the part of the Priory? Perhaps not, as Leonardo's name, at least, was already heavily featured in one—although as far as we can ascertain only one—of the esoteric orders that flourished in France at the end of the nineteenth century. (Botticelli had no parallel role, but presumably, as his patron was connected with the previous Nantonnier Iolande de Bar, his role in the list was to make the link between her and Leonardo.)

Da Vinci's latter-day esoteric connection comes from the Order of the Rose-Cross of the Temple and Grail (Ordre de la Rose-Croix du Temple et du Graal), of which Joséphin Péladan became Grand Master in 1891. (As previously mentioned, this Order was an offshoot of the Masonic La Sagesse lodge of Toulouse, in which the Hautpoul family were prominent.)

Péladan was one of the major figures in the nineteenth-century occult revival, a great scholar but also a devout Catholic (although he believed that the Church once possessed now-forgotten secret spiritual and esoteric knowledge). Péladan—whose secretary was Plantard's mentor Georges Monti—was closely involved with other major figures, such as Papus and Stanislas de Guaïta, in Rosicrucian circles of the time, although he distanced himself from them in 1890 after the Church condemned them. He then became Grand Master of the Rose-Cross of the Temple and Grail, which he reformed. According to its constitutions, which he drew up in 1893, new entrants were required to swear this oath to Leonardo da Vinci, "patron of the Rose-Cross":

> I swear on my eternal future, to seek, admire, and love Beauty . . . to praise, serve, and defend it even at my peril; to keep my heart from sexual love in order to give it to the ideal; and never to seek poetry in woman, who presents only the crude image.
>
> I swear it before Monseigneur Lionardo [*sic*] da Vinci, patron of the Rose-Cross.[21]

We have not been able to establish whether Péladan admired Leonardo because of something that was already known about him in the Order of the Rose-Cross of the Temple and Grail—founded some forty years before he took over—or whether he introduced the da Vinci theme. But Péladan certainly had a fascination with Leonardo, devoting two scholarly books to him besides being the first to translate Leonardo's notebooks and manuscripts in the Institut de France into French. One of his studies, *The Philosophy of Leonardo da Vinci from His Manuscripts* (1910), argues that the Florentine genius was essentially a great philosopher, likening his obsession with truth and perfection to Parsifal's Grail quest. To Péladan, Leonardo's "heresy" lay in his appropriation of subjects previously deemed solely the Church's province: "Leonardo secularized the idea of perfection and the notion of truth."[22]

The Priory, or at least Gino Sandri, still sticks by the list of Grand Masters since 1746: successively Charles de Lorraine (titular Duke of Lorraine), Maximilien de Lorraine (his nephew), Charles Nodier, Victor Hugo, Claude Debussy, and Jean Cocteau.

Nodier (1780–1844), the novelist and eclectic scholar, was Chief Librarian of the Arsenal Library in Paris, presiding over the cataloging of the archives Napoleon removed from the Vatican in 1810, a prodigious effort that inspired a boom in French historical scholarship. (One result was the first in-depth study of the trials of the Templars, based on Vatican records.) This helped kick-start a whole new trend that snowballed as the century progressed and that underpins our inquiry into the Priory's sources. This new wave of scholarship was partly thanks to Napoleon's keenness to establish France as the intellectual center of the world but also because of new methods of historical analysis imported from Germany. Archives suddenly assumed a new importance, and historians began delving into ever more abstruse subjects in increasingly minute detail. Learned societies—such as the Society of Arts and Sciences of Carcassonne, to which Abbé Henri Boudet belonged—mushroomed everywhere, and vast, multivolume historical works appeared on subjects from the most exotic to the terminally tedious.

When Abbé Faillon of St.-Sulpice produced his great work on Mary Magdalene in Provence (in 1848), he felt compelled to reproduce in full every passage from every text that even so much as mentioned her, followed by lengthy explanations and analyses. The result ran to two volumes totaling over fifteen hundred octavo pages. Faillon's work is a good example of another aspect of this explosion in historical scholarship—which even wormed its way into the Catholic Church, albeit by accident. As Baigent, Leigh, and Lincoln point out, the Catholic Modernist Movement, set up by the Church to protect its dogma from the challenges of the new, objective scholarship, actually embraced the opposition's methodology and began to pose its own searching questions about points of doctrine that are based not merely on faith but on supposedly real events. Perhaps predictably, one of the centers of this movement was St.-Sulpice in Paris.[23]

The new scholarship enjoyed a symbiotic relationship with the burgeoning esoteric scene: unearthed historical information on ancient religious or magical beliefs would be seized upon by the occult societies and incorporated into their practices. Conversely, many scholars—such as Nodier—would be prompted to delve into these subjects by their membership in Masonic or other initiatory societies.

Not only was Nodier one of the first of that generation of historians to write about the Merovingians but he also wrote about the 1188 affair of the Gisors elm,[24] perhaps because he was deeply interested in the occult—he was a close friend of the great French occult scholar Éliphas Lévi (1810–1875)—and secret societies. In fact, as Baigent, Leigh, and Lincoln note in *The Messianic Legacy,* he "made a point of inventing, and disseminating information about, a number of wholly fictitious secret societies."[25] Did that activity alone qualify Nodier to be included on the Priory's list?

Be that as it may, Nodier declared his allegiance to the Philadelphes, the secret society he claimed controlled all the others.[26] Given his habit of inventing shadowy organizations, it is hard to take him literally, but as we have seen, the Philadelphes was a real Masonic order—founded by the Marquis de Chefdebien—dedicated to the study of esoteric and Masonic secrets. Moreover, there is a connection, via the painter Jacques-Louis David (1748–1825), between Nodier and Armand, Marquis d'Hautpoul, the nephew—and heir—of Marie de Nègre d'Ablès, Dame d'Hautpoul et de Blanchefort. (David was a close friend of the former and art teacher to the latter.)[27]

As always, it would be a mistake to omit the arts from the symbiotic relationship between historians and occultists. Not only was it naturally the conjoined twin of the mystics' world but the new historical scholarship also directly inspired influential plays and novels. As a result, previously obscure historical characters and events came to the fore, and many of them emerge as themes in Priory material. For example, the Belgian dramatist Maurice Maeterlinck's *Pelléas et Mélisande* (1892), a "Merovingian drama,"[28] was followed eighteen years later by his *Mary Magdalene*—dealing with her role in the last days of Jesus.

Major Influences

The Dossiers Secrets' list of Templar Grand Masters up to 1188 had been published in the mid-1700s by the controversial German Karl Gotthelf, the Reichsfreiherr (Baron) von Hund und Altengrotkau (1722–1776), founder of a form of Freemasonry that explicitly claimed a direct kinship with the medieval Templars. Although his Strict Observance will be examined in detail shortly, as part of the proof of his claims he produced a document listing all the Templar Grand Masters—including those who came after Jacques de Molay, when the Templars went underground—with their dates, from the Order's origins all the way down to his day. As far as this investigation is concerned, the authenticity or accuracy of this list is immaterial. The relevant point is that the first eight Grand Masters, down to 1190 (after the "cutting of the Elm"), are identical to Henri Lobineau's *planche no. 41* with one exception (Von Hund's seventh Master, Théodore de Terroye, has become Théodore de Glaise).[29]

This can hardly be a coincidence. As the *Holy Blood* trio point out, because the records are scarce, there is no definitive and agreed list of Templar Grand Masters—no two lists are exactly alike.[30] So when two lists *are* identical, either one must have been copied from the other or both came from a third, original source. As the list's earliest known appearance was with von Hund in the 1750s, presumably that was the one Henri Lobineau copied it from. At least it shows that "They" had done their homework and must have been esoteric insiders—copies of the von Hund list are hardly ten a penny: it was available only in German Masonic works of von Hund's time and, slightly more accessibly, in an 1815 French history of Freemasonry by Claude Antoine Thory. (Paradoxically, in *The Temple and the Lodge,* Michael Baigent and Richard Leigh use the Dossiers Secrets' list to authenticate von Hund's, even though the latter predates the former by two hundred years.)[31]

Unfortunately, because of the absence of independent historical records, it is impossible to determine the accuracy or otherwise of von Hund's list. Baigent, Leigh, and Lincoln are convinced that it is at least as accurate as any other, and in our view it does stand up to scrutiny, with no obvious howlers. (In von Hund's day there had been little proper historical work on the Templars, so as the people he was trying to impress with the list were unlikely to know any better if it *was* made up, whoever fabricated it had done considerably more homework than was strictly necessary.)

But what of the third list, the Abbots of the Priory of Mount Sion? Although superficially it seems the least interesting—the heads of an obscure medieval priory—in fact, finding the Dossiers Secrets' source shows it to be the most revealing of all.

The Patriarch

In 1887 a short article—actually a transcript of a lecture—was published in the *Memoirs of the National Society of Antiquarians of France.* "Charters of the Abbey of Mount Sion" was the work of the eminent French historian and explorer Baron Emmanuel-Guillaume Rey (1837–1916), a specialist in the history of the Crusader kingdoms of the Middle East, and briefly told the story of the foundation of the Abbey of Notre-Dame de Mont Sion in Jerusalem by Godefroy de Bouillon, the transfer of its monks to Acre when Jerusalem was recaptured by the Saracens and then on to Sicily after the loss of the Holy Land. It also describes how some of its monks—returning to France with Louis VII—established themselves in the Priory of St. Samson of Orléans (now in the *département* of the Loiret), which was owned by the main abbey in Jerusalem. From local place-names, Rey believed there had also been a small Priory of Mount Sion close to Orléans, which in turn was dependent on the Priory of St.-Samson. Not only do these religious houses play a key part in the Dossiers Secrets but the link with the Priory of St.-Samson is there in the earliest reference to the Priory of Sion in a mainstream publication, Gérard de Sède's book of 1962.

Because of his enthusiasm for Crusader history, Baron Rey was excited to discover that the archives of Godefroy de Bouillon's original Jerusalem abbey had been transferred to the Priory of St.-Samson before ending up in Orléans's departmental archives at the Revolution. In this treasure trove Rey discovered documents listing all the extensive lands and property in Syria, Armenia, France, Italy, and Spain that had been donated to the mother house in Jerusalem, plus the names and details of the previously unknown Abbots of Notre-Dame de Mont Sion, which he neatly summarized in his article.

Clearly, as Rey's article is the basis for the Dossiers Secrets' list of Abbots, not only the names but also some snippets of information have been copied. For example, in the Dossiers, Girard, Abbot from 1239 to 1244, "ceded to the Teutonic Knights a piece of land at Acre," which in

Rey's original article was "ceded to the Teutonic knights, as Abbot of Mont Sion, in February 1239, a piece of land next to Acre."

Could the compiler of the Dossiers Secrets have drawn his information from separate records, from the Priory of Sion's secret archives? Unfortunately, even this remote possibility is highly unlikely because the Dossiers' author has made a major blunder, proving he was just copying Rey. Although Rey's list is of the abbots of the main house in Jerusalem and Acre, the Dossiers have mistakenly taken it to refer to the small Priory of Mount Sion in Orléans. No secret Priory archives were involved. Knowing this—and that the list of Templar Grand Masters was copied from Baron Von Hund—casts doubt (if any more were needed) on the third list.

However, although unearthing this somewhat obscure article of Rey's was no mean feat (even if the writer did get the wrong end of the stick), was this find the result of meticulous research—or did he just use a shortcut?

Describing his excitement on discovering the Jerusalem abbey's documents, Rey said, "Straightaway I began to explore, with the aid of M. Doinelle, archivist of the Loiret, the various boxes forming the said contents of St.-Samson."[32] This M. Doinelle is in fact Jules Doinel, a very significant figure indeed.

Jules Benoît Stanislas Doinel du Val-Michel (1842–1902) was an archivist and paleographer who worked in the departmental archives of Niort and the Cantal before moving to the Loiret.[33] Although typical of the new breed of dogged and methodical historians who bridged the gap with the burgeoning esoteric scene, Doinel was essentially a dilettante, restlessly searching for truth and perfection, constantly jumping from one interest to another, and spending years studying and promoting a subject only to drop it abruptly. Starting out a devout Catholic, he was later an equally committed Freemason, becoming an important official in a Grand Orient Masonic Lodge in Orléans—the Adepts of Isis Montyon—in 1884. From later clues in his correspondence, he seems to have shifted allegiance to one of the Scottish Rites, rivals to the "establishment" Grand Orient.

It was in the Loiret archives, at around the time of his collaboration with Baron Rey, that Doinel made a discovery that was to change his life yet again. This was an ancient document concerning the suppression of a heretical Gnostic sect, the Paulicians, in Orléans in the eleventh century. At least according to their enemies, they practiced sexual rituals and orgies, as well as sacrificing the unbaptized babies that resulted from these unions, and were accordingly rounded up and burned at the stake in the last days of December 1022.

This information fascinated Doinel, who began to study Gnosticism—naturally arriving at the Cathars, an open sesame to the esoteric salons. Seeing it as his mission to revive Gnosticism in the modern world, he established his own Gnostic Church in 1890, based on a wide spread of Gnostic doctrines and philosophies. The self-appointed Patriarch, Doinel developed the ceremonies—including a revival of the Cathar ritual, the Consolamentum—and organized his new religion, consecrating both male and female bishops. His new church met with immediate success, establishing twelve dioceses in France (including Paris, Bordeaux, Carcassonne, and Toulouse) and others in Italy, Bulgaria, and Bohemia. Besides being Patriarch, Doinel gave himself the titles Bishop of Montségur, the center of his church, and Bishop of Alet, close to Rennes-le-Château.

As this renewal of interest in Gnosticism proved popular with the spiritually inclined then flooding into the occult salons of Paris, there was both an overlapping membership and an affiliation with some of the other societies. For example, Papus was ordained a bishop in Doinel's church, and in September 1893 a formal link was established between the Gnostic Church and the Martinist Order.[34] Clearly Doinel mixed with all the major figures on the contemporary occult and esoteric scene: Papus (to whom he was particularly close), Péladan, Debussy, and Emma Calvé. He must also have known Péladan's secretary, Georges Monti. But once his new church was fully operative, Doinel flitted off again—this time, in 1894, to return to the Catholic Church and formally abjure his Gnostic creation (although it continued without him). The following year, under the pseudonym Jean Kotska, he published *Lucifer Unmasked* (*Lucifer démasquée*), in which he denounced Freemasonry as satanic, reserving special venom for the Rectified Scottish Rite and reproducing one of its rituals in his book as proof of its perfidy.[35] However, many researchers believe that Doinel's return to the bosom of the Church was little more than a cynical ploy, for appearance's sake.[36]

After his very public recantation and his pseudonymous denunciation of Freemasonry, he collaborated on the review *Gnosis,* edited by René Guénon. In fact, a Gnostic catechism developed by Doinel and Guénon has been praised by authorities such as René Nelli as one of the best and most consistent reconstructions of ancient Gnostic thinking.[37]

Doinel also pursued his professional career as an archivist, becoming in the 1890s curator of the departmental archives of the Aude at Carcassonne, where he remained until his death. Not only was he in the same area as Saunière while that mystery was unfolding but he was from 1898 Secretary of the Society of Arts and Sciences of Carcassonne, to which Henri Boudet belonged.

While at Carcassonne, Doinel wrote *Note on King Childeric III* (*Note sur le roi Hildéric III,* 1899), decrying the Merovingians' usurpation by the Carolingians. And he wrote *History of Blanche de Castile* (1887), as well as a study of Joan of Arc (1892), in which he argued that the angelic voices that had guided her were real "powers or manifestations of a spiritual order."[38] As we will see, this belief in the reality of communication with spirits to the shadowy figures involved in this story is more than an individual quirk—indeed, it will become surprisingly, perhaps even shockingly, central.

To a degree that certainly seems way beyond coincidence, Doinel is connected not only with virtually all the major themes of the Priory's Dossiers Secrets but also with their key players. He knew Abbé Boudet—and was presumably acquainted with his strange book *The True Celtic Language*—and had written on Blanche of Castile *and* the Merovingians. He knew Emma Calvé, Debussy, and Papus (and therefore presumably Émile Hoffet). He worked with Baron Rey on the research in the Loiret archives that prompted Rey's article on the Abbey of Notre-Dame de Mont Sion, which was borrowed for the Priory's foundation myth. One might be forgiven for supposing that the entire Dossiers Secrets were constructed from Doinel's personal library and archives.

Perhaps they were. After all, there was only one generation between the heyday of Paris's occult salons and the young Pierre Plantard's association with those same circles (admittedly by then somewhat less scintillating), and many individuals bridged the gap, such as Georges Monti and Camille Savoire.

Although the Priory of Sion was established in 1956, it draws almost exclusively on late-nineteenth-century material for its history and folklore, suggesting that whoever the shadowy figures were behind Plantard and the Priory, they belonged to that era. While the Priory might not have a pedigree going back to the Crusades, it does appear to go back to the golden age of Parisian occultism. But is it possible to identify those occult societies that shaped and controlled the Priory?

Throughout the first part of this book, we noted how certain Masonic and esoteric societies—especially the Rectified Scottish Rite (with its interior order of the Knights Beneficent of the Holy City, often referred to by its French acronym, CBCS) and the Martinist Order—recur.

It was the esoterically oriented Rectified Scottish Rite, rather than the establishment Grand Orient, to which members of the ostensibly anti-Masonic Alpha Galates Order, such as Camille Savoire and Robert Amadou (who was also a member of the interior Martinist order, the S.I.), belonged. The Priory of Sion's current General Secretary, Gino Sandri, is an authority on the history of the Rectified Scottish Rite and the Martinist Order, of which he is a leading member. (He also writes on the history of the German Order of the Gold and Rose Cross—which, as we will see, enjoyed a very close and specific relationship with the Rectified Scottish Rite.) We have linked the same societies with the Saunière affair at Rennes-le-Château.

Strictly Beneficent

Even a cursory delve reveals that the Rectified Scottish Rite and the Martinist Order are very closely related, and are also linked to other societies that have already assumed importance in our investigation. In particular, the Rectified Scottish Rite is essentially a rebranding of an earlier, and very controversial, form of Templarist Freemasonry—the Strict Observance.

We know that the Dossiers Secrets used material from documents that first appeared in the hands of the founder of the Strict Observance, Baron Karl von Hund. But did the Dossiers use it simply because it was convenient, or was there a genuine connection between the Priory of Sion and the Strict Observance?

Although much derided over the last couple of centuries, Baron von Hund was by no means insignificant or a credulous fool. The Lord of Lipse, in the Haute-Lusace, he was Chamberlain to the Elector of

Cologne, then to the Elector of Saxony, who when he became King Augustus III of Poland, retained von Hund as Intimate Counselor. He was also Councillor of State to the Habsburg Archduchess Maria Theresa and her husband, the Emperor Franz I.[39]

Initiated into a French Masonic lodge in Frankfurt an der Oder in 1742 at the exceptionally young age of nineteen, he received his famous initiation into a specifically Jacobite (Stuart Scottish exile) form of Freemasonry in Paris a year later. In this and subsequent meetings with chiefs of the Order in Flanders, the "true origins" of Freemasonry—as a continuation of the Knights Templar—were revealed to him, and he received the mission to "reform" Freemasonry by returning it to its Templar roots. He was also given documents that appeared to substantiate the Templar origins, most notably the list of Grand Masters discussed earlier. Von Hund also claimed to have been introduced to the Young Pretender, Charles Edward Stuart, himself one of the chiefs of the Order. Von Hund said later that he assumed Stuart to have been the Grand Master.[40]

According to von Hund's information (which he clearly passed on in good faith), certain French Templar knights, led by Pierre d'Aumont, Provincial Grand Master of the Auvergne, fled at the suppression to Scotland, where they disguised themselves as stonemasons. The order continued clandestinely in Scotland—becoming associated with the Stuarts after they were overthrown—and established itself among exiled Jacobite circles in Paris. (This is the Scottish transmission of Templar survival, rival to the Larmenius transmission discussed earlier.)

There is a certain paradox in all this. Since his death and the collapse of his Order, von Hund has been vilified as a charlatan and fraud, yet even his severest critics acknowledge that he seriously believed what he preached. The ultraskeptical historian J. M. Roberts writes in *The Mythology of the Secret Societies* (1972): "He cannot be dismissed merely as a huckster or a confidence-trickster; there is little doubt that he sincerely believed some of the rubbish he talked."[41] Neither was it a money-making scam: not only was he already extremely wealthy but he was happy to lavish money on the Strict Observance, even paying for the Masonic offices out of his own pocket—until 1766, when he finally had to plead poverty.[42]

The Baron genuinely believed in his experiences, and there is no reason to doubt that his initiation in Paris really happened as he described.

Basically von Hund was drawn into their circle, assigned his mission, and sent out into the world to accomplish it.

The problem—which would lead to his Order's downfall—was that those who initiated him into the Jacobite Order of the Temple remained anonymous, hiding behind Latin titles such as that of his initiator, the Eques a Penna Rubra, the Knight of the Red Feather. (The Strict Observance was fond of Latin noms de guerre—von Hund himself was Carolus, Eques ab Ense: Karl, Knight of the Sword.)

These mysterious individuals promised to contact von Hund again once he had established his new system, to instruct and direct the organization. As they retained their anonymity, the Baron called them his Unknown Superiors.

Poor von Hund. His Unknown Superiors failed to keep their promise; he never heard from them again. And after some years of success, the continued silence began to cause dark mutterings, even among his supporters. However, as Baigent and Leigh argue in *The Temple and the Lodge,* there is a perfectly logical explanation for the disappearance of the Unknown Superiors. As prominent Jacobites, most of them would have been dead or in hiding after the failed uprising of 1745, precisely the period between von Hund's initiation and the formal birth of the Strict Observance—as indicated by the fact that Baigent and Leigh identified the Knight of the Red Feather as Alexander Seton, the Earl of Eglinton, a leading Jacobite.[43]

(The arrival of the Unknown Superiors marked the introduction of an important new element into European esotericism, which was to develop into the idea of orders being under the guidance of spiritual or nonterrestrial entities rather than anonymous human beings—this notion eventually became more or less indispensable to magical orders.)

Because of the Seven Years' War between Prussia and Austria, von Hund had to wait for over a decade after his initiation before unveiling his new system of Rectified Masonry, before adopting the name Strict Observance. He founded its first lodge on one of his estates at Kittlitz in 1754. The Strict Observance quickly took Germany by storm and soon spread to France, Switzerland, and Russia.

Von Hund's strategy was to convince other Masons about his claims, then persuade them to recognize the superiority of the Strict Observance by signing an act of submission and obedience—essentially a takeover of Freemasonry. Besides the three grades common to other

Masonic systems, the Strict Observance possessed three others of an "interior order"—which were open to nonnobles, something fairly unusual in the higher grades of continental Masonry at that time.[44] (This is significant because skeptics often claim that the link between the Templars and Freemasonry was invented only to keep the nobility happy, arguing that members of the aristocracy wanted to become Freemasons but had no desire to join an organization that traced its origins back to plebeian workers in stone, which was the predominant theory of the origins of the Craft. So a new, more romantic foundation myth was invented, in which the Brotherhood really came from a chivalric order that merely *disguised* itself as Freemasons.)

This may be fine as far as it goes, but what were all these solemn and elaborate rites and systems *for*? Were they simply a matter of donning fancy regalia and handing out grandiose titles, or did they signify—or even obscure—a real objective, political, financial, or philosophical? In fact, the Strict Observance did have a definite agenda, which was originally the setting up of a state in Eastern Europe that would be run secretly by the Templars. But when it became apparent that this was unrealistic in the short term, the Order turned instead to the search for occult knowledge, particularly magical and mystical disciplines such as alchemy, the Cabala, and ceremonial magic.[45]

However, contrary to the common misapprehension, Baron von Hund was not the first to introduce a Templar rite into Freemasonry. In fact, the first *documented* account of the legend of the Templar origins of Masonry—dating from the mid-1750s—came not from within Freemasonry but from the German Order of the Gold and Rose Cross.[46] (Although this account came after von Hund claimed to have been told the same thing during his initiation in Paris, he did not make those claims public until after the Rosicrucian document.)

The Gold and Rose Cross (also variously known as the Cross of Gold and Red/Rose Cross, or the Gold and Rosicrucians) was the result of a second wave of interest in Rosicrucianism in Germany after the end of the Thirty Years' War, its main driving force being the Lutheran pastor Samuel Richter (Sincerus Renatus). Although the exact circumstances are unclear, this led to the formation of the Order of the Gold and Rose Cross, the first known identifiable Rosicrucian society, which possessed many Masonic elements, largely because Rosicrucianism and Freemasonry coexisted in the same milieu.[47]

However, because there was a close relationship between the Rosicrucian Order and Freemasonry in Germany—although rivals, they appealed to the same people and therefore had an overlapping membership—the Templar legend was quickly assimilated into Masonry. The first manifestation was within the important Berlin Lodge of the Three Globes, where some Masons began practicing rituals based on the Rosicrucian lore and some of the new chivalric grades imported from France. However, this new rite soon took over the Three Globes completely and spawned a new form of Masonry known as the Clermont System (after the Comte de Clermont, Grand Master of French Freemasonry).

The Clermont System expanded quickly, establishing fifteen chapters throughout Germany between 1760 and 1763—chapters rather than lodges, each presided over by a Prior rather than a Grand Master. However, very early in its history the new system was taken over by an outsider, an adventurer in the Masonic world under the alias Count Johnson, who took control of Clermont's second chapter in Jena and persuaded first its members and then those of the other chapters that he was privy to certain secret information about the Templar survival unknown even to the system's founders. As a result the Three Globes lost its authority and the Jena Chapter duly became Clermont's High Chapter. It was, in fact, Johnson who coined the term "Strict Observance" for the reinvented system. Significantly, the Jena lodge was called the Chapter of Sion—and as it was headed by a Prior, it could even be considered as the *Priory of Sion.*[48]

Von Hund targeted this system for conversion to that of his new, superior Templar rite, and essentially did to Johnson what Johnson had done to Clermont's leaders. Producing the documents that allegedly proved his system's descent from the medieval Order, including the list of Grand Masters discussed earlier, he challenged the Chapter of Sion to produce *its* credentials. As a result, after much internal discussion and argument, the Sion Chapter adopted the Strict Observance, throwing Johnson out.[49] In other words, the Strict Observance began with a secret Templar group called Sion. This makes our tracing of the origins of today's Priory of Sion back to the Strict Observance all the more significant and reinforces the idea of a direct connection between the two.

Added to this, because the Clermont System originated from a fusion between Masonry and the Gold and Rose Cross, a close connection remained between the latter and the Strict Observance. And significantly, in 1776 the legend of Ormus appeared in the mythology of the Gold and Rose Cross.[50]

So successful was the Strict Observance that by 1772 it was recognized in Germany as of equal status with the other (non-Templarist) stream of Freemasonry, the two being brought together as the United Lodges under the Grand Mastership of Ferdinand, Duke of Brunswick.

However, after a few years of runaway success, the Strict Observance began to run into trouble. The problem was not entirely von Hund's inability to prove the Templar origins of his rite (after all, mainstream Freemasonry could hardly prove its legendary history either) but instead his claim to be a representative of the Unknown Superiors without any proof of their existence. When he died, in 1776, he was still maintaining he had told the truth about his Unknown Superiors.[51] But the system he had worked so hard to create did not survive him long—at least in name.

After von Hund's death all the internal doubts and external hostilities came bubbling to the surface. First, there was the question of whether the Unknown Superiors had ever really existed and, if so, where they were now. But by claiming a connection with the medieval Templars, the Strict Observance had also attracted suspicion from the other establishment forms of Freemasonry and from the authorities, particularly in France, where Templars were still seen as both disgusting and *dangerous*. Hadn't the Order of the Temple been suppressed as a devilish and subversive organization? And wouldn't any organization descended from it be sure to seek revenge on the two institutions that had crushed and condemned it to centuries of twilight existence—the French monarchy and the Papacy?

As a result, some clarification was necessary, and it took the form of two major conferences or convents, the first in Lyons in 1778 and the second in Wilhelmsbad in Hesse-Kassel four years later. The Lyons gathering—the Convent of the Gauls—decided to reject the Strict Observance, at least in France, approving instead a new, reformed system, the Rectified Scottish Rite, with its interior order of the Knights Beneficent of the Holy City. (The Rectified Scottish Rite was essentially the Strict Observance repackaged—Scottish after the supposed Templar survival in Scotland, rectified at the Lyons Convent, and Knight of the Holy City [Jerusalem/Sion] being a not-so-subtle euphemism for Templar.) This was the initiative of Jean-Baptiste Willermoz (1730–1824), who after being initiated into the Strict Observance in 1774 had established the first of its French lodges, La Bienfaisance (Beneficence or Charity), in his hometown of Lyons. Willermoz had called the convent, and now he pressed the case for replacing the Strict Observance with the Knights Beneficent, partly, no doubt, as a power play in the wake of von Hund's death but also in order to protect the Order from growing suspicion among French officialdom. Indeed, one contemporary German commentator wrote: "The abjuration [of the Strict Observance] of the Convent of Lyons was made at the injunction of the police, who had declared that they opposed the propagation of any system which tended to recall the Templars and their customs, but this withdrawal was only simulated, and the Brothers remained in contact with the Lodges of the Strict Observance of Germany, as a province."[52]

At Wilhelmsbad in 1782, a second attempt was made to resolve the problem, this time for Germany as well as France.[53] Presided over by the Duke of Brunswick and the Landgrave of Hesse, the convent had to pacify the Masonic authorities, who had decided to make an end of the Strict Observance come what may. Basically, they asked its leadership to prove the existence of the Unknown Superiors and produce some indisputable proof of Freemasonry's Templar origins or else drop the whole business. When they failed to produce the proof, the convent officially repudiated both claims. However, in the words of the Masonic historian Claude Antoine Thory—no fan of von Hund or his Templar system—writing in 1815:

> It is certain that the convent had as an object only the separation from Freemasonry of the Templar system and placing Ferdinand of Brunswick at the head of the reformed lodges; also they took great care to keep away all those who they knew manifested a contrary opinion; refusing them entry to the assembly, particularly the deputation from the Chapter and Mother Lodge of the Crescent with Three Keys of Ratisbonne, and to the Brother Marquis de C.D.B. (Eques a Capite Galeato) as representative of the Lodge of the United Friends [Loge des Amis-Réunis] of Paris.54

(Brother Marquis de C.D.B. is François, Marquis de Chefdebien d'Armissan, or Franciscus, Eques a Capite Galeato,[55] founder of the

Philadelphes of Narbonne, with which Marconis de Nègre's Rite of Memphis was affiliated.) Thory also writes of a last-minute attempt to reverse these decisions, but the convent refused, declaring it was too late:

> A remarkable thing was that at the twenty-eighth session, the Scottish Lodge of Frédéric au Lion d'Or sent to the convent a memoir accompanied by a letter from Prince Frederick of Brunswick, in which it offered to communicate new information, to identify the major Unknown Superiors, to send shortly the Great Ritual manuscript kept by the Clerici Brothers [Clerks, the secretariat of the Strict Observance], et cetera, but the convent decided that the assembly had renounced all unknown and hidden superiors [and] that it had stopped new Rituals.[56]

It was the end of the Strict Observance, certainly as a major force in Freemasonry, although some brethren carried on independently. It still survives as a very small organization.

However, the convent recognized the Rectified Scottish Rite and Knights Beneficent. Thory writes in his dictionary of Masonry that the Rectified Scottish Rite is "the regime of the Strict Observance, rectified at the Convent of Wilhemsbad, in 1782,"[57] while A. E. Waite describes it as "the Strict Observance as transformed at Lyons and ratified at Wilhelmsbad."[58] It managed to do this by formally renouncing any connection with the medieval Templars while maintaining that it had a *spiritual* connection with the original Order (hence Knight of the Holy City).[59]

But the transition involved something more than simply crossing out "Strict Observance" and substituting "Rectified Scottish Rite." As Waite notes: "When the Strict Observance was transformed at Lyons, Martinism was the touchstone applied to it. The Secret Grades which lie behind it are permeated with Martinist elements."[60] All roads seem to lead to this mysterious but obviously crucial Martinism. But what exactly is it?

Voices from Beyond

The years leading up to the Revolution in the second half of the eighteenth century were particularly vibrant for French esotericism. One of the key figures, hugely influential for subsequent generations, was Louis-Claude de Saint-Martin (1743–1803), called the Unknown Philosopher (*Philosophe Inconnu*). Saint-Martin devoted himself to the search for esoteric knowledge and wisdom, eventually developing his own enormously seminal mystical and esoteric philosophy.

The scion of a noble French family, Saint-Martin became a Freemason more or less as a matter of routine in 1765, as soon as he reached the required age of twenty-one. However, his esoteric career began in earnest only through the niece of a fellow officer in his regiment at Foix, who happened to be married to another major figure in European occultism, Jacques Martines de Pasqually (1727–1774). Clearly, the Fates had arranged a rather roundabout way for Saint-Martin to encounter his mentor.

For a long time Martines de Pasqually's origins were disputed—it was thought he was either Spanish or Portuguese—but it is now largely agreed that he was born in or near Grenoble, his father a converted Spanish Jew (who held a Masonic patent or license of authority, bestowed on him by Charles Edward Stuart, linking him with the same forces that stood behind von Hund).[61] His mother was a French Catholic.[62]

Martines had established a semi-Masonic, semimagical order called—with an admirably ecumenical touch—the Order of the Elect Cohens (Ordre des Élus-Coëns), Cohen being Hebrew for "priest." Saint-Martin became a member of the Elect Cohens, rising to the status of Martines's secretary and establishing his own Temple Cohen in Toulouse, in which the du Bourg family—whom we met earlier—were prominent.[63]

The Elect Cohens' synthesis of Gnostic and magical thinking, blending Christianity with the Cabala and other occult systems, encouraged them to find the God within themselves—their union or reunion with the divine—through magical operations that invoked angelic and other spirit entities. Martines's basic ideas were developed from the philosophy of the great Swedish mystic Emanuel Swedenborg (1688–1772), which were based on an unshakable acceptance of the reality of an unseen world populated by spirits and other supernatural beings. In the words of J. M. Roberts, the Elect Cohens' philosophy "was expressed in a series of rituals whose purpose was to make it possible for spiritual beings to take physical shape and convey messages from the other world."[64] The secret of these processes was divulged to only the most elevated initiates of the Elect Cohens.

Although the lodges never practiced group magic, the higher grades learned magical exercises they were expected to perform alone. The exact details of these operations are unknown—they were jealously guarded—but they appear to have been a common enough form of ritual magic that aimed to put the adept in communion with other worldly intelligences, in a way similar to Dr. John Dee's angelic magic of the Elizabethan era. Not only did Martines de Pasqually himself take part in such operations but the whole purpose of the Elect Cohens was to develop a circle of similarly trained magi. Their ultimate aim was referred to simply as *la chose*—the thing—which Papus described as the manifestation of some form of intelligence or supernatural entity.[65]

From surviving correspondence, it appears that the future founder of the Rectified Scottish Rite, Jean-Baptiste Willermoz, followed this training between 1768 and 1772, although disappointingly he reported only "visions" of colors and "visible sparks."[66] Obviously he had expected unambiguous materializations of beings bearing revelatory messages from beyond.

Saint-Martin's time with Martines de Pasqually really just laid the foundation for his own quest, in which he explored various other disciplines and practices, studying Hermeticism and even setting up his own alchemical laboratory in Lyons.[67] Always a devout Christian—although no lover of the Church as an organization—he eventually developed his own mystical ideas, in which the power of Christ replaced the intervention of spirits. As the Unknown Philosopher, he outlined his thinking in a series of books beginning with *Errors and Truth* (*Des erreurs et de la Vérité*), which was published in Lyons in 1775 (although to add an air of mystery, it claimed an Edinburgh imprint). Another of his important works was *Natural Table of the Connections That Exist Between God, Man, and the Universe* (*Tableau naturel des rapports qui existent entre Dieu, l'Homme et l'Univers*, 1782, also with an Edinburgh imprint).

Essentially Saint-Martin's philosophy was fairly straightforward dualist Gnosticism, a theory of a battle between the opposing principles of good and evil coupled with a belief that a direct and personal relationship between man and God is not only possible but to be relentlessly sought as the highest good. He wrote, "*tous les hommes sont des C-H-R,*" "all men are Christs"[68]—at least potentially—and encouraged the belief that there are, and always have been, the select few destined secretly to perpetuate and transmit the universal truths of the true religion.[69] Even so, he remained spiritually restless, indefatigable in his search for useful mystical ideas, even joining one of Franz Mesmer's Societies of Harmony in 1784 to study "animal magnetism," although he later rejected it.[70]

The Austrian medical doctor Franz Anton Mesmer (1734–1815) caused an overnight sensation when he arrived in Paris in 1778. He claimed to have discovered what he called "animal magnetism"—a flow of "magnetic fluid," or in modern terms a current or energy, around and within the human body—which could be manipulated by a trained practitioner to cure both physical and mental ailments. Although derided by the medical profession of his day and ever since, essentially the theory bears a striking resemblance to the Eastern *qi* or Indian *prana,* still controversial concepts of a life force that nevertheless have been largely vindicated by the proven efficacy of acupuncture.

In Paris patients—mainly female—flocked to have themselves "stroked" by Mesmer's magnets in specially constructed tubs, often with dramatic results. Besides the cures—many of which appear to have been genuine, perhaps because they were psychosomatic—his process of magnetizing patients, by passes of either the hands or magnetized iron rods, also caused changes in their state of consciousness, sometimes resulting in shaking and convulsions or a sleeplike trance. Although technically not quite the discovery of hypnosis, as is often claimed, Mesmer's still mysterious process certainly paved the way for both hypnosis and psychoanalysis.

Despite the chorus of accusations both then and now, Mesmer was by no means a charlatan: he had discovered an authentic therapy that demonstrably worked, often with an immediate, visible effect, on many of those who came to him, even if he misinterpreted it. Apart from his healing "clinics," he established a network of Societies of Harmony to teach and experiment with animal magnetism. Although not widely known, these were actually Masonic lodges, also called Mesmerian Lodges of Harmony (Loges Mesmériennes de l'Harmonie) and were open only to Freemasons.[71] Mesmer was a member of the Order of the Gold and Rose Cross, which, as we have seen, was closely associated with the Strict Observance.[72] In fact, he and Saint-Martin moved in very much the same circles—for example, Mesmer stayed with Madame

Elizabeth du Bourg of Saint-Martin's Temple Cohen in Toulouse in March 1786.[73]

The Unknown Agent

Jean-Baptiste Willermoz also devoted himself to a passionate search for the truths behind Freemasonry, working his way through various systems and either discarding or synthesizing them. A member of the Strict Observance, as we have seen, he was the driving force behind the creation of the Rectified Scottish Rite in order to perpetuate it. But he had another motive in reforming von Hund's system, seeking to incorporate into its doctrines Martinist ideas—making the new Rite basically Strict Observance with an overlay of Martinist ideas and practices.

It is really only the interior order of the Rectified Scottish Rite, the Knights Beneficent of the Holy City, that is of interest to us, the other grades being effectively recruiting grounds for the higher grades, where the serious business took place. As we know, the Knights Beneficent itself possessed an inner circle, the Profession, which in turn had an inner core, called the Grand Profession (Grand Profès). Ostensibly, Willermoz established the Rectified Scottish Rite as a purely charitable organization—hence the emphasis on *bienfaisance*—but this was just a cover to divert attention and suspicion from the occultism of the Grand Profession.[74] Under his leadership, the Knights Beneficent began to explore some very strange areas of esotericism, pursuing the Elect Cohens' objective of establishing contact with spiritual beings of a higher order, usually believed to be angels or spirits. But rather than using the communications for personal improvement or enlightenment, as in Martines de Pasqually's system, Willermoz hoped they would pass on unique information and knowledge. (After all, he had taken the Elect Cohens' training specifically in order to manifest *la chose.*) No one knows whether this was Willermoz's own innovation or whether a similar aim already existed in the Strict Observance's higher grades. Mesmer may have been the key. Perhaps he honed his technique of magnetism within the Gold and Rose Cross—or did he even learn it there?

The Grand Profession definitely experimented with Mesmer's magnetism to put women into trance—this is where animal magnetism shades into hypnosis—to enable them to "channel" angels. In 1784, for example, a Grand Profession of Lyons called La Concorde, over which Willermoz presided, magnetized one Gilberte Rochette, who not only saw angels, saints, and deceased relatives of some of the Knights present but also channeled useful information on various subjects.[75] Questioned by the Knights, Gilberte passed on information about cures for various ailments and about the history of the Knights Templar, particularly its secret survival. In November 1784, Willermoz wrote to Prince Charles of Hesse that "the particular principles of La Concorde are leading to great discoveries in the most elevated metaphysics."[76] But a second, and perhaps more significant, series of revelations began in April 1785, apparently without the aid of Mesmerism. Suddenly the "other side" appears to have taken the initiative.

On the evening of April 5, 1785, Willermoz received a visitor—whose identity he kept secret in correspondence but who could only have been Alexandre de Monspey, a Commander of the Order of Malta and a member of the Grand Profession—who brought with him eleven remarkable notebooks, full of writings from an allegedly supernatural source. It transpired that they had been received via automatic writing by de Monspey's elderly sister, Madame Marie-Louise de Vallière, and according to the invisible guiding hand were specifically intended for Willermoz and his society.[77]

The communications instructed Willermoz to establish what would become essentially a yet more inner order of the Rectified Scottish Rite, comprising twelve chosen members of the Grand Profession, who would receive their instructions directly from this new source. As a result, he established a new lodge, the Elected and Beloved (Élue et Chérie), although he chose to confide in only two Brothers about the nature of the secret source of information[78]—which he code-named L'Agent Inconnu, the Unknown Agent, although opinions are divided on whether this referred to Madame de Vallière or the entity who supposedly communicated through her. (They never explained whether it was an angel, a spirit, or a discarnate human.) According to A. E. Waite, the Unknown Agent was the source itself, whereas Robert Amadou—the former Alpha Galates member, author of a study of L'Agent Inconnu—argues it was an alias for Madame de Vallière.[79] (In our mind it was probably both.)

The French historian René le Forestier writes in his monumental two-volume *Templar and Occultist Freemasonry of the Eighteenth and Nineteenth Centuries* (*Le franc-maçonneries templière et occultiste aux XVIIIe et XIXe siècles,* 1970): "For three full years, from the summer of 1784 to that of 1787, the most active members of the Metropolitan College of the Grand Profession occupied themselves exclusively with the revelations brought by Gilberte Rochette and the messages of the Unknown Agent."[80] A. E. Waite also notes: "I do not doubt that Willermoz and his circle received psychic communications in one and another psychic condition, induced by prolonged operations inspired by that intent, or with the aid of 'lucids' [mediums or channelers], the intervention of which is admitted."[81]

What was going on? Were these communications real, as far as one could tell, in any normal, objective way? Or was it all just an elaborately stage-managed trick? Was there a shadowy figure or group pulling the strings, attempting to control Willermoz and his Order by persuading Madame de Vallière to pass on these instructions? And, if so, why? Of course, any view will be critically colored by whether one considers such phenomena to be possible. But there are basically three options: genuine communication with real nonhuman intelligences, a psychological phenomenon, or outright fabrication. Whatever was going on, it proved crucial for Louis-Claude de Saint-Martin.

Outside of the Lyons group, the only members to be called to the new initiation, in Paris, were the Vicomte de Saulx-Tavannes and a German named Tieman—both close friends and followers of Saint-Martin,[82] who had himself corresponded with Willermoz since 1771. They met in September 1773, when Saint-Martin settled in Lyons for a year (during his alchemical research phase). Although after he left Lyons toward the end of the following year his and Willermoz's paths diverged, the two men continued to correspond. But the new development—the enticing prospect of communication with another dimension—brought Saint-Martin back to Lyons with "all possible speed."[83]

Papus and others have suggested that Saint-Martin's pseudonym, Unknown Philosopher, concealed the fact that his writings were actually dictated by the Unknown Agent. However, as Saint-Martin had already used the alias several years before the Agent's first known appearance, it seems rather to have been the other way round. But possibly the Agent's teaching found its way into his later works. As Papus claims:

> The "Unknown Agent or Philosopher" dictated 166 notebooks of instruction, of which Claude [*sic*] de Saint-Martin had knowledge and some of which he copied in his own hand. Of these notebooks, about 80 were destroyed in the first month of 1790 by the Agent himself, who wanted to avoid seeing them fall into the hands of Robespierre, who made extraordinary efforts to reach them.[84]

However, something about the Unknown Agent seems to have disconcerted Saint-Martin, although frustratingly—as we only have Saint-Martin's replies to Willermoz's letters—it is impossible to know exactly what it was. Willermoz had clearly informed Saint-Martin of some momentous breakthrough—from the timing (April 1785, within days of Commander de Monspey's visit) it must have been the arrival of those first notebooks—which threw Saint-Martin into a state of nervous excitement: asking for Willermoz's pardon, apologizing for having had the temerity to publish his works, and begging Willermoz to intercede on his behalf with, in Waite's words, "something which appears to be called *La chose,* whose place he has taken unasked"[85] (This suggests some continuity between Saint-Martin's practices and Willermoz's of fifteen years before and the appearance of the Unknown Agent, but tantalizingly no one knows what form it took.)

Saint-Martin's next letter implies that Willermoz had reassured him, and he was awaiting the latter's summons to Lyons.[86] Shortly after his arrival, he was initiated into the Rectified Scottish Rite as Eques a Leone Sidero (Knight of the Heavenly—or Starry—Lion), being quickly elevated to the Grand Profession. But five years later he requested that his name be removed from the Rite's register, although his reason remains unknown.[87]

Unfortunately, no other documentary evidence survives (or has been allowed to survive) on this critical period of Saint-Martin's life. The next we hear of him, at the end of 1786, he is back in Paris, and just weeks later he visited London, where he met various eminent people, including the astronomer Sir William Herschel. It was there that he wrote his most famous work, *The Man of Desire* (*L'homme du désir*), although it was not published for over a decade.

Because of the secrecy imposed by Willermoz and the "inner circle of the inner circle" of the Knights Beneficent, it is still hard to discover anything else about this curious episode. In any case, the French Revolution of 1789 soon gave people—particularly aristocrats—much more pressing matters to worry about.

Strangely, although Saint-Martin was in Paris during the Revolution and Reign of Terror, despite his noble origins he came through it unscathed, dying at Aulnay on October 13, 1803. As a predominantly aristocratic order, the Rectified Scottish Rite suffered heavily during the Revolution but was reconstructed in the early years of the nineteenth century by Willermoz, who also managed to survive the upheavals. Never likely to be a dominant order within Freemasonry, it is still nevertheless very much around and is particularly strong in Switzerland.

But what became of those 166 notebooks filled with information from the Unknown Agent? The fact that they obviously impressed influential figures such as Willermoz and Saint-Martin would no doubt have been enough also to impress their peers and subsequent generations of their followers, but without access to the notebooks themselves, we will never know how inspirational or revelatory they were. Although matters such as channeling and automatic writing are rather more familiar now, as either psychological or parapsychological phenomena (being treated with due caution in both fields), in the 1780s they were new, exciting, and considerably less subject to criticism. Pronouncements apparently from discarnate or even angelic entities, emanating inexplicably from the mouth or pen of an entranced medium, would be taken very seriously, as unique and possibly divine revelation. Those notebooks would have been treated with great reverence—and of course would have been much sought after by rival societies.

In his will, Willermoz left his Masonic and personal papers to a colleague, Joseph Antoine Pont, but they went missing for sixty years before being rediscovered in Lyons in 1894. Since 1935 they have been safe in Lyons Library and are a major source for occult and Masonic historians—but the fate of the Unknown Agent's notebooks after the Revolution and the disruption to the Knights Beneficent has never been ascertained. As we will see shortly, Papus claimed to possess Saint-Martin's copies of some of them and declared that most of the rest had been destroyed, but he never produced any evidence. Was he protesting too much? Was he cannily attempting to preempt further searches?

After the Revolution, the search for these scribblings of unearthly wisdom would have assumed the status of the quest for the Holy Grail among those who knew of their existence. But where to search? A good idea would have been either to follow the trail of Willermoz's archives or to investigate other documents belonging to individuals and societies with which he was connected, such as the Philadelphes, created by the Marquis de Chefdebien d'Armissan, or those of the Nègre and Hautpoul families, who were indirectly involved with the Knights Beneficent. Perhaps that explains the mysterious searches of the Saunière brothers a century afterward: after all, Alfred—who was dismissed for rummaging in the Chefdebien papers—is said to have had an affair with one of the descendants of the du Bourgs, who certainly knew the secret of *la chose.* Maybe the search continues, accounting for the misdirection of the Dossiers Secrets.

A Great Magus

In the 1880s, some eighty years after Saint-Martin's death, his great admirer Papus established an order dedicated to his philosophy. In fact, controversy rages in the esoteric world over whether Saint-Martin himself founded any kind of society or system of initiation—most think on the whole he avoided doing so because he was a philosopher, not an adept, although Robert Amadou, who edited the Martinist Order's review, *L'Initiation,* cites evidence that he did.[88] Papus claimed his Order's pedigree was established by the master himself, coming to him through one Henri Delaage, whose grandfather had supposedly been initiated by the Unknown Philosopher.

To bolster his claim that his Order was legitimately Saint-Martin's successor, Papus also maintained that it possessed several notebooks, in Saint-Martin's own hand, which he had copied directly from those containing the teachings of the Unknown Agent.[89] This assertion has never been substantiated, despite challenges made by Waite—among others—during his lifetime.

As Papus added other elements—particularly drawn from the Strict Observance—many esotericists dispute the validity of the Martinist Order, or even that it is properly Martinist. It represented Papus's own version of Martinism rather than Saint-Martin's original teachings. (Predictably, the Order founded by Papus experienced the usual schisms and breakaways, so today there are three major Martinist Orders).[90] Be that as it may, Papus's Order became very popular in Paris, and in 1891 a Supreme Council was created to oversee the burgeoning branches; by 1900 there were lodges in Britain, the United States, South America, and the Far East. The membership of the original Supreme Council is particularly intriguing: apart from Papus, it included Joséphin Péladan, Stanislas de Guaïta, and Maurice Barrès.[91]

Ostensibly, Papus's original Martinist Order possessed no particular doctrine but encouraged its members to undertake their own individual research and study. However, in reality considerable secrecy was involved—it even recruited by means of the cell system, deliberately modeled on the (newly discovered) physiological process of cell division, which is especially conducive to secrecy.[92] And in any case there are definite indications of an inner order that *did* uphold specific beliefs.

In 1902 the American branch, headed by Dr. Edouard Blitz, broke away from the Supreme Council's control, dubbing itself the American Rectified Martinist Order. Its first convocation, in Cleveland, Ohio, in June 1902, issued a manifesto that referred to "certain hidden grades which came out of the marriage between Martinism and the Rite of the Strict Observance."[93]

As we have seen, the Martinist Order did possess an interior order, called the S.I.—Silencieux Inconnus or Unknown Silent Ones (to which Robert Amadou belonged). Not much is known about it, its members being appropriately silent on the subject.

Increasingly, Papus emerges as a prime mover in the story. The real-life Gérard Encausse was a doctor and surgeon—taking the name Papus from a great physician in the works of Apollonius of Tyana—who died of tuberculosis contracted while serving in the medical corps on the front line in the First World War. A. E. Waite, often a critic of his claims about the Martinist connection but an admirer of the man, wrote, "He died for his country, literally worn out by his exertions on behalf of the wounded."[94]

So many of the threads of our story converge on Papus—whichever direction we might follow the trail. If we start at the modern end, with the Priory and the Dossiers Secrets, and follow the trail back, we end up at Papus, and if we start with von Hund and Saint-Martin and go forward, he is also at journey's end. Having founded the Martinist Order and been refused entry to the Grand Orient in 1899, he turned instead to the Rite of Memphis-Misraïm, of which he became Grand Master in France from 1908 until his death.[95] He was a Bishop in Jules Doinel's

Gnostic Church. Indeed, all roads do lead to Papus, whose son, Philippe (1906–1984), followed him into the medical profession, becoming Inspector-General in the Ministry of National Education, being awarded the Légion d'honneur for his public service. He also followed his father's esoteric interests, serving two periods as Grand Master of the Martinist Order, 1952–1971 and 1975–1979.[96]

Papus's whirlwind energy as a member and creator-director of so many orders means that ultimately it is impossible to be certain where his true allegiances lay. But his involvement with an even more secretive and closed society, the Swiss-based Hermetic Brotherhood of Light, is particularly intriguing. Although it was founded in Boston in about 1880, its headquarters were moved to Zurich, where it remains. The French authorities on Rosicrucianism Pierre Montloin and Jean-Pierre Bayard describe it as "strongly hierarchical, its adherents bound by dreadful oaths (which are not vain threats)."[97] According to Philippe Encausse, "From 1885, Papus was one of the agents of this society, in the sphere where he came to have authority in France."[98]

Behind the Priory

Gradually peeling away the accumulated layers of association and obfuscation, we are finally beginning to glimpse the identities of the shadowy groups behind the modern Priory of Sion. Recurring connections with the Masonic Rectified Scottish Rite and the Martinist Order confirm that they are indeed very closely related: the Rectified Scottish Rite being essentially the Strict Observance repackaged, with Martinist additions. And while it is by no means definite that Saint-Martin himself created a secret society or initiation, a century later Papus created the Martinist Order—explaining its overlapping membership with the Rectified Scottish Rite.

We have also identified the themes woven into the Priory's fictitious history in the mythology of the Rite of Memphis (later Memphis-Misraïm) and the Order of the Gold and Rose Cross. These, too, belong to the same family of secret societies. Although the Gold and Rose Cross was a separate, Rosicrucian society, it came to have a close relationship with the Strict Observance, at which time the legend of Ormus appeared in its lore.

Despite being an "Egyptian Rite," the Rite of Memphis—which used the Ormus theme—was also closely connected to the Strict Observance and its immediate predecessor, Misraïm (with which it later amalgamated). Misraïm actually owes its origin to the celebrated, or notorious, Count Cagliostro (Giuseppe Balsamo, 1743–1795)—a Strict Observance Mason who was initiated in London in 1777.[99] And Memphis maintained a close affiliation with the Philadelphes, founded by the Strict Observance (then Rectified Scottish Rite) Mason the Marquis de Chefdebien. So all these societies and orders that *seem* so different eventually turn out to be part of an interrelated, cross-fertilizing network, ultimately based on the Strict Observance.

There is one last member of the family of related secret societies and orders for which the Priory of Sion acted as a front or cover: Jules Doinel's Gnostic Church. Between 1917 and the end of the Second World War, this and the Martinist Order actually shared the same Grand Master—first Jean Bricaud, then Constant Chevillon.

Identifying this family of secret societies is one thing, but isolating what if anything lurks behind them sweeps us into much murkier waters. There seems to be something else underlying the Martinists' inner order, something more central, deeper, and perhaps darker than attempted communication with angels or spirits as a secret source of wisdom. Then there are the American schismatic Order's words about the "hidden grades" influenced by the Strict Observance, and the secrecy with which the ostensibly philosophical Martinist Order surrounded itself. In the words of the historian Richard F. Kuisel: "This modern Martinist order had its own rites and an unusual method of recruitment, the 'chain method,' which protected the society from exposure: each new member knew the identity of only the Martinist who had recruited him."[100] But exactly what exposure were they preventing? Are there any clues?

According to Papus's son, Philippe Encausse, the Martinist Order had *political* ambitions, its original aims—before the First World War—being "the Liberation of Poland [from czarist Russia], extinction of the Austro-Hungarian Empire, and a United States of Europe after the crushing of militarist feudalism."[101]

Obviously it would be essential to keep political objectives and activities, especially such radical ones as Philippe Encausse described, secret. But what connection could there possibly be between the Martinist

Order's political agenda and its weird communication with spirit entities? The answer is the person whom Papus regarded, even more than Saint-Martin, as his "intellectual master."[102] Although relatively unfamiliar outside France, this remarkable individual was actually the greatest influence on continental European esotericism in the late nineteenth and early twentieth centuries. And he provided us with an unexpected link back to the research for our 1999 book, *The Stargate Conspiracy.*

Inevitably, we found ourselves investigating the politico-occult school of synarchy, first formulated by Papus's intellectual master, the Frenchman who rejoiced in the name of Joseph Alexandre Saint-Yves, Marquis d'Alveydre (1842–1909).

Superficially, it might seem surprising that an occult school should be politically oriented or even inspire political ambitions. But if religious or philosophical beliefs often shape political views, or are expressed in political terms, why should occult or esoteric beliefs not do the same? As Pierre Plantard told the authors of *The Holy Blood and the Holy Grail,* politics is shaped by philosophy, not the other way round.[103] Not only did this line of research rush the Priory of Sion into sharp focus but it also took the story in a very disquieting direction.

The Prime Mover

In their *Encyclopedia of Sects of the World* (*Encyclopédie des sectes dans le monde,* 1984), Christian Plume and Xavier Pasquini describe Saint-Yves d'Alveydre as "one of the most outstanding figures of nineteenth-century esoterism,"[104] a sentiment echoed by other commentators, such as Emma Calvé's lover, the novelist Jules Bois, who knew Saint-Yves, describing him in his 1903 book, *The Invisible World* (*Le monde invisible*), as the "master of French occultists."[105]

Although Saint-Yves's ideas were to have an influence on mystical celebrities such as René Guénon, Rudolf Steiner, and G. I. Gurdjieff,[106] his major admirer and disciple, who passed his teachings on to the next generation, was undoubtedly Papus.

Saint-Yves's concept of synarchy was essentially a reaction to the rise of anarchy and therefore its opposite—a highly ordered method of government based on what he believed were universal laws and principles. Everything and everybody has its place and purpose; harmony is achieved by keeping to that place and fulfilling that purpose, whereas any circumvention of those natural laws leads to disaster. Everyone has to remain in his or her allotted station in life. (Papus likened the individual's relationship to a nation or race to the cells' relationship to the body. As each was preordained to fulfill a specific function, attempting to do anything else would only cause problems for both the individual and the organism as a whole.)[107]

His works outlined an ambitious, visionary program for establishing synarchy in France and beyond. Each state must be highly organized at every level, with everyone in his or her own specific place; otherwise anarchy would triumph. Challenging one's status would not be tolerated.

However, the concept that everyone has a preordained place and role means that some people are *naturally* intended to lead: in other words, Saint-Yves advocated government by a predestined elite. And although much of his work is about the practicality of applying synarchy to the government of society, at its core it is an essentially spiritual or mystical philosophy. The elite is spiritually attuned to the universal laws—effectively a priesthood. Synarchy is therefore a form of *theocracy,* rule by priests or priest-kings.

Synarchy even suggests that this enlightened elite is in direct contact with, and receives its instructions from, the spiritual intelligences that rule the universe—rather like the theocratic pharaohs of ancient Egypt, who were both secular rulers and intermediaries between the gods and the people. Saint-Yves himself believed he was in contact with invisible forces. But as André Ulmann and Henri Azeau point out in their 1968 *Synarchy and Power* (*Synarchie et pouvoir*), ultimately such elites are always self-selected.[108]

The son of a Breton doctor, the future political radical was born on March 26, 1842, plain Joseph Alexandre Saint-Yves; the title Marquis d'Alveydre was conferred on him by the Pope in 1880.[109] Despite his unconventional spiritual and mystical ideas, Saint-Yves remained a devout Catholic to the end of his life.

Abandoning the School of Naval Medicine in Brest in 1864 for health reasons, he went to Jersey in the Channel Islands, where he stayed until 1870, "living modestly as a professor of letters and sciences."[110] There Saint-Yves mixed with French expatriates and *proscrits*—"the banished," or political exiles from France—one of the most prominent being Victor Hugo, who lived in Guernsey between 1855 and 1870 (writing *Les Misérables* there). Saint-Yves and Hugo certainly met, introduced by their mutual friend Adolphe Pelleport. Perhaps this is why Hugo features in the Priory's list of Grand Masters.

It was in Jersey that Saint-Yves experienced an epiphany when he discovered the works of Antoine Fabre d'Olivet (1767–1825) through Pelleport's grandmother, who had known him in her youth.[111] Fabre d'Olivet—who was also famed for his abilities as a "magnetizer"—wrote a number of books on linguistics (including one on the Langue d'Oc) and on the esoteric aspects of remote history, proposing the existence of an ancient global civilization based on spiritual or occult principles.

While settled in the Channel Islands, Saint-Yves visited London to research at the British Museum, allegedly meeting the leading occultists Sir Edward Bulwer-Lytton and Éliphas Lévi. Although there is no direct evidence for such contacts, they would have been quite likely as he was a close friend of Bulwer-Lytton's son, also Edward (1831–1891), the late-1870s Viceroy of India. The incorporation of certain Eastern mystical ideas into Saint-Yves's system—which seems so at odds with his devout Catholicism—may well be due to Bulwer-Lytton's influence.

Returning to France at the onset of the Franco-Prussian War in 1870 to serve in the Army, Saint-Yves took part in the infamous suppression of the Paris Commune. According to his own account, it was at this time that he first talked about his social theory of synarchy, to his fellow soldiers.[112]

A year or so afterward he worked in a Ministry of the Interior department that kept a watchful eye on the Paris press, but he resigned in 1877 following his marriage in London to an aristocratic Polish divorcée, Marie-Victoire de Riznich, fifteen years his senior.[113] Even though this meant he could afford to give up work to pursue his interests and research, including alchemy, by all accounts it was a genuine love match, and he certainly never recovered from her death eighteen years later. In the same year as he married, Saint-Yves published his first major book, *Keys to the East* (*Clefs de l'Orient*), in which the term *synarchy* made its debut and its principles were outlined.[114]

But on the very first page Saint-Yves puts forward another concept that was to run parallel with the social theories of synarchy—the need for Europe to be united politically. Even more astonishing to modern eyes, on that very first page Saint-Yves states that, in his opinion, such a union was necessary because of the challenge created by the rise of Islam as a global force. He warns that a military conflict could break out at any time between a European nation and the Turkish Empire, "which will lead to, is already leading to, a religious awakening of all Islam."[115]

He considered that the two major crises confronting Europe were the emergence of Islam as a political force on the world stage—in his (very questionable) view, Muslims were united but Christendom was more fragmented than ever—and the political development of the European nations as a result of industrial progress and the rise of materialism, which he perceived as anti-Christian. The solution to both problems was for Europe to unite under a Christian banner, inspired by a "religious light" and a "fundamental or definitive revelation."[116] Saint-Yves also considered that the French Revolution had been a grave mistake: as the historian Olivier Dard notes, "Synarchy was supposed to allow France to surmount the conflicts born from the setting up of the Third Republic and Europe to unite."[117]

Throughout his series of books, Saint-Yves defined the three specific areas of society that needed to be governed—the law, the economy, and religion—proposing a European Council of National Communes, made up of economists, financiers, industrialists, and agriculturalists to regulate the economy; a European Council of National States of delegates from the member states' magistratures to govern international law; and a European Council of Churches to rule on religious matters.

However, Saint-Yves was not the first reformer, or even the first occulist, to think in terms of a united Europe, or at least to advocate that the secular rulers of Europe should be controlled by a single authority. (Although theoretically this had been the case before the Reformation, when the Pope claimed authority over all Christendom's kings and emperors, it had never actually produced a united Europe—except, arguably, for brief moments when attention turned outward during the Crusades. It rather dragged the Pope down to the level of just another secular ruler as he vied with them for power.)

An almost identical idea—in fact an "outline of synarchy"[118]—was proposed in the mid–seventeenth century by the Rosicrucian Jan Amos Comenius, who also suggested that three bodies should govern various aspects of society: a Council of Light would oversee learning and education, a Court of Justice would arbitrate in international disputes, and the World Consistory would oversee religious matters—an especially sensitive issue as Comenius wanted Christianity and Judaism to be reconciled. Besides seeing their apotheosis in Saint-Yves's philosophy, his ideas also influenced Rudolf Steiner—and even UNESCO, which paid tribute to Comenius in December 1958, as an inspiration of its ideal.

Louis-Claude de Saint-Martin shared this ideal to some extent, teaching "a sort of new theocracy established over all governments"[119] and that government should be in the hands of "divine commissioners."[120] The journalist Philippe Boudrel writes of the 1930s synarchist groups, which we will discuss later:

> The synarchist spirit, as much as its mode of thought, went back in particular to two philosophers . . . Louis de Saint-Martin (in the eighteenth century) and Saint-Yves d'Alveydre (in the following century). The one and the other extolled a vision of history through the will of Providence, man being only an instrument ruled by laws that are beyond him . . . But Providence, the "intelligence of the universe," delegated to some "divine commissioners," to the "sacerdotal man," the power to be the agents of a theocratic government.[121]

It was Saint-Yves, however, who developed and defined the idea in more or less modern political terms, directly inspiring Papus, who wrote: "France, which, in the Invisible, is the elder daughter of Europe and which, as a result, must always contain the center of the initiatory spirit."[122]

As with many idealists of his milieu, Saint-Yves projected his theories back into the distant past, believing that early civilizations had organized themselves according to the laws of "natural" leadership, which modern civilization had forgotten. His synarchist vision not only of the present but also of the past appeared in his series of "Mission" books: *Mission of the Sovereigns* (published anonymously in 1882), *Mission of the Workers* (also 1882), *Mission of the Jews* (1884), *Mission of the French* (1887), and the posthumously published *Mission of India in Europe, Mission of Europe in Asia* (1910).[123]

Inspired by the works of Fabre d'Olivet, Saint-Yves believed that in ancient times the whole of Asia, Europe, and Africa formed a single empire, under one religion and a theocratic system of rule; in other words, a synarchic golden age, which lasted from 7500 to 4000 B.C.E. The ancient religions of recorded history—especially those of Egypt, Greece, and Gaul—were merely the "dismemberment and dissolution" of that original global religion.[124] Saint-Yves invoked figures such as Apollonius of Tyana and Moses (founder of the "theocracy of Israel") as examples of initiates who had possessed the secret of the ancient global synarchy. He also argued that this sacred knowledge was known by the early Christian Church, which had a "secret initiation," but this was ruined by the formation of the Church of Rome, which became obsessed with political power. (Saint-Yves shared the thinking of many mystically inclined Catholics of the period, such as Péladan, that the Church was basically sound but had lost its way, forgetting its God-given secrets.)

Modern fans of "alternative history" will recognize in Saint-Yves's works many themes that were becoming popular in Theosophical and other circles—for instance, the existence of an ancient, advanced global civilization, unrecognized by conventional historians, of which the first acknowledged cultures, such as Egypt, were merely the heirs, besides the reality of the lost continent of Atlantis. (Saint-Yves claimed that the Great Sphinx of Giza was constructed by the Atlanteans many millennia earlier than historians believe.)

Most of this is outlined in his third Mission book, *Mission of the Jews*—which caused controversy by introducing such fringe ideas about ancient history into a series on social and political theory. (The title succinctly describes its purpose of winning the Jews over, on the grounds that Moses, like Jesus, had received the revelation of the ancient synarchy.)

In Saint-Yves's reconstruction, again based on Fabre d'Olivet's works, the revelation of synarchy had occurred three times in history, most recently to Jesus but previously to Moses and, the first time, to a heroic character named Ram—based on the Indian god Rama—who in 7500 B.C.E. had established the ancient global synarchist empire, which lasted until ancient Egypt (which represented the end of a civilization rather than the first flowering of a new one).[125] There was also an English pun involved, as Saint-Yves called this global civilization the Empire of the Ram (but *l'Empire du Bélier* in French) after the constellation and astrological sign of Aries.

(Tellingly, in the wake of *Mission of the Jews,* one of Saint-Yves's former mistresses, Claire Vautier, wrote a novel, *The Marquis: the Story of a Prophet* [*Monsieur le Marquis, histoire d'un prophète,* 1886], which was a thinly disguised account of her experiences with Saint-Yves. The prophet of the title, Saint-Emme, finds some of Fabre d'Olivet's writings and publishes them as his own—reflecting Jules Bois's later description of Saint-Yves as Fabre d'Olivet's "heir and even plagiarist."[126] Intriguingly, in Vautier's novel the youthful Saint-Emme claims to be the reincarnation of the mythical man-god Orpheus, presumably echoing Saint-Yves's own private belief.)

However, the "secret" of synarchy was not entirely lost to history, being kept alive through certain groups and brotherhoods. In *Mission of the French,* Saint-Yves particularly singled out the Templars as the "spiritual fathers of synarchy"—being a pan-European religious organization outside secular control that exercised considerable influence over religious, political, and economic matters.[127] For this reason, there was cross-fertilization between synarchy and neo-Templar orders, such as the Rectified Scottish Rite. Saint-Yves seems to have drawn on some of their deeper doctrines, and those groups in turn adopted his synarchist ideals. And of course all this came together perfectly in Papus, who synthesized all the disparate elements into a complete and coherent whole. As Ulmann and Azeau write (original emphasis):

> The Scottish reform of Freemasonry, . . . jointly with the source of Martinism, promoted some of the methods and some of the myths that later came to serve the inspirers of the Synarchic Movement. The reform first of all attributed an illustrious origin to Freemasonry, by making it the *continuator of the ancient orders of chivalry.* Subsequently, it added numerous new grades to the original three of the English rite, which allowed *hidden knowledge to be reserved for an elite,* as well as the possession of secrets that only sceptics qualify as imaginary.[128]

(The Synarchic Movement—more properly the Synarchic Empire Movement—was a synarchist society of the 1920s and '30s, which will be discussed later.)

Saint-Yves wrote of Freemasonry: "In our day, Freemasonry, the frame and skeleton of a theocracy, is the only initiation that bears the character of universality and which, from the thirty-third degree, recalls in a small way . . . the ancient intellectual and religious alliance."[129]

(There is, however, no evidence that Saint-Yves ever became any kind of Mason.[130] He seems to have avoided joining anything.)

Saint-Yves was not just some eccentric political theorist whose ideas were adopted by a handful of equally eccentric occultists. Not only did his vision come to dominate the whole of the French esoteric scene (thanks largely to Papus) but his ideas were also taken seriously within an influential political arena—at least for a time.

From 1882—when his first Mission books were published—Saint-Yves began to promote his thinking on lecture tours, speaking that year to a thousand-strong audience and later to a major conference in Amsterdam. In 1886 he created a pressure group, the Syndicate of the Professional and Economic Press (Syndicat de la Presse Professionnelle et Économique), made up of economists, businessmen, and politicians he had converted to synarchy. It lobbied government ministers, arranging meetings to discuss Saint-Yves's ideas, and disseminated literature. This group was fairly high powered, including Senators and Deputies, a government minister, François Césaire Demahy, Minister of the Navy and Colonies—and in 1899 one of the founders of Action Française[131]—and even a future President of the Republic, Paul Deschanel.[132]

Although Saint-Yves does not appear in today's records of members of the Légion d'honneur, the Légion's own publications show that he was made a Chevalier in 1893, under the sponsorship of a General Février. The researcher Jean Saunier suggests that the record was removed during the Nazis' anti-Masonic purges,[133] although, as we will see, there are reasons for the post-Liberation governments to suppress all and everything connected with synarchy.

In the end, however, Saint-Yves's ideal reorganization of French society and politics was simply too radical, too big a job, and too out of step with the existing order to have a realistic chance of succeeding—at least overtly. But as with many other ideologies, when it proves impossible to enter through the front door, other, back-door methods have to be employed, such as revolutions or coups d'état. Whether Saint-Yves himself thought along such lines is unknown, although from the evidence it seems unlikely—he seems to have given up the fight after 1890 and turned to rather more abstruse studies. But, as we will see, those who came after him had no such qualms, particularly after the First World War had torn the old Europe apart.

In 1890 Saint-Yves announced that his poem, *The Victorious Joan of Arc* (*Jeanne d'Arc victorieuse*) would be his last work, duly maintaining a low profile for the remaining nineteen years of his life. His beloved wife, Marie-Victoire, died in 1895 after a lengthy illness, and he turned their house in Versailles into a shrine to her memory, having her place at table set each day and claiming "that he does not cease conversing with her."[134] Although money was now tight, Saint-Yves devoted the last years of his life to developing his archeometer, a complex and abstruse system described as "an instrument of universal measure that will lay the foundations for the great renewal of the arts and sciences."[135] He died on February 5, 1909, in Pau, near the Pyrenees.

Although it was widely known only after his death, Saint-Yves had added another, very significant, element to his grand scheme. Not only was he advocating synarchy as the natural form of government and social organization for the modern world, and not only did he argue that it had been the universal system of world government in the ancient world, but, he claimed, the vestiges of that global empire still existed in the form of a synarchist utopia, hidden away from the rest of the world in a secret land in the Himalayas. He enlarged upon this claim in the last of his Mission books, *Mission of India,* which he wrote in 1886 (before the publication of *Mission of the French*) but suppressed during his lifetime. It was published, on Papus's initiative, in 1910.

With the full title of *Mission of India in Europe, Mission of Europe in Asia: The Question of the Mahatma and Its Solution,* this is one of the key texts of European esotericism. Saint-Yves introduced the idea of Agarttha (or Agartha, as it is now), a synarchically organized land somewhere in the Himalayas, where no Westerner is allowed and whose population of initiates is governed by Mahatmas, or spiritual masters. Both a sanctuary and a sacred center of learning, it has an underground library that stretches for thousands of miles, even under the sea.[136]

Saint-Yves wrote: "Before Ram, the metropolis of initiation had as its center Ayodha, the solar town. Subsequently, several times Agarttha moved its seat, which corresponds to a population of twenty million inhabitants, but around this center extends a synarchic confederation of peoples, corresponding to more than forty million souls."[137]

Agarttha is also mentioned in Saint-Yves's Joan of Arc poem, the reference explained in a note: "Following the revolutions that broke up the ancient synarchic organization revealed in *The Mission of the Jews,* this

Mother-University closed its Mysteries more and more. Its mystic name Agarttha, elusive to Violence, says very clearly that it conceals its location from the curious."[138]

Other occultists developed Saint-Yves's Agarttha, particularly the relationship between the sacred, hidden land and the rest of the world, as a key concept of European esotericism. Saint-Yves had claimed that its rulers were in psychic contact with certain individuals in the outside world—himself included—and that by this means they were trying to maneuver the planet so that more open contact could be established. If the world became synarchist, the Mahatmas would declare themselves openly. Agarttha therefore had only an indirect influence on the rest of the globe, through certain chosen individuals. However, soon the idea began to circulate that the Mahatmas had a direct influence on world events—and might even secretly control them.[139]

The knee-jerk, natural assumption is that Saint-Yves's detailed description of life in Agarttha is a fictional account of the workings of his perfect state, similar to Thomas More's *Utopia*—therefore his insistence that Agarttha was a real place may be taken with a large pinch of salt. Yet there is a central paradox: Saint-Yves claimed not only to have been in contact with Agartthan emissaries but to have suppressed the story on their instructions. As Plume and Pasquini relate: "In 1885, he received a visit from envoys of Agartha, a little time after he published his work *Mission of India in Europe, Mission of Europe in Asia.* But hardly was it printed when he ordered the destruction of all copies. He subsequently explained that he had been ordered to do so by superior powers, as he had revealed secrets in this work."[140] Why did he withdraw *Mission of India*? If he had second thoughts about foisting such a concept on the public, why tell his immediate circle the *reason* he had withdrawn it? Of course, there are psychological conditions that make it impossible for sufferers to know the difference between what they imagine and what is objectively real: Saint-Yves may have mistaken his own fantasies for input beamed in from elsewhere. But there may be more to it than that.

According to Papus's group the Friends of Saint-Yves (Les Amis de Saint-Yves), *Mission of India* was the product of "a double series of researches, first intellectual, then astral,"[141] suggesting that Saint-Yves utilized psychic or perhaps even magical means to discover more about Agarttha and the Mahatmas, corresponding neatly with *la chose* of the Elect Cohens and the Agent Inconnu of the Knights Beneficent.

Once again, the reality of what Saint-Yves himself experienced is unknowable and in any case is ultimately less important than his *belief* that the Mahatmas of Agarttha had made direct contact, not only confirming his synarchist ideology but perhaps even shaping his original ideas. These mysterious beings would communicate with and direct the synarchist elite.

This awe-inspiring new concept was enthusiastically embraced by occult orders and leaders: behind an Order's earthly chiefs hid spirit entities with whom they were in contact and who really were in control. A classic example is the Secret Chiefs of the seminal Hermetic Order of the Golden Dawn, which flourished in late-nineteenth-century Britain. They might be the spirits of the dead, "ascended masters" (humans so spiritually developed that they have been elevated to a new plane of existence), angelic or supernatural beings, or, more recently, extraterrestrials, but the basic idea remains the same. Only the heads of the Order can make contact with them, which gives them their authority—a tough concept for a subordinate to argue with! Baron von Hund's Unknown Superiors (a secret but mortal brotherhood directing from behind the scenes) had become first Saint-Yves's Mahatmas (spiritually advanced humans who can be contacted through psychic means) and then discarnate or extraterrestrial intelligences.

The inner secret of many of the groups behind this story—the Elect Cohens, the Knights Beneficent, and possibly the Strict Observance—was that they actively sought ways of contacting "higher intelligences" and, as in the case of the Unknown Agent of the Knights Beneficent, believed they had succeeded.

Whatever Saint-Yves really believed or knew, after his death it was on Papus's initiative that *Mission of India* was published, Papus having been a close friend and champion of Saint-Yves from 1887. When Papus established the Martinist Order, he offered Saint-Yves a seat on its Supreme Council, but—never one for joining groups—Saint-Yves declined.[142] (It is often claimed that Saint-Yves was Grand Master of the Martinist Order, but evidence is nonexistent.)

Papus obviously impressed the Czar's court in Russia, where he went in 1901, 1903, and 1906—with the backing of the French Foreign Ministry—with Saint-Yves's ideas. As a result several Russian aristocrats visited Saint-Yves, then living in Versailles.[143]

After Saint-Yves's death, synarchy developed in ways that would not necessarily have met with his approval. Whereas when his attempts to establish synarchy through overt means failed he gave up in favor of other pursuits, his successors simply turned to stealth. Revolution was out, elitist ideologies being largely unsuited to mass movements,[144] and with the rising popularity of democracy and the concept of individual liberty it became increasingly futile to attempt to win people over by debate to the notion of a fixed hierarchy—especially as by definition most people would find themselves in the lower orders. Synarchists therefore turned to cunning, seizing power from within by infiltration. Their only hope of success lay in taking control of the institutions of government by having members take key posts and then follow secret orders from the heads of the Order (or maybe even the "hidden powers"), propelling the state in the direction that would bring them even greater control. *Synarchy* came to stand for "rule by secret society"—not necessarily what Saint-Yves himself had advocated.

Synarchy is a very odd system that has no real place in the familiar left-to-right political spectrum. Its fundamental belief in hierarchy and an elite might make its natural home very much on the right, but the belief that each part of the social hierarchy—the cells of the body—has an important function, with which even the elite are not permitted to interfere, obviously reflects much more left-wing, socialist principles. (In fact synarchy's nearest counterpart is national socialism—which is why 1920s and '30s synarchists felt more comfortable working with Nazis and Italian Fascists, both of whom were to some degree influenced by synarchist thinking. Even so, basically synarchy remains outside the usual political categories.)

Synarchy became the underlying philosophy of many—if not all—of the esoteric societies and continued to inspire groups such as the Order of the Solar Temple, which unashamedly declared itself synarchist.[145]

The Egyptian Connection

We first came across synarchy through some quite separate research into certain ideas behind the "alternative Egypt" boom of the 1990s. Briefly, this led us to the grandfather of alternative Egyptology, the Alsatian mystical philosopher R. A. Schwaller de Lubicz (1887–1961), whose ideas on the religion of ancient Egypt and particularly the research he and his wife, Isha, carried out, underpin much of the more recent revisionist histories. They spent the years between 1938 and 1952 surveying and measuring the temple complex at Luxor, arriving at a complicated interpretation of its symbolism that Schwaller elaborated in his key three-volume work, *The Temple of Man* (*Le temple de l'homme*), published in 1957, which argues that the major achievements of the ancient Egyptian civilization, such as the Great Pyramid and Sphinx, are many thousands of years older than conventionally believed and are products of the science of a lost, advanced civilization—from where else but Atlantis.[146]

What intrigued us was that his modern admirers tend to refer to Schwaller de Lubicz as a philosopher or mathematician, rarely if ever mentioning his background as a leading light of the Parisian occult scene of the 1910s and '20s—he was another frequenter of the Bookshop of Independent Art with Debussy and Emma Calvé[147]—or, more important, that he was also a political activist: racist, anti-Semitic, and extremely right wing, not to say fascistic (Saul Bellow labels him a "protofascist"),[148] whose ideas significantly influenced the early Nazi Party. (He was particularly proud that he had designed the uniform adopted by the Nazi Brown Shirts.) Indeed, much of his interpretation of ancient Egyptian history and religion—cited so uncritically by his modern fans—was shaped by his political (and racial) views long before he set foot in Egypt.

We discovered that Schwaller de Lubicz's occult-influenced political ideals came directly from synarchy. His work on ancient Egypt was inspired by a belief that it was the perfect example of theocracy—essentially a synonym for synarchy—in action. Not only did he preach synarchist ideas but some of his reconstruction of the ancient world, even down to the dates, comes directly from Saint-Yves.

Born in Asnières in Alsace (then in Germany) in 1887, René Schwaller—as he was then—moved to Paris after qualifying as a chemist, becoming involved in the esoteric scene, particularly the Theosophical Society. In 1918 he and Isha formed their own group within it, called Les Veilleurs (The Watchers), and published its companion journal, *Le Veilleur.* But he broke with the Theosophists because they were wary of his ambitions to politicize their doctrines, making Les

Veilleurs—whose members included Camille Flammarion, Papus's former friend and colleague—an independent organization. Mixing politics and racial ideas with esotericism, *Le Veilleur* had as its slogan a new twist on the French Republic's call to arms: "Hierarchy! [instead of "Equality"] Fraternity! Liberty!"

Les Veilleurs was linked with similar groups in Germany, its ideas having a profound influence on the embryonic Nazi Party—particularly on Deputy Führer Rudolf Hess, who has often been linked to synarchy.[149] While there is no direct evidence that he belonged to a specifically synarchist group or society (although he certainly belonged to esoterically inclined organizations, such as the Munich-based Thule Society), his political thinking certainly ran smoothly along synarchist lines.

One of Les Veilleurs's most important members was the aristocratic Lithuanian poet Oscar Vladislav de Lubicz Milosz, who formally adopted Schwaller into his clan in 1919, dubbing him Chevalier de Lubicz. As Pierre Montloin and Jean-Pierre Bayard write in *The Rosicrucians, or the Sage's Plot* (1971): "O. V. de Lubicz Milosz was one of the rare initiates of the beginning of the twentieth century. He held the knowledge of the priest-kings of Lusace from whom he was descended, as well as, in his maternal line, Cabalists from the Baltic lands."[150] (Coincidentally, Lusace—which now straddles the border of Germany and the Czech Republic—was the original heartland of von Hund's Templarist Strict Observance.)

The newly elevated Schwaller de Lubicz apparently disbanded Les Veilleurs in 1920, instructing the members to use what they had learned in their chosen spheres. Perhaps rather than disbanding, the society was actually going underground.

It may also be significant that Schwaller de Lubicz claimed to his closest associates that he had access to what one of them later called "a mystic source . . . a private source of knowledge," or "Aor" (Hebrew for "Light").[151] The concept of the mystical light Aor also features in Saint-Yves's writings.

We were utterly astounded to discover that Schwaller de Lubicz and synarchy led us right back to the same groups—including the Martinist Order and the Knights Beneficent—which we had already identified as being behind the Priory of Sion. So we were intrigued to find that not only had Jean Cocteau and Schwaller de Lubicz corresponded for many years but Cocteau had stayed with the Lubiczes at Luxor during a tour of Egypt in 1949. The clearly awestruck Cocteau wrote in his journal: "I am a heretic by birth—may I be forgiven. I kneel down before the Lubicz family."[152] He also records his arrival in Luxor on April 4:

> I must warn the reader, if he is interested enough to follow me, that these three days will be of the utmost importance to me.
>
> My first impulse, after filling out the form at the hotel, will be to pay my respects to the Baron and Baroness de Lubicz, and to let them know I am in Luxor.[153]

Cocteau spent several days with the de Lubiczes, who showed him around the Temple, expounding their theories about its symbolism. Overwhelmed by his knowledgeable hosts, he can hardly praise them enough.

We were also struck by this statement in Cocteau's journal, about a nighttime visit to the pyramids of Giza:

> In the sky lies the unharnessed Wain, shafts pointing upwards. Strange stopping place! The Three Wise Men have struck their tents of stone, stretched from base to point, one side in the shadow and the other three smoothed by the moon. They sleep while their dog lies awake. Their watch dog is the Sphinx.[154]

"Three Wise Men" is the French term for the three stars we know as Orion's Belt. There was a media sensation when Robert Bauval and Adrian Gilbert's *The Orion Mystery* was published in 1994, arguing that the three pyramids of Giza were built specifically to represent Orion's Belt. Yet here we have Cocteau, in 1949, apparently taking the connection for granted! And he also describes the Sphinx as a watchdog; half a century later Robert Temple, in his 1999 revision of *The Sirius Mystery,* proposed that the Great Sphinx of Giza was originally a representation of the jackal-headed god Anubis. Presumably thanks to the influence of Schwaller de Lubicz, Cocteau was remarkably ahead of his time.

The fact that the Parisian artist should have known and admired Schwaller de Lubicz is not so odd. Cocteau had wide-ranging exotic interests, and Schwaller's ideas about the meaning of ancient Egyptian mythology would have had an irresistible allure. Synarchy as such may not have been on the agenda. But in Cocteau's journals (which, as we have seen, were intended for publication and therefore were sanitized), there is a single—isolated but telling—reference to the work of Saint-Yves d'Alveydre. In March 1953, lamenting the loss of some of his books, including Jacques Weiss's 1950 revival of Saint-Yves's ideas, Cocteau declares it to be "Sole important documentation on politics." [155] Obviously not only was he familiar with Saint-Yves's work but he approved of it. This may not be enough to identify him as an out-and-out synarchist, but he was certainly on the same wavelength. Could this be why Cocteau's name was included on the list of the Priory's Grand Masters? In fact, there are other intriguing connections between the Priory and synarchy.

The Secret of Alpha Galates

The most striking aspect of the wartime *Vaincre* and the Alpha Galates Order was their advocacy of the United States of Europe, or United States of the West. The postwar Priory has continued to insist on the importance of the European ideal—in fact, it is the one thing that has remained constant—and of course the United States of Europe is also at the heart of synarchist ideology. But in itself that does not necessarily mean Alpha Galates was synarchist—it is quite possible to believe in the desirability of a united Europe without being synarchist.

However, not only do *Vaincre*'s articles on Atlantis and the ancient past come straight out of Saint-Yves's historical reconstruction—for example, "The Legend of Ram" by Auguste Brisieux in the first issue—but Camille Savoire *explicitly* states that Alpha Galates's members are "resolute believers in synarchy . . . opposed to anarchy in all its forms." [156] This should hardly come as a great surprise. We have already traced Alpha Galates—and the later hollow shell that is the Priory of Sion—to the network of secret societies and "occult" Masonic orders that all end up with synarchy: under Papus's leadership, the Martinist Order was suffused with synarchist ideology; the Rectified Scottish Rite—the rebranded Strict Observance—enjoyed a cross-fertilizing relationship with synarchy, based on the concept that the original Templars were the prime medieval synarchists and the Rite being their modern incarnation.

Another highly intriguing aspect is the importance to Alpha Galates of the work of the esoteric philosopher (and Martinist) Paul Le Cour—which is repeatedly quoted in *Vaincre,* although there is no suggestion that he was actually a member.

Le Cour was certainly an admirer of Saint-Yves, his books including direct references to the Marquis's work, also incorporating Agarttha and so on. Le Cour also introduced some innovations that were to become central to Priory lore, one of the most important being the significance of Bourges, writing in a 1943 work: "At the centre of the hexagon [of France] is found Bourges, the mysterious capital of France . . ."[157] Another quotation from the same work links several themes:

> In the 12th century, Bourges was also fertilised by the tradition that raised its magnificent cathedral.
>
> But France also possessed the cathedrals of Paris, Chartres, Amiens and Mont Saint-Michel with the islet of Tambelaine, evokers of the Helleno-Christian tradition.
>
> From which were born the great Johannite Orders of the Hospitallers and Templars.
>
> Its [France's] royal château of the Val de Loire, dating from the Renaissance, was full of the symbols of Hellenic Christianity.
>
> To there came, to take refuge and to die, one of the greatest genuises of Christian esotericism, Leonardo da Vinci.[158]

The Hiéron du Val d'Or

In the Dossiers Secrets, the Priory of Sion associated itself obliquely with the strange Catholic society—or cult—the Hiéron du Val d'Or, founded in Paray-le-Monial in 1873 by Baron Alexis de Sarachaga y Lobanoff and the Jesuit Victor Dernon. The Priory makes the link by the inclusion of a single page of the June 24, 1926, issue of its journal, from an article dealing with the symbolism of the Sacred Heart, in *The Secret Files of Henri Lobineau.* There is no comment or explanation, but its very presence presumably implies that the Priory approves of the Hiéron du Val d'Or's own agenda.

The Hiéron was a very odd mixture of traditional Catholicism and occult philosophies, believing that, having originated in Atlantis, Christianity was the "universal tradition" so eagerly sought by esotericists. This conviction could easily be dismissed as crackpot were it not that Baron de Sarachaga counted two successive Popes, Pius IX and Leo XIII, among his personal friends. It was the Hiéron du Val d'Or that secured Pius XI's sanction for the initiation of the Feast of Christ the King, which honors Jesus as lord of creation, in December 1925.[159]

Jean-Luc Chaumeil describes its aims as the creation of "a theocracy in the eyes of which nations will be only provinces, their leaders only proconsuls in the service of an occult world government made up of an 'elite.' For Europe, this reign of the 'Great King' implies the double hegemony of the Papacy and the Empire, of the Vatican and the Habsburgs who are its right arm."[160] Its devotees also looked forward to the Millennium in 2000, when the Second Coming would bring about Jesus' rule on Earth. The society's great secret was the sacred name and "word of power" "Aor-Agni"—Hebrew for "Light-Fire." However, the project fell apart with the outbreak of the First World War and de Sarachaga's death in 1918, although the Hiéron du Val d'Or limped on until its dissolution in 1927.

But in its last years the Hiéron du Val d'Or greatly influenced Paul Le Cour, who was actively involved with the organization from 1923. After the Hiéron's demise, Le Cour founded an association called simply Atlantis (which numbers some three thousand members today) to continue its work. As he influenced the Alpha Galates Order, so therefore did the Hiéron. (The one page of the Hiéron's writing that is included in the Dossiers Secrets is dated June 24, 1926, the day on which Le Cour founded Atlantis).[161]

Ever more intriguingly, Paray-le-Monial seems to have been chosen by the Hiéron du Val d'Or as its base because it was also the center of the Catholic cult of the Sacred Heart (Sacré-Coeur). Revived as the symbol of Catholic monarchism in the latter half of the nineteenth century, the movement's immediate focus was the construction of the Sacré-Coeur basilica in Paris's Montmartre, the initiative of Hubert Rohault de Fleury, of the same family as Paul-Urbain de Fleury of Rennes-les-Bains. And, to make the circle of connections complete, the largest contributor of funds to the project was the Comte de Chambord.

It may also be significant that two of General de Gaulle's aunts were nuns in the Sacred Heart, while he himself was educated by Jesuits at the College of the Sacred Heart at Antoing in Belgium and remained a very devout Catholic whose religion profoundly molded his vision of France and his own destiny.[162] Perhaps control of the Sacred Heart was seen as a means of influencing political leaders. (Of course it would be utterly compelling if Jesus or the Virgin Mary—a variation of the "secret masters"—apparently issued orders to a devout Catholic President. Would he dare argue?)

The idea of an extremely conventional Catholic devotional movement working side by side with a group that linked Christianity with Atlantis might seem ridiculous, yet the connection went further than their just happening to have headquarters in the same town. In 1921 the Sacred Heart published a review called *Regnabit,* subtitled "The Universal Review of the Sacred Heart," the brainchild of an Oblate of Immaculate Mary named Félix Anizan, who worked closely not only with the Sacred Heart center in Paray-le-Monial but also with Gabriel de Noaillet, Baron de Sarachaga's successor as head of the Hiéron du Val d'Or. But Father Anizan had another close collaborator in *Regnabit:* a brother member of his order named Émile Hoffet.[163]

Despite its peculiar ideas, the Hiéron du Val d'Or makes sense of an otherwise fragmented picture, specifically: the esoteric philosophy underlying the Alpha Galates Order, of which Plantard was Grand Master; Émile Hoffet's friendship—or at least acquaintance—with Plantard's mentor Georges Monti, who is used (for no apparent reason) as the pivotal point of the Saunière story constructed in the Dossiers Secrets, obviously written by someone familiar with Hoffet's life and career. It is also clear that, despite its ostensibly Catholic orientation, the Hiéron was essentially synarchist—as Chaumeil's summary of its objectives reveals. Synarchy and Catholicism were by no means inimical: Saint-Yves himself was a committed Catholic—even honored by the Pope—who espoused many seemingly incongruous ideas about the ancient past and Eastern religions. In fact, the Hiéron du Val d'Or directly complements and expands Saint-Yves's work, carrying it into a practical arena.

Several researchers have suggested that the Hiéron du Val d'Or was the direct precursor of Opus Dei, the group of extreme Catholic activists made notorious by *The Da Vinci Code,* which was founded in Spain the year after the Hiéron's demise. Somewhat astonishingly, the authority on Rosicrucianism Jean-Pierre Bayard counts Opus Dei among the modern organizations that "could claim to belong [to Rosicrucianism] but which however do not seem to take advantage of this."

He adds, "Perhaps we can find a connection [of Opus Dei] with the 'Collège Historique du Hiéron du Val d'Or,' founded around 1890 at Paray-le-Monial and known also under the name of the 'Société du Règne' or again 'Société des Fastes.' "[164] Could it be that Opus Dei believes it is directly influenced by invisible entities—angels or saints, perhaps even Jesus himself?

By now we have arrived at a very consistent and clear picture: Alpha Galates was synarchist, and the Priory of Sion acts as a cover or front for synarchist societies. But how does this explain Alpha Galates' wartime activities—and those of the later Priory's?

Although happy to jump into bed with synarchy, Alpha Galates hardly shouted its affiliation from the rooftops. For those familiar with Saint-Yves's work, *Vaincre*'s inspiration is clear enough, but Savoire's brief mention of synarchy is its only overt reference. The Alpha Galates Order seems to have been playing down, if not actually concealing, its synarchist credentials. Why?

Perhaps the answer will lie in an examination of how synarchy transformed itself between the two world wars—into something very shady and sinister indeed.

CHAPTER SEVEN

The Shape-Shifters

Like most ideologies, synarchy underwent a radical shake-up and reorientation after the convulsions of the First World War had overturned all the old certainties and changed all the rules.

With no hope of establishing themselves overtly, the synarchists adopted a new contingency plan of "invisible revolution": infiltrating members into key positions in government—or converting top people—enabling their elite leaders to take control, one way or another, without being noticed. Once the stage was set for synarchists to exert an increasingly tight grip, the newly "enlightened" elite would forge ahead with the "revolution from above."

As it operates by controlling from within, synarchy can work inside any system of government, although it tends to favor totalitarian regimes, which have highly centralized governments and therefore fewer institutions to take control of. Democratic systems—with so many voices to be heard—inject an element of uncertainty into long-term planning. (In democracies, the synarchists' best strategy is to take control of the civil servants who remain in their jobs despite changes of government, but of course this limits their ability to influence the formulation of policy.)

Because they have no traditional political affiliations, synarchists are essentially the ultimate shape-shifters, with no qualms about taking on any disguise, from democrat to fascist and from New Age to Catholic traditionalist. In many ways, their watchword is expediency; converting the masses, or even overtly imposing their ideology on them, is relatively unimportant.

Synarchy's wider ambitions also changed radically. Although Saint-

Yves thought primarily in terms of France first, then Europe, his later followers—particularly between the two wars—sought to impose "a world government by an initiated elite" under "God's law for the organisation of society."[1]

Following Papus's death, there was a split within the Martinist Order, partly over the importance of synarchist ideology. Some, agreeing with Papus, thought it should be fundamental to the Order, while others were unconvinced that synarchy was necessarily synonymous with Saint-Martin's philosophy.

Papus was briefly succeeded as Grand Master by Charles Téder (also known as Charles Détre), who died in 1918. Then under Jean Bricaud (1881–1934) the Order took the major step of rejecting synarchy. He also completed the process begun by Téder whereby membership was open only to Freemasons. Women were excluded. Those who were unhappy with these reforms, especially the split from synarchy, formed the breakaway Martinist and Synarchic Order (Ordre Martiniste et Synarchique) in January 1921, under Victor Blanchard (1878–1953), otherwise known as Paul Yesir—who was actually head of the General Secretariat of the Presidency of the Chamber of Deputies. The new Order's journal was evocatively named *The Veil of Isis* (*Le Voile d'Isis*).[2]

It is entirely possible that the division of Martinism into two orders, one political and the other nonpolitical, was not as acrimonious or even as final as it was painted. The schism was probably a matter of public perception, providing the leaders with an escape route if their political activities backfired. Apparently Constant Chevillon, Grand Master of the nonpolitical Martinist Order from 1934 until his murder in 1944, was active in synarchist circles.[3] (Papus's son, Philippe Encausse, revived the original Order in the 1950s and so presumably remained faithful to his father's vision.)

In 1922 the Martinist and Synarchic Order formed the more obviously political Synarchic Central Committee (Comité Synarchique Central, or CSC), an organizing committee for study groups that aimed to recruit an elite of ambitious young civil servants. In 1930 the CSC adopted its better-known name, Synarchic Empire Movement (Mouvement Synarchique d'Empire, or MSE), and began recruiting by the chain method—each member having only limited contact with others—also employed by the Martinist Order.[4] A member of the Central Committee wrote later, anonymously:

> The true synarchs, if not synarchists, who we knew at the time and who were linked to the international movement, were not obviously part of the Committee; neither Jean Monnet, nor Clémentel, not Alexandre Millerand, to cite three men whose membership of the movement was never in doubt for the true initiates. The CSC was composed especially of young men, former polytechnicians, young inspectors of finances, younger members of great business families, gifted pupils of the Jesuits. It was in this way that [Yves] Bouthillier, who had passed the examination for the Inspectorate of Finances in 1921, really joined the Committee and was charged with canvassing in the Inspectorate; as were often members of the cabinets of the Ministers of Finance that followed one another, notably in the crucial period of 1926–27.[5]

The important names here are Jean Monnet and Yves Bouthillier, both of whom we will meet again later.

(*Polytechnician* refers to the synarchists' favored recruiting ground, the École Polytechnique, known as "the X": perhaps it is significant that one of Papus's closest friends—besides Emma Calvé, the noted astronomer Camille Flammarion, and the Nobel Prize–winning physiologish Charles Richet—was Colonel Albert de Rochas [1837–1914], its former Director of Studies. Calvé's biographer Jean Contrucci writes of him, "[He] would experience some trouble when they noticed that he gave himself over—outside course hours—to spiritist experiences in the sacrosanct enclosure of the X!"[6] De Rochas invested much time and energy investigating the mechanics of channeling and mediumship, of which Papus no doubt approved. But de Rochas's unconventional interests meant he was eventually forced to resign from his post at the École Polytechnique.)

According to an informant who had belonged to the MSE study group that met in Paris's Avenue du Coq:

> Sometimes men came to these meetings for a session on a particular subject, *all* of whom held an important place in the story of synarchy. I remember Baudoin, Bouthillier himself, Albertini. And, one day, the trio decided that I could meet a man who was introduced to me as one of their mentors "with whom they would do great things." They took me to him with some secrecy, and the conversa-

> tion was at first a dialogue, a little esoteric for me, between Lousteau and him. It was General Weygand, and this was a little after February 6 [1934].[7]

From the outbreak of the Second World War until the French surrender of 1940, Belgian-born General Maxime Weygand (1867–1965)—who was, incidentally, Saint-Yves d'Alveydre's great-nephew by marriage[8]—held the signally important position of Supreme Allied Commander of French and British forces. It was Weygand who called on the French government to ask Hitler for terms. After the surrender he was briefly Vichy's Minister of Defense before becoming head of French forces in North Africa—although he maintained direct, clandestine communication with Churchill.[9] If it could be proved he was a synarchist—although conclusive evidence is hard to find—it would be truly sensational.

It has been suggested that the MSE had some influence on the rise of Fascism in Italy in 1922. (There were certainly strong ties later between Mussolini's regime and French synarchist groups.) However, it was only in the 1930s that synarchy emerged as a political force, although as ever clandestinely. Its objectives and doctrines were set out in the notorious document known as the Synarchist Pact.

Pact with the Devil

"The Synarchist Revolutionary Pact for the French Empire" or "Synarchist Pact" for short, was explicitly the MSE's manifesto. Because it was kept strictly secret for several years, the precise circumstances surrounding its inception are unknown, but it opens with this ominous warning:

> All illicit possession of the present document opens one to sanctions without foreseeable limits, whatever the channel by which it was received.
>
> In such a case, it is best to burn it and at no point to speak of it.[10]

The earliest known copies are dated September 1936, although it was probably conceived in the wake of the upheavals of February 1934. However, its existence would not become known until 1941, when a copy was found among the possessions of a businessman who committed suicide under the Occupation, and although the existence of the Pact duly hit the headlines at that time, it was not published in an accessible form until 1946.

As a member of an MSE study group recognized their analyses in the text[11] the Pact was clearly collaborative, but the only specific names linked with its authorship are those of an esotericist named Vivian Postel du Mas and the businessman Jean Coutrot, both of whom will appear in this story later.[12]

In thirteen "fundamental points" and 598 "propositions," the manifesto sets out the basis for the "invisible revolution" or "revolution from above." The ultimate goal is "world synarchy," to be "instituted in each country according to the 'historical axis' of the country concerned": in other words, different methods will be employed in different countries, depending on their particular systems of government. However, the Pact itself is specifically geared to France, as it is France's mission to lead the world to the glories of synarchy.

The Pact utterly opposed the Third Republic's parliamentarianism ("that political potpourri issued from the Constitution of 1875") because it was a foreign import, essentially unsuited to France. Because in principle there is a correct form of government for each country and its people, individual interpretations will never work if transplanted elsewhere. Referring to the contemporary political climate of the 1930s, the Pact recognizes that "Bolshevism currently suits the Eurasian peoples, as Fascism the Italian people, Nazism the Germanic people, parliamentarianism the British people."

The Pact goes on: "Against all the relative forms of anarchy we struggle without mercy"—a phrase tellingly echoed in Alpha Galates's declaration in *Vaincre* that, as synarchists, they are "opposed to anarchy in all its forms." (Although even that comes second to synarchy's chameleon-like ability to change political color in order to further the cause. Remarkably, some of today's synarchist youth-oriented groups claim they are actually anarchist![13])

There is a major paradox. The Pact claims to act in the best interest of "the people"—as, of course, do all totalitarian regimes. Everything is expressed in terms of "the people": the revolution is for them, and the synarchist regime will be controlled by them—but by the people, *"not the masses."* This somewhat confusing notion is clarified by the proposition that all individuals will be allowed to participate in the running of the state *to the extent to which their position in society qualifies them.* In other words, it is a kind of graded democracy: some, quite literally, are more equal than others. For example, while the Pact acknowledges that "even the weakest has rights" that must be protected, because each "right" is counterbalanced by a "duty," all rights are defined by the service an individual is able to perform for society—"for the weakest the right relative to being of service, for the strongest the absolute right to serve." (This is a modification of Saint-Yves's original concept that although the officers of his proposed three assemblies would be elected by the people, in accordance with synarchy's hierarchical principles the voters' input would be greatly limited.) The historian Richard F. Kuisel writes: "The MSE pact described this synarchical state as 'democratic' because the elite served the people (although it was not controlled by the people) and the political influence of all special interests was suppressed." [14] Synarchy is founded on the idea that there is a "natural hierarchy" in everything—in the family, within professions and industries, and at every level in the state from commune to nation.

The empire after which the MSE was named is defined as the "organic grouping of major nations," of which there would be five: Eurafrica, the countries of the British Empire, the Americas, the "Pan-Eurasian nations" (the USSR), and the Asian nations. But all of them would be under the control of the Major Society of Nations—or world government. (Incidentally, many of the Synarchist Pact's principles are employed by the sinister regime in George Orwell's *1984.* As he lived in Paris in the 1930s, perhaps Orwell had seen or heard about the Pact.)

Participation is open to "all activists of goodwill, without distinction of origin, race, sex, religion, class, or party, who are or are prepared to be nationals of the French Empire" and who will commit themselves to the "revolutionary synarchist struggle" and uphold the "traditional values" of France—a nebulous term that can mean whatever one wants it to mean. And, of course, the Pact advocates a Federative Union of Europe—or European Union (Union Européene) for short.[15]

Composing and disseminating such a pact was one thing, but it would have been quite another for the MSE to have had any realistic chance of achieving its sworn ambitions. But disturbingly, synarchy did manage to exert real influence in France in the 1930s, through its association with two movements, one clandestine and shadowy, the other out in the open.

Under the Hood

The first is synarchy's covert association with the right-wing terrorist network known as the Cagoule, which we mentioned briefly when setting the scene for the young Plantard and Alpha Galates.

Although the somewhat stagy name Cagoule—the Hood—was an invention of the press, the organization itself was real and nasty enough: a coalition of extreme-right, anti–Popular Front, anti-Communist groups. Many similar organizations sprang up around that time, both within and outside the military, but it was the Cagoule that unified and coordinated them. The main groups were the CSAR (Comité Secret d'Action Révolutionnaire—Secret Committee for Revolutionary Action); OSARN (Organization Secrète d'Action Révolutionnaire Nationale—Secret Organization for National Revolutionary Action); the Spirale (a network within the army founded in 1937 by Major Georges Loustaunau-Lacau); UCAD (Union des Comités d'Action Defensive—Union of Committees of Defensive Action), created and led by the Air Force General Arthur Duseigneur; and the French Military Union (Union Militaire Française). The network called itself simply the Organization Marie, after its leader, Eugène Deloncle's, code name, Marie.[16] (His other code names were Mon Oncle and Ma Tante.)

The head of the CSAR and OSARN, besides being overall controller of the network, Deloncle (1890–1944) was the mastermind and driving force behind the Cagoule. Born in Brest, after studying at the seminal École Polytechnique and serving as an artillery officer in the First World War under General (later Marshal) Franchet d'Esperey, he became a naval engineer at Saint-Nazaire on the Atlantic coast. Until 1934 he was not a particularly active follower of Action Française, but during that fateful year his membership in its street gang, the Camelots du Roi, inspired him to create his own clandestine group to combat the left.

In the immediate aftermath of the upheaval of February 6, 1934, Deloncle and two fellow conspirators established a secret committee (their Superior Council) to coordinate the various clandestine right-wing organizations with common objectives. This endeavor, which would develop into the Cagoule, was funded by the industrialist Jacques Lemaigre-Dubreuil.[17]

Deloncle's two confederates in this enterprise were Colonel Georges Groussard and Dr. Henri Martin, one of France's great twentieth-century conspirators, a keen participant in everything from the uprising of February 6, 1934, to the OAS of the 1960s and who was also involved in de Gaulle's return to power in 1958. Martin (1895–1969), who was expelled from Action Française for violence in 1930, was the Cagoule's head of planning, with Colonel Groussard as chief of intelligence and liaison between the civilian Cagoule groups and clandestine army cells.

In fact, although (as far as can be established) Pétain was never personally a member of any of the military Cagoule organizations, he kept a watchful eye on them through Major Loustaunau-Lacau. According to one ex-Cagoulard, the sympathetic Pétain was biding his time—"waiting under the elm" (*attendait sous l'orme*)—for the moment when the Cagoule's program presented him with the opportunity to seize power. (This source explicitly likens Pétain's situation in the 1930s to the pre-1958 de Gaulle—both were former wartime leaders waiting for a crisis that would give them the power they needed to remold France according to their personal visions.)[18] In fact, the well-informed commentators Merry and Serge Bromberger, writing in 1959, bluntly describe the Cagoule as a "secret society whose design was to bring Marshal Pétain to power."[19] This is also what Henri Martin told the writer Roger Stéphane when they found themselves sharing a cell in 1942.[20]

Another future leader who was very well informed about the Cagoule was General Henri-Honoré Giraud, de Gaulle's great rival for leadership of the Free French during the Second World War. (Giraud was Roosevelt's preferred candidate as leader while de Gaulle was Churchill's, and the compromise proposed was shared power, but de Gaulle outmaneuvered them, succeeding in having Giraud sidelined).[21] The journalist Pierre Péan writes of a meeting in Lorraine in late 1936 between Giraud and members of his staff on the one side, and the Cagoule leaders Deloncle, Groussard, and Duseigneur on the other, to discuss their contingency plans in the case of a Communist uprising:

> He [Giraud] was evidently in agreement with working with the people of OSARN and wished the best success to Deloncle and Duseigneur. Two colonels assisted him at the meeting: one of them was called Charles de Gaulle.[22]

Active in both the Spirale network and the CSAR, Marshal Franchet d'Esperey is described by Péan as "the quasi official protector of the Cagoule,"[23] who was in direct contact with the Superior Council of Deloncle, Martin, and Groussard. As the front page of *Vaincre*'s first edition in September 1942 carried an endorsement by Franchet d'Esperey, we can deduce that at the very least the Cagoule were nibbling around Plantard and his cronies.

Funded by several wealthy industrialists, including members of the Michelin family and Eugène Schueller, the founder of L'Oréal,[24] the Cagoule were prime movers in the downfall of France. As Joseph Désert notes in his 1946 book, *The Whole Truth on the Cagoule Affair* (*Toute la vérité sur l'affaire de la Cagoule*): "The Cagoulards were the most active agents of Franco, Mussolini, and Hitler in France."[25] The distinguished American journalist William Shirer, a correspondent in Paris during the 1930s, describes the Cagoule as

> deliberately terrorist, resorting to murder and dynamiting, and its aim was to overthrow the Republic and set up an authoritarian régime on the model of the Fascist state of Mussolini, who furnished some of its arms and most of its funds and on whose behalf it murdered two leading anti-Fascist Italian exiles.[26]

The Italian exiles Carlo and Nello Rosselli were assassinated by the Cagoule in June 1937 at the request of the Italian Fascist government. (Mussolini's movement was taken as the great role model by the Cagoule, and so was Franco's regime in Spain after the Spanish Civil War of 1936–1939. But the Cagoule never idolized German Nazism in quite the same way.)

Another of their notable political murders was that of the Russian economist Dimitri Navachine—who settled France in 1927 and acted as adviser to politicians such as Charles Spinasse and Anatole de Monzie—in the Bois de Boulogne in January 1937.

In September that year bombs exploded at the headquarters of two employers' organizations in Paris. In their hunt for the culprits—Italian anarchists were initially suspected—the police arrested three arms traffickers, which led to the discovery of three caches of rifles and machine guns, ammunition, and grenades, smuggled in from Italy, at different

Paris addresses. There was a series of arrests in various parts of the country, including of Deloncle (in whose offices at the Caisse Hypothécaire Maritime et Fluviale the police found an incriminating list of four thousand members) and General Duseigneur and the Duc Pozzo do Borgo. Two newspaper offices—the *Courrier Royale,* the organ of the Comte de Paris, and *La Libre Parole* of Henry Coston, the anti-Semitic, collaborationist journalist who endorsed *Vaincre*—were raided. Finally, a "veritable arsenal" was discovered in a garage in the Boulevard de Picpus.

The Cagoule used the tunnels beneath Paris for their activities—their meetings were actually held beneath the Palais du Luxembourg, home of the Senate—and at the time of the 1937 roundup had advanced plans for a coup. The point of the coup was not to seize power but to precipitate a crisis that would allow Pétain and other military officers to take control "in the interests of public safety."

On November 23, 1937, Interior Minister Max Dormoy announced: "The documents seized [in Deloncle's office] establish that the culprits have assigned as their aim to substitute of the republican form, which our country has given itself freely, by a dictatorial regime, before proceeding to the restoration of the monarchy."[27] Once more there is a monarchist agenda lurking in the background. But what is the precise connection between the Cagoule and synarchy?

Richard F. Kuisel writes:

> The Cagoule bore a strong resemblance to the MSE. Both were conspiratorial societies, although the Cagoule differed in its reliance on violence. Strangely enough, although the Cagoule was an archenemy of Freemasonry, it imitated Masonic ritual, symbolism, and method of recruitment. The former head of the Cagoule, Eugène Deloncle, likened its recruiting procedures to the "chain method" of the *Illuminati.*[28]

As we have seen, this method was also used by the MSE and the Martinist Order. As William L. Shirer notes:

> That some Synarchists organized as far back as 1922 a secret society [the MSE] with revolutionary aims has been established. . . . That

at one time the MSE was linked to the terrorist Cagoule seems clear.[29]

Although denying that the MSE came close to revolution, Shirer nevertheless declares that "the Synarchists made a considerable, if subtle, contribution . . . to undermining the Republic.[30]

A secret report on the events of 1937, cited by J.-R. Tournoux in *Secret History* (*L'histoire secrète,* 1962), linked the CSAR/Cagoule with the MSE: "In 1937, affiliates of the Synarchic Movement were very numerous and already in place within, and at the head of, the major organs of the state. But the CSAR failed in its attempted insurrection (arrest of Deloncle on October 25, 1937)."[31]

Not every member of either the civilian or military organizations under the Cagoule umbrella was an ideological occult-minded synarchist—perhaps many had never even heard of synarchy—but it was certainly the ideal that motivated its *leaders,* such as Eugène Deloncle. One of his closest fellow Cagoulards recalled his enigmatic comment: "Now, I am sure: a circle exists, a coterie controlling considerable interests, which seems to have the same objectives as ourselves regarding the State and Europe. It is a very closed society of both thought and interests. I am looking for an opening. I want to know where these people are going. Besides, from a financial point of view, this alliance could bring us substantial help." Some time later, Deloncle told him momentously: "It's done. Now, I have a contact."[32]

In his 1970 book, *The Cagoule: Thirty Years of Plots* (*La Cagoule: 30 ans de complots*), Philippe Boudrel writes: "Eugène Deloncle, that lover of esotericism, found inspiration in the study of secret societies." Although Deloncle loathed Communism, Jews, and Freemasons, paradoxically, as Boudrel explains: "The detested Freemasons were nevertheless objects of admiration and envy. It was not forbidden to imitate them in trying to destroy them."[33]

Although Deloncle seems to have been an ideological synarchist, whether his fellow founders of the Cagoule network, Martin and Groussard, matched his enthusiasm remains an open question. (Martin's all-consuming passion for conspiracies makes it difficult to know what he really believed, certainly at that time.)

Deloncle has one other, very intriguing connection. His involvement with the Cagoule began while he was a marine engineer in Saint-

Nazaire, and according to the French researcher Roger-René Dagobert (cited in Patton and Mackness's *Web of Gold*), working alongside him there was one François Plantard—cousin of Pierre Plantard.[34] Coincidence? Perhaps, but as we will see, the connections between these and other prominent Cagoulard families are much more extensive.

The Poison Spreads

Synarchy was having an impact in another sphere of 1930s French life: the youth movements, especially under the inspiration of Vivian Postel du Mas—identified as one of the authors of the Synarchist Pact—and Jeanne Canudo. According to Jean-Pierre Monteils, those two were behind the "founding" of the MSE in 1930—presumably meaning its reorganization under that name.[35]

The widow of an Italian writer, Canudo (initiatory name Kryia) was described by the publisher Maurice Girodias as the "occult brain behind the radical and socialist parties, a militant adventuress of feminine Freemasonry and the cause of women in general."[36] She had met Postel du Mas in the 1920s in the Fraternity of the Polaires, latterly something of a star in esoteric circles, mainly because of its search for the Holy Grail around Montségur in the early 1930s, linked with the Nazi "Indiana Jones," Otto Rahn. (Fascinating though that story undoubtedly is, it is outside the scope of this book.)

Founded by the Italian Cesare Accomani (who styled himself Zam Bhotiva), the right-wing occultist Polaires boasted eminent members such as the poet Maurice Magre and, for a time, René Guénon. They followed the synarchist line in attributing the real control of the group to a nonhuman source called the Oracle. More significant, the Polaires' Grand Master was at one time Victor Blanchard, founder and leader of the Martinist and Synarchic Order.[37] In other words, the Polaires were another front for, or face of, synarchy.

Canudo and Postel du Mas left the Polaires in 1930 to form the Watchers' Group ("groupe des Veilleurs"), whose headquarters were a large and lavish apartment in Paris's Boulevard Saint-Germain.[38] Presumably the similarity of name to Schwaller de Lubicz's ostensibly disbanded organization of ten years before is no coincidence.

Despite Postel du Mas's fondness for pseudo-mystical trappings, he was not without real influence. Girodias writes:

> I saw at his feet men of science, company directors, and bankers, who drank in his words with the same expression of rapture—inscribed on masks nevertheless lined by mistrust and scepticism—that one could read on the fresh and naïve faces of juvenile members of the ashram.[39]

Postel du Mas and Canudo followed Saint-Yves's political aims, both for France and Europe: she began in 1933 by founding the journal *Terre d'Europe,* subtitled "Review of the Builders of the United Europe," and setting up the European Team (Equipe Européenne), to produce the journal and create a network of various other pro-European organizations. A leading investigator into synarchy, Raoul Hussan, points out that "the majority [of names on the Team's list] were found, after July 1940, either in the corridors of power in Vichy, or in the collaborationist circles in Paris."[40]

Jeanne Canudo founded one of the more important youth movements in the wake of the street violence of February 6, 1934, the Estates General of Youth (États Généraux de la Jeunesse). Three years later this was expanded into the Estates General of European Youth (États Généraux de la Jeunesse Européenne), aiming to mobilize European youth in support of a United States of Europe. Clearly, a major synarchist tactic was to propagate its ideals to the new generation. The Estates' first conference opened on September 21, 1937, with a speech by the Undersecretary of State for Foreign Affairs, François de Tessan. Canudo was also granted money by the French government to finance the youth congress. (Ultimately, of course, the movement foundered on the outbreak of war two years later—in the face of a very different attempt to unite Europe.)[41]

Canudo's project certainly involved some prominent names in pan-Europeanism, such as Anatole de Monzie, the former Minister of Education, and Gaston Riou, described by Olivier Dard as the "lyrical prophet of European union,"[42] the author of *Europe My Homeland* (*Europe ma patrie,* 1928) and *Unite or Die* (*S'unir ou mourir,* 1929) who was also active in the League for a United States of Europe, founded in 1934.

Tellingly, in 1936 Postel du Mas explained Kryia's idea of the Estates General of European Youth, as related by Maurice Girodias:

> Only the young people of Europe have the ability to do this work, to unify the continent. The foremost task to be carried out is to establish a constructive equilibrium in the world. This task we undertake under the direction of Kryia, with the support of superior forces. Kryia is assured of the necessary political assistance; in France itself, Justin Godard in the Senate, in the Chamber Gaston Riou, Anatole de Monzie in the government, Émile Roche on the Economic Council—the men who hold the real power. Abroad, we have Keyserling of course, but above all Coudenhove-Kalergi, and behind him a good number of statesmen and sympathetic diplomats or influential young economists such as Jean Monnet. But it is for youth to put life into it. It is for them to found the new international democracy, the United Europe.[43]

The above-mentioned Justin Godard (1871–1956) was the leading light of the Radical-Socialist Party and President of the Senate, who had maintained close relations with Canudo for a long time.[44] But the most significant name is Count Richard Coudenhove-Kalergi (1894–1972), an Austrian born of a Japanese mother, who in 1922 (the same year as the foundation of the MSE) launched the idea of Paneurope in Germany and Austria. Two years later he founded the organization Pan-Europe, together with a review of the same name. The true prime mover behind the European "project," Coudenhove-Kalergi was considered by another great promoter of the European ideal, Otto von Habsburg, as a "guide and prophet."[45] Jean Robin has no hesitation in describing him bluntly as "a 'synarch' of a high grade."[46] To find him backing Postel du Mas and Canudo's program is quite astonishing. However, in addition to advocating the union of Europe for practical and geopolitical reasons, Coudenhove-Kalergi may also have been motivated by more esoteric interests. He was, for example, a believer in Nostradamus's prophecies, writing in his 1953 book *An Idea Conquers the World* (to which, incidentally, Winston Churchill wrote the foreword):

> . . . we are mere puppets in the hands of God . . . a kind of microfilm of our entire life, from beginning to end, lies deposited in God's

> archives and . . . only a select few like Nostradamus possess the gift to gaze through the thick veil of the future at the shape of things to come.[47]

Another significant associate of Postel du Mas and Canudo is Jean Monnet (1888–1979), at the time an up-and-coming economist—the protégé of the great statesman Georges Clemenceau—who may not have been particularly well known then but very soon afterward became internationally renowned, although preferring to exercise his considerable influence from behind the scenes. As war loomed in 1939, he led a delegation to the United States to negotiate the purchase of American aircraft for France's emergency rearmament program, and during the conflict he was in charge of acquiring the Free French's supply of arms and equipment. He was also the prime mover in the—to modern eyes—highly improbable proposal for the union of Britain and France in June 1940, a desperate idea to keep the fight going during France's collapse. After the war Monnet's enthusiasm earned him the title Father of the Common Market.[48]

Some of these people supported Canudo's youth movement because they were already committed to the ideal of European union or, as it was called then, pan-Europeanism. But others, such as Monnet, were actually won over through her initiative. This is quite amazing: one of the most influential of the prewar United Europe organizations, from which some very key players—who literally shaped the destiny of Europe—were to emerge, was actually the creation of an occultist and synarchist!

Because of the secrecy with which Canudo and Postel du Mas surrounded themselves, and the postwar sweeping under the carpet of the synarchist conspiracy, firsthand information on the coconspirators is hard to find. However, one source—at first glance somewhat unlikely—is the autobiography of the celebrated publisher of erotica Maurice Girodias.

Girodias (1919–1990) was the son of Manchester-born Jack Kahane, founder of the Obelisk Press in Paris, which discovered hot literary properties such as Henry Miller, Anaïs Nin, and Lawrence Durrell between the wars. When his father died, Maurice Girodias became a publisher at the age of twenty—during the German Occupation—

specializing in books that horrified most other publishers. His hugely controversial successes over the years included *Zorba the Greek, Lolita,* and *The Story of O,* as well as the works of Samuel Beckett.

In his teens, Girodias was drawn into the world of Postel du Mas and Canudo, but it was through his Theosophist uncle that he became interested in esoteric matters, joining the Theosophical Society in Paris. Around 1935, when he was sixteen, he attended lectures by the religious philosopher Krishnamurti with his friends Claude and Édouard Delamere and was surprised to see in the audience "a group of people dressed as Knights of the Temple, a sort of mystic legion with long red capes and riding boots." Girodias goes on:

> Édouard told me about them: they are schismatic Theosophists with political designs, and they are linked to Count Coudenhove-Kalergi. . . . Their aim is to launch a pan-European political party and to institute in the entire world, commencing with Europe, a society obedient to a spiritualist ideal.[49]

The leaders of this group, Girodias learned, were Postel du Mas and Canudo, whose headquarters were in the Rue Serpente, although most of the activity took place in a large apartment in the nearby Boulevard Saint-Germain.

As Girodias became increasingly interested, Édouard Delamere arranged for him to attend one of its meetings. Impressed by Postel du Mas and his ideas, Girodias participated in the group's esoteric and political activities, joining its secret lodge Rahulla, besides working for Canudo's group, the Union of Young Cooperatives (Union des Jeunes Coopérateurs), which also operated from the Rue Serpente. Girodias admits that he got involved not only because of their lofty spiritual and political ideals but also because he got to meet their female members, particularly one young girl, Laurette, the group's "pythoness" or medium, who communicated with supernatural powers while in trance. Girodias has to marry her ten years after, Postel du Mas's hold over her—particularly his command to perpetual celibacy—had waned.

(Once again there is that disturbing and, to most people, unexpected link between a belief in the intercession of invisible entities and uncompromising political ambition. Of course what they have in common is a lust for *power,* even if it means suspending disbelief and harnessing the apparent potential of the occult realm.)

It is hard to know whether Postel du Mas or Canudo was the real driving force, or whether it was a genuinely equal partnership. Postel du Mas was a reclusive, gurulike character who rarely, if ever, left the Boulevard Saint-Germain apartment, where he was more or less permanently surrounded by his young disciples. He saw his mission as preparing for the coming of a political Messiah, Caesar reincarnated, likening himself to Christ's traditional forerunner, John the Baptist.[50] Their link with the outside world was the apparently haunting Canudo, whom Girodias describes in particularly high-flown terms: "Jeanne Canudo appeared more like a symbol than a human figure: she had the austere beauty of an allegory, and I could not prevent myself from imagining her engraved on the coins that the European Federation would one day strike."[51]

In the 1936 presidential elections, they backed Justin Godard as "our candidate," even consulting what Girodias described as "metaphysical forces" in the Rahulla lodge. Clearly the spirits were not on top form: Godard failed, and Albert Lebrun was reelected.[52]

From his firsthand experience, Girodias confirms that Postel du Mas wrote the Synarchist Pact (or at least had a hand in it).[53] Girodias himself was initiated into a Synarchist Order—mainly because Laurette was too.

Girodias records that Postel du Mas declared that synarchy would divide the population into four orders, based on the Hindu caste system: philosophers, artists, thinkers, and educators at the top; then administrators; next traders and industrialists; and finally, the workers. Each order would be organized hierarchically.[54]

Of course, all these plans for both synarchy in general and youth movements in particular were thrown out first by the gathering war clouds, then by the outbreak of war itself, and finally by the German Occupation, although almost instantly there was a typical synarchist fudging of sides. Girodias records that soon after the Nazis stormed into France, "Vivian and Kryia had made it known that their first impression of the troops of the Occupation was not so unfavorable."[55]

At that time, the reclusive Postel du Mas withdrew yet further from the world, moving to a house in the countryside with a coterie of disciples and taking little interest in outside events. Canudo, by contrast, continued to be both active and influential, launching her own publishing house, J. B. Janin, and cannily overcoming the problem of wartime paper shortage, in Laurette's words, "thanks to her friendships"[56]—which were apparently both controversial and extensive. She was known to dine at expensive restaurants with German generals.

Although as we have noted there was a certain amount of common ground between synarchy—or its manifestation under the harsh realities of the interwar period—and Nazism, there were also limits on their optimum relationship. The politically hyperactive side of synarchy, embodied in the Cagoule, preferred the Italian and Spanish regimes to Hitler's Germany as models. The chief barrier to full cooperation with Nazism was its overemphasis on German nationalism and superiority. Hitler, too, dreamed of a united Europe, but one that was united under the swastika, with Germany firmly in control, which was hardly acceptable either to many French fascists (though some thought a Franco-German axis possible) or to synarchists. Nazism was also too closed and authoritarian, refusing to tolerate any organization that promoted infiltration as a strategy to achieve power. The Nazis were suspicious of anything they stood no chance of controlling, routinely closing down all secret societies as soon as they occupied each successive country.

Predictably, therefore, under the Occupation there was a nervy relationship between the German authorities and the synarchists. The Germans might have approved of the Cagoule's activities during the 1930s, but they still kept a watchful eye on its former members. On the synarchist side, undeniably the Occupation and Vichy had brought their control of France closer—but they had no wish to draw too much attention to themselves while the Germans still had the upper hand.

This atmosphere of caution finally explains the contradictions in Plantard's *Vaincre*—advertising itself while downplaying its true, synarchist affiliation; appearing to be pro-German and yet attempting to rally the French people to its cause. Recent Priory researchers have perhaps tended to be too fixated on trying to pigeonhole Alpha Galates and *Vaincre* (and therefore Plantard) as either pro-Pétain or pro–de Gaulle—collaborationist or actively anti-Nazi. In fact, not only were there several other options but apparently the Order simply pursued its own agenda while making the right noises for expediency's sake. The truth about Alpha Galates is probably that it was exactly what it claimed to be: a neochivalric youth movement that would strive to create a united Europe for the postwar world, whatever shape it might take. But like all synarchist organizations, it had to contend with German suspicions in the Occupied zone, which led to *Vaincre*'s closure after just a few issues.

Another reason for downplaying Alpha Galates's synarchist credentials was that *Vaincre* was launched at the end of 1942—after synarchy had earned itself a terrible reputation by being behind a major scandal the previous summer, leading to hysteria about a synarchist plot to take over the Vichy government.

The Cagoulards' Comeback

After the Fall of France and the advent of the Vichy regime under Marshal Pétain, former Cagoulards staged a comeback. As we have seen, Pétain had been aware of the Cagoule's activities, even maintaining contact with them via his aide Major Loustaunau-Lacau, hoping they would help him to power by destabilizing the Third Republic so he could reform France according to his vision. (But was Pétain using the Cagoule, or had the Cagoule—or rather the synarchs—selected Pétain as its man?) Now the Nazi victory had given Pétain the power he sought, and with him as Head of the French State (Vichy's official name), his National Revolution was actively making his vision a reality. As Simone de Beauvoir wrote of that time:

> They were all lying: these generals and other notabilities who had sabotaged the war because they preferred Hitler to the Popular Front were now proclaiming that it was because of our "frivolous spirit" that we had lost. These ultrapatriotic characters were turning the defeat of France into a sort of pedestal on which they could stand, the better to insult Frenchmen . . . They took advantage of the German Occupation to impose a really tyrannous programme on the people, something that might have been thought up by a bunch of former Cagoulards.[57]

This is because—as we will now see—Vichy *was,* effectively, composed of former Cagoulards!

The historian John Hellman writes of the Cagoule as

> the pre-war secret organization whose members constituted an inner core of hard-line and ideologically committed anti-Communists and anti-Republicans active in the Vichy power centres. In July 1940 the most prominent *cagoulards,* whether in the occupied or nonoccupied zone, were well placed to plan the manipulation, control, and orientation of Pétainist France. . . . Ex-*cagoulards* helped create a political super-police, the Centre d'information et d'études (CIE), to gather information and keep tabs upon the perceived enemies of the National Revolution: Gaullists, Communists, Freemasons, and Jews.[58]

Former Cagoulards made up Pétain's bodyguard, going on to become the backbone of the dreaded Milice Française (French Militia, usually known simply as the Milice), "Vichy's political police and counterinsurgency unit"[59]—basically the Vichy French version of the Gestapo. The Milice evolved from the Service d'Ordre Légionnaire (SOL), created in December 1941 as a "paramilitary elite" to support the National Revolution. The SOL's doctrines endorsed "racial purity" and the defense and advancement of "Christian civilisation."[60] It has been described as "an elite organisation built upon veterans of the 1930s right-wing conspiratorial *cagoule.*" In January 1943 the SOL reincarnated as the Milice, which by 1944 had about fifteen thousand members and controlled several prefectures, all the French police, the media, prisons, and the justice system. (About fifteen hundred Miliciens were shot at the Liberation, but many others went into hiding in monasteries and convents in France and Canada.)[61]

Perhaps significantly, the Milice's insignia was the astrological sign for Aries, the Ram, supposedly because—as the sign is in the ascendant during spring—it symbolizes renewal and strength, but of course it also echoed Saint-Yves's English pun on the name of Ram, allegedly the great synarchist hero of ancient times.

Although not all Cagoulards were synarchists like Deloncle, the preeminence of Cagoulards in Vichy *must* have meant that synarchists, too, were in the ascendant. In fact, all three of the Cagoule's original Superior Council had important positions under the Vichy regime.

In March 1939, Eugène Deloncle created the pro-Pétain party, the Social Revolutionary Movement (Mouvement Social Révolutionnaire, or MSR). As its General Secretary, Deloncle declared that the MSR "succeeds on the visible level the secret organization I founded in 1936–1937." He explained the doctrines by saying that the MSR had

> chosen the new Europe, the national socialist Europe on the move, which nothing will stop. It will be national, the new Europe, because, in the new extension of the human group, the nation remains the basic unit, the elementary cell of the new world. The nation is the tutelary sheltering community that assures the free development of, and gives the measure of the original genius to, a people that has issued from the same blood, lives on the same soil, speaks the same tongue, [and] is penetrated by the same ideal. It will be socialist, this Europe, because the progress of modern technology has created an amount of wealth, [and] disciplined production allows the most humble worker to participate largely in the general well-being. Finally, it will, be racist, this new Europe, because economic anarchy and political division have only ever served the interests of a single caste: that of the Jews, that of the international bankers for whom the war is the principal source of profits.[62]

Along with Marcel Déat, in February 1941 Deloncle also founded the National Popular Rally (Rassemblement National Populaire, or RNP), the first plank of its constitution being that it stood for Franco-German collaboration, defense of the French Empire, the "economic, political, and spiritual construction of Europe," and the "development of Africa through European cooperation" (i.e., Euroafrica).[63]

A former Air Minister, Marcel Déat (1894–1955) was a socialist who turned collaborationist under the Occupation, editing the newspaper *L'Oeuvre.* At the Liberation he took refuge in a Catholic convent in Turin, where he lived for the rest of his life.[64] (Deloncle later became embroiled in a power struggle with him, as a result of which Deloncle was expelled from the RNP and, subsequently, the MSR.)

Deloncle also returned to his old Cagoule ways. Max Dormoy, the Interior Minister at the time of his arrest in 1937, was murdered in July 1941, and although it was never proven, it was—and still is—widely believed that Deloncle was responsible. He was also believed to have been behind an assassination attempt on Déat and the Vichy leader Pierre Laval a month later. In October 1941, with the approval of the SS, he and colleagues from the MSR blew up synagogues in Paris.

The other two founder members of the Cagoule network, Colonel Georges Groussard and Dr. Henri Martin, were involved in Vichy's intelligence network. Groussard became head of the security police, the Protection Groups (Groupes de Protection), while Martin—who later replaced Groussard—was given the task of watching and investigating "suspect" political groups and individuals in both the Vichy and Occupied zones, which was to have some interesting consequences as far as synarchy was concerned.

The Plot

Considerable though it undoubtedly was, it would be a mistake to overestimate the extent of the synarchists' power and influence. There were other factions, other interests, other agendas at play in France during the war years, and synarchy had to operate within the same framework as all of them. There were distinct limits on its possible achievements.

Although Marshal Pétain was Head of State and President of the Council of Ministers, giving him overall authority in Vichy-controlled France, it was still not *quite* a dictatorship. As the function of Prime Minister—i.e., head of the government—went with the post of Vice-President of the Council (later renamed Head of the Government), the Vichy years saw a power struggle between Admiral François Darlan and Pierre Laval for this post. While both supported the policy of collaboration (they would hardly have got where they were if they hadn't), they had very different agendas for how it could be turned to France's (or their own) advantage.

Laval (1883–1945), who began as a socialist but drifted further and further to the right over the years, had served three terms as Prime Minister in the 1930s. During that time he believed that France should side with Mussolini's Italy specifically to check Nazi Germany's strength in Europe.[65] After the French surrender, the new constitution that gave power to Pétain was Laval's initiative. (He was originally named as Pétan's successor in the case of the Marshal's death or incapacity.) Laval believed that collaboration with Germany was necessary in order to gain concessions for France: it was a matter of expediency, not choice. But in December 1940 a palace revolution saw him under house arrest: he had been trying to usurp Pétain, so a counterconspiracy, led by

Darlan and Finance Minister Yves Bouthillier, got rid of Laval first and Darlan became head of government. (It was another ex-Cagoulard, François Méténier, who arrested Laval on Pétain's orders.) However, in April 1942, Laval was restored to power, where he remained until the Liberation, when it was all over for him. He was tried and executed by firing squad in July 1945.

Admiral Darlan (1881–1942) was motivated much more by personal ambition, as demonstrated by his changes of side. He was an even greater enthusiast of collaboration with Germany, unlike Laval out of not expediency but *principle,* believing that, as Hitler was certain to win the war, France's future lay in working closely with Germany. Darlan would even consider France aiding Germany militarily, which both Pétain and Laval were desperate to avoid. After Laval's eclipse, Darlan steadily accumulated more power, eventually becoming Vice-President of the Council (i.e., Prime Minister). But ousted by Laval in April 1942, he began to make overtures to the Allies, hoping to return to power by being given charge of French North Africa when they took control, which would position him nicely for the leadership of the whole of France when it was liberated. He was in Algiers when the Torch landings took place, initially being put in charge of French North Africa—on an American initiative that appalled both the British and Free French—although not for long: he was assassinated on Christmas Eve 1942 by a young resistant, in a plot by a loyalist faction and probably with the backing of SOE and the Free French. (Their involvement had to be kept secret to avoid upsetting relations with the American Allies.)[66] Significantly, in his 1965 book *The Murder of Admiral Darlan,* Peter Tompkins—who took part in Operation Torch as an intelligence and psychological warfare officer—links Darlan's assassination directly with the synarchist conspiracy. Tompkins argues that Darlan was the synarchists' original choice as the leader of France whom they could control, but as this would not have been acceptable to all the Allies, they had thrown their weight behind General Giraud instead. Darlan's death cleared the way not only for Giraud to take command of North Africa but also for the Comte de Paris to assume authority. (In the event, de Gaulle managed to circumvent both.) (Curiously, Jean Cocteau was related by marriage to both Darlan and his killer, Fernand Bonnier de la Chapelle—Darlan's wife was Cocteau's cousin, and his sister was the Comtesse de la Chapelle.)[67]

Laval and Darlan had their own factions of supporters and backers. Darlan's clique in particular was composed of a new caste of industrialists and businessmen, the technocrats—mostly forty-something men who sought to apply modern management and production techniques to French industry and the economy but who badly needed political authority to carry out the necessary reforms. As the American historian Bertram M. Gordon notes about Jean Berthelot, Vichy's Minister of Communications: "[He] was typical of the technocrats in Vichy who were able to accommodate themselves to collaboration and the special circumstances of the Occupation in order to see their projects for the improvement of France brought to fruition."[68] Meanwhile, in Occupied Paris—technically under Vichy but in practice under German control—support was divided between Laval and Darlan.

"The disarray of spirits"

That hotbed of simmering factionalism provided the uneasy background to the major scandal of summer 1941—the exposure of an apparent synarchist plot to take control of Vichy, the moment when the word *synarchy* truly entered the French political vocabulary. The Vichy economist Pierre Nicolle captured the atmosphere of intrigue and suspicion in his diary:

> June 3, 1941: They speak in covered words of a secret organization (synarchy) that brings together the polytechnicians. At the head of this body are found Bouthillier and Berthelot as well as an important number of high officials in [the Ministries of] Finance and Public Works.[69]
>
> July 14, 1941: During the day, from very different sources, I learned that Synarchy will be unveiled and made known. This revelation will cause great difficulties for its members. After the inquiry conducted by the Marshal's entourage, they say that 140 people will be apprehended. There is now definitely a case against Bouthillier.[70]
>
> August 12, 1941: The Synarchic Movement, which some have not taken seriously, is a veritable enterprise of intrigues and conspira-

> cies. A strike would have been attempted in a few days but has been averted. From Limoges, they give me the following news; on Sunday, July 30, the prefecture prepares to guard against any revolutionary eventualities. The same facts are produced in different prefectures, in particularly Annecy, where at two o'clock in the morning, the alert was given to both police and legionnaires. All these rumors are disquieting and add to the disarray of spirits.[71]

Yves Bouthillier (1901–1977) was Minister of Finance in Paul Reynaud's War Cabinet of 1940, then Minister of Finance and the National Economy in the Vichy government from 1940 to 1942. And, as we have already seen, Bouthillier was involved with the MSE in the 1920s. Vichy's Minister of Communications, Jean Berthelot (1897–1985), resigned when Laval returned to power in April 1942 and was imprisoned for two years after the Liberation—an unusually severe sentence for a Vichy official.[72]

The turmoil described by Nicolle was the result of the death of the businessman Jean Coutrot on May 19, 1941, in a fall from the window of his Paris apartment. It was probably suicide, although confusion and contradictions—some reports said he was found dead in bed—and a certain vagueness in the registration of his death cast a shadow of conspiracy over the tragedy, causing some to speculate it was murder. But these suspicions came about because Coutrot was found to possess three copies of the Synarchist Pact, the manifesto of the MSE—the first time this document was revealed outside the restricted circle for which it was originally intended. So, although his death may have been unconnected with the conspiracy—apparently he had been depressed for some time—it certainly lifted the lid on it.[73]

However, Coutrot was already being investigated by Vichy's undercover intelligence network in Paris, under the control of Colonel Groussard, the ex–Cagoulard founder, now chief of Vichy's security police. In March 1941, Coutrot's brother-in-law Henri Brûlé, who hated him, had denounced him as a conspirator to one of Groussard's agents in Paris—giving him one of Coutrot's copies of the Synarchist Pact. Two more copies were found when Coutrot's apartment was searched after his death.

Some reject the idea that Coutrot was a synarchist or that his possession of the Pact reflected anything other than a casual interest—but after all, he possessed *three* copies. However, William Shirer was convinced of Coutrot's guilt, declaring that he "preferred to work in the shadows as a manipulator of men and movements."[74] But beyond owning the Pact, is there any hard evidence to link him with the synarchist movement?

The matter is complicated by the fact that once suggestions of a conspiracy circulate, events that are not necessarily connected begin to appear considerably more sinister. For example, deaths of individuals connected with Coutrot that occurred a few months before and after his suicide were seen as related, even though no evidence linked them, and some were undoubtedly due to natural causes. But even when these red herrings are eliminated, enough remains to show that at the very least Coutrot *thought* suspiciously like a synarchist.

Jean Coutrot (1885–1941), who lost a leg in the First World War, was the manager of a large paper company, but he was also an economic and political theorist, who in 1931 had cofounded the think tank X-Crise—affiliated with the ubiquitous École Polytechnique—which studied possible solutions to the global economic crisis caused by the Wall Street Crash of 1929. During the 1930s he created or was active in several other organizations dedicated to the study of the economy, industrial relations, and management. (Dimitri Navachine, the Russian economist who was murdered by the Cagoule in 1937, belonged to one of Coutrot's groups.) Perhaps appropriately, he was also friendly with Aldous Huxley, author of the chilling futuristic fable *Brave New World*.

Coutrot proclaimed that liberalism, socialism, and Communism were all outmoded, proposing instead what he called "economic humanism"—voluntary collectives regulating production and working conditions in each industry.[75] A journalist specializing in synarchy, Roger Mennevée (1885–1972), who produced the regular bulletin *Les Documents Politiques* (a major authority on the underside of French politics), pointed out that the principles of Coutrot's economic humanism—particularly as expressed in a series of articles for *La Journée Industrielle* in 1938—are virtually identical to those of the Synarchist Pact.[76] Indeed, there have been claims that Coutrot was one of its authors. According to his memoirs, Maurice Girodias, who—as we have seen—moved in synarchist circles in Paris before the war, knew Coutrot, although he never explains in what context.[77] However, Girodias was certain that Coutrot had been involved with synarchists *before* the war, although ascribing a less central role to him, describing the businessman as "that curious spirit who had founded a political group (made up exclusively of polytechnicians and named 'X-Crise'), [who] believed himself surrounded by synarchists and became a synarchist himself in order not to trail behind his troops."[78] Another of those whose involvement was inspired by the traumatic events of February 6, 1934, Coutrot later claimed that Jules Romains's "July 9 Plan," which tried to reconcile the various political youth movements, was his idea.[79]

In 1935 Coutrot was on the Economic Committee of the Ministry of Foreign Affairs under Laval; then a year later he joined the socialist Charles Spinasse in the Ministry of the National Economy. With that background, Spinasse's speech in the wake of France's capitulation in July 1940 can be seen in quite a different light. On that very day, Laval had made a bid to abolish Parliament and establish Pétain as a dictator. Spinasse spoke out in Laval's support, declaring:

> Parliament is going to indict itself for all its faults. This crucifixion is necessary to prevent the country from foundering in violence and anarchy. Our duty is to allow the government to make a revolution without bloodshed.[80]

This is a neat summary of the main themes of the Synarchist Pact—opposition to parliamentarianism, opposition to anarchy, and "revolution from above." But Coutrot extended his philosophy to society as a whole—and advocated some very disturbing ideas based on the then cutting-edge psychological theories. He wrote (emphasis in original):

> Already, it would not be impossible with the aid of what we have learned from the laws of collective psychology to specify a modern technique of Revolution. The barricades, the machine guns, the exiles, and the tortures are wasteful techniques, worthy only of the most primitive peoples, relics of the ancient rites of human sacrifice. A *methodical revolutionary* has as his precise objective the transformation of the social structure of his country, the modification to a certain degree of the minds and hearts of its citizens and *their conversion to his own opinion. . . .*
>
> We know about the extraordinary development of techniques

> of suggestion—education, propaganda, the press, books, reviews, the cinema, gramophone, wireless, television—which pursue the individual at all hours and into the greatest secrecy of his domicile, disturbing the development of his personality. The vast majority of our contemporaries receive all their facts, their sentiments, their ideas, in this way: it is possible to peel men from the inside as one hollows a melon, replacing the insipid pips with a flavorful port, and to graft onto them, without distress or waste, the chosen psychological contents. It is moreover what all the totalitarian governments at the present time do with masterly skill, in taking, for more safety, their subjects from the cradle. It will be inexcusable for an era that deploys the machine guns of suggestion to have recourse to those of Hotchkiss or Armstrong, which have the grave fault of making martyrs, those indestructible explosive caps, in France, of a resistance in the present, and of an inevitable reaction in the future. *The maximum violence that methodical revolutionaries can permit themselves . . . will, without doubt, be the concentration camp conceived of as a temporary sanatorium, with teachers and nurses, where in order to prevent them doing harm or evil, they temporarily isolate, until the cure is finished, those whom they cannot convince.*[81]

This vision is especially disturbing with the awful knowledge of hindsight, inevitably conjuring nightmarish images of the "Final Solution" and Stalin's gulags. Brave New World indeed.

As Coutrot certainly *sounds* like a synarchist and possessed copies of the Synarchist Pact, it is difficult to avoid the conclusion that he was involved with the MSE. Whether this affiliation was in any way connected with his death is unknown (although the fact that he was already under investigation for owning a copy of the Pact does suggest his suicide was related to his political activities). But to add a very curious—but typically synarchist—twist, it was the Vichy synarchists themselves who exposed the synarchist conspiracy. . . .

Dr. Henri Martin, founder of the Cagoule, was directly responsible for causing the panic. A couple of weeks after Coutrot's death, he circulated a brief report (the "Martin note") among Vichy officials about the "synarchist conspiracy" revealed by the suicide. The collaborationist press in Paris—primarily *L'Appel* and *Au Pilori*—began to run stories about Coutrot's "strange death" and the contingent conspiracy, turning it into a massive sensation.

What was going on? Was Martin actually unaware of the Cagoule's connections with the MSE? Was he blind to his former colleague Deloncle's synarchist orientation? There are clues, in the way Martin chose to present synarchy, to another explanation. Ludicrously, he claimed it was primarily concerned with checking the National Revolution; protecting Jewish, Anglo-Saxon, and other international business interests; and blocking efforts to organize Europe into a single economic entity—the polar *opposite* of the Pact's program. The fact that Martin, who knew it well, could present such a travesty suggests this was quite deliberate, to deflect attention away from synarchy's *real* goals, not to mention its presence in the Vichy administration. And these were exactly the allegations that would bring the wrath of the German authorities down on the synarchists—or rather those who would be *identified* as synarchists, who also happened to be Martin's political enemies.

Martin's actions appear to be a hasty damage limitation exercise, after the denunciation and death of Coutrot had brought synarchy to the attention of the authorities in the Occupied zone—but he also typically turned to it to synarchy's advantage by deflecting attention onto another group entirely.

His trick was to exploit Coutrot's connections to confuse synarchy with a conspiracy of technocrats, which many politicians and officials of the old school—concerned at the technocrats' influence on the Vichy government—already suspected. As the technocrats backed Darlan, this had the added advantage of playing into the hands of Laval's supporters, who enthusiastically embraced the conspiracy theory. At the time the synarchist panic first broke, Martin had already been investigating the technocrats for several months on behalf of Justice Minister Raphaël Alibert (another onetime Cagoulard).[82]

Another consequence of the Martin note was the Vichy police's report on synarchy, known as the Chavin report after their Secretary-General, Henri Chavin.[83] In fact, its main author was apparently Raoul Hussan (1901–1967), a left-wing Freemason, by profession a physiologist and statistician, who after the war—under the pseudonym of Geoffrey de Charnay, the medieval Templar leader executed with Jacques de Molay—wrote one of the major exposés of synarchy, which included the first full reproduction of the Synarchist Pact.

Linking MSE and Martinism, the report named Yves Bouthillier as the major synarchist figure in the Vichy government and cited the Banque Worms et Cie as a major player in the conspiracy. However, the Chavin report concluded that the MSE was part of an international banking conspiracy linked to both Jewish and American interests, which aimed to install ostensibly synarchist governments in every country that would actually be controlled by a bank. In the reverse of the true situation, synarchy is presented as a front for a conspiracy of international bankers.

Bêtes Noires and Scandale

On August 1, 1941, the Chavin report made banner headlines in Marcel Déat's *L'Oeuvre,* turning the synarchist conspiracy into a succès de scandale. (Ironically, Coutrot was a former contributor to *L'Oeuvre.*) Déat used it as a weapon with which to attack his particular bêtes noires, the technocrats and the Banque Worms, who backed Darlan.

It is significant that an American postwar analysis identified a powerful group of bankers and industrialists who supported Darlan and his policies, noting that the bank "particularly identified with the Darlan regime" was the Banque Worms, headed by Hippolyte Worms.[84] The study also identified Bouthillier and Berthelot (as well as Interior Minister Pierre Pucheu) as "members of the Worms clique."[85] As Hippolyte Worms—head of a family bank founded in 1848—had Jewish ancestry, and before the war his bank had boasted extensive interests in the United Kingdom, the Germans were very suspicious of both him and the bank.

But the immediate result of the Chavin report was that Pucheu sacked Chavin—who was duly exiled to the Bouches-du-Rhône as a prefect—and tried to silence the press in Paris (though the reporters were ultimately protected by the German authorities).

On August 12, 1941, Pétain broadcast an address about the "atmosphere of false rumors and intrigues," describing his disappointment with the progress of the National Revolution. He also declared his confidence in Darlan.

Tellingly, despite Pierre Nicolle's predictions, none of those named directly as conspirators in the synarchist Vichy plot suffered as a result—

Bouthillier and Bertholet remained in their ministerial posts until the great shake-up of Laval's return to power in April 1942. The only person whose career suffered was Chavin. (The loose cannon Henri Martin, too, was interned on the orders of Pucheu—under German pressure—in March 1942, but apparently this was more because of his dangerous capacity for intrigue than a result of his antisynarchy stance.)

But the media excitement provoked the Germans to order an investigation into synarchy, and specifically the MSE, by the Special Service of Dissolved Associations (Service Spécial des Associations Dissoutes), known as the "service Moerschell" after the police inspector who headed it, which was directly under Nazi control.[86]

The connection between MSE and Martinism lead swiftly in September 1941 to the Vichy police raid of the Order's headquarters and those of the Rite of Memphis-Misraïm, besides the Lyons home of their joint Grand Master, Constant Chevillon (1880–1944). A "writer, moralist, and philosopher,"[87] at the time of his arrest Chevillon was an official with the Banque Nationale du Commerce et de l'Industrie, but in his less public role, he was not only Grand Master of both the Martinist Order and Memphis-Misraïm but also Patriarch of the Gnostic Church founded by Jules Doinel.[88] Another copy of the Synarchist Pact, along with other documents relating to synarchist plans for the social organization of France, having been duly discovered in his home, Chevillon was hauled in for questioning. At first he declared that the document had been sent to him for his personal information only, several years before. A few days later he said he had been sent the Pact in strictest confidence by Jeanne Canudo so he could "compare its tenor to the synarchic principles of Saint-Yves d'Alveydre."[89]

But on October 3, Chevillon shifted his position slightly in a lengthy statement for the police in which he explained there were two separate Martinist Orders, the one of which he was Grand Master (the Martinist Order pure and simple) and the Martinist and Synarchic Order, which had Victor Blanchard as Grand Master. Chevillon elaborated, explaining that his Martinist Order "has always carefully avoided employing the word *synarchic,* in order to mark clearly the difference between the two organizations," adding that "regular Martinism, without scorning any of Saint-Yves d'Alveydre's ideas, does not especially occupy itself with them."[90]

Without being particularly convincing, at least this reinforces suspicions that the distance between the two Martinist Orders was not as significant as they liked to pretend. Why else would Canudo—so involved with the MSE, the creation of the "other" Martinist Order—have asked Chevillon to check the Pact against Saint-Yves's original synarchist doctrines? Certainly, Michel Gaudart de Soulages and Hubert Lamant, in their *Dictionary of French Freemasons,* unhesitatingly identify Chevillon as a member of the MSE itself.[91]

In any case, Chevillon's explanation seems to have sufficed: he was released without any further action—only to suffer a darker fate two and a half years later. In March 1944 four armed men burst into his house in Lyons and dragged him out, and a few days later his body was found; he had been shot in the neck. Who did it and why has never been established.

Scaremongering, Paranoia, and Conspiracy

Many historians, such as Pierre Péan, author of *The Mysterious Doctor Martin* (*Le mystérieux Docteur Martin,* 1993), believe that there was no synarchist conspiracy in Vichy and the events of 1941 were just a scare, a storm in a *tasse du thé*—a product of the heightened state of paranoia of the time or part of a dirty tricks campaign, perhaps to undermine the influence of the technocrats.

This view rests mainly on the denials of those named as conspirators, such as Bouthillier and Berthelot, when questioned after the war. But it ignores the fact that the Synarchist Pact had been around from at least 1936—probably two years earlier—and that synarchist groups had been incontestably active during the 1930s in several spheres of French political life, from the overt to the covert. The synarchist conspiracy was emphatically not invented in 1941.

Others—mostly journalists who were there at the time—such as William L. Shirer, readily acknowledge the reality of synarchy in Vichy, which Shirer describes as "a sort of first step towards the half-baked idea of the Fascist corporate state,"[92] acknowledging, "That its adherents infiltrated the highest posts in business and finance and in the government bureaucracy there can be no doubt."[93]

The "exposure" of 1941 is often presented as the discovery of a plot to take over the Vichy government and administration—by implication ousting Pétain—which was smartly nipped in the bud. However, no such plot was necessary: *Pétain's administration was already in the grip of the synarchists.* As Jean Saunier notes: "Synarchy was not a sabotage of Pétain's action; on the contrary, it is the explanation of the fact that Pétain had taken power."[94]

After all, Pétain had maintained contact with synarchists for several years before the war, via the Cagoule. Former Cagoulards, even those arrested and imprisoned following the abortive coup of 1937, returned to high office in Vichy. And although no action was taken against named conspirators such as Bouthillier, who belonged to a synarchist group in the late 1920s, the ax did fall—on the *investigators,* such as Chavin. Constant Chevillon was released. (He was murdered two years later, when circumstances were very different. Synarchy was not only very at home in Vichy but all set to flourish.)

In fact, according to the synarchy expert Roger Mennevée, Vichy marked the *climax* of the first phase of the plan outlined in the Pact, seizing power in France: Vichy's "National Revolution" *was* the synarchist "revolution from above." But by 1942 it was already moving on to the next phase: the domination of Europe.[95]

The researchers André Ulmann and Henri Azeau also point out that the French State was organized precisely on synarchist lines. Pétain had absolute power over the "trinity of synarchist powers: education, justice, and the economy" and presided over a revolution from above. They also note that although Pétain's program was originally called the National Renewal (Rénovation Nationale), it transmuted into the much more synarchist National Revolution.[96] The historian René Remond sums up the National Revolution's aim as being to "restore a hierarchical order in society,"[97] the fundamental principle of synarchy.

If synarchists were firmly established in the Vichy regime in 1941, then like all the other vested interests and factions, they were forced to react to three major turning points. The first was internal—the return to power of Pierre Laval in April 1942 and the consequent eclipse of Admiral Darlan (who began to woo the Allies instead), prompting a major overhaul of the regime. The second was the Allied landings in French North Africa in November 1942, precipitating the German takeover of Vichy (after which Pétain's regime truly became a puppet of the Nazis). After this it was much more difficult for any French faction to hold real power in Vichy. Finally, after the Allied successes in all theaters of war in early 1943, it was obvious that the tide had turned irrevocably against Hitler. Inevitably, the Germans would be kicked out of France and the Vichy regime would tumble; therefore the new priority was to jockey for power in whatever government followed—probably, though at that stage not inevitably, under de Gaulle. Consequently, the synarchist groups (like many others that had previously been all for Pétain) abruptly began working with the Resistance and forging alliances with Allied covert operations organizations such as SOE.

Ulmann and Azeau reproduce a lengthy report on synarchy, dated November 14, 1943, which was drawn up by the Committee of General Studies (Comité Général d'Études, or CGE)—a group of analysts established by Jean Moulin to advise on political affairs for the Liberation.[98] (Ulmann himself was a Resistance analyst, submitting political reports to London, working alongside François Mitterrand, who was—by then—with the Resistance.) While examining the question of why synarchists had begun collaborating with the Resistance, the experts reached the interesting conclusion that one of the Vichy synarchs' main objectives in 1941 was to make France an intermediary between Germany and the United States, particularly through certain American banks. (Although it has been studiously forgotten since the war, the United States continued to deal with the Vichy regime until November 1942—and even then it was *Vichy* that broke off diplomatic relations.) America's entry into the war after Pearl Harbor in December 1941 brought this plan to a shuddering halt. The significant thing about the CGE report was that it acknowledged the reality and seriousness of synarchy in Vichy France.

However, it is the carefully forged links between synarchists and Allied—particularly British—intelligence that are the most interesting. Henri Martin is a case in point. His eternal conspiring having finally caught up with him, under German pressure Interior Minister Pierre Pucheu had Martin imprisoned in Évaux in March 1942. In a drama of which wartime movie directors would have been proud, Martin was rescued in the wake of D-Day by his son and some confederates who cleverly persuaded the prison authorities they were just the vanguard of a huge Allied force that was close behind them—but that actually was nonexistent. Martin then joined the Resistance before working for the American Office of Strategic Services, or OSS, in the last months of the war.[99]

Just like Henri Martin, in the final stages of the war Eugène Deloncle made contact with the Allies—in his case with British intelligence, although he died before being able to make the most of it. Having roused the Germans' suspicions, he was briefly imprisoned in late 1942, when the Nazis took over the Vichy zone. Together with the tide turning in favor of the Allies, this lead him to establish contact with SOE. However, in January 1944 he was killed in a shoot-out with Gestapo officers who had arrived to arrest him.[100]

As Guy Patton and Robin Mackness write: "The Synarchists, in sympathy with the Resistance, had also established close contact with British Intelligence; the British made use of their secret lodge network for intelligence gathering."[101] This closes another loop. As we have seen, certain British individuals connected with SOE and other wartime intelligence activities in France have been linked to the Priory of Sion. There is no need to speculate too wildly to see these links being forged in France during the last twelve or eighteen months of the war.

After the Liberation, the spin doctors of de Gaulle's provisional government wanted to keep the story of the Fall of France simple. There was room only for collaborators and resistants—and none for the complication of synarchy. There was an official inquiry into the allegations of a synarchist conspiracy, but the file was quietly closed in April 1947. Pétain was even questioned in his cell about synarchy, but although admitting he had heard the rumors, he denied any knowledge of what it actually was.[102]

Significantly, in November 1945 the Grand Orient required its members to sign a declaration of whether they had (a) ever received a copy of the Synarchist Pact and (b) been part of any society "serving the propaganda of the major synarchic themes." If a Mason answered yes to (a), he had to supply full details of where, when, and how he had received the document—and where it was now.[103]

There are two extremes of opinion about synarchy in the Vichy years: either it was nonexistent—the synarchist scare of 1941 having been just the product of fevered imaginations—or it was behind *everything* that happened in France between 1940 and 1944. One of the most extreme views was that synarchists in the military command actively conspired to bring about the Fall of France in 1940 precisely in order to create the right conditions for them to take control.[104] But in our view that is simply—as Sherlock Holmes would say—theorizing ahead of the data. However, we believe the evidence for synarchy's very real influence on French political life, and particularly in the Vichy regime, is sufficiently solid—not to say downright disturbing.

Because synarchy works by adapting to any form of government, it can present itself to outsiders in many different guises, easily creating misinformation and cover stories, as we believe it did in order to deflect attention onto the technocrat clique. No doubt there were synarchists among the technocrats—such as Coutrot—but in itself that is hardly proof of a technocratic conspiracy. However, once the existence of the Synarchist Pact had been drawn to the attention of the authorities (particularly the German occupiers), it was a very convenient way of deflecting attention.

Tellingly, the confusion between technocrats and synarchists was maintained by Henry Coston, the anti-Semitic and pro-collaboration journalist who managed to reinvent himself after the war. Although he endorsed the synarchist *Vaincre* during the war, when he reemerged as a leading journalist and editor in the late 1950s, he was one of synarchy's most implacable enemies—at least in its guise as a technocrats' conspiracy. In February 1962 he produced a special edition of *Lectures Françaises* entitled *The Technocrats and Synarchy* (*Les technocrates et la Synarchie*), which effectively maintained Dr. Martin's 1941 cover story.

As for Martin himself, in 1950 he settled in French Indochina, where he worked with Army dissidents to engineer a crisis that would also cause disruption back home. Although arrested there for distributing seditious literature, he received an unexpectedly wide range of support in France: Jean-Paul Sartre asked Jean Cocteau to join in the chorus demanding his freedom.[105] Martin also received unlikely support from the journalist, critic, and one-time fellow prisoner Roger Stéphane, as Pierre Péan writes, "A man of the left, a Jew moreover, devoted numerous pages to testifying to his friendship with a man reputedly situated to the right of the extreme right."[106] (Perhaps it was not so unlikely after all: Stéphane—a friend of Cocteau and Malraux—had been born Roger Worms, from the banking family linked with the Vichy synarchist conspiracy.)[107]

Back in Paris, in 1956—Indochina having become independent—Martin turned his attention to Algeria, hoping to foment unrest that would lead to a military takeover, or at least a system of government more to the Army's liking, in Metropolitan France; "to snatch control of France from the politicians responsible for the nation's misfortunes."[108] This was the Grand O conspiracy (the "new Cagoule"), which he masterminded with Generals Cherrière, Chassin, and Salan, and another arch-conspirator, the Belgian journalist Pierre Joly.

From his base in Paris, Martin organized the planting of bombs in Algiers, and also established in France itself the network of Committees of Public Safety, which involved the Captain Way who turned out to be Pierre Plantard.

"Now you see it . . ."

Synarchy's ability to camouflage itself, coupled with the fact that it defies categorization as left- or right-wing, not only makes it hard to pin down but means it often shape-shifts into an outsider's worst nightmare. Those who looked with misgivings at the influence of the technocrats in Vichy saw it as a technocratic conspiracy. Those who believed that true power lay in the hands of international banks saw it as an international banking conspiracy. Left-wingers (such as Raoul Hussan) saw it as an international capitalist conspiracy. To cap it all, Henri Martin's son-in-law Pierre de Villemarest, also an extreme-right conspirator, believed synarchy to be a Soviet conspiracy! In reality it was all and none of these: depending on the perceived needs of the time, a synarchist can be a technocrat, banker, capitalist, Communist, or fascist.

Synarchy's now you see it, now you don't nature can also mean its influence can be vastly overestimated, as speculation gets mistaken for fact. This undoubtedly happened when the quite natural deaths of all manner of people who had ever been associated with Jean Coutrot became incorporated into the story as a veritable campaign of assassinations. Coutrot himself was spoken of—without any particular evidence—as the leader of the conspiracy. Sensationalizing a story in this way makes it easier to dismiss as mere wartime paranoia. However, we believe that once the overblown elements are removed, a hard core of evidence—which is quite sensational enough—remains. And in the end, although it appears that the evidence shows that synarchy was—and still is—a significant but unrecognized force in French life, the scale of the conspiracy should no more be overstated than it should be ignored. Although clearly it was enormously influential over Pétain and his program, synarchy had to contend with other political factors, besides the hostility of the Germans and the critically changing world situation.

Synarchy may not have got its own way in everything, but it still outlived Vichy's downfall, with serious repercussions for the modern world—as we are about to see.

CHAPTER EIGHT

A New United States

Throughout this investigation the one common and recurring thread is the United States of Europe. It was the motivating force behind Saint-Yves d'Alveydre's formulation of synarchy and remained at the core of the synarchist agenda up to Vichy and beyond. A "United States of the West" was at the center of Plantard's Alpha Galates Order—unsurprisingly, given its synarchist background—and it has been the one constant throughout the Priory of Sion's various convolutions and reinventions. Even during the Gisors affair, in the early 1960s, Plantard found time to compile and deposit in the Bibliothèque Nationale a small study of comparative social costs within what was then the European Economic Community or Common Market—which is usually ignored or dismissed because it lies completely outside the development of the Priory of Sion story.

Over the years, the Priory has chosen to associate itself with individuals such as Alain Poher, André Malraux, and Marshal Juin, although whether they have any genuine connection with the society or with the organizations behind it is open to debate. But what these people have in common is that they were passionate supporters of, and prime movers in, the move to forge an ever closer union of the European nations.

André Malraux advocated a "federal Europe" in 1941, and the idea was also espoused by Marshal Juin. As we saw in Chapter 2, Plantard and his confederates alleged that the secret group behind the Committees of Public Safety in 1958 was composed of Malraux, Juin, and Michel Debré, but the Priory claimed only the first two as actual members. Of the three, Debré was the only one who was lukewarm about European union, opposing ratification of the Maastricht Treaty in 1993.

The Priory's European ideal explains Victor Hugo's presence on the list of its Grand Masters. As we have seen, Pierre Plantard linked a reformation of the Priory with Hugo's planting of the "oak tree of the United States of Europe." This referred to a real event. On July 14, 1870, Hugo, with his two grandchildren, planted an acorn in the lawn of his house in Guernsey, telling them, "When this oak will have become mighty the United States of Europe will crown the old world."[1] (In 1966 a movement started to take acorns from this oak and plant them in European cities and towns.) A passionate advocate of a united Europe, Hugo also coined the term "United States of Europe."

It is tempting to speculate that this had some connection with his meeting with Saint-Yves d'Alveydre in the Channel Islands. Hugo (who made his family motto *Ego Hugo*) certainly has all the right connections: in Guernsey he took part in a long-term project to communicate with spirits—specializing in contact with great minds of the past such as Plato and Shakespeare—almost every day for two years from 1853,[2] he was married at St.-Sulpice in Paris,[3] and, according to Gaudart de Soulages and Lamant, he was, briefly before his death, a member of the Martinist Order.[4]

In September 1984, Plantard not only suggested to the *Holy Blood* authors that the United States of Europe was a higher priority to the Priory of Sion than the restoration of the Merovingians but also made the apparently grandiose claim that the election of François Mitterrand as President of the Republic three years earlier was in some way connected to the Priory's plans. However, Plantard said that whatever it was Mitterrand was supposed to do was now completed, and he had "served his purpose."[5] (Perhaps this was simply intended to preempt further research into the connection between the Priory and the President. Or perhaps Plantard was trying to find out if Baigent, Leigh, and Lincoln had discovered any links with Mitterrand.) But just how fanciful was his apparent suggestion that the French President was either a member of the Priory or at least significantly under its influence?

The Priory and the President

There may be more truth in Plantard's statement than one might even begin to imagine. One of the most dedicated advocates of closer European integration, Mitterrand took initiatives of which the synarchists would have been proud—even being responsible for changing the name of the European Community to the European Union, the very title used in the Synarchist Pact.

In this context perhaps it is significant that during his perambulations around the country on his presidential election campaign, on March 2, 1981, Mitterrand went out of his way to visit Rennes-le-Château, being shown round the church and Saunière's *domaine*—together with his companion, Patrice Pelat—as well as enjoying the view from the Tour Magdala. Afterward, at the Château de Joyeuse in Couiza, he spoke of his "proven fascination" for Rennes-le-Château.[6] (Amusingly—or perhaps revealingly—*L'Indépendant*'s report carried the headline "Mitterrand on the *Colline Inspirée.*") But was this well-publicized visit merely a cynical bid to win over the esoteric vote?

In fact, Mitterrand had paid rather more low-key visits to the area from at least two years previously, because his friend and political ally Robert Capdeville (who accompanied him on his tour of the village), a former deputy, lived there and represented Couiza on the Council General of Languedoc-Roussillon.[7] Capdeville (1919–2001) had a great passion for the Languedoc's heretical and Gnostic past, with a particular admiration for the work of Déodat Roché, and in 1982, together with René Nelli—who acclaimed Jules Doinel's Gnostic writings—founded the Center for Cathar Studies in Carcassonne.[8]

However, Plantard was to claim another connection with Mitterrand that was to backfire dramatically on him—or so we are supposed to believe. As we have seen, Plantard returned briefly to the "helm" in 1989, when he completely overturned the Merovingian survival story and offered a new, improved, and rather more mundane version of the history of the Priory of Sion that disowned any connections with Templars, Rosicrucians, or any of the esoteric usual suspects. His detractors explain this in one of two mutually exclusive ways. Some believe it was an attempt at a comeback, others that it proved he was panicking because of the publicity generated by *The Holy Blood and the Holy Grail,* particularly that resulting from the suggestion that he was Jesus' descendant, and was downplaying the whole business in order to distance himself from it. But neither explanation works. It was seven years since the publication of *The Holy Blood and the Holy Grail*—so this would have been an exceptionally delayed panic reaction. And if Plantard was attempting a comeback, not only would he have done far better sticking to the original Merovingian fable—by then well established around the world and with thousands, perhaps millions, of people eager to hang on his every word—but all he actually did was place some new documents in the Bibliothèque Nationale and disappear back into the shadows. Plantard even failed to alert researchers to the new Dossiers, instead just leaving them to be found. Still less did he try to generate any new publicity around them.

Plantard's actions in 1989 seem more like an attempt to close down the Priory of Sion cover story: the new version of its history was so *uninteresting,* and completely demolished the more romantic and intriguing one that people actually wanted to hear. Perhaps it was his retirement plan, a way of ensuring he could enjoy his remaining years in peace and quiet—he was, after all, nearly seventy by then. But if he wanted a quiet life, it was not exactly forthcoming.

Plantard explained his reappearance by the sudden death of the Priory's Grand Master. In a letter to "members" dated July 1989, he said that since his resignation in 1984, "two Nautonniers have tried to lead the Priory, but both failed and each died from heart attacks, one on July 17, 1985, the other on March 7, 1989." The first is clearly de Chérisey, but who was the second? Interviewed in *Vaincre* by Noël Pinot, supposedly on March 9, 1989, at Avignon, Plantard identified his immediate predecessor: Patrice Pelat, a name that also appears on *Vaincre*'s new list of Grand Masters.

Roger-Patrice—or just Patrice—Pelat had indeed died suddenly of a heart attack on March 7, 1989. He was not particularly well known to the French public (however, that would change because of his posthumous involvement in a major scandal), although he was exceedingly well known in political and commercial circles. He was a businessman who was so close to President Mitterrand—a friend since their POW days in the Second World War—both personally and financially, that he was known as the Vice President.

Whatever the truth about Pelat and the Priory, naming him as

Grand Master in 1989 was innocuous enough. (At the time of his death, Pelat was being investigated for alleged insider trading and corruption, but the inquiry failed to find any hard evidence on which he could have been prosecuted.) However, four years later the designation was to assume rather more importance in the fallout from one of France's greatest ever political sensations—the suicide, while in office, of the Prime Minister, Pierre Bérégovoy, on May 1, 1993. One of the major factors behind it was an investigation into government corruption that found Bérégovoy had received a million-franc "loan" from Pelat several years earlier. Inevitably, the claims that Pelat had been Grand Master of the Priory of Sion dragged Plantard into the furore.

Intent on seeing his reputation ground down as far as possible, Plantard's critics are not just an insignificant handful scattered thinly across the globe. Thanks to Dan Brown, there is now a whole new legion of hostile Christians, who believe that if they can posthumously destroy Plantard himself, then all those embarrassing questions about Mary Magdalene, Gnostic Gospels, and the decisions of the Council of Nicaea will conveniently disappear. They also do what they accuse the "believers" of doing: stretch the evidence way too far and report rumor as established fact without verifying it.

According to this faction, and widely reported on the Internet, as a result of Plantard's 1989 claims, four years later he was hauled in before the judge investigating "*l'affaire Pelat,*" and was forced to admit under oath that not just the Pelat connection but *everything* he had ever said about the Priory was a lie, resulting in a stern official rebuke for wasting investigators' time. We are told this was widely reported in the French media, and the humiliated Plantard crawled away to spend his remaining years in hiding.

It is emphatically not our job to defend Plantard. To put it in punchy London slang, he was a downright "dodgy" character—virtually everything he said was a lie or half-truth. Where we differ from his more dismissive critics is in the interpretation of the *purpose* of the lie and his ultimate role. We believe the Priory to be a cover and Plantard its front man, chosen precisely *because* he was a dodgy character who knew how to tell a good tale or skillfully evade a question. But our own investigation astonished us by revealing that the critics' version of this tale is, to say the least, considerably overstated.

Leaving aside the fact that we would *expect* the supposed protector of a secret society to deny its very existence, we were quite perplexed when the stories about the wave of publicity that turned Plantard into a national laughingstock started to circulate in the wake of *The Da Vinci Code.* All this is supposed to have happened in 1993, yet we had been researching the Priory and Plantard throughout the 1990s and had never even heard of it. And we had spent considerable time, particularly in the mid-nineties, mixing with many other researchers and enthusiasts, in both the United Kingdom and France, of all shades of opinion, including skeptics and Plantard opponents, and *none* of them had even so much as mentioned Plantard's public humiliation of '93. Nor is it mentioned in any of the books—including those by skeptics—written since then. But this is what we found.

In September 1993, the French Plantard detractor Roger-René Dagobert sent Thierry Jean-Pierre—the judge investigating the Pelat affair—copies of the 1989 *Vaincre* that named Pelat as the Priory's Grand Master. As a result, in October 1993, the judge visited Plantard at his home in the Paris suburb of Colombes to question him and, with the aid of gendarmes, to search his house. (After all, if the allegations surrounding Pelat were true, there could have been another P2-type scandal in the offing.) Plantard was *not* hauled up before the judge; the judge went to him. But in any case, Jean-Pierre went away unconvinced by both the claim of Pelat's membership and its relevance to his investigation. Apparently this was partly because of Plantard's age and failing memory (real or feigned—he was seventy-three by then), but mainly because the search had failed to find any documents relating to Pelat, anything bearing his signature or written in his hand. A few days later Jean-Pierre also interviewed Thomas Plantard, after which that avenue of inquiry was closed.

We have not found *any* evidence of an official reprimand (although in any case, Plantard could hardly have interfered in an official inquiry through material disseminated more than three years before it was set up) or of the tidal wave of publicity that turned Plantard into an overnight joke. There was a report of the Jean-Pierre–Plantard encounter in the daily *France-Soir* on October 27, 1993 which raised the question of a secret society lurking in the shadows of the Pelat affair before announcing that Jean-Pierre was unconvinced—and describing how the Pelat family lawyer had denied the Priory connection. If anything this report made Roger-René Dagobert the miscreant, for diverting Jean-Pierre's energies. The major nationals, such as *Le Figaro*—while attentively following the Pelat investigation—failed to mention the Plantard episode at all, even though they carried regular reports about other developments in the case in the days before and after it. Indeed on November 6, the weekly color supplement *Le Figaro Magazine* featured a lengthy interview with Jean-Pierre on the progress of the investigation, but nothing about the Priory of Sion was either asked or offered. The weekly magazine *L'Express* carried an article on the investigation on October 21—two days after Jean-Pierre's visit to Plantard—that dwelt solely on the fact that a number of Pelat's papers had disappeared. Most telling of all, the satirical *Le Canard Enchâiné*—a sort of French *Private Eye*—which surely would have loved the tale, thought it unworthy of newsprint. Instead of being a major public humiliation for Plantard, it seems to have been noticed by few in the media.

None of this vindicates Plantard or confirms Pelat's Grand Mastership, but it does mean that the question is rather more open than the debunkers would suggest. But why did they pick Pelat as an alleged Grand Master? We will return to the puzzle shortly.

Synarchy in the "United States"

Naturally Baigent, Leigh, and Lincoln pondered on the emphasis on the United States of Europe and its central place on the Priory's agenda, noting in *The Holy Blood and the Holy Grail* that its aims "would seem to include a theocratic United States of Europe—a trans- or pan-European confederation assembled into a modern empire and ruled by a dynasty descended from Jesus . . . [while] the actual process of governing would presumably reside with the Prieuré de Sion—which might take the form of, say, a European Parliament endowed with executive and/or legislative powers."[9]

The last comment is particularly prescient: in 1982, when they were writing, the European Parliament did not possess legislative powers—it had only the authority to adopt resolutions that were not actually binding on member nations. Those powers were not added until the Maastricht Treaty ten years later.

Many readers of *The Holy Blood and the Holy Grail* must have wondered how on earth the Priory could achieve such ambitious plans.

But as it is attached to an important esoteric stream with political ambitions in which the United States of Europe is absolutely central—i.e., synarchy—a movement with many faces, the idea begins to seem almost reasonable. Except for the reference to Jesus, and for "Prieuré de Sion" substitute "the network of synarchist societies that stand behind the Prieuré de Sion," the preceding quotation is a neat summary of our interpretation of the synarchists' plans: the Priory's emphasis on the United States of Europe is not surprising at all when set against its own synarchist background. But although anyone can make plans, no matter how grandiose, has the Priory come anywhere near achieving them?

As our investigation turned to other facets of the synarchist program, such as the organizations of the Synarchic Empire Movement members Jeanne Canudo and Vivian Postel du Mas in the 1930s, we found (unsurprisingly) that they too were working toward a European federation but (perhaps more surprisingly) that individuals who later played key roles in Europe's postwar development were also heavily involved.

Of course, there are many different reasons—political, financial, and/or idealistic—for considering a United States of Europe a good idea. But the more we delved, the more we began to wonder, because *all* the major initiatives that fostered the EU came from individuals who were *directly* connected with the synarchist groups we had been investigating. After a while, as one connection after another fell into place, we began to wonder if there *was* more to it than mere coincidence: was the creation of the EU actually the result of subtle, and sometimes not-so-subtle, guidance by synarchs?

Birth of a Federation

In his 1997 book, *The Tainted Source: The Undemocratic Origins of the European Ideal,* John Laughland notes that although the drive to ever greater European union is generally portrayed as a necessary "antidote" to the Second World War, "There are . . . some direct links between Nazi, Vichyite and fascist thought, and the ideology of European integration in our own day."[10] Before the war, a united Europe was the dream of the right-wing totalitarians, but afterward it became the goal of their opponents. Of course, not all those who advocate closer union are closet fascists, but Laughland argues that, with closer integration and enlarged membership, the political institutions of Europe will inevitably become less rather than more democratic and accountable, for purely practical reasons. Europe will have to be *less* responsive to the wishes of the population and unilateral in its decision making if it is to be able to function.

A federal Europe was also a cornerstone of the Nazis' long-term agenda—but, naturally, with Germany as the most powerful nation and the others ruled by national socialist or fascist governments. (To the prewar Hitler, Britain would have been excluded because it had its empire anyway.) During the Second World War, with the continent firmly under Axis domination, the dreaded SS—originally conceived as a kind of chivalric order made up of an Aryan elite—began to add divisions of nationals from conquered territories, with the aim of creating a pan-European military force.

Ironically, the one point on which Nazis and anti-Nazis agreed on was that the answer to their problems would be a united Europe. The anti-Nazi André Malraux called for a "federal Europe" in 1941; in 1944 the journal of the French SS, *Devenir* (subtitled *The Militant Journal of the European Community*), declared that it stood for "a federalist Europe." Perhaps the supreme expression of this irony is that both Churchill and Hitler published collections of their speeches in favor of European union: Churchill's *Europe Unite* in 1950 and Hitler's *Europa* in 1943. Churchill—directly inspired by Count Coudenhove-Kalergi—advocated a united Europe as early as 1930 (although he did not see Britain, with its Empire, as a part of it).[11] During the Second World War he began to see a United States of Europe as a way of preventing another conflict on the continent, particularly by creating a solid front against the Soviet Union. This culminated in his landmark speech at the University of Zurich in September 1946, in which he called for the creation of "a kind of United States of Europe."[12] In May 1948 the Committee for the International Co-ordination of Movements for the Unification of Europe, chaired by Churchill, met in The Hague.

The relationship between a putative united Europe and the United States created a sharp division in French attitudes to union. De Gaulle believed that Europe should unite to protect itself against the economic and political might of the United States, which had emerged from the

Second World War as a global superpower. (He even vetoed British membership of the EEC because he was wary of the United Kingdom's "special relationship" with America.) At the first meeting of the RPF's National Council in Paris in July 1948, de Gaulle set out his vision:

> In response to the disintegration of the Empire which has already begun, we have a solution to offer which is called French Union. To the grave dangers looming over Europe, the rest of the world, and ourselves, which are due to nothing other than Soviet Russia's ambitions for world domination, we have a solution called the European Federation, in both the economic and the defense areas . . .[13]

However, others, notably Jean Monnet, advocated a United States of Europe that would work together with the United States of America.

American attitudes to a United States of Europe varied depending on the vested interests involved—some saw it as a way forward, others as a potential threat. In the immediate postwar world and with the first chills of the Cold War swirling ominously ever closer, the Truman administration deemed a united Europe necessary for containing Soviet ambitions and actively encouraged a closer union.[14] As Baigent, Leigh, and Lincoln point out in *The Messianic Legacy,* this led to the creation in 1949 of the American Committee on a United Europe (ACUE)—the result of lobbying by Europeans, who included Churchill. However, U.S. funds for the pro-union organizations in Europe came at a price. As the three authors write: "With ACUE, a process was inaugurated whereby successive organisations working for European unity were effectively hijacked by American agencies working for American interests.[15] The chairman of ACUE was William J. (Wild Bill) Donovan, wartime head of the OSS, while its Vice Chairman was Allen Welsh Dulles, an important OSS officer who subsequently became Director of the CIA.

The Americans supported a united Europe provided it worked as they wanted. Because their primary reason for backing pan-Europeanism was defense against the USSR (which had to be carefully balanced against potential economic European competition), during the Cold War, U.S. administrations generally supported some measure of European integration. Since the ending of the Russian menace, however, economic considerations have taken priority.

Significantly, the American consensus gradually changed during the 1980s, when it became increasingly clear that the Cold War would never turn hot—indeed, by the end of the decade, with the fall of the Berlin Wall and the collapse, one by one, of Communist regimes in eastern and central Europe, it was over. This coincides exactly with the alleged friction between the Priory of Sion's European members and the "Anglo-American contingent," which had coexisted quite happily until the beginning of the eighties, and the tension was supposedly resolved in 1989, when Plantard split the society into two orders, European and American. Was this just a coincidence? In the absence of evidence that the Priory of Sion *as such* has any members, it might well be a mistake to take this literally, but at least Plantard put it into the correct political context for an organization whose priority was establishing a United States of Europe but whose members also had other political and economic concerns. In 1980 both the Europeans and the Americans would have agreed on the United States of Europe objective, but as the decade progressed, the Americans would have become less keen. The British membership would have been caught between Europe and America but probably inclined—as always—to side with the latter.

But in all the factions and groups with different reasons for advocating closer European integration, and different expectations of the outcome, the key question, then as now, was how far the process of integration should go: simple coordination of trade, industry, agriculture, and to some degree, economy, or a fully blown United States of Europe with a common currency and the power to affect the social structure of all member nations? (Churchill, for example, thought in terms of a Council of Europe that would decide matters affecting the continent as a whole, not a federal government to which the individual nations' domestic policies would be subordinate.)

The development of the European Union has been a process of gradual change punctuated by a few major steps—which have fundamentally changed its course, leading not just to closer economic union but to ever closer *political* cooperation. And every one of those great leaps forward was the initiative of an individual who was specifically linked to the groups we are investigating.

The first serious step on the path to integration was the creation of the Pan-European movement by Count Coudenhove-Kalergi in 1923, with its initial Pan-European Congress in Vienna three years later. As we have seen, he was a major supporter of Jeanne Canudo's Estates General of European Youth.

The European Union traces its birth to May 9, 1950, the day that France made the Schuman Declaration, the initiative of the politician Robert Schuman, which marked the first step toward Europe-wide industrial and economic cooperation. (May 9 is still the EU's official Schuman Day.) The Declaration announced that France and West Germany intended to combine their coal and steel industries and would welcome the participation of any other countries; Italy, the Netherlands, Belgium, and Luxembourg decided to join in. The result was the Treaty of Paris of April 1951, which created the European Coal and Steel Community and a "supranational" body, the High Authority under Jean Monnet, to control the industries in the six nations.

The successful cooperation among the six countries inspired the idea of working together in other areas, leading to an agreement for a mutual defense system (ratified by the European Defense Community Treaty of 1952). More significantly, in March 1957 the Treaty of Rome established the European Economic Community (EEC), removing trade barriers to form a "common market."

The European Parliament was set up in 1958. Schuman's protégé Alain Poher was President from March 1966 to March 1969—and it was under his presidency that the Parliament's powers enjoyed their first major extension.

All this began with the Schuman Declaration—which, as a matter of pure historical fact, was the result of a conspiracy to overcome the French Parliament's understandable reticence about a closer working relationship with France's great rival, Germany. And the éminence grise of the plot, customarily operating from deep in the background, was Jean Monnet. As René Lejeune writes in *Robert Schuman* (2000):

> During the course of the genesis of the Declaration of May 9, 1950, Robert Schuman did not stop tricking, maneuvering, concealing; he deployed a strategy of meanders, detours, subterfuges. Before the Council of Ministers on May 3, he feigned the insignificance of the project. He literally plotted with René Meyer and René Pleven; their intervention in favor of the project, in the Council on May 9, had to appear spontaneous. He himself unveiled his project to only three people: he nevertheless knew that it was an initiative of capital im-

> portance. Did he not apply Machiavelli's advice to the letter: to succeed in politics, one must know how to pretend and disguise?

Lejeune also notes sharply:

> Without trickery [*ruse*], there would have been no Declaration of May 9, 1950. And perhaps no European Community, without the stratagem deployed by Robert Schuman and Jean Monnet, throughout the ten days that preceded May 9, 1950, which history accepts as the communal Europe's birth.[16]

Monnet's presence was ubiquitous: as Merry and Serge Bromberger write in *Jean Monnet and the United States of Europe* (1968), "The Schuman plan was actually the Monnet plan; the Treaty of Rome, the Monnet Treaty."[17]

A devout Catholic, Jean-Baptiste Nicolas Robert Schuman (1886–1963) hailed from a famous cognac family of Alsace-Lorraine, although he himself was born in Luxembourg. He was therefore a German citizen but became French at the age of thirty-three when Alsace was returned to France at the end of the First World War. Alsace-Lorraine being an obvious crucible for the concept of political union—having been historically torn between France and Germany—it was natural for Schuman to embrace the ideal of a united Europe.

As he belonged to the prewar pro-Europe group Energie, founded by Alpha Galates's Louis Le Fur, Lejeune's phrase is particularly telling when describing Schuman's grave in Scy-Chazelles (just outside Metz): "From all parts, the tourists of Europe pour into the heights of Scy-Chazelles, destined to become the '*colline inspirée*' of Europe."[18] (There are even moves to beatify Schuman.)

As we saw in the last chapter, in the 1930s Jean Monnet was involved with the Estates General of European Youth, the brainchild of Jeanne Canudo, whose heavy involvement in the Synarchic Empire Movement meant she worked closely with one of the authors of the Synarchist Pact, Vivian Postel du Mas.

Although Monnet was vastly influential on France's history from the Second World War onward, as his biographers Merry and Serge Bromberger point out, he preferred to keep himself anonymous, as far as possible a shadowy figure. But in no way was he insignificant.

Through his close relationship with Harry Hopkins, Franklin Roosevelt's closest and most trusted adviser, Monnet even became the American President's "personal advisor on Europe."[19] As we have seen, because Roosevelt loathed de Gaulle both personally and politically, de Gaulle was the last person he wanted as Free French leader, favoring his rival General Giraud. Monnet cleverly maneuvered so he became the power broker in this internal struggle but in an abrupt move in August 1943 used the American President's own authority against him. As Robert Murphy, Roosevelt's envoy in French North Africa, explained: "Influenced by Hopkins, Roosevelt gave Monnet letters of credit that raised him almost to the status of a personal envoy of the United States to North Africa. He used the documents to put de Gaulle in power—the very opposite of Roosevelt's plan for the French empire."[20]

The impact of Monnet's actions on the course of world history can hardly be overestimated. The months after the Allied occupation of French North Africa were crucial for deciding who would govern France after the Liberation. With Darlan dead, the remaining candidates were de Gaulle and Giraud, but in the event—thanks to Monnet—Giraud was eclipsed (how many people have heard of him today?). Had it gone the other way, it would have been de Gaulle who was quietly forgotten. And if de Gaulle had not presided over the Liberation, establishing himself as France's protector and savior, then he would never have been called back in 1958. This was no mean achievement for Monnet. Neither was his acting as the driving force behind the 1950 Schuman Declaration. Monnet's influence over the postwar history of Europe is truly momentous—yet his is not a name that readily springs to mind.

Monnet was involved in the negotiations to prepare the ground in Algeria and Morocco for the Torch landings.[21] Although it is portrayed today as an invasion, a huge amount of careful and secret diplomatic work—involving the Resistance *and* the ostensibly Vichy authorities in those colonies, such as Marshal Juin—had taken place over several months to ensure minimum resistance to the Allies' arrival. The only, brief fighting occurred almost by accident, as the result of bad coordination between the various elements on the French side and Darlan's unexpected and divisive appearance in Algiers.[22]

Here we have two politicians, instrumental in creating the first step toward the EU, one of whom (Schuman) had belonged to a think tank organized by Louis Le Fur of Alpha Galates, and the other (Monnet) who had been involved in the prewar synarchist milieu. And disturbingly, it was those two who brought about the treaties of Paris and Rome that set the agenda for a united Europe. Another of Monnet's "protégés," at least as far as European policy was concerned, was François Mitterrand, whom he backed in the 1965 presidential election.

The very least that can be said is that through Canudo's influence over Monnet and Le Fur's influence over Schuman (even if it went no further than that), synarchy has indeed changed the face of Europe—and therefore, without the slightest exaggeration, the world. But *did* it go any further than that?

For many years the limit of the EEC's ambitions was to coordinate the elements of industry and the economy that worked best collectively—it was just a matter of refining and extending what had already been achieved, for example, adding new member nations or organizing more areas of influence (such as the Common Agricultural Policy, developed in the early 1960s) on a Europe-wide basis. During that decade the institutions that oversaw individual industries and other areas were merged into the European Commission, with a Council of Ministers. In 1973 the United Kingdom, Ireland, and Denmark were the first of the new wave of member nations.

Although the first direct elections to the European Parliament were held in 1979, the Parliament still possessed no real legislative powers, simply the authority to pass nonbinding resolutions. (The major extension of its power during the 1970s was greater control of the EEC's budget.) The process reached its culmination in the Single European Act of 1986, which extended the common market principles beyond the free trade of goods to the freedom of movement of individuals and money within the EEC. With that, the original concept of the united Europe—economic and financial cooperation kick-started by the Schuman Declaration—had gone just about as far as was possible.

The next major step increased the European Parliament's *political* power, with the Maastricht Treaty (properly the European Union Treaty) of 1992, which turned the EEC into the European Union. The Treaty gave the European Parliament extended powers over the domestic policies of the individual nations, for the first time beyond the areas of trade and economics—which was seen by many as the first step toward a European "superstate." Now the European Parliament had proper legislative powers. Now it had *teeth.*

Also in 1992 the EU decided in favor of full economic and monetary union—a single currency with a European Central Bank, leading to the adoption of the euro in twelve of the fifteen member nations, the initiative of the French President, François Mitterrand. Indeed, with his close political ally Jacques Delors and special relationship with German Chancellor Helmut Kohl, Mitterrand may be described as the architect of the Europe we have today. But although we may be initially inclined to take with more than a pinch of salt Plantard's claim that Mitterrand was either a Priory member or a patsy, an examination of his background and career does give serious pause for thought.

The French Pharaoh

In September 1994 there was a wave of "shock horror" in France when a sensational new book shone a spotlight on the skeletons in the closet of its President—then into his thirteenth year and second term in office. Pierre Péan's *A French Youth* (*Une jeunesse française*), for which Mitterrand himself had been interviewed, revealed that the socialist President not only had been a leading light in 1930s far-right circles but had also held an important post in the Vichy administration—even being awarded its highest decoration for his service to the French State. The ensuing furore saw Mitterrand trying to defend himself on national television: urbanely he explained his right-wing lapse as mere youthful folly, the important thing being that he had realized the error of his ways and crucially changed his political views. That was *then*, this is *now*.

Even so, Mitterrand's dubious past came as a real shock to most French voters, although it had been common knowledge in political circles for years. (After all, Henry Coston had been vociferous enough on the subject in the 1960s.)[23] The American historian John Hellman explains the full extent of Mitterrand's political treachery—and that of the French establishment:

> Both during and after the Vichy period he appears to have been a supreme opportunist for whom family and fraternal loyalties took precedence over principles, ideologies, and grand designs. . . . Like a number of his wartime allies. . . . Mitterrand was able to refashion his right-wing background into having been "of the left" when he

> began to challenge the influence of the French Communist party. . . . That France's dominant public figure could have so successfully concealed his beginnings is a revelation and leaves us wondering what his memories of his past actually were, how the entire French historical profession managed to avoid bringing the important facts to light, and why Mitterrand and his allies made such an effort to conceal what they had been thinking and doing.[24]

(We will examine the full importance of these "family and fraternal loyalties" shortly.)

François Mitterrand was born in 1916 in Jarnac, where one of the Priory of Sion's commanderies was allegedly based. The reasons for the Priory's claim are not particularly clear—unlike the other places, such as Bourges, Jarnac never otherwise features in Priory lore or the history of any associated movements.

In a 1969 interview, Mitterrand said he and his siblings had been instilled with a patriotism based on God's wrath, adding rather gnomically, "with, fortunately, a Barrès and *Colline inspirée* side."[25] At least during his youth, he was a very devout Catholic, with a special veneration for the nineteenth-century patron saint of missionaries, Thérèse of Lisieux. As he explained to his mentor Abbé Jobit in 1934: "Christian action does not preclude political action: it completes it."[26]

As a student in Paris, he joined the Croix de Feu (Cross of Fire), the right-wing nationalist organization founded and led by Colonel François de La Rocque; indeed, in January 1935 he gave two lectures on the virtues of the organization, which were reported in the press at the time. Mitterrand also contributed to the right-wing journal *Combat*.[27] As befits a frequenter of those circles, he was an ardent royalist—at Easter 1939 he and some friends visited Brussels to "seek counsel" from the pretender to the throne, the Comte de Paris.[28]

Unarguably, in his late teens and early twenties, Mitterrand played an active part in extreme-right politics at a street level, the same ground inhabited by the dreaded Cagoule. But the most extreme accusation was that the future French President himself was an active member of its terrorist network.

There are many rumors but few hard facts. Several people who knew him at the time stated that it was widely believed he was a Cagoulard, although none could produce concrete evidence. The most dramatic claim relates to the Cagoule's 1937 bombing campaign in Paris, targeting employers' organizations. According to the founder Cagoulard Dr. Henri Martin's family, Mitterrand himself was the bomb carrier.[29]

In fact, the allegation that Mitterrand was an active Cagoulard first surfaced in 1991 in the extreme-right magazine *Le Choc du Mois,* in a special edition on the President. By contrast, Pierre Péan stops short of making such an accusation because Mitterrand categorically denied any involvement—and in any case there was no compelling evidence to the contrary. (However, there is still room for argument: although his name may be conspicuous by its absence from the Cagoule membership lists seized in 1937, it seems that the identities of certain leaders were kept scrupulously secret. Was his one of them?) But the absence of evidence for Mitterrand's actual membership in the terrorist network is rather irrelevant compared with his personal and political closeness to certain fanatical Cagoulards.

Mitterrand was a close friend of Jean Bouvyer, who kept watch when the Rosselli brothers were assassinated and who was also involved in planning the murder of Dimitri Navachine.[30] Mitterrand and he were good friends from at least 1936—the year before the murders—although their paths were to cross most frequently in Vichy. Bouvyer was arrested in connection with the murders in January 1938, although the outbreak of war not only interrupted the investigation of the most prominent Cagoulards, including Deloncle, but allowed them to rise unimpeded in the Vichy administration. Mitterrand's sister Marie-Josèphe, divorced from the Marquis de Corlieu, became Bouvyer's lover during the Vichy years. Despite her pleas he refused to marry her, partly because he feared a postwar reopening of the investigation into his Cagoule activities.[31] He was right to be worried. Another friend and ally of the prewar and Vichy years was François Méténier, one of Deloncle's assistants and the man who arrested Laval in 1940, later sentenced to twenty years for the 1937 Paris bombings. And, as we will see, Mitterrand later used his influence to aid both men. In July 1939, after a whirlwind romance, his brother Robert married Edith Cahier—sister of Eugène Deloncle's wife, Mercedes.[32] This group from Mitterrand's prewar extreme-right days, to whom he either was related by blood or became related to by marriage, remorselessly built up into the "clan," the perfect example of blatant political nepotism in action. (As another example of the insularity of this group, Pétain's niece was married to Henri Martin's lawyer).[33]

From Villain to Hero

Mitterrand's biography in the 1964 *Nouveau dictionnaire national des contemporains* describes a history any true son of France would have been proud of: "Mobilized in 1939, he was wounded, taken prisoner, and escaped in 1942. He then became an active member of the Resistance and founded the National Movement of Prisoners of War (1942). After various missions in London and Algiers (1943), he became, at the Liberation, secretary-general of Prisoners of War."[34] Nothing in this summary is technically inaccurate—but something rather critical has been carefully omitted.

When war broke out, the future President became a sergeant in the infantry, and after being taken prisoner in June 1940, he was sent to a POW camp in Germany—his "pilgrimage." To him, the defeat was a kind of purgation of France's sins, particularly the blood-soaked antimonarchist Revolution. In the camp he forged a friendship that would have profound consequences decades later, with a former Young Communist named Roger-Patrice Pelat. A lifelong companion, Pelat introduced Mitterrand to Danielle Gouze-Rénal, whom he married in October 1944.[35]

Having been transferred to a camp in Occupied France, Mitterrand and Pelat escaped, making their way to the Vichy zone in December 1941. (Despite suggestions that Vichy cronies got him released, Péan presents evidence that Mitterrand actually did escape.)

In Vichy, Mitterrand was assigned to the documentation service of the Legion of Combatants and Volunteers for the National Revolution—a group of pro-Pétain former soldiers founded by the ex-Cagoulard and Bouvyer's onetime lawyer Xavier Vallat—which had just merged with Colonel de La Rocque's organization, the former Croix de Feu.[36] Mitterrand got this job through Colonel Cahier, his brother's father-in-law, but just a few months later he joined the Vichy administration's Board of Rehabilitation of Prisoners of War, thanks this time to Justice Minister Raphaël Alibert—also, predictably, an ex-Cagoulard.[37]

(The trauma of French prisoners of war—an incredible 1.8 million at one point—was a particularly hot issue. Not only did France want its young men back but such a large influx of ex-soldiers posed both opportunities and risks, depending on their attitude to the Occupation: would they rush to support Pétain or bolster the ranks of the Resistance? Despite its mundane-sounding title, therefore, the work of the Rehabilitation Board in deciding *who* was to be rehabilitated and what conditions were to be imposed was highly important.)

It was while in this post that Mitterrand wrote "Pilgrimage to Thuringia" for the Vichyite journal *France, Revue de l'État Nouveau,* founded by Gabriel Jeantet—director of Pétain's cabinet and formerly responsible for the Cagoule's arms supplies. (And, needless to say, he was also a member of Mitterrand's gilded circle.)[38] Pétain himself was a fellow contributor.

In Vichy "the former Cagoulards continued to move around and within the Mitterrand 'clan' "[39]—forming a dubious glitterati including Bouvyer, Méténier, and Deloncle.

At the beginning of 1943, with the tide turning against Hitler, the ever opportunistic Mitterrand and some colleagues put out feelers to the Resistance—but pledging their support to General Giraud, not his bitter rival de Gaulle. André Ulmann, the later writer on synarchy (who worked alongside Mitterrand in the Resistance), produced a report for de Gaulle on Mitterrand's "*attentiste* [those with a wait-and-see policy] and Giraudist" movement.[40] (Mitterrand was a longtime friend of Giraud's son.)

It was during this period that Mitterrand was awarded the Francisque Gallique, the highest honor the Vichy administration had to offer. There is a certain confusion—undoubtedly deliberate—about the date on which it was given. Mitterrand said it was awarded only in December 1943—after he had left France—but the evidence points to his receiving it in August.[41] The difference is crucial, because if it was the earlier date, he would have received it and been required to take the pledge: "I make a gift of my person to Marshal Pétain, as he has made a gift of himself to France. I commit myself to serve his disciplines and to remain faithful to his person and his work."[42] But worse for Mitterrand's postwar reputation is the fact that his sponsors had been Jeantet and the staunchly pro-Vichy Simon Arbellot, who said later that Mitterrand had actually *solicited* the award.[43]

After Giraud's eclipse, Mitterrand metamorphosed overnight into a staunch Gaullist and in November 1943, with a colleague, made the hazardous journey to London to meet with Colonel Maurice Buckmaster, head of SOE's French Section. Then he visited de Gaulle in Algiers; the General, exploiting his experience with the Prisoners of War board, assigned him the job of organizing Resistance among POWs. Mitterrand returned to Paris at the end of February 1944.[44]

Angels and Demons

Although prudently ending the war on the side of the angels, Mitterrand was still happy to mix with former Cagoulards, to whom he owed and by whom he was owed favors. In need of a job, he was duly made editor in chief for the review *Votre Beauté* (*Your Beauty*), of all things, by Eugène Schueller, founder and head of L'Oréal, who had previously financed the Cagoule and Deloncle's racist MSR party.[45] (Several ex-Cagoulards were similarly assisted after the fall of Vichy: Jacques Corrèze, one of Deloncle's assistants in the MSR—who married his widow after the war—became L'Oréal's representative in Spain.[46] Perhaps he was worth it.)

When the Cagoule investigation reopened after the Liberation, Jean Bouvyer and François Méténier were arrested once again and charged in connection with the bombings and murders. At least nothing if not a loyal friend, Mitterrand visited them frequently in prison.[47]

In Vichy, Jean Bouvyer had been an enthusiastic employee of the General Commission for Jewish Questions, with all that chilling euphemism now implies. In August 1945, when he was rearrested, Mitterrand wrote in his support, claiming that Bouvyer had provided forged documents for the Resistance and that his attitude during the Occupation had been "irreproachable." Challenged on this by Pierre Péan, Mitterrand claimed he had had no knowledge at that time about the true nature of Bouvyer's job in Vichy.[48] (As the latter was in a relationship with Mitterrand's sister, this is somewhat hard to believe.)

While he was out on bail in 1948, Bouvyer and his new wife fled to South America, although he was sentenced to death in absentia. Sentenced to twenty years in jail, Méténier was freed in 1951 on health grounds—thanks to Mitterrand's intervention.[49] A friend of Mitterrand's says that Méténier told him in 1950, "Whatever you ask Mitterrand in my name, you will have."[50] One wonders just how long Mitterrand's subservience to the ex-Cagoulards lasted, and how far it influenced his political decisions on behalf of France and Europe as a whole.

Entering politics after the war as a socialist, Mitterrand still presented himself as an implacable opponent of the Communists, who had considerable support at that time. In 1946 he joined the Rally of the Republican Left (Rassemblement des Gauches Républicains, or RGR) led by the prewar prime minister Daladier. In November he was elected a senator representing the *département* of Nièvre, rapidly becoming quite a high flyer: during the 1950s, while still in his late thirties and early forties, he held various top-level posts, even becoming Minister of the Interior and of Justice in 1954–55.

During those years of political success, Mitterrand made the infamous comment that he needed only "fifty well-placed friends to run the country."[51] This was no idle boast, as can be seen from his astonishing nepotism when he finally achieved the highest office in the Republic.

Sworn Enemies

It was all looking so promising for Mitterrand, until the triumph of Gaullism in 1958 summarily ejected him into the wilderness. He loathed de Gaulle, throughout the General's presidency even being his "sworn enemy."[52] (De Gaulle records that when he met the parliamentary leaders on May 31, 1958, the only one who "gave vent to his feelings" against the General's installation as Prime Minister was Mitterrand).[53] This gave Mitterrand common ground with the extreme right in the French Parliament, who also hated de Gaulle because of his volte-face over Algeria, and accounts for—or perhaps provides a convenient excuse for—his occasional alliances with them during the 1960s.[54]

(There may appear to be a contradiction in synarchists—or at least Plantard and the then Priory of Sion—appearing to have succeeded in getting de Gaulle into power and Monnet and Mitterrand being in conflict with him. But of course, as synarchy works in steps toward its final goal, de Gaulle may have been viewed as the safest pair of hands to carry the agenda forward to a certain point, after which the synarchists would switch their support to whoever would advance their cause most swiftly and efficiently. The perfect synarchist maneuver would be to establish influence over *opposing* electoral candidates.)

One of Mitterrand's most breathtaking stunts to reclaim his former high profile—and very telling it is about his character—was what became known as the Observatory Affair. On the night of October 15–16, 1959, as Mitterrand was driving by the Jardin du Luxembourg in Paris (outside the Palais du Luxembourg, the seat of the Senate at the top of the Avenue de l'Observatoire), a gunman opened fire on his car. Mitterrand jumped out, leapt over the hedge into the park, and ran off. He reported the incident to the police—and to the press, for whom he enacted a somewhat undignified replay of his hedge hopping. As to the identity of the would-be hit man and his backers, Mitterrand left that to the imagination—after all, everyone knew he was the major thorn in the side of General de Gaulle.

The investigation into the attempted assassination of one of France's best-known politicians rapidly led to the arrest of the alleged gunman, Abel Dahuron, as well as a right-wing politician, Robert Pesquet, who was supposedly behind it. (Pesquet belonged to a far-right party and was then a colleague of Jean-Marie Le Pen.) But in his defense Pesquet named as his coconspirator none other than *François Mitterrand.* He claimed that the whole thing was the "victim's" own idea—a blatant hoax designed to get publicity, win public sympathy, and cast suspicion on his enemies. Apparently his car was shot up *after* he had got out. Bizarre and incredible though it may seem, Pesquet could even prove it: as insurance against a debacle, he had sent himself letters to two separate post office boxes, describing the plan in elaborate detail and postmarked *before* the attempt took place. The investigating magistrate collected the letters and opened them in Mitterrand's presence. His last shred of dignity and, one would have assumed, credibility, gone, Mitterrand broke down in tears.[55]

In August 1966, Pesquet and Dahuron were acquitted on the grounds that the attempt had been made with the consent of the supposed victim. With either incredible arrogance or ignorance of his true position, Mitterrand appealed, but in November the verdict was upheld and he was compelled to pay the costs. (There was an attempt to prosecute him, but for some reason it never got to court.) Perhaps the only real winner, apart from Mitterrand himself, was French cynicism. It is hard to imagine British or American politicians even considering continuing their careers after such a spectacularly humiliating scandal, even if their peers—and the voters—would countenance their doing so.

It is also baffling how Mitterrand could pretend to be a socialist when he was well known for his right-wing views and regular contact with extremists such as Pesquet, especially as his opponents seem to have been fully aware of his political orientation. His bid for the presidency in the 1965 elections was actually backed by the extreme-right Republican Alliance (of which Le Pen was a member).[56] Yet still he rose to the top.

Presenting himself as the only real alternative to Gaullism, in the 1960s Mitterrand led a coalition of left-wing parties, then created the Socialist Party (Parti Socialiste—usually known by its initials, *PS*).

One of his influential coterie who helped him organize the PS was Hubert Beuve-Méry (1902–1989), founder and owner of *Le Monde*—he wrote under the pseudonym Sirius—and an intellectual leader of the wartime Uriage schools.[57] One of the great advocates of European union, Beuve-Méry even enjoyed a dinner with Goebbels and Himmler in Berlin in 1939.[58] (And he got Lionel de Roulet, leader of the prewar Merovingian Party, his job in Vienna—apparently a cover for intelligence operations.) Finally, on his third attempt, Mitterrand was elected President of the French Republic on May 10, 1981 (and reelected seven years later). One of his first acts as France's top man was to push through a law granting an amnesty to those in the military who had plotted against de Gaulle—in other words, the OAS.[59]

"Incontestably a monarch"

Although still hiding behind his caring socialist mask, Mitterrand adopted an aloof and regal style more fitting for a king—indeed, the Comte de Paris said of him in 1987: "He is incontestably a monarch."[60] As a socialist, Mitterrand had been an outspoken opponent of the kind of presidency created by de Gaulle, because it concentrated too much power in the President's hands, publishing his views in a broadside entitled *The Permanent Coup d'État* in 1964. But characteristically, once elected he changed his tune, breaking his manifesto pledges to reduce the presidential term from seven to five years and to limit the presidency to two terms.[61] John Laughland shrewdly assesses his presidency:

> While Mitterrand devoted his efforts to vain politicking, France drifted. During his fourteen years in office, French industry stood still. The rise in unemployment and poverty has been matched only by the multiplication of the favours and privileges accorded to Mitterrand's personal friends; he has preferred to govern through his private clan rather than through the public institutions of the state, and he pursues power for no other purpose than itself. If "Thatcherism" denotes an invigorating economic creed and a style of government which has left a significant legacy, "Mitterrandism" denotes opportunism, favouritism, corruption, and the substitution of illusions and talk for concrete action.[62]

Laughland also notes uncompromisingly of "King" Mitterrand:

> [His] whole political personality depends on the blurring of distinctions, political as much as moral, and on the refusal ever to be pinned down to any single position on anything. Few phrases, indeed, epitomize his moral cynicism better than when he refused to accept that there was anything wrong with his continuing to frequent his old friend, René Bousquet, the former Chief of Police under Vichy: "You think that life is black and white? No, it is light grey and dark grey."[63]

As the reference to the "private clan" underlines, Mitterrand was soon notorious for unashamedly favoring his and his wife's families. (Even so, the question niggles, who actually ran this little cabal? Was Mitterrand really in charge—or was he just its public face?) He also retained his connections with his Vichy comrades, arrogantly defying public opinion.

Mitterrand's most notorious associate was René Bousquet (1909–1993), Secretary-General of the Vichy Police—Henri Chavin's former post—from April 1942. A month later, when the Germans prepared to deport French Jews from the Occupied zone, Bousquet voluntarily offered them foreign Jews held in Vichy camps as well. He went on to supervise personally roundups of French Jews in Paris and the Vichy zone that summer, being responsible for deporting some 76,000 human beings to hell on Earth. The Nazis removed him from office in December 1943, and after D-Day he was deported to Germany, where he languished under house arrest. In 1949 he was sentenced to five years' loss of civil rights for his involvement in Vichy, but this was immediately commuted for "acts of resistance."[64]

After the war Bousquet joined the boards of directors of various companies, mainly banking interests connected with the Far East—particularly the Banque d'Indochine, of which he was Assistant Director General. In 1962 he became a director of the Toulouse-based newspaper *La Dépêche du Midi,* which was solidly pro-Vichy during the war and vociferously anti–de Gaulle after it.[65] Perhaps unsurprisingly, it supported Mitterrand in his 1965 presidential bid. Mitterrand remained lifelong friends with Bousquet, whom he received at the Élysée Palace shortly after becoming President.[66]

Although *L'Express* exposed Bousquet's wartime role in persecuting the Jews in 1979, it took a decade for charges to be brought against him. When he was indicted for crimes against humanity in 1991, the legal process was deliberately slowed by powerful friends, including Mitterrand. A verdict was never reached: he was shot dead in his apartment on June 8, 1993, by Christian Didier, described as a "deranged and unsuccessful writer"[67] (he had tried to kill the notorious war criminal Klaus Barbie five years before).

Apart from Mitterrand's continued associations with deeply dubious characters, corruption, coupled with often breathtakingly blatant cover-ups—and sometimes coinciding with "convenient" deaths—was undoubtedly the signature of his presidency. For example, François de Grossouvre, a friend since Vichy and then the Resistance, financed all four of Mitterrand's election campaigns. But during Mitterrand's second term, the relationship soured, and de Grossouvre was frozen out. He was writing his memoirs when, in April 1994, he shot himself—at least officially; there are grounds for suspecting he was murdered.[68]

The escalating scandals reached their climax with the "Urba Affair" of 1990, in which "consultancy" companies Mitterrand set up were found to have taken fees from contractors that disappeared into the "hidden finance" of the PS; later they would be given lucrative government or local authority contracts.

With staggering hypocrisy, in April 1992—in the wake of this furore—Mitterrand appointed Pierre Bérégovoy of his Socialist Party as Prime Minister, with a specific brief to root out corruption. But just over a year later, Bérégovoy shot himself, probably for several reasons: the Socialist Party had been virtually eliminated in the previous month's general election, Mitterrand had frozen him out (the removal of his patronage and protection was always devastating), and he himself was also about to be embroiled in a financial scandal.

This involved the dubious "Vice President" Patrice Pelat, one of the few whom Mitterrand addressed familiarly as *tu*[69] and an important source of funds for his presidential campaigns. In 1953, with the President's brother Robert, Pelat founded a company called Vibrachoc, for which—in the years leading up to his election—François Mitterrand acted as legal adviser, receiving "tens of thousands of francs" in fees. Little more than a year after his election, Vibrachoc was bought by a subsidiary of the recently nationalized electricity giant CGE—a sale that was expedited by the President. Although the company fetched 110 million francs, it rapidly became apparent to CGE that it had been grossly overvalued. But the sale made Pelat enormously rich—he even bought a château at Sologne, which he fitted out with a helipad specifically in order to receive his crony Mitterrand.[70]

In December 1988 another financial scandal involving Pelat broke, this time relating to insider trading. In the days before the takeover of an American company by the Péchiney group, Pelat, together with other friends and associates of the President, bought shares in it. Mitterrand approved the takeover. The possibility of insider trading—involving privileged information from Mitterrand himself—was being investigated when, on March 7, 1989, Pelat died of a heart attack, bringing some closure to that unsavory business.[71] (Although the Péchiney Affair never resulted in any prosecutions or definite findings of wrongdoing, it certainly raised an almighty stink of corruption. But at least the Urba business provided the much-needed impetus to change the French system, which until then had permitted politicians immense control over judicial investigations, even if they themselves were the ones being investigated.)

Five years later it was the continuing investigation of the Urba affair that plunged Pelat's loan to Pierre Bérégovoy into the spotlight, which (after its exposure in *Le Canard Enchaîné*) led to the French Prime Minister's suicide. And the investigation into *that,* by Thierry Jean-Pierre, prompted Plantard's questioning about Pelat's connection with the Priory of Sion.

But why had Plantard selected Pelat's name as his alleged predecessor as Grand Master back in 1989, without anticipating the unfortunate consequences? The most obvious explanation is that—returning to the favorite tactics of the Dossiers Secrets—Plantard simply utilized the recent, convenient death of a man whose closeness to Mitterrand would bestow the required gravitas on the newly reinvented Priory. However, there is a curious, if coincidental, connection between Mitterrand and Plantard, through André Rousselet, a close friend from the last months of the war who remained at the heart of his inner circle for the rest of Mitterrand's life, being director of his Cabinet from 1981 to 1982 and even the executor of his will in 1996. (Rousselet was also the founder of the influential Canal+ television station.) French researchers have found that his adopted daughter, Chantal, married Jean, son of François Plantard—Pierre's cousin. According to Guy Patton, Pierre Plantard kept in regular touch with his extended family over the years—so was he actually a member of the Mitterrand "clan," if only on its fringes?[72]

From Corruption to Subversion

Mitterrand may have been corrupt, opportunistic, and unprincipled, both personally and politically, yet his overriding concern—almost obsession—as President was foreign policy, particularly where Europe was concerned. Not only was it his personal priority but he insisted on keeping tight control of it, declaring: "Foreign policy is my affair. I define it, and I am going to keep it for myself."[73] One of his ministers agreed: "The only subject he is really interested in, the one to which he devotes the main part of his time, is foreign policy."[74] But his obsession was specific. As far as the man in the top job was concerned, there was no doubt that "European solidarity takes precedence over everything."[75]

Mitterrand's greatest change of traditional French policy on the subject of Europe was that he wanted to persuade the notoriously cautious United Kingdom to engage more fully with the EEC—which is why, controversially, he unhesitatingly declared his unconditional support for the Thatcher government during the Falklands war. He was also the most pro-American of French Presidents, seeking to allay American fears over a united Europe, matching Jean Monnet's original vision—although he was equally pro-Soviet. It is no coincidence that Monnet endorsed Mitterrand's 1965 presidential bid against de Gaulle.

It was Mitterrand's unique partnership with German Chancellor Helmut Kohl that allowed the European "project" to make its greatest advance in thirty years. He consolidated Franco-German relations—the two shook hands on it at Verdun in September 1984—and launched a joint initiative to create a common foreign and security policy. (Also that September, Mitterrand arranged for a wreath to be placed on Pétain's grave on the Île de Yeu; and from 1986 to 1992 a wreath was laid there annually on his orders.)[76]

As John Laughland explains: "In parallel with Chancellor Kohl, Mitterrand proposed that the national governments of the European Community be liquidated into a European Union with one currency managed by a single central bank."[77]

The major event that triggered the initiative was the historic fall of the Berlin Wall in November 1989. Six months later, Mitterrand and Kohl jointly proposed a conference that aimed to "transform the whole of the relations between the member countries into a real political Union."[78] This led to the Maastricht Treaty, which was signed by the member nations on February 7, 1992.

After Mitterrand's death from cancer on January 8, 1996, he was buried at his birthplace of Jarnac (somewhat surprisingly, as he had not been near it for decades)—but at the same time heads of state from around the world were gathered to honor him in Notre-Dame Cathedral in Paris.

The Initiate

Perhaps disappointingly, there is no specific evidence to link Mitterrand with any of the *esoteric* secret societies that we have identified lurking in the shadows behind the Priory of Sion, plotting to fulfill the synarchist agenda. But although he was not, as far as can be established, even a Freemason,[79] there is no doubt of his abiding interest in the esoteric in general.

According to those who met him, Mitterrand was extraordinarily charismatic, with a striking air of dignified and urbane superiority. Everything about him announced that here was someone who *knew* it was his place and destiny to rule—the elite of the elite. But although he was undoubtedly an unscrupulous opportunist for whom power itself was the ultimate glittering prize, he was not entirely a hardheaded cynic, a grasping materialist who had abandoned all principles. There was another side to him.

Mitterrand had a deep passion for the ancient world, especially the fabled civilizations of Europe, the Americas, and the Middle East, and he often visited evocative locations such as Mexico and Masada in Israel. But after his beloved France, above all his heart and soul belonged to ancient Egypt, earning him the nicknames "Republican Pharaoh" and "the Sphinx"—although the latter was probably only because of his aloof, inscrutable, and enigmatic presidential style. (Paying tribute to him after his death, Egyptian President Hosni Mubarak said that Mitterrand knew more about ancient Egypt than most archaeologists.)[80] It was this passion for ancient Egypt that inspired Mitterrand to oversee France's accumulation of Egyptian antiquities—which Dan Brown features in *The Da Vinci Code*. Mitterrand saw an affinity—even a similarity—between the early civilizations of Egypt and France.[81]

After the President's death, the French researcher Nicolas Bonnal's study *Mitterrand, the Great Initiate* (*Mitterrand, le grand initié,* 1996) showed that he had a genuine love of decidedly esoteric subjects and also revealed a profound knowledge of occult symbolism in the many public works for which he was responsible during his long presidency. Bonnal argues that Mitterrand's beliefs and interest in unconventional and "fringe" ideas make him more of a "New Ager" than an occultist—but then there is often a very thin dividing line. (On the whole, the New Age tends to take late-nineteenth/early-twentieth-century occult ideas and dilute them with hefty doses of näive "Love and Light," despite the fact that Victorian occultism usually makes no sense through rose-tinted spectacles.)

Mitterrand consulted the astrologer Elizabeth Teissier on matters of state—even about the First Gulf War and the outcome of the referendum on the Maastricht Treaty.[82] (But then de Gaulle, too, employed an astrologer, as do many heads of state, although they rarely advertise the fact.) As Marie Delarue, author of a study of Mitterrand's program of public works, *A Republican Pharaoh* (*Un pharaon républicain,* 1999), notes wryly: "presented as the light of rational, if not rationalist, thought, he who governed us for fourteen years spurned the aid of neither the stars nor religion."[83] Mitterrand also believed in reincarnation and was intrigued by the phenomenon of UFOs. But Mitterrand also possessed certain passions that are even more relevant to this investigation.

He had a particular veneration for the Mary Magdalene cult center of Vézelay (where her relics were worshiped until papal endorsement was switched to the newly discovered bones in Saint-Maximin in Provence in the fourteenth century). Judging by his autobiographical writings published in 1975, he had been a regular visitor since his first time there as, in his own words, a "pilgrim" thirty years before—around the end of the Second World War.[84] Another of Mitterrand's favorite religious centers was Bourges, the resting place of St. Sulpice, of which he said of his first visit at age 17, "The cathedral at Bourges was love at first sight."[85]

There was a reason for his fascination with Bourges—since the beginning of the eighteenth century, it had been his family's home, although he was born in Jarnac, where his father had moved. However, there is more than just sentiment in his passion for the town: he seemed to regard it not only as France's mystical center but also as the source of his own destiny. His family name (originally Mitterrant) was derived from "*milieu des terres*"—"middle of the land" (or even, Tolkien-style, "middle earth")—and Mitterrand himself pointed out that Bourges was the geographical center of France, adding that at the precise center of the land, some twenty miles south of Bourges at Bruère-Allichamp, there is a field called the Champs de Mitterrand.[86]

Not only would this explain why Mitterrand felt himself directly connected with his homeland and therefore fated to reign over it, but perhaps also why, as early as 1961, Plantard and the Priory of Sion were emphasizing (on their "mystic triangle" projected over France) two towns dear to Mitterrand's heart: Bourges and Jarnac.

Aside from foreign—and particularly European—policy, Mitterrand did have another passion that characterized his presidency. He oversaw a huge program of public works costing some 30 billion francs, particularly in Paris, echoing the burning desire—often amounting to a kind of frenzy—of the ancient Egyptian pharaohs to leave an enduring and visible reminder of their immortal greatness. He commissioned new architectural work and monuments, devised competitions for Europe's best architects, but above all exploited his authority to change the face of Paris according to his vision. Commenting on this burning desire to leave his mark on history, Marie Delarue observes: "It is from this angle, perhaps, that the Great Works must be considered as, when one looks closely, they do indeed seem to relate more to personal destiny and François Mitterrand's pronounced taste for hermeticism and the Sacred Science, than to the politics of socialist governments."[87] She also writes: "One could even . . . have sympathy for an old man—not a mason and still less free, but obsessed by magic, winsome astrologers, occultism, magical cures and sacred geography—finding it amusing to transform Paris into a journey for initiates."[88] There were many projects of all sizes—the remodeling of the Jardin du Palais-Royal, work at the Opéra, the new Bibliothèque Nationale—but the most obvious constructions he left to posterity are the Grande Arche of La Défense and, of course, the remodeling of the area in front of the Louvre museum.

The Grande Arche, in the area of skyscrapers and office blocks known as La Défense, is a breathtaking monument that was commissioned in 1982 and completed in 1989 (the result of an architectural competition won by the Dane Otto von Spreckelsen, who called it a "porte cosmique"—a stargate), although it was actually built by Christian Pellerin, a friend of Patrice Pelat. A cube-shaped thirty-five-story (360-foot-high) building with a huge square space in the middle, it was inaugurated on July 14, 1989, for a G7 summit.

To mark the two hundredth anniversary of the Revolution, the new-look Louvre was opened in October 1993, at which time Mitterrand said: "Transforming the Louvre demanded exceptional precautions. It is the heart of the city, the heart of our history. I wished for an architecture of purity and rigor that would combine boldness and respect."[89]

As millions are now aware, the most famous feature of the "new Louvre" is the great glass pyramid, seventy feet high and built to the same proportions as the Great Pyramid of Giza. (If anything symbolizes Mitterrand's belief in a mystical connection between ancient Egypt and France, this is it.) Fans should note that Dan Brown repeats the fallacy that the pyramid is composed of 666 panes of glass—but although it is actually 684, that is still an intriguing 666 + 6 + 6 + 6. In any case, Bonnal's close analysis of the numerical symbolism incorporated into the pyramid's design and dimensions demonstrates that all of it works perfectly.[90] But as always, as many of the mathematical and geometrical relationships in the pyramid are those that are naturally harmonious and pleasing, they could have been selected for aesthetic rather than esoteric reasons. It is equally difficult to know whether this symbolism was Mitterrand's initiative—as is often claimed—or the designers' (or indeed that of people behind Mitterrand). And if it is intended to be an esoteric statement, what does it mean? Here we have the same conundrum as in Saunière's work in Rennes-le-Château, but this time in the heart of Paris and on a much larger scale.

Frankly, most of the works for which Mitterrand was responsible *look* as if they are intended to convey something important at a symbolic or esoteric level. The Grand Arche and the Louvre pyramid are the two most obvious examples, but a smaller one also merits close attention.

Set in the Parc du Champs-de-Mars, which leads up to the Eiffel Tower, is the elaborate Monument to the Rights of Man and the Citizen, which was also commissioned to commemorate the bicentennial of the Revolution in 1989. Described by Delarue as "the most beautiful, most esoteric, and least known of the Mitterrandian Great Works,"[91] it consists of a central building, modeled on an Egyptian funerary temple or mastaba, surrounded by bronze statues and other decorations, such as the double-headed god Janus (often linked to the two Saints John in esoteric tradition). Even to most non-Masons, the plentiful Masonic symbolism is immediately recognizable: pairs of pillars—the Jachin and Boaz of the traditional lodge room—a triangle of three round holes in one wall, and all manner of symbols and signs. The monument is aligned to the summer solstice—the sun at noon on that day penetrates a shaft between the columns.

The Paris Mairie's own official pamphlet, *Walks of Discovery of the Municipal Artistic Commissions,* notes that "the monument raised on the Champs-de-Mars, the privileged site of the revolutionary celebrations, goes beyond just the celebration of the Declaration of the Rights of Man and the Citizen. It is composed of two obelisks, a stone temple and two figures in bronze inspired by Poussin's *Shepherds of Arcadia.*"[92] In fact, the two figures feature twice—on the bronze doors and on the columns. As Delarue points out, Poussin is decidedly out of place on a monument that it supposed to represent and symbolize the philosophical and political currents that led to the Revolution and Liberty.[93] But Poussin's tableau is clearly important, as revealed by the presence, on the monument's west face, of the legend *Et in Arcadia ego.*

This monument, though not on the scale of most of his Great

Works, was obviously very dear to Mitterrand's heart: although the fact was kept secret until after his death, he used to pay private nocturnal visits to this strange and haunting "temple."[94]

Undoubtedly the French President's psychological makeup—his unshakable belief that he was one of an elite born to rule, coupled with New Age or occult interests—and his sense of a spiritual connection to the heart of the land made him perfect potential for manipulation by synarchists. His actions where Europe was concerned certainly brought the synarchist dream of a United States of Europe a big step nearer to reality, but does that mean he was consciously acting in accordance with the synarchist agenda? Of course, conclusive evidence would never be easy to come by, but the facts are suggestive: his long association with members of the Cagoule, with its links to the Synarchic Empire Movement; his relationship by marriage, within the "clan," to Eugène Deloncle, the most easily identified synarchist of all the Cagoule leaders; the fact that Mitterrand showed no idealism or principle about anything *except* the European project, suggesting it was his greatest mission, even the reason he wanted to be President. And then there was the link between the Mitterrand "clan" and Pierre Plantard.

Stranger Than Fiction

Our detective work has led inexorably to certain bizarre—and even apparently incredible—conclusions about the true nature of the Priory of Sion, its influence, and its motives in the real world.

The Priory—the alleged upholders of the bloodline of Jesus that is so central to *The Holy Blood and the Holy Grail* and *The Da Vinci Code*—*is* a hoax, but in the same way that intelligence deceptions are hoaxes. What *really* matter are the groups behind it, the network of societies that include the Rectified Scottish Rite and Papus's Martinist Order, with their secret interior orders (of which most of their rank and file are probably unaware). And behind all this stands synarchy, at whose core is the drive to forge the United States of Europe.

However, it is important not to get swept along, way beyond the evidence. We are not saying that the Priory of Sion created or is behind the European Union. We are saying that the Priory is one manifestation of a movement—synarchy—which is more important than the society and that has exerted a significant but not exclusive influence over modern French history and the development of the European Union. Neither are we saying that Europe is solely the product of synarchists or that they are the secret controllers of Brussels—although they certainly have ambitions in that direction. Our intention is to stress that the synarchists' influence in the past and their presence today need to be recognized, not to suggest that they are all-powerful, everywhere.

The Priory was originally established in 1956 as a front for groups plotting Charles de Gaulle's return to power, either the network that would later become the notorious Gaullist "praetorian guard," the SAC, or the related Grand O conspiracy led by the arch-plotter Henri Martin. Later, in the 1960s, it was revived with a new purpose, a misinformation exercise aimed to divert other esoteric groups from seeking out certain archives by laying the bewildering false trail of the Merovingian bloodline. After *The Holy Blood and the Holy Grail* gave its cover story unexpected and unprecedented international publicity—whether it was welcome, unwelcome, or by the 1980s irrelevant, is unclear—it was quietly closed down by reinventing itself with a far less interesting history and purpose.

But of course it is still around, its public face now being Gino Sandri. Presumably it is being kept "warm" in case it is needed as a cover for something else. After all, it has been half a century in the making, and it would be a pity to lose all that hard work. Sandri insists that although today's Priory of Sion includes important figures from the world of high finance, business, and politics, it does not have political or financial objectives.[94] If our conclusions about the Priory being a convenient and versatile cover are correct, then at the moment that must be true. Where it will go in the future remains to be seen. Whether the Priory being thrust back into the international spotlight because of *The Da Vinci Code* will make it disappear or inspire a new phase in its development also remains to be seen.

However, delving into the Priory's murky history reveals even darker links with racist, collaborationist, and even terrorist groups. But in investigating the Priory of Sion's affiliations of decades ago, an astounding scenario is gradually revealed, which one hesitates to set down in black and white. Yet as we have seen from dozens of checkable associations and links, it seems that at least the *concept* of the European Union is the product of an occult conspiracy, inspired by individuals who believed they were in contact with spirit entities, with the ultimate aim of establishing a full-blown United States of Europe in line with Joseph Alexandre Saint-Yves d'Alveydre's original vision.

Clever, fanatical, and impossible to categorize as left- or right-wing, liberal or extremist—or even heretical, occult, *or* Catholic—the political and religious shape-shifting synarchists may be poised to take over the lives of millions by infiltrating the classrooms and the churches, by abusing simple patriotism and overturning democracy. Perhaps they already have.

Synarchy may appear to be a long way from da Vinci's paintings and the weird decoration in St. Mary Magdalene's church at Rennes-le-Château, but our journey through the extraordinary links spiraling through the arcane and often murky world of occult brotherhoods, religious intrigue, and even spirit contact leads inexorably to the stark world of modern politics. Where it will go next remains to be seen, but almost certainly sooner or later it will affect us all.

Notes and References

1. TRUE LIES

1. Purists might object that, in translating the society's name into English, "Sion" should be given as "Zion," the usual English spelling of the Old Testament name for Jerusalem. However, as we will see, there is considerable debate about why the Priory calls itself *of Sion.* It may be a reference to Jerusalem, but it may equally be to the Col du Mont Sion in the Haute-Savoie region of France or to the town of Sion in Switzerland or to Sion-Vaudémont in Lorraine—or none of the above. For this reason, we prefer the neutral "Sion."
2. Dan Brown, *The Da Vinci Code* (New York: Doubleday, 2003), p. 291.
3. Margaret Starbird, *The Woman with the Alabaster Jar* (Sante Fe: Bear & Co., 1993) and *The Goddess in the Gospels* (Sante Fe: Bear & Co., 1998).
5. See www.bletchleypark.org.
4. "Arcadia," "Entretien avec Gino Sandri." *La Lettre du Thot* webzine, part 1: no. 7, July 2003. http://62.212.97.214/thot/arcadia/webzine/webzine_no7.html.
5. Our own dealings with Plantard—who was by then (the mid-1990s) keeping a very low profile—were limited to a single letter, which was answered by Gino Sandri. See Lynn Picknett and Clive Prince, *The Templar Revelation* (New York: Touchstone, 1998), p. 56.
6. Michael Baigent, Richard Leigh, and Henry Lincoln, *The Holy Blood and the Holy Grail* (London: Arrow, 1976), p. 235.

7. Quoted in Pierre Jarnac, *Les archives du trésor de Rennes-le-Château* (Saleilles: Pierre Jarnac, 1985), p. 549.
8. Dan Burstein, ed., *Secrets of the Code* (New York: CDS Books, 2004), p. 353.
9. We will return to this interesting allegation in the last chapter.
10. Paul Smith's research and conclusions can be seen on his website, www.priory-of-sion.com.
11. Bill Putnam and John Edwin Wood, *The Treasure of Rennes-le-Château* (Stroud: Sutton Publishing, 2004), p. 185.
12. Dr. Steven Mizrach, "Priory of Sion," Florida International University. www.fiu.edu/~mizrachs/poseur3.html.
13. Frances A. Yates, *The Rosicrucian Enlightenment* (London: Routledge & Kegan Paul, 1972), p. 141.
14. Ibid., p. 143.
15. Foreword to Tobias Churton, *Gnostic Philosophy: From Ancient Persia to Modern Times* (Rochester, Vt.: Inner Traditions, 2005), p. xiii.
16. On René d'Anjou and Arcadia, see Baigent, Leigh, and Lincoln, *The Holy Blood and the Holy Grail*, pp. 140–43; and on his interest in Magdalene sites, see Picknett and Prince, *The Templar Revelation*, pp. 70–71.
17. Paul Digot, *Notice historique sur Notre-Dame-de-Sion (Vaudémont)* (Nancy, privately published, 1856), p. 8.
18. Alsace and Lorraine, bordering Germany, have been fought over throughout history and so can be seen as symbolic of French nationalism. The two regions were taken by France in the mid–seventeenth century, ceded to Germany in 1871 after the Franco-Prussian War, returned to France after the First World War, and taken back under German control from 1940 to 1945, since which they have been part of France. The Baillard brothers' activities took place under French rule.
19. Details taken from Joseph Barbier, *Les sources de La colline Inspirée de Maurice Barrès* (Nancy: Berger-Levrault, 1957). To add to the chain of connections, Vintras was backed by a group known as the Johannites, who linked themselves with John the Baptist and were led by a mysterious figure, Madame Bouche (alias Sister Salome), from the Rue Saint-Sulpice in Paris, bringing in two other major themes of the Priory of Sion mystery (which will be explained later). After Vintras's death, his Church of Carmel was taken over by the decidedly unsavory defrocked priest Abbé Joseph Boullan (1824–

1893), who added some extreme sexual practices, including bestiality, to its ceremonies. The evidence points to Boullan being an agent of Vintras's enemies—probably the Church—who was given the mission of, literally, perverting his order to bring about its downfall. See Picknett and Prince, *The Templar Revelation,* pp. 168–74.

20. Michael Baigent, Richard Leigh, and Henry Lincoln, *The Messianic Legacy* (London: Corgi, 1987), p. 233.
21. See Lynn Picknett and Clive Prince, *Turin Shroud—In Whose Image?* (London: Corgi, 2000), pp. 133–40, 146–50.
22. *Leonardo—The Man Behind the Shroud,* produced by Stefilm for The National Geographic Channel, directed by Susan Gray, 2001.
23. Ilse Hecht, "The Infants Christ and St. John Embracing: Notes on a Composition by Joos van Cleve," *Apollo* 113 (April 1981): 228–29.
24. Jean Markale, *The Templar Treasure at Gisors* (Rochester, Vt.: Inner Traditions, 2003), p. 69.
25. Estimates of the number of Mandaeans in Iraq very widely. The United Nations Economic and Social Council—which lists the Mandaeans as a threatened people—gives 15,000, while other sources give figures between 100,000 and 200,000.
26. The Mandaeans are discussed in more detail in chapter 15 of *The Templar Revelation.*
27. Jean-Pierre Bayard with Natacha Olejnik-Sarkissian, *Guide des Sociétés secrètes et des sectes* (Paris: Oxus, 2004), p. 128.
28. See pages 269–70.
29. Paul Smith, "The 1989 Plantard Comeback." www.priory-of-sion.com/psp/id.60.html, undated.
30. Picknett and Prince, *Turin Shroud—In Whose Image?,* pp. 144–45.
31. François Audigier, *Histoire du SAC* (Paris: Stock, 2003), p. 7.
32. See Serge Ferrand and G. Lecavelier, *Aux ordres du SAC* (Paris: Albin Michel, 1982), pp. 85–92.
33. Audigier, *Histoire du SAC,* p. 231.
34. Ferrand and Lecavelier, *Aux ordres du SAC,* p. 95.
35. Audigier, *Histoire du SAC,* p. 232.

2. BEHIND THE THRONE

1. Under a French law passed in 1901, every society and association must register itself with the local prefecture, declaring its purpose and aims and placing a copy of its rules on file (hence "law-of-1901 association"). Ostensibly this is to give it legal status (for activities such as taking subscriptions and owning property), but it also gives the authorities the opportunity to ensure that the society does not have an objective that is "illicit, contrary to the law or good morals, or which aims to undermine the integrity of the national territory or the republican form of the government."

   As the French researcher Jean-Pierre Monteils points out in *Sectes et sociétés secrètes* (1999), to avoid infringing this law, most "secret" societies elect to register themselves as law-of-1901 associations. However, they are often vague about their aims: the bland purpose of *study,* for example, can cover a multitude of sins.
2. Facsimile images of the original registration documents, taken from the St.-Julien-en-Genevois Sub-Prefectures file (reference KM94550), can be seen on Paul Smith's Priory of Sion website, www.priory-of-sion.com/psp/posd/regdoc.html.
3. Bonhomme's letter is reproduced in Pierre Jarnac, *Les archives du trésor de Rennes-le-Château* (Nice: Bélisane, 1988), p. 566.
4. In the BBC *Timewatch* program "History of a Mystery," broadcast on September 17, 1996.
5. See www.priory-of-sion.com/psp/posd/regdoc.html for reproductions of the statutes.
6. See pages 314–18.
7. *Circuit,* no. 1, May 27, 1956.
8. Ibid.
9. Michael Baigent, Richard Leigh, and Henry Lincoln, *The Messianic Legacy* (London: Corgi, 1987), pp. 361–62 and 366–67.
10. See www.priory-of-sion.com/psp/gap/feb41.html.
11. Jarnac, *Les archives du trésor de Rennes-le-Château,* p. 542.
12. Baigent, Leigh, and Lincoln, *The Messianic Legacy,* pp. 362, 482–83.
13. Jean Markale, *The Church of Mary Magdalene* (Rochester, Vt.: Inner Traditions, 2004), p. 198.
14. Burke's Peerage website, www.burkes-peerage.com/authority.htm.
15. From a profile of Giscard d'Estaing in *The Sunday Times,* May 11, 2003.

16. Plantard's association with Monti was first referred to in an article by Anne-Léa Hisler in 1960 (*Circuit,* 2nd series, no. 8, March 1960). This issue is missing from the collection in the Bibliothèque Nationale, but Hisler's article is quoted in *Le Charivari,* no. 18, 1973. Plantard gave more details of the circumstances of his association with Monti in the 1989 series of *Vaincre.*
17. Gérard de Sède, *Rennes-le-Château* (Paris: Robert Laffont, 1988), pp. 225–34.
18. Osmont's account is reproduced in Jean Robin, *Rennes-le-Château* (Paris: Guy Trédaniel, 1982), pp. 151–52.
19. Quoted in Jean Cocteau, *Journal d'un inconnu* (Paris: Bernard Grasset, 1953), pp. 85–86.
20. John Laughland, *The Death of Politics* (London: Michael Joseph, 1994), p. 191.
21. Ibid., p. 189. On the "subversive Right" generally, see ibid., chapter 10.
22. See William L. Shirer, *The Collapse of the Third Republic* (London: William Heinemann/Secker & Warburg, 1970), pp. 195–201, for his description of the battle. Shirer was then working as a journalist in Paris.
23. Michael Gaudart de Soulages and Hubert Lamant include Blum in their list of people reputed to be Freemasons but whose names do not appear in any Masonic records. *Dictionnaire des francs-maçons français* (Paris: Jean-Claude Lattès, 1995), p. 923.
24. Quoted in Henry Coston, *Les technocrates et la Synarchie* (Paris: special ed. of *Lectures françaises,* February 1962), p. 10.
25. February 1941 police report (see www.priory-of-sion.com/psp/gap/feb41.html); *Vaincre,* no. 1, September 1942.
26. February 1941 police report; Jarnac, *Les archives du trésor de Rennes-le-Château,* pp. 524 and 542; Jean-Luc Chaumeil, interviewed in December 2003 for the Gazette de Rennes-le-Château website (www.gazette.portail-rennes-le-chateau.com/intchaumeil.htm).
27. Chaumeil, 2003 interview.
28. Jean Blum, *Rennes-le-Château* (Monaco: Éditions du Rocher, 1994), p. 209.
29. See Lynn Picknett, Clive Prince, and Stephen Prior with Robert Brydon, *Friendly Fire* (Edinburgh: Mainstream Publishing, 2004), pp. 184–86.
30. Ibid., pp. 185 and 192–93.

31. On Maurras's influence on de Gaulle, see Laughland, *The Death of Politics,* p. 33.
32. Ibid., p. 211. On the similarity of ideals between de Gaulle and Pétain, the latter's biographer Richard Griffiths writes: "Pétain and de Gaulle shared many ideas and attitudes . . . An innate conservatism, a mistrust of politicians and the workings of parliamentary democracy, a belief in the military virtues, a vision of the leadership the nation required; all these they had in common. Added to this, however, there are certain other personal attitudes which link them: the personal conviction that France would call on them in its hour of need, for example." *Marshal Pétain* (London: Constable, 1994), p. 348.
33. Emmanuel Faux, Thomas Legrand, and Gilles Perez, *La main droite de Dieu* (Paris: Éditions du Seuil, 1994), p. 239.
34. The letter is reproduced at www.priory-of-sion.com/psp/gap/petain.html.
35. See www.priory-of-sion.com/psp/gap/feb41.html.
36. Some have seen significance in the fact that Georges Monti's last address, where he died in 1936, was also in the Rue du Rocher, but in our view this is reading too much into it.
37. The customary declaration of Alpha Galates' formation does not appear in the *Journal Officiel* on or around December 1937. However, this does not necessarily mean that the society was not registered with the relevant local prefecture, as the onus is on the society's officials to inform the *Journal Officiel* of the registration.
38. *Vaincre,* no. 4, December 21, 1942.
39. John Hellman, *The Knight-Monks of Vichy France* (Liverpool, U.K.: Liverpool University Press/Montreal: McGill-Queen's University Press, 1997), p. 243.
40. Paul Smith, "Pierre Plantard Profile," www.priory-of-sion.com/psp/id60.html, undated.
41. Baigent, Leigh, and Lincoln, *The Messianic Legacy,* pp. 484–85.
42. Louis Le Fur, *Races, nationalities, états* (Paris: Librairie Félix Alcan, 1922), p. 27.
43. Gaudart de Soulages and Lamant, *Dictionnaire des francs-maçons français,* p. 816.
44. Ibid., p. 70.
45. Ibid. In 1944 Amadou—again through his mentor Ambelain—was received into two other orders, the Réau-Croix of the Elect Cohens

and the Cabalistic Order of the Rose-Cross (Ordre Kabbalistique de la Rose-Croix).

46. Letter from Philippe de Chérisey to Geoffrey Basil-Smith, July 7, 1983. Our thanks to Geoffrey Basil-Smith for supplying us with a copy.
47. Henry Coston, *Dictionnaire de la politique française* (Paris: Publications Henry Coston/Librairie Française, 1967, 1972, 1979, 1982), vol. 1, p. 695; Nath Imbert, ed., *Dictionnaire national des contemporains* (Paris: Lajeunesse, 1936), p. 435.
48. Imbert, p. 179.
49. Coston, *Dictionnaire de la politique française,* vol. 1, p. 305.
50. X. de T., "Le complot juif contre la paix," in Henry Coston, ed., *Je vous hais!* (Paris: Bureau Central de Presse, 1944), p. 129.
51. Henry Coston, "De Talmud aux Protocols: Le plan juif de domination ne date pas d'hier," in ibid., p. 14.
52. Henry Coston, "L'enjuivement de la France," in ibid., p. 5.
53. Coston, *Dictionnaire de la politique française,* vol. 1, pp. 577–79.
54. Coston, "L'enjuivement de la France," in *Je vous hais!,* p. 4.
55. *Vaincre,* no. 5, January 21, 1943.
56. Michael Balfour and Julian Frisby, *Helmuth von Moltke* (London: Macmillan, 1972), p. 61, referencing a letter written by Helmuth James von Moltke.
57. Ger van Roon, *German Resistance to Hitler* (London: Van Nostrand Reinhold Co., 1971), p. 211.
58. Baigent, Leigh, and Lincoln, *The Messianic Legacy,* pp. 396–97.
59. There is little biographical information available on Murat or the date on which he was supposedly made a Chevalier of the Légion d'honneur. Details of those awarded the Légion d'honneur who died before 1954 can be found on the website of the French Ministry of Culture (www.culture.gouv.fr/documentation/leonore/pres.htm); Murat's name does not appear in this database. Our inquiries to the Grand Chancellerie of the Légion d'honneur, which holds details of all members, produced a negative result.
60. Baigent, Leigh, and Lincoln, *The Messianic Legacy,* pp. 392 and 485.
61. See p. 90.
62. See Christian Plume and Xavier Pasquini, *Encyclopédie des sectes dans le monde* (Paris: Henri Veyrier, 1984), pp. 215–20; Gaudart de Soulages and Lamant, *Dictionnaire des francs-maçons français,* pp. 36–37.

63. See Baigent, Leigh, and Lincoln, *The Messianic Legacy*, p. 371.
64. Coston, *Dictionnaire de la politique française*, vol. 1, p. 390.
65. André Figueras, *Pétain c'était de Gaulle* (Paris: André Figueras, 1979), p. 180.
66. Count Helmuth James von Moltke, *A German of the Resistance* (London: Oxford University Press, 1947), p. 22.
67. As we have seen, Georges Monti allegedly founded the Alpha Galates Order in 1934, but if so, it was truly a secret society, as it was never registered under the 1901 law. The statutes reproduced in *Vaincre* in 1942 are dated 1937—when they were supposedly submitted to the authorities. However, in October 1942 the Germans in the Occupied zone asked the French police to investigate Plantard and the organization, because its request for registration had been *turned down.*
68. See www.priory-of-sion.com/psp/id163.html.
69. In *Circuit*, no. 8, March 1960.
70. Jarnac, *Les archives du trésor de Rennes-le-Château*, p. 544.
71. The circular purported to be a flyer for a forthcoming book about the Priory of Sion by Jean-Luc Chaumeil, with whom Plantard was embroiled in a dispute, thereby implying that he was responsible for the allegations. There is, however, no evidence that Chaumeil was the author of the document, something he has strenuously denied. "Criminal court" is *tribunal correctionnel,* the court that tries serious criminal cases.
72. Baigent, Leigh, and Lincoln, *The Messianic Legacy*, pp. 343–44.
73. Paul Smith, "Priory of Sion Debunked," www.priory-of-sion.com/posd/posdebunking.html, undated.
74. Laughland, *The Death of Politics*, p. 33.
75. Charles de Gaulle, *Memoirs of Hope* (London: Weidenfeld & Nicolson, 1971), p. 16.
76. Jean-Pierre Rioux, "De Gaulle in Waiting, 1946–1958," in Hugh Gough and John Horne, eds., *De Gaulle and Twentieth-Century France* (London and New York: Edward Arnold, 1994), p. 49.
77. Quoted in Bernard Pujo, *Juin, Maréchal de France* (Paris: Albin Michel, 1988), pp. 333–34.
78. De Gaulle, *Memoirs of Hope*, p. 18.
79. Michael Kettle, *De Gaulle and Algeria 1940–1960* (London: Quartet, 1994), p. 194.
80. Laughland, *The Death of Politics*, p. 26.
81. De Gaulle, *Memoirs of Hope*, pp. 16–17.

82. Ibid., p. 17.
83. Merry Bromberger and Serge Bromberger, *Les 13 complots du 13 mai, ou la délivrance du Gulliver* (Paris: Librairie Arthème Fayard, 1959), p. 7.
84. Ibid., p. 9.
85. Pierre Péan, *Le mystérieux Docteur Martin* (Paris: Fayard, 1993), p. 427.
86. Bromberger and Bromberger, *Les 13 complots du 13 mai,* pp. 250–51.
87. Baigent, Leigh, and Lincoln, *The Messianic Legacy,* p. 405.
88. *Le Monde,* May 18–19, 1958.
89. *Le Monde,* June 6, 1958.
90. *Le Monde,* June 8–9, 1958.
91. *Le Monde,* July 29, 1958.
92. De Gaulle, *Memoirs of Hope,* p. 28.
93. Marshall Juin's three-volume memoirs cover his life only to 1956, so his own account of his movements at the time of de Gaulle's return is absent from the record.
94. André Malraux, *Antimemoirs* (London: Hamish Hamilton, 1968), p. 98.
95. Jania Magillivray, "Cocteau fut le dernier grand-maître; qui lui a succedé? L'énigme du Prieuré de Sion," in *Bonne Soirée,* August 14, 1980.
96. Interviewed for the Rennes-le-Château, Le Dossier website in October 2003 (www.rennes-le-chateau.org/rlctoday/int-sandri.htm).
97. Baigent, Leigh, and Lincoln, *The Messianic Legacy,* p. 412.
98. The Cocteau statutes are reproduced on the Le Temple d'Arcadia website, www.ekamp.club.fr/arcadia/statuts.htm.
99. Jean Robin, *Rennes-le-Château,* p. 86.
100. Magillivray, "Cocteau fut le dernier grand-maître," quoting Lord Blackford. Although this article is attributed to Magillivray, certain parts, including the interview with Blackford, were added by an unknown author.
101. Some support for this scenario can be found in Article VI of the original 1956 statutes, which states: "Admissions are valid only if they are carried out legally by three members, and in a Province having a regular patent from the Council. All other claimed admissions to the Association are struck with illegality." This suggests that some people claiming to be members are regarded by *this* Priory as illegitimate. However, the explanation that the 1956 Priory was created as a cover for political agitation fits the facts much more snugly: the

second set of statutes may have been a retrospective muddying of the waters—or perhaps evidence of a later change of the *purpose* of the cover.

102. "Visits to Maurice Barrès," in Jean Cocteau, *A Call to Order* (London: Faber & Gwyer, 1926).
103. Arthur King Peters, *Jean Cocteau and His World* (London: Thames & Hudson, 1987), p. 62.
104. Patrick Mauriès, *Jean Cocteau* (London: Thames & Hudson, 1998), p. 15.
105. Jean Cocteau, *Le passé défini,* vol. 1, Pierre Chanel, ed. (Paris: Gallimard, 1983), p. 206.
106. Jean Cocteau, *Le passé défini,* vol. 2 (Paris: Gallimard, 1985), p. 267 (Journal entry for September 8, 1953).
107. Jean Cocteau, *Le passé défini,* vol. 3 (Paris: Gallimard, 1989), p. 272.
108. Pierre Chanel, Introduction to Cocteau, *Le passé défini,* vol. 1, p. 10.
109. E.g., see Cocteau, *Le passé défini,* vol. 3, pp. 272, 284–85.
110. Mauriès, *Jean Cocteau,* p. 12.
111. Peters, *Jean Cocteau and His World,* p. 196.
112. Lynn Picknett and Clive Prince, *The Templar Revelation* (New York: Touchstone, 1998), pp. 43–47.
113. Jean Cocteau, "Chaque nuit la Joconde en soi-même se change," in Marcel Brion, ed., *Léonard de Vinci* (Paris: Librairie Hachette, 1959), pp. 282–83.
114. Cocteau, *Le passé défini,* vol. 3, p. 153.
115. Cocteau, *Journal d'un inconnu,* p. 143.
116. The first mention of these names in connection with the Priory was in the journal *Nostra* in October 1982, in a review of R. P. Martin's book *Le livre des compagnons secrets* (1982), signed Bayard.
117. Anthony Clayton, *Three Marshals of France* (London: Brassey's, 1992), p. 165.
118. Ibid., p. 189. Juin was disappointed to be overlooked for a senior post in de Gaulle's new government, although he accepted a seat on the Supreme Council of National Defense. Like many others, Juin turned against de Gaulle when he realized that the President was pursuing independence for Algeria. In March 1962, Juin was even courted by the OAS, but although he refused their advances, his letter to their leader, General Raoul Salan—in which he expressed sympathy for their cause but not their methods—was selectively edited

as propaganda by the OAS. The effect of this apparent treachery was dramatic: de Gaulle sentenced Juin to thirty days' house arrest, withdrawing his allowances and privileges. Despite this Juin still refused to lead, or even support, an anti-Gaullist movement. He was finally reconciled with de Gaulle when the President visited him in hospital during his final illness in December 1963. Juin was buried with full military honors on January 27, 1967.

119. William Righter, *The Rhetorical Hero* (London: Routledge and Kegan Paul, 1964), p. 2.
120. James Robert Hewitt, *André Malraux* (New York: Frederick Ungar Publishing, 1978), p. 115.
121. Righter, *The Rhetorical Hero,* p. 2.
122. Janine Mossuz, *Andre Malraux et le gaullisme* (Paris: Armand Colin, 1970), pp. 25–26.
123. See Guy Penaud, *André Malraux et le Résistance* (Périgneux: Pierre Fanlac, 1986), chapter 2.
124. Ibid., p. 62, from Penaud's interview with Ravanel in 1985. (Ravanel actually said MI5, but this is probably the result of a common confusion between the two British agencies—MI5 operates only in the United Kingdom.)
125. Malraux, *Antimemoirs,* p. 15.
126. See Hewitt, pp. 79–80.
127. Malraux, *Antimemoirs,* p. 8.
128. Mossuz, p. 162.
129. Quoted in Curtis Cate, *André Malraux* (London: Hutchinson, 1995), p. 406.
130. Mossuz, p. 213.
131. Righter, p. 30.
132. Ibid., p. 77.
133. François Gerber, *Malraux–de Gaulle: La nation retrouvée* (Paris: L'Harmattan, 1996), p. 123.
134. Herman Lebovics, *Mona Lisa's Escort* (Ithaca, N.Y., and London: Cornell University Press, 1999), p. xi.
135. Ibid., p. ix.
136. Quoted in Cate, *André Malraux,* p. 377.
137. Baigent, Leigh, and Lincoln, *The Messianic Legacy,* p. 312.
138. Ibid., pp. 480–81.

3. A TALE OF TWO TREASURES

1. Interviewed for the Octonovo website in August 2001 (www.octonovo.org/RlC/Fr/itw/itwaca.htm).
2. Jean Robin, *Rennes-le-Château* (Paris: Guy Trédaniel, 1982), p. 100.
3. Jean-Luc Chaumeil, *Le trésor du triangle d'or* (Nice: Alain Lefeuvre, 1979), p. 70, citing a letter written to him by Plantard in 1974.
4. René Descadeillas, *Mythologie du trésor de Rennes* (Carcassonne: J. M. Savary, 1988), p. 76.
5. Jean Markale, *The Templar Treasure at Gisors* (Rochester, Vt.: Inner Traditions, 2003), p. 28.
6. Gérard de Sède, *Les templiers sont parmi nous* (Paris: René Julliard, 1962), p. 16.
7. Michel Lamy, *Les templiers* (Bordeaux: Aubéron, 1994), pp. 304–6.
8. Quoted in Markale, *The Templar Treasure at Gisors,* p. 49.
9. Ibid., pp. 50–52.
10. E.g., Chaumeil, *Le trésor du triangle d'or,* p. 19.
11. Quoted in de Sède, *Les templiers sont parmi nous,* p. 26. Allegedly, Lhomoy subsequently confessed that he had invented the part about the coffers. However, this was not reported until after his death and was based, as Jean Markale points out (*The Templar Treasure at Gisors,* p. 60), on secondhand testimony, although it was gleefully picked up by Plantard's critics.
12. Markale, *The Templar Treasure at Gisors,* pp. 57–58.
13. Alain Lameyre, *Guide de la France templière* (Paris: Tchou, 1975), p. 232.
14. Markale, *The Templar Treasure at Gisors,* p. 62.
15. Ibid., p. 61.
16. Ibid., p. 19.
17. Quoted in Chaumeil, *Le trésor du triangle d'or,* p. 36.
18. De Sède, *Les templiers sont parmi nous,* pp. 40–42.
19. Markale, *The Templar Treasure at Gisors,* pp. 34–35.
20. Ibid., pp. 63–64.
21. Chaumeil, *Le trésor du triangle d'or,* p. 24.
22. Ibid., p. 25.
23. Quoted in Lameyre, *Guide de la france templière,* p. 235.
24. Quoted in ibid.
25. Ibid., p. 236.
26. Quoted in ibid., p. 239.

27. De Sède, *Les templiers sont parmi nous,* p. 284.
28. Ibid., p. 175.
29. Ibid., pp. 276–77. Dreux may have been chosen because it was the burial place of Louis-Philippe, the last king of France—1830–1848—who was interred in the family vault there in 1860, after a decade of exile in Surrey.
30. Ibid., p. 276.
31. Markale, *The Templar Treasure at Gisors,* pp. 39–41.
32. De Sède, *Les templiers sont parmi nous,* p. 284.
33. Leopold Sanchez, "Rennes-le-Château—vrai ou faux?," *Le Figaro,* July 7, 2001.
34. Quoted in ibid.
35. See Jean Markale, *The Church of Mary Magdalene* (Rochester, Vt.: Inner Traditions, 2004), pp. 74–75. Alet-les-Bains and Quillan are also candidates.
36. Markale (*The Church of Mary Magdalene,* p. 75) believes the John the Baptist church is the one that exists today, having been rededicated to the Magdalene.
37. Abbé Henri Boudet, *La vraie langue celtique et la Cromleck de Rennes-les-Bains* (Paris: Pierre Belfond, 1978), p. 58.
38. Ibid., pp. 228–29.
39. Markale, *The Church of Mary Magdalene,* p. 160.
40. Ibid., p. 27.
41. Claire Corbu and Antoine Captier, *L'Héritage de l'Abbé Saunière* (Cazilhac: Belisane, 1995), pp. 72 and 233.
42. In 1830 Charles X, rather than be forced to become a constitutional monarch, abdicated in favor of his grandson the Comte de Chambord. However, the Chamber of Deputies declared Louis-Philippe, the Duc d'Orléans—from another branch of the family—King. Louis-Philippe, who called himself "King of the French" rather than "King of France," and who repudiated the principle of divine right, was the more acceptable face of monarchy in post-Revolutionary France. This precipitated a split between the legitimists, who supported Chambord, and the Orléanists, who accepted Louis-Philippe; the division rumbles on today.

    Louis-Philippe reigned until 1848, when a new empire was proclaimed under Napoleon III, which lasted until 1870. A compromise was then proposed by which the childless Chambord, as Henri V, would reign as a constitutional monarch, and on his death the throne would pass to Louis-Philippe's grandson the Comte de Paris. (However, at the last minute Chambord refused even this, as he insisted that he would not reign under the republican Tricolore. This led to the formation of the Third Republic, with a figurehead president substituted for the King.) For this reason, when Chambord died in 1883, both monarchist streams accepted the Comte de Paris as the heir to the throne. Although a minority continued—and continue—to support the nearest legitimist successor (the succession is now with the Spanish branch of the Bourbon family), this did not include the monarchists, in whose support Saunière spoke out in 1885.

43. Descadeillas, *Mythologie du trésor de Rennes,* p. 43.
44. Markale, *The Church of Mary Magdalene,* pp. 179–80; Michael Baigent, Richard Leigh, and Henry Lincoln, *The Holy Blood and the Holy Grail* (London: Arrow, 1996), p. 481.
45. Baigent, Leigh, and Lincoln, *The Holy Blood and the Holy Grail,* p. 481, citing an 1851 source.
46. Descadeillas, *Mythologie du trésor de Rennes,* p. 48. For other parallels between the Sion-Vaudémont and Rennes-le-Château affairs, see Jean Robin, *Rennes-le-Château,* pp. 81–84.
47. The most valuable sources in this respect are Claire Corbu and Antoine Captier (based on Saunière's papers and Claire Corbu's memories of the village in the 1940s and '50s) and René Descadeillas, who had the advantage of interviewing villagers alive in the late 1950s who had known Saunière.
48. Corbu and Captier, *L'héritage de l'Abbé Saunière,* pp. 74–76.
49. See Robin, *Rennes-le-Château,* p. 144; Markale, *The Church of Mary Magdalene,* p. 38; Descadeillas, *Mythologie du trésor de Rennes,* p. 132.
50. Descadeillas, *Mythologie du trésor de Rennes,* p. 17.
51. See ibid., p. 134; Markale, *The Church of Mary Magdalene,* p. 44.
52. Corbu and Captier, *L'héritage de l'Abbé Saunière,* p. 74.
53. Descadeillas, *Mythologie du trésor de Rennes,* p. 19.
54. Ibid., p. 56.
55. Corbu and Captier, *L'héritage de l'Abbé Saunière,* pp. 75–76.
56. Jean Blum, *Rennes-le-Château* (Monaco: Éditions du Rocher, 1994), p. 84.
57. Corbu and Captier, *L'héritage de l'Abbé Saunière,* p. 95. The original French is *"Lettre de Granès. Découverte d'un tombeau. Le soir pluie."*

58. Ibid.
59. Bill Putnam and John Edwin Wood, *The Treasure of Rennes-le-Château* (Stroud, U.K.: Sutton Publishing, 2004), p. 163.
60. See Corbu and Captier, *L'héritage de l'Abbé Saunière*, pp. 269–72.
61. Ibid., pp. 78–79.
62. In rendering her name as "Marie de Nègre" we are following the convention used by Rennes researchers, rather than academic historians. Properly, her branch of the family used the spelling "Négri"—other branches used the variations "Nègre" and "Negré." In any case, the strictly correct short form of her name should be "Marie d'Ablès."
63. René Descadeillas, *Rennes et ses derniers seigneurs* (Toulouse: Édouard Privat, 1964), p. 64.
64. Putnam and Wood, *The Treasure of Rennes-le-Château*, pp. 59–62.
65. Markale, *The Church of Mary Magdalene*, pp. 93 and 97.
66. Ibid.
67. Ibid., p. 176.
68. Corbu and Captier, *L'héritage de l'Abbé Saunière*, pp. 85–86.
69. André Douzet, *Saunière's Model and the Secret of Rennes-le-Chateau* (Kempton/Enkhuizen: L'Adventures Unlimited Press/Frontier Publishing, 2001), pp. 67–80. Douzet argues that Saunière used Lyons as a base for visits to the nearby Le Pilat region, citing the similarity between a tableau of the Magdalene in a chapel there and the one Saunière had painted on his altar. However, the similarity is very much a matter of opinion.
70. Corbu and Captier, *L'héritage de l'Abbé Saunière*, pp. 84–85.
71. See Blum, *Rennes-le-Château*, p. 197.
72. Quoted in Markale, *The Church of Mary Magdalene*, p. 107.
73. Putnam and Wood, *The Treasure of Rennes-le-Château*, p. 89 and plate 14; Markale, *The Church of Mary Magdalene*, p. 41.
74. Markale, *The Church of Mary Magdalene*, p. 254, citing Courtaly's own testimony.
75. Ibid, p. 188.
76. J. Rivière, G. Tappa, and C. Boumendil, *Le fabuleux trésor de Rennes-le-Château!* (Cazilhac: Bélisane, 1996), pp. 17–20 and 37.
77. Descadeillas, *Mythologie du trésor de Rennes*, p. 28.
78. Markale, *The Church of Mary Magdalene*, pp. 150–51; Michel Gaudart de Soulages and Hubert Lamant, *Dictionnaire des francs-maçons français* (Paris: Jean-Claude Lattès, 1995), p. 351.

79. Corbu and Captier, *L'héritage de l'Abbé Saunière,* p. 151.
80. Ibid., p. 73.
81. Franck Marie, *Rennes-le-Château* (Bagneux: SRES, 1978), p. 20.
82. Jean Contrucci, *Emma Calvé, la diva du siècle* (Paris: Albin Michel, 1989), p. 130.
83. Ibid., p. 131.
84. Ibid., p. 216.
85. Ibid., pp. 130–31.
86. Ibid., p. 133.
87. Ibid.
88. Edward Lockspeiser, *Debussy,* vol. I, p. 109. On Debussy's esoteric interests and involvements, see Léon Guichard, "Debussy and the Occultists," Appendix E to Lockspeiser.
89. Contrucci, *Emma Calvé, la diva du siècle,* p. 311.
90. Emma Calvé, *My Life* (New York/London: D. Appleton & Co., 1922), p. 155.
91. Contrucci, *Emma Calvé, la diva du siècle,* p. 209, citing Pierre Borel, *Trésor des recherches et antiquités gauloises et françaises* (1655).
92. Emma Calvé, *Sous tous les ciels, j'ai chanté . . .* (Paris: Librairie Plon, 1940), p. 157.
93. Descadeillas, *Mythologie du trésor de Rennes,* p. 27.
94. Contrucci, *Emma Calvé, la diva du siècle,* p. 156.
95. Quoted in Corbu and Captier, *L'héritage de l'Abbé Saunière,* p. 20.
96. Ibid., p. 23.
97. Descadeillas, *Mythologie du trésor de Rennes,* p. 31.
98. Ibid., p. 32.
99. Quoted in Corbu and Captier, *L'héritage de l'Abbé Saunière,* p. 165.
100. Quoted in ibid., pp. 216–17.
101. Quoted in ibid., p. 253.
102. Ibid., p. 59.
103. Ibid.
104. Ibid., p. 254.
105. Ibid., p. 16.
106. See ibid., pp. 4–6.
107. Corbu and Captier, *L'héritage de l'Abbé Saunière,* p. 12.
108. Descadeillas, *Mythologie du trésor de Rennes,* pp. 56–57.
109. Jean-Luc Chaumeil, *Le trésor du triangle d'or* (Nice: Alain Lefeuvre, 1979), pp. 125–26.

110. Corbu and Captier, *L'héritage de l'Abbé Saunière*, p. 43.
111. De Sède, *Rennes-le-Château*, pp. 46–47.
112. From the France en Inflation website (www.lycos.fr/consommation/livre.php), which includes a useful calculator for relative values since 1901. Even the skeptics Bill Putnam and John Edwin Wood calculated a *minimum* of 1.5 million pounds (*The Treasure of Rennes-le-Château*, p. 25). Finally, the Rennes researcher and our friend Nigel Foster worked it out by estimating the modern costs of buying the land, materials, and labor, also arriving at a sum of between 1.5 and 2 million pounds.
113. Blanche of Castile was the mother of Louis IX; she ruled France when he was away on the Crusades and, incidentally, also ordered the attack on the Cathars' last stronghold at the citadel of Montségur.
114. Markale, *The Church of Mary Magdalene*, p. 237.
115. See Fernand Niel, *Les Cathares de Montségur* (Paris: Seghers, 1978), pp. 291–94.
116. Markale, *The Church of Mary Magdalene*, pp. 87–88. The Aniorts began the Crusade on the side of the heretics, and as a result Rennes-le-Château was given to one of the Crusade leaders, from the Voisins family. However, Pierre III de Voisins was careful to legitimize his claim by marrying Ramon d'Aniort's cousin Jordane (see ibid., pp. 89–93).
117. A hypothesis advanced most recently in Graham Phillips's *The Templars and the Ark of the Covenant* (Rochester, Vt.: Bear & Co., 2004).
118. Corbu and Captier, *L'héritage de l'Abbé Saunière*, p. 279; Andrew Collins, *Twenty-first Century Grail* (London: Virgin, 2004), pp. 54–55.
119. Blum, *Rennes-le-Château*, p. 43.
120. Ibid., pp. 62–63.
121. Descadeillas, *Mythologie du trésor de Rennes*, p. 29.
122. See Markale, *The Church of Mary Magdalene*, pp. 181–87.
123. Cassiel, *The Encyclopedia of Forbidden Knowledge* (London: Hamlyn, 1990), p. 12.
124. Rivière, Tappa, and Boumendil, *Le fabuleux trésor de Rennes-le-Château!*, p. 67.
125. Markale, *The Church of Mary Magdalene*, p. 180.
126. Descadeillas, *Mythologie du trésor de Rennes*, p. 47.
127. Quoted in Marie, *Rennes-le-Château*, p. 24.

128. Descadeillas, *Mythologie du trésor de Rennes,* p. 49.
129. Robin, *Rennes-le-Château,* p. 138.
130. Ibid., pp. 141–42.
131. Quoted in Corbu and Captier, *L'héritage de l'Abbé Saunière,* p. 257. The original French reads: "*As-tu des nouvelles de St. Jean? Moi, je ne sais rien depuis quelques temps. Après la mort de l'Abbé Bastide je voulais l'rettirer* [*sic*] *à Bonbania, mais il a refusé, me disant qu'il se contentait de St. Jean un des Consolations que lui donnais celle paroisse.*"
132. Quoted in ibid., p. 279: "*Maintenant, ma chère amie, puisque tu ne veux pas recevoir chez toi pour faire la besogne que tu sais Mr de St Jean, tu voudrais que je vienne.*"
133. Octonovo website interview (www.octonovo.org/RlC/Fr/itw/itwaca.htm).
134. Pierre Jarnac, *Les archives du trésor de Rennes-le-Château* (Nice: Bélisane, 1988), pp. 511–15. See also www.octonovo/RlC/Fr/bio/bioEdiv.htm.
135. After the Revolution the seat of the diocese moved to Carcassonne.
136. There is no doubt about this story: it appeared in a book by René Descadeillas—as we have seen, the leading academic debunker of the Saunière mystery—on the "straight" history of Rennes-le-Château, *Rennes and Its Last Lords* (*Rennes et ses derniers seigneurs*) pp. 7–8.
137. Ibid., p. 74.
138. Markale, *The Church of Mary Magdalene,* p. 94.
139. De Sède, *Rennes-le-Château,* p. 207, citing works by Gaston Martin and Jean-Claude Danis.
140. Ibid., pp. 207–8.
141. De Sède, *Rennes-le-Château,* p. 194.
142. A. E. Waite, *A New Encyclopaedia of Freemasonry (Ars Magna Latomorum) and of Cognate Instituted Mysteries* (London: William Rider & Son, 1923), vol. 2, p. 450.
143. Gaudart de Soulages and Lamant, *Dictionnaire des francs-maçons français,* p. 52. The grades are Apprentice, Companion, Master, Scottish Master of St. Andrew, Novice Squire, and Knight Beneficent of the Holy City.
144. Ibid., p. 48.
145. Ibid., pp. 48–49.

146. De Sède, *Rennes-le-Château,* p. 194.
147. Chaumeil, *Le trésor du triangle d'or,* p. 136.
148. Gaudart de Soulages and Lamant, *Dictionnaire des francs-maçons français,* p. 57.
149. One Rite of Memphis lodge was called the Philadelphes.
150. See pp. 323–25.
151. Jean-Pierre Monteils, *Sectes et sociétés secrètes* (Nîmes: C. Lacour, 1999), p. 128.
152. Quoted in de Sède, *Rennes-le-Château,* p. 206.
153. Jean-Luc Robin, *Rennes-le-Château* (Bordeaux: Sud Ouest, 2005), pp. 29–30. Originally from Brittany, the Chefdebiens settled in Narbonne in the eighteenth century.
154. De Sède, *Rennes-le-Château,* p. 218.
155. Contrucci, *Emma Calvé, la diva du siècle,* p. 218.
156. Arthur Edward Waite, *Saint-Martin the French Mystic and the Story of Modern Martinism* (London: William Rider & Son, 1922), p. 73.
157. Gaudart de Soulages and Lamant, *Dictionnaire des francs-maçons français,* p. 805.
158. Website of the Departmental Archives of the Haute-Garonne (www.archives.cg31.fr/Section_04/InventairesPDF/63J.pdf).
159. Markale, *The Church of Mary Magdalene,* pp. 148 and 252.
160. De Sède, *Rennes-le-Château,* pp. 193–94; Michel Lamy, *Jules Verne, initié et initiateur* (Paris: Pavot, 1984), p. 113. Antoine Captier's researchers have also linked Saunière with the Rectified Scottish Rite—see Lynn Picknett and Clive Prince, *The Templar Revelation* (New York: Touchstone, 1998), pp. 205–6.
161. Jarnac, *Les archives du trésor de Rennes-le-Château,* pp. 550–51.

4. "HIDDEN GOLD, HIDDEN BLOOD"

1. The complete Dossiers Secrets have been published by Pierre Jarnac as *Les mystères de Rennes-le-Château: Mélanges sulfureux,* 3 vols. (Couiza: Centre d'Études et des Recherches Templières, 1994–95).
2. Quoted in Pierre Jarnac, *Les archives du trésor de Rennes-le-Château* (Nice: Bélisane, 1988), p. 553.
3. Reproduced in ibid., p. 303.
4. Gérard de Sède, *Rennes-le-Château* (Paris: Robert Laffoont, 1988), p. 111.

5. Ibid., p. 123.
6. Ibid., p. 133.
7. Jean-Luc Chaumeil, August 2001 interview, at www.rennes-le-chateau.org/rlctoday/int-jlchaumeil.htm.
8. René Descadeillas, *Mythologie du trésor de Rennes* (Carcassonne: J. M. Savary, 1988), p. 83.
9. De Sède, *Rennes-le-Château,* p. 257.
10. Jean Markale, *The Church of Mary Magdalene* (Rochester, Vt.: Inner Traditions, 2004), p. 220.
11. Gino Sandri, October 2003 interview, at www.rennes-le-chateau.org/rlctoday/int-sandri.htm.
12. Reproduced in Jarnac, *Les mystères de Rennes-le-Château,* vol. 3, pp. 24–35.
13. Michael Baigent, Richard Leigh, and Henry Lincoln, *The Holy Blood and the Holy Grail* (London: Arrow, 1996), pp. 287–89.
14. S. Roux, "The Rennes-le-Château Affair: A Reply to Monsieur Lionel Burrus"—see pp. 204–207 in this book.
15. John C. Andressohn, *The Ancestry and Life of Godfrey of Bouillon* (Bloomington: Indiana University Publications, 1947), p. 5.
16. Quoted in Ian Wood, *The Merovingian Kingdoms 450–751* (London and New York: Longman, 1994), p. 235. Stephanus's *Life of St. Wilfrid,* concerning the Bishop of York who brought Dagobert back from exile, is about the only source on Dagobert's life, and even that was written a century and a half later.
17. This is according to Lobineau. Other sources have him aged seven.
18. De Sède, *Rennes-le-Château,* p. 137.
19. See Jarnac, *Les mystères de Rennes-le-Château,* vol. 2, pp. 3–19. In the meantime, a work not strictly classed as one of the Dossiers Secrets was deposited in the Bibliothèque Nationale in February 1965. This was Anne-Léa Hisler's *The Kings and Rulers of France: The Great Dynasties from the Beginning* (*Rois et gouvernants de la France: Les grandes dynasties depuis l'origine*). There is evidence that it was circulating as early as 1958, and in January 1960 it appeared under the byline of Louis Saurel in the periodical *Les Cahiers de l'Histoire* (with Hisler credited merely as the researcher). To add to the confusion, it was very similar to a 1906 work by Alfred Franklin, *The Kings and Rulers of France from Hugues Capet to 1906.* It has little connection with the unfolding story, though a second version appeared in 1969 with a new chapter on the Merovingians.

20. We have rendered *"gardent la clef"* as "have the key" rather than "hold the key" (as in the most widely used translation, that of Henry Lincoln), as this would be the more usual reading—and the latter has sent some researchers off looking for paintings that show somebody literally holding a key. *J'achève* is literally "I complete," but this is a common French euphemism for "kill"; "finish off" has a similar double meaning in English.
21. There are claims that the existence of the second stone—the slab—is at least partly confirmed in the works of the local engineer and amateur archaeologist Ernest Cros (1857–1946), not to be confused with the Abbé Cros who was Vicar-General of the diocese and Saunière's close friend. Ernest Cros, who knew Saunière, purportedly recorded some at least of the *Reddis Regis* part of the inscription. However, the description is based on what is alleged to be a typewritten transcription of Cros's handwritten notes, which are said to have disappeared. The preamble about Cros's life makes some elementary mistakes, so all in all it seems that this "evidence" is a later fabrication and that the second stone never existed. However, Franck Marie in *Rennes-le-Château* (Bagneux: SRES, 1978; p. 30) citing Abbé Mazières's private archives, has found evidence of Cros's adherence to the "Johannite ideology" (and membership in a Grand Orient Masonic lodge). Tantalizingly, that is all.
22. This is where the idea, referred to in the last chapter, of Marie Dénarnaud burning banknotes in 1945 came from. According to Blancasall, they were the 8 million francs gathered by Saunière in his last days, which had to be handed in during the post-Liberation issue of new currency. Rather than exchange them—and have to explain their provenance—she preferred to destroy them. There is no evidence outside the Dossiers Secrets for this act, which seems to be based on accounts of her burning *papers* after Saunière's death.
23. See, for example, Markale, *The Church of Mary Magdalene,* p. 87.
24. Descadeillas, *Mythologie du trésor de Rennes,* pp. 83–84.
25. Quoted in Ean Begg, *The Cult of the Black Virgin* (London: Arkana, 1985), p. 14.
26. Jean Contrucci, *Emma Calvé, la diva du siècle* (Paris: Albin Michel, 1989), p. 152.
27. Jean Robin, *Rennes-le-Château* (Paris: Guy Trédaniel, 1982), p. 151.
28. Charles de Gaulle, *Memoirs of Hope* (London: Weidenfeld & Nicolson, 1971), pp. 3–4.

29. Burgundy and Neustria being the possessions of one of his cousins.
30. Baigent, Leigh, and Lincoln, *The Holy Blood and the Holy Grail*, p. 265.
31. See Descadeillas, *Mythologie du trésor de Rennes*, pp. 77–78.
32. The French author Richard Bordes has devoted a book, *The Merovingians at Rennes-le-Château* (*Les mérovingiens à Rennes-le-Château*) (Rennes-le-Château: P. Schrauben, 1984), to the historical errors and implausibilities in the Dossiers Secrets' version of French history.
33. De Sède, *Rennes-le-Château*, p. 137, citing the work of the Carcassonne historian Louis Fédié.
34. Markale, *The Church of Mary Magdalene*, p. 80.
35. Andressohn, *The Ancestry and Life of Godfrey of Bouillon*, p. 9. Genealogies showing these lines of descent are on pp. 10 (maternal) and 19 (paternal).
36. Incidentally, the Comte du Boulogne was married to the daughter of King Malcolm of Scotland.
37. Jonathan Riley-Smith, *The Crusades* (London: The Athlone Press, 1987), p. 21.
38. Ibid., p. 21.
39. Andressohn, *The Ancestry and Life of Godfrey of Bouillon*, p. 52; John France, *Victory in the East: A Military History of the First Crusade* (Cambridge: Cambridge University Press, 1994), p. 85.
40. Andressohn, *The Ancestry and Life of Godfrey of Bouillon*, p. 105.
41. Later Dossiers say 1099.
42. Quoted in Robin, *Rennes-le-Château*, p. 123.
43. Simone de Beauvoir, *The Prime of Life* (Harmondsworth, U.K.: Penguin, 1965), p. 188.
44. Claudine Monteil, *Les amants de la liberté* (Paris: Éditions 1, 1999), p. 100.
45. Ibid., pp. 111–12.
46. See Jarnac, *Les mystères de Rennes-le-Château*, vol. 1, pp. 20–27.
47. Descadeillas, *Mythologie du trésor de Rennes*, pp. 75–76.
48. See Jarnac, *Les archives du trésor de Rennes-le-Château*, pp. 331–59; Descadeillas, *Mythologie du trésor de Rennes*, pp. 74–75.
49. Reproduced in Jarnac, *Les mystères de Rennes-le-Château*, vol. 1, pp. 17–19.
50. Descadeillas, *Mythologie du trésor de Rennes*, pp. 80–81.

51. The English-language edition appeared in 1964. Several other German and French editions were published from 1911 on.
52. *The Secret Files of Henri Lobineau;* see pp. 215–23.
53. Robin, *Rennes-le-Château,* pp. 119–22.
54. Jarnac, *Les archives du trésor de Rennes,* pp. 528–29.
55. Jean Blum, *Rennes-le-Chateau* (Monaco: Éditions du Rocher, 1994), p. 46.
56. Robin, *Rennes-le-Château,* pp. 32–33.
57. Ibid., p. 122; de Sède, *Rennes-le-Château,* p. 135, citing the testimony of the last Comte de Lénoncourt's niece.
58. Sandri, October 2003 interview.
59. Jarnac, *Les archives du trésor de Rennes-le-Château,* p. 24; Marie, *Rennes-le-Château,* pp. 200–201.
60. Reproduced in Jarnac, *Les mystères de Rennes-le-Château,* vol. 3, pp. 3–9.
61. Marie, *Rennes-le-Château,* p. 193.
62. Contrucci, *Emma Calvé, la diva du Siècle,* p. 133.
63. Work began in 1646, but it took over 130 years to finish it.
64. See Raoul Allier's *La cabale des dévots* (Paris: Armand Colin, 1902) and Abbé Alphonse Auguste's 1913 study of the company in Toulouse—one of the first places to which it expanded from Paris.
65. Abbé Alphonse Auguste, *La Compagnie du Saint-Sacrement à Toulouse* (Paris: A. Picard et Fils and Toulouse: Éduoard Privat, 1913), pp. 2–3.
66. Alain Tallon, *La Compagnie du Saint-Sacrement (1629–1667)* (Paris: Éditions du Cerf, 1990), p. 46.
67. Baigent, Leigh, and Lincoln, *The Holy Blood and the Holy Grail,* pp. 178–83.
68. Tallon, *La Compagnie du Saint-Sacrement,* p. 12.
69. On Notre-Dame de Marceille, see Lynn Picknett and Clive Prince, *The Templar Revelation* (New York: Touchstone, 1998), pp. 196–99.
70. The paintings are *Jacob Wrestling with the Angel, Heliodorus Chased from the Temple by the Angels,* and *The Archangel Michael Who Cast Down Lucifer.*
71. Jean Cocteau, *The Journals of Jean Cocteau,* Wallace Fowlie, ed. (London: Museum Press, 1957), p. 40.
72. Maurice Barrès, *Le mystère en plein lumière* (Paris: Librairie Plon, 1926), p. 93.

73. Reproduced in Jarnac, *Les mystères de Rennes-le-Château,* vol. 3, pp. 11–23. The identification of Lobineau as Schidlof is reaffirmed here—the later additional mystification of the alternative name of the Comte de Lénoncourt had yet to appear.
74. René Grousset, *Histoire des Croisades et du royaume franc de Jérusalem* (Paris: Librairie Plon, 1934–36), vol. 3, p. xiv.
75. Raymond Oursel, ed., *Le procès des templiers* (Paris: Denoël, 1955), p. 208; Baigent, Leigh, and Lincoln, *The Holy Blood and the Holy Grail,* p. 128.
76. Edward Burman, *Supremely Abominable Crimes* (London: Alison & Busby, 1994), pp. 226–28.
77. Baigent, Leigh, and Lincoln, *The Holy Blood and the Holy Grail,* pp. 467–68.
78. Gérard de Sède with Sophie de Sède, *Le trésor maudit de Rennes-le-Château* (Paris: J'ai Lu, 1968), p. 112.
79. For completeness, we should mention another, related work that appeared in October 1967: Nicolas Beaucéan's *In the Land of the White Queen.* This five-page booklet was published by Philippe de Chérisey (leaving very little doubt that he was the real author). (A year later it was republished, with a little extra material, as *Treasure in the Land of the White Queen,* this time attributed to Anne-Léa Hisler!) It is mainly concerned with Rennes-les-Bains and Boudet's book.
80. Sandri, October 2003 interview.
81. Paul Smith, "Pierre Plantard Profile," www.priory-of-sion.com/psp/id84.html, undated.
82. Chaumeil, August 2001 interview.
83. De Sède with de Sède, *Le trésor maudit de Rennes-le-Château,* pp. 19–20.
84. Ibid., p. 96.
85. Ibid., p. 107.
86. De Sède, *Rennes-le-Château,* p. 187.
87. Christopher Dawes, *Rat Scabies and the Holy Grail* (London: Sceptre, 2005), pp. 221–23.
88. De Sède with de Sède, *Le trésor maudit de Rennes-le-Château,* p. 110.
89. Descadeillas, *Mythologie du trésor de Rennes,* pp. 70–72.
90. Bill Putnam and John Edwin Wood, *The Treasure of Rennes-le-Château* (Stroud: Sutton Publishing, 2004), Appendix A.
91. Quoted in Robin, *Rennes-le-Château,* p. 100.

92. Jean-Loup Passek, ed., *Dictionnaire du cinéma français* (Paris: Librairie Larousse, 1987), p. 45.
93. The other Goons were the outrageous Spike Milligan, the Welsh singer and actor Harry Secombe, and originally, the former intelligence officer and later parapsychologist Michael Bentine.
94. Quoted in Jean-Luc Chaumeil, *Le trésor du triangle d'or* (Nice: Alain Lefeuvre, 1979), p. 80.
95. Ibid., p. 151.
96. Henry Lincoln, *The Holy Place* (London: Corgi, 1992), Appendix 1.
97. Markale, *The Church of Mary Magdalene,* p. 172.
98. Michel Lamy, *Jules Verne, initié et initiateur* (Paris: Payot, 1984), p. 95.
99. Ibid.
100. Jarnac, *Les archives du trésor de Rennes-le-Château,* p. 200.
101. Or, as all good Forteans would call them, "lexilinks."
102. Gaudart de Soulages and Lamant, *Dictionnaire des francs-maçons français,* p. 887.
103. See Chaumeil, *Le trésor du triangle d'or,* pp. 130–31; Markale, *The Church of Mary Magdalene,* pp. 227–28.
104. E.g., Markale, *The Church of Mary Magdalene,* pp. 279–80.
105. Maurice Barrès, *Le mystère en pleine lumière* (Paris: Librairie Plon, 1926), p. 34.
106. Ibid., p. 246.
107. Quoted in Markale, *The Church of Mary Magdalene,* p. 280.
108. Quoted in Jean Robin, *Le royaume du Graal* (Paris: Guy Trédaniel, 1992), p. 107.
109. The tomb is actually nearer Serres than Arques.
110. It was actually "discovered" by Gérard de Sède on a field trip to the area in 1972 and first appeared in print in an article written by de Sède (with Jean Pellet) in the July–August 1972 edition of the magazine *Le Grand-Albert.*

5. THE BLOODLINE MYTH

1. In 1968 de Chérisey did produce a 130-page novella entitled *Circuit,* which used many of the themes relating to Rennes-le-Château and the mythology outlined in the Dossiers Secrets—but although a copy was placed in the Bibliothèque Nationale, it was never published.

2. Michael Baigent, Richard Leigh, and Henry Lincoln, *The Holy Blood and the Holy Grail* (London: Arrow, 1996), p. xvii.
3. Ibid., pp. 37–38.
4. Euloge Boissonnade, *Jamais deux sans trois?* (Paris: France-Empire, 1986), p. 17.
5. Alain Poher, *Trois fois président* (Paris: Plon, 1993), p. 64.
6. Michael Baigent, Richard Leigh, and Henry Lincoln, *The Messianic Legacy* (London: Corgi, 1987), p. 394.
7. Quoted in Jean Robin, *Rennes-le-Château* (Paris: Guy Trédaniel, 1982), p. 90.
8. Baigent, Leigh, and Lincoln, *The Holy Blood and the Holy Grail,* pp. 532–33.
9. Pierre Jarnac, *Les archives du trésor de Rennes-le-Château* (Nice: Bélisane, 1988), p. 542.
10. Jean-Luc Chaumeil, December 2003 interview, at www.gazette.portail-rennes-le-chateau.com/intchaumeil.htm
11. Quoted in Jean-Luc Chaumeil, *Le trésor du triangle d'or* (Nice: Alain Lefeuvre, 1979), p. 172.
12. Chaumeil, December 2003 interview.
13. Quoted in Jean Robin, *Rennes-le-château,* p. 89.
14. Chaumeil, *Le trésor du triangle d'or,* p. 70.
15. Gino Sandri, October 2003 interview, at www.rennes-le-chateau.org/rlctoday/int-sandri.htm.
16. The "Delaude" work is reproduced in Pierre Jarnac, *Les mystères de Rennes-le-Château* (Couiza: Centre d'Études et des Recherches Templières, 1994–95), vol. 1, pp. 3–10.
17. Guy Patton and Robin Mackness, *Web of Gold: The Secret History of a Sacred Treasure* (London: Sidwick & Jackson, 2000), p. 207.
18. Gordon Thomas and Max Morgan-Witts, *Pontiff* (London: Panther, 1984), p. 61.
19. Ibid., pp. 64–66.
20. Baigent, Leigh, and Lincoln, *The Holy Blood and the Holy Grail,* pp. 222–23.
21. Thomas and Morgan-Witts, *Pontiff,* p. 501.
22. Dated June 24, St. John the Baptist's feast day, 1978.
23. Plantard de Saint-Clair's preface to Abbé Henri Boudet, *La vrai langue celtique et la Cromleck de Rennes-les-Bains* (Paris: Pierre Belfond, 1978), pp. 17–18.

24. Richard Andrews and Paul Schellenberger, *The Tomb of God* (London: Little, Brown, 1996), pp. 174–75.
25. Chaumeil, *Le trésor du triangle d'or,* p. 184.
26. Ibid., p. 185.
27. Jean Markale, *The Templar Treasure at Gisors* (Rochester, Vt.: Inner Traditions, 2003), pp. 66–67.
28. See Baigent, Leigh, and Lincoln, *The Holy Blood and the Holy Grail,* pp. 235–37.
29. See reproduction in Jarnac, *Les archives du trésor de Rennes-le-Château,* p. 551.
30. It also identified a British peer, Lord Blackford, as a member and even quoted from him. This is presumed to be the Second Baron Blackford (1887–1972), who before succeeding to the title, as Glyn Mason, was a Conservative MP from 1922 to 1940 (for Croydon in Surrey). He was later Deputy Speaker of the House of Lords.
31. Paul Smith, "Plantard's Secret Parchments," *Journal of the Pendragon Society* 17 (February 1986): 2.
32. Jarnac, *Les archives du trésor de Rennes-le-Château,* p. 497.
33. Details from *Who's Who in America.*
34. Some researchers have suggested that the Dossiers Secrets were inspired by the work of Walter Johannes Stein, in particular *The Ninth Century and the Holy Grail* (1928), in which he argued for the reality of a "Grail family" from which many later royal and noble houses were descended. However, although Stein included Godefroy de Bouillon as part of his "Grail lineage"—correctly as a descendant of the Carolingians (the Merovingians play no special part in Stein's reconstruction)—the similarities between the two end there. The Dossiers Secrets do not make a connection between their "bloodline" families and the Grail romances; that was an innovation of Baigent, Leigh, and Lincoln.
35. Baigent, Leigh, and Lincoln, *The Holy Blood and the Holy Grail,* pp. 319–21.
36. A. T. Hatto, Introduction to Wolfram von Eschenbach, *Parzival* (London: Penguin, 1980), p. 8.
37. Interviewed for the documentary *Da Vinci Code Decoded* (Disinformation Company productions, produced by Gary Baddeley and Richard Metzger, directed by Richard Metzger, 2004).

38. Lynn Picknett and Clive Prince, *The Templar Revelation* (New York: Touchstone, 1998), pp. 66–67. See also Lynn Picknett, *Mary Magdalene* (London: Robinson, 2004), pp. 93–101.
39. Gerard de Sède with Sophie de Sède, *Le trésor maudit de Rennes-le-Château* (Paris: J'ai Lu, 1968), p. 136.
40. An extract from the interview was included in the Channel 4 documentary *The Real Da Vinci Code,* produced and directed by Simon Raikes and broadcast in February 2005.
41. Jarnac, *Les archives du trésor de Rennes-le-Château,* p. 194.
42. *The Unexplained: Mysteries of Mind, Space and Time* was an early-1980s cult weekly publication that featured articles by Michael Baigent and Richard Leigh. Lynn was its Deputy Editor.
43. Baigent, Leigh, and Lincoln, *The Messianic Legacy,* pp. 328–29.
44. Chaumeil, *Le trésor du triangle d'or,* p. 150.
45. Baigent, Leigh, and Lincoln, *The Messianic Legacy,* p. 354.
46. See ibid., chapter 20.
47. Reproduced in Jarnac, *Les archives du trésor de Rennes-le-Château,* p. 554. Louis Vazart, who died in 2005, was an enthusiast for the Merovingian cause who founded the Cercle Saint-Dagobert II in the early 1980s and wrote two books on Dagobert II that were based heavily on the Dossiers Secrets.
48. Pierre Plantard de Saint-Clair, letter of July 6, 1989, reproduced on www.priory-of-sion.com/psp/vcr/p17.html. The new "official" list of Grand Masters appeared in *Vaincre,* no. 3, September 1989.
49. Gino Sandri, October 2003 interview, at www.rennes-le-chateau.org/rlctoday/int-sandri.htm.
50. Ibid.
51. Ibid.
52. Ibid.
53. Baigent, Leigh, and Lincoln, *The Messianic Legacy,* p. 447.
54. Ian Wood, *The Merovingian Kingdoms 450–751* (London and New York: Longman, 1994), p. 33.
55. Baigent, Leigh, and Lincoln, *The Holy Blood and the Holy Grail,* p. 254.
56. Ibid., pp. 434–38.
57. E.g., the Royal Stuart Society (see www.royalstuartsociety.com). See also the Jacobite Heritage website (www.jacobite.ca).
58. Jerry Jardine, "The Stuart Pretenders," *Scottish Journal,* May 1999.
59. Tracy R. Twyman, "Interview with Prince Michael Stewart of Al-

bany," Dragon Key Press website (www.dragonkeypress.com/articles/article_2004_10_23_5829.html).

60. See Sean Murphy, M.A., of the Centre for Irish Genealogical and Historical Studies, writing on the Irish Chiefs website in 2002 (www.homepage.eircom.net/~seanmurphy/chiefs/lafosse.htm); the detailed reports on the documents produced by Lafosse at www.sociologyesoscience.com/esoterica/michaell.html; and the comprehensive deconstruction of Prince Michael's claims on the Jacobite Heritage website (www.jacobite.ca/essays/lafosse.htm).
61. Prince Michael of Albany, *The Forgotten Monarchy of Scotland* (Shaftesbury: Element, 1998), pp. 312–13.
62. Both quotations are from Katka Krosnar, "Scot 'Prince' Seeks Czech EP Seat," *The Prague Post,* June 9–15, 2004.
63. From the Jacobite Heritage website (www.jacobite.ca/essays/lafosse.htm), citing comments from Otto von Habsburg to the genealogist David Willis.
64. Prince Michael of Albany, *The Forgotten Monarchy of Scotland,* pp. xix–xx.
65. Laurence Gardner, *Realm of the Ring Lords: Beyond the Portal of the Twilight World* (Ottery St. Mary: MediaQuest, 2000), p. 24.
66. Laurence Gardner, *Bloodline of the Holy Grail* (Shaftesbury: Element, 1996), p. 4.
67. In *Realm of the Ring Lords,* Gardner hedges between the Anunnaki being extraterrestrials and being an advanced terrestrial race, concluding (p. 26), "the chances are that both conclusions are correct."
68. Tracy R. Twyman, "My Kingdom Is Not of This World," Dagobert's Revenge website, www.dagobertstrevenge.com/devere/interview1.html.
69. Ascension Alchemy (www.asc-alchemy.com).
70. Reports on and discussions about Hudson's work, as well as transcripts of his lectures and interviews, abound on the Internet, but the most comprehensive source is the "Ormus" section of the Subtle Energies website (www.subtleenergies.com), compiled by Barry Carter.
71. www.subtleenergies.com/ormus/faq.htm.
72. Transcript of Hudson's Lecture in Denver, Colorado, August 1994, on the Subtle Energies website (ibid).
73. Twyman, "My Kingdom Is Not of This World."
74. The case for the Princess of Wales's assassination is discussed in

Lynn Picknett, Clive Prince, and Stephen Prior with Robert Brydon, *War of the Windsors* (Edinburgh: Mainstream Publishing, 2003), pp. 296–301.

75. Marilyn Hopkins, Graham Simmans, and Tim Wallace-Murphy, *Rex Deus* (Shaftesbury: Element, 2000), pp. 40–41.
76. Ibid., p. 109.
77. Ibid., p. 134.
78. Ibid., pp. 262–63.
79. Ibid., p. 35.
80. Baigent, Leigh, and Lincoln, *The Messianic Legacy,* pp. 367–68.

6. RETURN TO THE SOURCE

1. Quoted in Jean-Luc Chaumeil, *Le trésor du triangle d'or* (Nice: Alain Lefeuvre, 1979), p. 77.
2. The Magdalene was first declared a prostitute by Pope Gregory I in 690 C.E., but although this was repealed in 1969, most Christians still believe the slur. See Lynn Picknett, *Mary Magdalene* (London: Robinson, 2004), pp. 47ff.
3. See Lynn Picknett and Clive Prince, *The Templar Revelation* (New York: Touchstone, 1998), pp. 287–95, and Picknett, *Mary Magdalene,* pp. 147–48 and 161–62.
4. See Picknett and Prince, *The Templar Revelation,* pp. 94–95, and Picknett, *Mary Magdalene,* pp. 97–101.
5. Étienne Michel Faillon, *Monuments inédits sur l'apostolat de Sainte Marie-Madeleine en Provence, et sur les autres apôtres de cette contrée, Saint Lazare, Saint Maximin, Sainte Marthe et les Saintes Maries Jacobé et Salomé* (Paris: Abbé Migne, 1848), vol. 1, p. iv.
6. Gino Sandri, October 2003 interview, at www.rennes-le-chateau.org/rlctoday/int-sandri.htm.
7. These issues are explored in greater depth in Lynn Picknett, *Mary Magdalene,* chapter 4.
8. On the "Evangelist" Johannites, see Andrew Collins, *Twenty-first Century Grail* (London: Virgin, 2004), chapters 6 and 7.
9. Jean Markale, *The Templar Treasure at Gisors* (Rochester, Vt.: Inner Traditions, 2003), p. 4.
10. John 1:35–42.
11. Picknett and Prince, *The Templar Revelation,* pp. 147–49, 335–36.

12. To be strictly accurate, the Order's founder, the society doctor Bernard-Raymond Fabré-Palaprat, incorporated the Johannite elements into its doctrines some ten years after its foundation, thereby precipitating a split in the membership, the majority of whom were Catholics. This was resolved only on Fabré-Palaprat's death in 1838, when the Order rejected Johannitism. For more on Fabré-Palaprat, his revived Order of the Temple, and the Johannite Church, see Picknett and Prince, *The Templar Revelation*, pp. 143–46.
13. Jean-Pierre Bayard, *La symbolique de la Rose-Croix* (Paris: Payot, 1975), p. 192; Mildred J. Headings, *French Freemasonry under the Third Republic* (Baltimore: Johns Hopkins University Press, 1949), p. 108; Michel Gaudart de Soulages and Hubert Lamant, *Dictionnaire des francs-maçons français* (Paris: Jean-Claude Lattès, 1995), p. 131.
14. Gaudart de Soulages and Lamant, *Dictionnaire des francs-maçons français*, pp. 57 and 615.
15. Ibid., p. 615.
16. Ibid., p. 57.
17. Jean-Pierre Monteils, *Sectes et sociétés secrètes* (Nîmes: C. Lacour, 1999), pp. 129–30.
18. Egyptian Rite of Memphis, *Ritual of the A. & A. Egyptian Rite of Memphis 96°*, [London (Ontario): Sovereign Sanctuary of the Egyptian Rite of Memphis (Canada)], c. 1880.
19. See pp. 321–23.
20. Sandri, October 2003 interview.
21. (Joséphin) Péladan, *Constitutions de la Rose-Croix, le Temple et le Graal* (Paris: Secretariat of the Ordre de la Rose-Croix, le Temple et le Graal, 1893), pp. 28–29. Our thanks to Andrew Collins for bringing this to our attention and supplying us with a copy of the Constitutions.
22. (Joséphin) Péladan, *La philosophie de Léonard de Vinci* (Paris: Félix Alcan, 1910), p. 111.
23. Michael Baigent, Richard Leigh, and Henry Lincoln, *The Holy Blood and the Holy Grail* (London: Arrow, 1996), pp. 194–98.
24. Ibid., p. 156.
25. Michael Baigent, Richard Leigh, and Henry Lincoln, *The Messianic Legacy* (London: Corgi, 1987), p. 231.
26. Baigent, Leigh, and Lincoln, *The Holy Blood and the Holy Grail*, p. 157.
27. Ibid., pp. 477–79.

28. Jean Markale, *The Church of Mary Magdalene* (Rochester, Vt.: Inner Traditions, 2004), p. 172.
29. Von Hund's full list is reproduced in Claude Antoine Thory, *Acta Latomurum* (Paris: Pierre-Élie Dufart, 1815), vol. 1, pp. 282–3.
30. Baigent, Leigh, and Lincoln, *The Holy Blood and the Holy Grail,* pp. 129–32.
31. Michael Baigent and Richard Leigh, *The Temple and the Lodge* (London: Corgi, 1990), p. 267.
32. M. E. Guillaume Rey, "Chartes de l'Abbaye du Mont Sion, Mémoires de la Société Nationale des Antiquaires de France," vol. 48 (5th series, vol. 8) (1887), p. 33.
33. Biographical information on Doinel is from Pierre Jarnac, *Les archives du trésor de Rennes-le-Château* (Nice: Bélisane, 1988), pp. 397–401, and Gaudart de Soulages and Lamant, *Dictionnaire des francs-maçons francais,* pp. 338–9.
34. Jarnac, *Les archives du trésor de Rennes-le-Château,* p. 399.
35. René le Forestier, *La franc-maçonnerie templière et occultiste* (Paris: La Table d'Emeraude, 1987), vol. 1, p. 432.
36. See Jarnac, *Les archives du trésor de Rennes-le-Château,* p. 401, and Gaudart de Soulages and Lamant, *Dictionnaire des francs-maçons français,* p. 339.
37. René Nelli, *Dictionnaire des hérésies méridionales* (Toulouse: Éduoard Privat, 1968), p. 154.
38. Jules-Stanislas Doinel, *Jeanne d'Arc telle qu'elle est* (Orléans: H. Herluisen, 1892), p. 33.
39. Gaudart de Soulages and Lamant, *Dictionnaire des francs-maçons français,* p. 480; Jean Ursin, *Création et histoire du Rite Écossais Rectifié* (Paris: Dervy, 1993), pp. 61–62; le Foresher, *Le franc-maçonnerie templière et occultiste,* vol. 1, pp. 107–11.
40. René le Forestier, *Les illuminés de Bavière et la franc-maçonnerie allemande* (Paris: Librairie Hachette et Cie, 1914), pp. 107–11.
41. J. M. Roberts, *The Mythology of the Secret Societies* (London: Secker & Warburg, 1972), pp. 106–7.
42. Ibid., p. 107.
43. Baigent and Leigh, *The Temple and the Lodge,* pp. 265–69.
44. Le Forestier, *Le franc-maçonnerie templière et occultiste.* vol. 1, p. 118; Roberts, *The Mythology of the Secret Societies,* p. 107.
45. Le Forestier, *Les illuminés de Bavière et la franc-maçonnerie allemande,* pp. 163–74.

46. Ibid., pp. 148–50.
47. Pierre Montloin and Jean-Pierre Bayard, *Les Rose-Croix* (Paris: Grasset, 1971), pp. 95–110; Roberts, *The Mythology of the Secret Societies,* p. 102; le Forestier, *Le franc-maçonnerie templière et occultiste,* vol. 1, pp. 64–67.
48. Le Forestier, *Les illuminés de Bavière et la franc-maçonnerie allemande,* pp. 150–55.
49. Ibid., pp. 156–59. See also le Forestier's *La franc-maçonnerie templière et occultiste,* vol. 1, chapter 3.
50. Le Forestier, *La franc-maçonnerie templière et occultiste,* vol. 3, pp. 549–51.
51. Arthur Edward Waite, *A New Encyclopaedia of Freemasonry* (London: William Rider & Sons, 1923), vol. 2, p. 356.
52. Quoted in Thory, *Acta Latomurum,* vol. 1, p. 136. There are indications, in the correspondence that passed between Saint-Martin and Willermoz, that the Knights Beneficent was created in Lyons before the 1778 Convent. See Arthur Edward Waite, *Saint-Martin the French Mystic* (London: William Rider & Son, 1922), p. 55.
53. The proceedings of the Convent of Wilhelmsbad are dealt with exhaustively in the second volume of le Forestier's *La franc-maçonnerie templière et occultiste.*
54. Thory, *Acta Latomurum,* vol. 1, pp. 153–54.
55. See ibid., p. 136.
56. Ibid., p. 153.
57. Ibid., p. 299.
58. Waite, *Saint-Martin the French Mystic,* p. 59.
59. Gaudart de Soulages and Lamant, *Dictionnaire des francs-maçons français,* p. 49.
60. Waite, *A New Encyclopaedia of Freemasonry,* vol. 2, p. 403.
61. Robert Amadou, "Martines de Pasqually et l'Ordre des Élus Cohen," *L'Originel* 2, 1995, p. 54.
62. Michel Taillefer, "Les disciples toulousains de Martines de Pasqually et de Saint-Martin," in Michel Taillefer and Robert Amadou, eds., *Le Temple Cohen de Toulouse (1760–1792)* (Paris: Cariscript, 1986), p. 9.
63. On the relationship between Saint-Martin and the du Bourgs, see Taillefer and Amadou, *Le Temple Cohen de Toulouse (1760–1792).*
64. Roberts, *The Mythology of the Secret Societies,* p. 104.
65. See Waite, *Saint-Martin the French Mystic,* pp. 29–34.

66. Ibid., p. 31.
67. Papus, *Martinésisme, willermosisme, martinisme et franc-maçonnerie* (Paris: Chamuel, 1899), p. 20.
68. Quoted in Waite, *Saint-Martin the French Mystic,* p. 46.
69. Roberts, *The Mythology of the Secret Societies,* p. 104.
70. Gaudart de Soulages and Lamant, *Dictonnaire des francs-maçons français,* p. 84; Waite, *A New Encyclopaedia of Freemasonry,* vol. 2, p. 401.
71. Taillefer, "Les disciples toulousains de Martines de Pasqually et de Saint-Martin," in Taillefer and Amadou, *Le Temple Cohen de Toulouse (1760–1792),* p. 97; Gaudart de Soulages and Lamant, *Dictionnaire des francs-maçons français,* p. 644.
72. Roberts, *The Mythology of the Secret Societies,* p. 102. See also le Forestier, *Le franc-maçonnerie templière et occultiste,* vol. 1, pp. 64–67.
73. Taillefer, "Les disciples toulousains de Martines de Pasqually et de Saint-Martin," in Taillefer and Amadou, *Le Temple Cohen de Toulouse (1760–1792),* p. 111.
74. Roberts, *The Mythology of the Secret Societies,* p. 111.
75. The magnetizer was Canon Jean Antoine de Castellas, of St. John's Church in Lyons.
76. Quoted in le Forestier, *Le franc-maçonnerie templière et occultiste,* vol. 2, pp. 793–94.
77. Robert Amadou and Alice Joly, *De l'Agent Inconnu au Philosophe Inconnu* (Paris: Denoël, 1962), pp. 13–14.
78. Ibid., p. 14.
79. Waite, *Saint-Martin the French Mystic,* p. 35; Amadou and Joly, *De l'Agent Inconnu au Philosophe Inconnu,* p. 14.
80. Le Forestier, *Le franc-maçonnerie templière et occultiste,* vol. 2, p. 794.
81. Waite, *Saint-Martin the French Mystic,* p. 43.
82. Amadou and Joly, *De l'Agent Inconnu au Philosophe Inconnu,* p. 50.
83. Waite, *Saint-Martin the French Mystic,* p. 43.
84. Papus, *Martinésisme, willermosisme, martinisme et franc-maçonnerie,* pp. 15–16.
85. Waite, *Saint-Martin the French Mystic,* p. 56.
86. Ibid., p. 57.
87. Gaudart de Soulages and Lamant, *Dictionnaire des francs-maçons français,* p. 805.
88. Robert Amadou, *Louis-Claude de Saint-Martin et le martinisme* (Paris: Éditions du Griffon d'Or, 1946), pp. 42–43.

89. Papus, *Martinésisme, willermosisme, martinisme et franc-maçonnerie,* p. 20.
90. According to Gaudart de Soulages and Lamant (*Dictionnaire des Franç s-macons français,* p. 805), there are three major Martinist societies: the Martinist Order, the Initiatory Martinist Order, and the Traditional Martinist Order.
91. Christian Plume and Xavier Pasquini, *Encyclopédie des sectes dans le monde* (Paris: Henri Veyrier, 1984), p. 335.
92. Waite, *A New Encyclopaedia of Freemasonry,* vol. 2, p. 159.
93. Ibid., p. 161.
94. Ibid., p. 258.
95. Gaudart de Soulages and Lamant, *Dictionnaire des franç s-macons français,* p. 370.
96. Ibid., p. 371.
97. Montloin and Bayard, *Le Rose-Croix,* p. 212.
98. Quoted in ibid., p. 213.
99. J. G. Findel, *The History of Freemasonry from Its Origins Down to the Present Day* (London: George Kenning, 1869), p. 231.
100. Richard F. Kuisel, "The Legend of the Vichy Synarchy," *French Historical Studies* VI, no. 3 (Spring 1970): 378.
101. Quoted in Gérard de Sède, *Rennes-le-Château* (Paris: Robert Laffont, 1988), p. 212.
102. Quoted in Yves-Fred Boisset, *Les clés traditionelles et synarchiques de l'archéomètre* (Paris: JBJ, 1977), p. 5.
103. Baigent, Leigh, and Lincoln, *The Holy Blood and the Holy Grail,* p. 296.
104. Plume and Pasquini, *Encyclopédie des sectes dans le monde,* p. 397.
105. Jules Blois, *Le monde invisible* (Paris: Ernest Flammarion, 1902), p. 35.
106. See Monteils, *Sectes et sociétés secrètes,* p. 138.
107. Papus, *Anarchie, indolence et synarchie* (Paris: Chamuel, 1894), p. 7.
108. André Ulmann and Henri Azeau, *Synarchie et pouvoir* (Paris: Julliard, 1968), pp. 19–20.
109. Bois, *Le monde invisible,* p. 36.
110. Olivier Dard, *La synarchie, ou le mythe du complot permanent* (Paris: Perrin, 1998), p. 46.
111. Jean Saunier, *Saint-Yves d'Alveydre, ou une synarchie sans enigme* (Paris: Dervy-Livres, 1981), pp. 78–79; Dard, *La synarchie,* pp. 46–47.

112. Dard, *La synarchie,* p. 47; Saunier, *Saint-Yves d'Alveydre,* p. 102.
113. She had previously been married to Count Édouard Fédorovitch Keller, Vice Governor of Kiev and later an important official in the Czar's court. They divorced in 1876.
114. The term *synarchy* was actually borrowed from J. A. Vaillant's 1861 work *The Magic Key of Fiction and Fact* (*Clef magique de la fiction et du fait*), although Saint-Yves modified the concept in several respects. Vaillant, too, defined synarchy in opposition to anarchy, arguing that the principles of synarchy must shape the social order, which in turn would shape the "religion of the future." (See Saunier, *Saint-Yves d'Alveydre,* pp. 197–201.)
115. St. Yves d'Alveydre, *Clefs d'Orient* (Paris: Didier & Cie, 1877), p. 1.
116. Dard, *La synarchie,* p. 48.
117. Ibid., p. 43.
118. Montloin and Bayard, *Le Rose-Croix,* p. 85.
119. R. P. Martin, *Le livre des compagnons secrets* (Monaco: ACL Rocher, 1982), p. 140.
120. Ulmann and Azeau, *Synarchie et pouvoir,* p. 30.
121. Philippe Bourdrel, *La Cagoule* (Paris: Albin Michel, 1970), p. 164.
122. Papus, *Martinésisme, willermosisme, martinisme et franc-maçonnerie,* p. 40.
123. Matters are complicated by the fact that Saint-Yves kept changing the titles of his books. The first, for example, was originally entitled *Current Mission of the Sovereigns* (*Mission actuelle des souverains*), then *Current Mission of the Sovereigns by One of Them* (*Mission actuelle des souverains par l'un d'eux*), and finally *Mission of the Sovereigns by One of Them* (*Mission des souverains par l'un d'eux*). *Mission of the French* was originally entitled *The True France, or Mission of the French* (*La France vraie, ou mission des Français*). Most of Saint-Yves's books are today extremely hard to come by, but Jacques Weiss gives a detailed synopsis of them in *La synarchie selon l'oeuvre de Saint-Yves d'Alveydre* (Paris: Robert Laffont, 1976).
124. Dard, *La synarchie,* p. 50.
125. Saint-Yves d'Alveydre, *Mission des Juifs* (Paris: Calmann Lévy, 1884), chapter 6.
126. Bois, *Le monde invisible,* p. 38.
127. See Saint-Yves d'Alveydre, *Mission des Français,* chapter 8.
128. Ulmann and Azeau, *Synarchie et pouvoir,* p. 33.
129. Quoted in Saunier, *Saint-Yves d'Alveydre,* p. 211.

130. Gaudart de Soulages and Lamant, *Dictionnaire des francs-maçons français,* p. 923.
131. He subsequently left because of its antirepublican orientation.
132. Dard, *La synarchie,* p. 55; Saunier, *Saint-Yves d'Alveydre,* pp. 230–31.
133. Saunier, *Saint-Yves d'Alveydre,* p. 385.
134. Bois, *Le monde invisible,* p. 39.
135. Dard, *La synarchie,* p. 62.
136. Saint-Yves drew the idea from the writings of Louis Jacolliot (1837–1890), a diplomat in India who on his return to France wrote a series of books on its spirituality and religion, one of which mentions a cult center called Asgartha.
137. Quoted in Saunier, *Saint-Yves d'Alveydre,* p. 331.
138. Quoted in ibid., pp. 325–26.
139. The first appearance of this idea seems to have been in 1924, when the Russo-Polish chemist and journalist Ferdinand Ossendovski published a book on his travels in Mongolia in which he wrote of "Agarthi," where the "King of the World" was in contact with world leaders.
140. Plume and Pasquini, *Encyclopédie des sectes dans le monde,* p. 397.
141. Quoted in Dard, *La synarchie,* p. 61.
142. Ibid., p. 68. In 1883 the Theosophical Society in Madras (which then had only about fifty members in France) invited Saint-Yves to join, but he declined. (This seems to have been resented by the Society's founder, Madame Blavatsky, who wrote a hostile review of *Mission of the Jews* in *Le Lotus* of June 1888.)
143. Dard, *La synarchie,* p. 64.
144. With the exception of Mexico, where synarchy did, for a time in the 1930s, become a mass political movement. Synarchy was introduced into Mexico around 1914 by the occultist Tomás Rosales, a follower of Papus, and in 1937 the Unión Nacional Sinarquista, described by Jean Saunier (*Saint-Yves d'Alveydre,* p. 40) as "a curious movement of mass nationalism," was formed. It actually played a major part in Mexican politics for the next few years, winning seats in the Mexican Parliament and producing its own newspaper, *El Sinarquista.* (There were even sinarquiste colonies in California.) For a study of Mexican synarchy, see Jean Meyer, *Le sinarquisme* (Paris: Hachette, 1977).
145. See Peronnik, *Pourquoi la resurgence de l'Ordre du Temple?* (Monte Carlo: Éditions de la Pensée Solaire, 1975), pp. 307–14, on "Authority and Power: Synarchy in Politics." The Sovereign Order's ill-fated

spin-off, the Order of the Solar Temple, also aligned itself with synarchy—see, for example, Raphaël Aubert and Carl-A. Keller, *Vie et mort de l'Ordre du Temple Solaire* (Vevey: Éditions de l'Aire, 1994), p. 44.

146. See Lynn Picknett and Clive Prince, *The Stargate Conspiracy* (New York: Berkley, 2000), pp. 255–63.
147. Erik Sablé, *La vie et l'oeuvre de René Schwaller de Lubicz* (Paris: Dervy, 2003), p. 15.
148. In his introduction to Andre VandenBroeck, *Al-Kemi* (Great Barrington, Mass.: Lindisfarne Press, 1987).
149. For example, Ulmann and Azeau, *Synarchie et pouvoir,* p. 135.
150. Montloin and Bayard, *Le Rose-Croix,* p. 89.
151. VandenBroeck, *Al-Kemi,* p. 212.
152. Jean Cocteau, *Maalesh* (London: Peter Owen, 1956), p. 58.
153. Ibid., p. 56.
154. Ibid., p. 37.
155. Jean Cocteau, *Le passé défini,* vol. 2 (Paris: Gallimard, 1985), pp. 67–68.
156. In an article entitled "What Is the Alpha?," *Vaincre,* no. 4, December 21, 1942.
157. Paul Le Cour, *Hellénisme et christianisme* (Paris: Atlantis, 1943), p. 61.
158. Ibid., p. 62.
159. Pierluigi Zoccatelli, "De *Regnabit* au *Bestaire du Christ.* L'itinéraire intellectuelle d'un symboliste chrétien: Louis Charbonneau-Lassy." Transcript of lecture delivered on 7 December 1996 at the Sainte-Croix Collegiate Church, London. Centre for Studies on New Religions website www.cesnur.org/paraclet/loudon_01.htm.
160. Chaumeil, *Le trésor du triangle d'or,* pp. 139–40.
161. Jean-Pierre Bayard with Natacha Olejnik-Sarkissian, *Guide des sociétés sécrètes et des sectes* (Paris: Oxus, 2004), pp. 336–37.
162. See Jean-Marie Mayeur, "De Gaulle as a Politician and Christian," in Hugh Gough and John Horne, eds., *De Gaulle and Twentieth-Century France* (London and New York: Edward Arnold, 1994), pp. 96–97.
163. Zoccatelli, "De *Regnabit* au *Bestaire du Christ.*"
164. Bayard, *La symbolique de la Rose-Croix* (Paris: Payot, 1975), p. 274. See also Chaumeil, *Le trésor du triangle d'or,* p. 140.

7. THE SHAPE-SHIFTERS

1. Richard F. Kuisel, "The Legend of the Vichy Synarchy," *French Historical Studies* 6, no. 3 (Spring 1970), p. 378.
2. Ibid., pp. 379–80; Olivier Dard, *La synarchie, ou le mythe du complot permanent* (Paris: Perrin, 1998), p. 68.
3. See pp. 388–89.
4. André Ulmann and Henri Azeau, *Synarchie et pouvoir* (Paris: Julliard, 1968), p. 62; Christian Plume and Xavier Pasquini, *Encyclopédie des sectes dans le monde* (Paris: Henri Veyrier, 1984), pp. 421–22.
5. Quoted in Ulmann and Azeau, *Synarchie et pouvoir,* p. 63.
6. Jean Contrucci, *Emma Calvé, la diva du siècle* (Paris: Albin Michel, 1989), p. 129.
7. Quoted in Ulmann and Azeau, *Synarchie et pouvoir,* p. 116.
8. Jean Saunier, *Saint-Yves d'Alveydre, ou une synarchie sans énigme* (Paris: Dervy-Livres, 1981), p. 127.
9. See Lynn Picknett, Clive Prince, and Stephen Prior with Robert Brydon, *Friendly Fire* (Edinburgh: Mainstream Publishing, 2004), pp. 185–86 and 192–93. Weygand was never trusted by Hitler, who demanded his resignation in November 1941 and ordered his arrest and imprisonment in Germany a year later. He was acquitted of treason charges after the war.
10. The Synarchist Pact is reproduced in the Appendix to Geoffrey de Charnay, *Synarchie* (Paris: Médicis, 1946), from which this and the following quotations and extracts are taken.
11. Ulmann and Azeau, *Synarchie et pouvoir,* p. 112.
12. See, for example, Saunier, *Saint-Yves d'Alveydre,* p. 41.
13. For example, the Network Synarchique, which is active in the United Kingdom, France, and Belgium, and which bizarrely affiliates itself to the Anarchic Movement.
14. Kuisel, "The Legend of the Vichy Synarchy," p. 380.
15. De Charnay, *Synarchie,* Appendix, p. 102.
16. Joseph Désert, *Toute la vérité sur l'affaire de la Cagoule* (Paris: Librairie des Sciences et des Arts, 1946), pp. 5 and 15.
17. Pierre Péan, *Le mystérieux Docteur Martin* (Paris: Fayard, 1993), p. 97.
18. Cited in J.-R. Tournoux, *L'histoire secrète* (Paris: Plon, 1962), p. 30.
19. Merry Bromberger and Serge Bromberger, *Les 13 complots du 13 mai* (Paris: Librairie Arthème Fayard, 1959), p. 80.

20. Péan, *Le mystérieux Docteur Martin,* pp. 102–3.
21. See Picknett, Prince, and Prior, with Brydon, *Friendly Fire,* pp. 297–99 and 308–10.
22. Péan, *Le mystérieux Docteur Martin,* p. 140.
23. Ibid., p. 117. See also William L. Shirer, *The Collapse of the Third Republic* (London: William Heinemann/Seckers & Warburg, 1970), p. 209, and Tournoux, *L'histoire secrète,* pp. 307–9.
24. Ferand Fontenay, *La Cagoule contre la France* (Paris: Sociales Internationales, 1938), pp. 72–3; Pierre Péan, *Une jeunesse française* (Paris: Fayard, 1994), p. 503.
25. Désert, *Tout la vérité sur l'affaire de la Cagoule,* p. 3.
26. Shirer, *The Collapse of the Third Republic,* p. 209.
27. Quoted in Henry Coston, ed., *Dictionnaire de la politique française* (Paris: Publications Henry Coston/Librairie Française, 1967, 1972, 1979, 1982), vol. 1, p. 191.
28. Kuisel, "The Legend of the Vichy Synarchy," p. 385; see also Philippe Bourdrel, *La Cagoule* (Paris: Albin Michel, 1970), pp. 164–65.
29. Shirer, *The Collapse of the Third Republic,* p. 219.
30. Ibid.
31. Quoted in Tournoux, *L'histoire secrète,* p. 173.
32. Quoted in ibid. Tournoux keeps his informant anonymous.
33. Bourdrel, *La Cagoule,* p. 56.
34. Guy Patton and Robin Mackness, *Web of Gold* (London: Sidgwick & Jackson, 2000), p. 222. Dagobert owes his evocative name to descent from General Luc-Siméon Dagobert, an important general in the Republican Army formed after the French Revolution.
35. Jean-Pierre Monteils, *Sectes et sociétés secrètes* (Nimes: C. Lacour, 1999), p. 141.
36. Maurice Girodias, *Une journée sur la terre* (Paris: Éditions de la Différence, 1990), vol. 1, p. 402.
37. Monteils, *Sectes et sociétés secrètes,* p. 139.
38. Dard, *La synarchie,* pp. 69–70.
39. Girodias, vol. 1, p. 411.
40. Geoffrey de Charnay, *Synarchie* (Paris: Médicis, 1946), p. 67.
41. Dard, *La synarchie,* pp. 71 and 74–75.
42. Ibid., p. 73.
43. Girodias, *Une journée sur la terre,* vol. 1, p. 184.
44. Ibid., p. 198.

45. Quoted in Jean Robin, *Rennes-le-Château* (Paris: Guy Trédaniel, 1982), p. 141.
46. Ibid.
47. Count Richard N. Coudenhove-Kalergi, *An Idea Conquers the World* (London: Hutchinson, 1953), pp. 270–71.
48. I. C. B. Dear, ed., *The Oxford Companion to the Second World War* (Oxford and New York: Oxford University Press, 1995), p. 756; John McVickar Haight Jr., *American Aid to France, 1938–1940* (New York: Atheneum, 1970), p. 2.
49. Girodias, *Une journée sur la terre*, vol. 1, p. 149.
50. Ibid., p. 410.
51. Ibid., p. 208.
52. Ibid., p. 198.
53. Ibid., p. 238.
54. Ibid., p. 239.
55. Ibid., pp. 347–48.
56. Ibid., p. 401.
57. Simone de Beauvoir, *The Prime of Life* (Harmondsworth, U.K.: Penguin Books, 1965), p. 465.
58. John Hellman, *The Knight-Monks of Vichy France* (Liverpool, U.K.: Liverpool University Press/Montreal: McGill-Queen's University Press, 1997), p. 331.
59. Bertram M. Gordon, *Historical Dictionary of World War II France* (Westport, Conn.: Greenwood Press, 1998), pp. 243–44.
60. Ibid., pp. 326–27.
61. Ibid., pp. 243–44.
62. Quoted in Coston, *Dictionnaire de la politique française*, vol. 1, p. 735.
63. Claude Varennes, *Le Destin de Marcel Déat* (Paris: Janmaray, 1948), p. 111.
64. Gordon, *Historical Dictionary of World War II France*, pp. 98–99.
65. Dear, *The Oxford Companion to the Second World War*, p. 673.
66. See Picknett, Prince, and Prior, with Brydon, *Friendly Fire*, pp. 290–92.
67. Jean Cocteau, *Journal 1942–1945*, Jean Touzot, ed. (Paris: Gallimard, 1989), pp. 68 and 224.
68. Gordon, *Historical Dictionary of World War II France*, p. 35.
69. Pierre Nicolle, *Cinquante mois d'armistice* (Paris: André Bonne, 1947), vol. 1, p. 266.

70. Ibid., p. 285.
71. Ibid., p. 305.
72. In his memoirs (pp. 271–79), written in 1944–45 while he was awaiting trial but not published until 1968, Berthelot mocked the claims of a synarchist conspiracy in Vichy, saying that the society was so secret that even he didn't know he was a member!
73. See Kuisel, "The Legend of the Vichy Synarchy," pp. 384–93; Dard, *La synarchie,* p. 27; and Henry Coston, *Les technocrates et la Synarchie,* Special ed. of *Lectures françaises* (Paris: February 1962), pp. 19–20.
74. Shirer, *The Collapse of the Third Republic,* p. 218.
75. Kuisel, "The Legend of the Vichy Synarchy," pp. 376–77.
76. Coston, *Les technocrates et la Synarchie,* p. 19, citing Mennevée's *Documents politiques, diplomatiques et financiers,* April 1948.
77. Girodias, *Une journée sur la terre,* vol. 1, p. 402.
78. Ibid., p. 279.
79. Coston, *Les technocrates et la Synarchie,* p. 36.
80. Quoted in Shirer, *The Collapse of the Third Republic,* p. 897.
81. Quoted in Coston, *Les technocrates et la Synarchie,* pp. 31–32.
82. Alibert was a member of the Cagoule's Superior Council. See Péan, *Le mystérieux Docteur Martin,* p. 104.
83. The Chavin report is reproduced in the appendix to Nicolle, *Cinquante mois d'armistice.*
84. William L. Langer, *Our Vichy Gamble* (New York: Alfred A. Knopf, 1947), p. 168.
85. Ibid., p. 169.
86. Dard, *La synarchie,* pp. 30–31.
87. Michel Gaudart de Soulages and Aubert Lamant, *Dictionnaire des francs-maçons français* (Paris: Jean-Claude Lattès, 1995), p. 263.
88. The leadership of the Gnostic Church passed through the following succession: after Doinel's resignation to the poet Fabre des Essarts, who was also an official in the Ministry of Public Education; on his death in 1917 to Jean Bricaud, the writer on the occult, who took the title Patriarch Jean II; Chevillon took over on Bricaud's death in 1934. Bricaud, too, had been Grand Master of the Martinist Order.
89. Coston, *Les technocrates et la Synarchie,* pp. 13–15. Coston's source is the April 1944 edition of *Les Documentes Maçonniques,* published in Paris and Vichy.

90. Ibid., p. 15.
91. Gaudart de Soulages and Lamant, *Dictionnaire des francs-maçons français*, p. 263.
92. Shirer, *The Collapse of the Third Republic*, p. 897.
93. Ibid., p. 218.
94. Saunier, *Saint-Yves d'Alveydre*, p. 38.
95. Cited in Coston, *Les technocrates et la Synarchie*, p. 19, citing *Documents politiques, diplomatiques, et financiers* for April 1948.
96. Ulmann and Azeau, *Synarchie et pouvoir*, pp. 223–25.
97. René Remond, "Two Destinies: Pétain and de Gaulle," in Hugh Gough and John Horne, eds., *De Gaulle and Twentieth-Century France* (London and New York: Edward Arnold, 1994), p. 15.
98. Ullman and Azeau, *Synarchie et pouvoir*, pp. 293–310. See also Peter Tompkins, *The Murder of Admiral Darlan* (London: Weidenfeld and Nicolson, 1965), p. 254.
99. Péan, *Le mystérieux Docteur Martin*, p. 369.
100. Gordon, *Historical Dictionary of World War II France*, p. 102.
101. Patton and Mackness, *Web of Gold*, p. 170.
102. Tournoux, *L'histoire secrète*, p. 295.
103. Coston, *Les technocrates et la Synarchie*, p. 18, citing *Action*, November 2, 1945.
104. For a discussion, see Ulmann and Azeau, *Synarchie et pouvoir*, chapter 12.
105. Jean Cocteau, *Le passé défini*, Pierre Chanel, ed. (Paris: Gallimard, 1983), vol. 1, p. 390.
106. Péan, *Le mystérieux Docteur Martin*, p. 7.
107. Ibid., p. 313. Stéphane was the nephew of the bank's wartime owner, Hippolyte Worms.
108. Ibid.

8. A NEW UNITED STATES

1. A. D. Chauvel and M. Forestier, *The Extraordinary House of Victor Hugo in Guernsey* (St. Peter Port: Toucan Press, 1975), p. 34.
2. See Jean de Mutigny, *Victor Hugo et le spiritisme* (Paris: Fernand Nathan, 1981).
3. Samuel Edwards, *Victor Hugo* (London: New English Library, 1975), p. 47.

4. Michel Gaudart de Soulages and Hubert Lamant, *Dictionnaire des francs-maçons français* (Paris: Jean-Claude Lattès, 1995), p. 478.
5. Michael Baigent, Richard Leigh, and Henry Lincoln, *The Messianic Legacy* (London: Corgi, 1987), p. 367.
6. *L'Indépendant,* March 4, 1981.
7. Capdeville subsequently became President of the Council General.
8. www.cathares.org/cec/.
9. Michael Baigent, Richard Leigh, and Henry Lincoln, *The Holy Blood and the Holy Grail* (London: Arrow, 1996), pp. 435–36. Those authors explored the Priory's ambitions for Europe in more detail in chapter 22 of *The Messianic Legacy.*
10. John Laughland, *The Tainted Source* (London: Little, Brown & Co., 1997), p. 69.
11. Count Richard N. Coudenhove-Kalergi, in *An Idea Conquers the World* (London: Hutchinson, 1953; pp. 162–63), reproduces an article of Churchill's from the *Saturday Evening Post* of February 15, 1930, in which he argues for a United Europe.
12. Winston S. Churchill, *The Sinews of Peace,* Randolph S. Churchill, ed. (London: Cassell & Co, 1948), p. 199.
13. Quoted in Jean-Pierre Rioux, "De Gaulle in Waiting, 1946–1958," in Hugh Gough and John Horne, eds., *De Gaulle and Twentieth-Century France* (London and New York: Edward Arnold, 1994), pp. 42–43.
14. David Dimbleby and David Reynolds, *An Ocean Apart* (London: BBC Books/Hodder & Stoughton, 1988), p. 209.
15. Baigent, Leigh, and Lincoln, *The Messianic Legacy,* p. 419.
16. René Lejeune, *Robert Schuman (1886–1963), Père de l'Europe* (Paris: Fayard, 2000), p. 13.
17. Merry Bromberger and Serge Bromberger, *Jean Monnet and the United States of Europe* (New York: Coward-McCann, 1969), p. 10.
18. Lejeune, *Robert Schuman,* p. 199.
19. Bromberger and Bromberger, *Jean Monnet and the United States of Europe,* p. 33.
20. Quoted in ibid., p. 41.
21. Ibid., p. 38.
22. Lynn Picknett, Clive Prince, and Stephen Prior with Robert Brydon, *Friendly Fire* (Edinburgh: Mainstream Publishing, 2004), pp. 287–89.
23. See Henry Coston, ed., *Dictionnaire de la politique française* (Paris:

Publications Henry Coston/Librairie Française, 1967, 1972, 1979, 1982), vol. 1, p. 467.

24. John Hellman, *The Knight-Monks of Vichy France* (Liverpool, U.K.: Liverpool University Press/Montreal: McGill-Queen's University Press, 1997), p. 240.
25. François Mitterrand, *Ma part de vérité* (Paris: Fayard, 1969), p. 17.
26. Quoted in Hellman, *The Knight-Monks of Vichy France*, p. 241.
27. John Laughland, *The Death of Politics* (London: Michael Joseph, 1994) p. 205.
28. Pierre Péan, *Une jeunesse française* (Paris: Fayard, 1994), pp. 33–35; Hellman, *The Knight-Monks of Vichy France*, p. 241.
29. Péan, *Une jeunesse française*, p. 109.
30. Ibid., pp. 103–4.
31. Ibid., p. 533.
32. Ibid., p. 110.
33. Pierre Péan, *Le mystérieux Docteur Martin* (Paris: Fayard, 1993), p. 64.
34. *Nouveau dictionnaire national des contemporains* (Paris: Éditions du Nouveau Dictionnaire National des Contemporains, 1964), p. 685.
35. Péan, *Une jeunesse française*, p. 130; Laughland, *The Death of Politics*, p. 120.
36. Hellman, *The Knight-Monks of Vichy France*, p. 242.
37. Laughland, *The Death of Politics*, p. 208.
38. Ibid., pp. 208–9.
39. Péan, *Une jeunesse française*, p. 533.
40. Ibid., p. 326.
41. See Laughland, *The Death of Politics*, pp. 213–14.
42. Coston, *Dictionnaire de la politique française*, vol. 1, p. 467.
43. Laughland, *The Death of Politics*, p. 215.
44. Péan, *Une jeunesse française*, p. 348; Bertram Gordon, *Historical Dictionary of World War II France* (Westport, Conn.: Greenwood Press, 1998), p. 244.
45. Ibid., p. 503.
46. Coston, *Dictionnaire de la politique française*, vol. 1, p. 348.
47. Péan, *Une jeunesse française*, p. 108.
48. Ibid., p. 534. Mitterrand's letter of support is reproduced in an appendix of Péan's book.

49. Ibid., pp. 554–55.
50. Laughland, *The Death of Politics,* pp. 206–7.
51. Quoted in ibid., p. 60.
52. Serge Berstein, "De Gaulle and Gaullism in the Fifth Republic," in Hugh Gough and John Horne, eds., *De Gaulle and Twentieth-Century France,* p. 120.
53. Charles de Gaulle, *Memoirs of Hope* (London: Weidenfeld & Nicolson, 1971), p. 28.
54. Laughland, *The Death of Politics,* pp. 203–4.
55. See Jean Montaldo, *Lettre ouverte d'un "chien" à François Mitterrand au nom de la liberté d'aboyer* (Paris: Albin Michel, 1993), pp. 42–47; Laughland, *The Death of Politics,* pp. 152–53.
56. Laughland, *The Death of Politics,* pp. 203–4.
57. Gordon, *Historical Dictionary of World War II France,* p. 357.
58. Laughland, *The Tainted Source,* p. 67.
59. Laughland, *The Death of Politics,* pp. 204–5.
60. Quoted in ibid., p. 41.
61. Ibid., pp. 41–42.
62. Ibid., p. xiv.
63. Ibid., p. 117.
64. Richard J. Golsan, ed., *Memory, the Holocaust, and French Justice* (Hanover, N.H.: University Press of New England, 1996), p. 5.
65. From Gordon, *Historical Dictionary of World War II France,* pp. 43–44; Coston, *Dictionnaire de la politique française,* vol. 1, p. 165. Some researchers [(e.g., Guy Patton and Robin Mackness, *Web of Gold* (London: Sidgwick & Jackson, 2000), p. 211] have seen significance in Bousquet's association with *La Dépêche,* which took the lead in publicizing the Rennes-le-Château mystery. However, Bousquet became involved with the newspaper only some six years after that publicity.
66. Laughland, *The Death of Politics,* p. 218.
67. Golsan, *Memory, the Holocaust, and French Justice,* p. xxxii.
68. Laughland, *The Death of Politics,* p. 129.
69. Ibid., p. 120.
70. Ibid., pp. 121–23.
71. Ibid., pp. 123–24.
72. Patton and Mackness, p. 215.
73. Quoted in Laughland, *The Death of Politics,* p. 223.

74. Quoted in ibid.
75. Quoted in ibid., p. 227.
76. Ibid., p. 218.
77. Ibid., p. 247.
78. Quoted in Mitterrand's obituary on the Info Europe website (www.info-europe.fr/seb.dirr/seb03.dir/mitterrand/mitterrand.htm).
79. Gaudart de Soulages and Lamant, *Dictionnaire des francs-maçons français*, p. 924.
80. Nicolas Bonnal, *Mitterrand, le grand initié* (Paris: Albin Michel, 2001), p. 37.
81. Ibid., p. 36.
82. Ibid., p. 185.
83. Marie Delarue, *Un Pharaon républicain* (Paris: Jacques Grancher, 1999), p. 8.
84. François Mitterrand, *The Wheat and the Chaff* (London: Weidenfeld and Nicolson, 1982), p. 124.
85. Mitterrand, *Ma part de vérité*, p. 14.
86. Ibid., p. 21. See also Marie Balvet, *La roman familial de François Mitterrand* (Paris: Plon, 1994), p. 21.
87. Delarue, *Un Pharaon républicain*, p. 21.
88. Ibid., p. 55.
89. Quoted in Bonnal, *Mitterrand, le grand initié*, p. 71.
90. See ibid., pp. 71–74.
91. Marie Delarue, *Un Pharaon républicain*, p. 50.
92. Quoted in ibid., p. 52.
93. Ibid., p. 53.
94. Sandri, 2003 interview at www.rennes-le-chateau.org/rlctoday/int-sandri.htm.

BIBLIOGRAPHY

Main entries are for the editions cited in the text. Where this is not the first edition, details of the original publication (where known) follow.

Allier, Raoul. *La cabal des dévots, 1627–1666.* Paris: Armand Colin, 1902.

———. *Une société secrète au XVII siècle: La Compagnie du Très-Saint-Sacrement de l'Autel à Marseille.* Paris: Librairie Honoré Champion, 1909.

Amadou, Robert. *Louis-Claude de Saint-Martin et le Martinisme: Introduction à l'étude de la vie, l'ordre et de la dóctrine du Philosophe Inconnu.* Paris: Éditions du Griffon d'Or, 1946.

———. "Martines de Pasqually et l'Ordre des Élus Cohen." *L'Originel* 2 (1995).

———, ed. *Louis-Claude de Saint-Martin, le Philosophe inconnu: Lettres aux du Bourg (1776–1785).* Special edition of *L'Initiation.* Paris, 1977.

Amadou, Robert, and Alice Joly. *De l'Agent Inconnu au Philosophe Inconnu: Essais.* Paris: Denoël, 1962.

Ambelain, Robert, ed. *Cérémonies et rituels de la maçonnerie symbolique.* Paris: Bussière, 1966.

Andressohn, John C. *The Ancestry and Life of Godfrey of Bouillon.* Bloomington: Indiana University Publications, 1947.

Andrews, Richard, and Paul Schellenberger. *The Tomb of God: The Body of Jesus and the Solution to a 2000-Year-Old Mystery.* London: Little, Brown, 1996.

"Arcadia," "Entretien avec Gino Sandri." *La Lettre du Thot* webzine, part 1: no. 7, July 2003. http://62.212.97.214/thot/arcadia/webzine/

webzine_no7.html. Part 2: no. 8, August 2003. http://62.212.97.214/thot/arcadia/webzine/webzine_no8.html.

Aubert, Raphaël, and Carl-A. Keller. *Vie et mort de l'Ordre du Temple Solaire.* Vevey: Éditions de l'Aire, 1994.

Audigier, François. *Histoire du SAC: La part d'ombre du gaullisme.* Paris: Stock, 2003.

Auguste, Abbé Alphonse. *La Compagnie du Saint-Sacrement à Toulouse: notes et documents.* Paris: A. Picard et Fils and Toulouse: Éduoard Privat, 1913.

Baigent, Michael, and Richard Leigh. *Secret Germany: Claus von Stauffenberg and the Mystical Crusade Against Hitler.* London: Jonathan Cape, 1994.

———. *The Temple and the Lodge.* London: Corgi, 1990. First published in 1989 by Jonathan Cape.

Baigent, Michael, Richard Leigh, and Henry Lincoln. *The Holy Blood and the Holy Grail.* Updated ed. London: Arrow, 1996. First published in 1982 by Jonathan Cape.

———. *The Messianic Legacy.* London: Corgi, 1987. First published in 1986 by Jonathan Cape.

Balfour, Michael, and Julian Frisby. *Helmuth von Moltke: A Leader Against Hitler.* London: Macmillan, 1972.

Balvet, Marie. *Le roman familial de François Mitterrand.* Paris: Plon, 1994.

Barbier, Joseph. *Les sources de La colline inspirée de Maurice Barrès.* Nancy: Berger-Levrault, 1957.

Barrès, Maurice. *La colline inspirée,* critical edition, ed. by Joseph Barbier. Nancy: Berger-Levrault, 1962. First published in 1913 by Emile-Paul, Paris.

———. *Le mystère en pleine lumière.* Paris: Librairie Plon, 1926.

———. *Un renovateur de l'occultisme: Stanislas de Gauita (1861–1898).* Paris: Chamuel, 1898.

Bauval, Robert, and Adrian Gilbert. *The Orion Mystery: Unlocking the Secrets of the Pyramids.* London: William Heinemann, 1994.

Bayard, Jean-Pierre, *Le symbolique de la Rose-Croix.* Paris: Payot, 1975.

———. *Le symbolisme maçonnique traditionnel.* Paris: Éditions du Prisme, 1974.

———. *Le symbolisme maçonnique des haut grades.* Paris: Éditions du Prisme, 1975.

Bayard, Jean-Pierre, with Natacha Olejnik-Sarkissian. *Guide des sociétés secrètes et des sectes.* Paris: Oxus, 2004. Rev. ed. of *Le guide des sociétés secrètes.* Paris: Philippe Lebaud, 1989.

Beaucéan, Nicolas. *Au pays de la Reine Blanche.* Paris: Philippe de Chérisey, 1967.

Begg, Ean. *The Cult of the Black Virgin.* London: Arkana, 1985.

Bernadac, Christian, ed. *"Dagore": les carnets secrets de la Cagoule.* Paris: France-Empire, 1977.

Berthelot, Jean. *Sur les rails du pouvoir (de Munich à Vichy).* Paris: Robert Laffont, 1968.

Blum, Jean. *Rennes-le-Château: Wisigoths, cathares, templiers—le secret des hérétiques.* Monaco: Éditions du Rocher, 1994.

Bois, Jules. *Le monde invisible: Lettre de M. Sully-Prudhomme de l'Académie Française.* Paris: Ernest Flammarion, 1902.

———. *Le satanisme et la magie, avec un étude de J-K Huysmans.* Paris: Léon Chailley, 1895.

Boisset, Yves-Fred. *Les clés traditionelles et synarchiques de l'archéomètre.* Paris: JBG, 1977.

Boissonnade, Euloge. *Jamais deux sans trois? . . . ou l'étonnant destin d'Alain Poher.* Paris: France-Empire, 1986.

Bonnal, Nicolas. *Mitterrand, le grand initié.* Paris: Albin Michel, 2001.

Bord, Lucien-Jean. *Généalogie commenté des rois de France.* Vouillé: Éditions de Chiré, 1980.

———. *Les Mérovingiens: "Les rois inconnus."* Vouille: Éditions de Chiré, 1981.

Bordes, Richard. *Les mérovingiens à Rennes-le-Château—mythes ou réalités: Réponse à Messieurs Plantard, Lincoln, Vazart and Cie.* Rennes-les-Bains: Philippe Schrauben, 1984.

Boudet, Abbé Henri. *La vraie langue celtique et la cromleck de Rennes-les-Bains.* Paris: Pierre Belfond, 1978. Facsimile of original 1886 ed. with preface by Pierre Plantard de Saint-Clair.

Bourdrel, Philippe. *La Cagoule: 30 ans de complots.* Paris: Albin Michel, 1970.

Bouthillier, Yves. *Le drame de Vichy.* Vol. 1, *Face à l'ennemi, face à l'allié.* Paris: Librairie Plon, 1950; vol. 2, *Finances sous la contrainte.* Paris: Librairie Plon, 1951.

Brion, Marcel, ed. *Léonard de Vinci.* Paris: Librairie Hachette, 1959.

Bromberger, Merry, and Serge Bromberger. *Jean Monnet and the United States of Europe.* New York: Coward-McCann, 1969. First published as *Les coulisses de l'Europe* (Paris: Presses de la Cité, 1968).

———. *Les 13 complots du 13 mai, ou la délivrance du Gulliver.* Paris: Librairie Arthème Fayard, 1959.

Brown, Dan. *The Da Vinci Code: A Novel.* New York: Doubleday, 2003.

Burman, Edward. *Supremely Abominable Crimes: The Trial of the Knights Templar.* London: Alison & Busby, 1994.

Burstein, Dan, ed. *Secrets of the Code: The Unauthorized Guide to the Mysteries Behind The Da Vinci Code.* New York: CDS Books, 2004.

Calvé, Emma. *My Life.* New York/London: D. Appleton & Co., 1922.

———. *Sous tous les ciels, j'ai chanté . . .* Paris: Librairie Plon, 1940.

Carnac, Pierre. *L'Histoire commence à Bimini.* Paris: Robert Laffont, 1973.

Cassiel, *The Encyclopedia of Forbidden Knowledge.* London: Hamlyn, 1990.

Cate, Curtis. *André Malraux: A Biography.* London: Hutchinson, 1995.

Charroux, Robert. *Treasures of the World.* London: Frederick Muller, 1964. Originally published as *Trésors du monde, enterrés, emmurés, engloutis.* (Paris: Fayard, 1962).

Chaumeil, Jean-Luc. *La table d'Isis, ou le secret de la lumière.* Paris: Guy Trédaniel, 1994.

———. *Le trésor du triangle d'or.* Nice: Alain Lefeuvre, 1979.

Chaumeil, Jean-Luc, and J. Rivière. *L'alphabet solaire: Introduction à la Langue Universelle avec des inédits de l'Abbé Boudet.* Paris: Éditions du Borrego, 1985.

Chauvel, A. D., and M. Forestier. *The Extraordinary House of Victor Hugo in Guernsey.* St. Peter Port: Toucan Press, 1975.

Churchill, Winston S. *The Sinews of Peace: Post-War Speeches.* Edited by Randolph S. Churchill. London: Cassell & Co, 1948.

———. *Europe Unite: Speeches 1947 and 1948.* London: Cassell & Co. 1950.

Clayton, Anthony. *Three Marshals of France: Leadership after Trauma.* London: Brassey's, 1992.

Cocteau, Jean. *A Call to Order.* London: Faber & Gwyer, 1926.

———. *Journal d'un inconnu.* Paris: Bernard Grasset, 1953.

———. *Journal 1942–1945.* Edited by Jean Touzot. Paris: Gallimard, 1989.

———. *The Journals of Jean Cocteau.* Edited by Wallace Fowlie. London: Museum Press, 1957.

———. *Maalesh: A Theatrical Tour in the Middle-East.* London: Peter Owen, 1956. First published as *Maalesh: Journal d'une tournée de théâtre* (Paris: Librairie Gallimard, 1949).

———. *Le passé défini.* vol. 1, *1951–1952.* Edited by Pierre Chanel. Paris: Gallimard, 1983; vol. 2, *1953.* Paris: Gallimard, 1985; vol. 3, *1954.* Paris: Gallimard, 1989.

———. *Le requiem.* Paris: Gallimard, 1962.

Collins, Andrew. *Twenty-First Century Grail: The Quest for a Legend.* London: Virgin, 2004.

Contrucci, Jean. *Emma Calvé, la diva du siècle.* Paris: Albin Michel, 1989.

Corbu, Claire, and Antoine Captier. *L'Héritage de l'Abbé Saunière.* Cazilhac: Bélisane, 1995.

Coston, Henry. ed. *Dictionnaire de la politique française.* 4 vols. Paris: Publications Henry Coston/Librairie Française, 1967, 1972, 1979, 1982.

———. *La finance juive et les trusts.* Paris: Jean-Renard, 1942.

———, ed. *Je vous hais!* Paris: Bureau Central de Presse, 1944.

———. *Les Juifs contre la France. Les Dossiers de l'O.P.N.*, no. 1. Paris, June 1937.

———. *Le retour des "200 familles."* Paris: Librairie Française, 1960.

———. *Les technocrates et la Synarchie.* Special ed. of *Lectures françaises.* Paris: February 1962.

Coston, Henry, and Jacques Isorni, eds. *Pétain toujours présent.* Special ed. of *Lectures françaises.* Paris: June 1964.

Coudenhove-Kalergi, Count Richard N. *Pan-Europe.* New York: Alfred A. Knopf, 1926.

———. *Europe Must Unite.* Glarus: Paneuropa Editions, 1939.

———. *An Idea Conquers the World.* London: Hutchinson, 1953.

Cox, Simon. *Cracking the Da Vinci Code: The Unauthorized Guide to the Facts Behind the Fiction.* London: Michael O'Mara, 2004.

Dard, Olivier. *La synarchie, ou le mythe du complot permanent.* Paris: Perrin, 1998.

Dawes, Christopher. *Rat Scabies and the Holy Grail.* London: Sceptre, 2005.

Dear, I. C. B., ed. *The Oxford Companion to the Second World War.* Oxford and New York: Oxford University Press, 1995.

de Beauvoir, Simone. *The Prime of Life.* Harmondsworth, U.K.: Penguin Books, 1965. Originally published as *La force de l'âge* (Paris: Librairie Gallimard, 1960).

de Charnay, Geoffrey. *Synarchie: Panorama de 25 années d'activité occulte, avec la reproduction intégrale du Pacte Synarchique.* Paris: Médicis, 1946.

de Gaulle, Charles. *Memoirs of Hope: Renewal 1958–62; Endeavour 1962–.*

London: Weidenfeld & Nicolson, 1971. Originally published as *Mémoires d'espoir: Le renouveau 1958–62; L'effort 1962–*. (Paris: Librairie Plon, 1970).

de Kerillis, Henri. *De Gaulle dictateur: une grande mystification de l'histoire.* Montréal: Beauchemin, 1945.

Delarue, Marie. *Un Pharaon républicain: Enquêtes.* Paris: Jacques Grancher, 1999.

Delaude, Jean. *Le cercle d'Ulysse.* Toulouse: Dyroles, 1977.

Deloux, Jean-Pierre, and Jacques Brétigny. *Rennes-le-Château: capitale secrète de l'histoire de France.* Paris: Atlas, 1982.

de Mutigny, Jean. *Victor Hugo et le spiritisme.* Paris: Fernand Nathan, 1981.

Descadeillas, René. *Mythologie du trésor de Rennes: Histoire véritable de l'Abbê Saunière, curé de Rennes-le-Château.* Carcassonne: J. M. Savary, 1988. Originally published in *Mémoires de la Société des Arts et des Sciences de Carcassonne* (July 1974).

———. *Notice sur Rennes-le-Château et l'Abbé Saunière,* Carcassonne: written for the Departmental Archives of the Aude, 1962.

———. *Rennes et ses derniers seigneurs 1730–1820: contribution à l'étude économique et sociale de la baronnie de Rennes (Aude) au XVIII siècle.* Toulouse: Édouard Privat, 1964.

de Sède, Gérard. *L'incendie habitable.* Paris: Éditions de la Main à Plume, 1942.

———. *La race fabuleuse: Extra-terrestre et mythologie mérovingienne.* Paris: J'ai Lu, 1973.

———. *Rennes-le-Château: le dossier, les impostures, les phantasmes, les hypothèses.* Paris: Robert Laffont, 1988.

———. *Signé: Rose + Croix—L'énigme de Rennes-le-Château.* Paris: Librairie Plon, 1977.

———. *Les templiers sont parmi nous, ou l'énigme de Gisors.* Paris: René Julliard, 1962.

———. *Le trésor cathare.* Paris: René Julliard, 1966.

de Sède, Gérard, with Sophie de Sède. *L'occultisme dans la politique: de Pythagore à nos jours.* Paris: Robert Laffont, 1994.

———. *Le trésor maudit de Rennes-le-Château.* Paris: J'ai Lu, 1968. Originally published as *L'or de Rennes, ou la vie insolite de Bérenger Saunière, curé de Rennes-le-Château* (Paris: Julliard, 1967).

de Sède, Gérard, et al. *Pourquoi Prague?* Paris: Publications Premières/ Tallandier, 1968.

Désert. Joseph. *Toute la vérité sur l'affaire de la Cagoule: Sa trahison, ses crimes, ses hommes.* Paris: Librairie des Sciences et des Arts, 1946.

Digot, Paul. *Notice historique sur Notre-Dame-de-Sion (Vaudémont).* Nancy: privately published, 1856.

Dimbleby, David, and David Reynolds. *An Ocean Apart: The Relationship between Britain and America in the Twentieth Century.* London: BBC Books/Hodder & Stoughton, 1988.

Doinel, Jules-Stanislas. *Histoire de Blanche de Castille.* Tours: Alfred Mame et Fils, 1887.

———. *Jeanne d'Arc telle qu'elle est.* Orléans: H. Herluisen, 1892.

Douzet, André. *Saunière's Model and the Secret of Rennes-le-Château: The Priest's Final Legacy That Unveils the Location of His Terrifying Discovery.* Kempton/Enkhuizen: Adventures Unlimited Press/Frontier Publishing, 2001. Revised, translated edition of *Lumières nouvelles sur Rennes-le-Château* (Lyons: Benoist Rivière, 1995).

Duhamel, Alain. *De Gaulle–Mitterrand: La marque et la trace.* Paris: Flammarion, 1991.

Edwards, Samuel. *Victor Hugo: A Biography.* London: New English Library, 1975. First published in 1971 by David McKay.

Egyptian Rite of Memphis. *Ritual of the A. & A. Egyptian Rite of Memphis 96°, also Constitutions and By-Laws of the Sovereign Sanctuary, Valley of Canada.* London (Ontario): Sovereign Sanctuary of the Egyptian Rite of Memphis (Canada), c. 1880.

Faillon, Étienne Michel. *Monuments inédits sur l'apostolat de Sainte Marie-Madeleine en Provence, et sur les autres apôtres de cette contrée, Saint Lazare, Saint Maximin, Sainte Marthe et les Saintes Maries Jacobé et Salomé.* 2 vols. Paris: Abbé Migne, 1848.

Faux, Emmanuel, Thomas Legrand, and Gilles Perez. *La main droite de Dieu: Enquête sur François Mitterrand et l'extrême droite.* Paris: Éditions de Seuil, 1994.

Ferrand, Serge, and G. Lecavelier. *Aux ordres du SAC.* Paris: Albin Michel, 1982.

Figueras, André. *Pétain c'était de Gaulle.* Paris: André Figueras, 1979.

———. *Mitterrand dévoilé.* Paris: André Figueras, 1980.

Findel, J. G. *The History of Freemasonry from Its Origins Down to the Present Day.* London: George Kenning, 1869.

Fontenay, Fernand. *La Cagoule contre la France: Ses crimes, son organisation, ses chefs, ses inspirateurs.* Paris: Sociales Internationales, 1938.

France, John. "The Election and Title of Godfrey de Bouillon." *Canadian Journal of History* 18, no. 3 (December 1983).

———. *Victory in the East: A Military History of the First Crusade.* Cambridge, U.K.: Cambridge University Press 1994.

Friend, Julius W. *The Long Presidency: France in the Mitterrand Years, 1981–1995.* Boulder, Colo.: Westview Press, 1998.

Frohock, W. M. *André Malraux and the Tragic Imagination.* Palo Alto, Calif.: Stanford University Press, 1952.

Froment, Pascale. *René Bousquet.* Rev. ed. Paris: Fayard, 2001. First published in 1994 by Stock.

Gardner, Laurence. *Bloodline of the Holy Grail: The Hidden Lineage of Jesus Revealed.* Shaftesbury: Element, 1996.

———. *Genesis of the Grail Kings: The Pendragon Legacy of Adam and Eve.* London: Bantam Press, 1999.

———. *Lost Secrets of the Sacred Ark: Amazing Revelations of the Incredible Power of Gold.* London: Element, 2003.

———. *Realm of the Ring Lords: Beyond the Portal of the Twilight World.* Ottery St. Mary: MediaQuest, 2000.

Gaudart de Soulages, Michel, and Hubert Lamant. *Dictionnaire des francs-maçons français.* Paris: Jean-Claude Lattès, 1995.

Gaudino, Antoine. *L'enquête impossible.* Paris: Albin Michel, 1990.

Gerber, François. *Malraux–de Gaulle: la nation retrouvée.* Paris: L'Harmattan, 1996.

Girodias, Maurice. *Une journée sur la terre.* Vol. 1, *L'Arrivée.* Paris: Éditions de la Différence, 1990. Originally published as *J'arrive* (Paris: Stock, 1977).

———. *Une journée sur la terre.* Vol. 2, *Les jardins d'Éros.* Paris: Éditions de la Différence, 1990.

Golsan, Richard J., ed. *Memory, the Holocaust, and French Justice: The Bousquet and Touvier Affairs.* Hanover, N.H., and London: University of New England, 1996.

Gordon, Bertram M. *Historical Dictionary of World War II France: The Occupation, Vichy and the Resistance 1938–1946.* Westport, Conn.: Greenwood Press, 1998.

Gough, Hugh, and John Horne, eds. *De Gaulle and Twentieth-Century France.* London and New York: Edward Arnold, 1994.

Greene, Liz. *The Dreamer of the Vine.* London: The Bodley Head, 1980.

———. *The Puppet Master: A Novel.* London: Arkana, 1987.

Griffiths, Richard. *Marshal Pétain.* London: Constable, 1994 (first edition 1970).

Grousset, René. *Histoire des Croisades et du royaume franc de Jérusalem.* 3 vols. Paris: Librairie Plon, 1934–36.

Guinguand, Maurice, and Béatrice Lanne. *L'or des templiers: Gisors ou Tomar?* Paris: Robert Laffont, 1973.

Haight, John McVickar, Jr. *American Aid to France, 1938–1940.* New York: Atheneum, 1970.

Headings, Mildred J. *French Freemasonry under the Third Republic.* Johns Hopkins University Studies in Historical and Political Science, Series 66, no. 1. Baltimore: Johns Hopkins University Press, 1949.

Hecht, Ilse. "The Infants Christ and St. John Embracing: Notes on a Composition by Joos van Cleve." *Apollo* 113, no. 230 (April 1981).

Hellman, John. *The Knight-Monks of Vichy France: Uriage, 1940–1945.* 2nd expanded ed. Liverpool, U.K.: Liverpool University Press; Montreal: McGill-Queen's University Press, 1997 (first edition 1993).

Hewitt, James Robert. *André Malraux.* New York: Frederick Ungar Publishing, 1978.

Hopkins, Marilyn, Graham Simmans, and Tim Wallace-Murphy. *Rex Deus: The True Mystery of Rennes-le-Château and the Dynasty of Jesus.* Shaftesbury: Element, 2000.

Hutin, Serge. *Histoire des Rose-Croix.* Rev. ed. Paris: Le Courner du Livre, 1971 (first edition 1955).

Imbert, Nath, ed. *Dictionnaire national des contemporains.* Paris: Lajeunesse, 1936.

Isorni, Jacques. *Pétain a sauvé la France.* Paris: Flammarion, 1964.

Jardine, Jerry. "The Stuart Pretenders." *Scottish Journal,* May 1999.

Jarnac, Pierre. *Les archives du trésor de Rennes-le-Château.* Single-volume ed. Nice: Bélisane, 1988. Original two volumes published in 1987 and 1988.

———. *Histoire du trésor de Rennes-le-Château.* Saleilles: Pierre Jarnac, 1985.

———, ed. *Les mystères de Rennes-le-Château: Mélanges sulfureux.* 3 vols. Couiza: Centre d'Études et des Recherches Templières, 1994–95.

Jonas, Raymond. *France and the Cult of the Sacred Heart: An Epic Tale for Modern Times.* Berkeley and Los Angeles: University of California, 2000.

Kettle, Michael. *De Gaulle and Algeria 1940–1960: From Mers El-Kébir to the Algiers Barricades.* London: Quartet, 1994.

King, Jon, and John Beveridge. *Princess Diana—The Hidden Evidence: How M16 and the CIA Were Involved in the Death of Princess Diana.* Northam: Roundhouse, 2001.

Krosnar, Katka. "Scot 'Prince' Seeks Czech EP Seat." *The Prague Post,* 9–15 June 2004.

Kuisel, Richard F. "The Legend of the Vichy Synarchy." *French Historical Studies* 6, no. 3 (Spring 1970).

Lameyre, Alain. *Guide de la France templière.* Paris: Tchou, 1975.

Lamy, Michel. *Jules Verne, initié et initiateur: La clé du secret de Rennes-le-Château et le trésor des rois de France.* Paris: Payot, 1984.

———. *Les templiers: ces grands seigneurs aux blancs manteaux.* Bordeaux: Aubéron, 1994.

Langer, William L. *Our Vichy Gamble.* New York: Alfred A. Knopf, 1947.

Laughland, John. *The Death of Politics: France under Mitterrand.* London: Michael Joseph, 1994.

———. *The Tainted Source: The Undemocratic Origins of the European Ideal.* London: Little, Brown & Co., 1997.

Lebovics, Herman. *Mona Lisa's Escort: André Malraux and the Reinvention of French Culture.* Ithaca, N.Y., and London: Cornell University Press, 1999.

Le Cour, Paul. *L'Atlantide: Origine des civilisations.* Paris: Dervy, 1950.

———. *Hellénisme et christianisme.* Paris: Atlantis, 1943.

le Forestier, René. *Les Illuminés de Bavière et la franc-maçonnerie allemande.* Paris: Librairie Hachette et Cie, 1914.

———. *La franc-maçonnerie occultiste au VIII siècle et l'Ordre des Élus Coens.* Paris: Dorbon-Ainé, 1928.

———. *La franc-maçonnerie templière et occultiste aux XVIII et XIX siècles.* 2 vols. Paris: La Table d'Émeraude, 1987. First published in 1970 by Montaigne.

———. *L'occultisme et la franc-maçonnerie écossaise.* Paris: Perrin & Cie, 1928.

Le Fur, Louis. *État fédéral et confédération d'États.* Paris: Marchal & Billard, 1896.

———. *Races, nationalités, états.* Paris: Librairie Félix Alcan, 1922.

Lejeune, René. *Robert Schuman (1886–1963), Père de l'Europe: La politique, chemin de sainteté.* Paris: Fayard, 2000.

Lincoln, Henry. *The Holy Place: The Mystery of Rennes-le-Château—*

Discovering the Eighth Wonder of the Ancient World. London: Corgi, 1992. First published in 1991 by Jonathan Cape.

———. *Key to the Sacred Pattern: The Untold Story of Rennes-le-Château.* Moreton-in-Marsh: Windrush Press, 1997.

Lockspeiser, Edward. *Debussy: His Life and Mind.* Vol. 1, *1862–1902.* London: Cassell, 1962.

———. *Debussy: His Life and Mind.* Vol. 2, *1902–1918.* London: Cassell, 1965.

Lottman, Herbert R. *Pétain—Hero or Traitor: The Untold Story.* Harmondsworth, U.K.: Viking, 1985.

Magillivray, Jania. "Cocteau fut le dernier grand-maître; qui lui a succédé? L'énigme du Prieuré de Sion." *Bonne Soirée,* August 14, 1980.

Malraux, André. *Antimemoirs.* London: Hamish Hamilton, 1968. Originally published as *Antimémoires* (Paris: Gallimard, 1967).

———. *Fallen Oaks: Conversation with De Gaulle.* London: Hamish Hamilton, 1971. Originally published as *Les chênes qu'on abat* (Paris: Gallimard, 1971).

Marie, Franck. *Rennes-le-Château: Études critiques.* Bagneux: SRES, 1978.

———. *La résurrection du "Grand Cocu."* Bagneux: SRES, 1981.

Markale, Jean. *The Church of Mary Magdalene: The Sacred Feminine and the Treasure of Rennes-le-Château.* Rochester, Vt.: Inner Traditions, 2004. Originally published as *Rennes-le-Château et l'énigme de l'or maudit* (Paris: Pygmalion, 1989).

———. *The Templar Treasure at Gisors.* Rochester, Vt.: Inner Traditions, 2003. Originally published as *Gisors et l'énigme des templiers* (Paris: Pygmalion, 1986).

Martin, R.P. *Le livre des compagnons secrets.* Monaco: ACL Rocher, 1982.

Mauriès, Patrick. *Jean Cocteau.* London: Thames & Hudson, 1998.

Meyer, Jean. *Le sinarquisme: Un fascisme mexicain? 1937–1947.* Paris: Hachette, 1977.

Michael of Albany, Prince. *The Forgotten Monarchy of Scotland: The True Story of the Royal House of Stewart and the Hidden Lineage of the Kings and Queens of Scots.* Shaftesbury: Element, 1998.

Mitterrand, François. *Ma part de verité: De la rupture à l'unité.* Paris: Fayard, 1969.

———. *The Wheat and the Chaff.* London: Weidenfeld and Nicolson, 1982. Originally published as *La paille et le grain* (Paris: Flammarion, 1975) and *L'abeille et l'architecte* (Paris: Flammarion, 1978).

Mizrach, Dr. Steven. "Priory of Sion: The Facts, the Theories, the

Mystery." Florida International University. www.fiu.edu/~mizrachs/poseur3.html, undated.

Monier, Frédéric. *Le complot dans le République: Stratégies du secret, de Boulanger à la Cagoule:* Paris: Éditions La Découverte, 1998.

Montaldo, Jean. *Lettre ouverte d'un "chien" à François Mitterrand au nom de la liberté d'aboyer.* Paris: Albin Michel, 1993.

Monteil, Claudine. *Les amants de la liberté.* Paris: Éditions 1, 1999.

———. *Simone de Beauvoir: Le mouvement des femmes: Mémoires d'une jeune fille rebelle.* Quebec: Alain Stanké, 1995.

Monteils, Jean-Pierre. *Sectes et sociétés secrètes: le douloureux chemin vers la lumière—Église, franc-maçonnerie, Synarchie et pouvoirs à l'épreuve de l'Histoire.* Nîmes: C. Lacour, 1999.

Montloin, Pierre, and Jean-Pierre Bayard. *Les Rose-Croix, ou le complot des sages.* Paris: Grasset, 1971.

Mossuz, Janine. *André Malraux et le gaullisme (Cahiers de la fondation nationale des sciences politiques,* no. 177). Paris: Armand Colin, 1970.

Nelli, René. *Dictionnaire des hérésies méridionales et des mouvements hétérodox ou indépendants apparus dans le Midi de la France depuis l'établissement du christianisme.* Toulouse: Édouard Privat, 1968.

———. *Histoire secrète du Languedoc.* Paris: Albin Michel 1978.

———. Fernand Niel, Jean Duvernoy, and Déodat Roché. *Les Cathares.* Paris: Éditions du Delphes, 1965.

Nicolle, Pierre. *Cinquante mois d'armistice: Vichy 2 juillet 1940–26 août 1944—Journal d'un témoin.* 2 vols. Paris: André Bonne, 1947.

Niel, Fernand. *Les Cathares de Montségur.* Paris: Seghers, 1978. First published in 1973 by Robert Laffont.

Nouveau dictionnaire national des contemporains. 3rd ed. Paris: Éditions du Nouveau Dictionnaire National des Contemporains, 1964.

Oursel, Raymond, ed. *Le procès des templiers.* Paris: Denoël, 1955.

Paoli, Mathieu. *Le dessous d'une ambition politique: Nouvelles révélations sur le trésor du Razès et de Gisors.* Nyons: Associés, 1973.

Papus. *Anarchie, indolence et synarchie: les lois physiologiques d'organisations socials et l'ésotérisme.* Paris: Chamuel, 1894.

———. *Martinésisme, willermosisme, martinisme et franc-maçonnerie.* Paris: Chamuel, 1899.

Passek, Jean-Loup, ed. *Dictionnaire du cinéma français.* Paris: Librairie Larousse, 1987.

Patton, Guy, and Robin Mackness. *Web of Gold: The Secret History of a Sacred Treasure.* London: Sidgwick & Jackson, 2000.

Paxton, Robert O. *Vichy France: Old Guard and New Order 1940–1944.* New York: Columbia University Press, 2001 (first edition 1972).

Péan, Pierre. *Une jeunesse française: François Mitterrand, 1934–1947.* Paris: Fayard, 1994.

———. *Le mystérieux Docteur Martin.* Paris: Fayard, 1993.

Péladan, (Joséphin). *Constitutions de la Rose-Croix, le Temple et le Graal.* Paris: Secretariat de l'Ordre de la Rose-Croix, le Temple et le Graal, 1893.

———. *Les manuscrits de Léonard de Vinci: les 14 manuscrits de l'Institut de France.* Paris: E. Sansot & Cie, 1910.

———. *La philosophie de Léonard de Vinci d'après ses manuscrits.* Paris: Félix Alcan, 1910.

———. *Textes choisis de Léonard de Vinci: pensées, théories, préceptes, fables et facéties.* Paris: Mercure de France 1907.

Penaud, Guy. *André Malraux et la Résistance.* Périgueux: Pierre Fanlac, 1986.

Pennera, Christian. *Robert Schuman: La jeunesse et les débuts politiques d'un grand Européen, de 1886 à 1924.* Sarrequemines: Pierron, 1985.

Péronic. *Ma queste du Graal.* Vol. 1, *Le sang.* Monte Carlo: Éditions de la Pensée Solaire, 1967.

———. *Ma Queste du Graal.* Vol. 2, *La coupe ou le saint vase.* Monte Carlo: Éditions de la Pensée Solaire, 1969.

Peronnik. *Pourquoi la résurgence de l'Ordre du Temple?* Vol. 1, *Le corps.* Monte Carlo: Éditions de la Pensée Solaire, 1975.

Peters, Arthur King. *Jean Cocteau and His World.* London: Thames & Hudson, 1987.

Phillips, Graham. *The Templars and the Ark of the Covenant: The Discovery of the Treasure of Solomon.* Rochester, Vt.: Bear & Co., 2004.

Picknett, Lynn. *Mary Magdalene: Christianity's Hidden Goddess.* Rev. ed. London: Robinson, 2004 (first edition 2003).

Picknett, Lynn, and Clive Prince. *The Stargate Conspiracy: Revealing the Truth Behind Extraterrestrial Contact, Military Intelligence and the Mysteries of Ancient Egypt.* New York: Berkley, 2001. Originally published in 1999 by Little, Brown, London.

———. *The Secret History of Lucifer: The Ancient Path to Knowledge and the Real Da Vinci Code.* London: Constable & Robinson, 2005.

———. *The Templar Revelation: Secret Guardians of the True Identity of Christ.* New York: Touchstone, 1998.

———. *Turin Shroud—In Whose Image?* Rev. ed. London: Corgi, 2000. Originally published in 1994 by Bloomsbury.

Picknett, Lynn, Clive Prince, and Stephen Prior with Robert Brydon. *Double Standards: The Rudolf Hess Cover-up.* Rev. ed. London: TimeWarner Books, 2002. Originally published in 2001 by Little, Brown.

———. *Friendly Fire: The Secret War Between the Allies.* Edinburgh: Mainstream Publishing, 2004.

———. *War of the Windsors: A Century of Unconstitutional Monarchy.* Rev. ed. Edinburgh: Mainstream Publishing, 2003 (first edition 2002).

Plume, Christian, and Xavier Pasquini. *Encyclopédie des sectes dans le monde.* Paris: Henri Veyrier, 1984.

Poher, Alain. *Trois fois président: Mémoires.* Paris: Plon, 1993.

Pujo, Bernard. *Juin, Maréchal de France.* Paris: Albin Michel, 1988.

Putnam, Bill, and John Edwin Wood. *The Treasure of Rennes-le-Château: A Mystery Solved.* Stroud, U.K.: Sutton Publishing, 2004.

Rémond, René. *1958, le retour de de Gaulle.* Brussels: Complexe, 1998.

Rey, M. E. Guillaume. "Chartes de l'Abbaye du Mont-Sion." *Mémoires de la Société Nationale des Antiquaires de France.* Vol. 68 (5th series, vol. 8), 1887.

Righter, William. *The Rhetorical Hero: An Essay on the Aesthetics of André Malraux.* London: Routledge and Kegan Paul, 1964.

Riley-Smith, Jonathan. *The Crusades: A Short History.* London: Athlone Press, 1987.

———. *The First Crusaders, 1095–1131.* Cambridge, U.K.: Cambridge University Press, 1997.

Rivière, Jacques. *Le fabuleux trésor de Rennes-le-Château! Le secret de l'Abbé Saunière.* Nice: Bélisane, 1983.

Rivière, J., G. Tappa, and C. Boumendil. *Le fabuleux trésor de Rennes-le-Château!: Le secret de l'Abbé Gélis—le piste Corse.* Cazilhac: Bélisane, 1996.

Roberts, J. M. *The Mythology of the Secret Societies.* London: Secker & Warburg, 1972.

Robin, Jean. *Rennes-le-Château: La colline envoûtée.* Paris: Guy Trédaniel, 1982.

———. *Le royaume du Graal: Introduction au mystère de la France.* Paris: Guy Trédaniel, 1992.

Robin, Jean-Luc. *Rennes-le-Château: Le secret de Saunière.* Bordeaux: Sud Ouest, 2005.

Sablé, Erik. *La vie et l'oeuvre de René Schwaller de Lubicz.* Paris: Dervy, 2003.

Saint-Yves d'Alveydre. *Clefs d'Orient.* Paris: Didier & Cie, 1877.

———. *La France vraie.* Paris: Calmann Lévy, 1887.

———. *Mission actuelle des ouvriers.* Paris: E. Dentu, 1882.

———. *Mission actuelle des souverains.* Paris: E. Dentu, 1882.

———. *Mission de l'Inde en Europe, mission de l'Europe en Asie: La question du Mahatma et sa solution.* Paris: Dorbon, 1910.

———. *Mission des Juifs.* Paris: Calmann Lévy, 1884.

———. *La théogonie des patriarchs: Traduction archéométrique des saintes écritures.* Paris: La Librairie Hermétique, 1909.

Sanchez, Léopold. "Rennes-le-Château—vrai ou faux? Le trésor du curé." *Le Figaro,* July 7, 2001.

Sandri, Gino. "La ligne rouge." *La Lettre du Thot* webzine, no. 8, August 2003. http://62.212.97.214/thot/arcadia/webzine/webzine_no8.html.

Saunier, Jean. *Saint-Yves d'Alveydre, ou une synarchie sans énigme.* Paris: Dervy-Livres, 1981.

Schwaller de Lubicz, R.A. *Le temple de l'homme: Apet du sud à Louqsor.* 3 vols. Paris: Caractères, 1957.

Shirer, William L. *The Collapse of the Third Republic: An Enquiry into the Fall of France in 1940.* London: William Heinemann/Secker & Warburg, 1970.

Smith, Paul. "The 1989 Plantard Comeback." www.priory-of-sion.com/psp/id60.html, undated.

———. "Pierre Plantard Profile." www.priory-of-sion.com/psp/id84.html, undated.

———. "Plantard's Secret Parchments." *Journal of the Pendragon Society,* vol. 17, no. 4, February 1986.

———. "Priory of Sion Debunked." www.priory-of-sion.com/posd/posdebunking.html, undated.

Starbird, Margaret. *The Goddess in the Gospels: Reclaiming the Sacred Feminine.* Santa Fe: Bear & Co., 1998.

———. *The Woman with the Alabaster Jar: Mary Magdalen and the Holy Grail.* Santa Fe: Bear & Co., 1993.

Stein, Walter Johannes. *The Ninth Century and the Holy Grail.* London: Temple Lodge Press, 1988. Originally published as *Weltgeschichte im Lichte des Heiligen Grail: Das neunte Jahrhundert* (Stuttgart: Orient-Occident Verlag, 1928).

Stéphane, Roger. *André Malraux, entretiens et précisions.* Paris: Gallimard, 1984.

———. *Chaque homme est lié au monde: carnets (août 1939–août 1944).* Paris: Éditions de Sagittaire, 1946.

———. *Chaque homme est lié au monde.* Vol. 2, *Fin d'une jeunesse.* Paris: La Table Ronde, 1954.

Taillefer, Michel, and Robert Amadou, eds. *Le Temple Cohen de Toulouse (1760–1792).* Paris: Cariscript, 1986.

Tallon, Alain. *La Compagnie du Saint-Sacrement (1629–1667): Spiritualité et société.* Paris: Éditions du Cerf, 1990.

Temple, Robert. *The Sirius Mystery: New Scientific Evidence of Alien Contact 5,000 Years Ago.* Rev. ed. London: Century, 2000. Originally published in 1976 by Sidgwick & Jackson.

Thomas, Gordon, and Max Morgan-Witts. *Pontiff.* London: Panther, 1984. First published in 1983 in London by Granada.

Thory, Claude Antoine. *Acta Latomurum, ou chronologie de l'histoire de la franche-maçonnerie française et étrangère.* 2 vols. Paris: Pierre-Elie Dufart, 1815.

Tiersky, Ronald. *François Mitterrand: The Last French President.* New York: St. Martin's Press, 2000.

Tompkins, Peter. *The Murder of Admiral Darlan: A Study in Conspiracy.* London: Weidenfeld and Nicolson, 1965.

Tournoux, J.-R. *L'histoire secrète.* Paris: Plon, 1962.

———. *Pétain and de Gaulle.* London: Heinemann, 1966. Originally published as *Pétain et de Gaulle* (Paris: Librairie Plon, 1964).

Twyman, Tracy R. "Interview with Prince Michael Stewart of Albany." Dragon Key Press website, www.dragonkeypress.com/articles/article_2004_10_23_5829.html.

———. "My Kingdom Is Not of This World: Prince Nicholas de Vere von Drakenburg." Dagobert's Revenge website, www.dagobertsrevenge.com/devere/interview1.html.

Ulmann, André, and Henri Azeau. *Synarchie et pouvoir.* Paris: Julliard, 1968.

Ursin, Jean. *Création et histoire du Rite Écossais Rectifé.* Paris: Dervy, 1993.

VandenBroeck, André. *Al-Kemi: Hermetic, Occult, Political and Private Aspects of R. A. Schwaller de Lubicz.* Great Barrington, Mass.: Lindisfarne Press, 1987.

van Roon, Ger. *German Resistance to Hitler: Count von Moltke and the*

Kreisau Circle. London: Van Nostrand Reinhold Co., 1971. Originally published as *Neuordnung im Widerstand* (Munich: R. Oldenbourg, 1967).

Varennes, Claude. *Le destin de Marcel Déat.* Paris: Janmaray, 1948.

Vazart, Louis. *Abrégé de l'histoire des Francs: Les gouvernants et rois de la France.* Suresnes: Louis Vazart, 1978.

Verne, Jules. *Clovis Dardentor.* London: Sampson Low, Marston & Co., 1897. First published in Paris in 1896 by Hetzel.

Vinciguerra, Marie-Jean. "Garibaldi héros du Risorgimento et la maçonnerie italienne." *L'Originel* 2, 1995.

von Habsburg, Otto (Otto de Habsbourg). *Naissance d'un continent: Une histoire de l'Europe dite par Otto de Habsbourg à Guy de Chambure.* Paris: Bernard Grasset, 1975.

von Moltke, Count Helmuth James. *A German of the Resistance: The Last Letters of Count Helmuth James von Moltke.* Enlarged ed. London: Oxford University Press, 1947 (first edition 1946).

Waite, Arthur Edward. *A New Encyclopaedia of Freemasonry (Ars Magna Latomorum) and of Cognate Instituted Mysteries: Their Rites, Literature and History.* Rev. ed. 2 vols. London: William Rider & Son, 1923 (first edition 1921).

———. *Saint-Martin the French Mystic and the Story of Modern Martinism.* London: William Rider & Son, 1922.

Weber, Eugen. *Action Française: Royalism and Reaction in Twentieth-Century France* (Palo Alto, Calif.: Stanford University Press, 1962).

Weiss, Jacques. *La synarchie selon l'oeuvre de Saint-Yves d'Alveydre.* Paris: Robert Laffont, 1976.

Wolfram von Eschenbach. *Parzival.* Trans. and ed. A. T. Hatto. London: Penguin, 1980.

Wood, Ian. *The Merovingian Kingdoms 450–751.* London and New York: Longman, 1994.

Yates, Frances A. *The Rosicrucian Enlightenment.* London: Routledge & Kegan Paul, 1972.

Youssef, Ahmed. *Cocteau l'Egyptien.* Monaco: Éditions du Rocher, 2001.

Zoccatelli, Pierluigi. "De *Regnabit* au *Bestaire du Christ.* L'itinéraire intellectuelle d'un symboliste chrétien: Louis Charbonneau-Lassy." Transcript of lecture delivered on 7 December 1996 at the Sainte-Croix Collegiate Church, Loudon. Centre for Studies on New Religions website, www.cesnur.org/paraclet/loudon_01.htm.

Index